Java™ 2

Stephen Potts
Alex Pestrikov
Mike Kopack

Unleashed

Java™ 2 Unleashed

Copyright ©2002 by Sams Publishing

International Standard Book Number: 0-672-32394-x

Library of Congress Catalog Card Number: 2001099556

Printed in the United States of America

First Printing: July 2002

05 04 03 02   4 3 2 1

Trademarks

Warning and Disclaimer

ASSOCIATE PUBLISHER
Michael Stephens

EXECUTIVE EDITOR
Shelley Kronzek

ACQUISITIONS EDITOR
Michelle Newcomb

DEVELOPMENT EDITOR
Songlin Qiu

MANAGING EDITOR
Charlotte Clapp

PROJECT EDITOR
Andy Beaster

COPY EDITORS
Rhonda Tinch-Mize
Matt Wynalda

INDEXER
Erika Millen

PROOFREADERS
Bob LaRoche
Abby Van Huss

TECHNICAL EDITORS
Mike Kopack
Jeffrey Pajor
Craig Pfeifer
George Stones

TEAM COORDINATOR
Lynne Williams

INTERIOR DESIGNER
Gary Adair

COVER DESIGNER
Aren Howell

PAGE LAYOUT
Cheryl Lynch

Contents at a Glance

Contents

10 JDBC and Databases   371

11 Java Naming and Directory Interface (JNDI)   403

12 Processing Speech with Java   431

About the Authors

Steve Potts is an independent consultant, author, and Java instructor in Atlanta, Georgia (United States). Steve received his computer science degree in 1982 from Georgia Tech. He has worked in a number of disciplines during his 20-year career, with manufacturing being his area of greatest expertise. His previous books include *Special Edition Using Visual C++ 4* and *Java 1.2 How-To*. He can be reached via e-mail at stevepotts@mindspring.com.

Alex Pestrikov is an independent consultant specializing in J2EE technologies. He graduated from the University of Bridgeport in Connecticut. Alex has been involved in a number of J2EE projects in both the United States and Canada, most recently consulting for the government of Ontario. He lives with his fiancée, Stephanie, in Toronto and can be reached at pestrikov@yahoo.com.

Mike Kopack is a graduate of the Georgia Institute of Technology, where he earned a bachelor of science degree in computer science. Mike is a Sun Certified Java Programmer with experience dating back to JDK 1.0.2. He specializes in server-side Web technologies. His prior work has involved building dynamic Web site content management systems for multibillion-dollar corporations. Currently he works as a software engineer for ISX Corporation in Atlanta, Georgia.

Dedications

I would like to dedicate this book to Suzanne, my wife of twenty years. The hours required to produce a book of this size and scope place an additional burden on her in caring for our six children.

—Steve Potts

I want to dedicate this book to my family, who have always supported my dreams.

—Alex Pestrikov

Acknowledgments

I would like to thank all the editors who have worked on this book for their contributions. Shelley Kronzek guided me through the conceptual phases, and Michelle Newcomb helped me stay on schedule. Songlin Qiu has been a big help in keeping me focused on the details. I would also like to thank Mike Kopack, Craig Pfeifer, and George Stones, the technical reviewers, for their diligence. Finally, I want to thank Alex Pestrikov for being so easy to work with and so open to suggestions.

—*Steve Potts*

I want to thank all the people who have made this book a reality. Thanks to Shelley Kronzek for giving me the opportunity to work on this book. Steve Potts was an excellent mentor throughout the writing. Michelle Newcomb and Songlin Qiu helped me improve my contributions to the project. I would also like to thank the guys at the Middleware Lab for sharing their ideas with me.

—*Alex Pestrikov*

Tell Us What You Think!

As the reader of this book, *you* are our most important critic and commentator. We value your opinion and want to know what we're doing right, what we could do better, what areas you'd like to see us publish in, and any other words of wisdom you're willing to pass our way.

As an associate publisher for Sams, I welcome your comments. You can fax, e-mail, or write me directly to let me know what you did or didn't like about this book—as well as what we can do to make our books stronger.

Please note that I cannot help you with technical problems related to the topic of this book, and that due to the high volume of mail I receive, I might not be able to reply to every message.

When you write, please be sure to include this book's title and author as well as your name and phone or fax number. I will carefully review your comments and share them with the authors and editors who worked on the book.

Fax: 317-581-4770

E-mail: feedback@samspublishing.com

Mail: Michael Stephens
          Associate Publisher
          Sams Publishing
          201 West 103rd Street
          Indianapolis, IN 46290 USA

Introduction

Our goal in writing this book was to cover what Java programmers really do for a living. It is extremely rare that a company gives a programmer a project that involves only the Java language itself. Modern projects involve extensions to the core language such as JDBC, RMI, J2EE, JavaBeans, and serial port communications. Programmers commonly need different extensions for different projects.

We began by browsing the shelves of the mega-bookstores to determine what was missing from the total knowledge base. We found tons of beginning books, and lots of single-topic advanced books. What was missing was the intermediate range of books—those that explain advanced topics in plain language. This is what we set out to provide. There are several advantages to this approach:

- The book is written in plain language by programmers. The only assumption that we make about you is that you know Java well. For example, the chapter on Java Sound assumes that you know Java but it does not assume that you know anything about the Java Sound API. This makes it easy to get started.

- Each chapter contains code that you can use. All the code in this book is designed to be copied into your projects. There are no "code snippets" that appear in explanations but never run. You can copy or type in the examples from this book, run them, and modify them to fit your specific requirements.

- Output is shown for every example. If the result of an example is difficult to show, we've added `println()` calls so that you can be sure that you've set it up successfully.

- You will save time. Pulling this book off your shelf is much faster than signing up for a course or even surfing the Internet for hours looking for material that is easy to follow.

- This book is much less expensive than a set of single-topic books. Books that cover only one of the subjects of this book normally cost just as much as this book. Gathering 20 or 30 of them would require quite a budget. After working through the examples in one of our chapters, you might want to purchase a single-topic book on that subject. You might, however, discover that you have learned enough to enable you to comprehend the material that you can find on the Internet.

- The book covers 28 different topics in 28 chapters. This means that you can find information on a broad range of Java topics in a single book.

- The book is written as a reference. Every chapter can be read independently from the others. We tried to use similar examples from chapter to chapter, but you will be able to follow the reasoning in each chapter, even if it is the first one that you have read.

Intended Audience

This book is written for the intermediate Java developer. It is assumed that you know the basics of the Java language well and that you are looking for knowledge that goes beyond the syntax. We don't explain code features that don't pertain to the subject of a chapter.

A programmer with five or more years of experience, including at least two years of working with Java, should have no problem following the explanations and examples in this book. Those with less experience may benefit from reading this book, but they should be prepared to consult an introductory text when they have trouble following the examples.

Approach

The scope of this book is broad. A quick perusal of the table of contents will tell you that this book covers a lot of subject matter. The number of pages available for each topic is somewhat limited. As a result, each chapter's objective is to provide the information to jump-start you in each topic.

We chose the subject matter by answering the question, "What does a Java programmer need to know to take his career to the next level?" If you know Java, you will be able to understand all the examples in this book. If you work your way through them, modifying them here and there to see what happens, you will find that you can provide informed opinions about the topics that the book covers in meetings and conversations. Every chapter in this book provides a few pages of introduction and background followed by several examples of the technology in use, complete with a description of the output.

There is no substitute for working through examples. Before going into a meeting where suggestions will be made, grab this book and spend two hours working a few examples. When you propose a technical approach with which you have real, if limited, experience, your suggestions will be better received. If a picture is worth a thousand words, an example is worth ten thousand.

Most programmers keep their favorite introduction to Java book and an advanced Java programming book with them when they move from one job to another. It is our hope that this will be the third book that you keep on your shelf.

Organization of This Book

This book is organized into six parts:

- Part I—Programming with Distributed Objects
- Part II—Enterprise Java
- Part III—Java Integration Technologies
- Part IV—Java Media Technology
- Part V—Best Practices for Designing Java Classes
- Part VI—Appendixes

The contents of each part play a key role in making you a better and more respected programmer.

Part I—Programming with Distributed Objects

Many of our projects will require you to cross the boundaries between computers. The chapters in this section show you how to do so.

Chapter 1, "Programming Interconnected Computers," deals with the topic of connecting two computers together. It provides an overview of the technologies that can be used to accomplish this, along with some historical information to help you understand their origins. It also provides an explanation of how Transmission Control Protocol/Internet Protocol (TCP/IP) works. This is important because all the other technologies are built on top of TCP/IP.

Chapter 2, "Creating Applications with Remote Method Invocation (RMI)," teaches you how to use RMI. This is important because many distributed technologies are built on top of RMI.

Chapter 3, "Creating Applications with Java API for XML Parsing (JAXP)," provides an understanding of how Java processes XML. Many of the techniques described in this book can pass XML files as their data.

Chapter 4, "Application Development with JSP and Servlets," shows how to create systems using JavaServer Pages and servlets. For many applications, servlets provide a straightforward and effective approach.

Part II—Enterprise Java

If you need scalability, you need Enterprise Java. The chapters in this section show you the leading technologies in the J2EE suite and helps you decide which one of them fits your need best.

Chapter 5, "Enterprise JavaBeans (EJB)," talks about today's hottest technology, EJB. It provides examples that you can run to get you going, and covers both session and entity beans.

Chapter 6, "Message-Driven Beans (MDB)," covers a brand new type of EJB, the message-driven bean. This bean scales like an EJB, but communicates like a message queue.

Chapter 7, "Java Message Service (JMS)," covers a mature technology that provides a nice alternative for certain types of Enterprise systems. Many JMS applications have been written to communicate across heterogeneous programming environments.

Chapter 8, "Approaches for Choosing the Right Technology," compares available technologies and guides you toward making intelligent choices. It contains criteria for evaluating whether or not a technology fits your needs.

Part III—Java Integration Technologies

Java is a great gluing technology. The chapters in this section teach you about the different types of "glue" available to you as a programmer.

Chapter 9, "Web Services," provides an explanation of how you can use this new technology to create applications that communicate by way of XML files.

Chapter 10, "JDBC and Databases," teaches you how to interface with databases from Java programs. It also shows how to perform batch updates.

Chapter 11, "Java Naming and Directory Interface (JNDI)," explains one of the mysteries of Java programming. It pulls back the curtain and shows you how naming services really work.

Chapter 12, "Processing Speech with Java," provides examples of how you can use speech synthesis and recognition in your applications. This capability is becoming more important as portable devices become "hands-free."

Chapter 13, "JavaMail," teaches you how to use the JavaMail protocols to create asynchronous applications that don't have to be e-mail oriented.

Chapter 14, "Serial Port Communications," shows you how to use Java to communicate with devices using the serial port on your computer and the Java Communications Standard Extension.

Part IV—Java Media Technology

Java is a great platform for dealing with media. The chapters in this section introduce you to the stars of the Java Media packages.

Chapter 15, "Drawing with Java 2D," introduces you to this very important API and provides you with working examples of it in action. These examples show how to accomplish 2D animation also.

Chapter 16, "Java 3D Graphics," teaches you how to create objects in a 3D universe. It also shows you how to animate and light them.

Chapter 17, "The Java Media Framework (JMF) and the Java Advanced Imaging (JAI) API," shows you how to play motion video using Java. It also shows you how to use Java code to do the type of image manipulation that you find in editing tools.

Chapter 18, "Processing Sound with Java," shows you how to capture and play high quality sound from within your Java program. This sound can be in the form of either samples or musical instrument digital interface (MIDI) files.

Part V—Best Practices for Designing Java Classes

Senior developers are expected to understand certain concepts. The chapters in this section concentrate on those topics that we feel are not widely understood in the programming community.

Chapter 19, "JavaBeans and the Java Event Model," teaches you how to create JavaBeans. It also provides a detailed explanation of how events are communicated between classes in Java.

Chapter 20, "Architectural Models and Frameworks," explains how to create a framework for your application. It also discusses some commercial frameworks and what makes them successful.

Chapter 21, "Design Patterns in Java," teaches you how to improve your systems and make them more maintainable using design patterns. An understanding of these patterns is assumed in many higher-level design discussions.

Chapter 22, "Exceptions and Debugging," shows you how to use a comprehensive approach to handling exceptions. It provides a description of common pitfalls.

Chapter 23, "Java Security," shows you how to protect the information in your systems from theft and destruction.

Chapter 24, " Multithreading Applications in Java," shows you how to create applications that run in parallel. Much of the multimedia programming in Java uses threads extensively.

Chapter 25, "Java Internationalization," shows you how to create applications that can support multiple natural languages. It provides guidance on varying graphics also.

Chapter 26, "Persistence and Cloning," provides a run-through of the issues associated with serialization. This is key because most enterprise technologies rely on serialized objects.

Chapter 27, "Polymorphism and Inheritance," provides an explanation complete with examples of how Java inheritance works. This is critical to understanding the standard extensions.

Chapter 28, "Code Organization and Deployment," provides a convenient place for you to look up the syntax of JAR files, packages, and Javadocs.

Part VI—Appendixes

The appendixes help you work through this book. Appendix A contains code that is used in several of the chapters in the book. Appendix B explains how to obtain a copy of WebLogic Server, the J2EE-based application server used in many of the book's chapters.

Conventions Used in This Book

The following typographic conventions are used in this book:

- Code lines, commands, statements, variables, and any text that you type onscreen appear in a computer typeface. When lines of input and output are shown, **bold computer** typeface is often used to show the user's input.
- *Italics* highlight technical terms when they first appear in the text and are being defined.
- A special icon (➡) is used for lines of code that are too long for to fit on one line in the book. If you see ➡ before a line of code, remember that you should interpret that "line" as part of the line immediately preceding it.

The book also makes use of Notes, Cautions, and Tips. These special elements appear separately from the text and provide additional information about relevant topics.

> **Note**
>
> Notes are used to indicate that you might need additional information to understand the concept being discussed in the text. Because of its importance, it is given special treatment.

> **Caution**
>
> Cautions are used to make you aware of a potential pitfall associated with the subject being explained.

> **Tip**
>
> Tips are used to give you extra information that is not generally available. Often this information is something that the authors have learned from experience.

The Web Site

The chapter-by-chapter code files that are described in this book are available on the Sams Publishing Web site at http://www.samspublishing.com/. Enter this book's ISBN (067232394x) without the hyphens in the Search box and click Search. When the book's title is displayed, click it to go to a page where you can download all the code.

Contact Us

As authors, we welcome feedback from our readers. If you have praise, criticism, corrections, additional wisdom, or suggestions for future books, feel free to contact us. Steve Potts can be reached at stevepotts@mindspring.com. Alex Pestrikov can be reached at pestrikov@yahoo.com.

Programming with Distributed Objects

PART

I

IN THIS PART

Programming Interconnected Computers

CHAPTER 1

The desire to interconnect computers began the minute that the second computer was created. It seems as if the data that we need is always on another computer running a different operating system. In this chapter, you will learn about the technologies that enable us to connect computers to each other.

First, we will briefly cover the history of computer connectivity. Next, we will look at a few simple examples of TCP/IP, the technology that serves as the foundation for all the others. Understanding these examples will prove useful as you read chapters about technologies built on top of TCP/IP such as RMI, EJB, JNDI, and JMS.

Following that, we will take a high-level look at the technology, packages, and techniques that programmers currently use to connect computers and exchange information. Chapter 8, "Approaches for Choosing the Right Technology," compares technologies to determine which are best suited for specific requirements. The current chapter serves as a preview of the technologies that will be covered in detail in later chapters.

Finally, we will take a look at the design of a simple cruise ticketing system. This system is used as an example in later chapters. Later chapters will lay out the details of the application as it is built, but an overview of the system is provided here.

A Brief History of Connectivity

Back in the early days of computing, computers filled huge rooms and yet were strictly one-application-at-a-time systems; there was only one user running one program at any one time. All data used to solve the problem had to exist on the same machine. As computers became more powerful, it became possible to perform multiple tasks on a computer by swapping tasks very quickly. This allowed multiple applications to be run at virtually the same time.

Soon thereafter, engineers devised a way to allow multiple people to use the computer at the same time to run their own individual tasks, and the mainframe was born. The mainframe was the actual brain of the system, and each user used a terminal (usually a dumb CRT screen and keyboard or a Teletype) connected via a serial modem to the mainframe. The mainframe did all processing and controlled everything. Without the mainframe, the client terminals had no capabilities at all.

The mainframe worked well because all the data was in one place. If report processing was needed, the data was always on the same computer as the report-writing program. Mainframes had their drawbacks, however. It was expensive to purchase and operate these large computers. They required special cooling systems and a small army of technicians to monitor and program them. In addition, they didn't support remote users very well at all. If you were located in Atlanta and your mainframe computer was in St. Louis, a very expensive set of lines had to be leased and installed to provide connectivity.

Another problem was interoperability. Communication between two computers that were not from the same vendor was problematic. For the most part, mainframe vendors did not see any advantage in providing easy connectivity to their competitors' systems. Despite their shortcomings, mainframe computers did provide a platform for many sophisticated systems, some of which are still in production today.

One of the problems that still existed, though, was that every piece of relevant data had to exist on a single mainframe. If you needed data from another machine, you typically had save it to some medium (such as tape, punch card, or paper tape) and physically move it to the machine you were using. You were basically working with a complete copy of the data and not the original, so updates to the original were not on the copy and vice versa. This caused a lot of headaches.

In the 1960s, the Advanced Research Projects Agency (ARPA) started a project whose purpose was to find a way to connect mainframes together so data could be shared. This led to the first true network (the ARPANET), which would eventually evolve into the Internet that we have today.

With the ARPANET, mainframes could finally share data without users having to move the physical data tapes/cards between machines. Applications such as e-mail were created, the first databases were built, and files on one mainframe could be accessed by users on another mainframe.

Building on the networking technology that emerged from this work, a client/server approach became popular. Small companies needed a solution that was less expensive to acquire and run than a mainframe. Smaller computers from companies such as Digital Equipment, Sun Microsystems, and Hewlett-Packard became popular with smaller firms and individual departments within companies that needed more control over their computing resources.

These vendors were very advanced technically and they aggressively fought for market share. They provided connectivity that was far superior to that of the mainframe. Vendors such as Ingres and Oracle produced database management systems that allowed users to access their data from different computers. The database was placed on a server and the program that contained the business logic was placed on a client. This is the origin of the term *client/server*.

This approach solved some of the problems of the mainframe. The servers were less expensive to purchase, and they could be connected to even less expensive clients such as

X Window terminals or personal computers. The primary drawback of client/server systems was the difficulty of maintaining the code on the clients. In this model, if there are 100 clients accessing data on the same server, 100 installations have to be performed for every maintenance release of the client software. Nevertheless, many successful systems were written and deployed using this model.

To solve the problems caused by the client/server approach, engineers have devised a three-tiered approach in which the presentation is handled on the client and data is handled on the server. This approach creates another server (or tier) that runs programs containing business logic only. The presentation layer on the client is simplified, so it does not need much maintenance. In fact, many clients are small enough to download every time that they are run.

The n-tier model has become the favored approach because it allows the client end to handle issues such as data capture, validation, and presentation, while at the same time keeping the majority of the business processes and data inside a server where they can be better controlled, maintained, and secured. It's called the n-tier model because there can be any number of layers on the server side (the *n* indicates an indefinite number).

For instance, many corporate systems utilize an applet or HTML page running on a Web browser as the client, and a two-tiered server consisting of a Web server and a dedicated database server. This separation allows each machine to focus on a specific part of the system and do what it does best. Presently, we are using an n-tier thin-client model in designing our systems. In this model, the business logic and the database normally reside on servers. The client tends to be presentation oriented and contains very little logic except error checking. The technologies covered in this book use this model, generally speaking.

TCP/IP and Java

All the technologies that we describe in this chapter run on top of TCP/IP. Because of this, it is critical that you have an understanding of what TCP/IP is and how it works. You may have a set of requirements that begs for a TCP/IP socketed solution. In that case, this material is critical. Even if you don't actually program at this level, you will be better educated if you understand how every layer that you are using works. The reasoning here is the same as the reasoning behind learning something about cars when you begin to drive one. It is possible to go through life driving cars without a clue as to how they work. Those who do so are helpless in a breakdown. They allow simple problems to put them on foot. When major problems occur, they are frequently charged more for repairs because they don't know how to evaluate the story that a mechanic is giving them.

In programming, we see error messages constantly. It helps us tremendously if we have some idea of what error messages mean, because they give us clues as to where we went wrong.

How TCP/IP Works

TCP/IP is not actually a protocol, but rather a suite consisting of dozens of protocols that work together to effect data transfer from one computer to another. It is named for two of the most important protocols in the suite—Transmission Control Protocol and Internet Protocol. TCP/IP is divided into four layers. These layers can be visualized as APIs within the protocol suite. By establishing these APIs instead of coding one monolithic program to do everything, the designers of the suite preserved the possibility of replacing each layer without affecting the layers above and below it. Figure 1.1 shows the layers of the Internet Protocol model on which TCP/IP is based.

FIGURE 1.1
The Internet Protocol model.

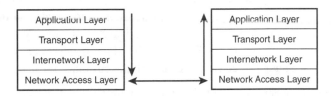

The stack of layers on one side represents one application on one computer. The other stack represents another layer on another machine. Conceptually, each of the layers talks to its counterpart on the other machine. This means that the programmer of the application layer programs based on the requirements and expectations of the application layer on the other machine. The transport layer is programmed to talk to the transport layer on the other machine. In addition, this layer is programmed to fulfill calls made by the application layer above it and to make requests of the internetwork layer below it. Each layer can be thought of as a service provider for the layers above and a customer of the layers beneath.

The layers in this model are listed and described here:

- Application layer—This layer can be as simple as a chat program or as complex as an EJB application.

- Transport layer—This layer is responsible for sending a set of data from one machine to another with data integrity and high reliability.
- Internetwork layer—This layer makes calls to the network access layer to pass what are called datagrams from one computer to another until they reach the final destination.
- Network access layer—This is the bottom layer in the model. This layer exchanges frames of data with other computers or routing devices on the same network.

Each of the layers below the application layer sends metadata to its counterpart on the other computer by encapsulating the message with a header and trailer. The contents of the headers and trailers in each level are different from those in the other layers, but they serve a similar purpose.

The process of sending a message over the Internet can be compared to sending an electric generator from Tulsa, Oklahoma to Shanghai, China. At the application level, the XYX Turbine Company creates a working electric generator at its factory in Tulsa and tests it. They sell this generator along with installation services to Shanghi Electric. The boss at XYX tells the operations manager to ship the generator to Shanghai. Because of the complexity and size of this generator, XYX will have to install it at the customer site and test it before turning it over to the customer. The XYX Company represents the application layer on the left side of Figure 1.1. The boss is interested in getting the generator installed at Shanghi Electric so he can bill the customer for it.

The operations manager takes the generator apart and packages it into numbered containers. His department represents the transport layer on the left side of Figure 1.1. The operations manager in Tulsa is responsible for making sure that every piece of the generator arrives in Shanghai, and his counterpart in Shanghai is responsible for putting it back together correctly. This is not a simple task because the 1,500 parts of the generator have a combined weight of about 100,000 pounds.

XYX does not have any trucks of its own, so it will contract with another company to take the pieces. The operations department calls the ACE Specialty Shipping Company and hands them all the containers. ACE is a global company with facilities in all of the world's important transportation hub cities.

ACE represents the internetwork layer on both sides of Figure 1.1. ACE's employees in the U.S. take all the containers from XYX and repackage them in ACE containers. They address them to be sent to Shanghai. ACE is responsible for figuring out how to get each package from one point to the next at every step along the path. This is complicated by the fact that some of the light parts can be sent by air, while heavy parts must be sent by ship. ACE subdivides the parts into air shipments and ocean surface shipments. It then hands each part to a North American seaport or airport for transportation.

The North American seaport and airport represent the network access layer on the left side of Figure 1.1. Seaports interact with a network of ships. The crews of these ships know nothing about the packages they carry except for the size and weight. The seaport personnel simply mark the containers that they receive with their own labels and move them to the next port. Airport personnel follow the same procedure, but they move the packages from one air terminal to the next.

Once all of the packages have arrived in Asia, the process reverses. The seaport and airport personnel take the packages off the ship or plane, remove their markings, and hand them to the ACE shipping agent. The Asian seaport and airport represent the network access layer on the right side of Figure 1.1.

ACE's employees in Asia represent the right side internetwork layer. They gather all the packages, place them into their trucks, and transport them to Shanghai. They don't worry about whether any of them got lost in the ocean, they just move them as quickly as possible. Other shippers offered to take responsibility for lost packages, but they were so expensive that XYX chose to use the less reliable shipper and handle reorders themselves. When the parts get to Shanghai, the ACE employees remove them from the ACE containers and hand them to the XYX Company's subsidiary in China.

The XYX operations department in China fills the role of the transport layer on the right side of Figure 1.1. When the parts arrive at Shanghai, the XYX shipping department takes inventory of them. If some parts are missing, a member of the operations department sends an e-mail to reorder the missing parts. Eventually, when all parts are received, the operations department puts them together and notifies the XYX boss in Shanghai that the generator has arrived and is ready to use.

The Shanghai Electric boss represents the application layer on the right side of the diagram. He accepts the generator as a whole and starts generating electricity with it.

Figure 1.2 shows this process graphically.

The movement of data through TCP/IP layers is much like the generator shipping analogy in that each layer plays a role that is distinct from those above and below it. In the following sections we will look at each of these layers in more detail.

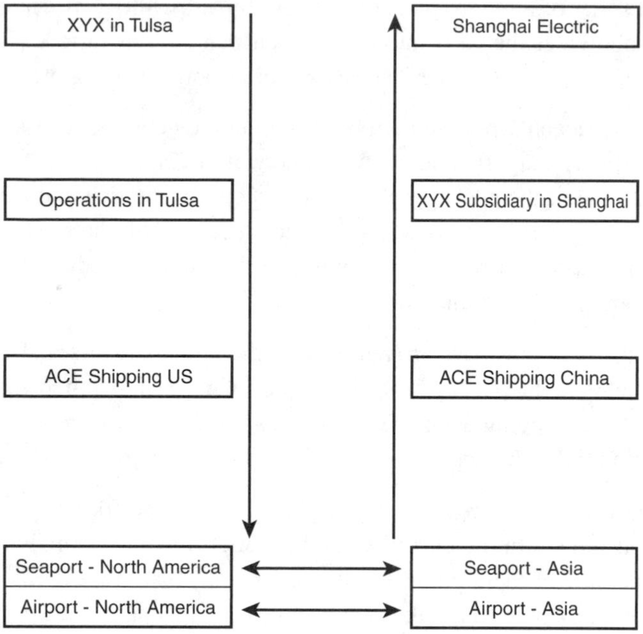

FIGURE 1.2

Sending a generator to Shanghai.

The Application Layer

The topmost layer in the model is the application layer. Encryption, compression, decryption, and decompression normally reside at this layer. This layer is often called the TCP/IP client or TCP/IP server. A TCP/IP server normally opens a socket and places a stream of data on it. A TCP/IP client listens on a socket and receives a stream from it.

Modern systems often contain sublayers in the application layer. Figure 1.3 shows how this sublayering works for Enterprise JavaBeans.

EJB is built on top of RMI and uses the services provided by it. The EJB client thinks that it is talking to an EJB server directly, when in reality it is making RMI calls, which are making transport layer calls, and so on. The EJB container's goal is still accomplished, though, because this complexity is hidden from the client programmer. She can follow the rules of EJB development and everything works fine.

FIGURE 1.3
The EJB architecture.

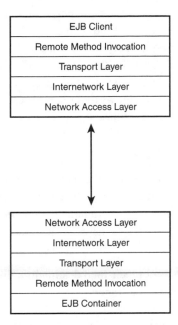

The Transport Layer

The transport layer is responsible for data integrity. It supports open and close commands and the concept of a connection. If one machine sends data to another machine and some of the data doesn't arrive intact, this layer of software is responsible for noticing that the data is missing and requesting that it be re-sent. Its counterpart on the sending side is responsible for performing the re-send. The transport layer receives data as a stream, and sends it out as packets by making calls to the internetwork layer. On the other side, its counterpart receives packets and reassembles them into a stream.

The Internetwork Layer

The internetwork layer is responsible for moving all the packets that it has been given to the correct destination. This layer lives on every computer in the network. It evaluates the IP address of the packet and determines whether it knows what computer to deliver the packet to. If it does not, it passes the datagram to another node according to an established hierarchy.

Datagrams are packets (strings of characters) that are composed of a header, the data, and a trailer. The header contains the IP address of the final destination, the source of the packet, and security information. The trailer usually contains a checksum that can be used to verify that the data has been sent correctly. The internetwork layer has no concept of a session or a connection. It sees data, packages it into a packet, sends it to the address in the header, and promptly forgets that it was ever sent. If a broken datagram arrives, it is discarded as defective. In this layer, throughput is the goal.

The Network Access Layer

At the bottom of the stack is the network access layer. This layer talks directly to the network cards via their drivers. It is responsible for transmitting frames of data from one computer to another computer over a connection. A frame may contain a whole datagram or just part of one. If a datagram is too large for the network, it is subdivided and sent in pieces.

If the computer that receives the frames is not their final destination, the internetwork layer will repeat the process by transmitting the frame of data to the next node on the path to its ultimate destination. This node uses the physical address of the ethernet card to transfer the data. This layer understands the physical characteristics of the network that it is using such as the packet structure, the maximum frame size, and the physical address scheme that is used.

Figure 1.4 shows this four-layer encapsulation and decapsulation strategy diagrammatically.

As you can see from the diagram, each layer adds its own header and trailer. Its peer layer on the other stack peels off the header and trailer added by that layer on the sending side. It then hands the slimmed down message to the layer above.

A simple example of a TCP/IP server is shown in Listing 1.1.

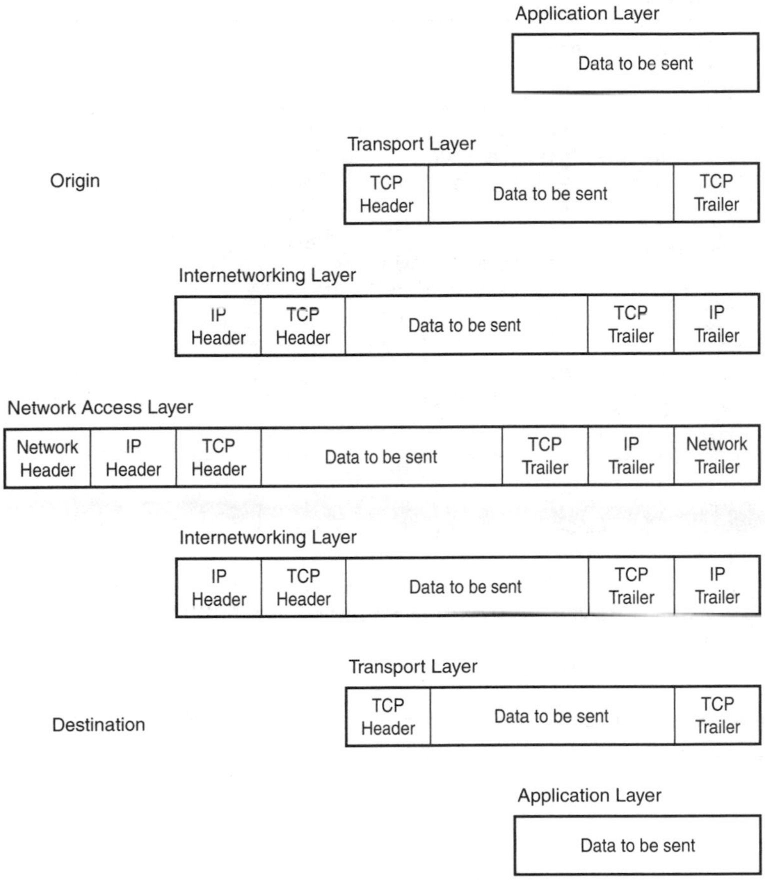

FIGURE **1.4**
*TCP/IP data
encapsulation and
decapsulation.*

Application Layer

Data to be sent

Transport Layer

Origin

TCP Header	Data to be sent	TCP Trailer

Internetworking Layer

IP Header	TCP Header	Data to be sent	TCP Trailer	IP Trailer

Network Access Layer

Network Header	IP Header	TCP Header	Data to be sent	TCP Trailer	IP Trailer	Network Trailer

Internetworking Layer

IP Header	TCP Header	Data to be sent	TCP Trailer	IP Trailer

Transport Layer

Destination

TCP Header	Data to be sent	TCP Trailer

Application Layer

Data to be sent

LISTING **1.1**   A Simple TCP/IP Server

```java
package unleashed.ch1;

import java.net.*;
import java.io.*;

public class TestSocketServer
{
    ServerSocket serverSocket;
    int portNumber = 9001;
    Socket socket;
    String str;
```

LISTING 1.1   continued

```
TestSocketServer()
{
    str = " <?xml version=\"1.0\" encoding=\"UTF-8\"?>";
    str += "<ticketRequest><customer custID=\"1001\">";
    str += "<lastName>Carter</lastName>";
    str += "<firstName>Joey</firstName>";
    str += "</customer>";
    str += "<cruise cruiseID=\"3005\">";
    str += "<destination>Alaska</destination>";
    str += "<port>Vancouver</port>";
    str += "<sailing>4/15/02</sailing>";
    str += "<numberOfTickets>4</numberOfTickets>";
    str += "</cruise>";
    str += "</ticketRequest>";

    // Create ServerSocket to listen for connections
    try
    {
        serverSocket = new ServerSocket(portNumber);

        // Wait for client to connect, then get Socket
        socket = serverSocket.accept();

        // Use ObjectOutputStream to send String to the client
        ObjectOutputStream oos =
        new ObjectOutputStream(socket.getOutputStream());

        oos.writeObject(str);

        oos.close();

        // Close Socket and go back to wait for next client
        socket.close();
    } catch (Exception e)
    {
        System.out.println("Exception " + e);
    }
}

public static void main(String args[])
{
    TestSocketServer tss = new TestSocketServer();
}
}
```

Considering the complexity of what happens in the layers of the TCP/IP protocol suite, the code to control it is amazingly simple. The first thing that we do is create a string that contains an XML document in text form. Next, we create a serverSocket object with a port number of 9001. (You, the programmer, choose this number.)

```
serverSocket = new ServerSocket(portNumber);
```

We then wait for a client program to try and connect to a server on port 9001:

```
// Wait for client to connnect, then get Socket
socket = serverSocket.accept();
```

As soon as a client connects to the server, we create a stream that can send the String object that contains the XML:

```
// Use ObjectOutputStream to send String to the client
ObjectOutputStream oos =
new ObjectOutputStream(socket.getOutputStream());
```

Armed with a stream that is connected to the socket, we write the XML string:

```
oos.writeObject(str);
```

Finally, we close the stream and the socket:

```
oos.close();

// Close Socket and go back to wait for next client
socket.close();
```

The other half of the program is the client. In TCP/IP parlance, a server is a program that sends data over a port and a client is one that receives it. It is easy to see that the same program could be both a client and a server.

Listing 1.2 shows a client that communicates with the server in Listing 1.1.

LISTING 1.2   A Simple TCP/IP Client

```
package unleashed.ch1;

import java.net.*;
import java.io.*;

public class TestSocketClient
{
    Socket socket;
    int portNumber = 9001;
    String str = "";

    public TestSocketClient()
    {
        try
        {
```

LISTING 1.2   continued

```
        socket = new Socket(InetAddress.getLocalHost(),
        portNumber);

        ObjectInputStream ois =
        new ObjectInputStream(socket.getInputStream());
        str = (String) ois.readObject();
        System.out.println(str);

    } catch (Exception e)
    {
        System.out.println("Exception " + e);
    }
}

public static void main(String args[])
{
    TestSocketClient tcp = new TestSocketClient();
}
}
```

The client is even simpler than the server. All that we have to do is create an object of the class `Socket` by passing in the IP address of the server and the port that the server is listening to. In this case, we are running both client and server on the same machine, so `LocalHost` is the server address:

```
        socket = new Socket(InetAddress.getLocalHost(),
            portNumber);
```

An input stream must be created to make the data accessible to this program:

```
        ObjectInputStream ois =
        new ObjectInputStream(socket.getInputStream());
```

We simply read the object, cast it to become a `String`, and print it out:

```
        str = (String) ois.readObject();
        System.out.println(str);
```

The result is a string that contains an XML document, as shown here:

```
<?xml version="1.0" encoding="UTF-8"?><ticketRequest>
<customer custID="1001"><lastName>Carter</lastName>
<firstName>Joey</firstName></customer><cruise cruiseID="3005">
<destination>Alaska</destination><port>Vancouver</port>
<sailing>4/15/02</sailing><numberOfTickets>4</numberOfTickets>
</cruise></ticketRequest>
```

Remember that the transport layer verifies that you receive the whole message, which makes it especially well suited for transferring XML.

Understanding Modern Interconnection Technologies

Currently, there are quite a few state-of-the-art technologies for interconnecting computers. Of course, the old ways will be around for years to come, but new systems are rarely created using them.

The important products and technologies that are currently used by the Java programming community are the subject of the rest of this chapter. Some of them are well established while others are still seeking broad acceptance. Taken as a whole, they represent the universe of choices available to you when designing an interconnected system. In the following sections, we will look at each technology at a high level and point you to the chapter that covers it in more detail. Keep in mind that many designs use more than one of these technologies.

All of these technologies share certain features. Each consists of a client, a server (or servers), and a mechanism for moving data from the client to the server or vice versa.

Java Database Connectivity (JDBC)

Java Database Connectivity (JDBC) offers one of the simplest ways of interconnecting two computers. JDBC was originally designed as an interface for executing SQL statements, not as a way to interconnect computers. Databases are frequently located on a server machine, not on the same computer as the application. This creates a need for JDBC to attack the data transportation problem as well as the database communication that it was intended for.

As a designer, you can take advantage of this functionality and create two or more applications that read and write to the same database. One of the applications can use JDBC to update a particular table or set of tables in a database located on a server. All other applications can use JDBC to access the data in these tables from other computers on the network.

The fact that this approach is not synchronous, and that it requires quite a bit of coordination between the programmers who are writing each of the applications, places limits on the type of system that you can design with JDBC. The amount of overhead associated with each transaction limits the throughput of the system as well. In certain cases, however, this might be your best choice. See Chapter 10, " JDBC and Databases," for a more detailed discussion of JDBC.

TCP/IP

Servlets, RMI, JDBC, EJB, MDB, and almost any other network-based technology that you can think of is really a TCP/IP application at its most basic level. This means that anything you can write using these other tools can be written using TCP/IP sockets. The java.net package makes this type of programming easy to write and debug. The fact that almost every modern computer can communicate using TCP/IP makes it a good candidate for interconnecting computers.

Application programming using sockets is not common, but software engineers use this package regularly when performance dwarfs all other requirements. This is often the case when creating products such as EJB containers and database management systems.

Quite often, application programmers find that some of the services provided by higher-level products such as RMI or EJBs provide cost savings compared to programming with TCP/IP directly. Some of these services are serializability, security, transaction support, and message queues. Understanding the TCP/IP layer is critical to diagnosing many errors that occur using higher-level products.

If a significant system that uses TCP/IP to interconnect computers is written in Java, all services needed beyond the guaranteed delivery of data must be written by hand. Even so, don't rule out this approach altogether, especially if what you are creating has performance problems or if it starts to resemble a software product. There is a tradeoff between coding raw sockets and using other technologies such as RMI or EJB. It's a matter of execution speed versus clarity and development time/cost.

Servlets

Servlets are Java programs that run on a Web server. They provide a way of using standard HTML Web pages to present and capture data. With servlets, the client is a Web browser. Data can be captured by the browser and sent to the server, where it can be manipulated by the servlet. This provides a way to easily deploy an application, because it really exists only on the Web server, not on each client machine. Servlets provide another fairly simple design for connecting two or more computers together. Using the Hypertext Transfer Protocol (HTTP), you can create a set of servlets that contain the business logic for the system that you are creating. These servlets may make calls to other popular technologies such as JDBC or the Java Message Service (JMS), thereby extending their reach even further.

Servlets can be scaled readily to respond to changing traffic patterns. Programmers can use JavaServer Pages (JSP) or HTML forms to gather data from clients and send it to servlets.

The fact that the clients run in a browser places some limits on this approach. Browsers tend to support fairly old versions of Java and the security model that they use limits the amount of work that they can do on the client side. In addition, maintaining a program's state is difficult (but not impossible) to achieve in a complex application. There are many systems in production today that use this approach. See Chapter 4, "Application Development with JSP and Servlets," for an in-depth look at programming servlets.

Remote Method Invocation (RMI)

Remote Method Invocation is a fundamental approach to exchanging serializable objects between programs written in Java. Remote Method Invocation over Internet Inter-Orb Protocol (RMI/IIOP) opens this technology to exchange objects with CORBA-based applications.

RMI has the advantage of being simple for an experienced Java programmer to use. In addition, it is now a part of the core Java download and therefore is supported on every platform that supports Java.

In some ways, the decision to write a system with RMI resembles the decision to write a system using TCP/IP and sockets. RMI offers more control over performance-related features than Enterprise JavaBeans or message-driven beans do. However, the limited nature of the services provided by RMI makes it an inferior choice for many systems. The cost of writing and debugging custom software makes most programmers want to use the highest-level software available.

A good understanding of RMI is critical to really getting the most out of Java 2 Enterprise Edition. When errors occur in programs using EJBs, they often contain RMI-level messages. The ability to interpret these messages is a valuable skill. You can quickly and efficiently write smaller systems using RMI if few or no additional services are needed. Chapter 2, "Creating Applications with Remote Method Invocation (RMI)," provides a detailed look at RMI programming.

Java Naming and Directory Interface (JNDI)

JNDI may seem like an odd topic to include in a list of technologies for interconnecting computers, but it fits. JNDI servers normally reside on a server. They are accessed by programs running on clients using a TCP/IP-based protocol. They accept serializable objects and throw exceptions when distributed transactions fail.

Normally, the JNDI server is used to provide handles to objects such as JMS queues or EJB containers. If you start putting application objects on the company's main name server, your manager will probably get a phone call from his boss about it. However, there is nothing to stop you from creating your own JNDI server that is separate from the name-lookup server and using it to exchange objects between applications running on different computers. Chapter 11, "Java Naming and Directory Interface (JNDI)," provides details on how to program using JNDI.

JavaMail

JavaMail is another topic that may seem out of place in a discussion of computer interconnection. You receive e-mails generated by programs frequently. The "out of the office" e-mail is a common one. Most of the spam that you receive was generated by a program instead of a person. You may have written systems that provide automatic notification of job completion or system failure via e-mail.

JavaMail systems contain a client that communicates with a server by sending it an e-mail. The server can be programmed to retrieve the e-mail, parse it, and perform some work. It can even send an e-mail back to the client telling it whether the transaction was successful.

This design is natural for systems that contain human and machine components. You could design a system in which messages that contain a certain phrase such as "unsubscribe" would be handled by a program. Other messages such as "help me please" would be passed on to the support staff mailbox. Chapter 13, "JavaMail," provides a detailed explanation of how to build such a system along with an example that implements it.

Java Message Service (JMS)

Messaging has a long and distinguished history of providing interconnection between computers. In the past, considerable effort was required to program these systems if the two computers being connected ran on different operating systems. Finding a person who could (and would) program in COBOL on a VAX as well as in C++ on a Unix platform was difficult. This necessitated the formation of very heterogeneous and difficult-to-manage teams of programmers.

JMS is a Java API that interacts with all the popular messaging products. A single Java programmer can write the code on both sides of the application regardless of the platform. Most programmers are particularly fluent in one operating system, but, with a little support, can learn enough to compile and run a Java program on another system.

Message queues provide persistent storage for messages. In addition, they provide guaranteed delivery and notification of delivery. These services allow part of a system to function when another part is down, making this a good design for companies that require high availability systems. Chapter 7, "Java Message Service (JMS)," examines this approach in detail and provides working examples of JMS-based Java programs.

Enterprise JavaBeans (EJB)

The most popular technology among programmers for interconnecting computer systems is Enterprise JavaBeans. EJBs are Java classes that contain business logic. These classes reside on a server in a special environment called a container. They can be accessed remotely as though they reside on the client, which makes them a very powerful abstraction mechanism. An application server's container notices their presence and loads a number of them into memory. Applications make calls to these classes via the container that is hosting them. This container provides many services such as connection pooling, security, transaction support, and persistence. A particular EJB may use one or all of these services depending on its function.

The primary use of EJBs is in the deployment of applications that must be able to scale rapidly. These systems come with a price tag that is higher than the other technologies on this list, but they save a lot of programmer hours that would otherwise be spent writing and debugging these services.

Programmers who have experience programming and administrating these containers are currently in high demand. Chapter 5, "Enterprise JavaBeans (EJB)," covers the creation and deployment of EJBs.

Message-Driven Beans (MDB)

One of the most exciting new technologies is the message-driven bean. MDBs are message-handling versions of EJBs. They are deployed in much the same way as ordinary EJBs, but they respond to messages sent to queues rather than to calls from a client program.

They have the same scalability, security, and transaction models as ordinary EJBs. They can serve as both message consumers and message creators, but they use ordinary message queue calls to accomplish this.

MDBs support both Topics and Queues. Chapter 6, "Message-Driven Beans (MDB)," provides instructions on how to create and deploy these new beans.

XML

The Extensible Markup Language (XML) has taken the Java world by storm. Even though this technology cannot be used to interconnect computers without some sort of transport, it is covered in this book. So many of the technologies discussed are capable of passing XML documents as their "cargo" that a discussion of Java's facilities for parsing and writing XML is essential.

JAXP is the Java API for XML Parsing. It provides classes that automate the parsing of XML documents. JAXP offers two approaches. The Simple API for XML (SAX) approach parses the XML sequentially as it is read. The other approach, which involves the Document Object Model (DOM), creates a treelike structure in memory and provides programmers with methods to traverse the tree.

XML can also be written using Java classes. Chapter 3, "Creating Applications with Java API for XML Parsing (JAXP)," provides examples of all these approaches.

Web Services

A Web service is an integration gateway that connects your application to the Internet or provides a window from the Internet into your application.

Web services follow a client/server model: A client sends a request to a server and the server returns a response to the client. In this model, the role of the server is played by a Web service.

Web services consist of three technologies: Simple Object Access Protocol (SOAP); Web Services Description Language (WSDL); and Universal Description, Discovery, and Integration (UDDI). The three technologies complement each other. UDDI is used to find a Web service, WSDL describes how to communicate with the Web service, and SOAP transfers data between the client and the Web service.

Chapter 9, "Web Services," covers this important topic and provides examples of how to get Web services to work in your programs.

The Design of the Cruise Ticket Application

In order to make this book easier to use, we decided to create a standard example and use it in several chapters. The goal of this is to reduce the amount of time you have to spend learning new example applications.

This does not mean that the chapters depend on each other. You should be able to start with any chapter in the book and follow its examples with no prerequisite. After you have worked through one chapter's examples, you should find the other chapters' examples easier.

The example application is a cruise ticket system. This application is a simplified version of a system that a travel agent would use to book a cruise.

The user interface is a Swing application called CruiseList. It reads the database, populates pick lists, and displays the result. The details change with every chapter. For example, in one chapter, CruiseList is an RMI client and in another it is a message producer and consumer.

The back end of the application is the TicketAgent. The TicketAgent is responsible for creating the ticket in the database and notifying the client that the ticket was successfully booked.

TicketAgent makes calls to a routine that verifies credit card numbers. If this method approves a credit card, a ticket is issued. If not, a message is created that tells the GUI that the request was denied.

Some of the chapters modify this design. Chapter 5, for example, moves the processing of a payment to a payment agent. You will see other variations, but the basic application remains unchanged.

> **Note**
>
> This book uses two different DBMSs, both via JDBC: MS Access (because it is so common) and Cloudscape (because it ships with the downloadable version of WebLogic Server). Prior to running many of the examples, you will be instructed to run either WlJDBC2.java or AccessJDBC2.java. All that these applications do is create tables and populate them so that the examples will have data to work with.
>
> Full listings of both of these applications are found in Appendix A, "Source Code Listings for Utility Programs Used in This Book." They are included with the source code files for each chapter where they are needed.
>
> Another Java class, TicketRequest2.java, is also found in Appendix A. This is a class that contains information about a request for a ticket. It also appears in the source file for each chapter that needs it, but does not appear by itself in the chapters.
>
> Many of the chapters use WebLogic Server. Appendix B, "Downloading and Installing WebLogic Server," provides instructions on how to download and install this product.

Summary

In this chapter, we covered the subject of interconnecting two or more computers and running applications that span them. We looked at the various Java technical solutions for interconnecting that are currently popular in the Java world.

You learned about the internal workings of the TCP/IP protocol suite, and the model on which it is based. We discussed in some detail the layers and their functions.

We worked through an example that transferred an XML document from one JVM to another using TCP/IP. Armed with the understanding you've gained from this chapter, you are in a good position to comprehend the internal workings of technologies that sit atop TCP/IP such as Remote Method Invocation (RMI) and Enterprise JavaBeans (EJB).

We gave a brief introduction to the technologies that are explained in the later chapters of this book along with a little background on each of them.

Finally, we introduced the cruise ticket system example that appears in several chapters in this book. This same example is implemented over and over again, each time using different technology.

Creating Applications with Remote Method Invocation (RMI)

CHAPTER 2

In the age of wooden ships, a captain could command everyone in his crew and execute a battle with great efficiency. The admiral, however, couldn't coordinate the actions of his fleet in the same fashion. Because of the distance between him and the captains of his ships, he could not shout orders. He had to communicate using flags. Needless to say, the baud rate for flags being waved by a seaman is slow, and if the flags had to be run up a brace on the mast, it was even slower.

Imagine what the effect might have been on the result of a sea battle if the admiral had possessed a real-time, high-bandwidth communications channel to all his subordinates.

Early computers were much like lone ships in an ocean. We learned quickly how to make that standalone computer race along, impressing the world with the programs that we could write. The minute we needed to jump to another computer, though, we were crawling.

None of us really wanted to connect computers together. We had to do it because the data in our enterprise was there. Our accounting department would purchase the latest and greatest Unisys computer and spend a few million dollars to put a lot of data on it. The engineering department would purchase a DEC/VAX and put all the designs on it. Manufacturing would purchase an HP and put the bill of material and the shop instructions on it. The president would purchase a PC and tell us to give him a view of all three departments' data on his desktop.

No sooner had we found ways to do this, than the departments developed business requirements for systems that required running a program on a different computer from the one that you were running on. This meant that we had to be able to receive a success or failure acknowledgement back from this computer. After we figured out how to do this, we were told to design systems that required entire objects to be moved from one platform to another.

The purpose of this chapter is to help you learn how to write applications that take advantage of RMI. We will start by looking at using RMI in a simple application. Next, we will create a real, if simple, database application. Finally, we will create a full-blown application that combines a user interface and RMI with database access.

Understanding RMI

Java has always been a network-oriented language. RMI has been present from the first release as a separate download. By JDK version 1.3, it had become a part of the core product.

The development goals for RMI were simple. It had to be easy to use, and it had to have that Java feel we all know and love. In other words, RMI had to be a real Java solution to the problem of how to call methods on another machine.

RMI is clearly of the *Remote Procedure Call (RPC)* lineage, but it is more advanced than RPC in that it can pass serialized methods back and forth. In addition, RMI is part of the Java Development Kit, not a feature of the operating system. This makes RMI much more accessible to programmers, and it maintains its platform independence.

RMI runs on top of the *Java Remote Method Protocol (JRMP)*. This Java-specific protocol handles issues such as finding the server, starting servers on remote boxes, and finding class files.

JRMP runs on top of a Transport layer that, in the past, was always *Transmission Control Protocol (TCP)*.

The essential operation of RMI is fairly simple. A server interface is created and a proxy, or stub, is generated from it. This stub is copied to every client computer that wants to communicate to the server. Client programs are written, which make calls to this stub. The stub is sophisticated enough to find the correct server on the correct computer and to pass it the serialized parameters. It then provides a return value to the client program.

This process is facilitated by the use of a naming service. A naming service returns a connection to the remote server. The RMIRegistry is a simple naming service that ships with the JDK, but other naming services such as JNDI can also be used.

RMI Features

RMI contains a surprisingly sophisticated set of features. Among the most important are these:

- RMI can pass serializable objects in both directions.
- It can dynamically load class files using the CodeBase. This is important because the process of unmarshaling an object requires the presence of the class file for that object type.
- Servers can be activated by request from the client. A non-running server can also be started remotely.
- Distributed garbage collection is supported. The client can tell the server when it has received an object successfully so that the server can garbage-collect it.
- RMI can operate through a firewall using HTTP.
- Socket protocols other than TCP can be used.

These features make RMI a practical solution for application programmers, as well as for tool developers.

Comparing RMI with CORBA

To the casual observer, RMI and CORBA look like directly competing technologies. If you dig below the surface, however, you will see that they fill two different niches. Table 2.1 shows a side-by-side comparison of the two.

TABLE 2.1 Comparing RMI and CORBA

RMI	*CORBA*
Normally free	Normally not free
Simple to implement	Not that simple
Passes objects	Can't pass objects
Lighter weight	Heavier weight
Java-centric	Not language-centric
Not governed by a standards body	Governed by a standards body

Typically, a CORBA product is normally purchased, although open source implementations are available. Many developers complain that implementing CORBA in their applications is difficult. RMI is straightforward for Java developers. Because of its language dependence on Java, RMI can be implemented in a more streamlined fashion.

Advantages to CORBA exist, however. CORBA is a widely accepted standard with a large installed base. If your project must support multiple programming languages, CORBA must be used. There is no support for RMI in C++, Visual Basic, C, and so on.

RMI Internals

Many subjects are easier to work with if we remove the cover and look inside the proverbial black box. Figure 2.1 shows a diagram that represents how RMI invokes methods remotely and sends objects as parameters to them.

Let's examine this document from the bottom up. At the bottom layer, RMI always runs the IP. At the next level, the diagram is the Transport Layer. This layer used to be TCP at all times, but now RMI has provided classes and interfaces that allow you to specify a custom transport protocol (custom socket). TCP is used as the Transport protocol for all examples in this chapter.

Remote Method Invocation Architecture

FIGURE **2.1**
*RMI is built on
top of the Internet
Protocol.*

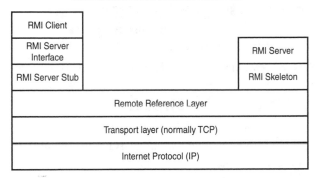

2

CREATING
APPLICATIONS
WITH RMI

The Transport Layer is responsible for managing the socket connection between the two computers involved in this RMI session. It is also responsible for ensuring that all packets arrive. This requires that it send retransmission requests for any packets that don't arrive (often because of network collisions or noise on the line).

The next level is called the Remote Reference Layer. This layer is responsible for finding the server, activating it (if needed), and initializing an RMI connection with it. RMI now supports two Remote Reference Layer implementations. One of them is the *Java Remote Method Protocol (JRMP)*. This is the original—and was for many years the only—protocol supported. The next layer on the client side is the RMI Server Stub. This stub is generated from the interface definition of the RMI server. It contains the magic that allows RMI to work. It provides a proxy implementation of the same interface that is implemented by the RMI Server. The RMI client makes calls to the proxy implementation as if it were the real server. The RMI Server Stub marshals any objects that it finds in the parameters of the method call into serialized packets that it hands to the Remote Reference Layer.

The RMI client is a program that looks and acts quite a bit like any other program on your system. It uses a handle to the RMI Server interface to make its calls. Beyond that, it does not do much that is special.

An additional class, the skeleton, is needed. The skeleton performs server-specific functions as well as the marshaling and unmarshaling of the parameters.

The Supporting Cast

In addition to the RMI classes that become part of the server and client programs, several other executables play a role in the RMI world:

- RMI Compiler (`rmic`)—A command-line utility that creates the stub and skeleton by reading the compiled RMI Server's code.

- RMI Registry (rmiregistry)—A RMI naming service that the clients use to locate servers. Servers are registered with this program.
- RMI Activation Daemon (rmid)—A program that manages the automatic activation of servers based on client requests.
- HTTP Server—RMI can use a server to download classes to servers.

Creating an RMI Application

Before we dive into the world of industrial-strength RMI, it is useful to work through the process of writing and implementing a minimal example. Listing 2.1 contains the client portion of the minimal example.

LISTING 2.1 The Client Portion of the Minimal Example Passes an Object to an RMI Server, Gets an Identical One Back, and Examines Its Contents

```
/*
 * GreetingClient.java
 *
 * Created on February 26, 2002, 4:03 PM
 */

package unleashed.ch2;

import java.io.IOException;
import java.rmi.*;
import java.util.*;
import javax.rmi.*;

/**
 *
 * @author  Stephen Potts
 * @version
 */
public class GreetingClient
{

    /** Creates new GreetingClient */
    public GreetingClient()
    {
    }

    public static void main(String[] args) throws Exception
    {
        try
        {
            //Create a server connection
            Greeter greeter = (Greeter)
```

LISTING 2.1 continued

```
            Naming.lookup("rmi://localhost:1099/GreeterService");

        //Create the object to send
        Greeting greeting1 = new Greeting("Bonjour, Monde");

        //Send the object and get another one back
        Object obj2 = greeter.translate(greeting1);
        System.out.println("Object obj2 = " + obj2);

        //Cast the return object to be of type Greeting
        Greeting greeting2 = (Greeting)obj2;
        System.out.println("The Original is " + greeting1.getStr1());
        System.out.println("The Translation is " +
                                    greeting2.getStr1());
    }catch (Exception e)
    {
        System.out.println("Exception " + e);
    }
    }
}
```

Even a minimal RMI program has several classes that have to be written. None of them are particularly complex, but the process of knitting them together can be confusing. The approach that we take here is to start with the client because it is the easiest one to understand.

This class is called `GreetingClient`. It wants to communicate with a server called `GreetingServer`. This server accepts an object of type `Greeting` as a parameter to its `translate()` method. The `translate()` method returns another `Greeting` object with a translation in it.

If we were operating in a non-distributed fashion, we would simply create an instance of the object here. In the world of RMI, the server is presumed to be located in another JVM. Thus, direct instantiation is not possible. As a substitute for direct instantiation, RMI requires the creation of an interface that contains the methods of the server. This interface definition is located in the client's classpath. We use this to assign a type to the handle returned by the naming service.

```
        Greeter greeter = (Greeter)
            Naming.lookup("rmi://localhost:1099/GreeterService");
```

In this program, the naming service used is `java.rmi.Naming`. In brief, a naming service stores key/object pairs. By using the `lookup()` method, you can locate objects that are represented by the string that you have passed in. In this case, we pass in the string `"rmi://localhost:1099/GreeterService"`. It returns the stub object for this class. You can use the stub to get access to the methods in the GreeterService. Before you can use the lookup() method, some program at some time has to call the bind(), or rebind() method, on the string that you need in the RMI server's VM. This is done in the GreeterServer class that you will see later.

Armed with a stub, we are prepared to make a method call on the remote class. We do this by creating an object of type Greeting. In its constructor, we pass a weak French translation of "Hello, World":

```
Greeting greeting1 = new Greeting("Bonjour, Monde");
```

We send the greeting1 object to the remote server's translate() method. Notice how similar this is to calling a method on a local server:

```
Object obj2 = greeter.translate(greeting1);
```

Next, we print out the object so that you can see that it is a real one:

```
System.out.println("Object obj2 = " + obj2);
```

Following that, we cast the returned object to be of type Greeting so that we can call its getStr1() method:

```
Greeting greeting2 = (Greeting)obj2;
```

Next, we print out the original string so that you can see that we have two objects—the one that we created initially and another one that we got from calling the server:

```
System.out.println("The Original is " + greeting1.getStr1());
```

Finally, we print out the contents of the object that was returned by the remote server:

```
System.out.println("The String is " + greeting2.getStr1());
```

Before we talk about how to make all the magic happen on your machine, we need to see the other classes that make up our application. Listing 2.2 shows the Greeting class.

LISTING 2.2   The Greeting Class Gives Us an Object to Toss Around

```
/*
 * Greeting.java
 *
 * Created on February 26, 2002, 4:24 PM
 */

package unleashed.ch2;
import java.io.*;
```

LISTING 2.2 continued

```
/**
 *
 * @author  Stephen Potts
 * @version
 */

public class Greeting implements Serializable
{
    String str1;

    /** Creates new Greeting */
    public Greeting()
    {
    }

    public Greeting(String str1)
    {
        this.str1 = str1;
    }

    public String getStr1()
    {
        return this.str1;
    }

    public void setStr1(String str1)
    {
        this.str1 = str1;
    }
}
```

The only thing noteworthy in this class is the fact that it implements the `Serializable` interface. You can learn more than you every wanted to know about `Serializable` classes in Chapter 26, "Persistence and Cloning." Briefly, the `Serializable` interface has no methods that you implement. It is a marker placed on a class by its author that certifies that its member variables and classes can be stored and retrieved without loss of data. The process of passing an object as a parameter to a remote server requires that it be stored and retrieved. Listing 2.3 shows the `Greeter` interface.

LISTING 2.3 The `Greeter` Interface Serves as a Contract Between the Remote Server and the Clients that Want to Call Its Methods

```
/*
 * Greeter.java
 *
```

LISTING 2.3 continued

```
 * Created on February 26, 2002, 5:15 PM
 */

package unleashed.ch2;

import java.rmi.*;


/**
 *
 * @author   Stephen Potts
 * @version
 */
public interface Greeter extends Remote
{
    Object translate(Object obj) throws RemoteException;
}
```

The interesting part of this interface is that it extends another interface, `java.rmi.Remote`. `Remote` is another marker interface that tells RMI that a class is eligible for remote access if it implements this interface either directly or by inheritance. Listing 2.4 shows the `GreeterImpl` class.

LISTING 2.4 The `GreeterImpl` Class Implements the `Greeter` Interface and Provides the Actual Code that Will Run Remotely

```
/*
 * GreeterImpl.java
 *
 * Created on February 26, 2002, 4:03 PM
 */

package unleashed.ch2;


import java.rmi.*;
import java.rmi.server.*;

/**
 *
 * @author   Stephen Potts
 * @version
 */
public class GreeterImpl extends UnicastRemoteObject
implements Greeter
{
```

LISTING 2.4   continued

```java
/** Creates new HelloServer */
public GreeterImpl() throws RemoteException
{
    super();
}

//Echo back what was sent
public Object translate(Object obj)
{
    Greeting greeting3 = (Greeting)obj;
    if (greeting3.getStr1().equals("Bonjour, Monde"))
    {
        greeting3.setStr1("Hello, World");
    }else
    {
        greeting3.setStr1("Huh?");
    }

    return greeting3;
}
}
```

GreeterImpl implements Greeter, but it also extends UnicastRemoteObject.
UnicastRemoteObject is descended from both the java.rmi.server.RemoteServer and
the java.rmi.server.RemoteObject classes. It provides support for point-to-point (one-
to-one) communications between a client and a server that is already active. It supports
method calling, parameter passing, and returning results. It is provided as a convenience
for programmers so that they don't have to implement valid toString(), equals(), and
hashCode() methods. (RMI requires that these methods be overridden.)

Finally, Listing 2.5 shows us the code for the GreeterServer class.

LISTING 2.5   The GreeterServer Class Registers the Server with the Naming Service
and Serves as a Factory for Creating Server Instances

```java
/*
 * GreeterServer.java
 *
 * Created on February 27, 2002, 10:20 AM
 */

package unleashed.ch2;

/**
 *
 * @author  Stephen Potts
```

2

CREATING
APPLICATIONS
WITH RMI

LISTING 2.5 continued

```java
 * @version
 */
import java.rmi.Naming;

public class GreeterServer
{

    public GreeterServer()
    {
        try
        {
            Greeter g = new GreeterImpl();
            Naming.rebind("rmi://localhost:1099/GreeterService", g);
        } catch (Exception e)
        {
            System.out.println("Exception: " + e);
        }
    }

    public static void main(String args[])
    {
        new GreeterServer();
    }
}
```

> **Note**
>
> It is possible to start up a registry inside the code using the `getRegistry()` method of the `java.rmi.registry.LocateRegistry` class.

The `GreeterServer` names the service and registers the `GreeterImpl` class object as having that name. It does this by doing a `rebind()` to the naming service. It instantiates the server in its `main()` method. We use a `rebind()` call here because it doesn't throw an `AlreadyBoundException` if the name already exists in the Registry.

Getting the Example to Run

After all that, this code still won't run unless you perform a few more procedures. The commands in this section assume that you have unzipped these files to a directory called `c:\unleashed\ch2`. Follow this procedure to get this example to run. For simplicity in development, we will run both the server and the client on the same computer during development. This is always a good idea during the early stages because it allows you to fix bugs in all the components on one machine.

1. Move to the directory containing all your classes and compile them.

2. Move to the root directory of your tree (c:\) and type

   `c:\> rmic unleashed.ch2.GreeterImpl`

   This will generate `GreeterImpl_Stub.class` and `GreeterImpl_Skel.class`.

3. Open one command window and type

   `c:\> rmiregistry`

   This will start up the naming service for this computer.

4. Open another command window and type

   `c:\> java unleashed.ch2.GreeterServer`

   This will start the server and binds the name of the service to the `RMIRegistry`.

5. Finally, open a third window and type

   `c:\> java unleashed.ch2.GreetingClient`

The output from this is minimal, but it proves that it did indeed send an object from one JVM to the other and receive a new object back:

```
C:\unleashed\ch2>java unleashed.ch2.GreetingClient
Object obj2 = unleashed.ch2.Greeting@86c347
The Original is Bonjour, Monde
The Translation is Hello, World
```

This example doesn't do any real work, but it does demonstrate how to get the plumbing working. In addition, you can copy and paste this application to give you a start on getting your own systems running.

Converting an Application to RMI

Now that we know how to create a functioning, if not very functional, RMI server, we can enhance our understanding by expanding it to do something useful. One of the most useful missions for an RMI server is to perform a lookup on a database that is located on the server and pass that information back to a client.

To make that task easier, we will preload a database with tables and rows. To perform this preload, run the following command:

```
java unleashed.ch2.AccessJDBC2
```

2

CREATING
APPLICATIONS
WITH RMI

> **Note**
>
> The listing for this program is located in Appendix A, "Source Code Listings for Utility Programs Used in This Book." For our purposes, all we need to understand is that it contains data we can access.

All distributed object technologies are hard to debug because the system is divided into pieces that normally run in different JVM and often in different computers. Because of that, it is wise to create your applications in a standalone fashion. After they are debugged to your satisfaction, they can be divided into parts and distributed where they can meet the requirements that specified that the objects be remote from each other.

We will develop a simple JDBC application in this section. After we prove that it works, we will go through the process of chopping it into the pieces necessary to make it an RMI application. Listing 2.6 shows this application in its non-RMI persona.

LISTING 2.6   It Is Often Useful to Implement a System as a Standalone Product Before Distributing It with RMI

```
/*
 * CreditCardFinder.java
 *
 * Created on January 14, 2002, 5:23 PM
 */

package unleashed.ch2;

/**
 *
 * @author  Stephen Potts
 * @version
 */

import java.io.*;
import java.util.*;
import javax.transaction.*;
import javax.naming.*;

import java.sql.*;
import javax.mail.*;
import javax.mail.internet.*;

/**
 * @author Steve Potts
 */
```

LISTING 2.6   continued

```java
public class CreditCardFinder
{
    //JDBC variables
    java.sql.Connection dbConn = null;
    Statement statement1 = null;


    public CreditCardFinder() throws Exception
    {
        init();
    }

    //The init() method moves real processing
    // out of the constructors where
    //Exception handling is simpler
    private void init() throws Exception
    {
        try
        {
            //Obtain connections to JDBC and JavaMail
            ConnectToServices();

        }catch(Exception e)
        {
            System.out.println("Exception thrown " + e);
        }
    }

    private void ConnectToServices()
    {
        try
        {
            //Get a connection to the datasource
            //load the driver class
            Class.forName("sun.jdbc.odbc.JdbcOdbcDriver");

            //Specify the ODBC data source
            String sourceURL = "jdbc:odbc:CruiseTicket";

            //get a connection to the database
            dbConn =DriverManager.getConnection(sourceURL);

            //If we get to here, no exception was thrown
            System.out.println("The database connection is " + dbConn);
            System.out.println("Making connection...\n");

            //Create the statement
            statement1 = dbConn.createStatement();
```

LISTING 2.6   continued

```java
        } catch (Exception e)
        {
            System.out.println("Exception was thrown: " + e);
        }
    }

    private void addCreditCardNumber(Customer cust) throws Exception
    {

        int custID = cust.getCustID();

        String ccNum = "";

        //Populate the creditcard string string
        String getCCString =
        "SELECT CreditCardNumber FROM CruiseCustomer " +
        "WHERE CustomerID = " + Integer.toString(custID);

        ResultSet ccResults = statement1.executeQuery(getCCString);

        while (ccResults.next())
        {
            ccNum = ccResults.getString("CreditCardNumber");
        }

        cust.setCreditCardNumber(ccNum);
    }


    private static void log(String s)
    {
        System.out.println(s);
    }

    /**
     * main() method.
     *
     * @exception  Exception if execution fails
     */
    public static void main(String[] args)
    {
        try
        {
            CreditCardFinder ccf = new CreditCardFinder();
            Customer cust1 = new Customer(1001);

            ccf.addCreditCardNumber(cust1);
            System.out.println("The credit card Number for " +
                        cust1.getCustID() + " = " +
```

LISTING 2.6 continued

```
                    cust1.getCreditCardNumber());
    }catch (Exception e)
    {
        System.out.println("Exception in main() " + e);
    }
  }
}
```

> **Note**
>
> The source code for this chapter contains a `readme.txt` file that contains instructions for setting up the ODBC data source for using MS Access in this example. It also contains instructions for how to use MySQL for the database management system.

This application is very straightforward. We are in possession of a database whose source URL is `jdbc:odbc:CruiseTicket`. It contains many tables, but the one that we are interested in is `CruiseCustomer`. This table contains a number of pieces of information about the customer, including his credit card number.

In the `main()` method for this class, we declare an object of type `Customer`. Listing 2.7 shows the code for the `Customer` class.

LISTING 2.7 The `Customer` Class Is Composed of Two Variables as well as the Getters and Setters for Each of Them

```
/*
 * Customer.java
 *
 * Created on February 26, 2002, 4:24 PM
 */

package unleashed.ch2;
import java.io.*;

/**
 *
 * @author  Stephen Potts
 * @version
 */

public class Customer implements Serializable
```

LISTING 2.7 continued

```java
{
    int custID;
    String creditCardNumber;

    /** Creates new Greeting */
    public Customer()
    {
    }

    public Customer(int custID)
    {
        this.custID = custID;
    }

    public int getCustID()
    {
        return this.custID;
    }

    public void setCustID(int custID)
    {
        this.custID = custID;
    }

    public String getCreditCardNumber()
    {
        return this.creditCardNumber;
    }

    public void setCreditCardNumber(String creditCardNumber)
    {
        this.creditCardNumber = creditCardNumber;
    }
}
```

This application passes an object to the server and back. Passing strings would work, but the real value of RMI is its ability to send any `Serializable` object as a parameter.

Creating the Server

The process of creating the server is straightforward. We first separate the parts of the application that provide the responses from the parts that make requests. The first ones will become the server. In our application, the `addCreditCardNumber()` method provides the responses.

Next, we identify all the methods that support the addCreditCardNumber() method. In our case, this would be the constructor, the init() method, and the connectToServices() method.

Having identified what we need to create the server, we need to repackage these methods into a class of their own. Listing 2.8 shows this class.

LISTING 2.8   CreditCardImpl Provides the Actual Database Lookup Functionality for This Application

```
/*
 * CreditCardImpl.java
 *
 * Created on February 26, 2002, 4:03 PM
 */

package unleashed.ch2;


import java.rmi.*;
import java.rmi.server.*;
import java.sql.*;

/**
 *
 * @author  Stephen Potts
 * @version
 */
public class CreditCardImpl extends UnicastRemoteObject implements Finder
{
    //JDBC variables
    java.sql.Connection dbConn = null;
    Statement statement1 = null;

    /** Creates new HelloServer */
    public CreditCardImpl() throws RemoteException, Exception
    {
        super();
        init();
    }


    //The init() method moves real processing
    // out of the constructors where
    //Exception handling is simpler
    private void init() throws Exception
    {
        try
        {
```

LISTING 2.8   continued

```java
            //Obtain connections to JDBC and JavaMail
            ConnectToServices();

        }catch(Exception e)
        {
            System.out.println("Exception thrown " + e);
        }
    }

    private void ConnectToServices()
    {
        try
        {
            //Get a connection to the datasource
            //load the driver class
            Class.forName("sun.jdbc.odbc.JdbcOdbcDriver");

            //Specify the ODBC data source
            String sourceURL = "jdbc:odbc:CruiseTicket";

            //get a connection to the database
            dbConn =DriverManager.getConnection(sourceURL);

            //If we get to here, no exception was thrown
            System.out.println("The database connection is " + dbConn);
            System.out.println("Making connection...\n");

            //Create the statement
            statement1 = dbConn.createStatement();

        } catch (Exception e)
        {
            System.out.println("Exception was thrown: " + e);
        }
    }

    public Object addCreditCardNumber(Object obj)
    throws RemoteException
    {
        try
        {
            Customer cust = (Customer)obj;
            int custID = cust.getCustID();

            String ccNum = "";

            //Populate the creditcard string string
            String getCCString =
            "SELECT CreditCardNumber FROM CruiseCustomer " +
```

LISTING 2.8   continued

```
                "WHERE CustomerID = " + Integer.toString(custID);

            ResultSet ccResults = statement1.executeQuery(getCCString);

            while (ccResults.next())
            {
                ccNum = ccResults.getString("CreditCardNumber");
            }

            cust.setCreditCardNumber(ccNum);

            return cust;
        }catch (Exception e)
        {
            System.out.println("Exception " + e);
            return null;
        }
    }
}
```

You will, no doubt, recognize all the methods that we identified earlier as providing functionality for our application. The class itself must implement the `UnicastRemoteObject` so that RMI can provide it service. The class also implements an interface called `Finder` that we will define shortly.

```
public class CreditCardImpl extends UnicastRemoteObject implements Finder
```

The signature of the `addCreditCardNumber` changed as well. It has been made public so that it can be called from outside the class itself. In addition, it must now return an object. In the standalone application, the object was passed by reference, and the changes made to it by `addCreditCardNumber()` were made to the object itself. RMI passed all objects as type `Object` in order for simplicity. It is the job of the class that receives the `Object` to cast it to its correct subclass.

In the world of distributed objects, the calling program has no idea of the state of the object that was passed in because it has been passed by value to another JVM. In order to learn about the state change, we have to receive the object back from the server and examine its contents:

```
public Object addCreditCardNumber(Object obj)
throws RemoteException
```

You will notice that this method throws a `RemoteException`. This class contains several methods that help the calling program determine the reason that a request failed. A new method, getCause(), has been added that allows the Exception object that was generated in the server to be passed back. This method was added in JDK 1.4.

We declared that CreditCardImpl implements an interface called Finder. Listing 2.9 shows this interface.

LISTING 2.9   The Finder Interface Describes the Public Methods that the Server Will Provide

```
/*
 * Finder.java
 *
 * Created on February 26, 2002, 5:15 PM
 */

package unleashed.ch2;

import java.rmi.*;


/**
 *
 * @author   Stephen Potts
 * @version
 */
public interface Finder extends Remote
{
    Object addCreditCardNumber(Object obj) throws RemoteException;
}
```

The only entry for this server is the addCreditCardNumber() method. This interface is used to create handles to the server on the client side. Because it is an interface, it can point to any object that implants this interface. Both the server's Impl file and the stub that we will generate for this server fit that description.

Somewhere, the server has to be started up. We need a file that contains a main() class that starts the server's implementation running inside a JVM on the server machine. The class that we have written to do this is shown in Listing 2.10.

LISTING 2.10   The CreditCardServer Class Informs the RMIRegistry About the Service and Instantiates the CreditCardImpl Class

```
/*
 * CreditCardServer.java
 *
 * Created on February 27, 2002, 10:20 AM
 */
```

LISTING 2.10   continued

```java
package unleashed.ch2;

/**
 *
 * @author  Stephen Potts
 * @version
 */
import java.rmi.Naming;

public class CreditCardServer
{

    public CreditCardServer()
    {
        try
        {
            Finder f = new CreditCardImpl();
            Naming.rebind("rmi://localhost:1099/FinderService", f);
        } catch (Exception e)
        {
            System.out.println("Exception: " + e);
        }
    }

    public static void main(String args[])
    {
        new CreditCardServer();
    }
}
```

RMI provides a junior naming service called the RMIRegistry. This service operates over the Internet and provides a handle to the server. Here we declared the Finder handle f. Next, we bound it to the RMIRegistry that is located on my machine at port 1099. We gave it the name of FinderService. We will see shortly how we can use this naming service to locate the server.

Now that we have all the classes we need, let's crank it up. We need two command windows to do this. In the first one, type the following command:

c:\> rmic unleashed.ch2.CreditCardImpl

This will generate the stubs and skeletons (depending on the JDK you are using). Next, type the following command:

C:\> RMIRegistry

This will start up the registry so that it will be there when we do the `rebind()` and `lookup()` method calls. In the next window, type the following:

C:\> java unleashed.ch2.CreditCardServer

This will actually start the server in the JVM. Now that we have a server and a naming service running, all that remains is to call it. Listing 2.11 shows us a client that calls this server.

LISTING 2.11   The `CreditCardClient` Is Able to Make Calls Outside Its Own JVM Using RMI

```
/*
 * CreditCardClient.java
 *
 * Created on February 26, 2002, 4:03 PM
 */

package unleashed.ch2;

import java.io.IOException;
import java.rmi.*;
import java.util.*;
import javax.rmi.*;

/**
 *
 * @author  Stephen Potts
 * @version
 */
public class CreditCardClient
{

    /** Creates new GreetingClient */
    public CreditCardClient()
    {
    }

    public static void main(String[] args) throws Exception
    {
        try
        {
            //Create a server connection
            Finder finder = (Finder)
            Naming.lookup("rmi://localhost:1099/FinderService");

            Customer cust1 = new Customer(1001);

            //Send the object and get another one back
```

LISTING 2.11 continued

```
        Object obj2 = finder.addCreditCardNumber(cust1);
        System.out.println("Object obj2 = " + obj2);

        //Cast the return object to be of type Customer
        Customer cust2 = (Customer)obj2;

        System.out.println("The credit card Number for " +
        cust2.getCustID() + " = " +
        cust2.getCreditCardNumber());
    }catch (Exception e)
    {
        System.out.println("Exception in main() " + e);
    }
  }
}
```

You will recognize several familiar lines of code here because it is simply the `main()` method from the `CreditCardFinder` program with a few additions. The most important addition is the code to find the server. Notice that the `Finder` interface is used here to get a handle to the server. The server, if you will recall, was bound to a string called `FinderService`. We use that fact to locate it:

```
        Finder finder = (Finder)
        Naming.lookup("rmi://localhost:1099/FinderService");
```

The implementation of the `addCreditCardNumber()` method is not present in this program, nor is it located anywhere in the classes that it has access to. It is, however, referenced by the `Finder` interface. Because we have a handle to this interface, we can follow the rules of polymorphism and make a call to `addCreditCardNumber()`. The magic of RMI is that we will actually be calling this method in the stub that must be in my classpath on my machine:

```
        //Send the object and get another one back
        Object obj2 = finder.addCreditCardNumber(cust1);
```

Now that we have a client, let's fire it up and see if it works:

```
C:> java unleashed.ch2.CreditCardClient
```

Lo and behold, we have communications taking place between two different virtual machines, as shown here:

```
Object obj2 = unleashed.ch2.Customer@45e044
The credit card Number for 1001 = 1234-1234-1234-1234
```

The output to the console proves that this program ran because the `CreditCardClient` has no way of knowing what the credit card number is without making the call to `CreditCardServer`.

This example is a bit more real-world than the minimal example that we worked on first. The initial example was to provide you with the smallest amount of code so that you can understand all the players in the production. It also provides a starting point for your programs. You can simply replace the trivial functionality with your own.

The credit card example was designed to throw in a few wrinkles such as database access and real data exchange via RMI. The final example that we will work on is designed to give you a real-world example that is not trivial, but one that performs a lot of tasks that are common to commercial systems.

Creating an RMI Version of the CruiseList Application

Throughout this book, we are working in a simple domain in which a travel agent uses a GUI to place an order for cruise tickets. The GUI acts as the client, and a server (in this chapter it is RMI-based) does the actual work of verifying the credit card information and creating the ticket. The GUI then displays the success or failure of the request.

The most remarkable thing about this version of the CruiseList is that it is about one hundred lines shorter than the equivalent JavaMail application. Almost no code is associated with sending and receiving messages. The simple call and return logic is all that is needed. Listing 2.12 shows the GUI portion of this application.

LISTING 2.12   The CruiseList GUI Fills the Role of the Client in the RMI

```
/*
 * CruiseList.java
 *
 * Created on January 14, 2002, 4:02 PM
 */

package unleashed.ch2;

import javax.swing.*;
import java.awt.event.ActionListener;
import javax.swing.border.EtchedBorder;
import java.awt.Container;
import java.awt.BorderLayout;
import java.sql.*;

import java.rmi.*;
import javax.rmi.*;
import java.util.*;
import java.io.*;
```

LISTING 2.12   continued

```java
/**
 *
 * @author   Stephen Potts
 * @version
 */
public class CruiseList extends JFrame implements ActionListener
{
    //RMI variables
    static TicketAgent ta;

    //JDBC variables
    java.sql.Connection dbConn = null;
    Statement statement1 = null;

    String server;
    String user;
    String password;

    //GUI Variables
    JList customerList;
    JList cruisesAvailable;
    JButton btnBook;
    JButton btnCheck;
    JButton btnExit;

    //Arrays to hold database information
    int[] custNums = null;
    String[] lastNames = null;
    String[] firstNames = null;

    int[] cruiseIDs = null;
    String[] cruiseDestinations = null;
    String[] cruisePorts = null;
    String[] cruiseSailings = null;

    /** Constructors for CruiseList */
    public CruiseList() throws Exception
    {
        init();
    }

    public CruiseList(String caption) throws Exception
    {
        super(caption);
        init();
    }
```

LISTING 2.12   continued

```java
//The init() method moves real processing out
//of the constructors where
//Exception handling is simpler
private void init() throws Exception
{
    try
    {
        //Obtain connections to JDBC
        ConnectToServices();

        //configure the Frame
        setBounds(150,200,500,250);
        setDefaultCloseOperation(JFrame.EXIT_ON_CLOSE);

        //set the layout
        BorderLayout border = new BorderLayout();
        Container content = getContentPane();
        content.setLayout(border);

        //Populate the customerNames string
        String getCustomerString =
        "SELECT CustomerID, LastName, FirstName FROM CruiseCustomer";
        ResultSet custResults =
                    statement1.executeQuery(getCustomerString);

        custNums = new int[20];
        lastNames = new String[20];
        firstNames = new String[20];
        int index = 0;

        while (custResults.next())
        {
            custNums[index] = custResults.getInt("CustomerID");
            firstNames[index] = custResults.getString("FirstName");
            lastNames[index] = custResults.getString("LastName");
            index += 1;
        }

        String[] customerNames = new String[index];

        for (int i=0;i<index;i++)
        {
            customerNames[i] = firstNames[i] + " " + lastNames[i];
        }
        int numCustomers = index;
        System.out.println("The number of customers " + index);

        //Populate the cruises string
```

LISTING 2.12   continued

```java
String getCruiseString =
"SELECT CruiseID, Destination, Port, Sailing FROM Cruises";
ResultSet cruiseResults =
        statement1.executeQuery(getCruiseString);

cruiseIDs = new int[20];
cruiseDestinations = new String[20];
cruisePorts = new String[20];
cruiseSailings = new String[20];
index = 0;

while (cruiseResults.next())
{
    cruiseIDs[index] = cruiseResults.getInt("CruiseID");
    cruiseDestinations[index] =
        cruiseResults.getString("Destination");
    cruisePorts[index] = cruiseResults.getString("Port");
    cruiseSailings[index] =
            cruiseResults.getString("Sailing");
    index += 1;
}

String[] cruises = new String[index];

for (int i=0;i<index;i++)
{
    cruises[i] = cruiseDestinations[i] +
    "      Departs: " + cruisePorts[i] +
    " " + cruiseSailings[i];
}

int numCruises = index;
System.out.println("The number of cruises" + index);


//More GUI components
String labelString = "                 Customer";
labelString += "                   Cruise";
JLabel label1 = new JLabel(labelString);
customerList = new JList(customerNames);
cruisesAvailable = new JList(cruises);
btnBook = new JButton("Book");
btnCheck = new JButton("Check");
btnExit = new JButton("Exit");
btnBook.addActionListener(this);
btnCheck.addActionListener(this);
btnExit.addActionListener(this);
```

2

CREATING
APPLICATIONS
WITH RMI

LISTING 2.12   continued

```
            JPanel bottomPanel = new JPanel();
            JPanel centerPanel = new JPanel();
            centerPanel.add(new JScrollPane(customerList,
                    JScrollPane.VERTICAL_SCROLLBAR_ALWAYS,
            JScrollPane.HORIZONTAL_SCROLLBAR_AS_NEEDED));
            centerPanel.add(new JScrollPane(cruisesAvailable,
            JScrollPane.VERTICAL_SCROLLBAR_ALWAYS,
            JScrollPane.HORIZONTAL_SCROLLBAR_AS_NEEDED));
            bottomPanel.add(btnBook);
            bottomPanel.add(btnCheck);
            bottomPanel.add(btnExit);
            content.add(label1, BorderLayout.NORTH);
            content.add(centerPanel, BorderLayout.CENTER);
            content.add(bottomPanel, BorderLayout.SOUTH);
            setVisible(true);
        }catch(Exception e)
        {
            System.out.println("Exception thrown " + e);
        } finally
        {
            try
            {
                //close all connections
                if (statement1 != null)
                    statement1.close();
                if (dbConn != null)
                    dbConn.close();

            } catch (SQLException sqle)
            {
                System.out.println(
                    "SQLException during close(): " +
                                    sqle.getMessage());
            }
        }

    }

    private void ConnectToServices()
    {
        try
        {

            //Get a connection to the datasource
            //load the driver class
            Class.forName("sun.jdbc.odbc.JdbcOdbcDriver");

            //Specify the ODBC datasource
```

LISTING 2.12 continued

```java
                String sourceURL = "jdbc:odbc:CruiseTicket";

                //get a connection to the database
                dbConn =DriverManager.getConnection(sourceURL);

                //If we get to here, no exception was thrown
                System.out.println("The database connection is " + dbConn);
                System.out.println("Making connection...\n");

                //Create the statement
                statement1 = dbConn.createStatement();


        } catch (Exception e)
        {
            System.out.println("Exception was thrown: " + e);
        }
    }

    /**
     * @param args the command line arguments
     */
    public static void main(String args[])
    {
        try
        {
            //create a handle to the TicketAgentService
            ta = (TicketAgent)Naming.lookup(
                    "rmi://localhost:1099/TicketAgentService");

            //create an instance of the GUI
            CruiseList mainWindow =
                    new CruiseList("Cruise Ticket System");
        }catch(Exception e)
        {
            System.out.println("Exception in main " + e);
        }
    }

    public void actionPerformed(java.awt.event.ActionEvent ae)
    {
        try
        {
            TicketRequest tickReq2 = null;
            Container c = btnExit.getParent();
            if (ae.getActionCommand().equals("Exit"))
```

LISTING 2.12 continued

```
        {
            System.exit(0);
        }

        //Try and book a ticket
        if (ae.getActionCommand().equals("Book"))
        {
            System.out.println("Book was clicked");
            int custIndex = customerList.getSelectedIndex();
            int cruiseIndex =
                    cruisesAvailable.getSelectedIndex();

            if (custIndex == -1 || cruiseIndex == -1)
            {
                JOptionPane.showMessageDialog(c,
                "You must choose a customer and a cruise");
            }else
            {
                //Pop up a dialog asking how many tickets
                //are requested
                String numTickets = JOptionPane.showInputDialog(c,
                "How many tickets?");
                int numberOfTickets = Integer.parseInt(numTickets);

                //create a ticket request object
                TicketRequest tickReq =
                        new TicketRequest(custNums[custIndex],
                lastNames[custIndex], firstNames[custIndex],
                cruiseIDs[cruiseIndex],
                cruiseDestinations[cruiseIndex],
                cruisePorts[cruiseIndex],
                cruiseSailings[cruiseIndex],
                numberOfTickets);

                System.out.println(tickReq);
                //Create a message using this object

                try
                {
                    Object obj2 = ta.createTicket(tickReq);
                    System.out.println("TicketRequest sent via RMI");

                    tickReq2 = (TicketRequest)obj2;
                    System.out.println(tickReq2);

                }catch (Exception e)
                {
                    log("Error making RMI call " + e);
                }
```

LISTING 2.12 continued

```
                    System.out.println("Ticket Request complete ");
                    if (tickReq2.isApproved())
                    {
                        displayResult("The ticket for " +
                                        tickReq2.getLastName() +
                                        " has been approved");
                    }else
                    {
                        displayResult("The ticket for " +
                                        tickReq2.getLastName() +
                                        " was not approved");
                    }
                }
            }

        }catch (Exception e)
        {
            System.out.println("Exception thrown = " + e);
        }
    }

    private void log(String s)
    {
        System.out.println(s);
    }

    public void displayResult(String str)
    {
        try
        {
            Container c = btnExit.getParent();

            //show the message in a dialog box
            JOptionPane.showMessageDialog(c, str);
        }catch (Exception e)
        {
            System.out.println("o Exception " + e);
        }
    }
}
```

Amid all the GUI code, there is a small amount of RMI logic that looks almost exactly like it does in every RMI client. The first part of the RMI code creates a handle to the TicketAgentService. We will use this handle to make calls to the method on the server:

```
ta = (TicketAgent)Naming.lookup(
        "rmi://localhost:1099/TicketAgentService");
```

All that we have to do to call the method is declare an Object handle and make the call. The object being passed is of type `TicketRequest`. It contains the details about the request that are gathered from the user's interaction with the GUI:

```
Object obj2 = ta.createTicket(tickReq);
System.out.println("TicketRequest sent via RMI");
```

Figure 2.2 shows what the GUI looks like.

FIGURE 2.2

The CruiseList GUI gathers information and passes it as a parameter to the server.

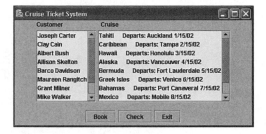

The returned object is cast as type `TicketRequest`.

```
tickReq2 = (TicketRequest)obj2;
```

We use this handle to call a method in the `TicketRequest` object called `isApproved()`. It returns a `boolean` value that indicates whether the request was approved. Disapproval can occur when a credit card is not accepted:

```
if (tickReq2.isApproved())
{
    displayResult("The ticket for " +
                        tickReq2.getLastName() +
                        " has been approved");
}else
{
    displayResult("The ticket for " +
                        tickReq2.getLastName() +
                        " was not approved");
}
```

The approval status is displayed in a modal dialog box, as shown in Figure 2.3.

FIGURE 2.3

A dialog box is displayed to notify the user of the approval status of the ticket request.

The `TicketRequest` class is fairly simple. It contains all the information needed for the server to create a ticket. It also contains a `boolean` field that will be set by the server indicating whether the request was approved. Listing 2.13 shows the code for this class.

LISTING 2.13 The `TicketRequest` Class Contains the Fields that the Server Needs to Process a Request

```java
/*
/ * TicketRequest.java
 *
 * Created on January 14, 2002, 4:13 PM
 */

package unleashed.ch2;

/**
 *
 * @author   Stephen Potts
 * @version
 */
public class TicketRequest implements java.io.Serializable
{
    //information about the customer
    int custID;
    String lastName;
    String firstName;

    //information about the cruise
    int cruiseID;
    String destination;
    String port;
    String sailing;

    int numberOfTickets;
    boolean approved;

    /** Constructor */
    public TicketRequest(int custID, String lastName, String firstName,
    int cruiseID, String destination,
    String port, String sailing, int numberOfTickets)
    {
        //set the information about the customer
        this.custID = custID;
        this.lastName = lastName;
        this.firstName = firstName;

        //set the information about the cruise
        this.cruiseID = cruiseID;
        this.destination = destination;
```

LISTING 2.13 continued

```java
        this.port = port;
        this.sailing = sailing;

        this.numberOfTickets = numberOfTickets;
        this.approved = false;
    }

    public int getCustID()
    {
        return this.custID = custID;
    }

    public String getLastName()
    {
        return this.lastName = lastName;
    }

    public String getFirstName()
    {
        return this.firstName = firstName;
    }

    public int getCruiseID()
    {
        return this.cruiseID;
    }

    public String getDestination()
    {
        return this.destination;
    }

    public String getPort()
    {
        return this.port;
    }

    public String getSailing()
    {
        return this.sailing;
    }

    public int getNumberOfTickets()
    {
        return this.numberOfTickets;
    }

    public boolean isApproved()
    {
```

LISTING 2.13   continued

```
        return approved;
    }

    public void approve()
    {
        approved = true;
    }

    public void disApprove()
    {
        approved = false;
    }

    public String toString()
    {
        String outString;
        outString = "--------------------------------" + "\n";

        //information about the customer
        outString += "custID = " + this.custID + "\n";
        outString += "lastName = " + this.lastName + "\n";
        outString += "firstName = " + this.firstName + "\n";
        outString += "----------------------------------" + "\n";

        //information about the cruise
        outString += "cruiseID = " + this.cruiseID + "\n";
        outString += "destination = " + this.destination + "\n";
        outString += "port = " + this.port + "\n";
        outString += "sailing = " + this.sailing + "\n";
        outString += "numberOfTickets = " + this.numberOfTickets + "\n";
        outString += "approved? = " + this.approved + "\n";

        outString += "------------------------------------------------" + "\n";
        return outString;
    }
}
```

The only RMI-specific part of this class is that it implements the `Serializable` interface. The server logic is contained in a file called `TicketAgentImpl`, which implements the `TicketAgent` interface. This interface is shown in Listing 2.14.

LISTING 2.14   The `TicketAgent` Interface Is Used to Communicate the Server's Methods to the Client

```
/*
 * TicketAgent.java
 *
```

LISTING 2.14 continued

```
 * Created on February 26, 2002, 5:15 PM
 */

package unleashed.ch2;

import java.rmi.*;


/**
 *
 * @author  Stephen Potts
 * @version
 */
public interface TicketAgent extends Remote
{
    Object createTicket(Object obj) throws RemoteException;
}
```

The implementation class for this interface is shown in Listing 2.15.

LISTING 2.15 The `TicketAgentImpl` Class Does the Real Work of the Server

```
/*
 * TicketAgentImpl.java
 *
 * Created on January 14, 2002, 5:23 PM
 */

package unleashed.ch2;
/**
 *
 * @author  Stephen Potts
 * @version
 */

import java.io.*;
import java.util.*;

import java.sql.*;
import java.rmi.*;
import java.rmi.server.*;

/**
*
 * @author Steve Potts
 */
public class TicketAgentImpl
```

LISTING 2.15   continued

```
                    extends UnicastRemoteObject
                    implements TicketAgent
{
    static int ticketID = 7000;
    private boolean quit = false;

    //JDBC variables
    java.sql.Connection dbConn = null;
    Statement statement1 = null;

    String server;
    String user;
    String password;


    public TicketAgentImpl() throws Exception
    {
        init();
    }

    //The init() method moves real processing
    // out of the constructors where
    //Exception handling is simpler
    private void init() throws Exception
    {
        try
        {
            //Obtain connections to JDBC
            ConnectToServices();

        }catch(Exception e)
        {
            System.out.println("Exception thrown " + e);
        }
    }

    private void ConnectToServices()
    {
        try
        {
            //Get a connection to the datasource
             //load the driver class
            Class.forName("sun.jdbc.odbc.JdbcOdbcDriver");

            //Specify the ODBC datasource
            String sourceURL = "jdbc:odbc:CruiseTicket";

            //get a connection to the database
```

LISTING 2.15 continued

```
                dbConn =DriverManager.getConnection(sourceURL);

                //If we get to here, no exception was thrown
                System.out.println("The database connection is " + dbConn);
                System.out.println("Making connection...\n");

                //Create the statement
                statement1 = dbConn.createStatement();

        } catch (Exception e)
        {
            System.out.println("Exception was thrown: " + e);
        }
    }


    public void respondToRequest(TicketRequest tr)
    {
        try
        {
            String msgText = "";

            //get the credit card number from the database
            String ccNum = getCreditCardNumber(tr.getCustID());
            System.out.println("The Credit Card Number is " + ccNum);

            //create a queue send to the Payment queue
            if (verifyCreditCard(ccNum))
            {
                buildTicket(tr);
                tr.approve();
            }else
                tr.disApprove();

            //if the queue receives a text message to quit
            if (msgText.equalsIgnoreCase("quit"))
            {
                synchronized(this)
                {
                    quit = true;
                    this.notifyAll(); // Notify main thread to quit
                }
            }
        }catch (Exception e)
        {
            e.printStackTrace();
        }
    }
```

LISTING 2.15 continued

```
//This method creates a database entry for the new ticket
private void buildTicket(TicketRequest tr) throws Exception
{
    String insertStatement;
    ticketID += 1;
    insertStatement = "INSERT INTO CruiseTicket VALUES(" +
                         ticketID + "," +
    Integer.toString(tr.getCustID()) + ", 'Unleashed Cruise Line'," +
    "'USS SeaBiscuit', '" + tr.getPort() + "','" +
        tr.getSailing() +"'," +
    "999.99," + "0,"+ "0,"+ "''')";

    statement1.executeUpdate(insertStatement);
    System.out.println("Update was successful CustID = " +
                                    tr.getCustID());
}

private String getCreditCardNumber(int CustID) throws Exception
{
    System.out.println("getCreditCard Making Db connection...\n");

    String ccNum = "";

    //Populate the creditcard string string
    String getCCString =
    "SELECT CreditCardNumber FROM CruiseCustomer " +
    "WHERE CustomerID = " + Integer.toString(CustID);

    ResultSet ccResults = statement1.executeQuery(getCCString);

    while (ccResults.next())
    {
        ccNum = ccResults.getString("CreditCardNumber");
    }

    return ccNum;
}

private boolean verifyCreditCard(String ccNum)
{
    int firstNum = Integer.parseInt(ccNum.substring(0,1));

    if ( firstNum > 4)
```

LISTING 2.15 continued

```
            return false;
        else
            return true;
    }

    private void log(String s)
    {
        System.out.println(s);
    }


    public Object createTicket(Object obj) throws RemoteException
    {
        TicketRequest tr = (TicketRequest)obj;
        respondToRequest(tr);
        return tr;
    }

}
```

This class evaluates the request and queries the database to see whether the credit card is valid. If it is, a ticket is created in the database. In any case, the status is communicated to the TicketRequest object by the approve() and disapprove() methods:

```
        if (verifyCreditCard(ccNum))
        {
            buildTicket(tr);
            tr.approve();
        }else
            tr.disApprove();
```

All that we have to do to communicate back to the client is pass the object via the remote method's return call:

```
    public Object createTicket(Object obj) throws RemoteException
    {
        TicketRequest tr = (TicketRequest)obj;
        respondToRequest(tr);
        return tr;
    }
```

We just cast the incoming object to be a TicketRequest object. This object can be returned, which automatically serializes it and sends it back to the client.

The final file that we need is the TicketAgentServer class as shown in Listing 2.16.

LISTING 2.16 The `TicketAgentServer` Class Allows Us to Instantiate the `TicketAgentImpl` Class and to Bind This Class to a Name in the `RMIRegistry`

```
/*
 * TicketAgentServer.java
 *
 * Created on February 27, 2002, 10:20 AM
 */

package unleashed.ch2;

/**
 *
 * @author  Stephen Potts
 * @version
 */
import java.rmi.Naming;

public class TicketAgentServer
{

    public TicketAgentServer()
    {
        try
        {
            TicketAgent ta = new TicketAgentImpl();
            Naming.rebind("rmi://localhost:1099/TicketAgentService", ta);
        } catch (Exception e)
        {
            System.out.println("Exception: " + e);
        }
    }

    public static void main(String args[])
    {
        new TicketAgentServer();
    }
}
```

This class instantiates the server so that it will be running when the client makes a call to it. To build the application, follow these steps:

1. Move to the directory containing all your classes and compile them.

2. Move to the root directory of your tree (c:\) and type

   c:\> rmic unleashed.ch2.TicketAgentImpl

   This will generate `TicketAgentImpl_Stub.class` and `TicketAgentImpl_Skel.class`.

3. Open one command window and type

   ```
   c:\> rmiregistry
   ```

   This will start up the naming service for this computer.

4. Open another command window and type

   ```
   c:\> java unleashed.ch2.TicketAgentServer
   ```

   This will start the server and bind the name of the service to the RMIRegistry.

5. Finally, open a third window and type

   ```
   c:\> java unleashed.ch2.CruiseList
   ```

   This will bring up the GUI and allow you to begin creating tickets to imaginary cruises for your imaginary customers.

This example was provided in the hope that you will find that it does some of the tasks needed by your programs. It shows how to create an RMI client that is also a GUI. In addition, it shows how an RMI server can retrieve data from a database and create rows in it also.

Summary

In this chapter, you learned about Remote Method Invocation. We first examined how RMI operates behind the scenes. Next, you learned how to create a minimal RMI example that can be used as a starting point for your own applications.

Following that, we created a more complicated application that had the server query a database and return a result. This example showed you how to do real work with RMI.

Finally, we wrote a program that was much more full-featured. It consisted of a GUI that queried a database to get the data that it displays. It created an object that contained the information necessary for booking a ticket on a cruise line. It passed this object to a remote server via RMI. This remote server retrieved the information that it needed from this object and created a ticket in the database if the credit card number was valid. It updated a status in the object that was passed in. It then returned the object to the client who examined its status and displayed the result to the user.

The goal of this chapter was to give you a jump-start on using RMI to create distributed objects. There is a lot more to know about RMI than we covered here. But if you understand this material, you will have a good working knowledge of Remote Method Invocation in Java.

Creating Applications with Java API for XML Parsing (JAXP)

CHAPTER 3

Most programs need to exchange data with other programs from time to time. Many techniques for making this exchange have been used over the years. Currently, the most popular approach to doing this is to create XML documents and transfer them to another computer where they can be parsed and the data processed.

Because XML documents are really text files, you can parse them any way that you like. Java programmers normally use the parsers that are found in the Java API for XML Parsing (JAXP). This chapter will introduce you to the use of these parsers.

XML is a set of rules that govern how you create a special language to describe your data. These rules provide a set of reserved characters and their usage in defining a set of tags that identify entities in your world. If you make up the tags according to the rules of XML, you will have access to a number of tools that will make parsing your data easier, once you are familiar with them. Getting you familiar with them is the main goal of this chapter.

Understanding XML

An XML document is a text document. It can be written using any tool that is capable of producing text. Your programs can also write XML as a form of output. While the purpose of creating an XML document is normally to provide data to software, a human with a trained eye can read it. This is very comforting to programmers because it makes debugging simpler. If you have a problem in the XML document, you can open it in any text editor and look at the characters that compose the file.

The textual representation of an XML document, in a nutshell, is a text file full of data and markup. *Markup* is just text surrounded very carefully by combinations of the ampersand (&), the less-than symbol (<), the greater-than symbol (>), the apostrophe ('), and the quotation mark ("). These characters have been taken out of common usage and forbidden in your data, and have been replaced by entity references:

- &amp replaces &
- &lt replaces <
- &gt replaces >
- &apos replaces '
- &quot replaces "

You can define your own entities that get expanded to the strings that you define. This is very useful for headers, footers, and other boilerplate items that you commonly include by reference.

Actually, this is not a very long list. Whenever you see one of these characters, know that you are looking at markup of some sort. The trick is to understand what sort of special instruction you are looking at. Conceptually, the process is very simple. One program combines its data with instructions (markup) that tell what the data means. Another program looks in that document and uses the markup to navigate through the data to find the part that it needs.

There is a set of rules associated with an XML document that it must follow:

- Each start tag must have a corresponding end tag.
- Attribute values must be enclosed in quotes.
- Some characters in data must be represented by entity references. If they appear in text as ordinary characters, the XML parser becomes confused.
- Overlapping tags are not permitted. If you start a tag sequence <a><b>, it must end <b><a>, not <a><b>.
- It must have the XML prolog: <?xml version='1.0'?>.

Documents that follow these rules are considered "well formed." If a document is not well formed, it will cause errors to be thrown during parsing.

XML Related Tools

You could, of course, ignore the XML world altogether and create your own markup language with its own set of reserved characters and rules about how markup is created. As long as all the other programs that you need to exchange data with are programmed using the same markup language, everything will work just fine.

One big advantage of cooperating with the XML world, however, is the toolset that is available. Many tools have been written that attempt to simplify the handling of XML documents in programs. These tools focus on various tasks:

- Editing—Most integrated development environments (IDEs) such as Forte, Visual Café, and JBuilder contain special editors to help you compose XML documents.
- Parsing—JAXP defines two ways of parsing XML documents: sequentially (processing the file in a line-by-line fashion) or objectively (using the Document Object Model [DOM]). JAXP contains parsers for both.
- Transforming—Extensible Stylesheet Language Transformations (XSLT) helps you transform documents from one grammar to another.
- Displaying—Extensible Stylesheet Language (XSL) allows you to describe how an XML document should be displayed or printed out.

- Verifying—Document Type Definitions (DTDs) allow you to define the grammar for your XML document. This allows the parser to verify that any document you receive is created in accordance to your instructions. XML Schemas can also be used to verify documents. They provide a more robust set of rules for defining a grammar.

If you chose to "roll your own" markup language, you would have to create an equivalent for each of these activities.

Creating an XML Document

XML is programming language–neutral. But because we are not neutral, we will be programming using the Java API for XML Parsing (JAXP) in all the examples in this chapter.

The important JAXP classes and interfaces are summarized here:

- `org.xml.sax.helpers.DefaultHandler`—This class is the default base class for SAX2 event handlers. It serves as a convenience class, which means that it provides a default handler for any events that you don't want to handle. When writing applications, you can extend this class and override the parts of the interface that you want to control.

- `javax.xml.parsers.DocumentBuilder`—This abstract class allows an application programmer to obtain a DOM version of an XML document.

- `javax.xml.parsers.DocumentBuilderFactory`—This class allows a programmer to get a handle to a concrete `DocumentBuilder` object.

- `org.w3c.dom.Document`—This interface provides a reference to the entire XML document tree. Using this handle, the contents of the tree can be analyzed.

- `javax.xml.transform.Transformer`—An instance of this abstract class provides us with a way to stream XML to a file.

- `javax.xml.transform.stream.StreamResult`—This class receives a stream representing the XML that is to be put in a file.

- `org.w3c.dom.Node`—This interface provides references to the nodes in the document tree. As a reference, it can serve as a handle to any type of node.

The simplest way to create an XML document is to type it in using a text editor such as Notepad or vi. This is a useful approach while you are learning XML because it gives you time to think about each reserved character and its purpose.

Listing 3.1 is a simple XML document that illustrates several of the points that we have discussed.

> **Note**
>
> All the code in this chapter can be found on the Sams Publishing Web site at
> www.samspublishing.com.

LISTING 3.1   A Simple XML File Representing a Request for a Cruise Ticket

```xml
<?xml version='1.0' encoding='utf-8' standalone='yes' ?>
<!--This XML document represents a request for a cruise ticket-->

<!DOCTYPE ticketRequest SYSTEM "ticketRequest.dtd">

<ticketRequest>
    <customer custID="10003" >
        <lastName>Carter</lastName>
        <firstName>Joseph</firstName>
    </customer>
    <cruise cruiseID="3004">
        <destination>Hawaii</destination>
        <port>Honolulu</port>
        <sailing>7/7/2001</sailing>
        <numberOfTickets>5</numberOfTickets>
        <isCommissionable/>
    </cruise>
</ticketRequest>
```

Let's take this example apart and figure out what each element in the file means. The first line is

```xml
<?xml version='1.0' encoding='utf-8' standalone='yes' ?>
```

This line starts with a <? character sequence. This line allows the parser or any other software that is looking at the file to detect that it is an XML file that is governed by the rules of version 1.0. This will become important as new versions are introduced. The encoding attribute tells us that the character set used in the document is utf-8, commonly known as text. The keyword standalone is set to yes, which indicates that this document is self-contained and references no other files.

The next line begins with <!--. This character sequence tells the processing program that this is a comment.

```xml
<!--This XML document represents a request for a cruise ticket-->
```

The drawback to this is the use of the comments to contain information that is processing-oriented. We see this in the very next line in the file:

```xml
<!DOCTYPE ticketRequest SYSTEM "ticketRequest.dtd">
```

3

CREATING
APPLICATIONS
WITH JAXP

This line associates the document with a more detailed definition of correctness called the Document Type Definition (DTD). We will see the DTD for this example in the next section. The word SYSTEM tells us to look for a file on our local file system relative to the location of this document. In this case, the DTD file, `ticketRequest.dtd`, would be in the same directory as this file. The word SYSTEM, if it appears here, tells the XML parser that the following string in quotes can be used to load the DTD. This can be used to provide a hyperlink to a DTD using a URL.

The next line is the root element of the document. You are only allowed to define one root element per XML document. The root element contains all other elements in the XML file. The `<ticketRequest>` form tells us that this is a user-defined tag with the name `ticketRequest` and that `ticketRequest` is in the default namespace. The tools that manipulate the XML document are oblivious to the fact that this is a request for tickets. Extracting meaningful information from the document is the job of the XML document consumer that we will create later in this chapter. All that the XML tools are able to do is notice whether the rules of XML are being followed and process the document according to those rules.

```
<ticketRequest>
```

Next, we see another tag named `customer`. The format is a little different, though, because we see extra characters before the > appears.

```
<customer custID="10003" >
```

The extra characters represent an attribute of the customer tag. Defining an attribute is one way of associating information with a tag name. The syntax is formed by simply placing the name of the attribute next to the name of the tag followed by = and a quoted string. Even if a number appears in an attribute, it still appears inside quotes. The > tells us that there are no more attributes for this tag.

The following line is associated with the `customer` tag because it appears before the closing tag for `customer`. Any element that appears before the closing tag is considered a nested element. Nested elements are associated logically with the enclosing element. This means that they will be considered part of the enclosing tag by the parser. In this case, `custID` is considered the `custID` of the `ticketRequest`.

```
<lastName>Carter</lastName>
```

There is another nested element in `customer`: the `firstName` element. We know that the `firstName` element is not nested inside the `lastName` element because the closing tag for `lastName`, `</lastName>` has already appeared in the file.

```
<firstName>Joseph</firstName>
```

Finally, we come to the closing tag for `customer`. This tells us that there will not be any more attributes or nested elements defined for `customer`.

```
</customer>
```

The next line creates a new element called `cruise`. It also has a `cruiseID` attribute defined:

```
<cruise cruiseID="3004">
```

There are several nested elements inside the `cruise` tag. Each of them provides some detail about the cruise: where it is going, when it departs, and so on.

```
<destination>Hawaii</destination>
<port>Honolulu</port>
<sailing>7/7/2001</sailing>
<numberOfTickets>5</numberOfTickets>
```

The following syntax is somewhat different. This character sequence represents an empty tag. An empty tag is one that will never have a subtree of nested elements. The fact that it is present communicates information to the document's consumer. When the consuming program sees this tag, it will know to pay a commission to a travel agent for booking this cruise. If the cruise has been booked online, this tag will be left off, indicating to the consuming program that no commission need be paid.

```
<isCommissionable\>
```

Next, the closing tag for `cruise` appears. After this line we could create another element if we chose to do so. This is because we have still not closed the root element, `ticketRequest`. However, we can only create elements that are allowed by the DTD that was referenced in the `DOCTYPE` declaration.

```
<cruises
```

Finally, we close `ticketRequest`.

```
</ticketRequest>
```

This line must be the last one in the document. If you attempt to create another tag after this, it will be a second root element and that is not allowed. Each XML document is a representation of exactly one root tag.

At this point, we have created a file that contains a `ticketRequest` in a special format. In essence, we have a little piece of persistent storage in character form that can be transmitted anywhere a text file can go. This is the central idea behind XML.

Creating a Document Type Definition (DTD)

Most programmers would rather be poked in the eye than read about how to create a grammar. The subject brings back memories of diagramming sentences and memorizing rules about present participles, gerunds, and tenses. This being said, the grammar validation facility defined in XML is your friend, not a return to seventh grade torture.

If you think of a parser as a type of compiler, you will see its value. The Java compiler finds problems in your code that are normally simple to fix. This keeps you from having to find these problems yourself whenever an error in processing occurs—a big time-saver.

When another program sends you a file containing a ticket request, how do you know that it is a valid XML document? The parsers can tell whether it is well formed, but that doesn't guarantee very much. It would be nice if you could specify which elements are required, which are optional, which ones can have more than one element of a tag, and so on. Then, whenever you receive an XML document, the parser can "compile" it for you and tell you whether it passes. Better still, the sender can run it through the same "compiler" (the XML parser using the same DTD) before sending it to you, thereby guaranteeing that it passes this inspection. This still doesn't guarantee that everything in the file is okay, but it does catch another whole class of potential problems.

The process of creating a DTD is fairly simple if a bit precise. You create a grammar and store it in a file. When you receive an XML document, you parse it with a validating parser. The validation process throws exceptions when it encounters problems. Your code can decide to reject the document in order to prevent introduction of garbage data into your system.

That being said, let's create a DTD for the ticket request. This example is simple and very short. Listing 3.2 shows the DTD for the `ticketRequest` element, which serves as a grammar that allows the parser to validate XML documents.

LISTING 3.2   The `ticketRequest` DTD File

```
<!ELEMENT ticketRequest (customer, cruise)>
<!ELEMENT customer ( lastName, firstName)>
<!ATTLIST customer custID NMTOKEN #REQUIRED>
<!ELEMENT lastName (#PCDATA)>
<!ELEMENT firstName (#PCDATA)>
<!ELEMENT cruise (destination, port, sailing, numberOfTickets,
➥isCommissionable?)>
```

LISTING 3.2   continued

```
<!ATTLIST cruise cruiseID NMTOKEN #REQUIRED>
<!ELEMENT destination (#PCDATA)>
<!ELEMENT port (#PCDATA)>
<!ELEMENT sailing (#PCDATA)>
<!ELEMENT numberOfTickets (#PCDATA)>
<!ELEMENT isCommissionable EMPTY>
```

Let's look at this file line by line to get a better understanding of how to create DTDs.

The ticket request must contain exactly one customer and one cruise. I could have placed qualifiers after each word if there were other options. customer+ means one or more, customer* means zero or more, and customer? means zero or one of these elements must be present in order for the request to be valid.

```
<!ELEMENT ticketRequest (customer, cruise)>
```

Likewise, a customer must have a lastName and a firstName:

```
<!ELEMENT customer ( lastName, firstName)>
```

Each lastName and firstName contains only PCDATA, also known as text:

```
<!ATTLIST customer custID NMTOKEN #REQUIRED>
<!ELEMENT lastName (#PCDATA)>
<!ELEMENT firstName (#PCDATA)>
```

The only attribute that the customer needs is a custID. Its attribute type is NMTOKEN, which is like CDATA but allows fewer special characters.

The cruise element must contain exactly one destination, port, sailing, and numberOfTickets. It might contain a single isCommissionable, and it might not. It is valid with no tag for isCommissionable, but it will be invalid if there are two of them.

```
<!ELEMENT cruise(destination, port, sailing, numberOfTickets,
➥isCommissionable?)>
```

The cruiseID is a required attribute of the cruise tag:

```
<!ATTLIST cruise cruiseID NMTOKEN #REQUIRED>
```

The destination, port, sailing, and numberOfTickets will contain only text. Notice that this is true even for numbers.

```
<!ELEMENT destination (#PCDATA)>
<!ELEMENT port (#PCDATA)>
<!ELEMENT sailing (#PCDATA)>
<!ELEMENT numberOfTickets (#PCDATA)>
```

3

CREATING APPLICATIONS WITH JAXP

Finally, the isCommissionable tag is designated as EMPTY. This means that it can have no text or other elements in it. This makes sense for flag type elements.

```
<!ELEMENT isCommissionable EMPTY>
```

This is all that we need to specify our document in a DTD. You might be wondering how you might specify that a value must be all characters and no digits, or all digits. Unfortunately, the DTD standard doesn't allow that level of specification past a certain point. A W3C XML Working Group committee called the Schema Working Group is working on expanding the DTD to the level of a schema, but that work has not been incorporated into JAXP as of this writing. Microsoft has also proposed an XML Schema.

Parsing with the Simple API for XML (SAX)

There are three ways of getting at the data contained in an XML document. The first is to write your own parser using a StringTokenizer object to navigate through the code. This approach has the advantage of being conceptually simple and thus it has a short learning curve. You start at the beginning of the file and look for certain tag combinations. When you find the tag that you want, you remove the data, use it or store it in a variable, and move on to the next tag. This works well for very simple XML documents, but it can become tedious to code when the number of tags gets large.

The second approach is to use a parser to create a Document Object Model, or DOM. A DOM is an in-memory treelike model of the document. The parser provides a number of methods to traverse the tree. You use these methods to find the data that you want, and having found it, you use the data or store it in a local variable. There are advantages and disadvantages to this approach that we will discuss after we have covered some coding examples.

The third approach is the one that we will use in this section. It is called the Simple API for XML (SAX). SAX is simple to use once you become familiar with it. It is based on an event-driven model in which the parser generates events that you write handlers for. This works fine in practice, but it is not especially intuitive.

> **Note**
>
> The SAX examples in this chapter are based on the SAX 2.0 standard. The J2EE JAR file may contain a SAX 1.x parser. The WebLogic installation comes with a SAX 2.0 parser in the weblogic.jar file. See the readme in the code zip file for this chapter for instructions on how to place the correct parser in your classpath.

Rather than provide a long-winded explanation of how SAX works, we'll work through an example that uses SAX to parse the `ticketRequest.xml` file that we created earlier. We need a class to represent a travel agent's request to a cruise line to book a cruise on behalf of one of his customers. We will use the `TicketRequest2` object that can be found in Appendix A, "Source Code Listings for Utility Programs Used in This Book." The code for this class is included with the code for this chapter on the Web site.

The program that processes the XML file is called TicketRequestParser. It converts an XML document into a `TicketRequest2` object using a SAX2 parser. It is shown in Listing 3.3.

LISTING 3.3 The TicketRequestParser

```java
//object using the SAX parser.
/*
 * TicketRequestParser.java
 *
 * Created on January 18, 2002, 3:01 PM
 */

package unleashed.ch3;

import unleashed.TicketRequest2;
import org.xml.sax.*;
import org.xml.sax.helpers.*;
import javax.xml.parsers.*;
import java.io.*;

/**
 *
 * @author   Stephen Potts
 * @version
 */
public class TicketRequestParser extends DefaultHandler
{
    private CharArrayWriter buffer = new CharArrayWriter();
    static TicketRequest2 tr2;
    String custIDString;
    String cruiseIDString;

    public void startDocument() throws SAXException
    {
        System.out.println("startDocument() called");
    }

    public void endDocument() throws SAXException
    {
        System.out.println("endDocument() called");
```

LISTING 3.3 continued

```java
    }

    public void startElement(String namespaceURI, String localName,
    String qName, Attributes attr) throws SAXException
    {

        for ( int i=0; i < attr.getLength(); i++)
        {
            String attrName = attr.getQName(i);
            if (attrName.equals("custID"))
            {
                custIDString = attr.getValue(i);
            }
            if (attrName.equals("cruiseID"))
            {
                cruiseIDString = attr.getValue(i);
            }
        }
        buffer.reset();
    }

    public void endElement( String nameSpaceURI, String localName,
    String qName) throws SAXException
    {
        storeElementValue(qName);
    }

    public void characters( char[] ch, int start,
                            int length) throws SAXException
    {
        buffer.write(ch, start, length);
    }

    private void storeElementValue(String elementName)
    {
        if (elementName.equals("ticketRequest"))
        {
        }

        if (elementName.equals("customer"))
        {
            tr2.setCustID(Integer.parseInt(custIDString));
        }

        if (elementName.equals("lastName"))
        {
            tr2.setLastName(buffer.toString());
        }
```

LISTING 3.3   continued

```
    if (elementName.equals("firstName"))
    {
        tr2.setFirstName(buffer.toString());
    }

    if (elementName.equals("cruise"))
    {
        tr2.setCruiseID(Integer.parseInt(cruiseIDString));
    }

    if (elementName.equals("destination"))
    {
        tr2.setDestination(buffer.toString());
    }

    if (elementName.equals("port"))
    {
        tr2.setPort(buffer.toString());
    }

    if (elementName.equals("sailing"))
    {
        tr2.setSailing(buffer.toString());
    }

    if (elementName.equals("numberOfTickets"))
    {
        String numberOfTicketsString = buffer.toString();
        int numberOfTickets =
                        Integer.parseInt(numberOfTicketsString);
        tr2.setNumberOfTickets(numberOfTickets);
    }

    if (elementName.equals("isCommissionable"))
    {
        tr2.setCommissionable(true);
    }
}

public String toString()
{
    return tr2.toString();
}

public static void main( String[] args)
{

    System.out.println("TicketRequestParser main()");
```

LISTING 3.3   continued

```
        DefaultHandler trp = new TicketRequestParser();

        tr2 = new TicketRequest2();
        SAXParserFactory factory = SAXParserFactory.newInstance();
        try
        {
            SAXParser saxParser = factory.newSAXParser();
            saxParser.parse( new File(
              "c:/unleashed/ch3/ticketRequest.xml"),
                        trp);
        }catch (Exception e)
        {
            System.out.println("Exception in main " + e);
        }
        System.out.println(trp);
    }
}
```

There are quite a few interesting lines of code in this example. The declaration of the class states that it extends DefaultHandler:

```
public class TicketRequestParser extends DefaultHandler
```

The `org.xml.sax.helpers.DefaultHandler` class is the default base class for SAX2 event handlers. It serves as a convenience class, which means that it provides a default handler for any events that you don't want to handle. When writing applications, you can extend this class and override the parts of the interface that you want to control.

The processing of text in SAX is done in character buffers. The easiest way to convert these characters to strings is to define a buffer that grows when data is written to it:

```
    private CharArrayWriter buffer = new CharArrayWriter();
```

There are five methods that we will override to process our document:

- startDocument()—Called when the document is opened.
- endDocument()—Called at the end of the document.
- startElement()—Called when each opening tag is encountered.
- endElement()—Called when each end tag is encountered.
- characters()—Called whenever the parser encounters characters that it cannot identify as a type of tag or instruction. This method assumes that the characters are data of some sort.

The start and end of the documents are not very interesting in this application, so we simply do a `println()` to show that the application occurred. The elements are processed by the `startElement()` method and the `endElement()` method. `startElement()` does two things: It resets the buffer to empty it and processes the attributes, if any, of the element. In the case of `custID`, the value is kept in an attribute, not in a subelement:

```
for ( int i=0; i < attr.getLength(); i++)
{
    String attrName = attr.getLocalName(i);
    if (attrName.equals("custID"))
    {
        custIDString = attr.getValue(i);
    }
    if (attrName.equals("cruiseID"))
    {
        cruiseIDString = attr.getValue(i);
    }
}
```

If a tag has attributes, they will be kept in a list that implements the `org.xml.sax.Attributes` interface. This list has methods to get the name and the value. These are stored in class level variables so that we can keep all the `TicketRequest2` class updates in one method, making the example easier to follow.

The `storeElementValue()` accepts as a parameter the name of the element to be stored. It then copies what is in the buffer and passes this to the mutator method for that value in the `TicketRequest2` object. Some data type conversion takes place to store the values in the `int` fields.

Notice that the attributes are retrieved from the class level variables and placed in the object when a closing tag is encountered for their element.

A slightly different processing takes place for the `isCommissionable` element. The presence of this element indicates that a commission will be paid on this booking. It has no value to store, so the code infers that `true` is the correct value and sets it accordingly.

The result is output using the `toString()` method of the `TicketRequestParser` class, which simply calls the `toString()` method of the `TicketRequest2` class.

Running the `TicketRequestParser`'s `main()` gives us the following results:

```
TicketRequestParser main()
startDocument() called
endDocument() called
----------------------------------------------
```

3

CREATING
APPLICATIONS
WITH JAXP

```
custID = 10003
lastName = Carter
firstName = Joseph
------------------------------------------------
cruiseID = 3004
destination = Hawaii
port = Honolulu
sailing = 7/7/2001
numberOfTickets = 5
isCommissionable = true
----------------------------------------------\
```

There are not a lot of surprises here. The TicketRequestParser is doing a lot of work, but its job is to translate an XML document that represents a specific object into that object. We will see later how this code can be used to create asynchronous processing of distributed objects.

Parsing with the Document Object Model (DOM)

There is another approach to parsing XML documents called the Document Object Model (DOM) approach. This API produces an in-memory treelike version of the XML document, as well as a number of methods for traversing the model and obtaining the data stored in it.

There are many nice things about the DOM approach from a processing point of view. The first is that it is more intuitive than the SAX approach. As object-oriented programmers, we like being given an object structure. In addition, we can make changes to this model and persist these changes back to the XML document as output. SAX 2.0 allows this as well. This opens a world of possibilities where you can use the XML document as a sort of database.

Following the same approach that we used with SAX, we will show an example and then explain the whys and what fors of the code.

We will solve the same problem with DOM as we did with SAX—translating an XML document into an object. The code for this example is shown in Listing 3.4. The DOM approach creates a treelike structure in memory representing the XML document.

LISTING 3.4 The Document Object Model Approach

```
/*
 * TicketRequestDOMParser.java
 *
```

LISTING 3.4   continued

```
 * Created on January 19, 2002, 5:33 PM
 */

package unleashed.ch3;

import unleashed.TicketRequest2;
import javax.xml.parsers.DocumentBuilder;
import javax.xml.parsers.DocumentBuilderFactory;
import javax.xml.parsers.FactoryConfigurationError;
import javax.xml.parsers.ParserConfigurationException;

import org.xml.sax.SAXException;
import org.xml.sax.SAXParseException;

import java.io.*;

import org.w3c.dom.Document;
import org.w3c.dom.DOMException;
import org.w3c.dom.Node;
import org.w3c.dom.*;

/**
 *
 * @author   Stephen Potts
 * @version
 */
public class TicketRequestDOMParser
{
    static Document document;
    TicketRequest2 tr2;
    String eleName;


    public TicketRequestDOMParser()
    {
        DocumentBuilderFactory factory =
            DocumentBuilderFactory.newInstance();
        try
        {
            tr2 = new TicketRequest2();
            DocumentBuilder builder = factory.newDocumentBuilder();
            document = builder.parse( new File(
            "C:/unleashed/ch3/ticketRequest.xml"));
            traverse(document);
        }catch (SAXException sxe)
        {
            Exception e = sxe;
            if (sxe.getException() != null)
                e = sxe.getException();
```

LISTING 3.4   continued

```
            e.printStackTrace();
        }
        catch (ParserConfigurationException pce)
        {
            pce.printStackTrace();
        }
        catch (IOException ioe)
        {
            ioe.printStackTrace();
        }
    }

    private void traverse(Node cNode)
    {
        switch (cNode.getNodeType() )
        {
            case Node.DOCUMENT_NODE:
                System.out.println("Element " + cNode.getNodeName());
                processChildren( cNode.getChildNodes());
                break;

            case Node.ELEMENT_NODE:
                eleName = cNode.getNodeName();
                System.out.println("Element " + eleName);
                NamedNodeMap attributeMap = cNode.getAttributes();
                int numAttrs = attributeMap.getLength();
                for (int i=0; i<attributeMap.getLength(); i++)
                {
                    Attr attribute = (Attr)attributeMap.item(i);
                    String attrName =  attribute.getNodeName();
                    String attrValue = attribute.getNodeValue();
                    storeElementValue(attrName, attrValue);
                }
                if (eleName.equals("isCommissionable"))
                {
                    storeElementValue("isCommissionable", "");
                }

                processChildren( cNode.getChildNodes());
                break;
            case Node.CDATA_SECTION_NODE:
            case Node.TEXT_NODE:

                System.out.println("Text " + cNode.getNodeValue());
                if (! cNode.getNodeValue().trim().equals(""))
                {
                    System.out.println("eleName " + eleName);
                    System.out.println("Text " + cNode.getNodeValue());
                    storeElementValue(eleName, cNode.getNodeValue());
```

LISTING 3.4   continued

```
                }
                break;
        }
    }

    private void processChildren(NodeList nList)
    {
        if(nList.getLength() != 0)
        {
            for (int i=0; i<nList.getLength(); i++)
                traverse(nList.item(i));
        }
    }


    private void storeElementValue(String elementName,
                                   String elementValue)
    {
        if (elementName.equals("ticketRequest"))
        {
        }

        if (elementName.equals("custID"))
        {
            tr2.setCustID(Integer.parseInt(elementValue));
        }

        if (elementName.equals("lastName"))
        {
            tr2.setLastName(elementValue);
        }

        if (elementName.equals("firstName"))
        {
            tr2.setFirstName(elementValue);
        }

        if (elementName.equals("cruiseID"))
        {
            tr2.setCruiseID(Integer.parseInt(elementValue));
        }

        if (elementName.equals("destination"))
        {
            tr2.setDestination(elementValue);
        }

        if (elementName.equals("port"))
```

3

CREATING
APPLICATIONS
WITH JAXP

LISTING 3.4   continued

```
        {
            tr2.setPort(elementValue);
        }

        if (elementName.equals("sailing"))
        {
            tr2.setSailing(elementValue);
        }

        if (elementName.equals("numberOfTickets"))
        {
            String numberOfTicketsString = elementValue;
            int numberOfTickets =
                Integer.parseInt(numberOfTicketsString);
            tr2.setNumberOfTickets(numberOfTickets);
        }

        if (elementName.equals("isCommissionable"))
        {
            tr2.setCommissionable(true);
        }
    }

    public String toString()
    {
        return tr2.toString();
    }


    public static void main(String args[])
    {
        TicketRequestDOMParser  tp = new TicketRequestDOMParser();
        System.out.println(tp);
    }

}
```

This program contains quite a few lines that require some explanation.

There are three main variables in this program:

```
static Document document;
TicketRequest2 tr2;
String eleName;
```

The stars of the show are the document object, which holds the DOM structure; the eleName, which contains the name of whatever element we are working on at the moment; and the TicketRequest2, which is the product of our efforts.

The good news about DOM is that tree building is automatic. All that you have to do is create a factory, which creates a builder. The builder's parse method is called, which translates the XML document into the DOM tree.

```
DocumentBuilderFactory factory = DocumentBuilderFactory.newInstance();
tr2 = new TicketRequest2();
DocumentBuilder builder = factory.newDocumentBuilder();
document = builder.parse(
   new File("C:/projects/sampledir/unleashed/ch3/ticketRequest.xml"));
```

Once we have created a DOM tree, we call the `traverse()` method and pass the document into it:

```
traverse(document);
```

The `traverse()` method is a big switch statement that contains three main cases: document, element, and text. Whenever an element is encountered, its attributes are processed with the following code:

```
        Attr attribute = (Attr)attributeMap.item(i);
          String attrName =  attribute.getNodeName();
          String attrValue = attribute.getNodeValue();
          storeElementValue(attrName, attrValue);
```

The `isCommissionable` switch requires special treatment because it has no value. Because it is a flag, its presence alone tells you that the `boolean` needs to be set to `true`.

```
        if (eleName.equals("isCommissionable"))
        {
            storeElementValue("isCommissionable", "");
        }
```

Whenever we find either an attribute or element text that corresponds to a field in our object, we make a call and pass in two strings:

```
        storeElementValue(eleName, cNode.getNodeValue());
```

Because some nodes contain other nodes, we have to process our tree recursively. The `processChildren()` method takes in the children of a node in a list. It tests to see whether any children really do exist. If so, it calls the `traverse()` method on that branch of the tree:

```
    private void processChildren(NodeList nList)
    {
        if(nList.getLength() != 0)
        {
            for (int i=0; i<nList.getLength(); i++)
                traverse(nList.item(i));
        }
    }
```

The main method of this program is very simple. It instantiates the object and prints the result:

```
TicketRequestDOMParser  tp = new TicketRequestDOMParser();
      System.out.println(tp);
```

The result of running this example is shown here:

```
----------------------------------------------
custID = 10003
lastName = Carter
firstName = Joseph
----------------------------------------------
cruiseID = 3004
destination = Hawaii
port = Honolulu
sailing = 7/7/2001
numberOfTickets = 5
isCommissionable = true
----------------------------------------------
```

Prior to seeing this output, you will see some tracing information to show you some of the program flow. (It is not shown here.) The `TicketRequest` object is shown via its `toString()` method.

You can see from this that it is a relatively straightforward process to transform an XML file into a Java object. Once you have a Java object in your program, you are back in familiar territory.

How do we move XML documents between servers to support distributed computing? That is the topic of the next section.

An XML Version of the CruiseList Application

Once we are comfortable with our ability to verify that an XML document is correct and turn it into an object that can be manipulated in a program, we begin to ask questions about how to integrate this technology into a real application.

The biggest question is how to move the XML document from where it was created to the server where it will be consumed. The answer is simply that the XML document is a file full of characters (ASCII, Unicode, or some similar character set). Any transport that can move a text file can move an XML file.

XML and the Java Message Service (JMS) are a nice fit. All that you have to do to send XML via JMS is to place the XML into a string. This string can then be sent as a message. Messaging provides guaranteed delivery across heterogeneous operating system platforms. For more information on using messaging, see Chapter 7, "Java Message Service (JMS)," and Chapter 6, "Message-Driven Beans (MDB)."

The goal of this chapter, though, is to present Java-based XML processing to you as clearly as possible. It would be unwise to mix a JMS discussion in the same chapter. Therefore, we will create the CruiseList application here as a shared directory application.

The CruiseList GUI will create the XML document and place it in a special directory. The TicketAgent application will wake up periodically and look for files in that directory. It will open each file that it finds, create the tickets in the database, and send a response back to the GUI. The GUI will display the response in a dialog whenever the Check button is pressed.

> **Note**
>
> Before running this application, first run the `AccessJDBC2` application included as part of Appendix A. This application drops and adds tables to the database along with enough data to make the application work. It can also be used to reset the database between successive runs of the program.

The code for the CruiseList GUI is shown in Listing 3.5.

LISTING 3.5   The CruiseList Application

```
package unleashed.ch3;

/*
 * CruiseList.java
 *
 * Created on December 31, 2001, 6:35 PM
 */

import unleashed.TicketRequest2;
import javax.swing.*;
import java.awt.event.ActionListener;
import javax.swing.border.EtchedBorder;
import java.awt.Container;
import java.awt.BorderLayout;
import java.sql.*;
import javax.naming.*;
import java.util.*;
```

3

CREATING
APPLICATIONS
WITH JAXP

LISTING 3.5 continued

```java
import java.io.*;
import org.w3c.dom.*;
import org.xml.sax.*;
import javax.xml.parsers.*;


import javax.xml.transform.Transformer;
import javax.xml.transform.TransformerException;
import javax.xml.transform.TransformerFactory;
import javax.xml.transform.TransformerConfigurationException;
import javax.xml.transform.dom.DOMSource;
import javax.xml.transform.stream.StreamResult;

/**
 *
 * @author   Stephen Potts
 * @version
 */
public class CruiseList extends JFrame implements ActionListener
{
    Document doc;

    //JDBC variables
    java.sql.Connection dbConn = null;
    Statement statement1 = null;

    //GUI Variables
    JList customerList;
    JList cruisesAvailable;
    JButton btnBook;
    JButton btnExit;
    JButton btnCheck;


    //Arrays to hold database information
    int[] custNums = null;
    String[] lastNames = null;
    String[] firstNames = null;

    int[] cruiseIDs = null;
    String[] cruiseDestinations = null;
    String[] cruisePorts = null;
    String[] cruiseSailings = null;

    /** Constructors for CruiseList */
    public CruiseList() throws Exception
    {
        init();
    }
```

LISTING 3.5   continued

```java
public CruiseList(String caption) throws Exception
{
    super(caption);
    init();
}

//The init() method moves processing out of the constructors where
//Exception handling is simpler
private void init() throws Exception
{
    try
    {
        //Obtain connections to JDBC and JMS via JNDI
        ConnectToServices();

        //configure the Frame
        setBounds(150,200,500,250);
        setDefaultCloseOperation(JFrame.EXIT_ON_CLOSE);

        //set the layout
        BorderLayout border = new BorderLayout();
        Container content = getContentPane();
        content.setLayout(border);

        //Populate the customerNames string
        String getCustomerString =
        "SELECT CustomerID, LastName, FirstName FROM CruiseCustomer";
        ResultSet custResults =
        statement1.executeQuery(getCustomerString);

        custNums = new int[20];
        lastNames = new String[20];
        firstNames = new String[20];
        int index = 0;

        while (custResults.next())
        {
            custNums[index] = custResults.getInt("CustomerID");
            firstNames[index] = custResults.getString("FirstName");
            lastNames[index] = custResults.getString("LastName");
            index += 1;
        }

        String[] customerNames = new String[index];

        for (int i=0;i<index;i++)
        {
            customerNames[i] = firstNames[i] + " " + lastNames[i];
        }
```

3

CREATING
APPLICATIONS
WITH JAXP

LISTING 3.5   continued

```java
int numCustomers = index;
System.out.println("The number of customers " + index);

//Populate the cruises string
String getCruiseString =
"SELECT CruiseID, Destination, Port, Sailing FROM Cruises";
ResultSet cruiseResults =
statement1.executeQuery(getCruiseString);

cruiseIDs = new int[20];
cruiseDestinations = new String[20];
cruisePorts = new String[20];
cruiseSailings = new String[20];
index = 0;

while (cruiseResults.next())
{
    cruiseIDs[index] = cruiseResults.getInt("CruiseID");
    cruiseDestinations[index] =
    cruiseResults.getString("Destination");
    cruisePorts[index] = cruiseResults.getString("Port");
    cruiseSailings[index] =
    cruiseResults.getString("Sailing");
    index += 1;
}

String[] cruises = new String[index];

for (int i=0;i<index;i++)
{
    cruises[i] = cruiseDestinations[i] +
    "       Departs: " +
    cruisePorts[i] + " " + cruiseSailings[i];
}

int numCruises = index;
System.out.println("The number of cruises" + index);


//More GUI components
String labelString = "                 Customer";
labelString += "                    Cruise";
JLabel label1 = new JLabel(labelString);
customerList = new JList(customerNames);
cruisesAvailable = new JList(cruises);
btnBook = new JButton("Book");
btnCheck = new JButton("Check");
```

LISTING 3.5   continued

```
            btnExit = new JButton("Exit");
            btnBook.addActionListener(this);
            btnExit.addActionListener(this);
            btnCheck.addActionListener(this);

            JPanel bottomPanel = new JPanel();
            JPanel centerPanel = new JPanel();
            centerPanel.add(new JScrollPane(customerList,
            JScrollPane.VERTICAL_SCROLLBAR_ALWAYS,
            JScrollPane.HORIZONTAL_SCROLLBAR_AS_NEEDED));
            centerPanel.add(new JScrollPane(cruisesAvailable,
            JScrollPane.VERTICAL_SCROLLBAR_ALWAYS,
            JScrollPane.HORIZONTAL_SCROLLBAR_AS_NEEDED));
            bottomPanel.add(btnBook);
            bottomPanel.add(btnCheck);
            bottomPanel.add(btnExit);
            content.add(label1, BorderLayout.NORTH);
            content.add(centerPanel, BorderLayout.CENTER);
            content.add(bottomPanel, BorderLayout.SOUTH);
            setVisible(true);
        }catch(Exception e)
        {
            System.out.println("Exception thrown " + e);
        } finally
        {
            try
            {
                //close all connections
                if (statement1 != null)
                    statement1.close();
                if (dbConn != null)
                    dbConn.close();

            } catch (SQLException sqle)
            {
                System.out.println("SQLException during close(): " +
                sqle.getMessage());
            }
        }

    }

    private void ConnectToServices()
    {
        try
        {
            // ============== Make connection to database ============

            //load the driver class
```

LISTING 3.5   continued

```java
            Class.forName("sun.jdbc.odbc.JdbcOdbcDriver");

            //Specify the ODBC data source
            String sourceURL = "jdbc:odbc:CruiseTicket";

            //get a connection to the database
            dbConn =DriverManager.getConnection(sourceURL);

            //If we get to here, no exception was thrown
            System.out.println("The database connection is " + dbConn);
            System.out.println("Making connection...\n");

            //Create the statement
            statement1 = dbConn.createStatement();


        } catch (Exception e)
        {
            System.out.println("Exception was thrown: " + e);
        }
    }

    /**
     * @param args the command line arguments
     */
    public static void main(String args[])
    {
        //create an instance of the GUI
        try
        {
            CruiseList mainWindow =
            new CruiseList("Cruise Ticket System");
        }catch(Exception e)
        {
            System.out.println("Exception in main " + e);
        }
    }

    public void actionPerformed(java.awt.event.ActionEvent ae)
    {
        try
        {
            Container c = btnExit.getParent();
            if (ae.getActionCommand().equals("Exit"))
            {
                System.exit(0);
            }
```

LISTING 3.5 continued

```
            //Try and book a ticket
            if (ae.getActionCommand().equals("Book"))
            {
                System.out.println("Book was clicked");
                int custIndex = customerList.getSelectedIndex();
                int cruiseIndex = cruisesAvailable.getSelectedIndex();

                if (custIndex == -1 || cruiseIndex == -1)
                {
                    JOptionPane.showMessageDialog(c,
                    "You must choose a customer and a cruise");
                }else
                {
                    //Pop up a dialog asking how many tickets
                    String numTickets = JOptionPane.showInputDialog(c,
                    "How many tickets?");
                    int numberOfTickets = Integer.parseInt(numTickets);

                    //create a ticket request object
                    TicketRequest2 tickReq =
                    new TicketRequest2(custNums[custIndex],
                    lastNames[custIndex], firstNames[custIndex],
                    cruiseIDs[cruiseIndex], cruiseDestinations[cruiseIndex],
                    cruisePorts[cruiseIndex], cruiseSailings[cruiseIndex],
                    numberOfTickets, false);

                    //create the xml file
                    createXMLDoc(tickReq);

                }
            }
            //See if you got a mail message back
            if (ae.getActionCommand().equals("Check"))
            {
                //Check to see if there are any email messages for us
                fetchMessages();
            }

        }catch (Exception e)
        {
            System.out.println("Exception thrown = " + e);
        }
    }

    private void fetchMessages()
    {
        try
        {
```

3

CREATING
APPLICATIONS
WITH JAXP

LISTING 3.5 continued

```java
        Container c = btnExit.getParent();

        //read the text message from the file
        String dirName = "c:/XML/response/";
        File dir = new File(dirName);
        File f1;
        String messageLine = "";
        String strToken = "";
        String message = "";
        String message2 = "";

        String[]  fileList = dir.list();
        for (int i=0;i<fileList.length;++i)
        {
            String fileName = dirName + fileList[i];
            BufferedReader br = new BufferedReader(
            new FileReader(fileName));

            while( (messageLine = br.readLine()) != null)
            {
                message += messageLine;
                System.out.println("messageLine = " + messageLine);
            }
            StringTokenizer st = new StringTokenizer(message , "<>");
            while (st.hasMoreTokens())
            {
                strToken = st.nextToken();
                if (strToken.equals("ticketResponse"))
                {
                    message2 = st.nextToken();
                    //show the message in a dialog box
                    JOptionPane.showMessageDialog(c, message2);
                }
            }

        }
    }catch (Exception e)
    {
        System.out.println(" Exception " + e);
    }
}


public void createXMLDoc(TicketRequest2 tr2) throws IOException
{
        try
        {

                DocumentBuilderFactory dFactory =
```

LISTING 3.5 continued

```
            DocumentBuilderFactory.newInstance();

            DocumentBuilder dBuilder = dFactory.newDocumentBuilder();

            doc = dBuilder.newDocument();

            //Create the root element
            Element ticketRequest = doc.createElement("ticketRequest");

            doc.appendChild(ticketRequest);

            //create the customer node
            Node customer = createCustomer(doc, tr2);
            ticketRequest.appendChild(customer);

            //create the cruise node
            Node cruise = createCruise(doc, tr2);
            ticketRequest.appendChild(cruise);


            //Create a transformer to write the file out
            TransformerFactory tFactory =
            TransformerFactory.newInstance();

            Transformer transformer = tFactory.newTransformer();
            DOMSource source = new DOMSource(ticketRequest);

            //Write out the file
            String filename = "c:/XML/request/request" +
                                tr2.getCustID() + ".xml";
            StreamResult result = new StreamResult(
            new FileOutputStream(filename));
            transformer.transform(source, result);


        }catch(Exception e)
        {
            System.out.println("Exception e" + e);
        }
    }

    private Node createCustomer(Document doc, TicketRequest2 tr2)
    {
        Element lastName = doc.createElement("lastName");
        Element firstName = doc.createElement("firstName");

        lastName.appendChild(doc.createTextNode(tr2.getLastName()));
        firstName.appendChild(doc.createTextNode(tr2.getFirstName()));
```

LISTING 3.5   continued

```java
        Element customer = doc.createElement("customer");

        Attr custIDAttribute = doc.createAttribute("custID");
        String s1 = String.valueOf(tr2.getCustID());
        custIDAttribute.setValue(s1);

        //append the attribute
        customer.setAttributeNode( custIDAttribute );
        customer.appendChild(lastName);
        customer.appendChild(firstName);

        return customer;
    }

    private Node createCruise(Document doc, TicketRequest2 tr2)
    {
        Element destination = doc.createElement("destination");
        Element port = doc.createElement("port");
        Element sailing = doc.createElement("sailing");
        Element numberOfTickets = doc.createElement("numberOfTickets");

        destination.appendChild(doc.createTextNode(tr2.getDestination()));
        port.appendChild(doc.createTextNode(tr2.getPort()));
        sailing.appendChild(doc.createTextNode(tr2.getSailing()));
        String s3 = String.valueOf(tr2.getNumberOfTickets());
        numberOfTickets.appendChild(doc.createTextNode(s3));

        Element cruise = doc.createElement("cruise");

        Attr cruiseIDAttribute = doc.createAttribute("cruiseID");
        String s2 = String.valueOf(tr2.getCustID());
        cruiseIDAttribute.setValue(s2);

        //append the attribute
        cruise.setAttributeNode(cruiseIDAttribute);
        cruise.appendChild(destination);
        cruise.appendChild(port);
        cruise.appendChild(sailing);

        cruise.appendChild(numberOfTickets);

        return cruise;
    }

}
```

This application is a little long, but it is not very difficult. It uses XML to communicate its requests. It is a simple GUI that populates the variables in a `TicketRequest2` object that we introduced earlier in the chapter. After the object is built, the method

```
public void createXMLDoc(TicketRequest2 tr2) throws IOException
```

is called. It takes the data in the `TicketRequest2` object and creates an XML document out of it. This document is saved in a file in a special directory.

The other interesting part is checking for responses. Whenever the Check button is clicked, a separate directory is examined, all the files in that directory are opened, and a message is created and then displayed. The code to do this is shown here:

```
String[]  fileList = dir.list();
for (int i=0;i<fileList.length;++i)
{
    String fileName = dirName + fileList[i];
    BufferedReader br =
            new BufferedReader(new FileReader(fileName));

    while( (messageLine = br.readLine()) != null)
    {
        message += messageLine;
        System.out.println("messageLine = " + messageLine);
    }
    StringTokenizer st = new StringTokenizer(message , "<>");
    while (st.hasMoreTokens())
    {
        strToken = st.nextToken();
        if (strToken.equals("ticketResponse"))
            message2 = st.nextToken();
    }

    //show the message in a dialog box
    JOptionPane.showMessageDialog(c, message2);
}
```

The entire contents of the file that it reads in are in the form

```
<ticketResponse>
The ticket to Hawaii for Skelton was successful
</ticketResponse>
```

This looks like XML, but there is no prolog before the data. In reality, this is a simple text file that borrows its syntax from XML. Notice how `StringTokenizer` can be used and <> set as the delimiter. You can step through the file looking for a tag called `ticketResponse`. When you find it, the next token will be the contents of that tag, complete with whitespace.

This technique is useful when your needs are so simple that using either SAX or DOM is overkill. You can quickly find what you are looking for as long as the file doesn't contain too many attributes and nested tags.

The other half of this application is the TicketAgent. This application has no GUI, and in this version, it runs through the request files just once. The code for the TicketAgent application is shown in Listing 3.6.

LISTING 3.6   The TicketAgent Application

```
/*
 * TicketAgent.java
 *
 * Created on January 21, 2002, 4:37 PM
 */

package unleashed.ch3;

import unleashed.TicketRequest2;
import java.io.*;
import java.util.*;
import java.sql.*;
import javax.xml.parsers.DocumentBuilder;
import javax.xml.parsers.DocumentBuilderFactory;
import javax.xml.parsers.FactoryConfigurationError;
import javax.xml.parsers.ParserConfigurationException;

import org.xml.sax.SAXException;
import org.xml.sax.SAXParseException;

import org.w3c.dom.Document;
import org.w3c.dom.DOMException;
import org.w3c.dom.Node;
import org.w3c.dom.*;
/**
 * The TicketAgent application.  It received an XML TicketRequest file
 * It uses JDBC to access the database to
 * get the credit card number.It then sends a message to the PaymentAgent
 * to request approval of a charge to the credit card.  When the
 * charge is approved TicketAgent updates the database and sends
 * a message to the CruiseList application.
 *
 *
 * @author Steve Potts
 */
public class TicketAgent
{
    static int ticketID = 7000;
    private boolean quit = false;
```

LISTING 3.6   continued

```java
//JDBC variables
java.sql.Connection dbConn = null;
Statement statement1 = null;
String sourceURL = "jdbc:odbc:CruiseTicket";

DocumentBuilderFactory factory;
DocumentBuilder builder;
Document document;

TicketRequest2 tr2;
String eleName;



public TicketAgent() throws Exception
{
    init();
}

//The init() method moves processing out of the constructors where
//Exception handling is simpler
private void init() throws Exception
{
    try
    {
        //Obtain connections to JDBC and JMS via JNDI
        ConnectToServices();

    }catch(Exception e)
    {
        System.out.println("Exception thrown " + e);
    }
}

private void ConnectToServices()
{
    try
    {
        // ============== Make connection to database ==============

        //load the driver class
        Class.forName("sun.jdbc.odbc.JdbcOdbcDriver");


        //connect to the XML parser factory and builder
        factory = DocumentBuilderFactory.newInstance();
        builder = factory.newDocumentBuilder();
```

LISTING 3.6   continued

```java
        } catch (Exception e)
        {
            System.out.println("Exception was thrown: " + e);
        }
    }

    public void checkForXMlDocs()
    {
        String dirName = "c:/XML/request/";
        File dir = new File(dirName);
        File f1;

        String[]  fileList = dir.list();
        for (int i=0;i<fileList.length;++i)
        {
            String s = fileList[i];
            if (s.startsWith("r"))
            {
                System.out.println(fileList[i]);
                parseFile(dirName + fileList[i]);
                System.out.println(tr2);
            }
        }

    }

    public void parseFile(String fname)
    {
        try
        {
            tr2 = new TicketRequest2();
            File f1 = new File(fname);
            document = builder.parse(f1);
            traverse(document);

            //get the credit card number from the database
            String ccNum = getCreditCardNumber(tr2.getCustID());
            System.out.println("The Credit Card Number is " + ccNum);

            //create a queue send to the Payment queue
            if (verifyCreditCard(ccNum))
            {
                createTicket(tr2);
                sendTicketResponse(tr2, true);
            }else
                sendTicketResponse(tr2, false);

        }catch (SAXException sxe)
```

LISTING 3.6 continued

```
        {
            Exception e = sxe;
            if (sxe.getException() != null)
                e = sxe.getException();
            e.printStackTrace();
        }
        catch (ParserConfigurationException pce)
        {
            pce.printStackTrace();
        }
        catch (IOException ioe)
        {
            ioe.printStackTrace();
        }
        catch (Exception e)
        {
            e.printStackTrace();
        }
    }//parseFile

    private void traverse(Node cNode)
    {
        switch (cNode.getNodeType() )
        {
            case Node.DOCUMENT_NODE:
                System.out.println("Element " + cNode.getNodeName());
                processChildren( cNode.getChildNodes());
                break;

            case Node.ELEMENT_NODE:
                eleName = cNode.getNodeName();
                System.out.println("Element " + eleName);
                NamedNodeMap attributeMap = cNode.getAttributes();
                int numAttrs = attributeMap.getLength();
                for (int i=0; i<attributeMap.getLength(); i++)
                {
                    Attr attribute = (Attr)attributeMap.item(i);
                    String attrName =  attribute.getNodeName();
                    String attrValue = attribute.getNodeValue();
                    storeElementValue(attrName, attrValue);
                }
                if (eleName.equals("isCommissionable"))
                {
                    storeElementValue("isCommissionable", "");
                }

                processChildren( cNode.getChildNodes());
                break;
```

3

CREATING
APPLICATIONS
WITH JAXP

Listing 3.6   continued

```java
        case Node.CDATA_SECTION_NODE:
        case Node.TEXT_NODE:

            System.out.println("Text " + cNode.getNodeValue());
            if (! cNode.getNodeValue().trim().equals(""))
            {
                System.out.println("eleName " + eleName);
                System.out.println("Text " + cNode.getNodeValue());
                storeElementValue(eleName, cNode.getNodeValue());
            }
            break;
    }
}

private void processChildren(NodeList nList)
{
    if(nList.getLength() != 0)
    {
        for (int i=0; i<nList.getLength(); i++)
            traverse(nList.item(i));
    }
}


private void storeElementValue(String elementName,
                                String elementValue)
{
    if (elementName.equals("ticketRequest"))
    {
    }

    if (elementName.equals("custID"))
    {
        tr2.setCustID(Integer.parseInt(elementValue));
    }

    if (elementName.equals("lastName"))
    {
        tr2.setLastName(elementValue);
    }

    if (elementName.equals("firstName"))
    {
        tr2.setFirstName(elementValue);
    }

    if (elementName.equals("cruiseID"))
    {
        tr2.setCruiseID(Integer.parseInt(elementValue));
    }
```

LISTING 3.6   continued

```java
        if (elementName.equals("destination"))
        {
            tr2.setDestination(elementValue);
        }

        if (elementName.equals("port"))
        {
            tr2.setPort(elementValue);
        }

        if (elementName.equals("sailing"))
        {
            tr2.setSailing(elementValue);
        }

        if (elementName.equals("numberOfTickets"))
        {
            String numberOfTicketsString = elementValue;
            int numberOfTickets =
                Integer.parseInt(numberOfTicketsString);
            tr2.setNumberOfTickets(numberOfTickets);
        }

        if (elementName.equals("isCommissionable"))
        {
            tr2.setCommissionable(true);
        }
    }

    public String toString()
    {
        return tr2.toString();
    }


    //This method sends a message to the response queue
    private void sendTicketResponse(TicketRequest2 tr,
                                    boolean isSuccessful)
    {
        try
        {
            //Create a message using this object
            String tickResp = "The ticket to " + tr.getDestination() +
             " for " + tr.getLastName();
            if (isSuccessful)
                tickResp += " was successful";
```

3

CREATING
APPLICATIONS
WITH JAXP

LISTING 3.6   continued

```java
        else
            tickResp += " was not successful";

        System.out.println(tickResp);

        //Write the response
        char quote = '"';
        BufferedWriter bw = new BufferedWriter(
        new FileWriter("c:/XML/response/response"
        + tr2.getCustID() + ".xml"));

        bw.write(System.getProperty("line.separator"));

        bw.write("<ticketResponse>");
        bw.write(System.getProperty("line.separator"));
        bw.write(tickResp);
        bw.write(System.getProperty("line.separator"));
        bw.write("</ticketResponse>");
        bw.flush();
        bw.close();

        System.out.println("Created  the Ticket Response Message");

    }catch(Exception e)
    {
        System.out.println("Exception " + e);
    }
}

//This method creates a database entry for the new ticket
private void createTicket(TicketRequest2 tr) throws Exception
{
    //get a connection to the database
    dbConn =DriverManager.getConnection(sourceURL);

    //If we get to here, no exception was thrown
    System.out.println("The database connection is " + dbConn);
    System.out.println("Making connection...\n");

    //Create the statement
    statement1 = dbConn.createStatement();

    String insertStatement;
    ticketID += 1;
    insertStatement = "INSERT INTO CruiseTicket VALUES("
    + ticketID + "," +
    Integer.toString(tr.getCustID()) + ", 'Unleashed Cruise Line'," +
    "'USS SeaBiscuit', '" + tr.getPort() + "','" + tr.getSailing() +
    "'," + "999.99," + "0,"+ "0,"+ "'')";
```

LISTING 3.6   continued

```java
        statement1.executeUpdate(insertStatement);
        System.out.println("Update was successful CustID = " +
                            tr.getCustID());

        statement1.close();
        dbConn.close();

}

private String getCreditCardNumber(int CustID) throws Exception
{
        //get a connection to the database
        dbConn =DriverManager.getConnection(sourceURL);

        //If we get to here, no exception was thrown
        System.out.println("The database connection is " + dbConn);
        System.out.println("Making connection...\n");

        //Create the statement
        statement1 = dbConn.createStatement();

        String ccNum = "";

        //Populate the creditcard string string
        String getCCString =
        "SELECT CreditCardNumber FROM CruiseCustomer " +
        "WHERE CustomerID = " + Integer.toString(CustID);

        ResultSet ccResults = statement1.executeQuery(getCCString);

        while (ccResults.next())
        {
            ccNum = ccResults.getString("CreditCardNumber");
        }

        statement1.close();
        dbConn.close();
        return ccNum;
}

private boolean verifyCreditCard(String ccNum)
{
        int firstNum = Integer.parseInt(ccNum.substring(0,1));

        if ( firstNum > 4)
            return false;
        else
            return true;
```

3

CREATING
APPLICATIONS
WITH JAXP

LISTING 3.6   continued

```
    }

    /**
     * main() method.
     *
     * @exception  Exception if execution fails
     */
    public static void main(String[] args) throws Exception
    {
        try
        {
            TicketAgent ta = new TicketAgent();

            ta.checkForXMlDocs();

        }catch (Exception e)
        {
            System.out.println("Exception in main() " + e);
        }
    }
```

> **Note**
>
> Please notice that there are two hard-coded filenames in Listing 3.6. If you are running on a non-Windows platform you will need to modify these references.

This application is a combination of a fairly simple extraction of data from a `TicketRequest2` object and the creation of a ticket in the database. It is combined with XML DOM parsing code that is almost identical to the `TicketRequestDOMParser` class that we looked at in great detail earlier in the chapter. After the processing is done, a new message is created and placed in a special directory where the CruiseList application will look for it.

Figure 3.1 shows the CruiseList GUI.

FIGURE 3.1

The CruiseList application uses XML to formulate the message requesting tickets.

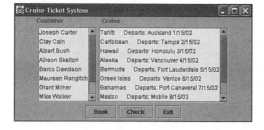

When the Check button is clicked, if a message is waiting, a dialog box will appear indicating whether the request was granted, as shown in Figure 3.2.

Message

The ticket to Alaska for Skelton was successful

OK

From this example, we see how XML can be created on the fly and written to a file. We also see how the document consumer can use JAXP to parse the document and update the database.

Summary

In this chapter we looked at how to use JAXP to process XML, one of the most exciting technologies in the computing world today. XML's combination of standardized processing on custom data is a powerful approach.

Early in the chapter, you learned how to parse an XML document and extract its information. We used the JAXP SAX approach to process the data sequentially. This approach has the advantage of performing better when large XML documents are parsed. The fact that only part of the document is contained in memory at any time during processing makes its memory requirements more manageable.

Then you learned how to parse the XML document using the JAXP's DOM approach. The DOM approach creates a treelike structure in memory that represents the document. Method calls and recursion are then used to traverse the tree and extract the data. This approach is nice in that the creation of the tree is automatic. Traversing it using recursion is a very comfortable approach for many programmers. In addition, the tree can be updated and written out, creating a database-like effect. The drawback to the DOM approach is the resource requirements of having the whole tree in virtual memory at the same time. For this reason, we can sometimes achieve better performance using SAX rather than DOM.

Finally, we created a real-world application that demonstrated how JAXP and XML could be used to facilitate distributed processing. We created an object in one application and translated it into an XML document. Another application opened the document, parsed it, and re-created the same object in its own JVM.

CHAPTER 4

Application Development with JSP and Servlets

In modern times, there are a large number of tools that allow developers to create dynamic Web pages in a fast and efficient manner. Java actually has two mechanisms. They are known as *JSP (JavaServer Pages)* and Java Servlets. These two tools directly compete with other dynamic page generation suites such as ColdFusion, PHP, and most notably Microsoft's ASP. Although ASP has gained a great deal of industry momentum over the past years, JSP in many ways holds technical advantages over ASP.

Both JSP and ASP are "scripting" languages, which means that, typically, they look more like HTML tags rather than actual code. The idea of both ASP and JSP is to simplify the process of Web page generation so that the people who typically do HTML writing can build dynamic pages without having to learn a language such as Java or C. JSP, however, holds a performance advantage over ASP in that JSP tagged pages are compiled into actual Java code. ASP pages are re-interpreted on the server on every page request. JSP code is also multithreaded. If 10,000 requests come in at the same time, there's still only a single Java runtime being executed: It just has 10,000 threads. This gives JSP the same performance advantages that Fast-CGI offered. However, unlike Fast-CGI that would only run on a specific vendor's Web server, JSP is an open platform that can be added to many different Web servers.

JSP and servlets are functionally similar. In fact, every JSP page you build actually gets converted into a servlet at compile time by the Web service container. JSP and servlets can be used to perform the same activities, but in practice each has its own special role in application development. JSPs tend to be easier to develop for the more HTML/Web designer community, whereas servlets tend to be easier for the more hard-core programmers. Functionally, though, at runtime, they both are compiled into very similar class files that behave the same.

In this chapter, we will first talk about JSP pages, introduce you to the tags that make up JSP, and show you how to build a few JSP pages. In the second half of this chapter we will walk through servlets, explain how to build them, and describe the differences between JSP and servlets. Finally, we'll build the familiar Cruise example using a combination of JSP and servlets.

HTTP Basics

Now that we've got you all pumped up about how wonderful JSPs are, you're probably wondering how to actually build a page by using them. Before we can do that, we need to talk briefly about how Web servers and the Hypertext Transfer Protocol (HTTP) actually work.

When a user opens a Web browser and types an address such as www.sams.com, the browser first looks to find out the numerical address of that URI. This is done through the Internet DNS service. Next, the browser puts together a small message that has in it a command that contains a *request* for the server to send back to this browser the page at www.sams.com. Next, the browser opens a socket connection to that server's numerical address and sends the text message containing the command to the server.

The Web server sees the request for the socket and opens it. The server then reads the message sent by the browser and examines the command that was included. In our example, the command asked for the default home page for this server. Depending on how the server is configured, the home page might be a static HTML encoded file on the disk or a call to a dynamic HTML code generation program (such as JSP, ASP, or CGI) on the server. In either case, the server opens a new socket connection back to the browser, gets the requested data, and sends it across the wire back to the browser. This information is called the *response*. When finished sending the data, the server closes the socket connection it opened to the browser, and the browser closes the socket it had opened to the server. The diagram in Figure 4.1 shows the steps in the HTTP transaction graphically.

FIGURE 4.1

Diagram of HTTP communication between a browser and a server.

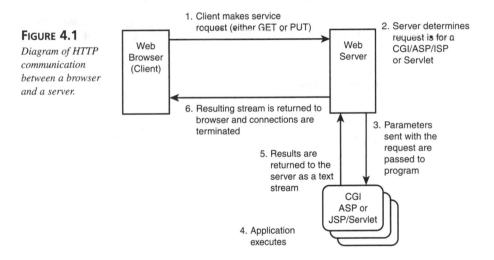

At this point, all connections are now gone and both the client and the server are free to go on their merry way. Neither is tied to the other any more. Because of this automatic termination of all connections, if the user were to ask for the same page from the server again, the exact same process would need to take place. The server does not remember who the browser is. We call this sort of processing *stateless* because neither the client nor the server remembers anything about what has taken place prior to the current request/response pair.

Your First JSP Page

We've all seen the standard "Hello World" HTML page. It usually looks something like Listing 4.1.

LISTING 4.1   The Standard Hello World HTML Page

```
<HTML>
<HEAD>
<TITLE>Standard Hello World HTML Example</TITLE>
</HEAD>
<BODY>
<FONT SIZE="3">Hello World!</FONT>
</BODY>
</HTML>
```

It's pretty basic and boring, huh? When the user requests this page from a Web server, the server simply reads the file from the Web server's disk and sends it back to the browser as a stream of text. The browser looks at the various HTML tags to determine how to format it. The browser will obviously return the expected message, which is shown in Figure 4.2.

FIGURE 4.2

Screenshot of the normal Hello World HTML page.

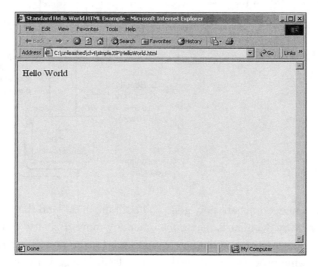

The interesting thing (or maybe the uninteresting thing) is that this never changes. If the author of the page wants something different to show up for every person, there's no way to do it with HTML alone. He would have to chain himself to the Web server and (really, really quickly) edit the HTML for the page between each page request for different people to see various responses.

Let's say that we wanted a way to count how many times a page has been hit. We've all seen page counters before on Web pages. Let's look at how we could build a (very rudimentary) one into our Hello World HTML page using JSP. The code to do this can be seen in Listing 4.2.

LISTING 4.2 A Simple Page Hit Counter with JSP

```
<%@ page language="java" %>
<HTML>
<HEAD>
<TITLE>Standard Hello World HTML Example</TITLE>
</HEAD>
<BODY>
<FONT SIZE="3">Hello World</FONT>
<BR>
<HR WIDTH="100%">
<BR>
This page has been accessed
<%! int pagecounter = 0; %>
<% ++pagecounter; %>
<%= pagecounter %>
 times
</BODY>
</HTML>
```

As you can see from this listing, there are a few more lines of code, as well as some strange looking tags that all start and end in <% and %>. Those tags are used to mark off JSP specific tags. In the first line, you see a tag that starts with <%@. Those are called directives. *Directives*, as you'll see later, give some instructions to the JSP container to explain how to process this page. In this case, we're telling the JSP container that throughout this page, we're going to be using Java code inside the page and that you need to make sure you use the Java compiler to process it.

Further down, you see a line that starts with <%!. Such lines are called JSP declarations. *Declarations* are used to define variables or even entire methods. The syntax within the declaration is no different from what you use within a Java program for defining a variable or a method.

Next, you see a line that starts with <%. This tag denotes a scriptlet. *Scriptlets* are just parts of Java code that perform a specific task. Scriptlet lines are executed at page request time, so they get processed over and over. In our example, every time this JSP page is called, our pagecounter variable gets incremented by 1. This scriptlet will evaluate to some number (for instance, if this is the third time the page has been requested, the scriptlet evaluates to "3") and that value will be stored in the variable pagecounter.

Finally, there is a line that starts with <%=. The <%= tag redirects the result to the output text stream. In this case, we're telling the JSP container to get the value of the pagecounter variable and print its value here. Hence, while the JSP container is processing this page request, it replaces our <%= pagecounter %> tag with the text "3" in the result text stream sent back to the browser.

Before we can run this example, we must package our JSP into a Web Archive file, commonly known as a WAR file. A WAR file is nothing more than a JAR that has a special directory containing an XML file in it. This XML file is a deployment descriptor that tells the JSP container about the application and how it should be set up to run.

We create a directory called WEB-INF at the same level as our JSP page file. Inside that directory, we'll need to create the web.xml file. That file can be found in Listing 4.3.

LISTING 4.3 The web.xml Deployment Descriptor for the simpleJSP Example

```
<!DOCTYPE web-app PUBLIC
"-//Sun Microsystems, Inc.//DTD Web Application 2.2//EN"
"http://java.sun.com/j2ee/dtds/web-app_2_2.dtd">

<web-app>
    <welcome-file-list>
        <welcome-file>HelloWorldCounter.jsp</welcome-file>
    </welcome-file-list>
</web-app>
```

The first line of this file specifies the encoding schema for this xml file. Next, we define our Web application with the <web-app> tag. A Web application can have a series of default pages that can be called if none is specified in the URI entered by the user. In this case, we want our HelloWorldCounter.jsp file to be called if the user doesn't explicitly state a file to run in our application.

Next, we will package our application into the WAR file. To do this, we execute the following command from the c:\unleashed\ch4\simpleJSP directory:

```
jar -cvf simpleJSP.war HelloWorldCounter.jsp WEB-INF
```

If everything went correctly, you should now see a file named simpleJSP.war in that directory. Now, we need to deploy the application. We'll do that by copying the WAR file into the WebLogic applications directory:

```
copy simpleJSP.war c:\bea\wlserver6.1\config\examples\applications
```

Finally, to test our JSP, we'll need a browser. Open the browser of your choice and point it to http://<yourweblogicserveraddr>:7001/simpleJSP, where <yourweblogicserveraddr> is replaced with the address that your WebLogic 6.1 Server is running at. If running the browser on your server, you can use `http://127.0.0.1:7001/simpleJSP`. If you've done everything correctly, you'll get a page that resembles Figure 4.3.

FIGURE 4.3

A screenshot of the `HelloWorldCounter.jsp`.

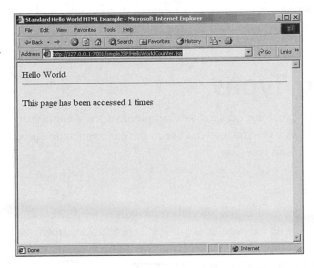

If you then refresh the page and have caching turned off in your browser, you'll find that it now reads `"2 times"`. Every visit to the page increments the counter. Congratulations! You've built your first dynamic Web page.

If, however, you had a bug in your JSP code (let's say that we left out the ; at the end of our `<%! Int pagecounter = 0; %>` line) when you go to run the application from the browser, you are presented with a page generated by the WebLogic Server showing that there was a compile error with your JSP code and what the nature of the error was. This is a good exercise to try now that you have the code working—just to prove that the code is actually compiled.

Another important thing to realize is that because this code is compiled, if you make a change to the JSP page in the `c:\unleashed\ch4\simpleJSP` directory, nothing changes on the actual application. You must repackage the JSP page into the WAR file and redeploy it. Only then is the JSP page recompiled, and the new executable code overwrites the old code.

You also might have noticed that the first time you made a call to the `simpleJSP` URL, the server took slightly longer to come back than all the subsequent times. This happened because the JSP container waits until the JSP has been requested before performing the compile. In most cases, this lag is not important because it only happens the very first time this version of the JSP is accessed. Every subsequent request of the JSP page calls

4

APPLICATION
DEVELOPMENT

the compiled class files. This is true even a year later, provided the WAR file hasn't been updated with a new version in that time.

You probably now have a bunch of ideas running through your head on how you can use this new knowledge. Before we get too far, let's talk about the various tag types in more detail.

JSP Tag Types

As you saw in the preceding simpleJSP example, JSP has a number of different tag types. Each type has a specific role and use in the page generation process. Let's quickly run through the various types.

Directives

Directives in JSP are used to give special commands to the JSP container regarding how to process or work with the page. In the JSP 1.2 specification, there are three possible directives: page, include, and taglib. By convention, directives usually appear at the beginning of a JSP file. You can create a directive using the following syntax:

```
<%@ directivename attribute="attribvalue" %>
```

If your page needs to follow XML encoding, you can also write the previous line as

```
<jsp:directive>
    directivename attribute="attribvalue"
</jsp:directive>
```

The page directive is by far the most extensive one, with the largest number of attributes. You can use any mixture of these attributes in your JSP pages, but only the import attribute can exist more than once in a page. The available attributes are

- autoFlush—Tells the JSP Container what to do when the buffer is full. Set to true to automatically flush and write the buffer to the output stream when full. A value of false will cause an exception to be thrown when the buffer fills up.

- buffer—Specifies a buffer size. Used when writing the output stream to the browser (for example, <%@ page buffer="16K" %>).

- contentType—Tells the browser how to interpret the character encoding of the page that will be returned. Usually, you'll set this using a mime type such as text/html.

- errorPage—Specifies the URL of some other JSP page that should be loaded if any sort of unchecked Java exceptions take place during the execution of this page. This URL must be specified relative to the current JSP file.

- `extends`—Allows the servlet generated by this JSP to be extended from whatever class you specify. This can sometimes cause problems in that the JSP container might need to extend from a specific class in order to operate correctly. In most cases, you should not need this attribute.

- `import`—Works the same as the import statement in a Java class file. By default, JSP pages automatically import the following packages: java.lang.*, javax.servlet.*, javax.servlet.jsp.*, and javax.servlet.http.*. If, for instance, we were to use the date class in our JSP code, we'd need to include the `<%@ page import="java.util.Date" %>` directive.

- `info`—Gives the descriptive information string for this JSP. One of the commands allowed by the HTTP protocol is `GETINFO`. If this command is sent to the server while requesting your JSP, the value you place into the `info` attribute is what gets returned.

- `isErrorPage`—Denotes whether this page is an error handler page. This attribute defaults to `false`. Set it to `true` if this JSP file is listed as the `errorPage` for some other JSP page.

- `isThreadSafe`—Specifies whether the code in your JSP is thread safe. By default, the value is assumed to be `true`. You must remember that every client request runs in a new thread on this code, not on separate copies. Hence, if your code is not thread safe, set this value to `false`.

- `language`—Specifies what language we're using inside our JSP code. In most cases, this will be set to `java`. Some JSP containers allow other languages to be used as well.

- `session`—Tells the JSP container whether session management should be invoked. JSP has a built-in object called `session` that can hold information about a client's interaction from one page to the next in attributes set and retrieved from one JSP page to another. Sessions are discussed later in the chapter. Setting this value to `true` turns on session management.

As you can see, a number of page attributes are available, and they can drastically change how a page is both generated and handled by a browser.

The `include` directive is a very powerful, and also somewhat dangerous, directive. When the JSP Container sees this directive, it looks for the file specified in the `file` attribute and replaces the directive with the complete text of the file. The `include` directive typically looks like this:

```
<%@ include file="relativefilename" %>
```

Unlike the page directive that usually appears at the start of your JSP files, include directives can take place anywhere. However, be aware that the included file will show up *exactly* where the directive is in the JSP file. If you're not careful about placement, you can very easily cause syntax errors by splitting tags in half or by having extra close tags unintentionally. The JSP container does the automatic equivalent of a copy and paste from the included file into this one. The file reference in the include directive must be listed relative to this JSP file.

Also, one caveat that should be noted: If you update the included file, you *must* also update any file that uses that included file. The include process only takes place at compile time. For instance, let's say we have a standard company footer that is in its own small partial JSP file, and it gets included in every JSP page in our site. If we were to make a small change to that footer JSP file, we'd have to update every other JSP page in our site to make sure that the new footer was re-included. On Unix systems, this can be easily performed by doing a *touch* on all the JSP files. On Windows, it's a bit more complicated. It usually involves opening, changing, and resaving each file.

The final directive is the taglib directive. One of the real strengths of JSP is the ability to create custom tag libraries that perform some sort of predefined functionality. In order to tell the JSP container that we're going to use a special custom tag library, we must include the taglib directive:

```
<%@ taglib uri=http://ourtaglibserver/ourtaglib.tld prefix="ours" %>
```

In the preceding line, we are telling the JSP container to go out to the ourtaglibserver and request the ourtaglib.tld tag library definition files. Whenever we use a tag in that library, we will prefix the tag with "ours:". For instance, if the tag library includes a tag named MyHeadline we would code the call to it in our JSP page as <ours:MyHeadline />. Addition of the prefix helps ensure unique tag names even if multiple libraries are used in the same JSP page. The taglib directive must appear before any uses of that library's tags in the JSP page. It's usually safest to place it near the top of the file with your page directives.

Declarations

Declarations are used in JSP to create new variables. We can use these variables to store information from one page execution to another. We can also use declarations to define special methods that can be called in our JSP page.

Say that we needed a way to repeatedly determine which was the greater of two numbers in a JSP page. We could create the following declaration in our page:

```
<%! int greaterInt(int number1, int number2)
    {
```

```
    if(number1>=number2) { return number1;}
    else {return number2;}
        }
%>
```

Then, wherever in our JSP page we needed to find which of two numbers was greater, we could simply make a call to our greaterInt method.

> **Note**
>
> Any variables created in JSP declarations are created only once and are shared among all threads running on this JSP. If you need a variable to only be defined for a specific thread instance, you should not declare them inside a JSP declaration, but inside a JSP Scriptlet instead.

JSP declarations can be coded in XML style by using the following pattern:

```
<jsp:declaration>
    the declaration code
</jsp:declaration>
```

Expressions

JSP expressions are used to place data into the resulting page. The result of the expression is converted into a string and placed into the output text stream of the HTML page as though it was typed in. Expressions take the following syntax:

```
<%= expression %>
```

Use expressions anytime you want to perform some processing and have the results added to the output of the page. Expressions are evaluated at page request time—not at deployment/compile time. Therefore, we could code an expression that gives the current date (on the server) just by performing a `<%= new java.util.Date() %>`. Every visit to the page will show the current time on the server. It's important to remember that this code runs *on the server*, not on the client. Therefore, if the client is in another time zone, the time might look wrong to her.

As with directives, expressions can be denoted in XML format also. You can use the following format instead of `<%=   expression %>`:

```
<jsp:expression>
    whatever the expression is
</jsp:expression>
```

4

APPLICATION
DEVELOPMENT

JSP Scriptlets

JSP scriptlets are where the bulk of your code processing takes place. A scriptlet can be partial or complete code, which means that you can mix and match Java code in with HTML code as long as you provide the correct <% and %> tags around the Java segments of the code. For example, the following is perfectly legal:

```
<% int anumber = 5000;
    if(anumber>6000)
    {
    %><Font size="7">It's bigger <%
    }
    else
    {
    %><Font size="2">It's smaller <%
    }
%></Font>
```

If we were to run this piece of code in a JSP page, we'd see It's smaller in a very small font in the output. This can be an extremely powerful feature because it allows you to perform operations such as conditional branching or loops with HTML output. How many times did you wish that were possible with HTML?

Notice that we declared a variable within our scriptlet example. Each thread instance of this JSP page will get its own unique copy of the variable anumber. If you need a variable value to be shared between thread instances, declare the variable inside of a JSP declaration, as noted earlier.

Again, the JSP scriptlet tag can be used in XML by adhering to the following pattern:

```
<jsp:scriptlet>
    your java code here
</jsp:scriptlet>
```

Finally, it should be noted that all JSP elements on a JSP page come together as if they were all written in one big class source code file. Therefore, it's possible to intermix these tags as much as you like and reference variables and code declared in one tag from within another.

Form Processing with JSP

The whole point of technologies such as JSP is to provide a means for the Web to be more interactive and dynamic. We've shown how JSP can facilitate the dynamic requirement, so now we need to work on the interactive. In HTML, the concept of the Form was created to give the Web user a way to enter information that she could then send to the

Web server for some sort of processing. That processing might, for instance, store the information into a database, perform a search of a telephone directory, or provide a mechanism for logging in to a system.

To demonstrate how to do this sort of processing with JSP, we'll create a small HTML Form that captures a person's first and last names, and then submits that data to a JSP page. That JSP will report back the number of characters in each segment of the name and the total length of the person's name.

A simple HTML Form to do the capture can be found in Listing 4.4.

LISTING 4.4   A Simple HTML Form

```
<HTML>
<HEAD>
<TITLE>JSP form Processing Example - Input</TITLE>
</HEAD>
<BODY>
<FORM NAME="JSPForm" METHOD="GET"
ACTION="http://127.0.0.1:7001/formProcessingJSP/nameCounter.jsp">
Enter First Name: <INPUT TYPE="text" NAME="FNAME" VALUE="">
<BR>
Enter Last  Name: <INPUT TYPE="text" NAME="LNAME" VALUE="">
<BR>
<INPUT TYPE="submit" VALUE="Continue">
</FORM>
</BODY>
</HTML>
```

In this form, we have a text field for capturing the First Name and one for capturing the Last Name. If you examine the HTML code, you'll see that we've named these fields "FNAME" and "LNAME". There is also a button labeled "Continue". We want the Web browser to send this data to our Web server and have a JSP page process that data and then return some result. Let's say that JSP page is called nameCounter.jsp.

In Listing 4.4, you'll need to modify the Form Action URL to point to your WebLogic Server. Replace 127.0.0.1 with the IP address or name of your server.

Now that we have our data source, let's focus on our JSP page that will be our data handler. In JSP, a number of built-in objects are always available on a page. One of these is the request object. Stored within the request object are all the parameter data elements that were passed to the server from the HTML Form. By simply querying the request object, we can find the values that were submitted and work with them. In Listing 4.5, you'll find the code for the nameCounter JSP page that does exactly that.

LISTING 4.5   The nameCounter.jsp Showing Simple Form Data Processing

```
<%@ page language="java" isErrorPage="false" %>
<%@ page buffer="16k" autoFlush="true" %>
<%@ page info="Name Counter JSP. Counts the number of "+
    "letters in the submitted name." %>
<%@ page contentType="text/html" %>

<HTML>
<HEAD>
<TITLE>Name Counter JSP Results</TITLE>
</HEAD>
<BODY>
<FONT SIZE="4">
<% int flen = request.getParameter("FNAME").length(); %>
<% int llen = request.getParameter("LNAME").length(); %>
<%= request.getParameter("FNAME") %>
has
<%= flen %>
characters </BR>
<%= request.getParameter("LNAME") %>
has
<%= llen %>
characters </BR>
<HR WIDTH="100%"></BR>

<% out.println("Your name is " + (flen + llen) +" long"); %>

</FONT>
</BODY>
</HTML>
```

As we look through the code, we see that this example has quite a few more JSP elements in it than the prior example does. In this example, we first set up the language and tell the JSP container that this is not an error page. Next, the buffer is set to be 16KB in size and the container is instructed to autoflush the buffer when it fills up. We also set up the information string and specify that our result will be an HTML page.

The normal HTML to start the returned page occurs next. We then have a scriptlet where we set up a pair of integer variables. In each, we query the implicit request object for a parameter with the name "FNAME" or "LNAME". Once we get the strings from the request, we find their lengths and store those lengths into the integer variables.

Next, we again request the First Name parameter from the request, but we simply write it to the page output stream, followed by the length count that we had previously stored in the flen variable. We repeat this process for the last name.

Finally, we create one more scriptlet. In this scriptlet, we make use of another of the JSP implicit objects—out. The out object is the JSP equivalent to a PrintWriter and is connected to the output response stream. In this example, we instructed out to print the total length of the two names put together (not counting the space between first and last names). We could just as easily have written this line as

```
Your name is <%= flen+llen %> long
```

We did it this way to demonstrate the use of the out implicit object.

Finally, we need the web.xml deployment descriptor file for this JSP application. That descriptor file can be seen in Listing 4.6.

LISTING 4.6   The web.xml Deployment Descriptor for the formProcessingJSP Application

```
<!DOCTYPE web-app PUBLIC
"-//Sun Microsystems, Inc.//DTD Web Application 2.2//EN"
"http://java.sun.com/j2ee/dtds/web-app_2_2.dtd">

<web-app>

    <welcome-file-list>
        <welcome-file>nameCounter.jsp</welcome-file>
    </welcome-file-list>
</web-app>
```

Package this application using the same procedure that you used earlier for the simpleJSP example, naming the WAR file formProcessingJSP.war. Deploy it to the same directory.

To run this example, simply open the HTML input page in your browser. You should see something like Figure 4.4.

Type your first name in the first field and your last name in the second field and click the Continue button. In my case, I typed "Mike" in the first field and "Kopack" in the second. When I clicked Continue, the JSP page was called and I got back the page shown in Figure 4.5.

If you look at the URL that shows up in your browser, you'll notice that it looks something like the following:

```
http://127.0.0.1:7001/formProcessingJSP/nameCounter.jsp?FNAME=Mike&LNAME=Kopack
```

4

**APPLICATION
DEVELOPMENT**

FIGURE 4.4

The example input HTML Form.

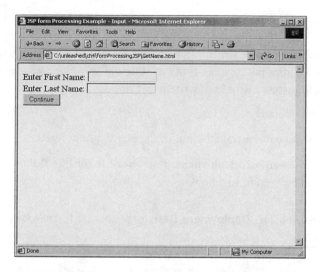

FIGURE 4.5

Results from the nameCounter.jsp *page.*

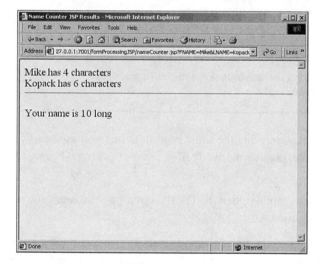

You're probably wondering what all that extra stuff is after nameCounter.jsp and how it got in there. After all, it wasn't part of our HTML Form action.

What you're seeing is the encoding of the Form data into the URL. This is what happens when we make use of the HTTP GET Form method. GET takes all the data elements in the form, puts them into name/value pairs, and places those pairs into the URL that is sent to the server at request time. If we were to go back into our HTML Form and change the Action parameter to POST, we would not see that additional information on the URL, but the process would work just fine. The POST mechanism still takes the data from the Form and places it into name/value pairs: It just sends data to the server in a different manner. In most cases, if you're working with large forms, you should use POST because GET has a limited size (because of URL length restrictions).

In either case, our nameCounter JSP doesn't care. The JSP container takes the data— coming from either GET or POST—and makes it available to the JSP page through the implicit request object. As you'll see later, servlets work in a similar manner, but allow for a bit more flexibility because they have separate mechanisms that get called when a GET happens rather than a POST.

Your First Servlet

Now that you've seen how JSPs work, we need to discuss the other way to build dynamic Web pages—using Java Servlets. As we stated earlier, JSP pages are actually compiled into Java Servlets, so the two are no different functionally. However, the manner in which they are written is very different. Recall the simple HelloWorldCounter.jsp that we built earlier in this chapter. To build the same functionality using a Java Servlet, we'd have to write code that looks like Listing 4.7.

LISTING 4.7   Java Servlet Version of the HelloWorldCounter

```
package unleashed.ch4.simpleServlet;

import javax.servlet.*;
import javax.servlet.http.*;
import java.io.*;

public class HelloWorldCounterServlet extends HttpServlet
{
    public static int pagecounter;
    public void init(ServletConfig config) throws ServletException
    {
        super.init(config);
        pagecounter =0;
    }
    public void doGet(HttpServletRequest request,
            HttpServletResponse response)
        throws ServletException, IOException
    {
        response.setContentType("text/html");
        PrintWriter out = response.getWriter();

        out.println("<HTML>");
        out.println("<HEAD>");
        out.println(
            "<TITLE>Hello World Servlet counter Example</TITLE>");
```

4

APPLICATION
DEVELOPMENT

LISTING 4.7   continued

```
            out.println("</HEAD>");
            out.println("<BODY>");
            out.println("<FONT SIZE=\"3\">Hello World</FONT>");
            out.println("<BR>");
            out.println("<HR WIDTH=\"100%\">");
            out.println("<BR>");
            out.println("This page has been accessed ");
            ++pagecounter;
            out.println(pagecounter);
            out.println(" times");
            out.println("</BODY>");
            out.println("</HTML>");
            out.close();
    }
}
```

Whoa! That's a lot more code to do the exact same thing as our simple JSP example, isn't it? Servlets are nothing more than Java classes that extend either the javax.servlet.Servlet class or the HttpServlet class. You'll notice that there is no constructor, but there is an init method. Typically, you won't need anything beyond the default constructor. The init method gets called when the servlet is first loaded into the servlet container. Therefore, init is a good place to do any sort of setup that is needed for later execution. In this case, we initialized our pagecounter variable to be 0.

The other method you see, doGet(), gets called when the browser asks for the page. Browsers usually send one of two commands: GET or POST. We'll discuss the differences more later, but for now just realize that when you type a URL into your browser's address line, you're performing a GET. The servlet container sees that GET command and routes control to the servlet's doGet() method, which is responsible for handling that command. doGet always takes two parameters: the HttpServletRequest, which contains the request command from the browser and any data associated with that request, and HttpServletResponse, which will be where we place any data we want to send back to the browser. In this case, we're going to send back an HTML page.

In this example, our doGet first sets up the response as an HTML page by setting the content type to "text/html". HTML is nothing more than a set of strings, so we're going to need a way to write those strings to the response stream. To do this, we get a PrintWriter named out and attach it to the response stream. This is doing the same work as the out implicit object found in JSP. Finally, we perform a series of out.println commands to write each part of the HTML for the page we want to construct. We must embed all the HTML inside the servlet because when we use a servlet (or CGI for that matter) the application/servlet is responsible for creating the complete response back to the browser. Finally, we close the response stream. This effectively closes the socket to the client browser and completes the communication process.

Now that we have our servlet code, we'll need to compile it. This can be done with the following command:

```
javac unleashed/ch4/simpleServlet/*.java
```

To deploy our `HelloWorldCounter` servlet, we'll first need a `web.xml` deployment descriptor, stored within a directory called `WEB-INF`. That deployment descriptor can be seen in Listing 4.8.

LISTING 4.8   The `web.xml` Deployment Descriptor for Our `HelloWorldCounterServlet`

```
<!DOCTYPE web-app PUBLIC
"-//Sun Microsystems, Inc.//DTD Web Application 2.2//EN"
"http://java.sun.com/j2ee/dtds/web-app_2_2.dtd">

<web-app>
    <display-name>Simple Servlet Example Application</display-name>
    <servlet>
    <servlet-name>simpleServlet</servlet-name>
    <servlet-class>
        unleashed.ch4.simpleServlet.HelloWorldCounterServlet
        </servlet-class>
    <load-on-startup>1</load-on-startup>
    </servlet>
    <servlet-mapping>
        <servlet-name>simpleServlet</servlet-name>
        <url-pattern>/HelloWorld</url-pattern>
    </servlet-mapping>
</web-app>
```

In this `web.xml` file, you'll see that a lot more is involved than what we had in the JSP version. The `<display-name>` tag simply sets up a descriptive string for helping us determine what this application is for while viewing it in our WebLogic Console. Next, we define the servlet and specify its name. The `<servlet-name>` should usually be set to the name of our WAR file. In this case, we set it as `simpleServlet`. Next, we must specify the full class file that will be invoked when this servlet is called. Finally, we tell the container that we want one thread started when the application is deployed so that a thread is waiting to start handling requests immediately.

4

APPLICATION
DEVELOPMENT

In the `<servlet-mapping>` section, we're attempting to set up a mapping between the URL that will call the servlet, as well as the servlet we defined earlier in our `web.xml` file. In this case, we're telling the container: Every time a request comes in for `simpleServlet/HelloWorld`, go launch the class file that was specified in the `simpleServlet` servlet configuration. In our case, this launches the `unleashed.ch4.simpleServlet.HelloWorldCounterServlet` class.

To package everything, we need a specific directory structure. Inside the `WEB-INF` directory, you'll need to have the following directory tree:

```
WEB-INF\
    classes\
        unleashed\
                ch4\
                    simpleServlet
```

Inside the `simpleServlet` directory should be the `HelloWorldCounterServlet.class` file.

Next, we'll need to create a WAR file, much as we did with `simpleJSP`. While in the parent directory above the `WEB-INF`, execute the following command:

```
jar -cvf simpleServlet.war WEB-INF
```

Finally, we need to copy the new WAR file into our WebLogic examples applications directory so that the servlet can be deployed. To do that, run the following command:

```
copy simpleServlet.war c:\bea\wlserver6.1\config\examples\applications
```

Now to test our servlet, we need to open a browser and point it to the following URL:

```
http://<yourweblogicserver>:7001/simpleServlet/HelloWorld
```

where `<yourweblogicserver>` is the name or IP address of the machine you're running WebLogic 6.1 on. If everything was done correctly, you should see a screen similar to the one shown in Figure 4.6.

You'll notice that the output is exactly the same as what we received from our simple JSP example earlier in the chapter. Refreshing the page will increment the page counter once per page request.

FIGURE **4.6**

Example output from HelloWorld-CounterServlet.

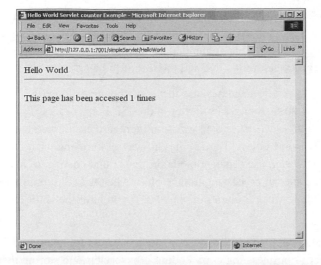

When Do We Use JSP and When Do We Use Servlets?

The previous servlet example did nothing more than what we saw earlier in our simple JSP example. Functionally, they are identical. So, why would anyone want to write a servlet when they can use JSP? The JSP looks easier to work with, looks more like HTML, and is shorter. What would be the advantage of servlets?

First of all, in most cases, you will want to use JSP when you're displaying data to a Web page. If you compare the two examples, you realize that the servlet example requires you to write all the HTML (and also any JavaScript or other code) within out.println() statements. This can be both tedious and error prone because you can't take advantage of any HTML generation tools. Also, if the look and feel of your Web site were to change, you'd need to go into every servlet, find the appropriate HTML code, change it, and then recompile. The average Webmaster is probably not going to be able or willing to go through servlet code to do that, but with JSP the code isn't very different from what he's used to working with. As a rule of thumb, you should tend to use JSP whenever you're dealing with look and feel.

Why use servlets at all then? That's a good question. Consider this: Every JSP that you write at deployment and request time gets compiled into a servlet. This compilation takes place automatically by a tool provided by the Application Server vendor, and you have very little control over the class file that is produced. When you write a servlet, however,

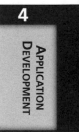

you have complete control. Also, because JSP pages don't get compiled until the first time they are requested, if any syntax errors exist in your JSP code, you won't know until then. Servlets, however, are compiled before they are deployed, so if a major problem exists, you know before it's live and the rest of the world can see it.

Servlets also have an advantage because they can operate differently if the data is sent in via a GET versus a POST. As we saw earlier in the JSP Form processing example, the JSP container simply takes whatever data was sent in, regardless of the mechanism, and stores it in the `request` object. The JSP has no way of knowing what mechanism was used. Servlets, however, use separate methods, `doGet` and `doPost`, to handle requests. As such, if you need special processing to take place when data is submitted via a GET that you don't need done when it comes in via a POST, you have the ability. With JSP, you don't.

Finally, it is usually a good idea to keep as much business logic out of JSPs as possible. If you have a lot of business logic, try coding it in servlets and storing the results in JavaBeans. As you'll see later in the cruise example, it is possible to have a servlet process the request, do the business logic, then store the data into a bean and pass that bean to a JSP to handle output of the data. This way, the Webmasters don't need to be concerned with business logic, they just make sure that everything looks good, whereas the Java developer can focus on the business logic and not worry about look and feel.

In a later chapter, you will also see how JSP and servlets can be used together to build what is known as the Model-View-Controller framework. In this framework, JSPs are used to handle HTML page generation, whereas servlets are used to do data processing and provide business logic.

Tip

For more information on the Model-View-Controller, see Chapter 20, "Architectural Models and Frameworks."

Using JSP and Servlets Together

Now that we've seen how to build simple JSPs and servlets, let's build a more complex application, making use of both technologies. Once again, we'll tackle our Cruise Ship system. Recall that in the cruise ship we needed a front-end application or client that the user would interact with to select a customer and a cruise to book tickets on. In other chapters, this application took the form of a simple Swing application. For this chapter, we'll use JSP to create a Web page–based client that will run in a browser.

Unlike other chapters in which the request was sent to a server to be processed and the results of the request were handled asynchronously, because we're working with HTTP and the Web, our solution will need to be synchronous. Therefore, our travel booking requests will wait until they can be approved or denied before we can return result information back to the user.

For our JSP and servlet solution, we'll need two JSP files. The first will be our main screen where the user will select the customer and cruise and enter the number of tickets to purchase. The other one will serve as our results screen, informing the user of the results of her ticket request. We'll also add an additional Banner file to demonstrate the `import` function. For the servlet side, we'll use just a single servlet class, plus a number of supporting JavaBeans and exception classes.

Listing 4.9 shows the code for `Cruises.jsp`. This will serve as our main interface screen to the user.

LISTING 4.9   The JSP for Rendering the Main Cruise Application Screen

```
<%@ page language = "java" %>
<%@ page import="unleashed.ch4.cruise.*" %>

<html>
<head>
<title>Cruise Listing Application for Chapter 4 of Java Unleashed</title>
</head>
<body>
<jsp:include page="Banner.jsp" flush="true" />
<form action="/ch4cruise/CruiseList" method="POST">

<input type="hidden" name="command" value="book">

<table border="0" width="90%" align="center">
<tr>
    <th bgcolor="#BBBBBB">Customers</th>
    <th bgcolor="#BBBBBB">Cruises</th>
</tr>

<tr>
<%
    CustomerListBean customerlist = (CustomerListBean)
        session.getValue("custList");
    Enumeration enum = customerlist.getCustomerList();
    CustomerBean aCustomer = null;
%>
    <td><select name="custid" size="10">
<%
    while(enum.hasMoreElements())
```

LISTING 4.9   continued

```
        {
            aCustomer = (CustomerBean) enum.nextElement();
%>
<option value="<%= aCustomer.getCustomerID() %>">
<%= aCustomer.getFirstName()+" "+aCustomer.getLastName() %>
</option>

<%  }%>

    </select>
    </td>

<%
    CruiseListBean cruiselist = (CruiseListBean)
        session.getValue("cruiseList");
    enum = cruiselist.getCruiseList();
    CruiseBean aCruise = null;
%>

    <td><select name="cruiseid" size="10">

<%
    while(enum.hasMoreElements())
    {
        aCruise = (CruiseBean) enum.nextElement();
%>
<option value="<%= aCruise.getCruiseID() %>">
<%= aCruise.getDestination()+"... Departs:"+aCruise.getPort()+
    " "+aCruise.getSailing() %>
</option>

<%      }%>
    </select>
    </td>
</tr>
<tr>
    <td colspan="2">
    <br>
    Number of Tickets to book:
    <input type="text" name="numbertickets" value="">
    </td>
</tr>

</table>
<br>
<br>
<center>
<input type="submit" value="Book">
</center>
```

LISTING 4.9   continued

```
</form>
</body>
</html>
```

As you see in the first few lines of the file, we import the classes that we'll later build. Some of these classes will be JavaBeans that we'll use to receive data from the servlet. This is done through the page import pragma.

The next line of interest is the `<jsp:include>`. This line instructs the JSP runtime to insert the contents of the specified file at runtime. Note that this is different from the include pragma. The pragma version inserts the specified file at compile time. In our case, we're attempting to read in a file that contains some HTML to draw a common banner on all of our application pages. In reality, this probably should be done with the include pragma, but we used the `jsp:include` action to demonstrate the feature.

Next, you'll see that we set up an HTML Form, set its `transmit` method to `POST`, and instructed it to send its data to our `CruiseList` servlet (which we'll build later in the chapter). We also set up a hidden HTML field called `"command"`. In most applications, you'll have multiple activities that the servlet will need to understand, so you'll normally set up this hidden field and then use JavaScript to set the command field's value based on the activity the user needs. In this application, we have only one command that we'll be worried about, `"book"`, so we'll hard-code it.

The really interesting work takes place inside the table cells where we set up the selection lists for the customer and cruise selection boxes. Although it would certainly be possible to place all the JDBC code to read these lists of data from the database inside this JSP, it would mean that our Webmaster would need to see and maintain all the code. Instead, we will let the servlet build the lists for us and simply pass that data to us. To achieve this goal, we'll make use of JavaBeans passed to us through the session by the servlet. The following line does this for us for the list of customers:

```
CustomerListBean customerlist = (CustomerListBean)
➥ session.getValue("custList");
```

In this line, we declare a JavaBean and set its value by requesting the data stored under the index name of `"custList"` inside the session context. We'll expect the servlet to place the data there for us.

After we have the list, we then loop through all the customer entries, pulling out the needed data elements to build up the options list for the HTML select field. We'll use the customer ID as the actual data element that is stored, and simply display the customer's name. You'll notice that we again mixed HTML code and scriptlets together to achieve the desired effect. This entire process is repeated for the cruise list selection box.

Finally, we also set up a field to capture the number of tickets. Because we're working with a browser, we don't have the ability to display a dialog box as we did with the Swing example. Therefore, we'll just ask for the number of tickets up front.

The second JSP page will be the one that displays the results of our ticket request. That code can be seen in Listing 4.10.

LISTING 4.10 The Results JSP Page Shows the Outcome of the Ticket Request

```
<%@ page language="java" %>
<%@ page import="unleashed.ch4.cruise.*" %>
<jsp:useBean id="message" scope="session"
    class="unleashed.ch4.cruise.ResponseMessage" />
<html>
<head>
<title>Cruise Listing Application for Chapter 4 of Java
Unleashed</title>
</head>
<body>
<jsp:include page="Banner.jsp" flush="true" />
<center>
<form action="/ch4cruise/CruiseList" method="POST">
<!--
    Notice that we don't put a command in.
    Instead, we want to return to the main screen
-->
<font color="#<%

// set color to black if it's a normal message,
// red if it's an error
  if(message.getMessageType()==0)
    out.println("000000");
  else
    out.println("FF0000");
%>">

<jsp:getProperty name="message" property="messageText" />
</font>
<br>
<input type="submit" value="Continue">
</form>
</center>
</body>
</html>
```

Again, in this code listing, we import the support classes that we build up later in the chapter. We then read in a JavaBean from the session that contains the result message we want to display to the user. We again import our common banner using the `<jsp:include>` action. You'll notice, however, that we did not get the bean data in the same way that we did in the Cruise screen. Instead, we made use of the JSP `getBean` call. This has the same effect as our other method and was used only to demonstrate the other way of pulling in and assigning bean data to a referenced object in the JSP code.

The `Form` tag is again set to submit all data back to the `CruiseList` servlet. This time, however, we don't create a hidden command field. This will have the same effect as if we had come into the application fresh from the start, and will therefore launch the initial screen. The servlet will look for a command parameter, it will not find one, and it will determine that we just typed in the URL to launch the application.

Next, we do a little bit of logic based on the type of message passed within the `ResponseMessage` bean. If the `messagetype` comes back as `"0"`, we set the text color to black because it's a normal message to the user. Otherwise, we set the color to red because it's an error message that we want to have stand out to the user. Finally, we write out the message text stored within the bean. You'll notice that we made use of the `<jsp:getProperty>` mechanism. With this mechanism, we are requesting that JSP get the bean property data and write it out to the result stream. Again, this is no different from what we were doing previously except that it means we don't really need the `getMessageText()` method in the bean class anymore. Similarly, JSP has a `setProperty` mechanism that allows you to store data in a bean.

The common banner file is very simple and is included only to demonstrate the `<jsp:include>` action. The code for the common banner is shown in Listing 4.11.

LISTING 4.11   The Banner JSP File Will Be Included at Runtime into the Other JSP Pages

```
<center>
<Font size="6" color="0000FF">Cruise Ticket System</FONT>
</center>
```

The next part of our application centers around the supporting classes and JavaBeans that both the servlet and the JSP will share. These include beans for storing client and cruise information, lists of both of these, the `ResponseMessage` bean to pass text messages between the servlet and the JSP pages, and the `IllegalCCException` class that we'll use when verifying the customer's credit card information.

Listings 4.12–4.15 show the code for the `CruiseBean`, `CruiseListBean`, `CustomerBean`, and `CustomerListBean` JavaBeans.

4

APPLICATION DEVELOPMENT

LISTING 4.12   The CruiseBean JavaBean Is Used to Hold Data About a Single Cruise

```
package unleashed.ch4.cruise;

public class CruiseBean implements java.io.Serializable
{
    int cruiseID;
    String destination;
    String port;
    String sailing;

    public CruiseBean(int id,String dest,String str,String date)
    {
        cruiseID = id;
        destination = dest;
        port = str;
        sailing = date;
    }

    public void setCruiseID(int id)
    {
        cruiseID = id;
    }
    public int getCruiseID()
    {
        return cruiseID;
    }

    public void setDestination(String str)
    {
        destination = str;
    }
    public String getDestination()
    {
        return destination;
    }
    public void setPort(String str)
    {
        port = str;
    }
    public String getPort()
    {
        return port;
    }
    public void setSailing(String str)
    {
        sailing = str;
    }
    public String getSailing()
    {
        return sailing;
```

LISTING 4.12   continued

```
    }
    public String toString()
    {
        String temp = cruiseID+" to "+destination+" from "+port+
            " on "+sailing;
        return temp;
    }
}
```

LISTING 4.13   The `CruiseListBean` JavaBean Holds a List of `CruiseBeans`

```
package unleashed.ch4.cruise;

import java.util.*;

public class CruiseListBean implements java.io.Serializable
{
    private Vector cruises;
    public CruiseListBean()
    {
        cruises = new Vector();
    }
    public void addCruise(CruiseBean acruise)
    {
        cruises.add(acruise);
    }
    public Enumeration getCruiseList()
    {
        return cruises.elements();
    }
}
```

LISTING 4.14   The `CustomerBean` Holds Partial Data About a Customer That Will be Needed for Rendering the `Cruises` JSP Page

```
package unleashed.ch4.cruise;

public class CustomerBean implements java.io.Serializable
{
    int customerID;
    String lastName;
    String firstName;

    public CustomerBean(int id, String last, String first)
    {
        customerID = id;
```

LISTING 4.14 continued

```
        lastName = last;
        firstName = first;
    }
    public void setCustomerID(int id)
    {
        customerID = id;
    }
    public int getCustomerID()
    {
        return customerID;
    }
    public void setLastName(String str)
    {
        lastName = str;
    }
    public String getLastName()
    {
        return lastName;
    }
    public void setFirstName(String str)
    {
        firstName = str;
    }
    public String getFirstName()
    {
        return firstName;
    }
    public String toString()
    {
        String temp = customerID+": "+firstName+" "+lastName;
        return temp;
    }
}
```

LISTING 4.15 The `CustomerListBean` JavaBean Stores a List of `CustomerBeans`

```
package unleashed.ch4.cruise;

import java.util.*;

public class CustomerListBean implements java.io.Serializable
{
    private Vector customers;

    public CustomerListBean()
    {
        customers = new Vector();
    }
```

LISTING 4.15   continued

```
public void addCustomer(CustomerBean acustomer)
{
    customers.add(acustomer);
}


public Enumeration getCustomerList()
{
    return customers.elements();
}
}
```

Next, we'll need the ResponseMessage JavaBean. This bean is used to pass message information between the servlet and the Results JSP page and can be seen in Listing 4.16.

LISTING 4.16   The ResponseMessage JavaBean Stores Both Message Information and a Type Code

```
package unleashed.ch4.cruise;


/*  A simple JavaBean to hold a message.
    This bean will be used to transfer a text
    message between the Controller Servlet and the JSP view.
    By using this mechanism, we can put a little bit of logic
    into a JSP page and only need a single JSP page instead of
    multiple ones for responses back to the user.
*/

public class ResponseMessage implements java.io.Serializable
{
    private int messageType;  // 0 is a normal message,
                              //1 is a warning,
                              //2 is an error message
    private String messageText; // The text of the message.

    public ResponseMessage()
    {
    }

    public ResponseMessage(int level, String str)
    {
        messageType = level;
        messageText = str;
```

LISTING 4.16   continued

```
    }
    public void setMessageType (int level)
    {
        messageType = level;
    }
    public int getMessageType()
    {
        return messageType;
    }
    public void setMessageText(String str)
    {
        messageText = str;
    }
    public String getMessageText()
    {
        return messageText;
    }

    public String toString()
    {
        String response = "Message level: "+messageType+
            "   Message is: "+messageText;
        return response;
    }
}
```

Finally, in Listing 4.17, we'll create a simple Exception class that we'll use while checking the customer's credit card number. We don't need it to do anything in particular, we just want to be able to distinguish it from some other type of exception. Therefore, we'll leave the body of the class blank and let it take on the default Exception characteristics.

LISTING 4.17   InvalidCCException Doesn't Actually Override Anything from Exception

```
package unleashed.ch4.cruise;

public class InvalidCCException extends Exception
{
    // We're not really going to do anything.
    // we're just using this class for
    // informational purposes.
}
```

Now that we have all of our supporting classes, we can build the servlet. This servlet will not be rendering any HTML pages itself. It will, however, be the piece of code that gets called whenever our application needs to move from one screen to the next. As such, we refer to this servlet as a *controller*. This controller will fetch any data that is passed in a request time, figure out what to do with it, perform the processing, and then hand off response page generation to the appropriate JSP page. By doing this, we will have a simple Model-View-Controller application.

> **Tip**
>
> For more information on the Model-View-Controller, see Chapter 20.

As you'll see, our servlet is rather lengthy. In a real application, you'll probably use separate classes and hand off processing responsibilities to them. For this example though, we've put all the code into the servlet in order to simplify our application. The code for the CruiseList servlet is in Listing 4.18.

LISTING 4.18 The CruiseList Servlet Does All the Actual Processing Work

```java
package unleashed.ch4.cruise;

import javax.servlet.*;
import javax.servlet.http.*;
import unleashed.*;
import java.io.*;
import java.sql.*;
import java.util.*;

public class CruiseList extends HttpServlet
{
    private java.sql.Connection dbConn = null;
    private CustomerListBean custList = null;
    private CruiseListBean cruiseList = null;
    public void init(ServletConfig config) throws ServletException
    {
        super.init();
        // now we'll get the connection to the database.
        try
        {
            // ==== Make connection to database =======

            //load the driver class
            Class.forName("sun.jdbc.odbc.JdbcOdbcDriver");

            //Specify the ODBC data source
            String sourceURL = "jdbc:odbc:CruiseTicket";
```

4

APPLICATION
DEVELOPMENT

LISTING 4.18 continued

```java
            //get a connection to the database
            dbConn =DriverManager.getConnection(sourceURL);
            custList = buildCustomerList();
            cruiseList = buildCruiseList();
            }
            catch (Exception e)
            {
                throw new ServletException(
                    "Could not create database " +
                    "connection in init(): "+e);
            }
}
public void destroy()
{
    try
    {
        if(dbConn!=null)
            dbConn.close();
    }
    catch(Exception e)
    {
        System.out.println(
            "error while closing down DB connection.");
    }
}


public String getServletInfo()
{
    return "Cruise List booking controller servlet.";
}

public void doGet( HttpServletRequest request,
        HttpServletResponse response)
    throws ServletException, IOException
{
    doPost(request,response);
}

public void doPost( HttpServletRequest request,
        HttpServletResponse response)
    throws ServletException, IOException
{
    System.out.println(
        "CruiseList servlet got a request...");
    ResponseMessage msg;
    String command = request.getParameter("command");
    HttpSession session = request.getSession();
```

Listing 4.18 continued

```
System.out.println("command is: "+command);
if(command == null || command.equals(""))
{
    try
    {
        //build up the CustomerList and CruiseLists from DB

        session.setAttribute("custList",custList);
        session.setAttribute("cruiseList",cruiseList);
    }
    catch(Exception e)
    {
        throw new ServletException(e);
    }

    response.sendRedirect("/ch4cruise/Cruises.jsp");
}

else if (command.equals("book"))
{
    String custid = request.getParameter("custid");
    String cruiseid = request.getParameter("cruiseid");
    String tickets = request.getParameter("numbertickets");

    System.out.println("Got parameters");
    try
    {
        if(custid.equals("") || cruiseid.equals(""))
        {
            System.out.println("Missing a parameter!");
            throw new Exception("Missing parameter");
        }
        else
        {
            int numtickets = Integer.parseInt(tickets);
            if(numtickets<=0)
                throw new NumberFormatException();
            try
            {
                if(makeReservation(custid,
                        cruiseid,
                        numtickets))
                    msg=new ResponseMessage(0,
                        "Cruise successfully booked.");
                else
                    msg=new ResponseMessage(2,
                        "Problem booking cruise.");
            }
```

LISTING 4.18 continued

```
                    catch (InvalidCCException cce)
                    {
                        msg = new ResponseMessage(2,
                            "That customer's credit card is"+
                            " invalid");
                    }
                }

            }
            catch(Exception e)
            {
                msg = new ResponseMessage(2,
                    "You must select a customer, "+
                    "a cruise and enter a valid number "+
                    "of tickets");
            }
            System.out.println(
                "Setting ResponseMessageBean for JSP use.");
            session.setAttribute("message",msg);
            System.out.println("Redirecting to JSP for output");
            response.sendRedirect("/ch4cruise/Results.jsp");

        } // if command

    } // doPost()


    private CruiseListBean buildCruiseList() throws Exception
    {
        CruiseBean aCruise = null;
        CruiseListBean cruiselist = new CruiseListBean();
        Statement statement = null;

        statement = dbConn.createStatement();

        String query = "SELECT CRUISEID, DESTINATION,PORT, "+
            "SAILING FROM CRUISES";
        ResultSet rs = statement.executeQuery(query);
        while(rs.next())
        {
            aCruise = new CruiseBean(
                rs.getInt(1),
                rs.getString(2),
                rs.getString(3),
                rs.getString(4));
            cruiselist.addCruise(aCruise);
            System.out.println("added :"+aCruise.toString());
        }
        statement.close();
```

LISTING 4.18 continued

```
        return cruiselist;
} // buildCruiseList

private CustomerListBean buildCustomerList() throws Exception
{
    CustomerBean aCustomer = null;
    CustomerListBean customerlist = new CustomerListBean();
    Statement statement = null;

    statement = dbConn.createStatement();

    String query = "SELECT CUSTOMERID, LASTNAME, FIRSTNAME "+
        "FROM CRUISECUSTOMER";
    ResultSet rs = statement.executeQuery(query);
    while(rs.next())
    {
        aCustomer = new CustomerBean(
            rs.getInt(1),
            rs.getString(2),
            rs.getString(3)
            );
        customerlist.addCustomer(aCustomer);
        System.out.println("added :"+aCustomer.toString());
    }
    statement.close();
    return customerlist;
} //buildCustomerList


// for simplicity sake we'll do the processing here.
// in a real application this work should be done in
// its own class
private boolean makeReservation(String custId,
    String cruiseId, int tickets) throws InvalidCCException
{
    System.out.println(
        "Attempting to make reservation for custid: "+custId);
    //first fetch the cc number of the customer
    Statement statement = null;
    String ccnum =null;
    boolean status = false;
    try
    {
        statement = dbConn.createStatement();

        String query = "SELECT CREDITCARDNUMBER "+
            "FROM CRUISECUSTOMER "+
            "WHERE (CUSTOMERID ="+custId+")";
        ResultSet rs = statement.executeQuery(query);
```

LISTING 4.18   continued

```
while(rs.next())
{
    ccnum = rs.getString(1);
}
statement.close();
System.out.println(
    "Credit card number for customer: "+
    custId+" is: "+ccnum);
if(!verifyCreditCard(ccnum))
    throw new InvalidCCException();


//Ok, valid CC number. Get the cruise info next

String destination = null;
String port=null;
String date=null;

statement = dbConn.createStatement();

query = "SELECT DESTINATION, PORT, SAILING "+
    "FROM CRUISES WHERE (CRUISEID="+cruiseId+")";
rs = statement.executeQuery(query);
while(rs.next())
{
    destination = rs.getString(1);
    port = rs.getString(2);
    date = rs.getString(3);
}
statement.close();
System.out.println("Got the cruise information. ");

// find the max ticketID in the system,
// if it's null, set to 1
statement = dbConn.createStatement();

int ticketID=0;
query = "SELECT MAX (TICKETID) FROM CRUISETICKET";
rs = statement.executeQuery(query);
while(rs.next())
{
    ticketID = rs.getInt(1);
}
statement.close();
ticketID++;

System.out.println("Next ticket ID is: "+ticketID);

System.out.println("Building reservation");
```

LISTING 4.18   continued

```
            // ok, now build the reservation in the ticket table

            statement=dbConn.createStatement();
            query = "INSERT INTO CRUISETICKET VALUES("+
                ticketID+","+custId+", 'Unleashed Cruise Line' , "+
                "'USS SeaBiscuit', '"+port+"','" +
                date+"',999.99,0,0,'CH4Servlet')";
            statement.executeUpdate(query);
            statement.close();
        }
        catch(SQLException sqle)
        {
            System.out.println("Had an SQL exception: "+sqle);
            status = false;
            return status;
        }
        status = true;
        return status;
    }
    private boolean verifyCreditCard(String ccnum)
    {
        int firstnum = Integer.parseInt(ccnum.substring(0,1));
        if(firstnum > 4)
            return false;
        else
            return true;
    }
} //class
```

Let's examine this code in detail because many new servlet concepts are being used.

First, you'll notice that the servlet contains an init() method. The container will exe-cute the code found within the init method only once. Usually, this takes place when the application is first deployed. In our servlet, we've gone ahead and created our data-base connection, as well as made calls to two methods that are responsible for building up lists of available customers and cruises. Because this data never changes in our appli-cation, we'll just read it in once and store it within the servlet for use later. In a full-fledged application, you'll probably want to fetch undated lists regularly, but this is outside the scope of our example. Notice that we did not close the connection. Instead, we'll keep it open and reuse that connection for every JDBC process in the servlet.

In order to make sure that we clean ourselves up correctly when the servlet is finally done, we use the destroy method. destroy is called whenever the servlet is deactivated and garbage collected. In our case, we close off our database connection so that we don't have any lingering open connections after the servlet is deactivated.

4

APPLICATION DEVELOPMENT

The servlet's doGet() method in this example has been set to simply pass on its data to the doPost(). We could set up the application to do something completely different when data is sent to it via a GET, but because we only are using the POST method in the HTML Forms found in our JSP pages, we have no need for this. Instead, we'll simply pass along processing responsibility to doPost.

Most of the real work takes place in doPost(). Every Form that gets submitted to our servlet will send its data to this method for processing. This method will be responsible for determining what activity needs to take place and what JSP page to call to generate the response to the user. As such, it will be the place where the first level of our business logic will go.

In our doPost, we first attempt to get the value of the "command" parameter from the HttpServletRequest. This is done with the getParameter method. The name of the variable we request must match the name of the HTML field set up in the submitting form. Using this mechanism, we can request any data element that the submitting Form has sent to the servlet. It should be noted that the value is always sent as a String, and will need to be converted to other types if needed by the servlet code.

The next line requests the current session information from the servlet context. This is the same session information that our JSP pages are given. By making use of this session object, we have a way of transferring data between the servlet and the JSPs.

We then perform a simple if-then check to find out what command was passed into the servlet by the form. In the event that the user typed the URL and we didn't have a command sent in, or the user decided to move on from the Results page, there won't be a command parameter passed. In either situation, we want to display the main Cruises page. That page needs the list of Customers and the list of Cruises in order to render, so we store both of those JavaBeans into the shared session object. That is accomplished with the session.setAttribute method. setAttribute takes any sort of object and stores it in the session with a key name associated to it. As you can see, we use the keys "custList" and "cruiseList". In the Cruises JSP, we referenced those lists by requesting the attribute objects by the same key names. The last part of the process for a null command is to actually call the Cruises JSP page so that it can render. This is accomplished by the HttpServlet Response.sendRedirect method. In this case, we instruct the servlet to hand off responsibility to the Cruises.jsp file. We could just as easily have passed off responsibility to another servlet or any other sort of application or file.

In the second command case, "book", we need to perform all the business logic to actually book a cruise. In such a case, we need a cruise ID, customer ID, and the number of tickets the customer wants to perform the processing. If we don't get one of those parameters, we set up an error message to be passed back to the Results JSP page through a ResultMessage bean.

In the event that we are sent all the required data, we call the makeReservation method. This method performs all the booking logic to check the customer's credit card and place the actual booking. In case the credit card for the selected customer is invalid, we throw an IllegalCCException, which is caught by the doPost() so that we can send a descriptive message back to the user. If, instead, everything went okay, we store the booking in the database and finally set up a message to the user that everything went through okay.

That's all there is to it! Now that we have all of our code, we'll need to make sure that we package it correctly. Place the code elements into the following structure, where ROOT is the base directory for our project:

```
ROOT\
    The .jsp files
    WEB-INF\
            web.xml
            classes\
                    unleashed\
                            ch4\
                                    cruise\
                                            all of the class files.
```

The web.xml file we'll need can be seen in Listing 4.19.

LISTING 4.19   The web.xml Deployment Descriptor for Our Cruise Application

```
<!DOCTYPE web-app PUBLIC
    "-//Sun Microsystems, Inc.//DTD Web Application 2.2//EN"
    "http://java.sun.com/j2ee/dtds/web-app_2_2.dtd">

<web-app>
    <display-name>Cruise List Application</display-name>
    <servlet>
    <servlet-name>ch4cruise</servlet-name>
        <servlet-class>unleashed.ch4.cruise.CruiseList
        </servlet-class>
    <load-on-startup>1</load-on-startup>
    </servlet>
    <servlet-mapping>
        <servlet-name>ch4cruise</servlet-name>
        <url-pattern>/*</url-pattern>
    </servlet-mapping>
</web-app>
```

Next, create the WAR file for the application using the following command from the ROOT directory:

```
Jar -cvf ch4cruise.war *.jsp WEB-INF
```

4

APPLICATION
DEVELOPMENT

Finally, copy the WAR file into the examples deployment directory:

```
Copy ch4cruise.war c:\bea\wlserver6.1\config\examples\applications
```

If you have the WebLogic Server running when you perform the copy and everything is correct, you should see the servlet loading in the customer and cruise information and storing it in the `CustomerListBean` and `CruiseListBean`. You should see something similar to Figure 4.7.

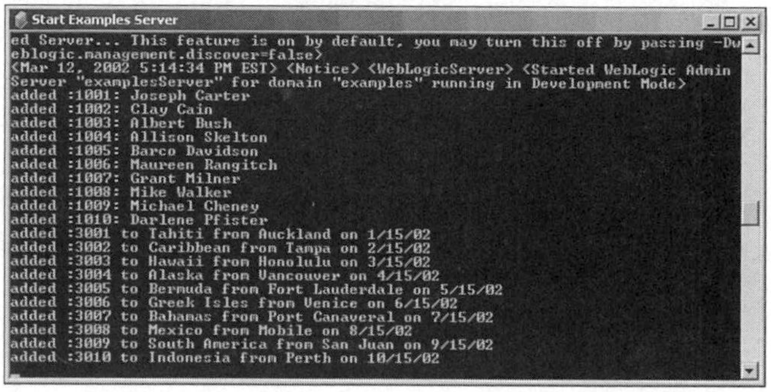

FIGURE 4.7

Example output to WebLogic Server console at servlet deployment.

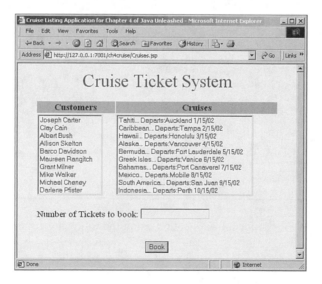

To launch our application, open a browser and point it to the following:

```
http://<yourweblogicServer>:7001/ch4cruise
```

You'll see a screen like the one in Figure 4.8.

FIGURE 4.8

The main screen of the Cruise application, rendered by the `Cruises.jsp` *using data fetched by the* `CruiseList` *servlet.*

By selecting a Customer and a Cruise, entering the number of tickets, and then pressing the Book button, we're invoking an HTTP request to our servlet and sending the data. The servlet processes the data according to the command passed and redirects to the Results JSP page with the appropriate message. If the booking request is successful, you'll see a page like the one shown in Figure 4.9.

FIGURE 4.9

The results of a successful cruise booking.

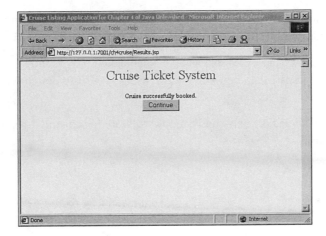

In this section, we've shown how you can use JSP and servlets together to solve a common problem, while at the same time leveraging the best of both technologies. By using JavaBeans to pass data to the JSP, we keep the level of Java coding experience needed by a Webmaster to a reasonable level, while allowing her maximum flexibility. At the same time, by placing our business logic into the servlet, we've abstracted that level of knowledge away from the Webmaster and put it into the hands of the Java developer who is better suited to the task. In Chapter 20, you'll see a commonly used framework for building applications using this type of mechanism.

Summary

In this chapter, we've discussed the evolution of dynamic page generation and shown where JSP and servlets fit into that history. We talked about the way in which Web-based applications operate and how HTTP sends data to the Web server on a page request.

We then looked at how to build a simple JSP that counted the number of times it was invoked. This JSP demonstrated how to package and run a JSP in WebLogic Server.

Next, we discussed the various elements that make up a JSP page. We looked at pragmas, declarations, expressions, and scriptlets.

We then showed how you could build a simple JSP page that handled Form data from another page.

We looked at a simple servlet and compared how to build the same page counter using a servlet instead of a JSP. We showed how the servlet needed to be packaged and deployed on the application server.

We then compared when it was appropriate to use JSP and when a servlet should be used. Remember, use JSP for presentation and servlets for data processing.

Finally, we built the Cruise example using a combination of JSP and servlets and demonstrated how we can pass data between the two using JavaBeans stored within the session object.

As we've seen, JSP and servlets can be a powerful tool for creating dynamic, interactive Web applications.

Enterprise Java

IN THIS PART

Enterprise
JavaBeans (EJB)

CHAPTER 5

In this chapter, we will cover Enterprise JavaBeans (EJBs) and discuss how to build various types of EJBs.

Building enterprise applications with EJBs is a large topic that certainly deserves many books. To make it easier for you to master the subject, we will cover it iteratively just like any enterprise project would be developed. We will start out with a simple view of EJB and build a *copy-and-paste* example to get you started. Then you will step back and look inside the EJB container to understand how EJBs work. When we have developed the basic understanding of EJB, we will talk about what kinds of EJBs exist, how they work, and how to develop each kind. In the last iteration, we will talk about what an EJB container is, what services it provides, and how you can use these services.

In the course of this chapter, we will build a Cruise Booking Application. Of course, the application will have a slightly different design to take advantage of EJBs. We will go over the changes in the design early on so you know what the big picture is.

I do not assume that you have any previous experience with EJBs, so the first section might seem oversimplified to some readers. Feel free to skip it and go to the implementation of the EJB type that is relevant to you. In the later sections, however, I do expect you to be familiar with J2EE services like JNDI, JTA, and JDBC. In the section "EJB Container Services," we only talk about various J2EE specifications in the context of EJBs, so you might have to refresh yourself on some of the APIs mentioned above.

> **Note**
>
> See Chapter 10, "JDBC and Databases," for a discussion on JDBC and Chapter 11, "Java Naming and Directory Interface (JNDI)," for a discussion on JNDI.

> **Note**
>
> This chapter covers version 2.0 of EJB specification. If for any reason some other version of the specification is mentioned, it will be specifically noted. Most of our examples will use server independent features. However, in some areas, the specification encourages the container to improvise. These places will be carefully noted.

Understanding the EJB Approach

Once I was presented with a Chinese puzzle. The puzzle consisted of a number of wooden bars with slots of different shape. It seemed pretty simple, yet it took a good deal of time before I figured out how the bars fit onto each other to produce the resulting figure.

Your enterprise application might look like a Chinese puzzle at times. Many different technologies are supposed to fit perfectly with each other to produce a cohesive system. An Enterprise JavaBean is just like a wooden bar in your puzzle that has a certain shape and is carved to hold a part of the whole structure. An Enterprise JavaBean is similar to some other technologies just like one bar in the puzzle is similar to some others. Yet EJB has its specifics that we have to understand to be able to use it.

Not surprisingly, Enterprise JavaBeans are Java objects just like almost everything else in Java. An object, however, must implement certain methods in order to become an EJB. These methods are called by an EJB container that creates and manages an EJB. These methods are also known as `callback` methods. They define how the EJB fits into the environment. The environment where each EJB exists is defined by an EJB container. The EJB container is responsible for creating, caching, and removing EJBs as well as other middleware services.

Implementing a set of defined callback methods is not a new concept in Java. A similar approach was taken earlier with Java Servlets. Java Servlets proved to be very successful because they hide the complexity of the HTTP protocol and present the developer with a simple object-oriented view of the client request.

> **Note**
>
> Enterprise JavaBeans, albeit similar in name, have nothing to do with JavaBeans. The two technologies serve different goals and are based on different specifications. In this book the words *bean*, *JavaBean*, and the like refer only to the Enterprise JavaBean specification and technology.

EJBs are similar to Java Servlets in that EJBs also hide the complexity of the communication between the client and the server. Just like Java Servlets, EJBs can only exist in the context of the container and must follow a certain protocol.

5

ENTERPRISE JAVABEANS (EJB)

Unlike Java Servlets, however, EJBs do not service HTTP requests. EJBs exist to contain business logic, implementing either model or controller pieces in the middle tier of the enterprise system. The word *enterprise* in the previous sentence assumes that the system has certain properties. It is beneficial to go over these properties briefly to understand why EJBs are needed. Typically, an enterprise application is expected to have these properties:

- Good scalability and reliability—Enterprise applications must be able to scale to large loads without performance degradation.

- High security—Most enterprise applications must pay attention to authentication and authorization of the clients.

- Easy integration with existing systems—Every new technology must bring new exciting features, yet it still has to peacefully coexist with many legacy applications.

In these and other requirements, EJBs provide an alternative that is superior to many earlier technologies. In the course of this chapter, we will talk about all these features.

There is no better explanation, however, than a demonstration. Let's see how a simple EJB can be developed.

EJB Strengths

If your manager has not done it already, she certainly will one day ask why you are using EJBs in your project. At that point, you will have to come up with the right answers quickly and be as relevant as possible. Saying that EJBs are cool probably won't help you. For every technology in a commercial project, there must be strong business reasons to use that technology. That is why we want to go over some of the reasons for and against using EJBs.

The business reasons to use EJBs are

- Industry approval—The whole industry supports EJBs as a part of J2EE. The EJB specification is being developed under the influence of the major players and is supported by a number of companies. This means that a lot of smart people are overseeing the technology to serve you better!

- Fast time to market—EJBs have features that make a developer very productive. The technology is also very flexible in that an EJB can be easily adapted to new business rules. This means that an EJB can be reused or bought from somebody else. EJBs allow you to build good systems quickly.

- Cost-effectiveness—Because there are a lot of EJB containers, a lot of competition exists between them, which means that you, as a customer, have a choice. You can buy an expensive EJB server or a cheap one (possibly free). What's even better, you can start with a cheap solution and grow to a more expensive one as your business grows. The EJB specification makes sure that all EJB containers provide the necessary level of portability.

There are also technical reasons to use EJBs that you can give to the technology leaders in your company:

- Technical leadership—EJB is the specification that is based on the latest advances in object-oriented design—patterns and best practices. Your developers will design a robust system without much pain.

- Maturity—The technology is the result of four years of hard work of many talented people. A number of projects are in production or coming to production in the near future. This means that the container vendors had time to fix initial bugs and improve usability. It also means that people have tried different features and know their way around the technology.

- Advanced container services—The EJB specification requires container vendors to implement certain services that we will discuss. It means that your developers will not need to implement these services, but rather use the best container implementation. Such a system has a better chance to be robust and adaptable to changing business rules.

EJB Weaknesses

Some of the EJB strengths are also its weaknesses. In some situations, these weaknesses might even cause you to turn to a competing technology.

Business reasons *not* to use EJBs:

- Harsh competition could fragment the market—There is no clear leader on the EJB container market at this point. The luck of the major players can change unexpectedly. This could result in a fragmented market in which different servers will have nonstandard features and extensions. This could potentially lock your business in a server that becomes obsolete and will require a costly change in your application. This issue can be mitigated by following the EJB specification and limiting the use of the container extensions.

- Total solution cost might be higher than that of some competing technologies— The flexibility and novelty of EJBs result in systems with many moving pieces. These systems require time and expensive people to make sure the system does not go awry. Similar arguments can be used against any other powerful and new technology.

5

ENTERPRISE
JAVABEANS (EJB)

You might also hear technical reasons *not* to use EJBs. The validity of these reasons depends on your specific project requirements:

- Performance—EJBs might be too slow for systems with strict performance requirements. However, you should be careful not to write off EJBs because of performance issues because this argument is used for almost any new technology. Often, this is based on feelings rather than concrete numbers.

- Interoperability—Problematic integration with Microsoft or legacy systems. If your project depends on integration with these different systems, it is worth uncovering the integration points first to see if EJB is the way to go.

- Discrepancy between the specification and different implementations—The EJB specification is being developed with unprecedented speed. Very few implementations are able to keep up with the new features. Choosing the right EJB container for your project is a technical challenge.

Writing a Simple EJB

In this section, we will write and run a simple EJB. We will go through all the necessary steps to develop a functional EJB on WebLogic Server. The source code for this chapter includes a readme file with instructions on how to compile and run this example.

> **Note**
>
> You can download the source code for this chapter at the Sams Publishing Web site (www.samspublishing.com).

Let us write a simple 'Hello World' EJB that is called by a Java client. To implement our 'Hello World' EJB, you will need to perform the following steps:

1. Declare an interface with business methods that we want to express.
2. Add a factory that will create the EJB.
3. Implement the bean.
4. Compile the bean classes.
5. Add a descriptor file called a *deployment descriptor*.
6. Put the deployment descriptors and the client files together in a JAR file.
7. The EJB container's EJB compiler can now generate the necessary network code for the EJB to become a remote object.

8. The output from the EJB compiler is ready to be deployed on your target EJB container.

9. Write a client to call the EJB.

Step 1: Declaring a Remote Interface

An EJB has to declare an interface with the business methods that we want to expose. This interface is called a *remote interface* because it allows an EJB to be running on a machine different from a client machine that calls the EJB. The remote interface is based on the Java *Remote Method Invocation (RMI)* technology. Java RMI is a technology that can send method calls over a network. Listing 5.1 shows the EJB remote interface.

LISTING 5.1   Simple EJB Remote Interface

```
package unleashed.ch5.simple;

import java.rmi.RemoteException;
import javax.ejb.EJBObject;

/**
 * Simple EJB.
 */
public interface HelloWorld extends EJBObject
{
    //declare our business method
    public  String sayIt() throws RemoteException;
}
```

The remote interface extends `javax.ejb.EJBObject`, and all its methods must have `java.rmi.RemoteException` in their `throws` clause. Because an EJB is using Java RMI to send the method calls, its remote interface methods must throw a `java.rmi.RemoteException` in case any communication error occurs.

> **Note**
>
> The Java RMI can be implemented over any communication protocol. The EJB specification requires every container vendor to support Java RMI over IIOP. This makes all EJB containers interoperable. In addition to RMI-IIOP, a vendor can implement any other communication protocol. Thus, using Java RMI for EJB communication makes them very flexible.

Step 2: Adding a Factory

Our simple EJB requires a factory that will create it. The factory interface is called the home interface in the EJB specification. The home interface is responsible for the creation of an EJB object on a remote server. Listing 5.2 shows the home interface for our simple EJB.

> **Note**
>
> A home interface is essentially a factory that creates EJBs remotely. Before creating an EJB a client needs to obtain a handle to the home interface.

LISTING 5.2 Simple EJB Home Interface

```
package unleashed.ch5.simple;

import java.rmi.RemoteException;
import javax.ejb.CreateException;
import javax.ejb.EJBHome;

/**
 * Simple EJB Home interface.
 */
public interface HelloWorldHome extends EJBHome
{
    //we need only create method
    public HelloWorld create() throws CreateException, RemoteException;
}
```

The home interface extends the `javax.ejb.EJBHome` interface and declares `create` methods. For our simple example, we only need a `create` method. Each `create` method has to throw `javax.ejb.CreateException` and `java.rmi.RemoteException`. The `java.rmi.RemoteException` must be declared on a home interface because it is also using Java RMI to communicate over a network.

Step 3: Implementing the Bean

Finally, we need to implement the bean—with the methods that are called callback methods by the EJB specification. The callback methods are the methods that are called by the EJB container. The callback methods are called at specific time—for example, when an EJB is created, removed, and so on. An EJB client never calls the callback methods explicitly; they are only called by the container. In addition to the callback methods, the bean implementation must also implement all the business methods. Business methods are the methods that an EJB client calls explicitly. Business methods are also declared on the remote interface. For example, we declared the sayIt method on the remote interface in step 1. Now we have to implement this method. Obviously, the method implementation has to follow the same signature; that is, it has to have the same arguments and throw the same exceptions as it declared on the remote interface. Listing 5.3 shows the implementation of the bean class.

LISTING 5.3   Simple EJB Implementation

```
package unleashed.ch5.simple;

import javax.ejb.CreateException;
import javax.ejb.SessionBean;
import javax.ejb.SessionContext;
import javax.naming.InitialContext;
import javax.naming.NamingException;

/**
 * Hello World bean implementation.
 */
public class HelloWorldBean implements SessionBean
{

  //callback method must be implemented
  public void ejbActivate() {}
  public void ejbRemove() {}
  public void ejbPassivate() {}
  public void setSessionContext(SessionContext ctx) {}
  public void ejbCreate () throws CreateException {}


  /**
   * Our hello world method
   */
   public String sayIt()
   {
       System.out.println("Hello World EJB is called");
       return "Hello World";
   }
}
```

Note that our implementation does not implement the HelloWorld interface but rather the javax.ejb.SessionBean interface. We will see a bit later how the interface is connected to the implementation.

In our simple example, we do not need to do anything inside the callback methods, so we just leave them empty. The only business method from the `HelloWorld` interface has these two lines of code:

```
System.out.println("Hello World EJB is called");
return "Hello World";
```

Step 4: Compiling the Classes

The next step is to compile these three classes. Compiling at this step is done by a regular Java compiler because we only want to generate normal Java classes. You can compile the example EJB by using the script provided with the source code for this chapter.

Step 5: Adding a Descriptor File

So far, developing an EJB was similar to many other framework implementations such as Java Servlets. We have created the remote and home interfaces and implemented the EJB. In this step, though, we need to do something different—our EJB needs a descriptor file called a *deployment descriptor*. The deployment descriptor glues the interfaces to the implementation classes and declares the JNDI name with which the bean is deployed in the EJB container. Additionally, the deployment descriptor carries the container-specific information that we will go over in the later sections of the chapter. Let's start with the simplest descriptor in Listing 5.4.

> **Note**
>
> JNDI is covered in Chapter 11.

LISTING 5.4   Simple EJB Deployment Descriptor

```xml
<?xml version="1.0"?>

<!DOCTYPE ejb-jar PUBLIC
'-//Sun Microsystems, Inc.//DTD Enterprise JavaBeans 2.0//EN'
'http://java.sun.com/dtd/ejb-jar_2_0.dtd'>

<ejb-jar>
  <enterprise-beans>
    <session>
      <ejb-name>HelloWorld</ejb-name>
      <home>unleashed.ch5.simple.HelloWorldHome</home>
      <remote>unleashed.ch5.simple.HelloWorld</remote>
      <ejb-class>unleashed.ch5.simple.HelloWorldBean</ejb-class>
      <session-type>Stateless</session-type>
```

LISTING 5.4   continued

```
      <transaction-type>Container</transaction-type>
    </session>
  </enterprise-beans>
</ejb-jar>
```

The preceding deployment descriptor must be located in the ejb-jar.xml file. As you can see, the descriptor is an XML file. The EJB specification defines the DTD for ejb-jar.xml, which ensures that all EJB containers follow the same format.

> **Note**
>
> In addition to ejb-jar.xml, every container might have its own specific deployment descriptors. The container-specific deployment descriptors need to be changed if you decide to port an EJB from one container to another. WebLogic Server 6.1 requires a weblogic-ejb-jar.xml descriptor. This is the weblogic-ejb-jar.xml file for our simple EJB:
>
> ```
> <?xml version="1.0"?>
> <!DOCTYPE weblogic-ejb-jar PUBLIC
> '-//BEA Systems, Inc.//DTD WebLogic 6.0.0 EJB//EN'
> 'http://www.bea.com/servers/wls600/dtd/weblogic-ejb-jar.dtd'>
> <weblogic-ejb-jar>
>     <weblogic-enterprise-bean>
>         <ejb-name>HelloWorld</ejb-name>
>         <jndi-name>HelloWorld</jndi-name>
>     </weblogic-enterprise-bean>
> </weblogic-ejb-jar>
> ```
>
> This is also an XML file, although it follows a proprietary DTD that is provided only for the Weblogic EJB container. So, the EJB that has this deployment descriptor will only run on the Weblogic EJB container.

Step 6: Packaging the Bean

When we have the EJB classes and the deployment descriptors, we have to put all these files together in a JAR file. You can use the jar utility that comes with the JDK to jar the files. You can use a script provided with the chapter to build the example. You can also just type a command similar to this:

```
jar -cvf simpleejb.jar META-INF unleashed\ch5\simple\*.class
```

The JAR file must have the following structure:

```
|-META-INF
   |-ejb-jar.xml
```

```
|-unleashed\
    |-ch5\
        |-simple\
            |HelloWorld.class
            |HelloWorldHome.class
            |HelloWorldBean.class
```

All EJBs must be packaged in a JAR file that follows the preceding structure. The deployment descriptors must reside in the `META-INF` directory. The class files follow their package structure. For example, the `unleashed.ch5.simple.HelloWorld` class must be located under directory `unleashed\ch5\simple`.

Step 7: Generating the EJB Container Code

Based on the JAR file created in the previous step, the EJB container's EJB compiler can generate the necessary network code for the EJB to become a remote object. Every EJB container provides its own EJB compiler because the generated code is container specific. The EJB compiler takes your JAR file and analyses the Java classes as well as the deployment descriptors to generate a final EJB. The compiler's output EJB can be deployed only on the container whose EJB compiler was used to generate it. If you decide to deploy your EJB on a different container, you will have to use that container's EJB compiler to regenerate the EJB.

> **Note**
>
> Our simple EJB is written for WebLogic Server 6.1, so we are calling the WebLogic EJB compiler in the `compilesimple.bat` file:
>
> ```
> java -cp %WL_HOME%\lib\weblogic_sp.jar;%WL_HOME%\lib\weblogic.jar;
> ➥ -Dweblogic.home=%WL_HOME% weblogic.ejbc  -compiler javac
> ➥.\simpleejbin.jar
> ```

Step 8: Deploying the Bean

The output from the EJB compiler is ready to be deployed on your target EJB container. The deployment procedure can be different from container to container. Typically, deployment involves copying the final EJB file to the container's deployment directory. After that, you often have to restart the container to force it to deploy the EJB. Most containers look in the deployment directory at the startup and try to deploy all JAR files as EJBs. Some containers have a feature that is called *hot deployment*. This means that you do not have to restart the container to deploy a new EJB. If the container is running, you can just copy an EJB to the hot deployment directory and the container will sense that there is a new EJB that needs to be deployed. This saves a lot of time during development because you do not have to restart the container every time you change the code. However, hot deployment is usually disabled on production servers because new EJBs do not get deployed there that often, and hot deployment takes some CPU cycles.

> **Note**
>
> You can use the script provided with the chapter to deploy this example. You can also do it by hand by copying your output JAR file to the applications directory under your domain of the running server. A new JAR in the applications directory will trigger a hot deployment if it is enabled. See the WebLogic Server documentation on how to enable hot deployment at http://edocs.bea.com/wls/docs61/index.html.

Step 9: Writing a Client

Let's write a client to call our 'Hello World' EJB. The client looks up a home interface, creates a bean, and calls its method. The lookup is done by using a standard JNDI lookup. Listing 5.5 shows the code for the client.

LISTING 5.5 Simple EJB Client

```
package unleashed.ch5.simple;

import java.rmi.RemoteException;
import java.util.Properties;
import javax.ejb.CreateException;
import javax.ejb.RemoveException;
import javax.naming.Context;
import javax.naming.InitialContext;
import javax.naming.NamingException;
import javax.rmi.PortableRemoteObject;

/**
 * Simple client
 */
public class SimpleEJBClient
{

    private static final String JNDI_NAME = "HelloWorld";


    public static void main(String[] args)
    throws Exception
```

LISTING 5.5   continued

```
    {
        try
        {
            //jndi properties
            Properties h = new Properties();
              h.put(Context.INITIAL_CONTEXT_FACTORY,
                "weblogic.jndi.WLInitialContextFactory");
              h.put(Context.PROVIDER_URL,
                "t3://localhost:7001");

              //lookup jndi initial context
            InitialContext ctx = new InitialContext(h);

            //lookup home
            Object obj = ctx.lookup(JNDI_NAME);

            //cast home
            HelloWorldHome home =
            (HelloWorldHome)PortableRemoteObject.narrow
➥ (obj, HelloWorldHome.class);

                //create the bean
                Object ejbObj = home.create();

                //cast the bean to our interface
                HelloWorld simpleEJB =
                (HelloWorld)PortableRemoteObject.narrow
➥ (ejbObj, HelloWorld.class);

                //call bean's method
                System.out.println("Calling Simple EJB "
➥ + simpleEJB.sayIt());

        } catch (Exception e)
        {
            System.out.println(e.getMessage());
            e.printStackTrace();
        }

    }
}
```

As you might have noticed, the client casts a retrieved object to an interface using
`PortableRemoteObject.narrow` method:

```
HelloWorldHome home =
(HelloWorldHome)PortableRemoteObject.narrow(obj, HelloWorldHome.class);
```

Such casting is required by the EJB specification for the client to be portable across various EJB containers. The reason not to use regular Java casting mechanisms is that it might not work with EJB containers that use RMI-IIOP as the communication transport.

You can try running the client to see if the EJB is called. Execute `runsimple.bat` to run the client. The client produces this output:

```
Calling Simple EJB: Hello World
```

As you can see, building an EJB is a little more involved than writing a Java class or a Java Servlet. Fortunately, you can increase your productivity by using various tools. Creating the remote and home interfaces, deployment descriptors, and JAR files can be automated. However, it is still common to change deployment descriptors by hand, so it is a good idea to become familiar with them.

EJB Internals

Let's step back a little and look at how EJBs work. This section covers the concepts that are used inside the container to give EJB its powerful features.

EJB Architecture

Java *Remote Method Invocation (RMI)* predates EJB as a way of building distributed systems. EJB borrows a lot from Java RMI to make the beans remote. Figure 5.1 shows how an RMI object would typically be created.

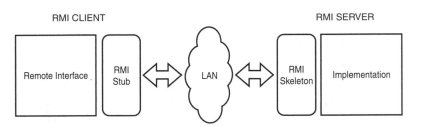

FIGURE 5.1
RMI uses stubs and skeletons to hide network code from the implementation.

In RMI, you have to write a remote interface, and the RMI compiler would produce the stub and skeleton with all the network code. Stubs and skeletons are essentially two Java classes that implement the networking code on a client and server. The stub is placed on the client and the skeleton on the server. The stub class implements the same remote interface, so the client code calls the stub just as if it were a real object. When the client calls the remote object, it actually calls the local stub object. The stub finds the machine where the object resides, opens a connection to that machine, and sends the method call to it. When the remote object on that machine responds, the stub gets the data from the connection and returns back to the client. Thus, the remote object looks just like a local one to the client because all the networking code is hidden in the stub class. The skeleton works on the other side of the communication. It is placed on the server so that the remote object gets all the calls from the skeleton. The skeleton accepts a connection from a remote machine, gets the method parameters, and calls the object. The skeleton also instantiates a remote object when needed. The calls from the skeleton look like local calls to the remote object. When the object returns from the call, the skeleton sends the return back to the client. Thus, the remote object does not have to contain the network code because it is provided by the skeleton.

> **Note**
>
> Stubs and skeletons are the Java classes that contain all the network code necessary to transmit the object over the network. The EJB framework borrowed these terms from Java RMI. Please see Chapter 2, "Creating Applications with Remote Method Invocation (RMI)," for the discussion of Java RMI.

Enterprise JavaBeans use a very similar architecture. In our simple EJB, we created the HelloWorld interface that is essentially a remote interface. Then, we created a bean implementation class that is logically similar to an implementation class in RMI. Finally, we compiled the classes using the EJB compiler. The EJB compiler generated the stub and skeleton code for our interfaces. The resulting architecture is shown in Figure 5.2.

FIGURE 5.2

In addition to stubs and skeletons, EJB calls are intercepted by the container.

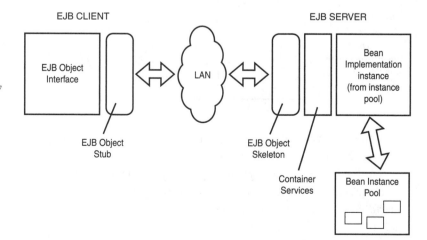

As you can see in the diagram, the client calls the remote interface without knowing the call is transmitted over the network. The interface is implemented by the stub code that sends the call to the EJB container. The EJB container locates the skeleton of the EJB interface that can handle all the communication with the client. This hides the network details from the bean developer.

The architecture of the home interface is similar to the EJB object. Unlike the EJB object, however, the home interface does not need any implementation class. All the implementation is done by the EJB compiler. The EJB compiler knows what EJB must be created by the return type of the `create` method.

Instance Pooling

Instance pooling is a concept that was not used in Java RMI, even though it is not new to distributed systems. Once the client's request reaches the EJB skeleton, the container can decide whether to create a new EJB instance or reuse an instance already in memory. The decision depends on the type of the EJB and the algorithm that the container employs. All the available EJBs are cached in the container in a so-called instance pool. An *instance pool* is really an array of already instantiated EJBs. Typically, the container finds an EJB in the pool and assigns it to handle the client. When the EJB is finished with a client, it is returned back to the pool. Thus, the container keeps reusing EJBs without instantiating new instances. Of course, if the pool is too small, and new requests keep coming in, the container will create more bean instances to increase the pool.

Instance pooling provides a powerful optimization for a distributed system. Typically, a user spends most of her time on the presentation and only a very short time actually calling the middle tier. As a result, a reasonably few middle-tier beans can service a large number of users.

> **Note**
>
> Instance pooling is conceptually very similar to connection pooling with JDBC. One of the most costly operations in Java is the instantiation and destruction of objects. With instance pooling, the EJB container does not have to create new beans for every request; it can just reuse the existing ones.

Typically, an EJB container creates a number of bean instances for the pool at startup, so they are ready to service the requests. You should be able to specify how many beans to have in the pool at startup. Also, when the container adds more instances to the pool, it can do it by creating a few every time. For example, you might set up the container to create 10 bean instances at startup and add another 10 instances whenever it runs out of available beans in the pool. This way, the container is ready for bursts of activity when the number of requests quickly increases. For example, your servers at work experience a sudden load increase when everybody decides to show up for work in the morning.

Deployment Descriptor Overview

In the section "Writing a Simple EJB," we created a simple deployment descriptor for our `'Hello World'` EJB. The deployment descriptors describe a bean's behavior in a runtime environment. The idea is that once the EJB is coded, certain aspects can be changed through the deployment descriptor to easily adapt the bean to a changing production environment.

The deployment descriptors include one or more XML files. The EJB specification mandates one deployment descriptor that is called `ejb-jar.xml`. However, EJB containers can have additional XML files to further customize the bean behavior.

The standard descriptor `ejb-jar.xml` has these elements:

- `<description>` (optional)—Description of the bean.
- `<display-name>` (optional)—Name used to identify the bean in container admin tools.
- `<small-icon>` (optional)—Small icon used to identify the bean in container admin tools.
- `<large-icon>` (optional)—Large icon used to identify the bean in container admin tools.
- `<enterprise-beans>` (required)—Contains the names of the interfaces and classes of the bean. It might also have persistent fields, schema, and other persistent information.
- `<relationships>` (optional)—Describes relationships between persistent bean if container-managed persistence is used.
- `<assembly-descriptor>` (optional)—Describes security roles, method permissions, and transaction demarcations for bean methods.
- `<ejb-client-jar>` (optional)—States the name of the client JAR file for this EJB JAR file.

As you can see, the `ejb-jar.xml` file contains a lot of information about EJB. Some of the important things seem to be missing though. The file does not declare a JNDI name for the bean, nor does it have actual mappings of the bean fields to the data storage. So it is necessary for an EJB container to have additional descriptor files to finish the work.

These additional descriptor files are container specific, so it will take time to change them if you decide to port an EJB from one container to another.

Types of EJBs

Enterprise JavaBeans are not born equal. They are meant to serve different purposes and, therefore, differ in certain aspects. You can distinguish them by the following features:

- Implemented interface
- Synchronous versus asynchronous
- Preserved state
- Remote versus local

EJB Types by Interfaces

Often, the beans are referred to by the interfaces that they implement. Most of the time, the implemented interface defines the bean's behavior. There are three types:

- Session beans—All session beans must implement the `javax.ejb.SessionBean` interface.
- Entity beans—Data persistent beans must implement `javax.ejb.EntityBean`.
- Message-driven beans—The beans that process messages from Message Queues must implement `javax.ejb.MessageDrivenBean`.

Figure 5.3 shows the base bean interfaces.

FIGURE 5.3
EJB Interfaces extend the `javax.ejb.EnterpriseBean` *interface.*

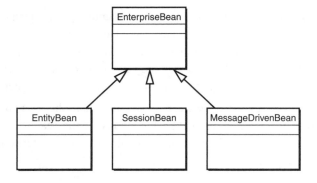

Synchronous Versus Asynchronous EJBs

EJBs can be called synchronously or asynchronously. Session beans and entity beans can only be called synchronously. This means that a client must wait for the EJB method to return. Essentially, your program will stop execution and wait for the EJB to do its processing. Only when the EJB is finished can your client continue.

On the contrary, with an asynchronous call, the client does not have to wait for the EJB method to return. The client can just drop a message to the server and continue its execution immediately. When the client makes an asynchronous call, it can usually pick up the result of the call later, for example, as a status in a database. The EJB specification added asynchronous EJBs in version 2.0. They are called message-driven beans. Message-driven beans can only be called asynchronously. Message-driven beans do not have a home interface and cannot be called directly. They are attached to a Message Queue and are called by a container when there is a message to process.

Preserving State in EJBs

We have three options to preserve an object state in an EJB:

- Stateless beans—A *stateless bean* is a session bean that cannot preserve a state from one method call to another. Each request that arrives at the container can potentially be sent to an arbitrary bean object from the instance pool. After the bean object services the request, it is returned back to the instance pool. The EJB container can use any algorithm to find the next available bean in the pool. In other words, there is no guarantee that the bean object will be called by the same client consecutively.

  Moreover, when the container sends a request to a stateless bean, it does not set any fields to their initial values. It is the bean developer's responsibility to reinitialize any instance variables.

- Stateful beans—A *stateful bean* is a session bean that can keep state between requests from the client. The container guarantees that the same bean object is called in this case. The client can also store a handle to a stateful bean. The handle can be serialized and used later to call the same bean object. However, a stateful bean cannot survive a container restart, so it is a true session object.

- Persistent beans—An *entity bean* can persist its state to the permanent data storage. The EJB specification provides callback methods for the bean to be notified when it is time to save its state. We will talk more about EJB persistence in the later sections of the chapter.

> **Note**
>
> There is nothing to stop you from acquiring a database connection in a stateless bean to save its state, but, generally, this is not what this type of bean is used for.

Remote EJBs Versus Local EJBs

In the first versions of the EJB specification, all EJBs were remote objects. This, of course, had an adverse effect on the performance of the systems. That's why version 2.0 of the specification introduced the notion of local EJB. A local EJB is a bean that exists in the same JVM as the client, and, therefore, does not require stubs and skeletons. The local EJB does not have to marshal any parameters or make any copies of the parameters. All the parameters in the call are passed by reference. The implementation of a local EJB is different from a remote EJB in the following:

- The local EJB interface must extend a `javax.ejb.LocalEJBObject` instead of `javax.ejb.EJBObject`.

- The home interface extends `javax.ejb.EJBLocalHome` instead of `javax.ejb.EJBHome`.

- The local EJB should not declare `java.rmi.RemoteException` in their remote methods.

- All arguments in local EJBs are passed by reference, which means that changing an argument can affect the caller of the bean.

- Deployment descriptors for local EJBs, although very similar, have slightly different element names. The new element names for local EJBs are specified in the DTD at `http://java.sun.com/dtd/ejb-jar_2_0.dtd`.

Developing the Cruise Booking Application with EJB

In the rest of this chapter, we will build a more involved application than the `'Hello World'` example. We will develop a program that allows you to buy cruise tickets. The Cruise Booking Application will have beans to make a booking and pay for the ticket.

As you might see in other chapters of the book, the ticketing application is a common example application that we use to compare different technologies. You can see the description of it in Chapter 1, "Programming Interconnected Computers."

We will build a ticketing application in this chapter using EJBs. The nature of the application will stay the same, although we will change some features in order to better demonstrate different aspects of EJBs.

Figure 5.4 depicts the object model that we will use for our ticketing example in EJB.

Figure 5.4 shows these objects:

- Presentation client—These are JSPs and servlets that present data to the user and collect input to send to the back-end EJBs.

- `TicketingAgent` EJB—This sends the available tickets to the presentation client. It also books a ticket for a customer.

- `PaymentAgent` EJB—This processes payment for the ticket.

- `Booking` EJB—This is an object that represents a booking. A booking is created and saved to a database when a use decides to buy a ticket. The `Booking` EJB will help us in our discussion of EJB persistence later in the chapter.

The sequence diagram in Figure 5.5 shows the messages that the components send to each other.

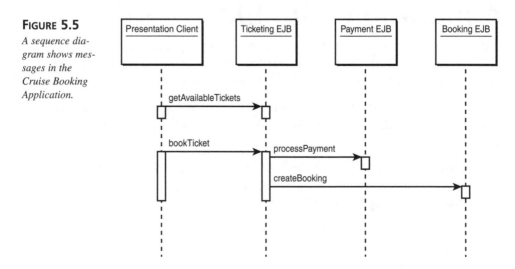

Developing Stateless Session Beans

Stateless session beans service a single request from different clients. They are typically kept in an instance pool and picked by the container to service only one request. A stateless session bean is not attached to the same client and cannot reliably keep the values of its instance variables. This means that after the bean is finished with a request, it is returned back to the instance pool by the EJB container.

Instance Pooling with Stateless Session Beans

The EJB container can keep a pool of bean instances. On each request, the container picks a bean from the pool and calls a business method. Appropriate callback methods are called when the instance is picked from the pool to service a request.

After the method returns, the bean instance is returned to the pool. The instance in the pool can be removed and destroyed at the discretion of the container.

Stateless Session Bean State Diagram

The EJB container calls methods in the bean's implementation class that are called *callback* methods. These methods are called at specific times during the life of the bean. As the bean transitions from one state to another, various methods are called. The states define the life cycle of the bean. Let's see when the callback methods are called by the container. This will help us understand how the bean instance is managed.

The stateless bean has a simple state diagram. It is shown in Figure 5.6. The bean instance can only exist in one state—when it is waiting to service a client's request.

FIGURE 5.6

A stateless session bean can exist in these states.

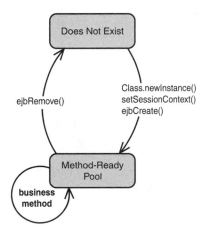

Callback Methods in Stateless Beans

The stateless session beans must implement the `javax.ejb.SessionBean` interface. The interface declares methods that the bean must implement. The methods are as follows:

- `ejbActivate` is never called in a stateless bean.
- `ejbPassivate` is never called in a stateless bean.
- `setSessionContext` is the first method called by the container after the instance is created. The instance variables should be initialized here.
- `ejbRemove` is called just before the instance is removed from the instance pool for garbage collection.

Writing a Stateless EJB for the Cruise Booking Application

In our Cruise Booking Application, we have a stateless session bean that shows available tickets and books a ticket. This is a `TicketingAgent` EJB. Showing what tickets are available for sale does not require remembering a state with a customer. Therefore, the `TicketingAgent` EJB can be stateless. Similarly, booking a ticket is a one method operation in the Cruise Booking Application. So, the bean does have to keep a conversational state with a client. To develop the `TicketingAgent` bean we have to create a remote interface as shown in Listing 5.6.

LISTING 5.6   `TicketingAgent` Remote Interface

```
package unleashed.ch5.cruise;

import java.rmi.RemoteException;
import javax.ejb.EJBObject;

/**
 * Ticketing Agent Remote Interface.
 */
public interface TicketingAgent extends EJBObject
{
    /**
     * Gets available tickets.
     */
    public Ticket[] getAvailableTickets() throws RemoteException;

    /**
     * Books a ticket.
     */
    public void bookTicket(String cruiseName)
```

LISTING 5.6 continued

```
    throws RemoteException, BookingFailedException;
}
```

The TicketingAgent remote interface can get available cruise tickets and book a ticket for a customer. Both methods must declare a RemoteException in their throw clauses because the EJB is deployed as a remote object using Java RMI. Every remote object in Java RMI must declare a RemoteException in all its public methods.

The TicketingAgent EJB also needs a home interface that a client can call to create a new bean. In reality, the EJB container might find an existing EJB instance in the instance pool instead of creating it. However, the client does not see that because the home interface hides the creation from it.

Listing 5.7 shows the home interface for the TicketingAgent EJB.

LISTING 5.7 TicketingAgent Home Interface

```
package unleashed.ch5.cruise;

import java.rmi.RemoteException;
import javax.ejb.CreateException;
import javax.ejb.EJBHome;

/**
 * Ticketing Agent Home interface.
 */
public interface TicketingAgentHome extends EJBHome
{
    public TicketingAgent create()
    throws CreateException, RemoteException;
}
```

Let's implement the TicketingAgent EJB. In addition to the callback methods, the EJB implements the business methods that we declared on the remote interface. Listing 5.8 shows the TicketingAgent implementation.

LISTING 5.8 TicketingAgent Bean Implementation

```
package unleashed.ch5.cruise;

import javax.ejb.*;
import javax.naming.*;
import java.util.*;
import javax.rmi.*;
```

LISTING 5.8 continued

```java
/**
 * Ticketing Agent Bean Implementation.
 */
public class TicketingAgentBean implements SessionBean
{

  //callback method must be implemented
  public void ejbActivate() {}
  public void ejbRemove() {}
  public void ejbPassivate() {}

  public void setSessionContext(SessionContext ctx)
  {

      //retrieve environment entry ApplicationName
      try
      {
          //get environment initial context
          InitialContext env = new InitialContext();
          String appName = (String)env.lookup("ApplicationName");
          System.out.println("Application Name entry is: " + appName);


      }catch(Exception e)
      {
          System.out.println(e.getMessage());
          e.printStackTrace();
      }
  }

  public void ejbCreate () throws CreateException {}


  /**
   * Gets all available tickets
   */
  public Ticket[] getAvailableTickets()
  {
      Ticket[] tickets = new Ticket[3];
      Ticket ticket = new Ticket("Aruba", "Sunny Cruise",
      5, "New York");

      Ticket ticket1 = new Ticket("Alaska", "Chilly Cruise",
      5, "San Francisco");

      Ticket ticket2 = new Ticket("Spain", "", 8, "New York");

      tickets[0] = ticket;
      tickets[1] = ticket1;
```

LISTING 5.8   continued

```
        tickets[2] = ticket2;
        return tickets;
    }

    /**
     * Books a ticket
     */
    public void bookTicket(String cruiseName)
    throws BookingFailedException
    {
        //Book the tickets
        try
        {
            //get JNDI initial context
            Properties h = new Properties();
            h.put(Context.INITIAL_CONTEXT_FACTORY,
                "weblogic.jndi.WLInitialContextFactory");
            String url = "t3://localhost:7001";
            h.put(Context.PROVIDER_URL, url);
            InitialContext itc = new InitialContext(h);

            //get booking home
        Object obj = (BookingHome) itc.lookup("Booking");
            BookingHome bHome = (BookingHome)
➥ PortableRemoteObject.narrow(obj, BookingHome.class);

            bHome.create(cruiseName);
        }catch(Exception e)
        {
            System.err.println("Exception creating a Booking Bean: "
              + e.getMessage());
            e.printStackTrace();
            throw new BookingFailedException(e.getMessage());
        }
    }
}
```

The getAvailableTickets method returns three available tickets to the client. The
bookTicket method takes the name of a cruise as an argument and creates a Booking
EJB. The Booking EJB will be explained later, but for now, think of it as another EJB
that stores and retrieves data from a database for us. The method looks up the Booking
EJB home interface using JNDI. After getting the home interface, the method calls the
create method on the home interface. The Booking EJB is saved in the database at the
time of creation. The bookTicket method throws a BookingFailedException if any of
the operation fails. For example, if the Booking EJB home interface is not found,
BookingFailedException will be thrown.

All the Cruise Booking Application EJBs must be declared in the `ejb-jar.xml` deployment descriptor. This deployment descriptor states the beans' interfaces and implementation classes. It also contains other information that the container uses to provide various services during the bean's life cycle. We will talk more about various portions later in this chapter. Let's look at the portion of the descriptor that deals with the `TicketingAgent` EJB. The descriptor is shown in Listing 5.9, and the portion in bold pertains to the `TicketingAgent` EJB.

LISTING 5.9   TicketingAgent Bean Deployment Descriptor

```
<?xml version="1.0"?>

<!DOCTYPE ejb-jar PUBLIC
'-//Sun Microsystems, Inc.//DTD Enterprise JavaBeans 2.0//EN'
'http://java.sun.com/dtd/ejb-jar_2_0.dtd'>

<ejb-jar>
  <enterprise-beans>
    <session>
      <ejb-name>TicketingAgent</ejb-name>
      <home>unleashed.ch5.cruise.TicketingAgentHome</home>
      <remote>unleashed.ch5.cruise.TicketingAgent</remote>
      <ejb-class>unleashed.ch5.cruise.TicketingAgentBean</ejb-class>
      <session-type>Stateless</session-type>
      <transaction-type>Container</transaction-type>
     <env-entry>
         <env-entry-name>ApplicationName</env-entry-name>
        <env-entry-type>java.lang.String</env-entry-type>
       <env-entry-value>Cruise Booking Application</env-entry-value>
     </env-entry>
     </session>

<session>
      <ejb-name>PaymentAgent</ejb-name>
      <home>unleashed.ch5.cruise.PaymentAgentHome</home>
      <remote>unleashed.ch5.cruise.PaymentAgent</remote>
      <ejb-class>unleashed.ch5.cruise.PaymentAgentBean</ejb-class>
      <session-type>Stateless</session-type>
      <transaction-type>Container</transaction-type>
     </session>

<entity>
      <ejb-name>Booking</ejb-name>
      <home>unleashed.ch5.cruise.BookingHome</home>
      <remote>unleashed.ch5.cruise.Booking</remote>
      <ejb-class>unleashed.ch5.cruise.BookingBean</ejb-class>
      <persistence-type>Container</persistence-type>
      <prim-key-class>java.lang.Integer</prim-key-class>
```

LISTING 5.9   continued

```
      <reentrant>False</reentrant>
      <cmp-version>2.x</cmp-version>
      <abstract-schema-name>BookingBean</abstract-schema-name>
    <cmp-field>
       <field-name>bookingID</field-name>
    </cmp-field>
    <cmp-field>
       <field-name>cruiseName</field-name>
    </cmp-field>
    <primkey-field>bookingID</primkey-field>
    <query>
       <query-method>
         <method-name>findAllBookings</method-name>
         <method-params>
         </method-params>
       </query-method>
       <ejb-ql>
         <![CDATA[SELECT OBJECT(b) FROM BookingBean as b]]>
       </ejb-ql>
    </query>
 </entity>
 </enterprise-beans>
<assembly-descriptor>

   <container-transaction>
     <method>
       <ejb-name>PaymentAgent</ejb-name>
   <method-name>*</method-name>
     </method>
     <trans-attribute>Required</trans-attribute>
   </container-transaction>


 </assembly-descriptor>
</ejb-jar>
```

In addition to the `ejb-jar.xml` file, we need to provide a WebLogic-specific deployment descriptor file. This file is called `weblogic-ejb-jar.xml`. It has the declarations required by the WebLogic Server to deploy a stateless session bean. Listing 5.10 shows a `TicketingAgent` WebLogic deployment descriptor. The portion of the listing in bold deals with the `TicketingAgent` EJB.

LISTING 5.10   `TicketingAgent` Bean WebLogic Deployment Descriptor

```
<?xml version="1.0"?>
<!DOCTYPE weblogic-ejb-jar PUBLIC
```

LISTING 5.10   continued

```
'-//BEA Systems, Inc.//DTD WebLogic 6.0.0 EJB//EN'
'http://www.bea.com/servers/wls600/dtd/weblogic-ejb-jar.dtd'>

<weblogic-ejb-jar>
    <weblogic-enterprise-bean>
        <ejb-name>PaymentAgent</ejb-name>
        <jndi-name>PaymentAgent</jndi-name>
    </weblogic-enterprise-bean>

<weblogic-enterprise-bean>
        <ejb-name>TicketingAgent</ejb-name>
        <jndi-name>TicketingAgent</jndi-name>
</weblogic-enterprise-bean>

 <weblogic-enterprise-bean>
    <ejb-name>Booking</ejb-name>
    <entity-descriptor>
      <persistence>
        <persistence-type>
        <type-identifier>WebLogic_CMP_RDBMS</type-identifier>
        <type-version>6.0</type-version>
        <type-storage>META-INF/weblogic-cmp-rdbms-jar.xml</type-storage>
      </persistence-type>
      <persistence-use>
        <type-identifier>WebLogic_CMP_RDBMS</type-identifier>
        <type-version>6.0</type-version>
      </persistence-use>
        </persistence>
    </entity-descriptor>
    <jndi-name>Booking</jndi-name>
  </weblogic-enterprise-bean>

</weblogic-ejb-jar>
```

The WebLogic deployment descriptor maps the `TicketingAgent` EJB name to a JNDI name. A client uses this JNDI name to find the beans home interface. After the client obtains a handle to the home interface, it can get an instance of the bean.

create<METHOD> Methods in Stateless Session Beans

For each `create<METHOD>` method on the home interface, there must be an `ejbCreate<METHOD>` method with the same parameters on the bean implementation class, where `<METHOD>` denotes a common suffix. A common suffix can be any name allowed in Java. For example, your home interface can have a method `createMyBean`. Then your bean implementation must have an `ejbCreateMyBean` method. `MyBean`, in this case, is a common suffix. The `ejbCreate<METHOD>` methods play the role of constructors for EJBs because EJBs do not have any Java constructors other than the no-argument constructor provided by the compiler. As a matter of fact, the bean implementation must not have any constructors. The reason for this is that the container uses only the default no-arguments constructor at runtime to instantiate the object.

Developing Stateful Session Beans

Stateful session beans are capable of keeping the state from one request to another. The EJB specification calls it *conversational state* and defines it as the values of all the instance's fields plus the trees of objects that can be reached from the instance's fields.

A stateful session bean is created by a client, and the client can obtain a handle to the bean using the `getHandle` method on `javax.ejb.EJBObject`. When the client needs the bean again, it can obtain the bean from the handle by calling its `getEJBObject` method. The container guarantees to retrieve the same bean instance. The handle can even be serialized and passed around to other objects.

Because stateful session beans preserve the conversational state, their methods can be called in a specific order—for example, if the application needs to gather information from a user about her preferences for a cruise, the client can call the stateful bean's multiple methods to set the meal preference, the room preference, and the payment choice. When the user is ready to book the ticket, the client can call the stateful bean again to submit all the user's preferences to the ticketing agent. In other words, the stateful bean can store the information on the server on behalf of the client.

The stateful session beans are not pooled. Moreover, if every client has a stateful bean associated with it, it might lead to many beans existing on the server. The server then must be able to swap the beans in and out of the process memory. The EJB specification calls this process `Passivation` and `Activation`. The bean is *passivated* when it is written to the disk. This happens when the server decides that it is running out of memory. If the client calls the bean, the container needs to bring back in to memory the bean that is being activated. The container can use any method to save the bean's conversational state. However, some resources—such as database connections, and so on—cannot be saved, so the container calls the `ejbPassivate` method for the developer to release these resources. When the bean is activated, its `ejbActivate` method is called so that the resources can be acquired again.

5

ENTERPRISE
JAVABEANS (EJB)

Stateful Session Bean State Diagram

The stateful session bean life cycle is slightly different from that of the stateless bean. In addition to the does-not-exist and method-ready states, the stateful session bean can exist in a passive state. The `ejbPassivate` method is called on the bean before it gets to this state. The bean is in the passive state when it is taken out of server memory and stored on disk. Typically, the container decides to passivate a stateful bean that is not being currently used when it needs additional memory for the active beans. However, the algorithm that decides when to passivate the bean is container specific. The stateful session bean state diagram is shown in Figure 5.7.

FIGURE 5.7

The life cycle defines states and callback methods for a stateful session bean.

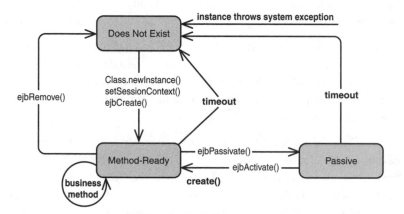

SessionSynchronization Interface

Stateful session beans are capable of caching the updates and writing them to the database only if the transaction is complete. To be notified by the container at various stages of the transaction, the bean has to implement the `javax.ejb.SessionSynchronization` interface. The interface adds more callback methods and changes the state diagram of the bean. Figure 5.8 shows how the new state diagram looks.

Callback Methods in Stateful Beans

Stateful session beans implement the same interface as stateless session beans—
`javax.ejb.SessionBean`:

- `ejbActivate` is called when the bean is activated.
- `ejbPassivate` is called just before the bean is passivated to disk.
- `setSessionContext` is called after the bean instance is created.
- `ejbRemove` is called just before the bean is destroyed.

FIGURE 5.8

The life cycle of a stateful session bean with the `javax.ejb.Session-Synchronization` *interface.*

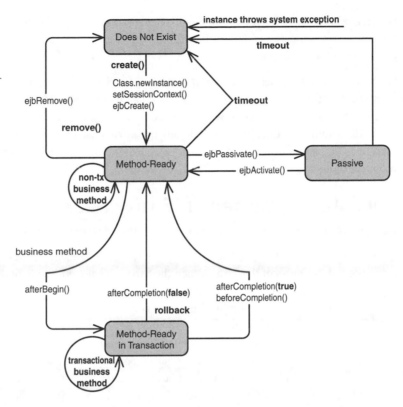

Note

Both stateless and stateful session beans implement the same interface `javax.ejb.SessionBean` and, therefore, have the same callback methods. Also, the `ejbCreate<METHOD>` methods work the same for stateful and stateless beans.

Developing Entity Beans

Entity beans are the beans that generally represent the data of the system. They abstract the model and help developers think of data in an object-oriented fashion. Before entity beans, the developers had to worry about how the data was actually stored and often wrote the database specific code inside the objects. This is no longer the case. The software architects can design a system in terms of objects. Then the developers can implement the objects and the business logic of the system. And only later, the objects have to be mapped to a specific production data storage system through the deployment descriptors. What is even better is that porting the system to a different database is only a matter of changing the deployment descriptors.

Of course, the system designers can still choose to write database code if required. The entity beans provide the callback methods that can be implemented to control the bean persistence. However, this code will not be portable from one database to another. Also, the EJB container will not be able to do any optimizations. Basically, the EJB specification gives you a choice to use the container's capability to generate the code for you or write the code yourself.

Persistence Models in Entity Beans

Entity beans can be persisted using either of the two persistence models:

- Container-managed persistence (CMP)—The persistence is declared in the deployment descriptors of the bean. When the bean is deployed, the container studies the deployment descriptors and generates the actual SQL code for the specific database. The code can be optimized by the container for that particular database. The bean developer cannot intervene or change this code. CMP entity beans are much easier to build and deploy because the EJB container generates all the database queries. This can save a lot of time during development, and gives the developer a chance to spend more time writing business logic code. Also, CMP code is portable across multiple databases. Every time the bean is deployed on a different database, the container will generate all the database queries for that database.

- Bean-managed persistence (BMP)—The bean developer writes all persistence code herself. The container does not generate or optimize any code; it just calls the bean callback methods when it is time to load or save the data. BMP is used when the developer wants to handle all the database code. This might be the case if the application needs optimized queries for better performance. The database code written for BMP entity beans only works with that database, so you have to change it every time you decide to change a database in your application.

Tip

Although some developers are skeptical about CMP because of possible performance issues, it can be very beneficial for the design of a complex system. Try designing the system with CMP in mind, and then see if your requirements make it necessary for you to use BMP.

Entity Bean State Diagram

The entity bean state diagram has similar states to those of the stateless session bean diagram. Entity beans also have a Pooled state when an instance of the bean exists but is not assigned to any clients. When a client calls a `create` method on the home interface, the instance is called an `ejbCreate` method and transitioned to the Method-Ready state. At this time, the bean's fields are assigned values that have to be persisted, so the `ejbLoad` and `ejbStore` methods are called to load and save these values.

The diagram also shows that a bean can execute an `ejbHome` method without getting to the Method-Ready state. In this case, the entity beans behave similarly to the stateless session beans because they do not get any permanent data associated with them. The diagram is shown in Figure 5.9.

FIGURE 5.9

An entity bean is called by the container each time the bean needs to be synchronized with a database.

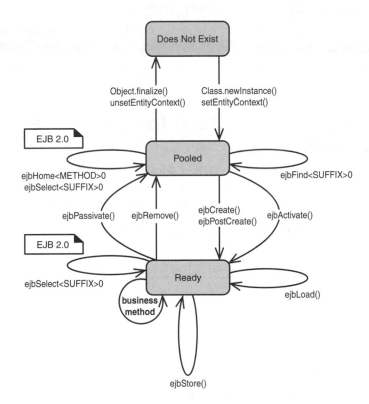

Callback Methods in Entity Beans

An entity bean implements the `javax.ejb.EntityBean` interface, which has the following methods:

- `ejbActivate` is called just before the `ejbLoad` method.
- `ejbPassivate` is called just after the `ejbStore` method.
- `ejbRemove` is called just before the instance is destroyed.
- `ejbStore` is called when the instance has to save itself to the database. This method is relevant to BMP beans. CMP beans do not have to do anything in it as the container does everything for them.
- `ejbLoad` is called when the bean needs to retrieve its data from the database. Again, this method is only useful to BMP beans.
- `setEntityContext` is the first method called by the container after the instance is created.
- `unsetEntityContext` is called by the container just before the instance is destroyed.

Writing an Entity Bean for the Cruise Booking Application

The Cruise Booking Application creates a `Booking` object when the customer buys a ticket. The booking must be saved to a database for later use. This is a good candidate for an entity bean. We will use CMP to store the booking in a database.

Listing 5.11 shows the `Booking` object remote interface.

LISTING 5.11   Booking Entity Bean Remote Interface

```
package unleashed.ch5.cruise;

import javax.ejb.*;
import java.rmi.RemoteException;

/**
* Remote interface for Booking EJB
*/
public interface Booking extends EJBObject
{
    public String getCruiseName()throws RemoteException;
}
```

The only public method is `getCruiseName`. The remote interface of an entity bean also extends `javax.ejb.EJBObject`.

The home interface is shown in Listing 5.12.

LISTING 5.12   Booking Entity Bean Home Interface

```
package unleashed.ch5.cruise;

import javax.ejb.CreateException;
import javax.ejb.EJBHome;
import javax.ejb.FinderException;
import java.rmi.RemoteException;
import java.util.*;

/**
 * Booking Home interface.
 *
 * @author Alex Pestrikov
 */
public interface BookingHome extends EJBHome
{

    public Booking create(String name)
    throws CreateException, RemoteException;

    public Booking findByPrimaryKey(Integer id)
    throws FinderException, RemoteException;


    public Collection findAllBookings()
    throws FinderException, RemoteException;
}
```

In addition to the familiar `create` method, the entity bean home interface can also contain a `findByPrimaryKey` method. `findByPrimaryKey` is a required method for entity beans and is implemented by the container.

Listing 5.13 shows the bean implementation class.

LISTING 5.13   Booking Entity Bean Implementation

```
package unleashed.ch5.cruise;

import javax.ejb.*;

/**
 * Booking Entity Bean.
```

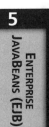

LISTING 5.13   continued

```
*
* @author Alex Pestrikov
*/
public abstract class BookingBean
implements javax.ejb.EntityBean
{
    /**
    * Entity context
    */
    private EntityContext ctx;

    /**
    * Business methods
    */
    public abstract Integer getBookingID();
    public abstract void setBookingID(Integer id);
    public abstract String getCruiseName();
    public abstract void setCruiseName(String name);

    /**
    * This method is required by the EJB Specification,
    * but is not used by this example.
    *
    */
    public void ejbActivate(){}

    /**
    * This method is required by the EJB Specification,
    * but is not used by this example.
    *
    */
    public void ejbPassivate(){}

    /**
    * This method is required by the EJB Specification,
    * but is not used by this example.
    *
    */
    public void ejbLoad(){}

    /**
    *
    */
    public void ejbStore(){}

    /**
    * This method is required by the EJB Specification,
    * but is not used by this example.
    *
```

LISTING 5.13   continued

```java
 * @exception              javax.ejb.RemoveException
 *                         if the EJBean does not allow removing the EJBean
 */
public void ejbRemove()throws RemoveException{}

/**
 *
 * @param id       String Booking id
 * @param name      String cruise name
 * @exception              javax.ejb.CreateException
 *                         if there is a problem creating the bean
 */
public Integer ejbCreate(String name)
throws CreateException
{
    setCruiseName(name);
    return null;
}

/**
 * This method is required by the EJB Specification,
 * but is not used by this example.
 *
 * @param id       String Booking id
 * @param name       String cruise name
 */
public void ejbPostCreate(String name){}

/**
 * Sets the EntityContext for the EJBean.
 *
 * @param ctx   EntityContext
 */

public void setEntityContext(EntityContext ctx)
{
   this.ctx = ctx;
}

/**
 * Unsets the EntityContext for the EJBean.
 *
 */
public void unsetEntityContext()
{
    this.ctx = null;
}
}
```

Even though I called this class an implementation class, it is implemented only partially. The get and set methods for the persistent fields are actually abstract. The implementation for these fields will be provided by the container later. Therefore, we cannot declare instance variables to keep the value. All access to the persistent fields are accomplished though the get and set methods.

Deployment descriptors for the CMP entity bean carry all the information necessary to map the persistent fields to the database tables. Listing 5.14 shows how our `ejb-jar.xml` file looks after adding the `Booking` EJB.

LISTING 5.14   Booking Entity Bean `ejb-jar.xml` File

```xml
<?xml version="1.0"?>

<!DOCTYPE ejb-jar PUBLIC
'-//Sun Microsystems, Inc.//DTD Enterprise JavaBeans 2.0//EN'
'http://java.sun.com/dtd/ejb-jar_2_0.dtd'>

<ejb-jar>
  <enterprise-beans>
    <session>
      <ejb-name>TicketingAgent</ejb-name>
      <home>unleashed.ch5.cruise.TicketingAgentHome</home>
      <remote>unleashed.ch5.cruise.TicketingAgent</remote>
      <ejb-class>unleashed.ch5.cruise.TicketingAgentBean</ejb-class>
      <session-type>Stateless</session-type>
      <transaction-type>Container</transaction-type>
    <env-entry>
        <env-entry-name>ApplicationName</env-entry-name>
       <env-entry-type>java.lang.String</env-entry-type>
      <env-entry-value>Cruise Booking Application</env-entry-value>
    </env-entry>
     </session>

<session>
     <ejb-name>PaymentAgent</ejb-name>
     <home>unleashed.ch5.cruise.PaymentAgentHome</home>
     <remote>unleashed.ch5.cruise.PaymentAgent</remote>
     <ejb-class>unleashed.ch5.cruise.PaymentAgentBean</ejb-class>
     <session-type>Stateless</session-type>
     <transaction-type>Container</transaction-type>
     </session>

<entity>
     <ejb-name>Booking</ejb-name>
     <home>unleashed.ch5.cruise.BookingHome</home>
     <remote>unleashed.ch5.cruise.Booking</remote>
     <ejb-class>unleashed.ch5.cruise.BookingBean</ejb-class>
```

LISTING 5.14 continued

```
        <persistence-type>Container</persistence-type>
        <prim-key-class>java.lang.Integer</prim-key-class>
        <reentrant>False</reentrant>
        <cmp-version>2.x</cmp-version>
        <abstract-schema-name>BookingBean</abstract-schema-name>
        <cmp-field>
            <field-name>bookingID</field-name>
        </cmp-field>
        <cmp-field>
            <field-name>cruiseName</field-name>
        </cmp-field>
        <primkey-field>bookingID</primkey-field>
        <query>
            <query-method>
              <method-name>findAllBookings</method-name>
              <method-params>
              </method-params>
            </query-method>
            <ejb-ql>
            <![CDATA[SELECT OBJECT(b) FROM BookingBean as b]]>
            </ejb-ql>
        </query>
  </entity>
 </enterprise-beans>
<assembly-descriptor>

    <container-transaction>
      <method>
        <ejb-name>PaymentAgent</ejb-name>
    <method-name>*</method-name>
      </method>
      <trans-attribute>Required</trans-attribute>
    </container-transaction>


   </assembly-descriptor>
</ejb-jar>
```

You can see the entity bean declaration in bold. The XML element <entity> specifies the bean interfaces and the implementation class. The <persistence-type> element states that the persistence type is CMP. The element <prim-key-class> states the data type of the primary key. Multiple <cmp-field> elements declare what fields we want the container to save. Finally, the <primkey-field> element allows us to specify what persistent field should be the primary key.

WebLogic Server 6.1 deployment descriptors define additional information for CMP entity beans. Listing 5.15 shows how weblogic-ejb-jar.xml looks after we add the Booking entity bean elements.

LISTING 5.15   Booking Entity Bean `weblogic-ejb-jar.xml` File

```xml
<?xml version="1.0"?>
<!DOCTYPE weblogic-ejb-jar PUBLIC
'-//BEA Systems, Inc.//DTD WebLogic 6.0.0 EJB//EN'
'http://www.bea.com/servers/wls600/dtd/weblogic-ejb-jar.dtd'>

<weblogic-ejb-jar>
    <weblogic-enterprise-bean>
        <ejb-name>PaymentAgent</ejb-name>
        <jndi-name>PaymentAgent</jndi-name>
    </weblogic-enterprise-bean>

<weblogic-enterprise-bean>
        <ejb-name>TicketingAgent</ejb-name>
        <jndi-name>TicketingAgent</jndi-name>
    </weblogic-enterprise-bean>

 <weblogic-enterprise-bean>
    <ejb-name>Booking</ejb-name>
    <entity-descriptor>
      <persistence>
        <persistence-type>
        <type-identifier>WebLogic_CMP_RDBMS</type-identifier>
        <type-version>6.0</type-version>
        <type-storage>META-INF/weblogic-cmp-rdbms-jar.xml</type-storage>
      </persistence-type>
      <persistence-use>
        <type-identifier>WebLogic_CMP_RDBMS</type-identifier>
        <type-version>6.0</type-version>
      </persistence-use>
        </persistence>
      </entity-descriptor>
      <jndi-name>Booking</jndi-name>
  </weblogic-enterprise-bean>

</weblogic-ejb-jar>
```

The portion in bold shows how an entity bean is declared in a WebLogic specific descriptor. In addition to the EJB name, <persistence> element specifies the type of persistence and a mapping file.

The database mapping is specified in yet another Weblogic specific file—weblogic-cmp-rdbms-jar.xml. Listing 5.16 shows the weblogic-cmp-rdbms-jar file for the Cruise Booking Application. This file declares CMP mappings for the Booking entity bean.

LISTING 5.16 Booking Entity Bean `weblogic-cmp-rdbms-jar` File

```
<!DOCTYPE weblogic-rdbms-jar PUBLIC
 '-//BEA Systems, Inc.//DTD WebLogic 6.0.0 EJB RDBMS Persistence//EN'
 'http://www.bea.com/servers/wls600/dtd/weblogic-rdbms20-persistence-600.dtd'>

<weblogic-rdbms-jar>

  <weblogic-rdbms-bean>
    <ejb-name>Booking</ejb-name>
    <data-source-name>examples-dataSource-demoPool</data-source-name>
    <table-name>Booking</table-name>
    <field-map>
      <cmp-field>bookingID</cmp-field>
      <dbms-column>id</dbms-column>
    </field-map>
    <field-map>
      <cmp-field>cruiseName</cmp-field>
      <dbms-column>CruiseName</dbms-column>
    </field-map>

  <automatic-key-generation>
      <generator-type>NAMED_SEQUENCE_TABLE</generator-type>
      <generator-name>NAMED_SEQUENCE_TABLE</generator-name>
      <key-cache-size>10</key-cache-size>
    </automatic-key-generation>

  </weblogic-rdbms-bean>
  <create-default-dbms-tables>True</create-default-dbms-tables>
</weblogic-rdbms-jar>
```

create<METHOD> Methods in Entity Beans

Like a session bean, an entity bean must provide an `ejbCreate<METHOD>` on a bean implementation class for each `create<METHOD>` method on the entity bean home interface. In addition to that, an entity bean must provide an `ejbPostCreate<METHOD>` on the bean implementation class for each `create<METHOD>` method on a home interface.

Listing 5.17 shows the `ejbCreate` method for the Booking EJB.

LISTING 5.17 Example `ejbCreate` and `ejbPostCreate` Methods

```
public Integer ejbCreate(String name)
throws CreateException
{
    setCruiseName(name);
    return null;
}
```

LISTING 5.17 continued

```
/**
 * This method is required by the EJB Specification,
 * but is not used by this example.
 *
 * @param id        String Booking id
 * @param name       String cruise name
 */
public void ejbPostCreate(String name){}
```

In the example `ejbCreate` method, we set the persistent fields using the set methods. The method returns the primary key of the bean. For CMP entity beans, the primary key is created by the container, so their `ejbCreate` methods must return null.

EJB Query Language

To define database queries in a database-neutral way, the specification had to come up with a EJB query language (EJB QL). EJB QL is used to express business queries in the deployment descriptors of the CMP entity beans. When the bean is deployed, its EJB QL statements are mapped to the native query language of the specific database—for a relational database, it is typically a version of SQL; for an object-oriented database, it can be a version of OOQL.

EJB QL is easy to figure out for anybody who has dealt with SQL because these two query languages are very similar.

find<METHOD> Methods

In the CMP entity beans for each `find<METHOD>` on a home interface, there must be an EJB QL query declared in the bean deployment descriptor. The EJB container generates a database query in the database native language at deployment time based on the declaration in the deployment descriptor. In the BMP entity beans for each `find<METHOD>`, the bean implementation class must have a `ejbFind<METHOD>` method with the same parameters and `throws` clause. The implementation method on a BMP bean has to contain database code to locate an instance or a collection of instances in the database.

The `findByPrimaryKey` method is an exception to this. The behavior of `findByPrimaryKey` is unambiguous and, therefore, the implementation is supplied by the container. Moreover, the bean developer cannot provide her own implementation to change the method's behavior.

ejbSelect<METHOD> Methods

The ejbSelect<METHOD> method is a recent addition to the specification. It complements find<METHOD> and is declared only on the bean implementation class. Thus, it is not visible to the bean clients, but used by the bean itself. The ejbSelect<METHOD> must have a query in the descriptor for a CMP bean or implemented by the developer for a BMP bean.

ejbHome<METHOD> Methods

The ejbHome<METHOD> method or a home method is declared on an entity bean home interface and implemented on the bean implementation class. ejbHome<METHOD> methods are created to implement business logic that might include multiple entity beans. Home methods are used to calculate totals, averages, and so on for entity beans instead of writing separate session beans. Home methods can use ejbSelect<METHOD> method internally to perform necessary database queries.

CMP Fields

CMP fields are entity bean fields that are mapped directly to a database tables. A CMP field is declared by an abstract get and set method on the bean implementation class. It is further specified in the deployment descriptors for the container to generate SQL code.

CMP fields can be types that the container can map directly to a database column type. These include Java primitive types, java.lang.String, java.util.Date, as well as the wrappers for the primitive types like java.lang.Short, and so on.

CMP fields are only relevant to the container-managed persistence model.

Let's see how a cruise name CMP field is defined on the Booking EJB. The bean implementation has abstract get and set methods:

```
public abstract String getCruiseName();
public abstract void setCruiseName(String name);
```

Both get and set methods are required to have a common portion—CruiseName for the container to be able to determine what CMP field these methods are for.

Listing 5.18 shows how a CMP field can be declared in the ejb-jar.xml file.

LISTING 5.18   A CMP Field in an ejb-jar.xml File

```
<entity>
     <ejb-name>Booking</ejb-name>
     <home>unleashed.ch5.cruise.BookingHome</home>
```

LISTING 5.18   continued

```
    <remote>unleashed.ch5.cruise.Booking</remote>
    <ejb-class>unleashed.ch5.cruise.BookingBean</ejb-class>
    <persistence-type>Container</persistence-type>
    <prim-key-class>java.lang.String</prim-key-class>
    <reentrant>False</reentrant>
    <cmp-version>2.x</cmp-version>
    <abstract-schema-name>BookingBean</abstract-schema-name>
  <cmp-field>
     <field-name>bookingID</field-name>
  </cmp-field>
  <cmp-field>
     <field-name>cruiseName</field-name>
  </cmp-field>
    <primkey-field>bookingID</primkey-field>
</entity>
```

The element `<cmp-field>` declares a CMP field as the common portion of the get and set methods—`CruiseName`—with the first letter in lowercase.

> **Note**
>
> The preceding rules for get and set methods are originated by the Java reflection API, which the container uses to discover CMP fields.

CMR Fields

In addition to CMP fields, a container-managed entity bean can also have container-managed relationship (CMR) fields. A CMR field declares the relationship of an entity bean to another entity bean. The CMR field also has abstract get and set methods that operate on the remote interface of another entity bean. CMR fields are declared in a separate section of the `ejb-jar.xml` file.

Primary Key

The primary key of an entity bean can be any of the following:

- A single-field primary key is mapped directly to a bean CMP field and, therefore, represents a column in a database table. Single-field primary keys are atomic—they cannot be further decomposed. They can be implemented by `java.lang.String` and the primitive type wrapper classes such as `java.lang.Short`, and so on. The example Booking EJB has a single-field primary key that is declared in the deployment descriptors using the <prim-key-class> element that specifies the data type of the primary key and the <prim-key> element that specifies the CMP field of the bean. Listing 5.19 shows these two fields in the descriptor.

LISTING 5.19   Single-Field Primary Key

```
<entity>
    <ejb-name>Booking</ejb-name>
    <home>unleashed.ch5.cruise.BookingHome</home>
    <remote>unleashed.ch5.cruise.Booking</remote>
    <ejb-class>unleashed.ch5.cruise.BookingBean</ejb-class>
    <persistence-type>Container</persistence-type>
    <prim-key-class>java.lang.String</prim-key-class>
    <reentrant>False</reentrant>
    <cmp-version>2.x</cmp-version>
    <abstract-schema-name>BookingBean</abstract-schema-name>
    <cmp-field>
       <field-name>bookingID</field-name>
    </cmp-field>
    <cmp-field>
       <field-name>cruiseName</field-name>
    </cmp-field>
    <primkey-field>bookingID</primkey-field>
</entity>
```

- A compound primary key is a Java object that consists of several fields. The compound primary key must implement java.io.Serializable. Further, the primary key class's fields must be public for the container to be able to access them. It also must have a no-argument constructor and implement equals and hashCode methods.

- An undefined primary key is a primary key that is declared as java.lang.Object in the deployment descriptor and all relevant methods like findByPrimaryKey. The undefined primary key does not assume the persistent storage mechanism, so the container can adapt the bean to a particular environment.

Note

In reality, it is difficult to operate on a primary key that is implemented as java.lang.Object. Also, most systems are created with a specific requirement for the data storage, whether it is a relational or object-oriented database. Consequently, undefined primary keys are rarely used.

Building and Running the Cruise Booking Application

The Cruise Booking Application consists of two modules: an EJB module that contains all EJBs, and a Web application module that contains JSPs and a Java Servlet. You can run a script for each of these modules. The scripts are provided with the source code for this chapter. Run the `compilecruise.bat` file to build and deploy the EJB module. The script compiles the classes, archives them with the deployment descriptors, and calls the WebLogic EJB compiler to generate deployable EJBs. After the EJBs are generated, the script copies the JAR file to the WebLogic deployment directory. If hot deployment is enabled on your server, the server will automatically find new EJBs and deploy them.

You can compile the Web application module by executing the `compilecruisewar.bat` file. This script compiles the Java Servlets, assembles all the files in a war file, and deploys the war file to the WebLogic deployment directory. A war file is a deployable file for Web applications. It contains the presentation pages, Java Servlet classes, images, and other files that are displayed in a Web browser. The Cruise Booking Application has two JSP files that display available tickets and bookings. The `tickets.jsp` file calls the `TicketingAgent` EJB to retrieve available cruise tickets. Figure 5.10 shows the `tickets.jsp` page.

FIGURE 5.10

The `tickets.jsp` *page.*

If you click on a cruise name, the browser calls the `BookTicketServlet`. The servlet calls the `TicketingAgent` EJB to book a ticket for a cruise. `TicketingAgent` creates a

`Booking` entity EJB for every booking. The booking is stored in a database that comes with your WebLogic Server installation. After the servlet made a booking, you can view the `bookings.jsp` page to see all the bookings that you have already made. Figure 5.11 shows the `bookings.jsp` page.

FIGURE 5.11

The `bookings.jsp` *page.*

The Cruise Booking Application is certainly far from a real commercial system. Yet, it uses all the concepts that we studied in the chapter and then some. It has a stateless session bean to display available tickets and book a ticket. It also has a CMP entity bean to save a booking in a relational database. Plus, you get the scripts that build and deploy the application in a popular EJB container.

EJB Container Services

So far we have talked about EJBs as remote stateless, stateful, and persistent server-side components. These features give EJBs the power to play an important role in the enterprise applications. There are, however, additional services that add even greater value to the technology. These services are provided by the EJB container according to the EJB specification. All the containers that follow the specification must have the same level of support for the services discussed in this section. We will cover security and transactional support that the EJB containers provide.

Declarative Security in EJB

Security is a very important aspect of any enterprise technology. EJBs provide a declarative authorization mechanism to assign permissions to your bean methods.

First we have to specify security roles in the `ejb-jar.xml` file. The security role declarations would look similar to Listing 5.20.

LISTING 5.20   Security Role Declaration

```
<security-role>
    <description>
    Travel Agent security role
    <description>
    <role-name>TravelAgent</role-name>
</security-role>
```

Once we declare security roles, we can assign roles to the bean methods. Only users from the assigned roles will be able to execute these methods. The container guarantees that the user is authenticated and belongs to an assigned role.

Listing 5.21 shows how a role assignment looks in the `ejb-jar.xml` descriptor.

LISTING 5.21   Method Permission in EJB Deployment Descriptor

```
<method-permission>
    <role-name>TravelAgent</role-name>
    <method>
        <ejb-name>PaymentAgent</ejb-name>
        <method-name>*</method-name>
    </method>
</method-permission>
```

The role name `TravelAgent` is assigned to all methods (`*`) in the `PaymentAgent` bean. This means that only the users that belong to the role `TravelAgent` will be able to execute methods on `PaymentAgent`.

Note

Roles are further assigned to individual users and user groups in a container-specific descriptor. Weblogic Server 6.1 has an element in the `weblogic-ejb-jar.xml` descriptor for this purpose.

User authentication is not provided by EJBs directly. Users can be authenticated through JNDI using the `Context.SECURITY_PRINCIPAL` property. Often users are authenticated when they access URI resources like JSPs and servlets. If a user is authenticated in the Web application, the authentication context is propagated when a servlet calls an EJB.

We can also designate EJB methods as `unchecked`. This means that the authorization is not verified at all, and anybody can execute the method. Listing 5.22 illustrates how a method can be declared as `unchecked`.

LISTING 5.22   unchecked Methods

```
<method-permission>
    <unchecked/>
    <method>
        <ejb-name>PaymentAgent</ejb-name>
        <method-name>*</method-name>
    </method>
</method-permission>
```

This example basically allows anybody to call any method on a `PaymentAgent` bean. The `unchecked` method declaration overrides any other security role assignment.

Declarative Transactions in EJB

One of the powerful features of Enterprise JavaBeans is transaction demarcation of EJB methods. An EJB method can be declared to be executed by the container in a specific type of transaction.

Declarative transactions spare bean developers from putting transaction logic inside the bean code. They also make the bean more flexible because transaction declarations can be changed in the descriptors without changing the bean code.

The deployment descriptor can specify what type of transaction the method requires. These are the available types:

- `NotSupported`—The bean method is not enrolled in a transaction.

- `Supports`—The method will be included in a transaction if it is executed within a transaction. However, if the method is called without a transaction, it continues without one.

- `Required`—The method must be executed within a transaction, so the client calls the method within a transaction and the bean will join it. If, however, there is no transaction, the bean will start a new one.

- `RequiresNew`—The method will always start a new transaction regardless of whether it is being called within one or not. This new transaction will cover this method and everything called from it but will end as this method ends.

- `Mandatory`—The method must always be invoked within a transaction, or `javax.ejb.TransactionRequiredException` will be thrown.

- Never—The method must only be invoked without a transaction, or `java.rmi.RemoteException` will be thrown.

The declarative transactions work only for a method scope. If your application requires more control, you can still manage transactions explicitly by calling JTA. It is not recommended though because in most cases you can design your bean methods to use declarative transaction demarcation.

Let's see how we can declare a transactional behavior for all methods of our `PaymentAgent` session bean. All you need to do is add an element to your `ejb-jar.xml` descriptor as shown in Listing 5.23.

LISTING 5.23   Transaction Declaration in the Deployment Descriptor

```xml
<?xml version="1.0"?>
<!DOCTYPE ejb-jar PUBLIC
'-//Sun Microsystems, Inc.//DTD Enterprise JavaBeans 2.0//EN'
'http://java.sun.com/dtd/ejb-jar_2_0.dtd'>

<ejb-jar>
  <enterprise-beans>
 <session>
      <ejb-name>PaymentAgent</ejb-name>
      <home>unleashed.ch5.cruise.PaymentAgentHome</home>
      <remote>unleashed.ch5.cruise.PaymentAgent</remote>
      <ejb-class>unleashed.ch5.cruise.PaymentAgentBean</ejb-class>
      <session-type>Stateless</session-type>
      <transaction-type>Container</transaction-type>
      </session>

  </enterprise-beans>
 <assembly-descriptor>
    <container-transaction>
      <method>
        <ejb-name>PaymentAgent</ejb-name>
    <method-name>*</method-name>
      </method>
      <trans-attribute>Required</trans-attribute>
    </container-transaction>
  </assembly-descriptor>
</ejb-jar>
```

There are two parts to adding a transaction to a method. In the `<session>` element of the descriptor, we have to specify that we want to use container-managed transactions:

```xml
<transaction-type>Container</transaction-type>
```

In the <assembly-descriptor> element, we specify transaction attributes for each method or use the wildcard character (*) to use one attribute for all the bean methods. The <method-name> element is the same as the method name on the bean implementation class.

For session beans, only business methods can have transaction attributes.

EJB Environment

EJBs can be customized by so-called environment entries. An environment entry is a name-value property that can be specified in the bean deployment descriptor. The bean can look up an environment entry using JNDI methods. Let's change our TicketingAgent bean to look up an environment entry that provides it with the name of our application—Cruise Booking Application. To specify this environment entry, we have to change a portion of the ejb-jar.xml deployment descriptor, as shown in bold in Listing 5.24.

LISTING 5.24 TicketingAgent Environment Entry

```
<session>
     <ejb-name>TicketingAgent</ejb-name>
     <home>unleashed.ch5.cruise.TicketingAgentHome</home>
     <remote>unleashed.ch5.cruise.TicketingAgent</remote>
     <ejb-class>unleashed.ch5.cruise.TicketingAgentBean</ejb-class>
     <session-type>Stateless</session-type>
     <transaction-type>Container</transaction-type>
   <env-entry>
       <env-entry-name>ApplicationName</env-entry-name>
       <env-entry-type>java.lang.String</env-entry-type>
       <env-entry-value>Cruise Booking Application</env-entry-value>
   </env-entry>
</session>
```

We can retrieve the value of the environment entry inside the setSessionContext method after the bean is instantiated but before any bean method is called, as shown in Listing 5.25.

LISTING 5.25 TicketingAgent Retrieves the Environment Entry

```
try
{
     InitialContext env = new InitialContext();
   String appName = (String)env.lookup("ApplicationName");
   System.out.println("Application Name entry is: " + appName);
}catch(Exception e)
{
```

LISTING 5.25   continued

```
        System.out.println(e.getMessage());
    }
```

The bean uses the JNDI `lookup` method to retrieve the value of the environment entry.

Summary

In this chapter, you learned about a very powerful technology—Enterprise JavaBeans. EJBs are a new way of creating distributed systems—they are concurrent, remote, secure, transactional server-side components that can be easily built and reused.

We started with an example of a simple stateless session EJB and went over all the steps required to code and deploy it. We looked at the big picture—the EJB strengths and weaknesses that you might encounter during your next project.

We briefly covered the architecture of the EJB—how the remote architecture is similar to Java RMI, as well as how EJBs became to be a scaleable solution through instance pooling.

For each type of EJB, we looked at its callback methods, life cycle, and other type related features. With that knowledge, we developed our Cruise Booking Application using EJBs. We created the `TicketingAgent` as stateless session beans. Later, we developed a persistent entity bean to store our bookings in a database. In the last section, we discussed additional container services that set EJBs apart from other distributed architectures. It is these services that make EJBs more productive and more adaptable to a quickly changing business environment. We talked about security, transactions, container environment, and other services.

With more than a dozen EJB containers available on the market, you have a choice to use the best ideas. This is a powerful thing that you should use wisely. The EJB specification should be your guide to finding the environment with which you can be most productive today and least vulnerable to the changing business requirements.

Message-Driven Beans (MDB)

CHAPTER 6

The Java world is ever changing. A few years ago, servlets and JavaServer Pages (JSP) were the new kids on the block. When Enterprise JavaBeans (EJB) 1.0 was announced, the Java community was very exited. Now these technologies have matured and new technologies are emerging to extend and complement them.

One of the most exciting of these new technologies is the message-driven beans (MDB) announced as part of the EJB 2.0 standard. MDBs are more the marriage of two existing technologies, Java Message Service (JMS) and EJB, than a totally new concept. That fact, though, should not diminish your enthusiasm because this marriage has strengthened both JMS and EJB.

EJB is strengthened because there are now three types of beans to choose from: stateful entity beans; stateless, synchronous session beans; and stateless, asynchronous message-driven beans. Before EJB 2.0, programmers had no good way to implement asynchronous processing inside the container.

JMS is strengthened because message processing can now take place inside the EJB container where all the services such as concurrency control, automatic transaction processing, and pooling are readily available.

This chapter addresses two audiences: EJB developers who want to understand messaging and MDB, and JMS developers who want to understand EJB as well as MDB. We will try to address the needs of both groups.

JMS developers will be taught only enough about EJB to understand MDBs. For a deeper understanding of EJB, turn to Chapter 5, "Enterprise JavaBeans (EJB)."

EJB developers will be taught only enough messaging to understand MDBs. For a deeper understanding of JMS, turn to Chapter 7, "Java Message Service (JMS)."

Caution

If you are unfamiliar with either JMS or EJB, the information in this chapter will be hard to understand. Gain a basic understanding of the foundation technologies before delving too deeply into MDBs.

The goal of this chapter is to provide you with a set of examples to cut and paste into your projects. Emphasis will be placed on keeping the examples business-oriented, even if a simpler example could have been written using fruits, pets, or geometric shapes.

This chapter will show you how to create and deploy MDBs in your system. It will provide examples of how a JMS application can put messages to a Queue whose messages are being removed and processed by MDBs.

Understanding Message-Driven Beans (MDB)

In order to understand the importance of MDBs, let's compare them both to ordinary EJBs and to ordinary JMS applications.

When we compare MDBs to normal EJBs, we find advantages in certain areas:

- Simplicity—MDBs are EJBs with a little added and a lot removed. The descriptors for an MDB include a description of the destination from which they will retrieve messages. However, MDBs have no home or remote interfaces, so they are, on the whole, simpler to implement.

- Non-blocking—MDBs are asynchronous message processors, which means that they do not block a client by making him wait for a response. Many applications wait for a response from a call to an EJB method only because it is required. Using MDBs, these same applications can proceed with other tasks after sending the message.

- Publishing—MDBs can subscribe to a Topic that a client is publishing to. This allows for a one-to-many relationship between clients and MDBs.

There are some disadvantages of MDBs when compared to EJBs, however:

- Error processing—There is no direct way to send an error message to a client from an MDB. Errors such as "invalid account number" and "no such address" require that a separate Queue be created for error messages.

- Stateless behavior—There is no concept of conversational state between the MDB and the client. The MDB processes the message and moves on to the next one.

There are also many advantages of using MDBs versus traditional JMS applications:

- Scalability—One of the prime motivations for creating application servers was to improve scalability. Because MDBs are really EJBs, you can set parameters in the server to specify the minimum and maximum number of instances that can exist simultaneously.

- Concurrency—You do not have to write thread-safe code; the server manages concurrency.

- Load balancing—If an EJB server supports clustering, you can deploy your MDBs over several physical machines. This allows you to balance the load and give your users more predictable performance.

- Fault tolerance—MDBs automatically provide fault tolerance for your Queues.

- Automatic startup—At startup, the MDBs are loaded into the server. This relieves you of the burden of starting these programs by hand.

- Transaction management—MDBs can be set to automatically provide transaction management via the container. This relieves your program of having to do so.

There are still areas where traditional JMS is superior to MDBs:

- Error handling—You cannot send an error message back to the client from an MDB. You have to create another Queue to do this.

- Message order—No order of message delivery can be guaranteed. Though messages are removed from a Queue in a First In/First Out (FIFO) fashion, transaction processing and multiple instances of the MDB can cause message processing to occur out of order.

- Single Queue or Topic—A traditional JMS application can consume messages from several Queues and/or Topics in the same application. This is not allowed in MDB. The rule is one Queue (or Topic) per MDB.

- Stateless behavior—There is no concept of conversational state in an MDB as there is in a normal JMS application. (If conversational state is important, messaging might not be the best approach anyway.)

The conclusion is that MDBs fill an important niche, but they are not a replacement for either traditional EJBs or for traditional JMS applications. They do, however, play a role where the services of the container are needed in an asynchronous system.

Developing and Deploying MDBs

Now that you have been told how wonderful your life can be if you start designing your projects with message-driven beans, you are, no doubt, wondering what is involved in getting these gems to work. Actually, the writing of an MDB is much simpler than deploying it in the container. Luckily, deployment is not very hard either. There are five basic steps to creating an MDB:

1. Write code that implements both the `javax.ejb.MessageDrivenBean` and the `javax.jms.MessageListener` interfaces. Compile it to a class file.

2. Create a Queue or Topic using the WebLogic GUI. See the `readme` file for instructions. The Queue or Topic name is always the destination in the `weblogic-ejb-jar.xml` file.

3. Create an `ejb-jar.xml` descriptor. This XML file is required by the EJB specification.

6

4. Create the `weblogic-ejb-jar.xml` descriptor file. WebLogic requires this XML file.

5. Create a `.jar` file that contains all three of these files. Move the `.jar` file into the server's application directory.

At this point you can begin sending messages to the Queue or Topic and the MDB will start receiving them. Sounds easy, doesn't it?

Writing the MDB Java File

The first step is to compose the Java code for the MDB. The Java file must implement two interfaces: `javax.ejb.MessageDrivenBean` and `javax.jms.MessageListener`. The `MessageDrivenBean` interface requires that two methods be implemented:

- `setMessageDrivenContext()`—The container calls this method during initialization and passes a context object in as a parameter. The MDB has an opportunity to store the context in case it is needed later in the program. This is not a client context (it is message-driven, remember?) Rather, it is a handle that allows your code to call several methods, none of which is commonly used. In practice, include this method and save the context to maintain good form.

- `ejbRemove()`—The container invokes this method before it ends the life of the MDB instance. The container decides when to kill the bean instance.

The `MessageListener` interface requires that only one method be implemented, the `onMessage()` method. This method is passed an object of type `Message`. It is the job of this method to process the message. The actual business logic associated with the application resides in this `onMessage()` method.

Manually Creating Deployment Descriptors

The code for the MDB is simple because we do not have to provide all of the "plumbing" information that we are used to providing in the class file of a traditional JMS application. Because of this, we have to create a couple of deployment descriptors. Deployment descriptors take the place of all this setup code. You will see that MDBs do not declare a connection factory, a connection, a session, or a Queue in the MDB code. That sort of detail is placed in the descriptor files.

The descriptor file is part of the contract between the container and the person who writes the class file. The descriptor files are ASCII text files that implement DTDs. The DTD describes the valid format for the XML document. The DTD for the `ejb-jar.xml` file is shown here:

```
<!ELEMENT message-driven (description?, display-name?,
small-icon?, large-icon?, ejb-name?, ejb-class, transaction-scope?,
```

```
jms-message_selector?, jms-acknowledge-mode?, message-driven-destination?,
env-entry*, ejb-ref*, security-identity?, resource-ref*, resource-env-ref*)>cx
```

The important thing to understand about this DTD is that not everything is required in your MDB descriptor. In fact, the only required field in the description is the `ejb-class` file that tells the container where to find the actual class file to load. Rather than take you through a long-winded explanation of each of the fields in the DTD, we'll show you a sample `ejb-jar.xml` file in Listing 6.1.

LISTING 6.1   `ejb-jar.xml` File

```
<!DOCTYPE ejb-jar PUBLIC "-//Sun Microsystems, Inc.//DTD
 Enterprise JavaBeans 2.0//EN" "http://java.sun.com/dtd/ejb-jar_2_0.dtd">


<ejb-jar>
 <enterprise-beans>

    <message-driven>
      <ejb-name>myCoolBean</ejb-name>
      <ejb-class>unleashed.message.MyCoolBean</ejb-class>
      <transaction-type>Container</transaction-type>
      <message-driven-destination>
        <destination-type>javax.jms.Queue</destination-type>
      </message-driven-destination>
    </message-driven>

 </enterprise-beans>

</ejb-jar>
```

There are several interesting points to be made about this file:

- The first line contains a `DOCTYPE` tag. This provides the DTD of the document. The DTD in this case is located at `java.sun.com`.

- In the `<enterprise-beans>` section, we have a `<message-driven>` tag. This indicates that the EJB described here is an MDB.

- The `<transaction-type>` tag states that the container will do transaction management. In stating this, we are asking the container to start a transaction when the message is handed to the MDB. If the MDB code finishes without throwing an uncaught exception, the transaction is to be committed; otherwise, roll it back.

- The `<message-driven-destination>` tag tells the container that this MDB listens to Queue rather than Topic. You might recall from JMS that the syntax is used to remove a message from a Topic or a Queue. The differentiation was all done in the connection and session. Because we have no connection or session setup in an MDB, we state whether this is a Queue or a Topic here.

That seems simple enough. The EJB 2.0 specification states that the container may provide its own descriptor file, and WebLogic does. It is called `weblogic-ejb-jar.xml`. It provides additional information about how the MDB is to be deployed in the container. Let's look at a sample of this file in Listing 6.2.

LISTING 6.2   The `weblogic-ejb-jar.xml` File for `myCoolBean`

```xml
<?xml version="1.0"?>

<!DOCTYPE weblogic-ejb-jar PUBLIC "-//BEA Systems, Inc.//
DTD WebLogic 6.0.0 EJB//EN"
"http://www.bea.com/servers/wls600/dtd/weblogic-ejb-jar.dtd">

<!-- MessageDriven bean Weblogic deployment descriptor -->

<weblogic-ejb-jar>

  <weblogic-enterprise-bean>
    <ejb-name>myCoolBean</ejb-name>
    <message-driven-descriptor>
      <pool>
        <max-beans-in-free-pool>200</max-beans-in-free-pool>
        <initial-beans-in-free-pool>20</initial-beans-in-free-pool>
      </pool>

      <destination-jndi-name>ticketRequestQueue</destination-jndi-name>
    </message-driven-descriptor>
    <jndi-name>myCoolBean</jndi-name>
  </weblogic-enterprise-bean>

</weblogic-ejb-jar>
```

The following list highlights several interesting features of this file:

- This XML file contains its own reference to a DTD. Observe that this DTD resides in a document at `www.bea.com`. BEA is the vendor of WebLogic.

- Note that the `<ejb-name>` in both of these files is `myCoolBean`. This provides the linkage between the files.

- The `<max-beans-in-free-pool>` tag tells the container not to create more than 200 instances of this MDB regardless of demand for them. Any messages that come into the Queue or Topic when all MDBs are busy will wait in the Queue until an MDB is freed up.

- The `<initial-beans-in-free-pool>` tag tells the container how many beans to create at startup. The MDBs will be idle if the message load is not sufficient to keep them all busy. Often this number is set to 0 to allow the container the maximum freedom in deciding how many MDBs of this type are needed at a given time.

- The `<destination-jndi-name>` tells the container the name of the Queue or Topic to get messages from.

- The `<jndi-name>` tag tells the container the name of this MDB in JNDI.

Deploying the Message-Driven Bean

Writing the code for the MDB is actually the easiest part of the whole process. The deployment of the MDB can be done either using Ant or by hand. We will do this by hand.

> **Tip**
>
> Avoid tools that keep you ignorant of what is really happening. Build tools should be used to speed up processes that you understand.

The process that we will follow is the one outlined in the WebLogic documentation. The goal of the deployment process is to prepare a JAR file that contains the MDB class file, the `ejb-jar.xml` file, and the `weblogic-ejb-jar.xml` file.

The XML files must be in a subdirectory called META-INF. The .class files must be in a directory structure to match the package statement in the files. This JAR file must be placed in the application directory of the WebLogic installation. (If you are running Windows XP or 2000 and WebLogic 6.1, the default location of this directory is `C:\bea\wlserver6.1\config\examples\applications`.)

Follow these steps to deploy the MDB:

1. Create a staging directory called `build` underneath your source directory.
2. Create a subdirectory of `build` called `META_INF`.
3. Copy both of the XML files into `META_INF`.
4. Compile the Java source files with the following command:
   ```
   javac –d build xyz.java abc.java mno.java
   ```
5. This will create a tree structure under the `build` directory that matches the package statements in the source files.

6. Package the files in a JAR with the following commands (`unleashed` is the top package name directory):

```
cd build
jar cv0f myCoolStuff.jar META-INF unleashed
```

This will place everything under the build into the JAR file that will appear in the `build` directory. (Name the JAR file something meaningful in your domain.)

Copy the resulting JAR file into the `applications` directory:

```
C:\bea\wlserver6.1\config\examples\applications
```

If discovery is set to `true` (the default) in your WebLogic Server, your MDB will be pulled into the container automatically in just a few seconds. Once it appears, you can begin sending messages to the MDB.

Programming a Simple MDB

Now that you have been introduced to the process of creating an MDB, let's go through the steps and produce a simple Topic example.

The first thing that we need is a Topic. Let's go into WebLogic and create one as shown in Figure 6.1.

FIGURE 6.1

You can use the WebLogic console to create Topics and Queues.

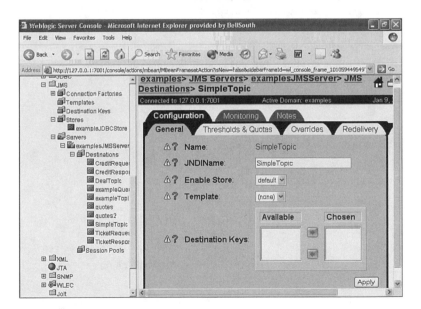

We now have a Topic called `SimpleTopic`. The next step is to create a program that is capable of publishing messages to `SimpleTopic`. Listing 6.3 contains such a program.

LISTING 6.3   The SimpleTopicClient

```java
/*
 * SimpleTopicClient.java
 *
 * Created on January 9, 2002, 2:05 PM
 */

package unleashed.ch6.SimpleTopic;

import java.rmi.RemoteException;
import java.util.Properties;
import javax.jms.JMSException;
import javax.jms.Message;
import javax.jms.Session;
import javax.jms.TextMessage;
import javax.jms.Topic;
import javax.jms.TopicConnection;
import javax.jms.TopicConnectionFactory;
import javax.jms.TopicPublisher;
import javax.jms.TopicSession;
import javax.ejb.CreateException;
import javax.ejb.RemoveException;
import javax.naming.Context;
import javax.naming.InitialContext;
import javax.naming.NamingException;
import javax.rmi.PortableRemoteObject;

/**
 * This class illustrates calling a Message-Driven bean and publishing
 * quotes on a topic.
 *
 * @author Steve Potts
 */

public class SimpleTopicClient
{
    private Context context;
    private TopicConnection tConnection;
    private TopicSession tSession;
    private Topic simpleTopic;
    private TextMessage tm;


    public SimpleTopicClient() throws NamingException
    {
        try
        {
            context = getInitialContext();

            // Create the connection
```

LISTING 6.3 continued

```java
        TopicConnectionFactory cf =
        (TopicConnectionFactory) context.lookup(
                                "weblogic.jms.ConnectionFactory");
        tConnection = cf.createTopicConnection();
        tConnection.start();


        //Get a handle to a topicSession
        tSession =
        tConnection.createTopicSession(false,
                                Session.AUTO_ACKNOWLEDGE);
        simpleTopic = (Topic) context.lookup("SimpleTopic");
        TopicPublisher tp = tSession.createPublisher(simpleTopic);
        tm = tSession.createTextMessage("This is the first message");
        tp.publish(tm);
        log("message1 sent");
        tm = tSession.createTextMessage("This is the second message");
        tp.publish(tm);
        log("message2 sent");
        tm = tSession.createTextMessage("This is the third message");
        tp.publish(tm);
        log("message3 sent");

    }catch (Exception e)
    {
        log("Exception " + e);
    }
}

//main()
public static void main(String[] args) throws Exception
{

    log("main() started");

    try
    {
        SimpleTopicClient stc = new SimpleTopicClient();
    }catch (Exception e)
    {
        log("Exception " + e);
    }
}

//get the jndi context
private Context getInitialContext() throws NamingException
{
    try
    {
```

LISTING 6.3 continued

```
            // Get an InitialContext
            Properties h = new Properties();
            h.put(Context.INITIAL_CONTEXT_FACTORY,
            "weblogic.jndi.WLInitialContextFactory");
            h.put(Context.PROVIDER_URL, "t3://127.0.0.1:7001");
            return new InitialContext(h);
        }
        catch (NamingException ex)
        {
            log("can't connect to the  server " + ex);
            throw ex;
        }
    }


    private static void log(String s)
    {
        System.out.println(s);
    }

}
```

There are several interesting elements in this listing:

- This program is an ordinary JMS application. The fact that the consumer of the messages that this program creates will be an MDB is of no concern to the `SimpleTopicClient`. A message published to a Topic is a message published to a Topic.

- The program has to obtain its `InitialContext` from JNDI. For more information on JDNI and the role of the `InitialContext`, see Chapter 11, "Java Naming and Directory Interface (JNDI)."

- The JMS setup is done by obtaining the usual set of connections, sessions, and Topics. For more information on connecting to JMS resources, see Chapter 7.

- The connection between this program and the Topic that we created in the WebLogic console can be found in this line:

```
simpleTopic = (Topic) context.lookup("SimpleTopic");
```

Now that we have a client and a Topic, we need a consumer. The consumer for this example is the message-driven bean called `SimpleTopicBean`. The `SimpleTopicBean` MDB can be written to comsume messages from any Topic that the deployment descriptor specifies.

The code for this MDB is shown in Listing 6.4.

LISTING 6.4   The `SimpleTopicBean` MDB

```java
/*
 * SimpleTopicBean.java
 *
 * Created on January 9, 2002, 2:04 PM
 */

package unleashed.ch6.SimpleTopic;

import weblogic.rmi.RemoteException;

import javax.ejb.CreateException;
import javax.ejb.MessageDrivenBean;
import javax.ejb.MessageDrivenContext;

import javax.jms.JMSException;
import javax.jms.Message;
import javax.jms.MessageListener;
import javax.jms.TextMessage;

import javax.naming.InitialContext;
import javax.naming.NamingException;

/**
 *
 * @author Steve Potts
 */
public class SimpleTopicBean implements MessageDrivenBean, MessageListener
{
    private MessageDrivenContext context;

    public void ejbActivate()
    {
        log("SimpleTopicBean ejbActivate called");
    }


    public void ejbRemove()
    {
        log("SimpleTopicBean ejbRemove called");
    }

    public void ejbPassivate()
    {
        log("SimpleTopicBean ejbPassivate called");
    }

    /**
     * Sets the session context. We don't
     * do anything with it in this example
```

LISTING 6.4   continued

```
 *
 * @param ctx        MessageDrivenContext Context for session
 */
public void setMessageDrivenContext(MessageDrivenContext ctx)
{
    log("SimpleTopicBean setMessageDrivenContext called");
    context = ctx;
}


public void ejbCreate() throws CreateException
{
    log("SimpleTopicBean ejbCreate called");

}

/////
// Implementation of MessageListener
//
public void onMessage(Message msg)
{
    TextMessage tm = (TextMessage) msg;
    try
    {
        String text = tm.getText();
        log("SimpleTopicBean : " + text);
    }
    catch(JMSException ex)
    {
        ex.printStackTrace();
    }
}


// logging
private void log(String s)
{
    System.out.println(s);
}

}
```

Here are several of the interesting aspects of this listing:

- This program implements two interfaces: `MessageDrivenBean` and `MessageListener`. The `MessageDrivenBean` interface allows the program to be created by the container and the `MessageListener` interface allows it to receive messages from a Queue or Topic.

- The program contains a required method called `setMessageDrivenContext()`. This method stores the context handle that it is given by the container to a variable, but makes no use of it.

- The MDB contains no connection information. It obtains no `InitialContext`. The container does this for it.

- The `onMessage()` method is the only place where any real work is done. This is not uncommon in MDBs with no database connections.

The next step in our example is to create the `ejb-jar.xml` file, which provides instructions to the container about the MDB being deployed. This file is shown in Listing 6.5.

LISTING 6.5   The `ejb-jar.xml` File for `SimpleTopicBean`

```
<!DOCTYPE ejb-jar PUBLIC "-//Sun Microsystems, Inc.//DTD
 Enterprise JavaBeans 2.0//EN" "http://java.sun.com/dtd/ejb-jar_2_0.dtd">

<ejb-jar>
 <enterprise-beans>

   <message-driven>
     <ejb-name>SimpleTopicBean</ejb-name>
     <ejb-class>unleashed.ch6.SimpleTopic.SimpleTopicBean</ejb-class>
     <transaction-type>Container</transaction-type>
     <message-driven-destination>
       <destination-type>javax.jms.Topic</destination-type>
     </message-driven-destination>
   </message-driven>

 </enterprise-beans>

</ejb-jar>
```

The connection is made in this file between the EJB name `SimpleTopicBean` and the classname `unleashed.ch6.SimpleTopic.SimpleTopicBean`. The fact that the EJB name is the same as the lowest level of the classname is not significant. These names may be different.

The `destination-type` is specified here, but the name of the destination is not. It will be specified in the `weblogic-ejb-jar.xml` file, which provides additional information to the container about how to deploy the MDB (see Listing 6.6).

LISTING 6.6   The `weblogic-ejb-jar.xml` File for `SimpleTopicBean`

```
<?xml version="1.0"?>

<!DOCTYPE weblogic-ejb-jar PUBLIC "-//BEA Systems, Inc.//
```

LISTING 6.6   continued

```
DTD WebLogic 6.0.0 EJB//EN"
"http://www.bea.com/servers/wls600/dtd/weblogic-ejb-jar.dtd">

<!-- Sample MessageDriven bean Weblogic deployment descriptor -->

<weblogic-ejb-jar>

  <weblogic-enterprise-bean>
    <ejb-name>SimpleTopicBean</ejb-name>
    <message-driven-descriptor>
      <pool>
        <max-beans-in-free-pool>20</max-beans-in-free-pool>
        <initial-beans-in-free-pool>5</initial-beans-in-free-pool>
      </pool>

      <destination-jndi-name>SimpleTopic</destination-jndi-name>
    </message-driven-descriptor>
    <jndi-name>SimpleTopicBean</jndi-name>
  </weblogic-enterprise-bean>


</weblogic-ejb-jar>
```

The connection between ejb-jar.xml and weblogic-ejb-jar.xml is found in the
ejb-name. The designation of the Topic to associate with this MDB is found in the
destination-jndi-name. This name must match the one specified when the Topic was
created using the console.

Next, we create the SimpleTopic.jar file using the procedure outlined earlier in this
chapter. When it is finished, we move it to the container's application directory.

The WebLogic container will notice the presence of the new MDB within a few seconds.
It will open the JAR file and find everything that it needs to proceed with the deployment. It will look into <initial-beans-in-free-pool> and determine how many MDBs
to create. In our case, we specified five.

If you look at the console for the WebLogic Server, you will see the five initial beans
being instantiated. This happens before the client is ever run. Notice that the methods
setMessageDrivenContext() and ejbCreate() are run for each instance of the MDB:

```
SimpleTopicBean setMessageDrivenContext called
SimpleTopicBean ejbCreate called
SimpleTopicBean setMessageDrivenContext called
SimpleTopicBean ejbCreate called
SimpleTopicBean setMessageDrivenContext called
SimpleTopicBean ejbCreate called
```

```
SimpleTopicBean setMessageDrivenContext called
SimpleTopicBean ejbCreate called
SimpleTopicBean setMessageDrivenContext called
SimpleTopicBean ejbCreate called
```

Now run the `SimpleTopicClient` from a command line. You will see the following lines appear in the application's console:

```
main() started
message1 sent
message2 sent
message3 sent
```

If you look in the console for the WebLogic Server, you will see the following:

```
SimpleTopicBean : This is the first message
SimpleTopicBean : This is the second message
SimpleTopicBean : This is the third message
```

This proves that our deployment of the MDB was done correctly.

How MDBs Work

Now that you are familiar with the process of creating MDBs, let's look at the internal workings of the container during deployment and message processing.

When you have created an MDB, placed it in a JAR along with its descriptor files, and moved that JAR file into the server's application directory, magical things happen. Within just a few seconds the container becomes aware of its existence. At that point, the container will create the MDBs in memory in accordance with your instructions to it in the `initial-beans-in-free-pool` parameter that you set in the `weblogic-ejb-jar.xml` file or through the GUI for WebLogic.

If there are any messages on the Queue for that MDB, the container will assign the first message to it, the second one to the next MDB, and so on. If the `initial-beans-in-free-pool` setting for this MDB is `0`, each message on the Queue will cause another MDB to be created until the container decides that it has enough to manage the flow, or the `maximum-beans-in-free-pool` limit is reached, whichever comes first.

When the MDB is being constructed, the container makes several method calls on it. First, the container will call the default constructor, though it is not common to create one for an MDB. (Initialization code is normally placed in an `ejbCreate()` method.) Next, the `setMessageDrivenContext()` method is called and an object of type `javax.ejb.MessageDrivenContext` is passed to the MDB. This context provides a handle to the services of the container. (Simple MDBs don't make much use of these services.) Finally, an `ejbCreate()` method is called. This is where you do most of the initialization work.

The newly created MDB sits quietly until the `weblogic-ejb-jar.xml` file places a message on the Queue or Topic that it is assigned to. When the container spots a message on the Queue, it picks an MDB out of the pool and makes a call to the `onMessage()` method in the MDB, passing it an object that contains a message.

> **Note**
>
> It is the MDB's job to apply whatever business logic the programmer has given to it. This may be a database update, the generation of another message on a different Queue, or any of the hundreds of things that Java programs do.

If the `onMessage()` method fails with an uncaught exception or error, the container automatically performs a rollback. This will cause the message to be returned to the Queue for reprocessing. If the cause of the error is in the message itself, the same bad message will be processed over and over again. The programmer is responsible for testing the message and generating an error message either to a log or to another message Queue. Otherwise, the message redeliveries will harm performance. The `OnMessage()` event is the right place to deal with it.

After the message is processed, the MDB sits there until the container decides that it is no longer needed in memory. Before the MDB is destroyed, the container will call the `ejbRemove()` method. This method contains any code that needs to be run before the destruction occurs. This normally includes handles to resources.

At that point, the container waits for the message arrival frequency to change. If the frequency increases, it may add additional instances of the MDB to memory, up to the maximum. If the frequency decreases, it may remove MDBs from memory down to the initial value, which serves as a minimum.

Setting the minimum and maximum numbers of MDBs in the container serves as a performance tuning opportunity for the system administrator. Having idle MDBs in the container consumes resources, but it avoids the overhead of having to create new instances every time a message arrives. On the other hand, letting the number of active MDBs go to zero lowers the overhead, but it consumes considerable resources when messages arrive.

The Point-to-Point Model

Two other issues need to be addressed before we move on to creating more complicated applications. We need to see an example that uses a Queue and we need to learn how to

configurc an MDB using the console. In order to do this, we will modify our
`SimpleTopicClient` to form the `SimpleQueueClient`. Then we will modify our
`SimpleTopicBean` to form a `SimpleQueueBean`. Finally, we will deploy this bean and use
the console to modify the behavior of the MDB.

The `SimpleQueueClient` program shown in Listing 6.7, which generates messages on the
Queue named `SimpleQueue`, is quite similar to the `SimpleTopicClient` version (see
Listing 6.3).

LISTING 6.7   The SimpleQueueClient Queue

```
/*
 * SimpleQueueClient.java
 *
 * Created on January 9, 2002, 7:39 PM
 */


package unleashed.ch6.SimpleQueue;

import java.rmi.RemoteException;
import java.util.Properties;
import javax.jms.JMSException;
import javax.jms.Message;
import javax.jms.Session;
import javax.jms.TextMessage;
import javax.jms.Queue;
import javax.jms.QueueConnection;
import javax.jms.QueueConnectionFactory;
import javax.jms.QueueSender;
import javax.jms.QueueSession;
import javax.ejb.CreateException;
import javax.ejb.RemoveException;
import javax.naming.Context;
import javax.naming.InitialContext;
import javax.naming.NamingException;
import javax.rmi.PortableRemoteObject;

/**
 * This class illustrates calling a message-driven bean and publishing
 * quotes on a Queue.
 *
 * @author Steve Potts
 */

public class SimpleQueueClient
{
    private Context context;
    private QueueConnection qConnection;
```

LISTING 6.7   continued

```
private QueueSession qSession;
private Queue simpleQueue;
private TextMessage tm;


public SimpleQueueClient() throws NamingException
{
    try
    {
        context = getInitialContext();

        // Create the connection
        QueueConnectionFactory cf =
        (QueueConnectionFactory) context.lookup(
                          "weblogic.jms.ConnectionFactory");
        qConnection = cf.createQueueConnection();
        qConnection.start();


        //Get a handle to a QueueSession
        qSession =
        qConnection.createQueueSession(false,
                          Session.AUTO_ACKNOWLEDGE);
        simpleQueue = (Queue) context.lookup("SimpleQueue");
        QueueSender ts = qSession.createSender(simpleQueue);
        tm = qSession.createTextMessage(
                          "This is the first Queue message");
        ts.send(tm);
        log("q message1 sent");
        tm = qSession.createTextMessage(
                          "This is the second Queue message");
        ts.send(tm);
        log("q message2 sent");
        tm = qSession.createTextMessage(
                          "This is the third Queue message");
        ts.send(tm);
        log("q message3 sent");

    }catch (Exception e)
    {
        log("Exception " + e);
    }
}

//main()
public static void main(String[] args) throws Exception
{

    log("main() started");
```

LISTING 6.7   continued

```java
        try
        {
            SimpleQueueClient stc = new SimpleQueueClient();
        }catch (Exception e)
        {
            log("Exception " + e);
        }
    }

    //get the jndi context
    private Context getInitialContext() throws NamingException
    {
        try
        {
            // Get an InitialContext
            Properties h = new Properties();
            h.put(Context.INITIAL_CONTEXT_FACTORY,
            "weblogic.jndi.WLInitialContextFactory");
            h.put(Context.PROVIDER_URL, "t3://127.0.0.1:7001");
            return new InitialContext(h);
        }
        catch (NamingException ex)
        {
            log("can't connect to the  server " + ex);
            throw ex;
        }
    }


    private static void log(String s)
    {
        System.out.println(s);
    }

}
```

The primary difference between this client and the `SimpleTopic` client is in the factory. To create a Queue, you need a `QueueConnectionFactory` object. The message Queue will then offer guaranteed delivery to a single message consumer.

Listing 6.7 only differs from Listing 6.3 in that the connections are all to a Queue instead of to a Topic. Likewise, `SimpleQueueBean`, which consumes messages from `SimpleQueue`, is very straightforward, as shown in Listing 6.8.

LISTING 6.8   The `SimpleQueueBean` Queue

```java
/*
 * SimpleQueueBean.java
 *
 * Created on January 9, 2002, 7:39 PM
 */

package unleashed.ch6.SimpleQueue;

import weblogic.rmi.RemoteException;

import javax.ejb.CreateException;
import javax.ejb.MessageDrivenBean;
import javax.ejb.MessageDrivenContext;

import javax.jms.JMSException;
import javax.jms.Message;
import javax.jms.MessageListener;
import javax.jms.TextMessage;

import javax.naming.InitialContext;
import javax.naming.NamingException;

/**
 *
 * @author Steve Potts
 */
public class SimpleQueueBean implements MessageDrivenBean, MessageListener
{
    private MessageDrivenContext context;

    public void ejbActivate()
    {
        log("SimpleQueueBean ejbActivate called");
    }


    public void ejbRemove()
    {
        log("SimpleQueueBean ejbRemove called");
    }

    public void ejbPassivate()
    {
        log("SimpleQueueBean ejbPassivate called");
    }

    /**
     * Sets the session context.
     *
```

Listing 6.8 continued

```
    * @param ctx        MessageDrivenContext Context for session
    */
   public void setMessageDrivenContext(MessageDrivenContext ctx)
   {
       log("SimpleQueueBean setMessageDrivenContext called");
       context = ctx;
   }


   public void ejbCreate() throws CreateException
   {
       log("SimpleQueueBean ejbCreate called");

   }

   /////
   // Implementation of MessageListener
   //
   public void onMessage(Message msg)
   {
       TextMessage tm = (TextMessage) msg;
       try
       {
           String text = tm.getText();
           log("SimpleQueueBean : " + text);
       }
       catch(JMSException ex)
       {
           ex.printStackTrace();
       }
   }


   // logging
   private void log(String s)
   {
       System.out.println(s);
   }

}
```

Notice that EJBActivate() and EJBPassivate() are not implemented in MDB. The reason for this is that the container manages the creation and deletion of the instances of the beans. Notice also the explicit cast of the message to the TextMessageObject. This is done so that we can display the message in the console.

It is necessary to create an ejb-jar.xml file for deployment purposes. The ejb-jar.xml file is shown in Listing 6.9.

LISTING 6.9 The `SimpleQueueBean` ejb-jar.xml

```
<!DOCTYPE ejb-jar PUBLIC "-//Sun Microsystems, Inc.//
 DTD Enterprise JavaBeans 2.0//EN"
"http://java.sun.com/dtd/ejb-jar_2_0.dtd">

<ejb-jar>
 <enterprise-beans>

    <message-driven>
      <ejb-name>SimpleQueueBean</ejb-name>
      <ejb-class>unleashed.ch6.SimpleQueue.SimpleQueueBean</ejb-class>
      <transaction-type>Container</transaction-type>
      <message-driven-destination>
        <destination-type>javax.jms.Queue</destination-type>
      </message-driven-destination>
    </message-driven>

</enterprise-beans>

</ejb-jar>
```

Notice the reference to the `java.jms.Queue` destination. The actual name of the Queue will not appear until the `weblogic-ejb-jar`.

The `weblogic-ejb-jar.xml` file is shown in Listing 6.10.

LISTING 6.10 The `SimpleQueueBean` weblogic-ejb-jar.xml

```
<?xml version="1.0"?>

<!DOCTYPE weblogic-ejb-jar PUBLIC "-//BEA Systems, Inc.//
DTD WebLogic 6.0.0 EJB//EN"
"http://www.bea.com/servers/wls600/dtd/weblogic-ejb-jar.dtd">

<!-- Sample MessageDriven bean Weblogic deployment descriptor -->

<weblogic-ejb-jar>

  <weblogic-enterprise-bean>
    <ejb-name>SimpleQueueBean</ejb-name>
    <message-driven-descriptor>
      <pool>
        <max-beans-in-free-pool>20</max-beans-in-free-pool>
        <initial-beans-in-free-pool>5</initial-beans-in-free-pool>
      </pool>

      <destination-jndi-name>SimpleQueue</destination-jndi-name>
    </message-driven-descriptor>
    <jndi-name>SimpleQueueBean</jndi-name>
```

LISTING 6.10 continued

```
    </weblogic-enterprise-bean>

</weblogic-ejb-jar>
```

We deploy the example in the manner described in the section titled "Developing and Deploying MDBs." When we run the `SimpleQueueClient`, we see the following in the command window or shell:

```
main() started
q message1 sent
q message2 sent
q message3 sent
```

The WebLogic Server responds to the messages by creating this output in its standard output window or shell:

```
main() started
q message1 sent
q message2 sent
q message3 sent
```

In WebLogic Server, we can also change (but not create) the deployment descriptors for an MDB using the Web-based console that ships with the product. Let's change `SimpleQueueClient`'s `max-beans-in-free-pool` value to `30`. To do this, open the WebLogic console and choose deployments, then EJB, then `SimpleQueue`. Click on the Edit EJB Descriptor label at the top of the contents area (see Figure 6.2).

FIGURE 6.2

The WebLogic console can be used to change some characteristics of Topics and Queues.

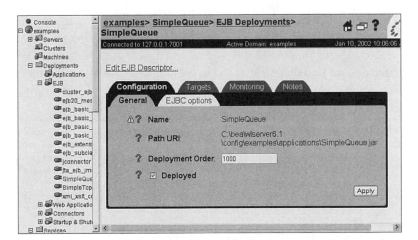

Navigate through the tree until it looks like Figure 6.3.

FIGURE 6.3

The WebLogic console can be used to change the maximum number of beans in the free pool as well as a number of other deployment descriptor parameters.

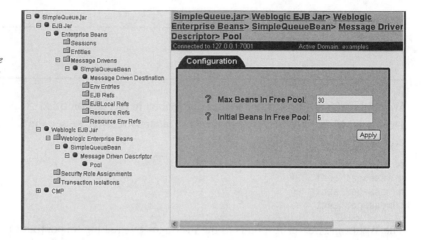

Now you can change the maximum to 30 and click on Apply. At this point, more beans can be created if the container needs them to handle the message load coming to the Queue.

Caution

Be sure to click the Back button and persist the changes if you want them to be there when you restart the WebLogic Server.

The container actually writes the changes to the JAR file containing the value just changed. In the case of the maximum number of beans in the pool, that value is set in the `weblogic-ejb-jar.xml` file. If we examine the contents of that file in the `applications` directory, we find that the change has been made as shown in Listing 6.11.

LISTING 6.11   The Changed `weblogic-ejb-jar.xml` File

```
<!DOCTYPE weblogic-ejb-jar PUBLIC '-//BEA Systems, Inc.//
DTD WebLogic 6.0.0 EJB//EN'
 'http://www.bea.com/servers/wls600/dtd/weblogic-ejb-jar.dtd'>


<!-- Generated XML! -->

<weblogic-ejb-jar>
  <weblogic-enterprise-bean>
    <ejb-name>SimpleQueueBean</ejb-name>
    <message-driven-descriptor>
```

LISTING 6.11   continued

```
    <pool>
      <max-beans-in-free-pool>30</max-beans-in-free-pool>
      <initial-beans-in-free-pool>5</initial-beans-in-free-pool>
    </pool>

    <destination-jndi-name>SimpleQueue</destination-jndi-name>
  </message-driven-descriptor>

  <jndi-name>SimpleQueueBean</jndi-name>
  </weblogic-enterprise-bean>
</weblogic-ejb-jar>
```

Notice that the XML file looks slightly different from the ones that you created by hand. It now contains a `<!-- Generated XML! -->` line. Other than that, the new `<max-beans-in-free-pool>` value is the only difference. This feature keeps you from having to edit the XML files by hand to make small changes.

Creating a GUI-Based Application

Flushed and heady with success in getting small programs to work, we must now attack a bigger problem. What would happen if we had the MDB receive a message that is an Object rather than simply text? We could make it hit a database and send a response back over another Queue to the client program telling it whether the request could be fulfilled. If we can get this to work, it will be a piece of code worth cutting and pasting.

The GUI for this will be the CruiseList program from the familiar cruise ticket system.

The first part of the application is the GUI, which provides a way for a travel agent to match a customer with a cruise. It is a Java application that uses Swing, as shown in Listing 6.12.

LISTING 6.12   The CruiseList GUI

```
/*
 * CruiseList.java
 *
 * Created on January 10, 2002, 12:06 PM
 */

package unleashed.ch6.CruiseList;

import javax.swing.*;
import java.awt.event.ActionListener;
import javax.swing.border.EtchedBorder;
```

LISTING 6.12 continued

```java
import java.awt.Container;
import java.awt.BorderLayout;
import java.sql.*;
import javax.naming.*;
import javax.jms.*;
import java.util.*;

/**
 *
 * @author  Stephen Potts
 * @version
 */
public class CruiseList extends JFrame implements ActionListener,
                                                  MessageListener
{
    //JDBC variables
    java.sql.Connection dbConn = null;
    Statement statement1 = null;

    //JMS variables
    QueueConnectionFactory qconFactory;
    QueueConnection qcon;
    QueueSession qsession;
    QueueSender qTicketRequestSender;
    QueueReceiver qTicketResponseReceiver;
    Queue ticketRequestQ;
    Queue ticketResponseQ;

    //GUI Variables
    JList customerList;
    JList cruisesAvailable;
    JButton btnBook;
    JButton btnExit;

    //Arrays to hold database information
    int[] custNums = null;
    String[] lastNames = null;
    String[] firstNames = null;

    int[] cruiseIDs = null;
    String[] cruiseDestinations = null;
    String[] cruisePorts = null;
    String[] cruiseSailings = null;

    /** Constructors for CruiseList */
    public CruiseList() throws Exception
    {
        init();
    }
```

LISTING 6.12 continued

```java
public CruiseList(String caption) throws Exception
{
    super(caption);
    init();
}

//The init() method moves real processing out of the constructors
//Exception handling is simpler
private void init() throws Exception
{
    try
    {
        //Obtain connections to JDBC and JMS via JNDI
        ConnectToServices();

        //configure the Frame
        setBounds(150,200,500,250);
        setDefaultCloseOperation(JFrame.EXIT_ON_CLOSE);

        //set the layout
        BorderLayout border = new BorderLayout();
        Container content = getContentPane();
        content.setLayout(border);

        //Populate the customerNames string
        String getCustomerString =
        "SELECT CustomerID, LastName, FirstName FROM CruiseCustomer";
        ResultSet custResults =
                statement1.executeQuery(getCustomerString);

        custNums = new int[20];
        lastNames = new String[20];
        firstNames = new String[20];
        int index = 0;

        while (custResults.next())
        {
            custNums[index] = custResults.getInt("CustomerID");
            firstNames[index] = custResults.getString("FirstName");
            lastNames[index] = custResults.getString("LastName");
            index += 1;
        }

        String[] customerNames = new String[index];

        for (int i=0;i<index;i++)
        {
            customerNames[i] = firstNames[i] + " " + lastNames[i];
        }
```

LISTING 6.12   continued

```java
int numCustomers = index;
System.out.println("The number of customers " + index);

//Populate the cruises string
String getCruiseString =
"SELECT CruiseID, Destination, Port, Sailing FROM Cruises";
ResultSet cruiseResults =
                statement1.executeQuery(getCruiseString);

cruiseIDs = new int[20];
cruiseDestinations = new String[20];
cruisePorts = new String[20];
cruiseSailings = new String[20];
index = 0;

while (cruiseResults.next())
{
    cruiseIDs[index] = cruiseResults.getInt("CruiseID");
    cruiseDestinations[index] =
                cruiseResults.getString("Destination");
    cruisePorts[index] = cruiseResults.getString("Port");
    cruiseSailings[index] =
                cruiseResults.getString("Sailing");
    index += 1;
}

String[] cruises = new String[index];

for (int i=0;i<index;i++)
{
    cruises[i] = cruiseDestinations[i] + "       Departs: " +
                    cruisePorts[i] + " " + cruiseSailings[i];
}

int numCruises = index;
System.out.println("The number of cruises" + index);


//More GUI components
String labelString = "                    Customer";
labelString += "                    Cruise";
JLabel label1 = new JLabel(labelString);
customerList = new JList(customerNames);
cruisesAvailable = new JList(cruises);
btnBook = new JButton("Book");
btnExit = new JButton("Exit");
btnBook.addActionListener(this);
btnExit.addActionListener(this);
```

LISTING 6.12   continued

```java
        JPanel bottomPanel = new JPanel();
        JPanel centerPanel = new JPanel();
        centerPanel.add(new JScrollPane(customerList,
                        JScrollPane.VERTICAL_SCROLLBAR_ALWAYS,
        JScrollPane.HORIZONTAL_SCROLLBAR_AS_NEEDED));
        centerPanel.add(new JScrollPane(cruisesAvailable,
                        JScrollPane.VERTICAL_SCROLLBAR_ALWAYS,
        JScrollPane.HORIZONTAL_SCROLLBAR_AS_NEEDED));
        bottomPanel.add(btnBook);
        bottomPanel.add(btnExit);
        content.add(label1, BorderLayout.NORTH);
        content.add(centerPanel, BorderLayout.CENTER);
        content.add(bottomPanel, BorderLayout.SOUTH);
        setVisible(true);
    }catch(Exception e)
    {
        System.out.println("Exception thrown " + e);
    } finally
    {
        try
        {
            //close all connection
            if (statement1 != null)
                statement1.close();
            if (dbConn != null)
                dbConn.close();

        } catch (SQLException sqle)
        {
            System.out.println("SQLException during close(): " +
                                            sqle.getMessage());
        }
    }

}

private void ConnectToServices()
{
    try
    {
        // Make connection to database
        // Obtain a Datasource connection from JNDI
        Context ctx = null;

        // Put connection properties in a hashtable.
        Hashtable ht = new Hashtable();
        ht.put(Context.INITIAL_CONTEXT_FACTORY,
        "weblogic.jndi.WLInitialContextFactory");
```

LISTING 6.12   continued

```java
            ht.put(Context.PROVIDER_URL,
            "t3://localhost:7001");

            // Get a context for the JNDI lookup
            ctx = new InitialContext(ht);

            //Get a connection to the datasource
            javax.sql.DataSource ds
            = (javax.sql.DataSource) ctx.lookup(
                                      "examples-dataSource-demoPool");
            dbConn = ds.getConnection();
            System.out.println("Making Database connection...\n");

            //Create the statement
            statement1 = dbConn.createStatement();

            //Get a connection to the naming service
            qconFactory = (QueueConnectionFactory)
            ctx.lookup("weblogic.examples.jms.QueueConnectionFactory");
            qcon = qconFactory.createQueueConnection();
            qsession = qcon.createQueueSession(
                        false, Session.AUTO_ACKNOWLEDGE);
            ticketRequestQ = (Queue)ctx.lookup("TicketRequestQueue");
            ticketResponseQ = (Queue)ctx.lookup("TicketResponseQueue");

            //create a sender
            qTicketRequestSender = qsession.createSender(ticketRequestQ);
            qTicketResponseReceiver = qsession.createReceiver(ticketResponseQ);
            qTicketResponseReceiver.setMessageListener(this);

            qcon.start();
            System.out.println("JMS Connections created");

        } catch (Exception e)
        {
            System.out.println("Exception was thrown: " + e);
        }
    }

    /**
     * @param args the command line arguments
     */
    public static void main(String args[])
    {
        //create an instance of the GUI
        try
        {
            CruiseList mainWindow = new CruiseList("Cruise Ticket System");
        }catch(Exception e)
```

LISTING 6.12 continued

```java
        {
            System.out.println("Exception in main " + e);
        }
    }

    public void actionPerformed(java.awt.event.ActionEvent ae)
    {
        try
        {
            Container c = btnExit.getParent();
            if (ae.getActionCommand().equals("Exit"))
            {
                //close all JMS Connections
                try
                {
                    if (qcon != null)
                        qcon.close();
                    if (qsession != null)
                        qsession.close();
                    if (qTicketRequestSender != null)
                        qTicketRequestSender.close();
                    if (qTicketResponseReceiver != null)
                        qTicketResponseReceiver.close();
                }catch(Exception e)
                {
                    System.out.println("Exception in main " + e);
                }
                System.exit(0);
            }

            //Try and book a ticket
            if (ae.getActionCommand().equals("Book"))
            {
                System.out.println("Book was clicked");
                int custIndex = customerList.getSelectedIndex();
                int cruiseIndex = cruisesAvailable.getSelectedIndex();

                if (custIndex == -1 || cruiseIndex == -1)
                {
                    JOptionPane.showMessageDialog(c,
                    "You must choose a customer and a cruise");
                }else
                {
                    //Pop up a dialog asking how many tickets
                    String numTickets = JOptionPane.showInputDialog(c,
                    "How many tickets?");
                    int numberOfTickets = Integer.parseInt(numTickets);
```

LISTING 6.12   continued

```java
                    //create a ticket request object
                    TicketRequest tickReq =
                            new TicketRequest(custNums[custIndex],
                    lastNames[custIndex], firstNames[custIndex],
                    cruiseIDs[cruiseIndex],
                    cruiseDestinations[cruiseIndex],
                    cruisePorts[cruiseIndex], cruiseSailings[cruiseIndex],
                    numberOfTickets);

                    //System.out.println(tickReq);
                    //Create a message using this object
                    ObjectMessage oMessage =
                                qsession.createObjectMessage(tickReq);
                    System.out.println(
                            "Created  the Ticket Request Message");

                    //put the message on the Queue
                    qTicketRequestSender.send(oMessage);
                    System.out.println("Sent the ticket Request Message");
                }
            }
        }catch (Exception e)
        {
            System.out.println("Exception thrown = " + e);
        }
    }

    /**
     * Message listener interface.
     * @param msg   message
     */

    // MessageListener interface
    public void onMessage(Message msg)
    {
        Container c = btnExit.getParent();
        try
        {
            //read the text message from JMS
            String msgText = "";
            if (msg instanceof TextMessage)
                msgText = ((TextMessage)msg).getText();
            else
                msgText = msg.toString();
            System.out.println(msgText);

            //show the message in a dialog box
            JOptionPane.showMessageDialog(c, msgText);
        }catch (Exception e)
```

6

LISTING 6.12   continued

```
    {
        System.out.println("onMessage() Exception " + e);
    }
  }
}
```

This application is a standard JMS client. Notice that it creates a connection to a Queue using a `QueueConnectionFactory`. Notice also that it receives its message by implementing the `onMessage()` method. The great thing about MDB from a client's standpoint is that it can't tell the difference between a message sent by an MDB and one sent by a JMS server.

The next part of this application is the MDB. It is called `TicketAgentBean`. The word *agent* implies that it is an automated process that issues tickets if the request is approved. If a client's credit card number is good, the ticket is created and stored in a database. The code for this MDB is shown in Listing 6.13.

LISTING 6.13   `TicketAgentBean`

```java
/*
 * TicketAgentBean.java
 *
 * Created on January 10, 2002, 12:10 PM
 */

package unleashed.ch6.CruiseList;

import weblogic.rmi.RemoteException;

import javax.ejb.CreateException;
import javax.ejb.MessageDrivenBean;
import javax.ejb.MessageDrivenContext;

import java.io.*;
import java.util.*;
import javax.transaction.*;
import javax.naming.*;
import javax.jms.*;
import java.sql.*;

/**
 *
 *
 * @author Steve Potts
 */
public class TicketAgentBean implements MessageDrivenBean,
                                        MessageListener
```

LISTING 6.13   continued

```java
{
    private MessageDrivenContext mdContext;

    static int ticketID = 7000;
    private boolean quit = false;
    //JDBC variables
    javax.sql.DataSource ds = null;
    java.sql.Connection dbConn = null;
    Statement statement1 = null;

    //JMS variables
    QueueConnectionFactory qconFactory;
    QueueConnection qcon;
    QueueSession qsession;

    Queue ticketResponseQ;

    //create the senders
    QueueSender qTicketResponseSender;


    public TicketAgentBean() throws Exception
    {
    }

    //The init() method moves real processing out of the
    // constructors where
    //Exception handling is simpler
    private void ejbActivate() throws Exception
    {
        log("TicketAgentBean ejbActivate entered");
    }

    private void ConnectToServices()
    {
        try
        {
            // Make connection to database
            // Obtain a Datasource connection from JNDI
            Context ctx = null;

            // Put connection properties in a hashtable.
            Hashtable ht = new Hashtable();
            ht.put(Context.INITIAL_CONTEXT_FACTORY,
            "weblogic.jndi.WLInitialContextFactory");
            ht.put(Context.PROVIDER_URL,
            "t3://localhost:7001");
```

LISTING 6.13   continued

```
                // Get a context for the JNDI lookup
                ctx = new InitialContext(ht);

                //Get a connection to the datasource
                ds= (javax.sql.DataSource) ctx.lookup(
                                     "examples-dataSource-demoPool");

                //Get a connection to the naming service
                qconFactory = (QueueConnectionFactory)
                ctx.lookup("weblogic.examples.jms.QueueConnectionFactory");
                qcon = qconFactory.createQueueConnection();
                qsession = qcon.createQueueSession(false,
                                         Session.AUTO_ACKNOWLEDGE);

                //get handles to all of the Queues
                ticketResponseQ = (Queue)ctx.lookup("TicketResponseQueue");

                //create the senders
                qTicketResponseSender =
                            qsession.createSender(ticketResponseQ);


                qcon.start();
                System.out.println("JMS Connections created");

        } catch (Exception e)
        {
            System.out.println("Exception was thrown: " + e);
        }
    }

    /**
     * Message listener interface.
     * @param msg   message
     */

    // MessageListener interface method. This method is run whenever a
    // Queue that we are listening for receives a new message
    public void onMessage(Message msg)
    {
        try
        {
            String msgText = "";
            TicketRequest tr = null;
            Object o;
            ObjectMessage om;
            if (msg instanceof ObjectMessage)
            {
                //DeQueue the message
                om = (ObjectMessage)msg;
```

LISTING 6.13   continued

```
            o = om.getObject();
            //cast the message to the correct object type
            if (o instanceof TicketRequest)
            {
                tr = (TicketRequest)o;
                msgText = tr.toString();

                //get the credit card number from the database
                String ccNum = getCreditCardNumber(tr.getCustID());
                System.out.println(
                        "The Credit Card Number is " + ccNum);

                //create a Queue send to the Payment Queue
                if (verifyCreditCard(ccNum))
                {
                    createTicket(tr);
                    sendTicketResponse(tr, true);
                }else
                    sendTicketResponse(tr, false);
            }
        }

        //if the Queue receives a text message to quit,
        if (msgText.equalsIgnoreCase("quit"))
        {
            synchronized(this)
            {
                quit = true;
                this.notifyAll(); // Notify main thread to quit
            }
        }
    } catch (JMSException jmse)
    {
        jmse.printStackTrace();
    }
    catch (Exception e)
    {
        e.printStackTrace();
    }
}

//This method sends a message to the response Queue
private void sendTicketResponse(TicketRequest tr,
                                boolean isSuccessful)
{
    try
    {
        //Create a message using this object
        String tickResp = "The ticket to " +
```

LISTING 6.13   continued

```
                        tr.getDestination() + " for " +
        tr.getLastName();
        if (isSuccessful)
            tickResp += " was successful";
        else
            tickResp += " was not successful";

        System.out.println(tickResp);
        TextMessage tMessage =
                    qsession.createTextMessage(tickResp);
        System.out.println("Created  the Ticket Response Message");

        //put the message on the Queue
        qTicketResponseSender.send(tMessage);
        System.out.println("Sent the ticket Response Message");
    }catch(Exception e)
    {
        System.out.println("Exception " + e);
    }
}

//This method creates a database entry for the new ticket
private void createTicket(TicketRequest tr) throws Exception
{
    dbConn = ds.getConnection();
    System.out.println(
                "createTicket Making Database connection...\n");

    //Create the statement
    statement1 = dbConn.createStatement();

    String insertStatement;
    ticketID += 1;
    insertStatement = "INSERT INTO CruiseTicket VALUES(
                                        " + ticketID + "," +
    Integer.toString(tr.getCustID()) + ", 'Unleashed Cruise Line'," +
    "'USS SeaBiscuit', '" + tr.getPort() + "','" +
                        tr.getSailing() +"'," +
    "999.99," + "0,"+ "0,"+ "'')";

    statement1.executeUpdate(insertStatement);
    System.out.println("Update was successful CustID = " +
                                        tr.getCustID());

    statement1.close();
    dbConn.close();
}

private String getCreditCardNumber(int CustID) throws Exception
```

LISTING 6.13   continued

```java
{
    dbConn = ds.getConnection();
    System.out.println(
                "getCreditCard Making Database connection...\n");

    //Create the statement
    statement1 = dbConn.createStatement();

    String ccNum = "";

    //Populate the creditcard string string
    String getCCString =
    "SELECT CreditCardNumber FROM CruiseCustomer " +
    "WHERE CustomerID = " + Integer.toString(CustID);

    ResultSet ccResults = statement1.executeQuery(getCCString);

    while (ccResults.next())
    {
        ccNum = ccResults.getString("CreditCardNumber");
    }

    statement1.close();
    dbConn.close();
    return ccNum;
}

private boolean verifyCreditCard(String ccNum)
{
    int firstNum = Integer.parseInt(ccNum.substring(0,1));

    if ( firstNum > 4)
        return false;
    else
        return true;
}

private void log(String s)
{
    System.out.println(s);
}

public void ejbRemove()
{
    try
    {
        log("TicketAgentBean ejbRemove() called");
        if (qsession != null)
            qsession.close();
```

LISTING 6.13   continued

```
            if (qcon != null)
                qcon.close();
        }catch (JMSException jmse)
        {
            log("JMSException thrown " +jmse);
        }
    }

    public void ejbPassivate()
    {
        log("TicketAgentBean ejbRemove() called");
    }

    public void ejbCreate()
    {
        log("TicketAgentBean ejbCreate() called");
        try
        {
            //Obtain connections to JDBC and JMS via JNDI
            ConnectToServices();

        }catch(Exception e)
        {
            System.out.println("Exception thrown " + e);
        }
    }

    public void setMessageDrivenContext(MessageDrivenContext ctx)
    {
        log("TicketAgentBean setMessageDrivenContext() called");
        mdContext = ctx;
    }
}
```

There are a number of points that we should make about this listing:

- This MDB implements the `MessageDrivenBean` and `MessageListener` interfaces. The `MessageDrivenBean` interface communicates with the container and the `MessageListener` communicates with JMS.

- The class has no constructor. MDBs have two routines that are automatically called when they are created: `ejbCreate()` and `setMessageDrivenContext()`. Constructor type code should be placed in `ejbCreate()`.

- We still have to make a call to get a context and a connection to the `TicketResponseQueue`. The automatic features of the MDB only apply to the Queue that is specified in the `weblogic-ejb-jar.xml` file. If additional Queues are needed, as one is here, they must be created the old-fashioned way.

- The JDBC connections are made and released as soon as they are done with the query. These connections are pooled in the container, so they are not expensive to create. It is a good strategy to obtain and release the handles when needed to allow the container the maximum flexibility in managing scarce resources.

- The message being deQueued by the onMessage() method is of type ObjectMessage. This requires us to downcast the object to its original type in order to gain access to the member variables.

- It is critical that ejbRemove() contain code to remove all of the JMS connections when the MDB is being removed from the container. If it doesn't, you risk running out of resources.

Another class that is needed is TicketRequest. The message being passed into the MDB is an object, not just text. This means that a cast will be done on the object as it is removed from the Queue. The class file is needed to perform this cast, as shown in Listing 6.14.

LISTING 6.14   The TicketRequest Class

```
*
 * TicketRequest.java
 *
 * Created on January 10, 2002, 12:08 PM
 */

package unleashed.ch6.CruiseList;

/**
 *
 * @author   Stephen Potts
 * @version
 */
public class TicketRequest implements java.io.Serializable
{
    //information about the customer
    int custID;
    String lastName;
    String firstName;

    //information about the cruise
    int cruiseID;
    String destination;
    String port;
    String sailing;

    int numberOfTickets;
```

LISTING 6.14 continued

```java
/** Constructor */
public TicketRequest(int custID, String lastName, String firstName,
int cruiseID, String destination,
String port, String sailing, int numberOfTickets)
{
    //set the information about the customer
    this.custID = custID;
    this.lastName = lastName;
    this.firstName = firstName;

    //set the information about the cruise
    this.cruiseID = cruiseID;
    this.destination = destination;
    this.port = port;
    this.sailing = sailing;

    this.numberOfTickets = numberOfTickets;
}

public int getCustID()
{
    return this.custID = custID;
}

public String getLastName()
{
    return this.lastName = lastName;
}

public String getFirstName()
{
    return this.firstName = firstName;
}

public int getCruiseID()
{
    return this.cruiseID;
}

public String getDestination()
{
    return this.destination;
}

public String getPort()
{
    return this.port;
}
```

LISTING 6.14   continued

```
    public String getSailing()
    {
        return this.sailing;
    }

    public int getNumberOfTickets()
    {
        return this.numberOfTickets;
    }

    public String toString()
    {
        String outString;
        outString = "---------------------------------" + "\n";

        //information about the customer
        outString += "custID = " + this.custID + "\n";
        outString += "lastName = " + this.lastName + "\n";
        outString += "firstName = " + this.firstName + "\n";
        outString += "---------------------------------" + "\n";

        //information about the cruise
        outString += "cruiseID = " + this.cruiseID + "\n";
        outString += "destination = " + this.destination + "\n";
        outString += "port = " + this.port + "\n";
        outString += "sailing = " + this.sailing + "\n";
        outString += "numberOfTickets = " + this.numberOfTickets + "\n";
        outString += "-------------------------------------" + "\n";
        return outString;
    }
}
```

This MDB will be deployed in the container in the same way that the `SimpleQueueBean` and the `SimpleTopicBean` were. The `ejb-jar.xml` file is needed to alert the container of the existence of the TicketAgent MDB. It is shown in Listing 6.15.

LISTING 6.15   The `ejb-jar.xml` File

```
<!DOCTYPE ejb-jar PUBLIC "-//Sun Microsystems, Inc.//
            DTD Enterprise JavaBeans 2.0//EN"
                "http://java.sun.com/dtd/ejb-jar_2_0.dtd">

<ejb-jar>
 <enterprise-beans>

    <message-driven>
      <ejb-name>TicketAgentBean</ejb-name>
```

LISTING 6.15 continued

```
     <ejb-class>unleashed.ch6.CruiseList.TicketAgentBean</ejb-class>
     <transaction-type>Container</transaction-type>
     <message-driven-destination>
       <destination-type>javax.jms.Queue</destination-type>
     </message-driven-destination>
   </message-driven>


 </enterprise-beans>

</ejb-jar>
```

All that this XML document does is connect the name of the MDB with the class and designate that it is connected to a Queue. The `weblogic-ejb-jar.xml` file, which instructs the container on the details of this MDB, is shown in Listing 6.16.

LISTING 6.16 The `weblogic-ejb-jar.xml` File

```
<?xml version="1.0"?>

<!DOCTYPE weblogic-ejb-jar PUBLIC "-//BEA Systems, Inc.//
                   DTD WebLogic 6.0.0 EJB//EN"
 "http://www.bea.com/servers/wls600/dtd/weblogic-ejb-jar.dtd">

<!--Unleashed  MessageDriven bean Weblogic deployment descriptor -->

<weblogic-ejb-jar>

  <weblogic-enterprise-bean>
    <ejb-name>TicketAgentBean</ejb-name>
    <message-driven-descriptor>
      <pool>
        <max-beans-in-free-pool>20</max-beans-in-free-pool>
        <initial-beans-in-free-pool>2</initial-beans-in-free-pool>
      </pool>

      <destination-jndi-name>TicketRequestQueue</destination-jndi-name>
    </message-driven-descriptor>
    <jndi-name>TicketAgentBean</jndi-name>
  </weblogic-enterprise-bean>


</weblogic-ejb-jar>
```

The main function of this file is to connect the Queue name with the MDB and to specify the minimum and initial number of MDBs to create in the container.

> **Note**
>
> Appendix A, "Source Code Listings for Utility Programs Used in This Book," contains a program called `W1JDBC2.java` that deletes and re-creates the tables for this example and several others. Run it each time before running the application to avoid duplicate primary key errors.

Running this program is very simple. Once the JAR file is placed in the container's application directory, it will pull the MDB into its control and create an initial set of `TicketAgentBeans` in memory. You can see where this was done by looking at the console:

```
TicketAgentBean setMessageDrivenContext() called
TicketAgentBean ejbCreate() called
JMS Connections created
TicketAgentBean setMessageDrivenContext() called
TicketAgentBean ejbCreate() called
JMS Connections created
```

Notice that the JMS connections are created immediately. It might be necessary in some MDBs to acquire the JMS connections on a just-in-time basis. These connections are pooled, so the cost of obtaining them when needed is not that great.

With the MDBs safely tucked inside the container, we are ready to start requesting tickets. We do this by running the CruiseList application. Figure 6.4 shows the initial screen displayed by this application.

FIGURE 6.4

The CruiseList GUI can be used to associate customers with cruises.

Whenever a selection is made and the number of tickets specified, the CruiseList application sends a message to the MDB. `TicketAgentBean` does its work and decides whether the request is valid. The following code shows the output to the container shell while this is happening. This output is for several bookings. You will see one chunk for each booking that you perform.

```
getCreditCard Making Database connection...

The Credit Card Number is 3234-3234-3234-3234
createTicket Making Database connection...

Update was successful CustID = 1003
The ticket to Bermuda for Bush was successful
Created  the Ticket Response Message
Sent the ticket Response Message
getCreditCard Making Database connection...

The Credit Card Number is 2234-2234-2234-2234
createTicket Making Database connection...

Update was successful CustID = 1002
The ticket to Caribbean for Cain was successful
Created  the Ticket Response Message
Sent the ticket Response Message
getCreditCard Making Database connection...

The Credit Card Number is 8234-8234-8234-8234
The ticket to Tahiti for Walker was not successful
Created  the Ticket Response Message
Sent the ticket Response Message
```

This proves to us that the message is getting to the MDB and that access to the database is available. It also indicates that the MDB thinks that it has created a response message and placed it on the `TicketResponseQueue`. The proof that the message was placed successfully is found in Figure 6.5.

FIGURE 6.5

A Message dialog is displayed to indicate the success of the request.

This provides proof that the application is working correctly, at least for messages sent in behalf of customers with valid credit card numbers.

Handling Errors in MDBs

How should errors be handled in message-driven beans? The answer depends on a couple of things. The container is managing transactions in this example according to the instructions that we gave it in the `ejb-jar.xml` file. The container will automatically roll back any message to the Queue if the MDB generates an exception out to the EJB level. That will take care of errors such as power outages or crashes in the container software.

The MDB may choose to define its own JTA transaction. In MDBs such as `TicketAgentBean`, where a message is received and an update is made to the database, a bean-managed transaction could make sure that both the message consumption and the database update take place together or they both will be rolled back. The TicketAgent application is vulnerable in the area of transaction processing.

There is, however, another type of error that cannot be handled properly by the container or JTA: the poison message. A poison message is a message that will fail every time that it is submitted because there is something wrong with the data. The `TicketAgentBean` received customer requests for customers who had no valid credit card.

If a normal exception is generated, the container or JTA will roll back the message and try again later. The problem is that the credit card is not likely to become valid in the near future, so the same message will be consumed and rolled back over and over again.

The correct strategy for dealing with this type of problem is for the MDB to create a test as we did here with the `validateCreditCard()` method. If the credit card fails the test, we send a message to a special Queue for responses (in our case, the `TicketResponseQueue`). This message is now consumed, no database entry is made, and a message is sent to a special Queue where the system can find it. In our case, CruiseList listens to this Queue and examines its contents. If a message is sent back with a rejection, CruiseList produces a message to the operator, as shown in Figure 6.6.

Figure 6.6

A Message dialog is displayed to indicate the failure of the request made by the CruiseList GUI.

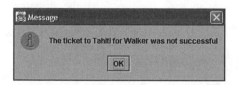

It is up to the receiver of the message to decide what the proper course of action should be. In our case, the operator would need to call the customer back and obtain a valid credit card number, if the customer has one.

Summary

In this chapter we looked at MDB as an alternative way of receiving messages from a messaging system. We looked at the advantages and disadvantages of this approach when compared to the alternatives.

You saw how to write a simple Topic example and a simple Queue example. You also learned how to deploy MDBs by placing the correct files into a JAR file.

Later, you learned how to create an MDB that could accept messages that are Objects, update a database, and send a response message to another Queue.

Java Message
Service (JMS)

CHAPTER 7

Many of us have become fond of e-mail. How many times have you asked for something on the phone, and the person you're talking to asks you to send him the request via e-mail? In many ways, e-mail and the telephone are similar—they both enable you to communicate information to another party. But in several fundamental ways, they are different, and these differences make e-mail a superior communication medium for a certain class of messages.

The telephone is synchronous. You call someone and she answers. If she doesn't answer, you don't complete the call. In the programming world, synchronous communications take place through services such as CORBA and session beans.

E-mail is asynchronous. You can send a message at any time, day or night. When the receiver is ready to process your message, he opens it and acts accordingly. In the programming world, asynchronous communications take place through message services.

Telephone messages can be lost; e-mails provide a permanent record. Telephone messages left on voice mail don't provide proof of receipt; e-mails can. Telephone messages are normally one-to-one communications; e-mails can be multicast to several recipients.

Message services are like e-mail between programs, and they provide the same set of advantages to programs that e-mails provide to humans:

- A sender program can send a message to a receiver program. If the receiver program cannot process the message immediately, it will process it when it can.
- Message services can guarantee message delivery. Messages can be persistent and they can participate in transactions.
- They can provide proof of receipt to the sender.
- They can multicast messages to several receivers.

There are disadvantages to message services also. By their very nature, messages are not processed in real time—there is no guarantee that they will be delivered right away. In addition, message services don't guarantee that the messages will be processed in any particular order. (They are removed in First In/First Out (FIFO) order, but multithreading may cause them to finish out of sequence.) These drawbacks make them unsuitable for certain types of systems.

Message services are not a recent development. IBM introduced its messaging product, MQ Series, years before Java even existed. Other commercial messaging products include Fiorano Message Server, Progress SonicMQ, and SilverStream JBrokerMQ. In addition to these, the EJB specification now requires that all J2EE-compliant servers support the JMS specification.

Conceptually, message queuing is very simple. A message queue is created. Message senders place messages on the queue and message receivers remove them from the queue as shown in Figure 7.1.

FIGURE 7.1

Message senders place messages on queues and message receivers remove them.

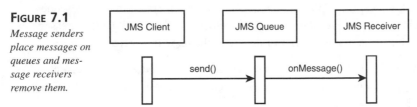

In this chapter, we will implement the Cruise Ticket System as a traditional point-to-point Java Message Service (JMS) system. You will learn how to establish communications between a message provider and the message queue. You will also learn how to remove a message from a Queue and process it. Figure 7.2 shows a diagram of this system.

FIGURE 7.2

Communication takes place between the message provider and the queues, then between the queues and the message consumer.

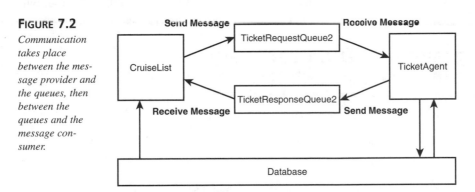

Then we will implement a `DealAnnouncer` system that uses the publish/subscribe model. We will also discuss considerations important to each approach as we develop the examples.

Understanding JMS

The Java Message Service (JMS) is a product of the Java Community Process. Message-queuing products were already in place by the time Java was introduced. What these products lacked, from a Java perspective, was a consistent, object-oriented Java interface. JMS provides that consistent interface to the variety of messaging products that are on the market. It contains enough features to support the richness of the underlying products, and it is easy for Java programmers to learn.

JMS supports two message models: point-to-point (PtP) and publish/subscribe (pub/sub). In the PtP model, a message is placed on a queue with the intention that exactly one message consumer will remove it. In the pub/sub model, a client will place a message in a topic with the intention that a number of different clients will receive it.

PtP is normally used to provide programmatic communication between the separate processes in a system. Pub/sub is normally used as a notification mechanism to communicate information.

Building the Cruise Ticket System with JMS

In order to illustrate the power of JMS, we will implement part of the Cruise Ticket System. We will create a GUI that has both a customer list and a cruise list. The user will select a customer and a cruise and click a button to process the request.

Programming The User Interface

The user interface for the JMS version of the system will be a Java application using Swing. We chose this interface to provide variety to the examples in this book and to focus on the JMS issues that we are covering in this chapter.

The first screen matches customers to the cruise that they requested, as shown in Figure 7.3.

FIGURE 7.3

The Cruise Ticket System uses JMS to book tickets on cruises.

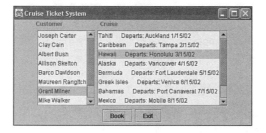

The Cruise Ticket System is a simplified version of what your travel agent uses to book you on a cruise. The agent has your name in the database already because he has worked with you before. He picks your name out of the list on the left and matches you with a cruise on the right. When he has done that, he presses the Book button. This causes the Input dialog box to appear, as shown in Figure 7.4.

FIGURE 7.4

The Input dialog allows a travel agent to specify the number of tickets to request for the client.

Once the user has entered the number of tickets needed, the message can be prepared and sent.

The message will be of type `javax.jms.ObjectMessage`. An `ObjectMessage` can contain any serializable object. This allows you to create a serializable object in one process, send it to a queue, and remove it in another process. The other process can then treat the object as if it were originally created there. This provides a lot of power beyond what can be accomplished with a simple text message. It is simpler to implement because the JVM does the marshaling and unmarshaling for you.

The object that we will be sending to request tickets is called `TicketRequest2`. Its code is shown in Appendix A, "Source Code Listings for Utility Programs Used in This Book." It can also be found in the source code download for this chapter.

There is nothing very remarkable about this class. It contains data fields, a constructor to set the values, and a set of accessor methods to provide public access to the member variables. We added a `toString()` method as a convenience.

Notice that this class implements the `java.io.Serializable` interface. This interface contains no method specifications, but it serves as a declaration that objects of this class can be written to a stream and recreated from that stream without information loss.

The body of the code is contained in the `CruiseList` class. This class contains not only the GUI, but also the code to create and send the `TicketRequest` objects in JMS messages, as shown in Listing 7.1.

LISTING 7.1 The `CruiseList` Class

```
/*
 * CruiseList.java
 *
 * Created on December 31, 2001, 6:35 PM
 */

package unleashed.ch7;
```

7

JAVA MESSAGE
SERVICE (JMS)

LISTING 7.1 continued

```java
import javax.swing.*;
import java.awt.event.ActionListener;
import javax.swing.border.EtchedBorder;
import java.awt.Container;
import java.awt.BorderLayout;
import java.sql.*;
import javax.naming.*;
import javax.jms.*;
import java.util.*;

/**
 *
 * @author  Stephen Potts
 * @version
 */
public class CruiseList extends JFrame implements ActionListener,
                                                  MessageListener
{
    //JDBC variables
    java.sql.Connection dbConn = null;
    Statement statement1 = null;

    //JMS variables
    QueueConnectionFactory qconFactory;
    QueueConnection qcon;
    QueueSession qsession;
    QueueSender qTicketRequestSender;
    QueueReceiver qTicketResponseReceiver;
    Queue ticketRequestQ;
    Queue ticketResponseQ;

    //GUI Variables
    JList customerList;
    JList cruisesAvailable;
    JButton btnBook;
    JButton btnExit;

    //Arrays to hold database information
    int[] custNums = null;
    String[] lastNames = null;
    String[] firstNames = null;

    int[] cruiseIDs = null;
    String[] cruiseDestinations = null;
    String[] cruisePorts = null;
    String[] cruiseSailings = null;

    /** Constructors for CruiseList */
    public CruiseList() throws Exception
```

LISTING 7.1   continued

```java
{
    init();
}

public CruiseList(String caption) throws Exception
{
    super(caption);
    init();
}

//The init() method moves real processing out of the constructors
//Exception handling is simpler
private void init() throws Exception
{
    try
    {
        //Obtain connections to JDBC and JMS via JNDI
        ConnectToServices();

        //configure the Frame
        setBounds(150,200,500,250);
        setDefaultCloseOperation(JFrame.EXIT_ON_CLOSE);

        //set the layout
        BorderLayout border = new BorderLayout();
        Container content = getContentPane();
        content.setLayout(border);

        //Populate the customerNames string
        String getCustomerString =
        "SELECT CustomerID, LastName, FirstName FROM CruiseCustomer";
        ResultSet custResults =
                statement1.executeQuery(getCustomerString);

        custNums = new int[20];
        lastNames = new String[20];
        firstNames = new String[20];
        int index = 0;

        while (custResults.next())
        {
            custNums[index] = custResults.getInt("CustomerID");
            firstNames[index] = custResults.getString("FirstName");
            lastNames[index] = custResults.getString("LastName");
            index += 1;
        }

        String[] customerNames = new String[index];
```

LISTING 7.1   continued

```java
                for (int i=0;i<index;i++)
                {
                    customerNames[i] = firstNames[i] + " " + lastNames[i];
                }
                int numCustomers = index;
                System.out.println("The number of customers " + index);

                //Populate the cruises string
                String getCruiseString =
                "SELECT CruiseID, Destination, Port, Sailing FROM Cruises";
                ResultSet cruiseResults =
                            statement1.executeQuery(getCruiseString);

                cruiseIDs = new int[20];
                cruiseDestinations = new String[20];
                cruisePorts = new String[20];
                cruiseSailings = new String[20];
                index = 0;

                while (cruiseResults.next())
                {
                    cruiseIDs[index] = cruiseResults.getInt("CruiseID");
                    cruiseDestinations[index] =
                                cruiseResults.getString("Destination");
                    cruisePorts[index] = cruiseResults.getString("Port");
                    cruiseSailings[index] =
                                cruiseResults.getString("Sailing");
                    index += 1;
                }

                String[] cruises = new String[index];

                for (int i=0;i<index;i++)
                {
                    cruises[i] = cruiseDestinations[i] +
                                "     Departs: " + cruisePorts[i] +
                    " " + cruiseSailings[i];
                }

                int numCruises = index;
                System.out.println("The number of cruises" + index);


                //More GUI components
                String labelString = "                Customer";
                labelString += "                Cruise";
                JLabel label1 = new JLabel(labelString);
                customerList = new JList(customerNames);
                cruisesAvailable = new JList(cruises);
```

LISTING 7.1 continued

```
            btnBook = new JButton("Book");
            btnExit = new JButton("Exit");
            btnBook.addActionListener(this);
            btnExit.addActionListener(this);

            JPanel bottomPanel = new JPanel();
            JPanel centerPanel = new JPanel();
            centerPanel.add(new JScrollPane(customerList,
            JScrollPane.VERTICAL_SCROLLBAR_ALWAYS,
            JScrollPane.HORIZONTAL_SCROLLBAR_AS_NEEDED));
            centerPanel.add(new JScrollPane(cruisesAvailable,
            JScrollPane.VERTICAL_SCROLLBAR_ALWAYS,
            JScrollPane.HORIZONTAL_SCROLLBAR_AS_NEEDED));
            bottomPanel.add(btnBook);
            bottomPanel.add(btnExit);
            content.add(label1, BorderLayout.NORTH);
            content.add(centerPanel, BorderLayout.CENTER);
            content.add(bottomPanel, BorderLayout.SOUTH);
            setVisible(true);
        }catch(Exception e)
        {
            System.out.println("Exception thrown " + e);
        } finally
        {
            try
            {
                //close all connections
                if (statement1 != null)
                    statement1.close();
                if (dbConn != null)
                    dbConn.close();

            } catch (SQLException sqle)
            {
                System.out.println("SQLException during close(): " +
                                            sqle.getMessage());
            }
        }

    }

    private void ConnectToServices()
    {
        try
        {
            // Make connection to database
            // Obtain a Datasource connection from JNDI
            Context ctx = null;
```

LISTING 7.1   continued

```java
                // Put connection properties in a hashtable.
                Hashtable ht = new Hashtable();
                ht.put(Context.INITIAL_CONTEXT_FACTORY,
                "weblogic.jndi.WLInitialContextFactory");
                ht.put(Context.PROVIDER_URL,
                "t3://localhost:7001");

                // Get a context for the JNDI lookup
                ctx = new InitialContext(ht);

                //Get a connection to the datasource
                javax.sql.DataSource ds
                = (javax.sql.DataSource) ctx.lookup(
                                        "examples-dataSource-demoPool");
                dbConn = ds.getConnection();
                System.out.println("Making Database connection...\n");

                //Create the statement
                statement1 = dbConn.createStatement();

                //Get a connection to the naming service
                qconFactory = (QueueConnectionFactory)
                ctx.lookup("weblogic.examples.jms.QueueConnectionFactory");
                qcon = qconFactory.createQueueConnection();
                qsession =
                    qcon.createQueueSession(false, Session.AUTO_ACKNOWLEDGE);
                ticketRequestQ = (Queue)ctx.lookup("TicketRequestQueue2");
                ticketResponseQ = (Queue)ctx.lookup("TicketResponseQueue2");

                //create a sender
                qTicketRequestSender = qsession.createSender(ticketRequestQ);
                qTicketResponseReceiver =
                            qsession.createReceiver(ticketResponseQ);
                qTicketResponseReceiver.setMessageListener(this);

                qcon.start();
                System.out.println("JMS Connections created");

        } catch (Exception e)
        {
            System.out.println("Exception was thrown: " + e);
        }
    }

    /**
     * @param args the command line arguments
     */
    public static void main(String args[])
```

LISTING 7.1 continued

```java
{
    //create an instance of the GUI
    try
    {
        CruiseList mainWindow =
                new CruiseList("Cruise Ticket System");
    }catch(Exception e)
    {
        System.out.println("Exception in main " + e);
    }
}

public void actionPerformed(java.awt.event.ActionEvent ae)
{
    try
    {
        Container c = btnExit.getParent();
        if (ae.getActionCommand().equals("Exit"))
        {
            //close all JMS Connections
            try
            {
                if (qcon != null)
                    qcon.close();
                if (qsession != null)
                    qsession.close();
                if (qTicketRequestSender != null)
                    qTicketRequestSender.close();
                if (qTicketResponseReceiver != null)
                    qTicketResponseReceiver.close();
            }catch(Exception e)
            {
                System.out.println("Exception in main " + e);
            }
            System.exit(0);
        }

        //Try and book a ticket
        if (ae.getActionCommand().equals("Book"))
        {
            System.out.println("Book was clicked");
            int custIndex = customerList.getSelectedIndex();
            int cruiseIndex = cruisesAvailable.getSelectedIndex();

            if (custIndex == -1 || cruiseIndex == -1)
            {
                JOptionPane.showMessageDialog(c,
                "You must choose a customer and a cruise");
```

LISTING 7.1   continued

```java
                }else
                {
                    //Pop up a dialog asking how many tickets
                    String numTickets = JOptionPane.showInputDialog(c,
                    "How many tickets?");
                    int numberOfTickets = Integer.parseInt(numTickets);

                    //create a ticket request object
                    TicketRequest tickReq =
                     new TicketRequest(custNums[custIndex],
                    lastNames[custIndex], firstNames[custIndex],
                    cruiseIDs[cruiseIndex], cruiseDestinations[cruiseIndex],
                    cruisePorts[cruiseIndex], cruiseSailings[cruiseIndex],
                    numberOfTickets);

                    //System.out.println(tickReq);
                    //Create a message using this object
                    ObjectMessage oMessage =
                            qsession.createObjectMessage(tickReq);
                    System.out.println(
                            "Created  the Ticket Request Message");

                    //put the message on the queue
                    qTicketRequestSender.send(oMessage);
                    System.out.println(
                            "Sent the ticket Request Message");
                }
            }
        }catch (Exception e)
        {
            System.out.println("Exception thrown = " + e);
        }
    }

    /**
     * Message listener interface.
     * @param msg   message
     */

    // MessageListener interface
    public void onMessage(Message msg)
    {
        Container c = btnExit.getParent();
        try
        {
            //read the text message from JMS
            String msgText = "";
            if (msg instanceof TextMessage)
                msgText = ((TextMessage)msg).getText();
```

LISTING 7.1 continued

```
        else
            msgText = msg.toString();
        System.out.println(msgText);

        //show the message in a dialog box
        JOptionPane.showMessageDialog(c, msgText);
    }catch (Exception e)
    {
        System.out.println("onMessage() Exception " + e);
    }
  }
}
```

This listing contains quite a few interesting sections of code. The application is essentially a GUI that communicates with a database via JDBC and with a message server via JMS. There are a number of interesting GUI features that we won't cover in this chapter. Instead, we will confine our discussion to message-related topics.

The constructors for this application do very little by design, as shown here:

```
public CruiseList(String caption) throws Exception
{
    super(caption);
    init();
}
```

The `init()` method does mostly GUI work, and it makes a call to the `ConnectToServices()` method. This method is responsible for obtaining a database connection and a message connection. Both of these connections are obtained using the Java Naming and Directory Interface (JNDI). The JDNI API contains method calls that provide naming services to your applications.

Naming services associate names with objects in the JVM. Two objects of interest to us are the `DataSource` object, which serves as a factory for creating connections to databases via JDBC, and the `QueueConnectionFactory`, which creates connections to message services via JMS. These associations are provided by the JNDI `InitialContext` object.

> **Note**
>
> If you desire a deeper explanation of naming services, see Chapter 11, "Java Naming and Directory Interface (JNDI)."

The code for obtaining this object is shown here:

```
// Obtain a Datasource connection from JNDI
Context ctx = null;

// Put connection properties in a hashtable.
Hashtable ht = new Hashtable();
ht.put(Context.INITIAL_CONTEXT_FACTORY,
"weblogic.jndi.WLInitialContextFactory");
ht.put(Context.PROVIDER_URL,
"t3://localhost:7001");

// Get a context for the JNDI lookup
ctx = new InitialContext(ht);
```

In brief, the initial context needs the address of a JNDI server to communicate with and a class with which to create the `InitialContext` object on the local machine. With these, you can create an `InitialContext` object. This object will act like a hotel front desk. You ask for an object by name and receive the object in the form of a handle.

Armed with the context, we can obtain a `DataSource` object. From that we obtain a `java.sql.Connection` object and a `java.sql.Statement` object. We will need these to connect to the database:

```
//Get a connection to the datasource
javax.sql.DataSource ds
= (javax.sql.DataSource) ctx.lookup(
            "examples-dataSource-demoPool");
dbConn = ds.getConnection();
System.out.println("Making Database connection...\n");

//Create the statement
statement1 = dbConn.createStatement();
```

> **Note**
>
> If you'd like a fuller explanation JDBC, see Chapter 10, "JDBC and Databases."

We create the connection to the JMS service in the same way:

```
//Get a connection to the naming service
qconFactory = (QueueConnectionFactory)
ctx.lookup("weblogic.examples.jms.QueueConnectionFactory");
qcon = qconFactory.createQueueConnection();
```

Using the `InitialContext`, we look for the object associated with the name:

```
"weblogic.examples.jms.QueueConnectionFactory"
```

The `QueueConnectionFactory` is a class that is capable of creating a connection to the queues inside WebLogic. If you use another JMS vendor, that vendor will supply you with the string that goes in the `lookup()` call. The JMS vendor will always supply this class. We use the factory to create the `QueueConnection` object that connects us to the JMS provider. Now we are prepared to create the `QueueSession`, which provides methods for creating `QueueReceivers` and `QueueSenders`:

```
qsession = qcon.createQueueSession(false,
                            Session.AUTO_ACKNOWLEDGE);
```

The first argument, `false`, indicates that this session is not transacted; it can't be rolled back later. The second argument, `Session.AUTO_ACKNOWLEDGE`, indicates that the session will acknowledge any messages that it receives.

> **Note**
>
> Chapter 10 provides an in-depth explanation of transactions.

We are now ready to get a handle to the queues where we will place the message and receive responses:

```
ticketRequestQ = (Queue)ctx.lookup("TicketRequestQueue");
ticketResponseQ = (Queue)ctx.lookup("TicketResponseQueue");
```

We use the `InitialContext` to look up the names `TicketRequestQueue` and `TicketResponseQueue`. This implies that these queues already exist. Queues can be created in several ways, but WebLogic, our message service provider for this example, wants us to create them using the console user interface, as shown in Figure 7.5.

FIGURE 7.5

The WebLogic console is used to add new queues to the provider.

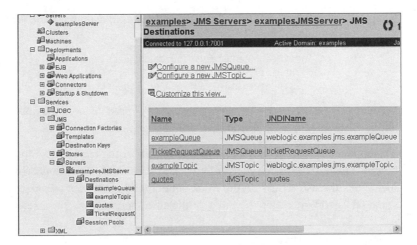

Using the Windows Explorer–like panel on the left, select "Destinations." You can then choose "Configure a new JMSQueue" from the right panel. This brings up a new right panel like the one shown in Figure 7.6.

FIGURE 7.6

The JNDIName is the one that you will use in the program.

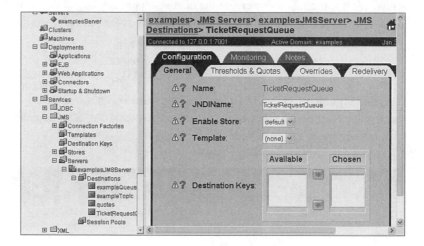

You may enter any names that you want in the Name and JNDIName fields. You can accept the defaults for everything else and the application will still work.

At this point, we are ready to create the senders and receivers:

```
//create a sender

//create a sender
qTicketRequestSender = qsession.createSender(ticketRequestQ);
qTicketResponseReceiver =
        qsession.createReceiver(ticketResponseQ);
```

Next, we need to set a message listener to this to indicate that the onMessage() method will be found in this class:

```
qTicketResponseReceiver.setMessageListener(this);
qcon.start();
System.out.println("JMS Connections created");
```

We will use the receiver to remove messages from the queue. This application both sends and receives messages, but from two different queues.

The application will display the screen and wait for the travel agent to click on the Book button. This GUI uses the standard ActionListener interface to provide event processing. When the user clicks on the Book button, the actionPerformed() method does some GUI work to obtain the index of the customer and the cruise selected. Combining this information with the `numberOfTickets` variable gives us the information needed to create the `TicketRequest` object:

```
//create a ticket request object
TicketRequest tickReq =
          new TicketRequest(custNums[custIndex],
lastNames[custIndex], firstNames[custIndex],
cruiseIDs[cruiseIndex],
          cruiseDestinations[cruiseIndex],
cruisePorts[cruiseIndex], cruiseSailings[cruiseIndex],
numberOfTickets);
System.out.println(
  "Created  the Ticket Request Message");
```

Finally, the moment that we have been waiting for arrives; we are ready to send the message to the queue:

```
//put the message on the queue
qTicketRequestSender.send(oMessage);
System.out.println("Sent the ticket Request Message");
```

Here is where the serialization mechanism in the JVM shows its worth. All that we have to do is place the serializable object handle in the method call, and voilà, the object is placed on the queue. There are performance implications, however, because getting messages to and from the queue requires a network hop and message serialization each way.

Because JMS is an asynchronous service, the travel agent can go on to other tasks. The message processing can take place as soon as the resources are available. Eventually, the request will be processed and the success or failure will be reported back. This reporting will be done via another queue, the `ticketResponseQueue`. In order to remove the message from a queue, we have to declare that the class implements the `MessageListener` interface. This interface requires that the `onMessage()` method be implemented. This method will be automatically called when a message is put on the `ticketResponseQueue`. The code for the `onMessage()` is fairly straightforward. We have to get a Container handle to place the message dialog on the screen:

```
Container c = btnExit.getParent();
```

Notice that this message is of type `TextMessage`. The response is much simpler than the request, so a simple text message is all that is needed:

```
String msgText = "";
if (msg instanceof TextMessage)
    msgText = ((TextMessage)msg).getText();
else
    msgText = msg.toString();
System.out.println(msgText);
```

We will show the message on the screen in a dialog box using the `JOptionPane`:

```
JOptionPane.showMessageDialog(c, msgText);
```

The application indicates the success of the ticket request by displaying a dialog box like the one shown in Figure 7.7.

FIGURE 7.7

A Message dialog appears when the response message arrives asynchronously.

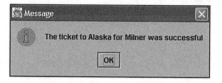

Because this program implements the `ActionListener` interface, it waits for events automatically. If it did not have the `ActionListener`, the program would exit and it would not be around when the message arrived from the queue. In that case, you would issue a `wait()` method call. Additionally, if there were several servers that could generate messages for this `MessageListener`, it would be necessary to synchronize access to maintain thread safety. For more information on threads, see Chapter 24, "Multithreading Applications in Java."

The basic difference between JMS and other methods of communicating between processes is that there is no actual connection between the message requesting the tickets and the response that the tickets have been obtained. There is not a call-and-return relationship between the CruiseList application and the TicketAgent application, but rather a request-and-response relationship.

You may have seen this type of model used on the Web by bid-oriented Web sites. You name a price for a hotel room in a certain town and the site takes your request. You come back to the site 15–20 minutes later and find out whether your bid was accepted.

Building the Ticketing Agent Application with JMS

The second part of our application is the `TicketAgent` class. This class has no user interface and it can be started from the command line. It provides some feedback on the console for monitoring purposes.

The `TicketAgent` is responsible for deciding whether to issue a ticket, issuing a ticket, and notifying the CruiseList that the request has either succeeded or failed. The criterion for deciding that a ticket can be issued is a call to the `verifyCreditCard()` method.

The `verifyCreditCard()` method accepts a credit card number and returns an approval/rejection. It is programmed to approve all cards with a first digit less than 5 and reject all others. In production, this method would make an encrypted call to a credit card server to get the answer. If the card number is approved, the `TicketAgent` creates the ticket in the `CruiseTicket` table. If the number is rejected, no ticket is created. In either case, a message is created and placed on the queue. The code for this example is shown in Listing 7.2.

Listing 7.2   The `TicketAgent` Class

```java
package unleashed.ch7;

import java.io.*;
import java.util.*;
import javax.transaction.*;
import javax.naming.*;
import javax.jms.*;
import java.sql.*;

/**
 *
 *
 * @author Steve Potts
 */
public class TicketAgent implements MessageListener
{
    static int ticketID = 7000;
    private boolean quit = false;
    //JDBC variables
    javax.sql.DataSource ds = null;
    java.sql.Connection dbConn = null;
    Statement statement1 = null;

    //JMS variables
    QueueConnectionFactory qconFactory;
    QueueConnection qcon;
    QueueSession qsession;

    Queue ticketRequestQ;
    Queue ticketResponseQ;

    //create the senders
    QueueSender qTicketResponseSender;

    //create the receivers
    QueueReceiver qticketRequestReceiver;

    public TicketAgent() throws Exception
```

LISTING 7.2   continued

```java
{
    init();
}

//The init() method moves real processing out of the constructors
//Exception handling is simpler
private void init() throws Exception
{
    try
    {
        //Obtain connections to JDBC and JMS via JNDI
        ConnectToServices();

    }catch(Exception e)
    {
        System.out.println("Exception thrown " + e);
    }
}

private void ConnectToServices()
{
    try
    {
        // Make connection to database
        // Obtain a Datasource connection from JNDI
        Context ctx = null;

        // Put connection properties in a hashtable.
        Hashtable ht = new Hashtable();
        ht.put(Context.INITIAL_CONTEXT_FACTORY,
        "weblogic.jndi.WLInitialContextFactory");
        ht.put(Context.PROVIDER_URL,
        "t3://localhost:7001");

        // Get a context for the JNDI lookup
        ctx = new InitialContext(ht);

        //Get a connection to the datasource
        ds= (javax.sql.DataSource) ctx.lookup(
                            "examples-dataSource-demoPool");

        //Get a connection to the naming service
        qconFactory = (QueueConnectionFactory)
        ctx.lookup("weblogic.examples.jms.QueueConnectionFactory");
        qcon = qconFactory.createQueueConnection();
        qsession = qcon.createQueueSession(false,
                            Session.AUTO_ACKNOWLEDGE);

        //get handles to all of the queues
```

Listing 7.2 continued

```
            ticketRequestQ = (Queue)ctx.lookup("TicketRequestQueue2");
            ticketResponseQ = (Queue)ctx.lookup("TicketResponseQueue2");

            //create the senders
            qTicketResponseSender =
                        qsession.createSender(ticketResponseQ);

            //create the receivers
            qticketRequestReceiver =
                        qsession.createReceiver(ticketRequestQ);

            //Set the message listeners
            qticketRequestReceiver.setMessageListener(this);

            qcon.start();
            System.out.println("JMS Connections created");

        } catch (Exception e)
        {
            System.out.println("Exception was thrown: " + e);
        }
    }

    /**
     * Message listener interface.
     * @param msg   message
     */

    // MessageListener interface method.  This method is run whenever a
    // queue that we are listening for receives a new message
    public void onMessage(Message msg)
    {
        try
        {
            String msgText = "";
            TicketRequest tr = null;
            Object o;
            ObjectMessage om;
            if (msg instanceof ObjectMessage)
            {
                //Dequeue the message
                om = (ObjectMessage)msg;
                o = om.getObject();
                //cast the message to the correct object type
                if (o instanceof TicketRequest)
                {
                    tr = (TicketRequest)o;
                    msgText = tr.toString();
```

LISTING 7.2   continued

```java
                    //get the credit card number from the database
                    String ccNum = getCreditCardNumber(tr.getCustID());
                    System.out.println("The Credit Card Number is " +
                                                                   ccNum);

                    //create a queue send to the Payment queue
                    if (verifyCreditCard(ccNum))
                    {
                        createTicket(tr);
                        sendTicketResponse(tr, true);
                    }else
                        sendTicketResponse(tr, false);
                }
            }

            //if the queue receives a text message to quit,
            if (msgText.equalsIgnoreCase("quit"))
            {
                synchronized(this)
                {
                    quit = true;
                    this.notifyAll(); // Notify main thread to quit
                }
            }
        } catch (JMSException jmse)
        {
            jmse.printStackTrace();
        }
        catch (Exception e)
        {
            e.printStackTrace();
        }
    }

    //This method sends a message to the response queue
    private void sendTicketResponse(TicketRequest tr,
                                        boolean isSuccessful)
    {
        try
        {
            //Create a message using this object
            String tickResp = "The ticket to " + tr.getDestination() +
                                                            " for " +
                tr.getLastName();
            if (isSuccessful)
                tickResp += " was successful";
            else
                tickResp += " was not successful";
```

LISTING 7.2 continued

```
            System.out.println(tickResp);
            TextMessage tMessage = qsession.createTextMessage(tickResp);
            System.out.println("Created  the Ticket Response Message");

            //put the message on the queue
            qTicketResponseSender.send(tMessage);
            System.out.println("Sent the ticket Response Message");
        }catch(Exception e)
        {
            System.out.println("Exception " + e);
        }
    }

    //This method creates a database entry for the new ticket
    private void createTicket(TicketRequest tr) throws Exception
    {
        dbConn = ds.getConnection();
        System.out.println(
                "createTicket Making Database connection...\n");

        //Create the statement
        statement1 = dbConn.createStatement();

        String insertStatement;
        ticketID += 1;
        insertStatement = "INSERT INTO CruiseTicket VALUES(" +
        ticketID + "," +
        Integer.toString(tr.getCustID()) +
        ", 'Unleashed Cruise Line'," +
        "'USS SeaBiscuit', '" + tr.getPort() +
        "','" + tr.getSailing() +"'," +
        "999.99," + "0,"+ "0,"+ "'')";

        statement1.executeUpdate(insertStatement);
        System.out.println("Update was successful CustID = " +
                                        tr.getCustID());

        statement1.close();
        dbConn.close();

    }

    private String getCreditCardNumber(int CustID) throws Exception
    {
        dbConn = ds.getConnection();
        System.out.println(
                "getCreditCard Making Database connection...\n");

        //Create the statement
```

LISTING 7.2   continued

```
        statement1 = dbConn.createStatement();

        String ccNum = "";

        //Populate the creditcard string string
        String getCCString =
        "SELECT CreditCardNumber FROM CruiseCustomer " +
        "WHERE CustomerID = " + Integer.toString(CustID);

        ResultSet ccResults = statement1.executeQuery(getCCString);

        while (ccResults.next())
        {
            ccNum = ccResults.getString("CreditCardNumber");
        }

        statement1.close();
        dbConn.close();
        return ccNum;
    }

    private boolean verifyCreditCard(String ccNum)
    {
        int firstNum = Integer.parseInt(ccNum.substring(0,1));

        if ( firstNum > 4)
            return false;
        else
            return true;
    }

    /**
     * main() method.
     *
     * @exception   Exception if execution fails
     */
    public static void main(String[] args) throws Exception
    {
        try
        {
            TicketAgent ta = new TicketAgent();

            synchronized(ta)
            {
                while (!ta.quit)
                {
                    System.out.println("waiting on a message");
                    ta.wait();
                    System.out.println("received a message");
```

LISTING 7.2 continued

```
            }
        }
    }catch (Exception e)
    {
        System.out.println("Exception in main() " + e);
    }
  }
}
```

Quite a few features of this example warrant explanation. The class itself implements the MessageListener interface. This interface enables a class to specify that it is a listener for a specific queue. Two queues are declared:

```
Queue ticketRequestQ;
Queue ticketResponseQ;
```

This application communicates with both queues. It gets requests from the ticketRequestQ. It places the response on the ticketResponseQ. It is not unusual to have many queues in a single application. In fact, these queues and the message types that are sent over them are the only contracts between the different parts of the system.

This casual relationship between the parts of the system is one of the outstanding features of message-based systems. For all we care, an IBM mainframe running COBOL and CICS could be receiving our requests.

One of the queues is used to send messages. In order to enable it to do this, we have to declare a sender for the queue:

```
//create the senders
QueueSender qTicketResponseSender;
```

Similarly, we need to declare one receiver for each of the queues that we need to receive messages from:

```
//create the receivers
QueueReceiver qticketRequestReceiver;
```

The TicketAgent class creates the connections to the message services. We declared the Queue handles earlier and now we have to connect them to the actual queues in the message service:

```
        //get handles to all of the queues
        ticketRequestQ = (Queue)ctx.lookup("TicketRequestQueue2");
        ticketResponseQ = (Queue)ctx.lookup("TicketResponseQueue2");
```

Notice that Queue objects are never created using new. This is because the process of performing a lookup in JNDI allocates the memory and creates the object that you have requested. All four of the queues shown here were created earlier in the user interface of the message service. In our case, this service is WebLogic.

We use the session object to create the senders. These classes do the actual work of taking a message in your JVM and creating a message that represents it on the queue:

```
//create the senders
qTicketResponseSender = qsession.createSender(ticketResponseQ);
```

We also use the session object to create receivers. Receivers remove messages from the queues and create message objects in your JVM:

```
//create the receivers
qticketRequestReceiver = qsession.createReceiver(ticketRequestQ);
```

Finally, the message listener is set on the receiver queue. Notice that it is set to `this`, indicating that the `TicketAgent` class itself contains the `onMessage()` method for the receiver queue:

```
//Set the message Listeners
qticketRequestReceiver.setMessageListener(this);
```

The `main()` method is not as simple as you might imagine. We first create a `TicketAgent` object, but we immediately put it in a wait state. This allows the thread to sleep until it is notified by some other process that there is work to do. This notification takes place whenever a message is placed on a queue that this class is listening for. The `onMessage()` method is immediately called. Synchronization guarantees that only one instance of this class will be asked to handle each message:

```
TicketAgent ta = new TicketAgent();

synchronized(ta)
{
    while (!ta.quit)
    {
        System.out.println("waiting on a message");
        ta.wait();
        System.out.println("received a message");
    }
}
```

The `onMessage()` method also contains a few twists. The logic of the method must sort out what type of message it is being asked to handle:

```
TicketRequest tr = null;
Object o;
ObjectMessage om;
```

Pulling an object out of a message is a little tricky. You need to use the `instanceof` operator to ensure that the downcast of the object type is done correctly:

```
if (msg instanceof ObjectMessage)
{
    //Dequeue the message
```

Next, we want to get the object out of the message:

```
        om = (ObjectMessage)msg;
        o = om.getObject();
```

Then we want to cast it to the correct object type. In this case, we have received a `TicketRequest2` object. The type of this object serves to tell us how to react. If we receive a `TicketRequest2` object in a message, it is logical to assume that the sender wants to request a ticket or tickets, even though, strictly speaking, we received no method call telling us that he wants us to order tickets:

```
        //cast the message to the correct object type
        if (o instanceof TicketRequest)
        {
            tr = (TicketRequest2)o;
            msgText = tr.toString();
```

One criticism of message solutions is that they contain no explicit commands. In truth, this is a small point. Those advocating synchronous approaches have labeled this lack of verbs in message-based systems a weakness. Practically speaking, you can write code that can infer the correct action, so the objection is easily addressed. Other considerations, such as synchronous versus asynchronous requirements, should drive your decisions.

Inferring that a ticket is being requested, the method gets a credit card number from the database and makes a call to verify it:

```
            //get the credit card number from the database
            String ccNum = getCreditCardNumber(tr.getCustID());
            System.out.println(
                "The Credit Card Number is " + ccNum);

            //create a queue send to the Payment queue
            if (verifyCreditCard(ccNum))
            {
                createTicket(tr);
```

```
                    sendTicketResponse(tr, true);
            }else
                    sendTicketResponse(tr, false);
    }
```

This is a good example of how message systems can send messages to each other in Ping-Pong ball fashion. Using this strategy, you can create some pretty sophisticated systems.

Integration Testing

Getting a message application to work in a demonstration is not as easy as getting a simple application or servlet to work. By definition, the senders and receivers are running in different processes, as is the JMS provider. In addition, they are often running on different platforms. To address these difficulties, follow this procedure to run this example:

1. Install WebLogic 6.1 and follow the instructions for starting the example server.

2. Create the queues using the process described earlier in this chapter.

3. Compile the source code for WlJDBC2 from Appendix A, "Source Code Listings for Utility Programs Used in This Book," and place the class file in the classpath.

4. Run WlJDBC2. This will clean out the database and create a set of tables with data for this example to run against.

5. Copy the source code from this chapter and compile it. Place the class files in the classpath.

6. Run CruiseList.

7. In another window, run the TicketAgent.

8. Use the GUI and watch the messages on the command windows to see the application's progress.

Alternately, you could run the examples from an environment such as Forte for Java.

The Publish/Subscribe Model

The point-to-point model of messaging is very common, but it is not the only one. An alternative is the publish/subscribe(pub/sub) model. The pub/sub model assumes that there are many listeners for every message that you will send. This makes it better suited for systems where distributing information to applications is the primary objective.

An example of this is a last-minute discount cruise system. In this system, an operator gets a phone call from headquarters with a price reduction on a specific cruise. It is important that all telemarketers be notified of this so that they can have a chance to sell these tickets before they are all gone. The operator uses the `DealAnnouncer` user interface to publish this information. The code for the message publisher is shown in Listing 7.3.

LISTING 7.3   The `DealAnnouncer` Class

```
/*
 * DealAnnouncer.java
 *
 * Created on January 4, 2002, 6:55 PM
 */

package unleashed.ch7;


import javax.swing.*;
import java.awt.event.ActionListener;
import javax.swing.border.EtchedBorder;
import java.awt.Container;
import java.awt.BorderLayout;
import javax.naming.*;
import javax.jms.*;
import java.util.*;

/**
 *
 * @author   Stephen Potts
 * @version
 */
public class DealAnnouncer extends JFrame implements ActionListener
{

    //JMS variables
    TopicConnectionFactory tConFactory;
    TopicConnection tCon;
    TopicSession tSession;
    TopicPublisher tDealPublisher;
    Topic dealAnnounceTopic;
    JButton btnPublish;
    JButton btnExit;
    JTextArea jta;

    /** Constructors for CruiseList */
    public DealAnnouncer() throws Exception
    {
        init();
    }
```

LISTING 7.3   continued

```java
public DealAnnouncer(String caption) throws Exception
{
    super(caption);
    init();
}

//The init() method moves real processing out of the constructors
//Exception handling is simpler
private void init() throws Exception
{
    try
    {
        //Obtain connections to JMS via JNDI
        ConnectToServices();

        //configure the Frame
        setBounds(150,200,500,250);
        setDefaultCloseOperation(JFrame.EXIT_ON_CLOSE);

        //set the layout
        BorderLayout border = new BorderLayout();
        Container content = getContentPane();
        content.setLayout(border);


        //More GUI components
        String labelString =
                        "                                        " +
        "                        Message";
        JLabel label1 = new JLabel(labelString);
        btnPublish = new JButton("Publish");
        btnExit = new JButton("Exit");
        btnPublish.addActionListener(this);
        btnExit.addActionListener(this);

        JPanel bottomPanel = new JPanel();
        JPanel centerPanel = new JPanel();
        jta = new JTextArea(15,30);
        jta.setLineWrap(true);
        jta.setWrapStyleWord(true);
        centerPanel.add(new JScrollPane(jta,
        JScrollPane.VERTICAL_SCROLLBAR_ALWAYS,
        JScrollPane.HORIZONTAL_SCROLLBAR_AS_NEEDED));
        bottomPanel.add(btnPublish);
        bottomPanel.add(btnExit);
        content.add(label1, BorderLayout.NORTH);
        content.add(centerPanel, BorderLayout.CENTER);
        content.add(bottomPanel, BorderLayout.SOUTH);
        setVisible(true);
```

LISTING 7.3   continued

```java
    }catch(Exception e)
    {
        System.out.println("Exception thrown " + e);
    }
}

private void ConnectToServices()
{
    try
    {
        // Obtain a Datasource connection from JNDI
        Context ctx = null;

        // Put connection properties in a hashtable.
        Hashtable ht = new Hashtable();
        ht.put(Context.INITIAL_CONTEXT_FACTORY,
        "weblogic.jndi.WLInitialContextFactory");
        ht.put(Context.PROVIDER_URL,
        "t3://localhost:7001");

        // Get a context for the JNDI lookup
        ctx = new InitialContext(ht);


        //Get a connection to the naming service
        tConFactory = (TopicConnectionFactory)
        ctx.lookup("weblogic.examples.jms.TopicConnectionFactory");
        tCon = tConFactory.createTopicConnection();
        tSession = tCon.createTopicSession(false,
                            Session.AUTO_ACKNOWLEDGE);
        dealAnnounceTopic = (Topic)ctx.lookup("dealTopic");

        //create a sender
        tDealPublisher = tSession.createPublisher(dealAnnounceTopic);
        tCon.start();
        System.out.println("JMS Connections created");

    } catch (Exception e)
    {
        System.out.println("Exception was thrown: " + e);
    }
}

/**
 * @param args the command line arguments
 */
public static void main(String args[])
{
    //create an instance of the GUI
```

LISTING 7.3   continued

```java
        try
        {
            DealAnnouncer mainWindow =
                new DealAnnouncer("Deal Announcer System");
        }catch(Exception e)
        {
            System.out.println("Exception in main " + e);
        }
    }

    public void actionPerformed(java.awt.event.ActionEvent ae)
    {
        try
        {
            Container c = btnExit.getParent();
            if (ae.getActionCommand().equals("Exit"))
            {
                //close all JMS Connections
                try
                {
                    if (tCon != null)
                        tCon.close();
                    if (tSession != null)
                        tSession.close();
                    if (tDealPublisher != null)
                        tDealPublisher.close();
                }catch(Exception e)
                {
                    System.out.println("Exception in main " + e);
                }
                System.exit(0);
            }

            //Try and book a ticket
            if (ae.getActionCommand().equals("Publish"))
            {
                System.out.println("Publish was clicked");
                String message1 = jta.getText();
                JOptionPane.showMessageDialog(c,
                message1);


                //Create a message using this object
                TextMessage message =
                        tSession.createTextMessage(message1);
                System.out.println(
                        "Created  the Cruise Discount Message");

                //put the message on the Topic
```

LISTING 7.3   continued

```
            tDealPublisher.publish(message);
            System.out.println(
                "Published the Cruise Discount Message");
        }

    }catch (Exception e)
    {
        System.out.println("Exception thrown = " + e);
    }
  }
}
```

You will notice several things about this code that are different from the point-to-point examples that you saw earlier in this chapter:

- A Topic is a queue that delivers its messages to every application that has subscribed to receive it. In the pub/sub world, sending is called publishing. Instead of creating a sender, we have to create a publisher:

```
tDealPublisher = tSession.createPublisher(dealAnnounceTopic);
```

- Instead of sending a message, we publish it. This analogy comes from the print publishing world, where a published article is intended for multiple readers:

```
tDealPublisher.publish(message);
```

- Notice that there is no listener declared in this example. When we are publishing, there is no concept of waiting for a response on another queue. These applications normally publish messages and forget them.

The subscribers to this topic use a parallel syntax to queue receivers, as shown in Listing 7.4.

LISTING 7.4   The `DealSubscriber` Class

```
/*
 * DealSubscriber.java
 *
 * Created on January 4, 2002, 8:17 PM
 */

package unleashed.ch7;

import javax.swing.*;
import java.awt.event.ActionListener;
import javax.swing.border.EtchedBorder;
import java.awt.Container;
```

LISTING 7.4   continued

```java
import java.awt.BorderLayout;
import java.sql.*;
import javax.naming.*;
import javax.jms.*;
import java.util.*;

/**
 *
 * @author   Stephen Potts
 * @version
 */
public class DealSubscriber extends JFrame implements ActionListener,
                                                    MessageListener
{

    //JMS variables
    //JMS variables
    TopicConnectionFactory tConFactory;
    TopicConnection tCon;
    TopicSession tSession;
    TopicSubscriber tDealSubscriber;
    Topic dealAnnounceTopic;

    //GUI Variables
    JButton btnExit;


    /** Constructors for CruiseList */
    public DealSubscriber() throws Exception
    {
        init();
    }

    public DealSubscriber(String caption) throws Exception
    {
        super(caption);
        init();
    }

    //The init() method moves real processing out of the constructors
    //Exception handling is simpler
    private void init() throws Exception
    {
        try
        {
            //Obtain connections to JDBC and JMS via JNDI
            ConnectToServices();
```

LISTING 7.4   continued

```
            //configure the Frame
            setBounds(150,200,500,250);
            setDefaultCloseOperation(JFrame.EXIT_ON_CLOSE);

            //set the layout
            BorderLayout border = new BorderLayout();
            Container content = getContentPane();
            content.setLayout(border);

            //More GUI components
            String labelString = "                    Customer";
            labelString += "                          Cruise";
            JLabel label1 = new JLabel(labelString);
            btnExit = new JButton("Exit");
            btnExit.addActionListener(this);

            JPanel bottomPanel = new JPanel();
            JPanel centerPanel = new JPanel();
            bottomPanel.add(btnExit);
            content.add(label1, BorderLayout.NORTH);
            content.add(centerPanel, BorderLayout.CENTER);
            content.add(bottomPanel, BorderLayout.SOUTH);
            setVisible(true);
        }catch(Exception e)
        {
            System.out.println("Exception thrown " + e);
        }

    }

    private void ConnectToServices()
    {
        try
        {
            // Make connection to database
            // Obtain a Datasource connection from JNDI
            Context ctx = null;

            // Put connection properties in a hashtable.
            Hashtable ht = new Hashtable();
            ht.put(Context.INITIAL_CONTEXT_FACTORY,
            "weblogic.jndi.WLInitialContextFactory");
            ht.put(Context.PROVIDER_URL,
            "t3://localhost:7001");

            // Get a context for the JNDI lookup
            ctx = new InitialContext(ht);
```

7

JAVA MESSAGE
SERVICE (JMS)

LISTING 7.4   continued

```java
                //Get a connection to the naming service
                tConFactory = (TopicConnectionFactory)
                ctx.lookup("weblogic.examples.jms.TopicConnectionFactory");
                tCon = tConFactory.createTopicConnection();
                tSession = tCon.createTopicSession(false,
                            Session.AUTO_ACKNOWLEDGE);
                dealAnnounceTopic = (Topic)ctx.lookup("dealTopic");

                //create a listener
                tDealSubscriber =
                        tSession.createSubscriber(dealAnnounceTopic);
                tDealSubscriber.setMessageListener(this);
                tCon.start();
                System.out.println("JMS Connections created");

        } catch (Exception e)
        {
            System.out.println("Exception was thrown: " + e);
        }
    }

    /**
     * @param args the command line arguments
     */
    public static void main(String args[])
    {
        //create an instance of the GUI
        try
        {
            DealSubscriber mainWindow =
                    new DealSubscriber("Deal Subscriber System");
        }catch(Exception e)
        {
            System.out.println("Exception in main " + e);
        }
    }

    public void actionPerformed(java.awt.event.ActionEvent ae)
    {
        try
        {
            Container c = btnExit.getParent();
            if (ae.getActionCommand().equals("Exit"))
            {
                //close all JMS Connections
                try
                {
                    if (tCon != null)
```

LISTING 7.4   continued

```
                         tCon.close();
                  if (tSession != null)
                         tSession.close();
              }catch(Exception e)
              {
                  System.out.println("Exception in main " + e);
              }
              System.exit(0);
        }
    }catch (Exception e)
    {
        System.out.println("Exception thrown = " + e);
    }
}

/**
 * Message listener interface.
 * @param msg   message
 */

// MessageListener interface
public void onMessage(Message msg)
{
    Container c = btnExit.getParent();
    try
    {
        //read the text message from JMS
        String msgText = "";
        if (msg instanceof TextMessage)
            msgText = ((TextMessage)msg).getText();
        else
            msgText = msg.toString();
        System.out.println(msgText);

        //show the message in a dialog box
        JOptionPane.showMessageDialog(c, msgText);
    }catch (Exception e)
    {
        System.out.println("onMessage() Exception " + e);
    }
  }
}
```

The interesting points in this example are as follows:

- This class implements the MessageListener interface. This interface allows us to receive messages from the Topic.

- We declare a `TopicSubscriber` object. A subscriber fills the same role as a receiver object in a queue model.

```
TopicSubscriber tDealSubscriber;
```

- We create a Topic named `dealTopic` using the WebLogic console. We connect to it in our code:

```
dealAnnounceTopic = (Topic)ctx.lookup("dealTopic");
```

- In this case, we set a listener because the purpose of this class is to get messages from the Topic:

```
//create a listener
tDealSubscriber = tSession.createSubscriber(dealAnnounceTopic);
tDealSubscriber.setMessageListener(this);
```

- The most surprising part of this example is the `onMessage()` method. Notice that the code for a subscribed message is the same as the code for the received message in the queue examples:

```
public void onMessage(Message msg)
{
    Container c = btnExit.getParent();
    try
    {
        //read the text message from JMS
        String msgText = "";
        if (msg instanceof TextMessage)
            msgText = ((TextMessage)msg).getText();
        else
            msgText = msg.toString();
        System.out.println(msgText);

        //show the message in a dialog box
        JOptionPane.showMessageDialog(c, msgText);
    }catch (Exception e)
```

To run this example, create one instance of the `DealAnnouncer` class and three or more instances of the `DealSubscriber` class. Create a message and click the Publish button. Figure 7.8 shows the result of doing this.

A message box pops up in the `DealAnnouncer` GUI. When this is closed, the dialogs appear in each of the `DealSubscriber` GUIs. In the real world, the `DealSubscriber` applications would be full-blown reservation system front ends. The details have been omitted here to make the example easier to understand.

FIGURE **7.8**

*A message dialog
will arrive for
each subscriber to
the Topic.*

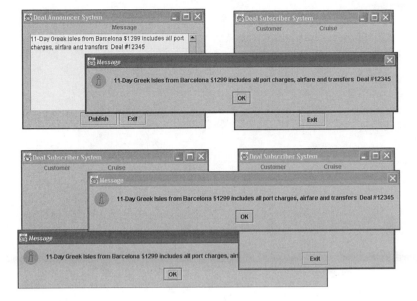

Summary

In this chapter we looked at JMS as a way of constructing distributed applications. We examined the features of the point-to-point approach and the publish/subscribe approach.

We created an example system that used two queues to communicate. One queue was used to send `ObjectMessage` instances and the other was used to send `TextMessage` instances. These two types of messages communicated with each other.

Later, we created an example based on the publish/subscribe model. This application used Topics instead of Queues to communicate with the subscribers. The application sent messages to all the applications that had subscribed to the Topic.

Messaging is a viable alternative to CORBA, EJB, and RMI for a certain class of systems. It requires a very small amount of coordination between processes, which can be a plus.

Approaches for Choosing the Right Technology

CHAPTER 8

The chief technical officer of a prominent software firm once asked, "Why is it that every time I find a so-called expert in a field, he is asking himself the same questions that I am asking myself?" Sound familiar? Customers, both internal and external to your organization, depend on the senior technical staff to "draw the pictures" that tell them how to solve a business problem with computer hardware and software. They are often frustrated when dealing with us because of our reluctance to describe a course of action, enumerate the cost, and create a schedule that we will commit to.

Some of this reluctance is understandable. At times, the people who manage the budgets for our projects don't have an appreciation for the number of unknown factors that we are trying to consider. At other times, the amount of detail provided is not sufficient to define the project. At other times, however, our reluctance is based on a lack of knowledge about the available technology. The purpose of this chapter is to address this lack of knowledge.

We will start off by covering the challenges that we face in selecting software. Following that, we will look at some of the characteristics that make one technology preferable to another. Finally, we will compare some of the competing technologies in order to guide you through the decision-making process.

The Challenge of Technology Selection

There are many challenges that face us when we are given the task of selecting the middleware for our project. Often when we are approached by a customer who has a budget and a problem, we feel that we have been handed an "insurmountable opportunity." Usually, customers are energized by the prospect of finding a solution to their problem. However, they often fail to clearly define the problem that they want solved. This doesn't stop them from wanting us to provide a detailed development plan, complete with an architecture, a schedule, and a fixed price quote right away. The challenge is to keep their enthusiasm high while gathering enough information to define a project that can be completed on schedule.

Instead of drawing a picture on a napkin during lunch, picking a date, and guessing how much the total cost will be, we would be wise to use a methodical approach that leads us to ask all the right questions before making commitments. In the project world, you lose credibility when you answer a question incorrectly, but you lose 10 times as much credibility if you never ask the right questions.

The following list consists of questions that you must be able to answer before you can even begin to decide on the architecture for your projects. The questions are grouped into several categories:

- Money—Do you have a budget? How big is it? How much of it is for acquiring hardware and software? How much of it is for staffing?

- Expertise—Do you know any of the candidate technologies well? Does your staff know any? Do you have authorization to hire? Can you pay the big money that it takes to hire some experienced people? Are those people available in your area? Will they take a job with your company? Can you pay a headhunter to find them? Do you have money to run advertisements in the paper? Do you have money to pay relocation expenses if they live far away? Do you have any money to fly them in for an interview? Can you bring in a consultant? Are any consultants available in your area? Can you afford them?

- Customer buy-in—How long is the attention span of your customer? Can they fund a large effort for the length of time that this project will last? Do they understand the uniqueness of software development or are they the brick and mortar type of management? How much pain are they in? How likely is it that they will be around for the life of the project? If they leave, who will replace them?

- Changing requirements—How much do you know about the business that you are automating? How good is your access to the people who *do* know? Can you write a complete requirement specification today? If not, when will you be able to write it? Will the specification be stable, or will you be inundated with change requests?

- Scalability—How many users/hits/transactions will the system have to handle in the first six months after deployment? How many in the following year? How many at full rollout? How likely is it that you will really get this big? What happens if you don't? What is your peak load? What is your average load? What do you do when your peak load is exceeded? Can your business model tolerate denial of service?

- Security—How secure do your transactions have to be? How much security validation can you place on your users before they balk? How many different applications do you interface with that require authentication?

- Transaction management—Are your transactions naturally atomic or do they require transaction management? Could you implement your own commit/rollback strategy if you wanted to? Can you rely on the database to handle this?

- Legacy systems—What are the legacy systems written in? Do you have to communicate with them? What is the nature of this communication? Do you have to call methods in them? Will they be calling methods in this system? Do you control both ends of all interfaces or are some of them out of your control?

- Hardware constraints—What hardware do you have to run on? Can you choose it? What hardware is planned for the future? What is the likelihood that the hardware platform will change during the life of the system?

The answers to these questions can be used to design the architecture. These questions alone are not sufficient, though, because we have not yet created a framework with which to evaluate the alternatives. If we are going to say that approach A is superior to approach B, we need to state what standard we used to perform the evaluation. The sections that follow will give us a standard for comparison.

Measuring Software Characteristics

Most of us can label something *good* or *bad* in an instant, and we often do. This is hazardous because it can lead us to make some decisions poorly because we don't fully understand what constitutes goodness or badness. When you set out to evaluate technologies that you might recommend to a customer, it is important to consider both the strengths and weaknesses of each technology. This section describes a set of 11 criteria by which you can judge each option in order to form a sound opinion about its suitability to your project.

Cost

The cost of a solution seems like a simple concept at first glance, but it can be quite complex. When you say that a project will cost a certain amount of money, are you talking about the cost of procurement, or the total life-cycle cost? How long is this life cycle? What are the tax implications of what you are asking for? If you are working in the United States, you will have to ask how much of the cost is going to be capital expenditure and how much of it can be expensed. If your customer has a customer, can this cost be charged through to his customer?

Are you asking for money this year, or is the cost spread out over several years? Are the savings that you project from this system available in the first year or will the customer have to wait several years for them to materialize?

> **Note**
>
> One cost that is often overlooked is the cost of doing nothing. Normally, the customer has a good idea of how much money she is losing each week, month, or year without the new system. Knowing this number can be a great help in keeping your customer on board when the project hits rough spots.

> **Tip**
>
> Cost can be measured in terms of the amount of money expended to solve a business problem (adapted to the customer's time frame).

Risk

Risk is defined on dictionary.com as "the possibility of suffering harm or loss." In the world of software projects, it can be defined as "the possibility of spending the money budgeted for solving a problem, but not solving it." When this happens, harm to companies and your career is the result. In an ideal world, a customer would simply describe a problem and the developers would complete the system on time and for exactly the amount of money quoted.

> **Tip**
>
> Risk can be measured in terms of the probability that a system will solve the customer's problems, will be ready on time, and will cost what was estimated.

Maintainability

A car that did not have a hood release would run well only until it got low on oil or water. It would then require a major effort to pry open the hood to add water or oil. Many software systems resemble such a car. They work well when delivered, but they do not tolerate alteration well. Simple modifications result in major expense and numerous side effects.

> **Tip**
>
> Maintainability can be measured in terms of the ease with which a system can be modified after it is delivered.

Reliability

A system that is not available for use has no value. We programmers have convinced the business and government worlds to allow us to automate almost everything that you can think of. The last thing we want is for them to wish for a pencil and a pad of paper.

> **Tip**
>
> Reliability can be measured in terms of the percentage of time that the system is actually available for use.

Scalability

A recent advertisement on television showed a group of programmers launching their Web site. They cheered wildly as the number of hits moved upward until the number got too high. They then fell silent and stared at the screen. Many systems are funded as research projects, but later turn into blockbusters. If a system cannot be enlarged, it will limit your customer's growth.

> **Tip**
>
> Scalability can be measured in terms of the maximum load a system can bear without a major rewrite.

Interoperability

Some systems get along well with other systems and some do not. Some only cooperate well with software written in the same language and others interact easily with software written in any language.

> **Tip**
>
> Interoperability can be measured in terms of the number of other system types that a system can interface with without requiring you to write special modules.

Simplicity

The complexity of the solution should not exceed the complexity of the problem. Many of us have worked on systems in which the solution seemed like the board game Mouse Trap. It seemed like the designers did everything the hard way, which made the system larger and harder to learn than it needed to be.

> **Tip**
>
> Simplicity can be measured in terms of how well the complexity of the solution matches the complexity of the problem.

Extensibility

Enhancing some systems is like stretching a rubber band. At first you can add length easily, but over time the process becomes so difficult that you give up and start over. Software systems vary greatly in their ability to accept changes. With some systems, the changes are easy to make at first and they generate few side effects. Over time, however, the expense of making a change and the number of bugs generated by each change become overwhelming.

Other systems tolerate change well. Classes can be replaced by newer versions that are duplicates or supersets of the original interface. It is rare to encounter a bug outside the code that was changed. These systems can be enhanced indefinitely.

> **Tip**
>
> Extensibility can be measured in terms of the number and size of the enhancements that can be made to a system before it becomes unmanageable.

Verifiability

Whenever we consider building a system with a certain technology, we have to ask ourselves how we plan to test and debug it. This involves both unit testing and integration testing. When we discover defects, how will they be fixed? What tool will we use to do the fixes?

> **Tip**
>
> Verifiability can be measured in terms of the percentage of bugs that can be discovered during testing and the ease of fixing those bugs.

Staffability

This is one "ility" that is often overlooked. Many business people are tied closely to their industry and their employers. Historically, this has not been true of programmers. Most of us have worked in more than one industry and many consultants have worked in a dozen. Programmers also change jobs more often than people in other fields, often voluntarily. As a result, you have to ask yourself who will design, create, test, and maintain the system you are architecting.

This is a tricky problem. When technology is new and exciting, everyone wants to work on it but almost no one is qualified. Once a technology matures, almost everyone is qualified to work on it, but no one will do it voluntarily. Additionally, some technologies are considered out of the mainstream, such as proprietary fourth-generation languages. It is very difficult to get programmers to accept these assignments because they fear that they will not be employable if they use such languages too long.

> **Tip**
>
> Staffability can be measured in terms of the number of qualified, affordable programmers available who would voluntarily work with a given technology.

Learnability

A study performed a few years ago on college campuses asked why there were so few computer science majors when the number of jobs for graduates was so high. The most common answer that students gave was, "Those courses are hard." Likewise, in the field of computer programming, some technologies are harder to learn than others. Many programmers are limited in their background and technical ambition. Others are not interested in learning technologies that have limited applicability. If a technology is hard to learn, it will take too long to bring in programmers who aren't familiar with it and get them up to speed. Your only choice is to bring in programmers who already have the skills you need, sometimes at a premium price.

> **Tip**
>
> Learnability can be measured in terms of how long it would take a qualified programmer to learn a technology well enough to be productive.

Evaluating Distributed Technologies

When setting out to evaluate technologies, be sure to include every technology that you can think of in your initial list. You can always remove items from the list once you find that they cannot meet your requirements. By doing this, you can avoid the embarrassment of having no answer if you are later asked why you didn't choose this or that technology. (This is especially important if your project bombs out.)

The remainder of this chapter is devoted to looking at Java-related technologies that you can use to create a system that spans more than one computer. I considered possibilities other than the normal two or three choices in order to provide as much food for thought as possible. The remainder of the chapter is based for the most part on opinion and personal experience. You may disagree with some of my conclusions; this is to be expected. The goal is to express an educated opinion that might prove helpful.

The basic order of the technologies is from simplest to most complex.

Java and Java Database Connectivity (JDBC)

Perhaps the simplest way to create a distributed system in Java is to place the data in a database on one computer and access the data from another computer that has a JDBC driver installed on it. The clients can be fairly simple Java programs. Chapter 10, "JDBC and Databases," covers how this is done and provides running examples complete with output.

The biggest advantage of using this approach is its cost. Your company probably already owns a DBMS. If it doesn't, you can download MySQL and a JDBC driver free from www.mysql.com. A second advantage of the JDBC approach is that expertise in this area is plentiful. This is considered an orthodox approach and it is generally acceptable to management. In addition, the technology is very mature.

This approach scales well because the DBMS engines are pretty powerful. In addition, DBMSs provide security and transaction management as built-in features.

On the flip side, there are serious negatives associated with placing a database in the middle of your application. The biggest drawback is in performance. The DBMS software is a large, complex piece of middleware that provides a lot of services but consumes a lot of cycles.

Another area where you might find this approach lacking is its tolerance to changing requirements. Projects written to use JDBC contain a lot of SQL code. This code takes time to get right, and it might have to be modified when the requirements change. Maintenance releases may have to be moved to each client and installed there. This is no small problem when you have 500 or 1,000 clients.

Synchronizing the client and server portions of the application can also be difficult. Normally, this places you in a polling situation where you look for changes to the data periodically.

Figure 8.1 shows a typical JDBC implementation.

FIGURE 8.1

All the clients access the same tables in the DBMS to exchange data.

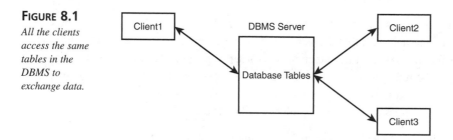

Here are a few successful implementations that have used this strategy:

- Manufacturing tracking system—This system enables factory workers to report the completion of tasks online. About 60 clients on the factory floor run with low volume.

- Hospital operating room system—This system provides a way for hospital personnel to report on what consumable items were used in each operation.

- EDI system—This system is updated every time an EDI message is received. This allows for the production of detailed bills that include date, time, and length of message.

In the past, JDBC was widely used because it works and it is well understood. Before you commit to using it, however, you would be wise to consider whether a more modern solution would be better.

TCP/IP Programming (Sockets)

Programming with the socket classes in the java.net package has many advantages, the primary one being performance. Because almost all other Java technologies are built on top of TCP/IP, you can cut out the middleman and program your own application layer. Chapter 1, "Programming Interconnected Computers," discusses socket programming and provides a simple example.

All the software that you need to do socket programming ships with the JDK, so you don't need money for software licenses. Socket technology is very mature. In addition, sockets run on every platform that Java runs on, so they may be a good choice when communicating with a "classic" computer.

There are considerable disadvantages to programming at the socket level for the application programmer. There are not many experienced socket programmers available, so they tend to be expensive. This solution may be viewed by management as a "roll you own" system and therefore not very "modern." All change traffic will cause you pain. You will have to write your own security and transaction support, and you will have to decide on your own protocol.

Because of the large amount of code that typically has to be written, the risk of failure can be high. Figure 8.2 shows a typical socket-based system.

FIGURE 8.2

Normally two sockets are used, one for incoming messages and one for outgoing messages.

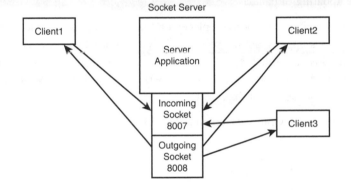

Successful implementations that have used this strategy include the following:

- EDI system—This system enables a message to be received on one computer and moved quickly to another computer for delivery on another network.
- Custom Web servers—The socket model is ideal for middleware applications that have throughput as their primary requirement.
- Credit card validation—This system takes an encrypted request containing a credit card number, validates it against a database, then sends an unencrypted confirmation code back.

There are rare situations where no middleware products are available on an obsolete platform. In these cases, you may not have any choice but to write socket programs. In general, socket programming is more of a software engineering tool than it is an application programming tool.

Servlets

Servlets were the workhorse technology for the late 1990s. The simplicity of the approach combined with the rapid spread of browsers made servlets the technology of choice for Web site development. Chapter 4, "Application Development with JSP and Servlets," gives a good overview of this technology.

Servlets are also a good choice when money for paying licensing fees is hard to get. You can find good servlet engines that ship with an operating system or are in the public domain. Many companies are already familiar with this mature technology and they consider it to be a wise choice.

On the downside, servlet development is not for the novice. There are many issues such as sessions, cookies, and variable life cycles that can trip you up. Web servers don't provide nearly the services that newer J2EE technologies do, such as container security and automatic updating of databases.

Another drawback is the limitation placed on the user interface by the browser. Front ends can be Java applets, but the version of Java supported by browsers tends to be out-of-date. Plug-ins are available, but many systems can't assume that their user base has installed them. As a result, many clients are written using HTML, which is a weaker language for GUI development than Java.

Figure 8.3 shows the CruiseList application architecture that is used in Chapter 4.

FIGURE 8.3

The Web server is able to create additional copies of the TicketAgent servlet to handle peak volumes.

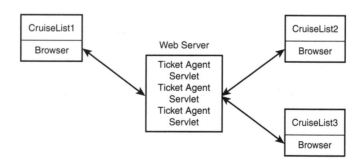

Here are a few successful implementations that have used this strategy:

- Custom order system—HTML user interfaces are used to coordinate projects that have multiple vendors, such as kitchen remodeling.
- Customer reports system—Customers access reports about their assets by going to a database.

- Online camera store—Customers buy directly from inventory using a credit card number, which is communicated over a secure HTTP connection (HTTPS).

If you have hundreds or perhaps thousands of potential users, servlets enable you to operate without installing client software on the user's machine. This may be the critical factor in deciding to go with a servlet approach.

Remote Method Invocation (RMI)

During Java's formative years, RMI was the primary method of communication between JVMs. Recently, EJBs and MDBs have surpassed RMI in popularity because they offer features such as scalability, security, and transaction processing that you must create yourself in RMI.

RMI development appeals to Java developers because it is very easy for them to learn. It ships along with the JDK, so it is free. Customers normally like it as a solution because of the cost and the fact that it is part of Java. You can use RMI to communicate with CORBA through the Internet Inter-Orb Protocol (IIOP). It is synchronous, so you can get an immediate response.

RMI has its drawbacks, though. It uses the serialization facilities of Java, which are a security risk. It also places you in a position to write a lot of code. This gives you control, but at a higher development cost than with higher-level middleware such as EJB or JMS.

Figure 8.4 shows the CruiseList application architecture that is used in Chapter 2, "Creating Applications with Remote Method Invocation (RMI)."

8

APPROACHES FOR
CHOOSING THE
RIGHT TECHNOLOGY

FIGURE 8.4

RMI enables the CruiseList client to communicate with the TicketAgent server as if it were local by using the stub that was generated.

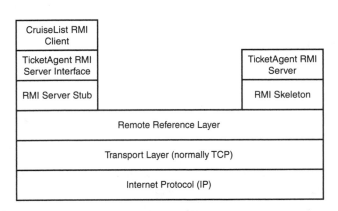

Successful implementations that have used this strategy include the following:

- Video file transfer system—This system enables an RMI client to request that a server stream a video file to it.

- Factory machine controller—This system allows a user to start a machine tool from a computer located in an office above the shop floor.

- Remote sensor reading—This system enables a user to monitor the activity in a factory from his office.

If your requirements are synchronous, but not large enough to justify the purchase of an EJB server, RMI may be a good option.

Java Naming and Directory Interface (JNDI)

JNDI is not often used to deliver data from one computer to another. It is possible to use it for this purpose because JNDI entries are serializable objects. You can create a program that places an object in the naming service. Another program can look for that object periodically and deserialize it into its own JVM and process it there. Chapter 11, "Java Naming and Directory Interface (JNDI)," covers this technology thoroughly.

If you have an EJB server or a JMS server, you most likely have a naming service installed at your site. In addition, Sun provides the reference implementation at no charge. JNDI is easy to learn, though many programmers have not used it much. It is mature, and it can be used to communicate information across platforms. The development of the object transfer is very easy because it uses Java serialization technology.

On the downside, using a JDNI server as an object swapper is a bit unorthodox, so plan on selling your idea. Many middleware applications such as the EJB server and the JMS server use a JNDI server. If you use the same JNDI server that they are using, you might degrade their performance. Remember that serializable objects often show private member variables in clear text when viewed in a text editor. Remember also that anyone with access to the server can obtain a list of the objects stored on it and the contents of any of them. For these reasons, you need to encrypt private data before placing it on the server.

Figure 8.5 shows the JNDI architecture. JNDI is covered in detail in Chapter 11.

Here are a few implementations that might use this strategy:

- Request for conference rooms—A GUI can place a request object on the server and a reservation agent program can honor the request.

- Low volume reports—A weekly report object can be placed on the server and removed after it is retrieved.

- Machine status—A machine can post its status to the JNDI server, where the monitor program can check it.

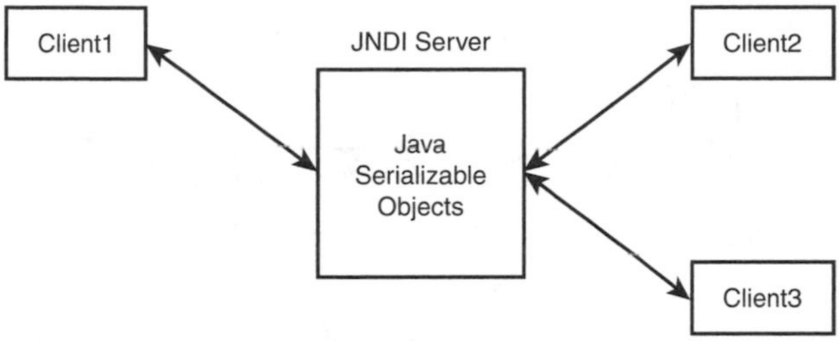

FIGURE 8.5

JNDI can serve as a repository for any serializable object.

If your requirements are asynchronous, but not large enough to justify the purchase of a JMS server, JNDI may be a good option.

JavaMail

JavaMail is composed of a pair of protocols that are able to exchange information across computer boundaries. JavaMail uses SMTP to send mail and POP to receive it. You can post nonserialized messages that contain attachments using SMTP. A program can access a POP server to retrieve them. Chapter 13, "JavaMail," shows examples of how this is done.

JavaMail and the Post Office Protocol (POP) can be used to create asynchronous applications. Almost everyone with a computer has access to mail services, so there is no incremental cost to using this mailbox to exchange information across computers. JavaMail is easy to learn, mature, and reliable. Also, complex attachments may be sent using e-mail.

Your program can leverage the built-in security of your e-mail provider to authenticate users, but transaction support is missing and would be very hard to implement. E-mail is a natural way to send computer-generated information to a human or to a heterogeneous computer.

The downside of JavaMail is its scalability. If you get too much traffic going, your e-mail provider will likely start charging you more money. In addition, JavaMail may seem like a strange solution to management if no human interaction is involved.

Figure 8.6 shows the JavaMail architecture.

Successful implementations that use this strategy include the following:

- Machine down notification—This system sends e-mail to the administrator when one of his machines does not respond.

- Unsubscribe system—This system reads all e-mail and deletes anyone from the list who has typed the word *Unsubscribe* in the subject field of an e-mail.

- Notification generator—This sends notices of upcoming meetings to a mailing list.

FIGURE 8.6

JavaMail can be used to communicate between computers and humans.

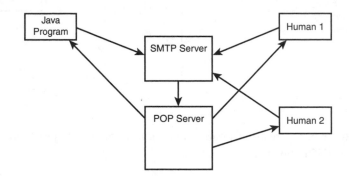

If your requirements are asynchronous and include human interaction, JavaMail may be a good option. This may also be a good solution if sending attachments is critical.

Java Message Service (JMS)

Messaging is a good way to move data from one computer to another. JMS is especially good at crossing the boundaries between platforms and programming languages. Chapter 7, "Java Message Service (JMS)," covers this technology in detail.

JMS provides guaranteed delivery of messages regardless of whether the recipient's computer is up when the message is sent. Much of the functionality needed to perform the transfer of the messages is provided with the JMS server software. Messaging is a mature and widely accepted way of communicating between machines. In addition, it scales very well.

JMS servers must be purchased. Developers with JMS experience are not especially common, but a fair number of developers know this technology. JMS is asynchronous and cannot guarantee the order in which messages will be delivered, which makes it unsuitable for some applications.

Figure 8.7 shows the JMS architecture.

Successful implementations that use JMS include the following:

- EDI message transfer—This system transfers EDI messages between a VAX and a Windows NT server.

- Video database update—This system updates a database whenever a new video is added to a library.

- CruiseList application—This example in Chapter 7 shows how to create a client-server application using JMS.

FIGURE 8.7

JMS can be used to communicate easily between heterogeneous computers.

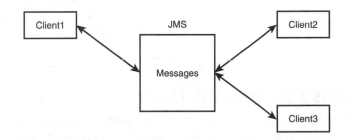

If your requirements are asynchronous and you have a lot of data and a budget to purchase software, JMS may be a good option.

Message-Driven Beans (MDB)

Message-driven bean technology is a hybrid of Java Message Service and Enterprise JavaBeans. MDBs are essentially EJBs that listen to message queues and respond when a message is posted. Chapter 6, "Message-Driven Beans (MDB)," covers this topic in detail.

If your requirements are a good fit for a JMS application and you have already purchased an EJB server such as WebLogic or WebSphere, you will likely want to use MDBs. MDBs provide the same functionality as JMS, but they scale well because of the EJB container that they reside in. You also get all the transaction, security, and database pooling services that regular EJBs receive.

If you don't already own an EJB server, the decision to use traditional JMS or MDB hinges on the scalability that you need. If scalability is not an issue, MDB is likely the more expensive route. Maturity of technology is also an issue, as MDBs were only recently introduced. Another limitation of MDBs is that they can only receive messages via the container. They must send messages using ordinary JMS classes.

Figure 8.8 shows the CruiseList MDB architecture.

Successful implementations that use MDB have yet to be written. In brief, any application that uses JMS can be converted to MDB.

If your requirements are asynchronous, you have a budget to purchase J2EE software, and you need scalability, MDB may be a good option.

FIGURE 8.8

MDBs can only receive messages via the EJB container. They must use JMS to send messages.

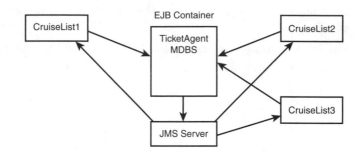

Enterprise JavaBeans (EJB)

EJBs are distributed business components that are managed by an EJB container. The container provides outstanding scalability, transactions, persistence, and security. EJBs are covered in Chapter 5, "Enterprise JavaBeans (EJB)."

EJBs are considered leading-edge technology for applications in which scalability is critical. The existence of entity beans allows the container to manage persistence to a database. This makes database applications much easier to develop. The container can also manage security and transaction support for you, so you save time in development. In general, the appeal of EJBs is that an experienced developer can use them to create a system in a very short amount of time compared to traditional approaches. They are also tolerant of change because so much of the functionality is provided by the container, presenting you with less code to change.

A budget is required if you want to use EJB technology, as the containers do carry a licensing fee. Experienced developers are in short supply and are therefore relatively expensive. Not all vendors' EJB containers are stable yet, so evaluate carefully when selecting a vendor.

Figure 8.9 shows the EJB architecture.

FIGURE 8.9

EJBs are called via the EJB container.

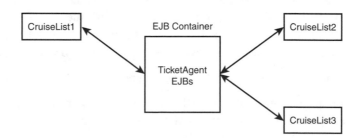

Here are a few successful implementations that use EJB:

- Hotel reservation system—This system uses JMS in a browser to enable customers to book their own rooms and rental cars.
- Airline reservation system—This system uses EJB to provide all business logic, then calls a mainframe-based system to reserve the tickets.
- Electronic commerce site—This site offers a wide variety of merchandise to customers, who use credit cards to make purchases.

If you have a budget to purchase J2EE software and if your requirements are synchronous and you need scalability, security, and transaction support, EJB may be a good option.

Web Services

Web services use the Simple Object Access Protocol (SOAP) to transfer data between heterogeneous systems. SOAP is based on XML, which makes it easy to read for both humans and machines. Chapter 9, "Web Services," covers this technology in detail.

Web services represent the very leading edge in technology. The services are free from a license standpoint. They are based on XML, so the learning curve is short for XML programmers.

The technology is not very mature and therefore not ready for large projects. Pilot projects and small implementations are feasible at the present time. Scalability, security, and transaction support are not built into the specification, so you are on your own to write them. Acceptance of this technology among programmers is building, but expect to have to convince management if you want to choose this route.

Figure 8.10 shows the Web services architecture.

FIGURE 8.10

The Web services architecture can provide a Web interface to applications.

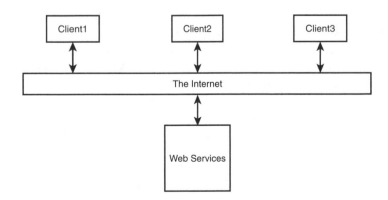

8
APPROACHES FOR
CHOOSING THE
RIGHT TECHNOLOGY

Large, successful implementations that use Web services have yet to be written. There are several areas where pilot systems are beginning to appear:

- Stock quote service—An investor retrieves a near real-time quote on his favorite stock.
- Driving directions service—A tourist retrieves directions on how to get from his hotel to points of interest.
- Raw materials service—A factory uses the service to find vendors with product available for immediate purchase.

If you want your system to be an integration gateway that connects your application to the Internet or provides a window from the Internet into your application, Web services are a good choice.

Comparing Java Technologies with CORBA

We examined all the technologies discussed in this chapter from a Java programmer's perspective. Some of them, such as JMS or JNDI, can provide asynchronous interconnection to programs written in other languages. Web services are totally agnostic about the languages that are used to create each service. Servlets, EJBs, and MDBs can use JDBC to communicate with other-language programs by sharing database tables. All these solutions are asynchronous by nature.

None of the solutions discussed in this book can provide a synchronous call and return to a program written in another language. To do this, you must use CORBA.

Java provides two ways of interfacing with CORBA—RMI/IIOP and Java/IDL. You can use either of these to call other-language subroutines and methods.

Absent the need to communicate synchronously with other-language programs, there is really no need to use these technologies. If you control all parts of the application, one of the Java-only solutions will be your best bet. If your connection to the legacy system can be asynchronous, technologies such as JDBC and JMS are easier to implement than RMI/IIOP or Java/IDL and CORBA.

Summary

In this chapter, we discussed the difficulties associated with selecting the best technology as the basis for a distributed system written in Java. We looked at the factors that you must consider when doing an evaluation.

Following that, we established a set of measurements that can be used to decide whether an approach is good for us or not. We described these criteria and explored the reasoning behind them.

Next, we looked at the most common technical approaches used by Java programmers. We considered both the outstanding qualities and the weaknesses of each technology so that you can make a fully informed decision and choose the solution that best suits your requirements. We also looked at examples of typical systems that use each approach.

Finally, we talked about the role of CORBA in the architecture of your system. We looked at situations that require one of the CORBA-friendly Java technologies.

Java Integration Technologies

PART

III

IN THIS PART

Web Services

CHAPTER 9

There is a very good chance that you have already heard something about Web services, SOAP, and their related technologies. Indeed, Web services are creating a lot of marketing hype in the industry. They are yet another technology that is presenting a rosy picture of the future of computing: the world of the Internet where any system is capable of discovering, identifying, and cooperating with any other system regardless of its underlying architecture. Of course, it is the world where we all want to be! In this chapter, we will uncover the technology underneath the hype and see how it can be used to solve your business problems today.

In the first few sections, we will see what a Web service is as well as how to create a simple Web service without getting in to too much detail. Later, we will talk about the technologies that compose a Web service: SOAP, WSDL, and UDDI. We will pay special attention to SOAP because it is the protocol that moves data from one Web service to another. We will see how the data inside a SOAP message is structured and the different types of messages that can exist. We will consider how SOAP handles various data types, exceptions, security, and so on.

Similar to other chapters of the book, we will use Cruise Booking application to demonstrate a technology. We will enhance the Cruise Booking Application to have a Web service that can process payments for the cruise tickets. The payment Web service will be built on the top of an Enterprise JavaBean (EJB). We will create a Java client that sends payments to the payment Web service. Of course, the value of our payment Web service is that it can be also accessed by systems other than Java. This will prompt us to write a .NET client that also can send payments to the payment Web service. In the process, we will talk about various interoperability issues.

Web services rely heavily on XML as the data protocol. Knowledge of XML can very helpful if you want to pay attention to how data is actually exchanged between two systems. If you have never touched XML, it would be helpful to look through an XML overview in this or any other book. The required experience with XML is minimal though because Web services have reached the point of maturity when it is possible to build them without intimate knowledge of XML. Therefore, we will not cover XML in this chapter for the sake of brevity: Such discussion would require a separate chapter.

Even though we will build a .NET client for our Web service, this chapter's goal is building Web services with Java. Therefore, the coverage of .NET technologies is very basic and is here only to show that it is in fact possible to get Java and .NET to work together.

Understanding the Web Service Approach

The world of enterprise computing has seen many distributed architectures from simple client-server TCP/IP models to elaborate leaders of today such as EJB and CORBA. Because new distributed technologies appear every few years, many companies have accumulated a bouquet of various applications running on diverse platforms and using different distributed architectures. Integration is becoming more and more difficult and is a core business for some software companies.

The situation has become even more complex with the proliferation of the Internet. Businesses have much less control over how distributed architectures are used by other businesses. Even though we can exercise some control over what is happening on our intranet, it would be impossible to do that on the Internet. Undoubtedly, the Internet has greatly increased the number of different architectures having to cooperate.

Almost all distributed architectures are based on a specific application protocol that moves data from one machine to another. For example, IIOP plays this role in CORBA, whereas Java JRMP is usually used in EJB or Java RMI systems. The application protocols are usually running on top of TCP/IP and might be responsible for a variety of things—mainly for sending method calls in a binary format along with some context data, such as security or transactional information.

Many application protocols tried to abstract away from a particular programming language. CORBA IIOP is an example of such a protocol. Unfortunately, all current application protocols either failed or were only marginally successful in interconnecting different systems. The reasons are that these protocols usually assumed advanced language features, were difficult to implement, or did not have wide support in the industry.

The situation started to change when Extensible Markup Language (XML) entered the world of computing. XML was recognized as an integration protocol from the beginning. It is simple and easily transformed by technologies like Extensible Stylesheet Language Transformations (XSLT). XML is a text protocol and can easily be interpreted by humans and parsed by the machines. XML was initially meant to substitute HTML to transfer data to the Internet browsers, so it was created to run on top of HTTP. It was quickly realized that XML needs only minor additions to be used to connect applications. These additions were made by Simple Object Access Protocol (SOAP) and other technologies. The resulting set of technologies was quickly adopted by many companies and named Web services.

9

WEB SERVICES

What Is a Web Service?

Web services is not another distributed architecture. You do not generally expect to see it to take over something like J2EE. Rather, a Web service is an integration gateway that connects your application to the Internet or provides a window from the Internet into your application.

Web services follow a client-server model: A client sends a request to a server, and the server returns a response back to the client. In this model, the role of the server is played by a Web service. Consequently, in the context of a client-server model, we might use names *Web service* and *server* interchangeably.

Web services consist of three technologies: SOAP application protocol, Web Service Description Language (WSDL), and Universal Discovery, Description, and Integration (UDDI). The three technologies complement each other. UDDI is used to find a Web service, WSDL describes how to communicate with the Web service, and SOAP transfers data between the client and the Web service.

These three core technologies are based on XML. SOAP defines XML messages that carry data, WSDL defines an XML schema that describes a Web service, and UDDI defines an XML schema that indicates where the Web service is located.

Communication between a client and a Web service is done primarily using HTTP—the same protocol that delivers Web pages to your browser. HTTP carries XML data inside its body using standard MIME messages. The Web server opens an HTTP message and passes the XML payload to whoever can handle it—our Web service. Basically, our XML data is piggybacking on top of existing HTTP Web servers.

The Web services do not necessarily have to be transmitted by HTTP. A variety of other protocols could be used and will probably be used in the future. As long as a protocol can handle text messages like XML, it can be used for Web services. However, the capability of Web services to run on top of HTTP is key to their popularity. HTTP is the engine of the Internet that moves the data from the Web server to the client Web browser. HTTP can carry text through the corporate firewalls, and it is implemented by multiple vendors.

Here is a typical flow of events that take place between a client and a Web service:

1. A client searches a UDDI server for a type of Web service—for example, a book-seller.

2. After the client decides to use a particular Web service, it goes to a location specified in UDDI to retrieve a WSDL file.

3. The client retrieves a WSDL file and generates a proxy object that can convert all Web service requests to the language of the client whether it is Java or Visual Basic.

4. The client application calls the proxy without knowing that it is a remote Web service. The proxy takes care of all translations of SOAP calls.

5. The Web service processes the SOAP messages that come from the client and translates them into the application method calls. The server application does not have to be aware of the fact that it is exposed as a Web service. It can be implemented by any existing technologies such as Java, COM+, or C.

Some of the steps might be different depending on the business scenario. For example, the UDDI step can be omitted if a WSDL file can be accessed by some other means. Imagine that company A decides that it will use company's B Web service to process credit card payments. Company B gives company A its WSDL file to describe the credit card processing Web service. Company A generates a proxy object from the WSDL file using some proxy generation tool. Once the proxy object is generated, the programmers at company A can start calling it in their development environment as if it were one of their own objects. They do need to know what language the Web service is implemented in or where the Web service resides. In this example, the UDDI registry is not used because company A only wants to integrate with company B and can do it during development time.

Web Services Strengths

Before studying the details of Web services, let's consider why they have become a popular integration technology in the enterprise. We will start with the strong points of Web services:

- Interoperability—The primary reason why Web services are stirring up the industry is that they allow different systems to work together. Interoperability of Web services is based on the ubiquity of XML and HTTP. Any company that has a Web server supports HTTP protocol. Moreover, most companies let HTTP pass through their corporate firewalls. Therefore, XML can easily pass through the firewalls inside of HTTP messages. Often, the Web server filters out any binary attachments, but XML is a text message and not considered harmful (unless the message is too large).

- Simplicity—The SOAP specification defines a relatively simple application protocol with minimal features in the spirit of the Internet itself. This was a prerequisite for many implementations to appear on the market in a relatively short time. The simplicity of SOAP is a good guarantee that we will have a choice of many cheap,

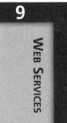

9

WEB SERVICES

stable implementations of Web services. Indeed, there are implementations of SOAP in almost any programming language that is used to process HTTP requests, such as Perl, Python, C, Java, and so on.

- Industry support—Web services (unlike Java or CORBA) are strongly supported by Microsoft. The SOAP specification is developed by a group of industry leaders. Different companies see Web services as a chance to connect different systems through a very simple mechanism on the Internet.

Tip

As with many other technologies, industry support does not necessarily lead to interoperability between different implementations. The features of the adopted specification should be your guide when deciding on whether you want to use a particular implementation of Web services.

Web Services Weaknesses

Surprisingly, Web services have their weak points. Here are some of the weaknesses that might affect your decision on whether to use them:

- Performance—This is a usual argument that is used against all new technologies, so you should look at what the performance problems might arise from. Performance of Web services is tied to these negative aspects of XML:

  XML is a text protocol; therefore, it has larger messages. This can overload the network much easier than a typical binary protocol. The text messages are easier to read for humans, but they create a burden for the machines. The SOAP specification might undertake efforts to compress messages in the future to improve the situation.

  Parsing messages is another negative side of XML. A Web service must convert binary objects to XML before sending then to the client. On the other side, the client must parse XML to create binary objects. Consequently, a lot of parsing is happening on both ends. Parsing of the text message is slower than serializing binary data, and it is memory consuming as well. The good thing is that XML has been around for a few years, and XML parsers have improved in their speed and stability.

- Lack of enterprise features—The simplicity of SOAP is its weakness in this regard. SOAP does not define any support for security, transactions, distributed garbage collection, and so on. Web services are made to serve one request at a time. This weakness prevents Web services from being called a distributed architecture. In other words, you do not really want to build your whole enterprise system as a collection of Web services—at least not at the time of this writing. There are attempts to add enterprise features to SOAP, so Web services might become better suited for the enterprise in the future.

- Novelty—Web services are going through development at the time of writing. Different SOAP implementations have interoperability problems because they interpret the specification differently. In addition, the SOAP specification is changing and other add-on specifications are evolving. This might create headaches for anybody who tries to integrate different implementations. In this fast changing environment, you are better off using a product that has an implementation of Web services proven to be interoperable with other implementations by following the specification.

Creating a Simple Web Service

In this section, we will build a simple "Hello World" Web service. This will give us a feel of what the important steps are. We will also learn how to use a Web service toolkit in order to build a Web service.

Multiple Web service toolkits are available. Some toolkits only include SOAP implementations, whereas others encompass WSDL generation, UDDI registry implementation, and utilities. CapeStudio and CapeConnect, two products offered by Cape Clear Software, can help you get your Web services running quick. CapeStudio is a graphical integrated development environment to create and deploy Web services. CapeConnect is a platform that can be used to integrate Web services with the back-end components like Java classes and Enterprise JavaBeans (EJB). We will use CapeConnect to deploy our Web services. CapeConnect has a deployment wizard that generates all the necessary plumbing code for a Java class, EJB, and so on for a Web service. The Web services are deployed on the CapeConnect server, whereas your EJBs can be located in an EJB container of your choice.

In addition to CapeConnect and CapeStudio, we will use a utility called tcp-tunnel that comes with CapeConnect. tcp-tunnel intercepts HTTP messages and displays them in a graphical screen. This utility is indispensable when you are developing and debugging a Web service because you can see XML for requests and responses.

9

WEB SERVICES

> **Note**
>
> The code for this chapter provides a readme file with instructions on how to configure and run the examples. Additionally, you can see the CapeClear documentation (located at `http://www.capeclear.com`) on how to get and set up CapeStudio and CapeConnect.
>
> You can download the code for this chapter at the Sams Publishing Web site.

> **Note**
>
> Even though all the Web services examples in this chapter are created with CapeClear products, it is possible to take the Java code and do the same steps using any other Web services toolkit.

Let's see how a simple Web service can be created. Our Web service will be based on a Java class with only one method that returns a `'Hello World Web Service'` string. We will create a Java client that calls the `hello-world` Web service.

First, we need to write a Java class. Our Web service class looks just like any other Java class. In fact, the class has no knowledge that it will be used as a Web service. Listing 9.1 shows the Java class for the simple Web service.

LISTING 9.1   A Simple Web Service Class

```
package unleashed.ch9.simple;
/**
* Simple Hello World java class
*/
public class HelloWorldWebService
{
    public String sayIt()
    {
        return "Hello Web Service";
    }
}
```

Second, the Java class that is used as a back-end component for a Web service should be archived in a JAR file with all the other classes that it might need. Our class does not need any other classes, so we will place only it into the JAR file. Use the `jar` utility to create the archive, or you can call `jarsimple.bat`, which is provided with the example:

```
jar cvf HelloWorldWS.jar unleashed/ch9/simple/HelloWorldWebService.class
```

Third, when we have a JAR file, we can create a Web service using a CapeStudio
Developer Center. As is the case with some other tools, the CapeStudio Developer Center
is capable of taking a Java class and creating all the necessary SOAP code for the Web
service. CapeStudio Developer Center bundles a WSDL generator that can create a
WSDL file from a Java class.

Open CapeStudio Developer Center, create a new project, and open Design/Generate
WSDL from the Java menu. On this screen, you need to specify the name of the Web
service, the location of the JAR file, and the location to put the WSDL file. Figure 9.1
shows the first screen.

FIGURE 9.1

*The first screen
shows the Java
classes that are
used to create a
Web service.*

The next screen shows what Java class will be exposed as a Web service. If you have
many Java classes in one JAR file, you will have to choose which classes to expose.
However, in case of our Web service, the WSDL generator determines that the only
available class in the JAR file is `unleashed.ch9.simple.HelloWorldWebService`. Figure
9.2 shows the screen of the WSDL generator.

As you click Finish, the WSDL Generator displays what files are being generated. Figure
9.3 shows the final screen of the WSDL Generator.

If the WSDL Generator reports success, you should have a WSDL file in the directory
that you specified. The WSDL file describes the Web service that we need to package
and deploy. Listing 9.2 shows the WSDL file that is generated by the CapeStudio WSDL
Generator.

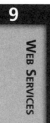

FIGURE 9.2

The component information screen shows information about a Web service.

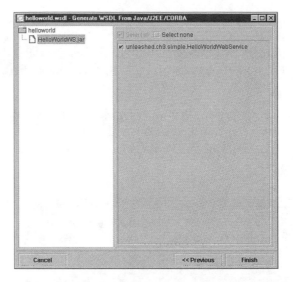

FIGURE 9.3

The final screen of the WSDL Generator shows the location of the generated WSDL file.

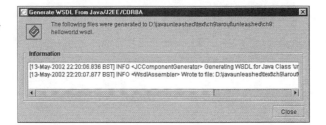

LISTING 9.2 WSDL File for a Simple Web Service

```
<?xml version="1.0" encoding="UTF-8"?>
<definitions
    name="hello"
    targetNamespace="http://www.capeclear.com/hello.wsdl"
    xmlns="http://schemas.xmlsoap.org/wsdl/"
    xmlns:soap="http://schemas.xmlsoap.org/wsdl/soap/"
    xmlns:tns="http://www.capeclear.com/hello.wsdl"
    xmlns:xsd="http://www.w3.org/2001/XMLSchema"
    xmlns:xsd1="http://www.capeclear.com/hello.xsd">
    <message name="sayIt"/>
    <message name="sayItResponse">
        <part name="return" type="xsd:string"/>
    </message>
    <portType name="HelloWorldWebService">
        <operation name="sayIt">
```

LISTING 9.2   continued

```
                <input message="tns:sayIt"/>
                <output message="tns:sayItResponse"/>
        </operation>
    </portType>
    <binding name="HelloWorldWebServiceBinding" type="tns:HelloWorldWebService">
        <soap:binding style="rpc" transport=
                ➥"http://schemas.xmlsoap.org/soap/http"/>
        <operation name="sayIt">
            <soap:operation soapAction=
                    ➥"capeconnect:hello:HelloWorldWebService#sayIt"/>
            <input>
            <soap:body
                encodingStyle="http://schemas.xmlsoap.org/soap/encoding/"
                namespace="capeconnect:hello:HelloWorldWebService"
                use="encoded"/>
            </input>
            <output>
        <soap:body
                encodingStyle="http://schemas.xmlsoap.org/soap/encoding/"
                namespace="capeconnect:hello:HelloWorldWebService"
                use="encoded"/>
        </output>
    </operation>
    </binding>
    <service name="hello">
        <documentation>hello</documentation>
        <port binding="tns:HelloWorldWebServiceBinding" name=
                ➥"HelloWorldWebService">
            <soap:address location="http://localhost:8000/ccx/hello"/>
        </port>
    </service>

</definitions>
```

In the next step, we have to package the Web service. In the CapeStudio Developer Center, click in the Deploy/Package menu. You do not have to type anything on this screen; CapeStudio will package the Web service as a WSAR file. Figure 9.4 shows the package screen.

After packaging a Web service, we can deploy it on a running CapeConnect server. First, you should start the CapeConnect server. You can do it by clicking on the CapeConnect Server shortcut in your Start menu. After you have started the server, you can go back to the Developer Center and open Deploy/Deploy Service. Figure 9.5 shows the Web service deployment screen.

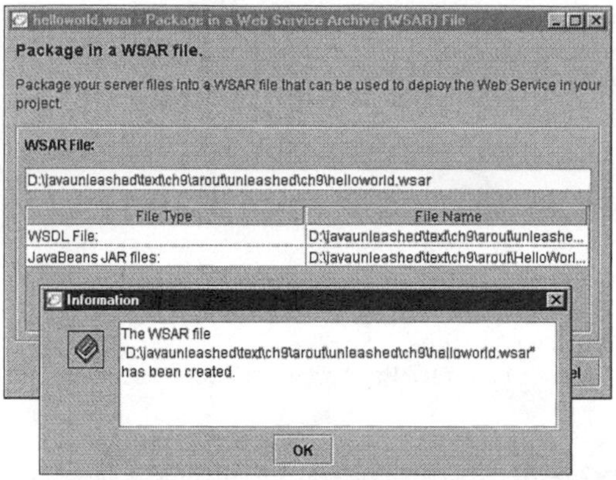

FIGURE 9.4

*The package
screen shows the
summary of
archiving the Web
service as a
WSAR file.*

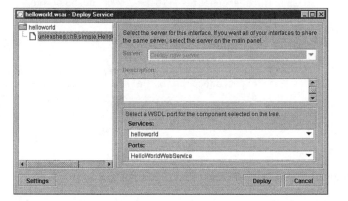

FIGURE 9.5

*The deployment
screen shows
which Web service
is being deployed.*

Finally, when the simple Web service is running on the CapeConnect server, we can create a client for it using the CapeStudio Java client generator. The client generator accepts a WSDL file from the Internet or your local machine and generates a proxy in the language of your choice. It can generate either Java or Visual Basic clients. Let's see how to create a Java proxy using the CapeStudio client generator. Open the Java client generator in the Developer Center by going to the Develop/Generate Java Client menu. Figure 9.6 shows the client generator for the "Helloworld" Web service.

CapeStudio generated four Java classes for our client:

`HelloWorldWebServiceBindingClient.java`

`HelloWorldWebServiceBindingClientFactory.java`

`HelloWorldWebServiceBindingClientImpl.java`

`HelloWorldWebServiceBindingClientMainline.java`

We can compile these classes and use them in our Java application. First, we need to call the factory class to create the Web service proxy. Once the proxy is created, we can call the Web service. Listing 9.3 shows how the Web service is called from Java.

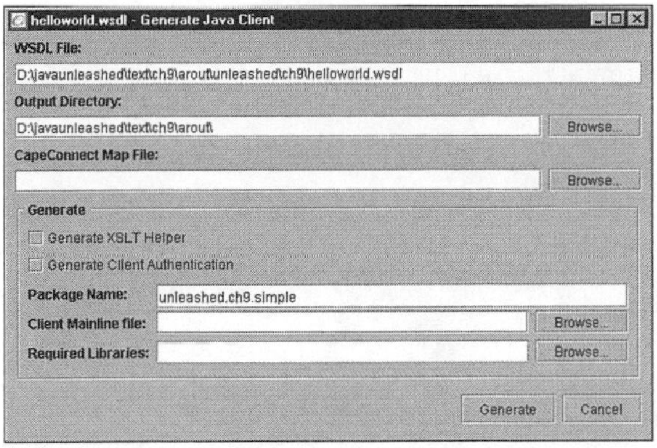

FIGURE 9.6

CapeStudio client generator creates a Java proxy for a Web service.

LISTING 9.3 Simple Web Service Client

```
package unleashed.ch9.simple;
/**
* Hello World Web Service Client
*/
public class HelloWorldWebServiceClient
{
    public static void main(String[] args)
    {
        try
        {
            callWS();
        }catch(Exception e)
        {
            e.printStackTrace();
        }

    }

    /**
    * This method calls web service proxy factory
    * to create a proxy. After the proxy is created it
    * calls its methods as if it is a local object.
    * The proxy takes care of all SOAP relevant code.
    */
    private static void callWS()
    throws Exception
    {
        System.out.println("Creating web service");


        HelloWorldWebServiceBindingClient ws =
            HelloWorldWebServiceBindingClientFactory.create();
```

LISTING 9.3 continued

```
        System.out.println("Calling web service");

        String result = ws.sayIt();

        System.out.println("Web Service returned " + result);

    }
}
```

You can see that calling the Web service is a matter of a few lines of code and is not any more difficult than calling a simple Java object.

The client runs to produce the output shown in Figure 9.7.

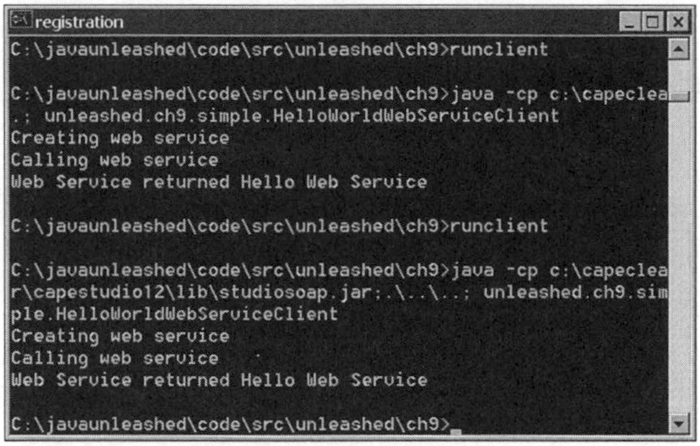

FIGURE 9.7

Calling a simple Web service produces this output.

Understanding SOAP

Web services are based on three technologies: SOAP, WSDL, and UDDI. SOAP is an XML-based protocol that moves data between a Web service and its client.

Web services do not include provisions for the secure transmission of data between the client and the server. The SOAP specification states the secure transmission is the responsibility of the underlying transport protocol whether it is HTTP or any other protocol.

Naturally, with HTTP you have an option to use the *Secure Sockets Layer (SSL)* protocol to encrypt your HTTP messages. SSL is a widely used protocol for secure transactions over the Internet. SSL can authenticate and encrypt the data that is transmitted inside HTTP packets. Because the SOAP messages are transmitted inside HTTP messages, they can get encrypted using SSL.

Let's examine the actual SOAP calls between a client and the Web service. CapeConnect includes a utility called `tcp-tunnel` that can be used to intercept SOAP messages. Use the CapeConnect documentation to configure it. Also, the `readme` file that is provided with the chapter source code explains how to configure `tcp-tunnel`. Figure 9.8 shows the intercepted SOAP messages from the `helloworld` Web service.

FIGURE 9.8

The `tcp-tunnel` *utility shows SOAP messages.*

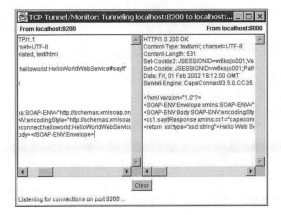

On the left side of the `tcp-tunnel` window, you can see the a SOAP request. The request is shown in Listing 9.4.

LISTING 9.4   HTTP Request with a SOAP Message

```
POST /ccx/SOAPServlet HTTP/1.1Content-Type: text/xml;
➥ charset=UTF-8accept: text/xml, multipart/related,
text/htmlContent-Length: 458SOAPAction:
➥ "capeconnect:helloworld:HelloWorldWebService#sayIt"User-Agent:
Java1.3.1Host: 142.107.253.41:8200Connection: keep-alive
<?xml version="1.0"?>
<SOAP-ENV:Envelope xmlns:SOAP-ENV="http://schemas.xmlsoap.org/soap/envelope/"
                   xmlns:xsd="http://www.w3.org/2001/XMLSchema"
                   xmlns:xsi="http://www.w3.org/2001/XMLSchema-instance"
                   xmlns:SOAP-ENC="http://schemas.xmlsoap.org/soap/encoding/">

<SOAP-ENV:Body SOAP-ENV:encodingStyle=
➥ "http://schemas.xmlsoap.org/soap/encoding/">
<cc1:sayIt xmlns:cc1="capeconnect:helloworld:HelloWorldWebService">
</cc1:sayIt></SOAP-ENV:Body></SOAP-ENV:Envelope>
```

Let's spend a little time studying the message. The top portion of Listing 9.4 is actually an HTTP header. The HTTP header has regular HTTP fields: type of request is POST,

9

WEB SERVICES

content type is text/xml, and so on. Under the HTTP header, we can see an HTTP message body that contains an XML document with a typical XML header:

```
<?xml version="1.0"?>
```

The XML header specifies the version of XML and can have the type of encoding. The SOAP message is included under the XML header. The SOAP message is shown in Listing 9.5.

LISTING 9.5   SOAP Message

```
<SOAP-ENV:Envelope
    xmlns:SOAP-ENV="http://schemas.xmlsoap.org/soap/envelope/"
    xmlns:xsd="http://www.w3.org/2001/XMLSchema"
    xmlns:xsi="http://www.w3.org/2001/XMLSchema-instance"
    xmlns:SOAP-ENC="http://schemas.xmlsoap.org/soap/encoding/">

  <SOAP-ENV:Body SOAP-ENV:encodingStyle=
  ➥ "http://schemas.xmlsoap.org/soap/encoding/">

    <cc1:sayIt xmlns:cc1="capeconnect:helloworld:HelloWorldWebService">
    </cc1:sayIt>
  </SOAP-ENV:Body>
</SOAP-ENV:Envelope>
```

The message is easy to read. In addition to XML namespace information, it has the name of the method that is called on our Java class.

```
<cc1:sayIt xmlns:cc1="capeconnect:helloworld:HelloWorldWebService"></cc1:sayIt>
```

On the right side of the tcp-tunnel window, you can see the response that the Web service sends back to the client. Listing 9.6 shows the whole response.

LISTING 9.6   HTTP Response with a SOAP Message

```
HTTP/1.0 200 OKContent-Type: text/xml;
➥ charset=UTF-8Content-Length: 531Set-Cookie2:
JSESSIONID=r23fm3xet1;Version=1;Discard;Path="/ccx"Set-Cookie:
➥ JSESSIONID=r23fm3xet1;Path=/ccxDate: Tue, 15 Jan
2002 19:15:23 GMTServlet-Engine: CapeConnect/3.5.0.CC35.651
➥ (Orcas/4.4.0, Tomcat Web Server/3.2.4)

<?xml version="1.0"?>
<SOAP-ENV:Envelope
      xmlns:SOAP-ENV="http://schemas.xmlsoap.org/soap/envelope/"
      xmlns:xsd="http://www.w3.org/2001/XMLSchema"
      xmlns:xsi="http://www.w3.org/2001/XMLSchema-instance"
      xmlns:SOAP-ENC="http://schemas.xmlsoap.org/soap/encoding/">
```

LISTING 9.6   continued

```
    <SOAP-ENV:Body SOAP-ENV:encodingStyle=
➡ "http://schemas.xmlsoap.org/soap/encoding/">

    <cc1:sayItResponse xmlns:cc1="capeconnect:helloworld:HelloWorldWebService">
        <return  xsi:type="xsd:string">Hello Web Service</return>
    </cc1:sayItResponse>

    </SOAP-ENV:Body>
</SOAP-ENV:Envelope>
```

> **Note**
>
> Our discussion of SOAP is based on version 1.1. Although this is the version used in most products, the next version of the spec is currently being developed. You can see the current version of the specification at `http://www.w3.org/TR/SOAP/`.

Again, you can see the HTTP header on the top. The HTTP header might look different from Web server to Web server, and it is not important to us. It only shows that SOAP messages do reside inside an HTTP message. The last line of Listing 9.6 actually carries the `Hello Web Service` string to our client.

You can see that even our trivial Web service produces a significant overhead in the message headers for HTTP and SOAP. The good thing is that we can easily see how the data is being represented inside the message. It will help us during development.

We have already looked at how a SOAP message gets to travel inside an HTTP message. We have also seen that a SOAP message is basically an XML document. A SOAP message consists of a few XML elements shown on Figure 9.9.

FIGURE 9.9

A SOAP message consists of these elements.

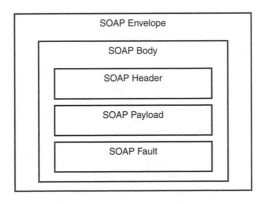

9

WEB SERVICES

The message has these parts:

- SOAP envelope—This is the top XML element that includes the whole message.
- SOAP body—This contains the data being transmitted. The body can contain the payload or an error message. Error messages are called SOAP faults.
- SOAP header—This can contain security information such as the session ID for the SOAP client, username, password, and so on.
- SOAP payload—This contains the actual data.
- SOAP fault—This contains an error code, description, and details. You'll see an example of the SOAP error messages in the upcoming "SOAP Error Messages" section.

> **Tip**
>
> Use the SOAP 1.1 message validator at `http://validator.soapware.org` to identify potential interoperability problems. You should test your server for SOAP 1.1 specification compatibility before exposing your system to your clients.

Creating a Payment Web Service

As you saw with the simple Web service example, Web services can be easily built on top of Java technologies. Naturally, Web services are good at providing gateways for other systems. The Cruise Booking Application is used throughout the book to demonstrate various Java technologies. This application is composed of a number of components that we develop in different chapters. One of the Cruise Booking Application components is a credit card payment component. In this chapter, we will separate the credit card payment component as a Web service. Implementing it as a Web service will help us see more advanced features of SOAP, WSDL, and UDDI.

A credit card payment system is a good candidate for a Web service. When a cruise ticket is booked, all we want is to pass the credit card number, the cardholder's name, expiration date, and the amount to some other service that will credit the card for that amount. The component might be located somewhere on the Internet to accept payments from many subscribers—for example, book retailers. The component can also charge a small fee for each transaction so that it can bring us additional revenue. Because we want our payment component to be contacted by any system on the Internet, it is well-suited to be implemented as a Web service. The payment component in the Cruise Booking can exist as a standalone Web service and be called by various clients including Java and Microsoft .NET.

The payment component is an EJB that processes credit card transactions. Follow the steps provided in the `readme` file to compile and deploy the payment EJB on a WebLogic Server 6.1. The WebLogic Server should be referenced in CapeConnect so that we can point to it when we are deploying the payment Web service. In order to reference the WebLogic Server, you need to open the CapeConnect Server console and go to the Edit\Server Settings menu. Select the weblogic_61 server entry and click on the Edit button. Figure 9.10 shows the configuration screen for WebLogic 6.1. The name of the host machine will be different for your installation of WebLogic.

FIGURE 9.10

Configuring CapeConnect to call an EJB that is deployed on a WebLogic Application Server.

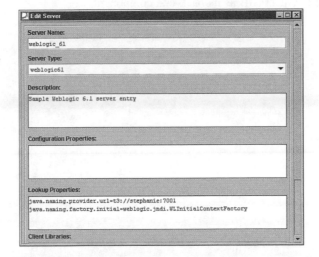

Note

See the `readme` file provided with this chapter source code on how to build and deploy the payment EJB.

After the payment EJB is deployed on your WebLogic Server and running, we need to generate a WSDL file for the Payment Web service. We can expose the payment EJB as a Web service using CapeStudio Developer Center. We will follow the steps outlined in the preceding simple Web service example to create a WSDL file, package and deploy the Web service on the CapeConnect server. We will also register the payment component in our UDDI registry.

9

WEB SERVICES

> **Note**
>
> See Chapter 5, "Enterprise JavaBeans (EJB)," for information on how to write and deploy Enterprise JavaBeans. The source code for this chapter provides a working payment EJB.

Figure 9.11 shows the CapeStudio WSDL Generation Wizard. As you can see, this Web service uses the payment EJB as its back-end component.

FIGURE 9.11

The WSDL Generator in CapeStudio.

After the WSDL file is generated, you can package and deploy the Web service following the steps in the `"Hello World"` example or using the `readme` file provided with the chapter source code. Deploying a Web service that calls an EJB in WebLogic is slightly different from the `"Hello World"` example because you have to specify the server. Figure 9.12 shows that we need to select weblogic_61 from the list of servers in the Deploy Service screen.

After the Web service is deployed, you can publish it in the CapeConnect UDDI registry. To log in to the UDDI registry, click on the Deploy/Publish to UDDI menu in the CapeStudio Developer Center. The login screen is shown in Figure 9.13.

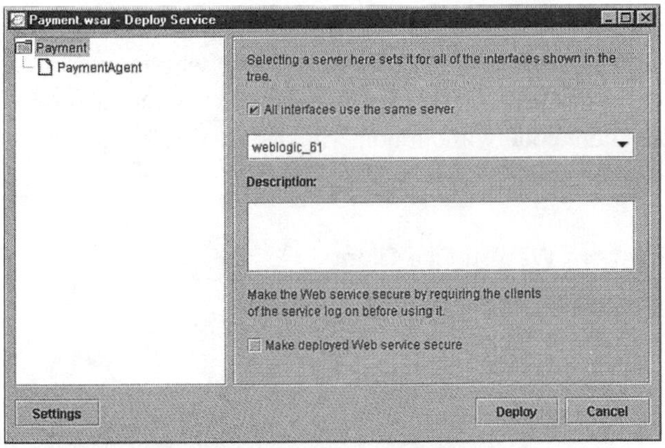

FIGURE 9.12

Selecting the WebLogic Server in the Deploy Service screen tells CapeConnect server to call our Payment EJB.

FIGURE 9.13

The login and publish payment Web service in the UDDI registry.

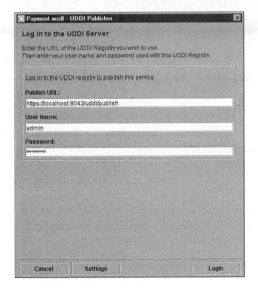

To test the payment Web service, we use the CapeStudio Developer Center to generate a Java client. You need to go to the Develop\Generate Java Client menu to generate all the necessary classes. This step is similar to the `"HelloWorld"` Web service example.

Similarly to the `"HelloWorld"` Web service, CapeStudio generates four proxy classes: `PaymentAgentBindingClient`, `PaymentAgentBindingClientFactory`, `PaymentAgentBindingClientImpl`, and `PaymentAgentBindingClientMainline`. You are free to change the names or code in these classes. Specifically, you might want to change the URL or port number of your Web service in the `PaymentAgentBindingClientFactory` class.

All we need to do now is write a client that calls the payment Web service. The client, as well as the generated classes, can be sent to anybody who is interested in calling the payment Web service from Java. Of course, potential clients can also find our UDDI registry and generate the client code without bothering us. Listing 9.7 shows the code for our payment Web service client in Java.

LISTING 9.7   Payment Web Service Client

```java
package unleashed.ch9.payment;
/**
 * PaymentAgentBindingClient
 */
public class PaymentAgentClient
{
    public  static void main(String args[])
    {
        if (args.length != 4)
        {
            System.out.println("USAGE: PaymentAgentClient CreditCardName
➡ CreditCardNumber ExpiryDate Amount");
            System.exit(1);
        }
        try
        {
            CreditCardInfo info = new CreditCardInfo(args[0], args[1],
➡args[2], Double.parseDouble(args[3]));
            PaymentAgentClient client = new PaymentAgentClient();

            client.processPayment(info);

        }catch(Exception e)
        {
            e.printStackTrace();
        }
    }


    public void processPayment(CreditCardInfo info)
    throws java.rmi.RemoteException, java.net.MalformedURLException
    {
        PaymentAgentBindingClient client =
➡ PaymentAgentBindingClientFactory.create();
        System.out.println("PaymentAgent web service proxy is created");
        System.out.println("Processing payment for " + info.toString());
        client.processPayment(info);
    }

}
```

The client calls the Web service in the processPayment method. It calls the factory to create a proxy object. Then it calls the proxy to actually process the payment.

Execute the runpaymentclient.bat file to run the payment client on Windows. Listing 9.8 shows the client output.

LISTING 9.8 Payment Client Output

```
PaymentAgent web service proxy is created
Processing payment for Credit Card Name: VISA Credit Card
Number: 1234567890123456 Expiry Date 12122004 Amount 30.0
```

On a console that runs our WebLogic Server, we can see the output produced by the payment EJB:

```
Processing CreditCard VISA Number: 1234567890123456 Amount: 30.0
```

We will create a Microsoft client using .NET in the "Integrating with .NET" section of the chapter.

SOAP Error Messages

The SOAP error message can be returned inside the SOAP body. A SOAP error message is returned if the server cannot process the request for a number of reasons. The errors are generally classified as follows:

- VersionMismatch—This error is caused by some problem with the envelope namespace. For example, the XML namespace in the SOAP envelope can be incorrect. You can see several namespaces provided in the SOAP Envelope message element. A namespace declaration looks like this:

      xmlns:SOAP-ENV="http://schemas.xmlsoap.org/soap/envelope/"

- Client—The server cannot process the XML in the request. The XML might be invalid, or there is no component that can process this request on the server.

- MustUnderstand—If the SOAP attribute mustUnderstand is set to 1 but the server cannot process the request, this type of error will occur. The problem could be with a server's SOAP processing capabilities or security concerns. Basically, this means that the client and the server do not understand each other.

- Server—The request is valid, but the server cannot process it because of some server-side problems. For example, lack of resources on the server could cause this type of error.

The payment Web service returns a SOAP fault if the credit card number does not have the correct length. Listing 9.9 shows a portion of the error message:

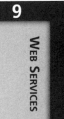

9

WEB SERVICES

LISTING 9.9 SOAP Fault

```
<?xml version="1.0"?>

<SOAP-ENV:Envelope
    xmlns:SOAP-ENV="http://schemas.xmlsoap.org/soap/envelope/"
    xmlns:xsd="http://www.w3.org/2001/XMLSchema"
    xmlns:cc1="http://www.capeclear.com/Payment.xsd"
    xmlns:xsi="http://www.w3.org/2001/XMLSchema-instance"
    xmlns:SOAP-ENC="http://schemas.xmlsoap.org/soap/encoding/">

<SOAP-ENV:Body
    SOAP-ENV:encodingStyle="http://schemas.xmlsoap.org/soap/encoding/">

<SOAP-ENV:Fault>
    <faultcode  xsi:type="xsd:string">SOAP-ENV:Client</faultcode>
    <faultstring  xsi:type="xsd:string">Credit Card Number Invalid&#xa;
        &#xa;Start server side stack trace:&#xa;
        unleashed.ch9.payment.PaymentException: Credit
➥ Card Number Invalid&#xd;&#xa;
        at unleashed.ch9.payment.PaymentAgentEJB.processPayment
➥ (PaymentAgentEJB.java:31)&#xd;&#xa;
        ......
    </faultstring>

    <faultactor  xsi:type="xsd:string">capeconnect:dispatch:dispatcher
    </faultactor>
  <detail>
   <exception>
   <type  xsi:type="xsd:string">unleashed.ch9.payment.PaymentException</type>
   <value>
   <detailMessage  xsi:type="xsd:string">Credit Card Number Invalid&#xa;
        &#xa;Start server side stack trace:&#xa;
        unleashed.ch9.payment.PaymentException:
➥ Credit Card Number Invalid&#xd;&#xa;
        at unleashed.ch9.payment.PaymentAgentEJB.processPayment
➥ (PaymentAgentEJB.java:31)&#xd;&#xa;
        ....
        End  server side stack trace&#xa;
   </detailMessage></value>
   <stacktrace  xsi:type="xsd:string">
        unleashed.ch9.payment.PaymentException:
➥ Credit Card Number Invalid&#xa;
        &#xa;Start server side stack trace:&#xa;
        unleashed.ch9.payment.PaymentException:
➥ Credit Card Number Invalid&#xd;&#xa;
        at unleashed.ch9.payment.PaymentAgentEJB.processPayment
➥ (PaymentAgentEJB.java:31)&#xd;&#xa;
        ....
   </stacktrace>
```

LISTING 9.9   continued

```
    </exception>
    </detail>
</SOAP-ENV:Fault>
</SOAP-ENV:Body>
</SOAP-ENV:Envelope>
```

The error message has these elements:

- `faultcode`—This element contains the code of the error. The code uses the preceding error classification. For example, all client codes start with the prefix `Client`. After the error classification, the code can further append additional error codes: `Client.XMLERROR`.

- `faultstring`—This is a description for the error.

- `faultactor`—This element points to the URI of the source of the error. This is necessary to determine the exact location of the server that has generated the error.

- `detail`—The detail element can specify additional information about the error. For example, it might contain an exception trace.

> **Tip**
>
> Unfortunately, SOAP error messages are not always translated correctly into exceptions on your client. It is a good idea to intercept SOAP messages to see the exact error description. You can use the `tcp-tunnel` utility provided with CapeConnect to see the SOAP messages. The CapeConnect documentation explains how to set up and use `tcp-tunnel`.

SOAP Data Types

Because SOAP is used primarily to transfer data, it is important to know what data types are supported. SOAP supports a pretty standard set of simple data types that are described in the SOAP encoding schema at `http://schemas.xmlsoap.org/soap/encoding`. You will find support for `boolean`, `int`, `short`, `long`, `string`, `float`, `date`, and so on.

In addition to the simple data types, the SOAP specification describes how to handle complex data types. Complex data types are typical objects that any Java application operates on. Our payment Web service has a class `CreditCardInfo` that is described in SOAP as a complex data type. Listing 9.10 shows how the credit card info is represented in SOAP.

LISTING 9.10   Credit Card Info as a SOAP Complex Data Type

```
<SOAP-ENV:Body SOAP-ENV:encodingStyle=
➡ "http://schemas.xmlsoap.org/soap/encoding/">
<cc3:processPayment xmlns:cc3="capeconnect:Payment:PaymentAgent">

<arg0  xsi:type="cc1:CreditCardInfo">
<ccName  xsi:type="xsd:string">VISA</ccName>
<ccNumber  xsi:type="xsd:string">1234567890123456</ccNumber>
<ccExpiry  xsi:type="xsd:string">12122004</ccExpiry>
<amount  xsi:type="xsd:double">30.0</amount>
</arg0>

</cc3:processPayment>
</SOAP-ENV:Body>
</SOAP-ENV:Envelope>
```

As you can see, the complex data type is based on simple ones. Our credit card info uses strings to represent the credit card name, credit card number, and expiration date. `double` represents the amount.

Complex data types are defined in the WSDL file so that the client knows how to handle them. We will see how credit card info is defined in the payment WSDL file in the next section.

> **Tip**
>
> Be sure to check what simple data types are supported by the specific SOAP toolkit you are planning to use. Also test support for complex data types. Various toolkits might have interoperability issues because they implement complex data types support differently.

Understanding WSDL

Web Service Description Language (WSDL; often pronounced *wizdel*) is a mechanism to describe any network services, including Web services. The WSDL specification defines Web service as an endpoint. WSDL describes endpoints that can operate on document-oriented or procedure-oriented messages.

WSDL is created to be extensible enough to describe endpoints regardless of the transmission protocol. However, the current specification defines only how to use WSDL with SOAP 1.1, HTTP GET/POST, and MIME.

Listing 9.11 illustrates the payment Web service WSDL file.

LISTING 9.11   Payment Web Service WSDL File

```
<?xml version="1.0" encoding="UTF-8"?>
<definitions
    name="Payment"
    targetNamespace="http://www.capeclear.com/Payment.wsdl"
    xmlns="http://schemas.xmlsoap.org/wsdl/"
    xmlns:soap="http://schemas.xmlsoap.org/wsdl/soap/"
    xmlns:tns="http://www.capeclear.com/Payment.wsdl"
    xmlns:xsd="http://www.w3.org/2001/XMLSchema"
    xmlns:xsd1="http://www.capeclear.com/Payment.xsd">
    <types>
        <xsd:schema
            targetNamespace="http://www.capeclear.com/Payment.xsd"
            xmlns:SOAP-ENC="http://schemas.xmlsoap.org/soap/encoding/"
            xmlns:wsdl="http://schemas.xmlsoap.org/wsdl/"
            xmlns:xsd="http://www.w3.org/2001/XMLSchema">
            <xsd:complexType name="CreditCardInfo">
                <xsd:sequence>
                    <xsd:element
                        maxOccurs="1"
                        minOccurs="1"
                        name="ccName"
                        nillable="true"
                        type="xsd:string"/>
                    <xsd:element
                        maxOccurs="1"
                        minOccurs="1"
                        name="ccNumber"
                        nillable="true"
                        type="xsd:string"/>
                    <xsd:element
                        maxOccurs="1"
                        minOccurs="1"
                        name="ccExpiry"
                        nillable="true"
                        type="xsd:string"/>
                </xsd:sequence>
            </xsd:complexType>
        </xsd:schema>
    </types>
    <message name="processPayment">
        <part name="arg0" type="xsd1:CreditCardInfo"/>
    </message>
    <message name="processPaymentResponse"/>
    <portType name="PaymentAgent">
        <operation name="processPayment">
            <input message="tns:processPayment"/>
            <output message="tns:processPaymentResponse"/>
        </operation>
    </portType>
```

9

WEB SERVICES

LISTING **9.11** continued

```
    <binding name="PaymentAgentBinding" type="tns:PaymentAgent">
        <soap:binding style="rpc"
➥ transport="http://schemas.xmlsoap.org/soap/http"/>
        <operation name="processPayment">
            <soap:operation soapAction="capeconnect:Payment:
➥ PaymentAgent#processPayment"/>
            <input>
                <soap:body
➥ encodingStyle="http://schemas.xmlsoap.org/soap/encoding/"
                    namespace="capeconnect:Payment:PaymentAgent"
                    use="encoded"/>
            </input>
            <output>
                <soap:body
➥encodingStyle="http://schemas.xmlsoap.org/soap/encoding/"
                    namespace="capeconnect:Payment:PaymentAgent"
                    use="encoded"/>
            </output>
        </operation>
    </binding>
    <service name="Payment">
        <documentation>Payment service</documentation>
        <port binding="tns:PaymentAgentBinding" name="PaymentAgent">
<soap:address location="http://142.107.253.41:8000/ccx/SOAPServlet"/>
        </port>
    </service>

</definitions>
```

As you can see, it is an XML document that has a typical XML header:

```
<?xml version="1.0" encoding="UTF-8"?>
```

The rest of the document consists of the following elements:

- `types`—This element describes all data types that are used in the messages. The simple types are defined in `xsd` namespace in this line:

  ```
  xmlns:xsd=http://www.w3.org/2001/XMLSchema
  ```

  Complex types are broken down to the simple types, so the WSDL document carries the definition of all complex types used for communication. This makes a Web service independent of any particular type definition. Our `CreditCardInfo` type is shown in Listing 9.12.

LISTING 9.12   A Complex Data Type in WSDL

```
<xsd:complexType name="CreditCardInfo">
            <xsd:sequence>
                <xsd:element
                    maxOccurs="1"
                    minOccurs="1"
                    name="ccName"
                    nillable="true"
                    type="xsd:string"/>
                <xsd:element
                    maxOccurs="1"
                    minOccurs="1"
                    name="ccNumber"
                    nillable="true"
                    type="xsd:string"/>
                <xsd:element
                    maxOccurs="1"
                    minOccurs="1"
                    name="ccExpiry"
                    nillable="true"
                    type="xsd:string"/>
            </xsd:sequence>
        </xsd:complexType>
```

- message—The message element describes all messages that a Web service accepts.

- portType—This element describes operations in which each operation can have input and output messages. These basically are the methods that can be called by the client, and their possible responses.

- binding—This element specifies what protocol is used for each operation.

- service—This element represents a set of communication endpoints, where each endpoint is represented by a single port element:

```
<port binding="tns:PaymentAgentBinding" name="PaymentAgent">
<soap:address location="http://142.107.253.41:8000/ccx/SOAPServlet"/>
</port>
```

In this case, the port element has a URL of the payment Web service.

Understanding UDDI

Basically, UDDI is a mechanism that can be used to locate and describe Web services. UDDI is supposed to serve a sort of business directory on the Internet. UDDI can be used and viewed by humans if the directory has a front end to it. It can also be called by applications because it has Application Programming Interfaces (APIs). UDDI provides a lookup capability to resources across the Internet.

> **Note**
>
> UDDI is not the only standard that aspires to be the yellow pages of the Internet. Similar technologies are being promoted by different companies and groups. You might run across Discovery of Web services (DISCO), ebXML, and other acronyms. Nonetheless, this chapter concentrates on UDDI because it seems to be the leading standard as of this writing.

UDDI is associated with a UDDI registry in which a business can enlist itself. The following three types of entries are available:

- White pages represent an alphabetical list of businesses in a very similar manner to the regular white pages. Each entry can have a name, address, contact information, and so on.

- Yellow pages list businesses by categories just like the phone yellow pages. The categories are following a set of standard codes like industry codes, geography codes, and business identification codes. The categories are well suited for indexing and searching.

- Green pages describe technical information about Web services. They would typically contain a URL of the WSDL file.

UDDI registries can propagate their entries to other registries, creating a net of nodes. The system is distributed and decentralized just like the Internet itself. This is one of the appealing features because the registry does not have to depend on one particular server or location.

UDDI is based on XML in the way that its internal structure is represented by XML. All entries are essentially XML elements.

XML is also used to access UDDI. The API for UDDI is defined in terms of SOAP messages, which makes UDDI another Web service.

The next sections discuss these two features in more detail.

UDDI Data Structures

The UDDI registry is described in XML elements. UDDI 2.0 defines these five elements:

- `businessEntity` is a top-level data element that contains descriptive information about a business for white and yellow pages. The `businessEntity` element contains a unique key for the registry entry.

- `businessService` represents a service that the business provides. Multiple `businessService` elements can belong to one `businessEntity` element. The `businessService` element contains a unique identifier for the service, a readable name, and a `bindingTemplate` element.

- `bindingTemplate` structure describes how a Web service can be invoked. The `bindingTemplate` includes a unique binding key, the `accessPoint`, and `tModelInstanceDetails`. The `accessPoint` can be any of the possible ways to access the Web service, like a URL.

- `tModel` contains a technical specification of a Web service. UDDI specification defines `tModel` as a broad set of metadata for any type of a Web service. However, `tModel` typically contains a URL of the WSDL file that can give a more precise description.

- `publisherAssertion` is essentially a link to another `businessEntity` entry in the directory. This is a structure that was introduced in the latest UDDI specification. It exists because many businesses can have multiple `businessEntity` entries—for example, for each company division or product line. In this case, different `businessEntity` entries want to point to each other using the `publishedAssertion` structure.

All the UDDI elements are combined in a structure as shown in Figure 9.14.

FIGURE 9.14
The UDDI registry contains five elements.

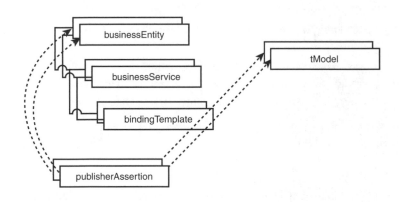

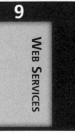

A UDDI registry contains XML elements of five different types. The 3D effect in Figure 9.14 shows that there can be multiple instances of every XML element in the registry.

UDDI APIs

UDDI API is slightly different from a typical programming language API. The API is a set of XML messages that a UDDI server should be able to process. The UDDI APIs are defined as two sets of messages: publish and inquiry.

Publish messages have these subtypes:

- Update messages save or update an entry in a UDDI registry. There is an update message for each type of UDDI data structure in which the name of a message differs based on the type that it updates. For example, the save_business message saves businessEntity, and the save_service message updates businessService. Each type of message contains an authentication token plus the data structure—for example, businessEntity. Alternatively, the update message can pass a URL that returns an HTTP response with a data structure inside. The HTTP response must only contain an XML of the relevant data structure—for example, businessService.

- Delete messages do exactly that—delete UDDI entries. There are also different types of delete messages for all types of data structures. The type of data structure is in the name of the message. For example, delete_business deletes businessEntity, and delete_service deletes businessService. Delete messages contain unique keys that identify the data structures: for example, delete_ business accepts the businessKey element.

Additionally, a UDDI registry can process these authentication messages:

- get_authToken returns an authentication token that can be used in update messages. This message authenticates the client and is conceptually similar to a user login.

- discard_authToken informs a UDDI registry that the authentication token is not valid.

- get_registeredInfo returns information about the entries that a client has saved or deleted in the registry. It returns a unique identifier of the data elements—for example, business key for a business entity data element.

Implementation of these is optional, and a registry can have other authentication mechanisms.

Inquiry messages are used to find a UDDI entry. Inquiry messages have these subtypes:

- Find messages represent simple queries that can be issued against a registry. For example, find_business can be issued to search for a businessEntity entry. The find_business message can contain any partial information about a business entity. The registry returns a businessList message that contains one or more business keys for business entities found by the query. The default behavior of a query can be changed by an optional findQualifiers element. For example, exactNameMatch specifies to search for an exact match, and so on. The find messages can also specify the number of results to be returned by a maxRow attribute.

- Get messages provide a method to retrieve an element by the unique key. After a client issues a find message, it might decide to use a get message to retrieve the entry. There are get messages for all types of elements: `get_businessDetail`, `get_serviceDetail`, `get_bindingDetail`, and `get_tModelDetail`.

By using the preceding update messages, a Web service can register itself in a UDDI registry. To find a Web service in a UDDI registry, a client application would issue a find message. Then the client would issue a get message to retrieve particular entry about a Web service. The client is particularly interested in a `bindingTemplate` entry because it describes how to call the Web service and gives a WSDL file that the client needs to generate a proxy.

Integrating with .NET

Microsoft markets .NET as a primary platform to create Web services. The platform encompasses changes to the well-known tools for the Windows family of operating systems: Visual Basic, Visual C++, and so on. Plus, .NET has some very important additions: the new programming language C# that looks very much like Java, a common language runtime—again, conceptually similar to JVM—and other technologies. Undoubtedly, .NET is promoting very popular ideas, like language independence, advanced object-oriented features, and so on. Much of what .NET is promising has already existed in Java for some time though. So Microsoft will have to try hard to lure developers from the existing features of Java to the new features of .NET.

> **Note**
>
> This section, dedicated to the .NET platform, is not an attempt to cover it in any sufficient detail. It is a very a short overview on how to write a payment Web service client in .NET. Please see Microsoft's Web site at `http://msdn.microsoft.com/net` for more information about .NET.

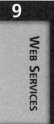

Microsoft has been playing a major role in making Web services a popular new technology. For many, Web services is a hope to put Microsoft solutions under one roof with the rest of the distributed architectures such as EJB and CORBA. Consequently, integration of a Java Web service with a .NET client is a very important proof of concept.

Let's write a simple Visual Basic application that sends credit card payments to our payment Web service. This is pretty easy, even for somebody who only writes Java for a living. We will use Visual Studio .NET to create a new project as a standalone Visual Basic Windows application.

First thing that we need to do is to create a Web Reference for our payment Web service. Web Reference is a proxy object that hides all SOAP code from you. Remember, when we created a Java client for a Web service, we had proxy files generated by CapeStudio. Visual Basic's Web reference is conceptually very similar to those Java proxy classes.

Click on the Project/Add Web Reference menu to create a Web reference. It will open a UDDI browser that you can use to see any Web services available on the Internet. We only need to go to our local CapeClear UDDI registry and search for Web service Payment. The entry in UDDI has a link to the WSDL file. Figure 9.15 shows the WSDL file for the payment Web service.

FIGURE 9.15

The payment WSDL file in .NET.

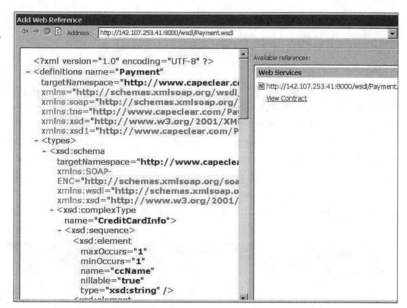

After we create the Web reference, we need to place the necessary controls on to the form. We will need controls for all the fields in our CreditCardInfo class: credit card name, credit card number, expiration date, and amount. See Figure 9.14 for the final look of the form. Visual Basic provides a user-friendly interface to arrange the controls, so user interface design is an easy step. Once you get the controls in order, double-click on the Submit button. This will open the event handler portion of the code. The code in Listing 9.13 shows the event handler that calls the payment Web service and shows the resulting message.

LISTING 9.13 Calling a Web Service from .NET

```
Private Sub Button1_Click(ByVal sender As System.Object, ByVal e
➥As System.EventArgs) Handles Button1.Click
        Dim ccName As String
        Dim ccNumber As String
        Dim ccExpiryDate As String
        Dim amount As Double
        ccName = ComboBox1.Text

        Dim paymentAgent As New WebReference1.Payment()
        Dim cci As New WebReference1.CreditCardInfo()
        cci.ccName = ComboBox1.Text
        cci.ccNumber = TextBox1.Text
        cci.ccExpiry = exDatePicker.Value
        cci.amount = TextBox2.Text
        paymentAgent.processPayment(cci)

        MsgBox("Payment Processed")
    End Sub
```

The code is doing things that are similar to the Java clients that we had written before. We create a new Web reference, get the data from the text boxes, and call the Web reference's `processPayment` method. As you can see, the Web reference looks like another object in Visual Basic.

That's it. We can run our Visual Basic and submit a payment or two. Figure 9.16 shows the running client.

FIGURE 9.16

The .NET client calling a payment Web service.

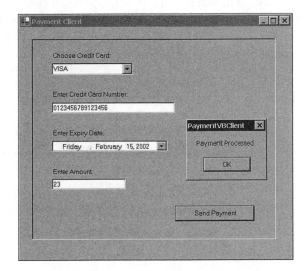

9

WEB SERVICES

Of course, our code does not handle any exceptions or error checking, but all in all integrating a Visual Basic client with a Java Web service is a relatively painless exercise.

Summary

Web services have taken the industry by storm. They have offered an enticing model that connects business application across the Internet. They are based on powerful, simple, and ubiquitous technologies: XML and HTTP. XML is an ASCII data protocol that is based on an open and easy-to-use specification. XML organizes data in Web services. HTTP is an application protocol that serves Web pages on the Internet. It is also simple and can carry a text message to any Web server. HTTP has been assigned a standard port that is not closed by corporate firewalls. This makes it one of the best-suited media to transfer business data. HTTP can also use SSL to encrypt messages, providing security for Web services.

Web services consist of three cooperating technologies: SOAP, WSDL, and UDDI. All three are based on open specifications that are developed by a group of companies. They are based on XML.

SOAP is an application protocol that defines how the data is organized in a request and response. SOAP can transmit both simple and complex data types.

WSDL is an XML structure that describes a Web service. It specifies exactly what the names of methods are, what argument it needs, and what the return data type is.

Finally, UDDI is a mechanism to locate Web services. UDDI can have white pages in which businesses are presented by their names, yellow pages in which businesses are categorized according to a known taxonomy, and green pages in which technical information about Web services is given. UDDI simply describes a Web service and points to a URL of the service WSDL file.

Web services are a promising integration architecture. The simplicity of all three technologies has resulted in many implementations of SOAP processors, WSDL generators, and UDDI registries. In this chapter, we used the products provided by CapeClear Software to create a payment Web service for our Cruise Booking application. We created a payment EJB, configured it as a Web service on a CapeConnect server, and used CapeStudio to create Java and Visual Basic .NET clients.

JDBC and Databases

CHAPTER 10

IN THIS CHAPTER

A few innovations in the computing world stand out above the rest. Hard drives allowed machines to boot without an operator. Online access got rid of paper tape and punch cards. GUIs opened the world of computing to the masses.

Right up there with these innovations is the database management system (DBMS). The DBMS is a marvel of software engineering. It allows an amazing amount of data to be stored and retrieved quickly. It is hard to spend a day in the modern world without causing some database somewhere to be accessed. If you write a check, a database looks you up in the deadbeat table. If you buy gas, the credit card company database is hit. If you get cash to buy the gas, the bank's database is hit to make the withdrawal.

To Java programmers, a database is a great friend. By using the logic that already resides in the DBMS, we can bypass many concurrency and security issues that would swamp our projects. JDBC, sometimes called Java Database Connectivity, makes programmatic access to databases simple.

There are many good books that cover basic JDBC. In this chapter we will concentrate on such topics as batch processing, using J2EE servers with JDBC, and transaction processing.

Why JDBC?

In the days of MS-DOS, printing was a real problem. Every program that you purchased talked directly to the printer. This meant that every time you installed new software, you were thrust (kicking and screaming) into the world of printer drivers. It was such a relief when the Windows operating system took over responsibility for these drivers. System administrators could set up the printer once and all other programs could use it via this setup.

At the same time, the world of database integration was just as difficult for the programmer. Each DBMS provided an API (if we were lucky) to the programmer. The programmer learned the API and wrote programs using it. If he needed to work with another database management system, it meant learning another API.

The solution to this problem was similar to the printer driver solution. An open standard called Open Database Connectivity (ODBC) was created. This enabled the installation of one driver for each DBMS that you needed to communicate with. Your program could then make a connection to the driver and the driver would handle the details of the connection for you. At first this connection was slower, but over time the drivers improved and programmers got better at using them wisely.

When Java came on the scene in the mid-1990s, the lessons learned from ODBC were applied to the design of JDBC, but with a Java flavor, of course. Special driver classes were written that created connections between programs and DBMSs. Java programmers placed commands in their code to instantiate the drivers, which were then used to instantiate the connection.

JDBC doesn't implement its own SQL version the way that some ODBC drivers do. It allows you to pass SQL to the database without translation. This is good in that it avoids introducing yet another dialect of SQL. It does limit the portability of the code across DBMS platforms if you use some of the unique features of a DBMS, such as stored procedures.

How JDBC Works

Most of us learned to write JDBC programs by copying or typing a few strange-looking lines of code that somehow got us a connection to the database. Then we added our own DBMS access command logic to get the data that we needed. In this section we will look at those mystery lines and attempt to make sense of them. First, let's look at the example shown in Listing 10.1.

LISTING 10.1   The JDBCConnection Class

```
/*
 * JDBCConnection.java
 *
 * Created on December 26, 2001, 2:27 PM
 * This program makes a connection to a database
 * using a JDBC driver
 */

package unleashed.ch10;
import java.sql.*;

/**
 *
 * @author   Stephen Potts
 * @version 1.0
 */
public class JDBCConnection
{

    /** Default Constructor */
    public JDBCConnection()
    {
    }

    public static void main(String[] args)
```

LISTING 10.1 continued

```
{
    try
    {
        //load the driver class
        Class.forName("sun.jdbc.odbc.JdbcOdbcDriver");

        //Specify the ODBC data source
        String sourceURL = "jdbc:odbc:authors";

        //get a connection to the database
        Connection databaseConnection =
            DriverManager.getConnection(sourceURL);

        //If we get to here, no exception was thrown
        System.out.println("The database connection is " +
                                        databaseConnection);

    }catch(ClassNotFoundException cnfe)
    {
        System.err.println(cnfe);
    }
    catch (SQLException sqle)
    {
        System.err.println(sqle);
    }
}
}
```

There are several interesting aspects of this simple example:

- The first actual command is Class.forName(). The fact that Class is capitalized indicates that the method forName() is static. Whenever forName() is passed a String, it instantiates the class named by the String. You could use the following syntax:

  ```
  Class xClass = Class.forName("sun.jdbc.odbc.JdbcOdbcDriver");
  ```

  In JDBC, however, there is no need for the xClass handle, so it is not often included.

- The sourceURL String doesn't look much like a normal URL. It is valid, however, even though it doesn't start with http, https, or FTP. The syntax for these URLs is often vendor-specific. In this case the code is saying that the database can be found via ODBC, and that it is called authors. The connection information can be found in the ODBC manager. The odbc section of the name is called the subprotocol, and jdbc is the primary protocol.

- The Connection handle is actually a handle to an interface. The object that is referenced by this handle is of class sun.jdbc.odbc.JdbcOdbcConnection. When getConnection() is called, the DriverManager will try and locate a suitable driver from those loaded.

- The DriverManager is a singleton class that manages the drivers in Java the same way that an ODBC manager manages them in Windows. In the true Java tradition, however, there is no user interface to DriverManager; we communicate with it in our code.

The output from running this program is

```
The database connection is sun.jdbc.odbc.JdbcOdbcConnection@41cd1f
```

This Connection class will be different for each JDBC driver. The fact that the handle is to the Connection interface and not to the class specifically enables the same code to work with different drivers loaded.

Batch Processing

Whenever you are making updates to a database through JDBC, it is better to process them as a batch rather than as individual transactions. The primary reason for this is performance. The overhead required to take a lock and release it for each insert into the database is prohibitive. Autocommitting every transaction is also expensive. Quite a bit of work takes place in the rollback log each time a transaction commits.

If you process your transactions in batches, you can reduce the number of locks taken and the amount of work that takes place on the rollback log. The combination of these improvements will have a positive effect on performance. Listing 10.2 shows how to perform an update using batch processing.

LISTING 10.2 The BatchCreator Class

```
/*
 * BatchCreator.java
 *
 * Created on December 27, 2001, 5:40 PM
 */

package unleashed.ch10;
import java.sql.*;
/**
 *
 * @author  Stephen Potts
 * @version
```

10

JDBC AND
DATABASES

LISTING 10.2   continued

```java
 */
public class BatchCreator
{

    /** Creates new BatchCreator */
    public BatchCreator() {
    }

    public static void main(String[] args)
    {
        try
        {
            //load the driver class
            Class.forName("sun.jdbc.odbc.JdbcOdbcDriver");

            //Specify the ODBC data source
            String sourceURL = "jdbc:odbc:CruiseTicket";

            //get a connection to the database
            Connection dbConn =
                DriverManager.getConnection(sourceURL);

            //If we get to here, no exception was thrown
            System.out.println("The database connection is " + dbConn);


            String createStatement;
            String insertStatement;


            //Create the statement
            Statement statement1 = dbConn.createStatement();

            ///////////////////////////////////////////////////////
            //            Create the tables in the database        //
            ///////////////////////////////////////////////////////

            //   Create the tables in the database                 //
            ///////////////////////////////////////////////////////////
            try
            {
                statement1.execute("drop table CruiseReservation");
                statement1.execute("drop table CruiseCustomer");
                statement1.execute("drop table CruiseTicket");
                statement1.execute("drop table TravelAgency");
                statement1.execute("drop table CruiseBooking");
                System.out.println("all tables dropped.");
            } catch (SQLException e)
            {
```

LISTING 10.2   continued

```
            System.out.println("table doesn't need to be dropped.");
}


//Add the customer data
createStatement =
  "CREATE TABLE CruiseReservation(resID int PRIMARY KEY,"
+ " CustomerID int, CruiseLine VARCHAR(30)," +
    " Ship VARCHAR(30), Port VARCHAR(30), "
+ "Sailing Date, AgencyID int, AgentName VARCHAR(30))";
statement1.executeUpdate(createStatement);
System.out.println("Table CruiseReservation created.");
createStatement =
  "CREATE TABLE CruiseCustomer(CustomerID int PRIMARY KEY, "
+ "LastName VARCHAR(30), FirstName VARCHAR(30), " +
    " MI VARCHAR(30), Address1 VARCHAR(30),"
+ " Address2 VARCHAR(30), City VARCHAR(30), " +
  " StateProv VARCHAR(30),"
+ " PostalCode VARCHAR(30), Country VARCHAR(30), " +
    " CreditCardType VARCHAR(30),"
+ " CreditCardNumber VARCHAR(30), "
+ " isGambler BIT, isDrinker BIT, isShortTourist BIT, " +
    " isPitchable BIT)";
statement1.executeUpdate(createStatement);
System.out.println("Table CruiseCustomer created.");
createStatement =
  "CREATE TABLE TravelAgency(AgencyID int PRIMARY KEY,"
+ " AgencyName VARCHAR(30), Address1 VARCHAR(30), " +
  " Address2 VARCHAR(30), City VARCHAR(30),"
+ " StateProv VARCHAR(30), PostalCode VARCHAR(30), " +
      " Country VARCHAR(30),"
+ " Telephone VARCHAR(30))";
statement1.executeUpdate(createStatement);
System.out.println("Table TravelAgency created.");
createStatement =
  "CREATE TABLE CruiseTicket(TicketID int PRIMARY KEY,"
+ " CustomerID int, CruiseLine VARCHAR(30), " +
  " Ship VARCHAR(30), Port VARCHAR(30),"
+ " Sailing Date, Price FLOAT, AgencyID int, " +
  " BookingID int, AgentName VARCHAR(30))";
statement1.executeUpdate(createStatement);
System.out.println("Table CruiseTicket created.");
createStatement =
  "CREATE TABLE CruiseBooking(BookingID int PRIMARY KEY,"
+ " TicketID int, CustomerID int, Smoking BIT, " +
  " DiningPreference VARCHAR(30), "
+ "LangPref VARCHAR(30))";
statement1.executeUpdate(createStatement);
System.out.println("Table CruiseBooking created.");
```

10

**JDBC AND
DATABASES**

LISTING 10.2   continued

```
//Add the customer information
insertStatement = "INSERT INTO CruiseCustomer VALUES(" +
        " 1001, 'Carter', 'Joseph', 'D', "
+ "'123 4th St.', '', 'Kennesaw', 'GA', '10064', " +
        "  'USA', 'MC', '1234-1234-1234-1234',"
+ "'0','0','0','0')";
statement1.addBatch(insertStatement);

insertStatement = "INSERT INTO CruiseCustomer VALUES(" +
        " 1002, 'Cain', 'Clay', 'F',"
+ " '1203 5th St.', '', 'Macon', 'GA', '20064', " +
        " 'USA', 'MC', '2234-2234-2234-2234', "
+ " '0','0','0','0')";
statement1.addBatch(insertStatement);
insertStatement = "INSERT INTO CruiseCustomer VALUES(" +
        " 1003, 'Bush', 'Albert', 'R',"
+ " '1523 6th St.', '', 'Cincinnati', 'OH', '30064', " +
        "  'USA', 'MC', '3234-3234-3234-3234', "
+ " '0','0','0','0')";
statement1.addBatch(insertStatement);
insertStatement = "INSERT INTO CruiseCustomer VALUES(" +
        " 1004, 'Skelton', 'Allison', 'T',"
+ " '1523 7th St.', '', 'Middletown', 'AL', '40064', " +
        " 'USA', 'MC', '4234-4234-4234-4234', "
+ "'0','0','0','0')";
statement1.addBatch(insertStatement);
insertStatement = "INSERT INTO CruiseCustomer VALUES(" +
        " 1005, 'Davidson', 'Barco', 'G',"
+ " '1823 8th St.', '', 'Dayton', 'OH', '50064', " +
        "  'USA', 'MC', '5234-5234-5234-5234', "
+ " '0','0','0','0')";
statement1.addBatch(insertStatement);
insertStatement = "INSERT INTO CruiseCustomer VALUES(" +
        " 1006, 'Rangitch', 'Maureen', 'B',"
+ " '1223 9th St.', '', 'Cairo', 'KA', '60064', " +
        "  'USA', 'MC', '6234-6234-6234-6234', "
+ " '0','0','0','0')";
statement1.addBatch(insertStatement);
insertStatement = "INSERT INTO CruiseCustomer VALUES(" +
            " 1007, 'Milner', 'Grant', 'V', "
+ "'1293 14th St.', '', 'Auberna', 'TN', '70064', " +
        "  'USA', 'MC', '7234-7234-7234-7234', "
+ " '0','0','0','0')";
statement1.addBatch(insertStatement);
insertStatement = "INSERT INTO CruiseCustomer VALUES(" +
            " 1008, 'Walker', 'Mike', 'C',"
+ " '1223 24th St.', '', 'Spokane', 'WA', '80064', " +
        "  'USA', 'MC', '8234-8234-8234-8234', "
```

LISTING 10.2   continued

```
+ " '0','0','0','0')";
statement1.addBatch(insertStatement);
insertStatement = "INSERT INTO CruiseCustomer VALUES(" +
        " 1009, 'Cheney', 'Michael', 'L',"
+ " '1723 25th St.', '', 'Orlando', 'FL', '90064', " +
    "   'USA', 'MC', '9234-9234-9234-9234', "
+ " '0','0','0','0')";
statement1.addBatch(insertStatement);
insertStatement = "INSERT INTO CruiseCustomer VALUES(" +
  " 1010, 'Pfister', 'Darlene', 'D',"
+ " '1233 9th St.', '', 'Bangor', 'MA', '10064', " +
                "   'USA', 'MC', '0234-0234-0234-0234', "
+ " '0','0','0','0')";
statement1.addBatch(insertStatement);

//Execute the batch
statement1.executeBatch();

//add the Travel Agents
insertStatement =
"INSERT INTO TravelAgency VALUES(" +
        " 2001, 'Cruise Junction', '1233 Sego St.', "
+ "'', 'Miami', 'FL', '10064', 'USA', '(800)242-4242')";
statement1.addBatch(insertStatement);
insertStatement =
"INSERT INTO TravelAgency VALUES(" +
        " 2002, 'Cruise and Snooze', '9387 Atlantic Ave.', "
+ "'', 'New York', 'NY', '00064', 'USA', '(800)343-3434')";
statement1.addBatch(insertStatement);
insertStatement =
"INSERT INTO TravelAgency VALUES(" +
            " 2003, 'Pokeys Cruises', '98223 Baltic Dr.', "
+ "'', 'Los Angeles', 'CA', '20064', 'USA', '(800)565-6565')";
statement1.addBatch(insertStatement);
insertStatement =
"INSERT INTO TravelAgency VALUES(" +
    " 2004, 'Cruise Animal', '2345 Lester Rd.', "
+ "'', 'New Orleans', 'LA', '40064', 'USA', '(800)787-8787')";
statement1.addBatch(insertStatement);
insertStatement =
"INSERT INTO TravelAgency VALUES(" +
    " 2005, 'Cruisy Dot Com', '5435 Spring St.', "
+ " '', 'Atlanta', 'GA', '30064', 'USA', '(800)879-6543')";
statement1.addBatch(insertStatement);

//Execute the batch
statement1.executeBatch();

System.out.println("The TravelAgent batch has been executed");
```

LISTING **10.2**   continued

```
        //Flush and close
        dbConn.close();

    }catch(ClassNotFoundException cnfe)
    {
        System.err.println(cnfe);
    }
    catch (SQLException sqle)
    {
        System.err.println(sqle);
    }
    catch (Exception e)
    {
        System.err.println(e);
    }
}//main
}
```

This listing has several interesting features:

- We get a connection and create a statement in the traditional way. Instead of using the Statement object to update the database, we use it to add to a batch.

  ```
  statement1.addBatch(insertStatement);
  ```

- When we get all of the inserts added to the batch, we call the executeBatch() method to do the actual work.

- We create two batches, one for each table that we want to update. Batches that span multiple tables are not allowed. The same statement is used twice, once for each batch:

  ```
  statement1.executeBatch();
  ```

The output from running Listing 10.2 is as follows:

```
The database connection is sun.jdbc.odbc.JdbcOdbcConnection@e53108
all tables dropped.
Table CruiseReservation created.
Table CruiseCustomer created.
Table TravelAgency created.
Table CruiseTicket created.
Table CruiseBooking created.
```

As you can see, using a batch update only requires a little additional work. One possible issue stems from the fact that a failure in the middle of a batch will cause all remaining items to fail and you won't know where in the batch the failure occurred. It's a trade-off between speed and safety. Given the performance advantages of this approach compared to the Autocommit approach, there may be advantages to using the batch if you are sure that your data is good.

JDBC and WebLogic Server

There are some differences between working with JDBC by itself and working with it through an application server such as WebLogic. Because the server provides its own environment for connection pooling, it requires that you get a connection in a special way. JDBC 2.0 added a new class called `javax.sql.DataSource`. The `DataSource` object encapsulates the details of making a connection to a database through JDBC.

One of these details is the creation of connection pools. *Connection pools* are sets of connections that are created when the server starts up. The application server keeps these connections open. When your program needs to communicate with a database, it asks for and receives a connection from the pool. There are several advantages of using this approach:

- Connection creation is an expensive operation. Keeping a connection open reduces the overhead associated with database access.
- It removes the driver name, DBMS `userid`, and `password` from your code. The application server administrator maintains this sensitive information behind the scenes.
- You can change DMBS vendors with minimal changes to your code.
- Database tuning is easier. One of the tuning parameters in most DBMSs is the number of open connections. This is much easier to manage if you maintain a connection pool.

The following example, Listing 10.3, shows how we obtain a pooled connection to a Cloudscape database via WebLogic Server.

LISTING 10.3   The W1JDBC Class

```
package examples.jdbc.datasource;

import java.sql.*;
import java.util.*;
import javax.naming.*;

public class WlJDBC
{
```

10

**JDBC AND
DATABASES**

LISTING 10.3   continued

```java
public static void main(String argv[])
throws Exception
{
    java.sql.Connection dbConn = null;
    Statement statement1 = null;
    String createStatement;
    String insertStatement;

    try
    {
        // ============== Make connection to database ==============
        // Obtain a Datasource from the WebLogic JNDI tree.
        Context ctx = null;

        // Put connection properties into a hashtable.
        Hashtable ht = new Hashtable();
        ht.put(Context.INITIAL_CONTEXT_FACTORY,
        "weblogic.jndi.WLInitialContextFactory");
        ht.put(Context.PROVIDER_URL,
        "t3://localhost:7001");

        // Get a context for the JNDI lookup
        ctx = new InitialContext(ht);
        javax.sql.DataSource ds
        = (javax.sql.DataSource) ctx.lookup(
                    "examples-dataSource-demoPool");
        dbConn = ds.getConnection();
        System.out.println("Making connection...\n");


        //Create the statement
        statement1 = dbConn.createStatement();

        ///////////////////////////////////////////////////////////
        //     Create the tables in the database                 //
        ///////////////////////////////////////////////////////////
        try
        {
            statement1.execute("drop table CruiseReservation");
            statement1.execute("drop table CruiseCustomer");
            statement1.execute("drop table CruiseTicket");
            statement1.execute("drop table TravelAgency");
            statement1.execute("drop table CruiseBooking");
            System.out.println("all tables dropped.");
        } catch (SQLException e)
        {
            System.out.println("table doesn't need to be dropped.");
        }
```

LISTING 10.3 continued

```
//Add the customer data
createStatement =
  "CREATE TABLE CruiseReservation(resID int PRIMARY KEY,"
+ " CustomerID int, CruiseLine VARCHAR(30)," +
    " Ship VARCHAR(30), Port VARCHAR(30), "
+ "Sailing Date, AgencyID int, AgentName VARCHAR(30))";
statement1.executeUpdate(createStatement);
System.out.println("Table CruiseReservation created.");
createStatement =
  "CREATE TABLE CruiseCustomer(CustomerID int PRIMARY KEY, "
+ "LastName VARCHAR(30), FirstName VARCHAR(30), " +
    " MI VARCHAR(30), Address1 VARCHAR(30),"
+ " Address2 VARCHAR(30), City VARCHAR(30), " +
   " StateProv VARCHAR(30),"
+ " PostalCode VARCHAR(30), Country VARCHAR(30), " +
    " CreditCardType VARCHAR(30),"
+ " CreditCardNumber VARCHAR(30), "
+ " isGambler BIT, isDrinker BIT, isShortTourist BIT, " +
    " isPitchable BIT)";
statement1.executeUpdate(createStatement);
System.out.println("Table CruiseCustomer created.");
createStatement =
  "CREATE TABLE TravelAgency(AgencyID int PRIMARY KEY,"
+ " AgencyName VARCHAR(30), Address1 VARCHAR(30), " +
   " Address2 VARCHAR(30), City VARCHAR(30),"
+ " StateProv VARCHAR(30), PostalCode VARCHAR(30), " +
     " Country VARCHAR(30),"
+ " Telephone VARCHAR(30))";
statement1.executeUpdate(createStatement);
System.out.println("Table TravelAgency created.");
createStatement =
  "CREATE TABLE CruiseTicket(TicketID int PRIMARY KEY,"
+ " CustomerID int, CruiseLine VARCHAR(30), " +
   " Ship VARCHAR(30), Port VARCHAR(30),"
+ " Sailing Date, Price FLOAT, AgencyID int, " +
  " BookingID int, AgentName VARCHAR(30))";
statement1.executeUpdate(createStatement);
System.out.println("Table CruiseTicket created.");
createStatement =
  "CREATE TABLE CruiseBooking(BookingID int PRIMARY KEY,"
+ " TicketID int, CustomerID int, Smoking BIT, " +
   " DiningPreference VARCHAR(30), "
+ "LangPref VARCHAR(30))";
statement1.executeUpdate(createStatement);
System.out.println("Table CruiseBooking created.");
```

LISTING 10.3   continued

```
//Add the customer information
insertStatement = "INSERT INTO CruiseCustomer VALUES(" +
        " 1001, 'Carter', 'Joseph', 'D', "
+ "'123 4th St.', '', 'Kennesaw', 'GA', '10064', " +
    "  'USA', 'MC', '1234-1234-1234-1234',"
+ "X'0',X'0',X'0',X'0')";
statement1.addBatch(insertStatement);

insertStatement = "INSERT INTO CruiseCustomer VALUES(" +
        " 1002, 'Cain', 'Clay', 'F',"
+ " '1203 5th St.', '', 'Macon', 'GA', '20064', " +
    "  'USA', 'MC', '2234-2234-2234-2234', "
+ " X'0',X'0',X'0',X'0')";
statement1.addBatch(insertStatement);
insertStatement = "INSERT INTO CruiseCustomer VALUES(" +
        " 1003, 'Bush', 'Albert', 'R',"
+ " '1523 6th St.', '', 'Cincinnati', 'OH', '30064', " +
  "  'USA', 'MC', '3234-3234-3234-3234', "
+ " X'0',X'0',X'0',X'0')";
statement1.addBatch(insertStatement);
insertStatement = "INSERT INTO CruiseCustomer VALUES(" +
        " 1004, 'Skelton', 'Allison', 'T',"
+ " '1523 7th St.', '', 'Middletown', 'AL', '40064', " +
  "  'USA', 'MC', '4234-4234-4234-4234', "
+ "X'0',X'0',X'0',X'0')";
statement1.addBatch(insertStatement);
insertStatement = "INSERT INTO CruiseCustomer VALUES(" +
        " 1005, 'Davidson', 'Barco', 'G',"
+ " '1823 8th St.', '', 'Dayton', 'OH', '50064', " +
  "  'USA', 'MC', '5234-5234-5234-5234', "
+ " X'0',X'0',X'0',X'0')";
statement1.addBatch(insertStatement);
insertStatement = "INSERT INTO CruiseCustomer VALUES(" +
    " 1006, 'Rangitch', 'Maureen', 'B',"
+ " '1223 9th St.', '', 'Cairo', 'KA', '60064', " +
  "  'USA', 'MC', '6234-6234-6234-6234', "
+ " X'0',X'0',X'0',X'0')";
statement1.addBatch(insertStatement);
insertStatement = "INSERT INTO CruiseCustomer VALUES(" +
            " 1007, 'Milner', 'Grant', 'V', "
+ "'1293 14th St.', '', 'Auberna', 'TN', '70064', " +
      "  'USA', 'MC', '7234-7234-7234-7234', "
+ " X'0',X'0',X'0',X'0')";
statement1.addBatch(insertStatement);
insertStatement = "INSERT INTO CruiseCustomer VALUES(" +
          " 1008, 'Walker', 'Mike', 'C',"
+ " '1223 24th St.', '', 'Spokane', 'WA', '80064', " +
      "  'USA', 'MC', '8234-8234-8234-8234', "
+ " X'0',X'0',X'0',X'0')";
statement1.addBatch(insertStatement);
```

LISTING 10.3   continued

```
insertStatement = "INSERT INTO CruiseCustomer VALUES(" +
        " 1009, 'Cheney', 'Michael', 'L',"
+ " '1723 25th St.', '', 'Orlando', 'FL', '90064', " +
    "  'USA', 'MC', '9234-9234-9234-9234', "
+ " X'0',X'0',X'0',X'0')";
statement1.addBatch(insertStatement);
insertStatement = "INSERT INTO CruiseCustomer VALUES(" +
    " 1010, 'Pfister', 'Darlene', 'D',"
+ " '1233 9th St.', '', 'Bangor', 'MA', '10064', " +
            "  'USA', 'MC', '0234-0234-0234-0234', "
+ " X'0',X'0',X'0',X'0')";
statement1.addBatch(insertStatement);

//Execute the batch
statement1.executeBatch();

//add the Travel Agents
insertStatement =
"INSERT INTO TravelAgency VALUES(" +
        " 2001, 'Cruise Junction', '1233 Sego St.', "
+ "'', 'Miami', 'FL', '10064', 'USA', '(800)242-4242')";
statement1.addBatch(insertStatement);
insertStatement =
"INSERT INTO TravelAgency VALUES(" +
        " 2002, 'Cruise and Snooze', '9387 Atlantic Ave.', "
+ "'', 'New York', 'NY', '00064', 'USA', '(800)343-3434')";
statement1.addBatch(insertStatement);
insertStatement =
"INSERT INTO TravelAgency VALUES(" +
            " 2003, 'Pokeys Cruises', '98223 Baltic Dr.', "
+ "'', 'Los Angeles', 'CA', '20064', 'USA', '(800)565-6565')";
statement1.addBatch(insertStatement);
insertStatement =
"INSERT INTO TravelAgency VALUES(" +
    " 2004, 'Cruise Animal', '2345 Lester Rd.', "
+ "'', 'New Orleans', 'LA', '40064', 'USA', '(800)787-8787')";
statement1.addBatch(insertStatement);
insertStatement =
"INSERT INTO TravelAgency VALUES(" +
    " 2005, 'Cruisy Dot Com', '5435 Spring St.', "
+ " '', 'Atlanta', 'GA', '30064', 'USA', '(800)879-6543')";
statement1.addBatch(insertStatement);

//Execute the batch
statement1.executeBatch();
System.out.println("All rows added successfully");

} catch (Exception e)
```

10

JDBC AND DATABASES

LISTING 10.3   continued

```
        {
            System.out.println("Exception was thrown: " + e.getMessage());
        } finally
        {
            try
            {
                if (statement1 != null)
                    statement1.close();
                if (dbConn != null)
                    dbConn.close();
            } catch (SQLException sqle)
            {
                System.out.println("SQLException during close(): " +
                                                    sqle.getMessage());
            }
        }
    }
}
```

This example is the application server version of the batch update program that we saw earlier in the chapter. There are several interesting elements in this code:

- Instead of using the `Class.forName()` method to instantiate a driver object, this program obtains a handle to the JNDI `InitialContext` object.

- This program uses the JNDI handle to obtain a `DataSource` object. The `DataSource` object is a factory for database connections. This object is created when the server is started and it contains all of the information needed to provide connections.

- The `DataSource` object makes pooling simpler because it hides the pool management code from your program, making pooling automatic.

- The `getConnection()` method is used to return a handle to the database connection.

The output of the program is shown here:

```
Making connection...

all tables dropped.
Table CruiseReservation created.
Table CruiseCustomer created.
Table TravelAgency created.
Table CruiseTicket created.
Table CruiseBooking created.
All rows added successfully
```

This approach to connection pooling is much simpler than creating and managing it yourself. The only tricky part is obtaining a handle to the `InitialContext`. If this part seems unfamiliar to you, read Chapter 11, "Java Naming and Directory Interface (JNDI)," for a more complete explanation of JNDI.

JDBC Transaction Management

The basic concept of a transaction is really quite simple—a certain group of activities must take place before the transaction is acceptable. If any of the activities can't be accomplished, none of them should be done.

The classic example of a transaction is that of a funds transfer. If you want to transfer money from your savings to your checking account, you don't want to complete half a transaction. If your savings account balance is reduced by $100, you need your checking account balance to increase by $100. This is the best result. The worst result is for the $100 to be deducted from your savings account but not deposited to your checking account because of a power outage or some other problem. If this happens, you are $100 poorer. If the transaction fails, you want the money put back in savings and you want to be told that the transfer wasn't successful.

From a computing standpoint, the deduction of the money from your savings account worked fine. The DBMS has no intrinsic understanding of what has to happen to the money. It just knows that the code to make the deduction finished without error.

Determining the boundaries of a transaction is the job of the application programmer. The DBMS programmer, the operating system programmer, and the hardware engineer lack the information necessary to make that determination.

To facilitate the solution to this problem, DBMS programmers introduced the concept of a transaction. A transaction must finish in its entirety, or it must be rolled back as if it never occurred. Listing 10.4 shows how this can be done.

LISTING 10.4 The Creator Class

```
/*
 * Creator.java
 *
 * Created on December 27, 2001, 10:25 AM
 */

package unleashed.ch10;
import java.sql.*;
```

10

JDBC AND DATABASES

LISTING 10.4 continued

```java
/**
 *
 * @author  Stephen Potts
 * @version
 */
public class Creator
{

    /** Creates new Creator */
    public Creator()
    {
    }

    public static void main(String[] args)
    {
        String createStatement;
        try
        {
            //load the driver class
            Class.forName("sun.jdbc.odbc.JdbcOdbcDriver");

            //Specify the ODBC data source
            String sourceURL = "jdbc:odbc:CruiseTicket";

            //get a connection to the database
            Connection dbConn =
            DriverManager.getConnection(sourceURL);

            //If we get to here, no exception was thrown
            System.out.println("The database connection is " + dbConn);

            //Turn Autocommit off
            dbConn.setAutoCommit(false);

            //Create the statement
            Statement statement1 = dbConn.createStatement();
            String insertStatement;

            ////////////////////////////////////////////////////////////
            //    drop the tables in the database                      //
            ////////////////////////////////////////////////////////////
            try
            {
                statement1.execute("drop table CruiseReservation");
                statement1.execute("drop table CruiseCustomer");
                statement1.execute("drop table CruiseTicket");
                statement1.execute("drop table TravelAgency");
                statement1.execute("drop table CruiseBooking");
                System.out.println("all tables dropped.");
            } catch (SQLException e)
```

LISTING 10.4   continued

```
{
    System.out.println("table doesn't need to be dropped.");
}

//Add the tables
createStatement =
"CREATE TABLE CruiseReservation(resID int PRIMARY KEY,"
+ " CustomerID int, CruiseLine VARCHAR(30)," +
" Ship VARCHAR(30), Port VARCHAR(30), "
+ "Sailing Date, AgencyID int, AgentName VARCHAR(30))";
statement1.executeUpdate(createStatement);
System.out.println("Table CruiseReservation created.");
createStatement =
"CREATE TABLE CruiseCustomer(CustomerID int PRIMARY KEY, "
+ "LastName VARCHAR(30), FirstName VARCHAR(30), " +
" MI VARCHAR(30), Address1 VARCHAR(30),"
+ " Address2 VARCHAR(30), City VARCHAR(30), " +
" StateProv VARCHAR(30),"
+ " PostalCode VARCHAR(30), Country VARCHAR(30), " +
" CreditCardType VARCHAR(30),"
+ " CreditCardNumber VARCHAR(30), "
+ " isGambler BIT, isDrinker BIT, isShortTourist BIT, " +
" isPitchable BIT)";
statement1.executeUpdate(createStatement);
System.out.println("Table CruiseCustomer created.");
createStatement =
"CREATE TABLE TravelAgency(AgencyID int PRIMARY KEY,"
+ " AgencyName VARCHAR(30), Address1 VARCHAR(30), " +
" Address2 VARCHAR(30), City VARCHAR(30),"
+ " StateProv VARCHAR(30), PostalCode VARCHAR(30), " +
" Country VARCHAR(30),"
+ " Telephone VARCHAR(30))";
statement1.executeUpdate(createStatement);
System.out.println("Table TravelAgency created.");
createStatement =
"CREATE TABLE CruiseTicket(TicketID int PRIMARY KEY,"
+ " CustomerID int, CruiseLine VARCHAR(30), " +
" Ship VARCHAR(30), Port VARCHAR(30),"
+ " Sailing Date, Price FLOAT, AgencyID int, " +
" BookingID int, AgentName VARCHAR(30))";
statement1.executeUpdate(createStatement);
System.out.println("Table CruiseTicket created.");
createStatement =
"CREATE TABLE CruiseBooking(BookingID int PRIMARY KEY,"
+ " TicketID int, CustomerID int, Smoking BIT, " +
" DiningPreference VARCHAR(30), "
+ "LangPref VARCHAR(30))";
statement1.executeUpdate(createStatement);
System.out.println("Table CruiseBooking created.");
```

10

**JDBC AND
DATABASES**

LISTING 10.4 continued

```java
//Add the customer information
insertStatement = "INSERT INTO CruiseCustomer VALUES(" +
" 1001, 'Carter', 'Joseph', 'D', "
+ "'123 4th St.', '', 'Kennesaw', 'GA', '10064', " +
"  'USA', 'MC', '1234-1234-1234-1234',"
+ "'0','0','0','0')";
statement1.executeUpdate(insertStatement);
insertStatement = "INSERT INTO CruiseCustomer VALUES(" +
" 1002, 'Cain', 'Clay', 'F',"
+ " '1203 5th St.', '', 'Macon', 'GA', '20064', " +
"  'USA', 'MC', '2234-2234-2234-2234', "
+ " '0','0','0','0')";
statement1.executeUpdate(insertStatement);
insertStatement = "INSERT INTO CruiseCustomer VALUES(" +
" 1003, 'Bush', 'Albert', 'R',"
+ " '1523 6th St.', '', 'Cincinnati', 'OH', '30064', " +
"  'USA', 'MC', '3234-3234-3234-3234', "
+ " '0','0','0','0')";
statement1.executeUpdate(insertStatement);
insertStatement = "INSERT INTO CruiseCustomer VALUES(" +
" 1004, 'Skelton', 'Allison', 'T',"
+ " '1523 7th St.', '', 'Middletown', 'AL', '40064', " +
"  'USA', 'MC', '4234-4234-4234-4234', "
+ "'0','0','0','0')";
statement1.executeUpdate(insertStatement);
insertStatement = "INSERT INTO CruiseCustomer VALUES(" +
" 1005, 'Davidson', 'Barco', 'G',"
+ " '1823 8th St.', '', 'Dayton', 'OH', '50064', " +
"  'USA', 'MC', '5234-5234-5234-5234', "
+ " '0','0','0','0')";

//Commit the first part of these inserts
dbConn.commit();

statement1.executeUpdate(insertStatement);
insertStatement = "INSERT INTO CruiseCustomer VALUES(" +
" 1006, 'Rangitch', 'Maureen', 'B',"
+ " '1223 9th St.', '', 'Cairo', 'KA', '60064', " +
"  'USA', 'MC', '6234-6234-6234-6234', "
+ " '0','0','0','0')";
statement1.executeUpdate(insertStatement);
insertStatement = "INSERT INTO CruiseCustomer VALUES(" +
" 1007, 'Milner', 'Grant', 'V', "
+ "'1293 14th St.', '', 'Auberna', 'TN', '70064', " +
"  'USA', 'MC', '7234-7234-7234-7234', "
+ " '0','0','0','0')";
```

LISTING 10.4   continued

```
statement1.executeUpdate(insertStatement);
insertStatement = "INSERT INTO CruiseCustomer VALUES(" +
" 1008, 'Walker', 'Mike', 'C',"
+ " '1223 24th St.', '', 'Spokane', 'WA', '80064', " +
"  'USA', 'MC', '8234-8234-8234-8234', "
+ " '0','0','0','0')";
statement1.executeUpdate(insertStatement);
insertStatement = "INSERT INTO CruiseCustomer VALUES(" +
" 1009, 'Cheney', 'Michael', 'L',"
+ " '1723 25th St.', '', 'Orlando', 'FL', '90064', " +
"  'USA', 'MC', '9234-9234-9234-9234', "
+ " '0','0','0','0')";
statement1.executeUpdate(insertStatement);
insertStatement = "INSERT INTO CruiseCustomer VALUES(" +
" 1010, 'Pfister', 'Darlene', 'D',"
+ " '1233 9th St.', '', 'Bangor', 'MA', '10064', " +
"  'USA', 'MC', '0234-0234-0234-0234', "
+ " '0','0','0','0')";
statement1.executeUpdate(insertStatement);


//add the Travel Agents
insertStatement =
"INSERT INTO TravelAgency VALUES(" +
" 2001, 'Cruise Junction', '1233 Sego St.', "
+ "'', 'Miami', 'FL', '10064', 'USA', '(800)242-4242')";
statement1.executeUpdate(insertStatement);
insertStatement =
"INSERT INTO TravelAgency VALUES(" +
" 2002, 'Cruise and Snooze', '9387 Atlantic Ave.', "
+ "'', 'New York', 'NY', '00064', 'USA', '(800)343-3434')";
statement1.executeUpdate(insertStatement);
insertStatement =
"INSERT INTO TravelAgency VALUES(" +
" 2003, 'Pokeys Cruises', '98223 Baltic Dr.', "
+ "'', 'Los Angeles', 'CA', '20064', 'USA', '(800)565-6565')";
statement1.executeUpdate(insertStatement);
insertStatement =
"INSERT INTO TravelAgency VALUES(" +
" 2004, 'Cruise Animal', '2345 Lester Rd.', "
+ "'', 'New Orleans', 'LA', '40064', 'USA', '(800)787-8787')";
statement1.executeUpdate(insertStatement);
insertStatement =
"INSERT INTO TravelAgency VALUES(" +
" 2005, 'Cruisy Dot Com', '5435 Spring St.', "
+ " '', 'Atlanta', 'GA', '30064', 'USA', '(800)879-6543')";
statement1.executeUpdate(insertStatement);
```

10

**JDBC AND
DATABASES**

LISTING 10.4   continued

```
                //roll back the second part of these inserts
                dbConn.rollback();

                //Flush and close
                dbConn.close();

        }catch(ClassNotFoundException cnfe)
        {
            System.err.println(cnfe);
        }
        catch (SQLException sqle)
        {
            System.err.println(sqle);
        }
        catch (Exception e)
        {
            System.err.println(e);
        }
    }//main
}//class
```

The following list highlights a few key points in this example:

- The first thing that we do is call the `setAutoCommit()` method and set it to `false`. Unless we do this, an implicit commit will take place after every insert.

- After four of the customers are inserted, we execute a `commit()` method on the connection. This caused these inserts to become permanent. You may be wondering what happened to the fifth row added, as only four of them are shown onscreen in Figure 10.1. Notice that the commit takes place after the statement is composed but before it is inserted, as shown here. No additional commit is executed before the rollback:

```
//Commit the first part of these inserts
dbConn.commit();

statement1.executeUpdate(insertStatement);
```

- After all of the inserts are complete, we call the `rollback()` method on the connection. This causes all of the uncommitted transactions to be discarded.

The result of running this code can be seen in the database itself. The CruiseCustomer table has only four rows in it, as shown in Figure 10.1.

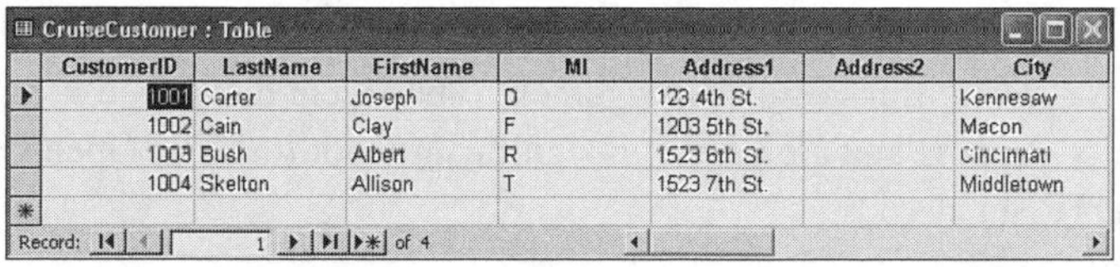

FIGURE 10.1

The rollback()
method of the con-
nection object
causes any
changes to the
database that
haven't been com-
mitted to be
undone.

The inner workings of a DBMS transaction manager are not especially complex. The DBMS keeps a log of all transactions that have taken place. This log is normally kept on a persistent medium such as a hard drive. Whenever a rollback() command is issued, the DBMS examines the log to locate the uncommitted transaction. It then performs the converse operation for every entry in the log (an addition for a subtraction, a delete for an insert, and so on).

Likewise, if a failure has taken place, there will be an uncommitted transaction on the log. When a DBMS is instantiated, it checks for uncommitted transactions. It performs the converse operations for each of these entries as well.

Java Transaction Management with the JTA API

The JDBC commit() and rollback() methods work well. But they are limited in what they can do. What happens when the transaction spans multiple databases? What happens if the transactions are against message queues and EJBs? In order to span multiple DBMSs, EJBs, and JMS queues, we need something stronger.

Strong transaction support must implement the classic ACID characteristics:

- Atomicity—a transaction must be atomic or indivisible. This means that the whole transaction must be completed or none of it must be completed.

- Consistency—data can be restored to its original state if a failure (such as a power outage) occurs during the transaction.

- Isolation—data that has not been committed cannot be viewed by other transactions.

- Durability—data that has been committed can survive a failure and maintain its correctness.

In addition, this stronger transaction management must be able to span multiple DBMSs on multiple (heterogeneous) servers, EJBs, and JMS queues. An additional requirement is that it must be fairly simple for an application programmer to use.

10

JDBC AND DATABASES

The Java Transaction API (JTA) and the Java Transaction Server (JTS) meet all the qualifications for strong transaction management. They were developed using the Java Community Process and are based on significant work that The Open Group did on the X/Open DTP standard.

JTA enables applications to access transaction services in a platform-independent way. The JTA specification defines how the application will communicate with the J2EE server and the managers responsible for each shared resource. The application programmer uses the JTA to designate the transaction boundaries in the application.

> **Note**
>
> JTS specifies the implementation of the transaction manager. This manager must provide transaction demarcation, transactional resource management, synchronization, and transaction context propagation.
>
> JTS implements a two-phase commit for a transaction:
>
> - Phase 1—The transaction manager sends a prepare-to-commit message to every one of the individual resource managers and waits to hear back.
> - Phase 2—If all of the resource managers indicate that they are prepared to commit, the transaction manager issues the command to commit, and the transaction is complete.

Similarly, if any of the resource managers fail to respond, or respond in the negative, a rollback message is sent to each resource manager. Each of them is responsible for rolling back its part of the transaction.

J2EE server programmers have a lot of responsibilities in the area of transactions. Because of this, application programmers have very few tasks and can add JTA support to their code very simply.

The `UserTransaction` interface provides us with the method calls such as `begin()` and `commit()` that we need to communicate with the J2EE server. The following example, Listing 10.5, shows how this is done.

LISTING 10.5   The W1JTA Class

```
/*
 * W1JTA.java
 *
 * Created on December 29, 2001, 11:39 AM
 */
```

LISTING 10.5   continued

```java
package examples.jdbc.datasource;

import java.sql.*;
import java.util.*;
import javax.naming.*;
import javax.transaction.*;

public class WlJTA
{
    public static void main(String argv[])
    throws Exception
    {
        java.sql.Connection dbConn = null;
        Statement statement1 = null;
        String createStatement;
        String insertStatement;

        try
        {
            // ============== Make connection to database =============
            // Obtain a Datasource from the WebLogic JNDI tree.
            Context ctx = null;

            // Put connection properties into a hashtable.
            Hashtable ht = new Hashtable();
            ht.put(Context.INITIAL_CONTEXT_FACTORY,
            "weblogic.jndi.WLInitialContextFactory");
            ht.put(Context.PROVIDER_URL,
            "t3://localhost:7001");

            // Get a context for the JNDI lookup
            ctx = new InitialContext(ht);
            javax.sql.DataSource ds
            = (javax.sql.DataSource) ctx.lookup(
                                "examples-dataSource-demoPool");
            dbConn = ds.getConnection();
            System.out.println("Making connection...\n");

            //Get a handle to a UserTransaction object
            UserTransaction tx =
                    (UserTransaction)ctx.lookup(
                        "javax.transaction.UserTransaction");
            System.out.println("Creating the transaction");


            //Create the statement
            statement1 = dbConn.createStatement();
```

LISTING 10.5   continued

```
//////////////////////////////////////////////////////////
//   Create the tables in the database                    //
//////////////////////////////////////////////////////////
try
{
    statement1.execute("drop table CruiseReservation");
    statement1.execute("drop table CruiseCustomer");
    statement1.execute("drop table CruiseTicket");
    statement1.execute("drop table TravelAgency");
    statement1.execute("drop table CruiseBooking");
    System.out.println("all tables dropped.");
} catch (SQLException e)
{
    System.out.println("table doesn't need to be dropped.");
}

//Begin the transaction
tx.begin();
System.out.println("transaction has begun");

//Add the customer data
createStatement =
  "CREATE TABLE CruiseReservation(resID int PRIMARY KEY,"
+ " CustomerID int, CruiseLine VARCHAR(30)," +
    " Ship VARCHAR(30), Port VARCHAR(30), "
+ "Sailing Date, AgencyID int, AgentName VARCHAR(30))";
statement1.executeUpdate(createStatement);
System.out.println("Table CruiseReservation created.");
createStatement =
    "CREATE TABLE CruiseCustomer(CustomerID int PRIMARY KEY, "
+ "LastName VARCHAR(30), FirstName VARCHAR(30), " +
    "  MI VARCHAR(30), Address1 VARCHAR(30),"
+ " Address2 VARCHAR(30), City VARCHAR(30), " +
   " StateProv VARCHAR(30),"
+ " PostalCode VARCHAR(30), Country VARCHAR(30), " +
    " CreditCardType VARCHAR(30),"
+ " CreditCardNumber VARCHAR(30), "
+ " isGambler BIT, isDrinker BIT, isShortTourist BIT, " +
    " isPitchable BIT)";
statement1.executeUpdate(createStatement);
System.out.println("Table CruiseCustomer created.");
createStatement =
    "CREATE TABLE TravelAgency(AgencyID int PRIMARY KEY,"
+ " AgencyName VARCHAR(30), Address1 VARCHAR(30), " +
   " Address2 VARCHAR(30), City VARCHAR(30),"
+ " StateProv VARCHAR(30), PostalCode VARCHAR(30), " +
      " Country VARCHAR(30),"
+ " Telephone VARCHAR(30))";
```

LISTING 10.5   continued

```java
statement1.executeUpdate(createStatement);
System.out.println("Table TravelAgency created.");
createStatement =
    "CREATE TABLE CruiseTicket(TicketID int PRIMARY KEY,"
+ " CustomerID int, CruiseLine VARCHAR(30), " +
    "  Ship VARCHAR(30), Port VARCHAR(30),"
+ " Sailing Date, Price FLOAT, AgencyID int, " +
    "  BookingID int, AgentName VARCHAR(30))";
statement1.executeUpdate(createStatement);
System.out.println("Table CruiseTicket created.");
createStatement =
    "CREATE TABLE CruiseBooking(BookingID int PRIMARY KEY,"
+ " TicketID int, CustomerID int, Smoking BIT, " +
    "  DiningPreference VARCHAR(30), "
+ "LangPref VARCHAR(30))";
statement1.executeUpdate(createStatement);
System.out.println("Table CruiseBooking created.");

//Add the customer information
insertStatement = "INSERT INTO CruiseCustomer VALUES(" +
        " 1001, 'Carter', 'Joseph', 'D', "
+ "'123 4th St.', '', 'Kennesaw', 'GA', '10064', " +
    "  'USA', 'MC', '1234-1234-1234-1234',"
+ "X'0',X'0',X'0',X'0')";
statement1.addBatch(insertStatement);

insertStatement = "INSERT INTO CruiseCustomer VALUES(" +
    " 1002, 'Cain', 'Clay', 'F',"
+ " '1203 5th St.', '', 'Macon', 'GA', '20064', " +
    " 'USA', 'MC', '2234-2234-2234-2234', "
+ " X'0',X'0',X'0',X'0')";
statement1.addBatch(insertStatement);
insertStatement = "INSERT INTO CruiseCustomer VALUES(" +
    " 1003, 'Bush', 'Albert', 'R',"
+ " '1523 6th St.', '', 'Cincinnati', 'OH', '30064', " +
    " 'USA', 'MC', '3234-3234-3234-3234', "
+ " X'0',X'0',X'0',X'0')";
statement1.addBatch(insertStatement);
insertStatement = "INSERT INTO CruiseCustomer VALUES(" +
        " 1004, 'Skelton', 'Allison', 'T',"
+ " '1523 7th St.', '', 'Middletown', 'AL', '40064', " +
    " 'USA', 'MC', '4234-4234-4234-4234', "
+ "X'0',X'0',X'0',X'0')";
statement1.addBatch(insertStatement);
insertStatement = "INSERT INTO CruiseCustomer VALUES(" +
        " 1005, 'Davidson', 'Barco', 'G',"
+ " '1823 8th St.', '', 'Dayton', 'OH', '50064', " +
    " 'USA', 'MC', '5234-5234-5234-5234', "
+ " X'0',X'0',X'0',X'0')";
```

10

**JDBC AND
DATABASES**

LISTING 10.5   continued

```
statement1.addBatch(insertStatement);
insertStatement = "INSERT INTO CruiseCustomer VALUES(" +
   " 1006, 'Rangitch', 'Maureen', 'B',"
+ " '1223 9th St.', '', 'Cairo', 'KA', '60064', " +
   "  'USA', 'MC', '6234-6234-6234-6234', "
+ " X'0',X'0',X'0',X'0')";
statement1.addBatch(insertStatement);
insertStatement = "INSERT INTO CruiseCustomer VALUES(" +
               " 1007, 'Milner', 'Grant', 'V', "
+ "'1293 14th St.', '', 'Auberna', 'TN', '70064', " +
      "  'USA', 'MC', '7234-7234-7234-7234', "
+ " X'0',X'0',X'0',X'0')";
statement1.addBatch(insertStatement);
insertStatement = "INSERT INTO CruiseCustomer VALUES(" +
            " 1008, 'Walker', 'Mike', 'C',"
+ " '1223 24th St.', '', 'Spokane', 'WA', '80064', " +
      "  'USA', 'MC', '8234-8234-8234-8234', "
+ " X'0',X'0',X'0',X'0')";
statement1.addBatch(insertStatement);
insertStatement = "INSERT INTO CruiseCustomer VALUES(" +
         " 1009, 'Cheney', 'Michael', 'L',"
+ " '1723 25th St.', '', 'Orlando', 'FL', '90064', " +
      "  'USA', 'MC', '9234-9234-9234-9234', "
+ " X'0',X'0',X'0',X'0')";
statement1.addBatch(insertStatement);
insertStatement = "INSERT INTO CruiseCustomer VALUES(" +
   " 1010, 'Pfister', 'Darlene', 'D',"
+ " '1233 9th St.', '', 'Bangor', 'MA', '10064', " +
            "  'USA', 'MC', '0234-0234-0234-0234', "
+ " X'0',X'0',X'0',X'0')";
statement1.addBatch(insertStatement);

//Execute the batch
statement1.executeBatch();

//add the Travel Agents
insertStatement =
"INSERT INTO TravelAgency VALUES(" +
      " 2001, 'Cruise Junction', '1233 Sego St.', "
+ "'', 'Miami', 'FL', '10064', 'USA', '(800)242-4242')";
statement1.addBatch(insertStatement);
insertStatement =
"INSERT INTO TravelAgency VALUES(" +
      " 2002, 'Cruise and Snooze', '9387 Atlantic Ave.', "
+ "'', 'New York', 'NY', '00064', 'USA', '(800)343-3434')";
statement1.addBatch(insertStatement);
insertStatement =
"INSERT INTO TravelAgency VALUES(" +
         " 2003, 'Pokeys Cruises', '98223 Baltic Dr.', "
```

LISTING 10.5 continued

```
              + "'', 'Los Angeles', 'CA', '20064', 'USA', '(800)565-6565')";
              statement1.addBatch(insertStatement);
              insertStatement =
              "INSERT INTO TravelAgency VALUES(" +
                   " 2004, 'Cruise Animal', '2345 Lester Rd.', "
              + "'', 'New Orleans', 'LA', '40064', 'USA', '(800)787-8787')";
              statement1.addBatch(insertStatement);
              insertStatement =
              "INSERT INTO TravelAgency VALUES(" +
                   " 2005, 'Cruisy Dot Com', '5435 Spring St.', "
              + " '', 'Atlanta', 'GA', '30064', 'USA', '(800)879-6543')";
              statement1.addBatch(insertStatement);

              //Execute the batch
              statement1.executeBatch();

              //commit the transaction
              tx.commit();
              System.out.println(
                        "All rows added successfully and committed");

      } catch (Exception e)
      {
              System.out.println("Exception was thrown: " +
                                            e.getMessage());
      } finally
      {
          try
          {
              if (statement1 != null)
                  statement1.close();
              if (dbConn != null)
                  dbConn.close();
          } catch (SQLException sqle)
          {
              System.out.println("SQLException during close(): " +
                                            sqle.getMessage());
          }
      }
    }
}
```

There are several aspects of this code that are worth highlighting:

- We get a handle to the UserTransaction object by making a call to
  ctx.lookup("javax.transaction.UserTransaction")

- Once this handle (tx) is obtained, we issue a begin() method for the transaction. Notice that all JTA transactions need an explicit begin() method call.

- After all of the work is done, we issue an explicit commit() command.

The result is predictable:

```
Making connection...

Creating the transaction
all tables dropped.
transaction has begun
Table CruiseReservation created.
Table CruiseCustomer created.
Table TravelAgency created.
Table CruiseTicket created.
Table CruiseBooking created.
All rows added successfully and committed
```

That's all there is to it! Transaction management is a big part of what you pay for when you write a check to a J2EE server vendor.

From this discussion, several best practices emerge as worthy of remembering:

- Stop using Autocommit completely. Explicit commit statements can greatly increase throughput by allowing your program to "keep moving" for longer periods of time.

- Use batch updates. Batch updates take a table lock once and hold it until all the updates have taken place. This is much more efficient than taking a lock over and over again.

- Do as much as you can in each transaction. Much of the processing associated with executing a command to the database involves setting up and releasing the communication resources. Once you start to access the data, access a lot of it, even if you never use some of it. This approach is similar to the read-ahead caching that many CPUs use.

- Release statements and connections yourself by issuing a close() method call in a finally block. This signals clearly that you are done with these resources.

- Release your connections quickly. Programs used to hold on to connections to avoid the overhead of re-creating them later. Connection pooling performs that function for you now, so give the connection up as soon as you can and get it back just before you are going to use it.

- Never allow a transaction to span a user-generated event such as a button click or text input. Humans are very slow compared to computers, and human involvement will slow everything to a crawl.

Enhancements in JDBC 3.0

JDBC 3.0 was released in conjunction with JDK 1.4. JDBC 3.0 contains the JDBC 2.0 classes as well as the JDBC optional download packages. JDBC 3.0 is now part of the core JDK. The parts of the SQL99 that JDBC 3.0 implements are consistent with the new SQL99.

Three new rowsets are supported:

- `JDBCRowSet` makes the JDBC driver act like a JavaBean.
- `CachedRowSet` is a snapshot of the data at a point in time. It has to be resynchronized at a later date.
- `WebRowSet` is an XML document that contains the data.

In addition to the rowsets, there are a few other new features that you need to be aware of:

- `Savepoint` support for subtransaction rollbacks. Some situations make it desirable to roll back partway instead of to the start of a transaction.
- Connection pool configurations. Previously, connection pools were handled in code.
- Reuse of prepared statements. This is a performance enhancement.
- Retrieval of prepared statement parameter metadata.
- Retrieval of automatically generated key columns.
- A `Boolean` data type. This provides a better way of representing `true` and `false` fields than the `BIT` data type.
- Updatable BLOB, CLOB, and ARRAY. Previously, these could only be added and deleted.
- Transform groups.
- A `DataLink` data type to external data. This allows you to query data that is not in database tables.
- `DatabaseMetaData` APIs.

These features were added in response to requests from the user community. They provide some added power to JDBC applications.

Summary

This chapter covered a number of advanced features of Java database access. We studied how traditional JDBC works by looking at the classes that operate behind the scenes to manage connections. We also studied how to put our updates in a batch to improve throughput.

We discussed the advantages of connection pooling over manual database connection creation.

We then looked at how application servers such as WebLogic change our approach to JDBC in general and to connection pooling specifically.

Finally, we discussed how to use JTA to create transactions that span multiple databases and services.

Java Naming and Directory Interface (JNDI)

There's a scene in the movie *Pretty Woman* in which Richard Gere picks up a lady (Julia Roberts) on a street corner. When she gets in the car he asks, "What's your name?" She answers, "What do you want it to be?" Sometimes the world of distributed object development feels like that. We seek definition and clarity, but what we find is indirection and fuzziness.

One of the fuzziest areas of the programming world is naming services. Nearly every book or chapter that you can find treats the topic as a sideshow. You get a simple formula for how to get it to work, but you never get a full understanding of what is going on.

The concept of a naming service is quite simple. It is a networkwide repository of name/object pairs. If you want others to be able to find an object, just give it a name and put it in a naming service. Tell others the name and they can get it at any time. The only thing hard about using a naming service is the fact that it has to be networkwide. This introduces some interesting complications that we will explore in this chapter.

Naming services provide several advantages:

- They provide remote administration of name/object pairs.
- They provide access to multiple naming services from the same program.
- They allow you to work with human-readable names instead of bizarre strings of special characters.
- They provide indirection. This means that the object can change over time but the name that it is known by stays the same.
- They can store serializable objects of arbitrary complexity. This allows your program to move objects across the network very simply.
- They can store handles to remote objects. This allows your program to find and obtain stubs to these objects and run them.
- They provide namespaces called contexts. If the same name is used twice but in two different contexts, all is well. This reduces the number of potential name conflicts.

The programming world is full of programmers who "get by" in naming technology. What we need are programmers who have a deep understanding of it, especially in the fuzzy areas. The goal of this chapter is to remove at least some of the fuzz from the Java Naming and Directory Interface (JNDI).

The Need for a Naming Service API

In the world of distributed programming, the hardest program to write is "Hello, World." Once you get it to work, other programs are fairly straightforward. Distributed programming means that at some point you have to obtain a handle to an object that is located on some other machine. How do you obtain that handle?

In a program that is running in one virtual machine, you obtain handles at the time that you create objects, as shown here:

```
StringBuffer sb1 = new StringBuffer();
```

The handle sb1 is an address in your own JVM. Now look at the following line:

```
MysteryObject mo1 = ?
```

If the mystery object is located on another machine, how will you get a handle to it? Will you get it from a naming provider via JNDI? How will you get a handle to a JNDI provider? The answer for the average programmer is to cut and paste code that he doesn't understand from a book or from someone else's program. A good programmer wants to know why something works every bit as much as he wants to understand how to make it work. You are probably reading this chapter because you are unwilling to take shortcuts.

The ability of one Java object to find another is fundamental to getting any real work done. Services that help us do this are called naming services. Naming services associate a name with an object. If you want a handle to the object, you hand the service the name and it gives you the handle that you asked for.

Directory services go one step further and also associate a set of properties with the name. The primary focus of this chapter is naming services because they are of greater interest in the context of J2EE.

The white pages section of the telephone book is like a naming service. You use a name such as "Jeremy Crosby" to perform a lookup. It returns a phone number object to your eyeball object. This phone number is really a handle. You don't get any information from the 10 digits. You pass that handle to another device, the telephone, and that device connects you.

Naming services act the same way. You type in the name of a Web site in the address line of the browser and press Enter. Domain Name Service (DNS) translates the name into an IP address of a site and sends a request for the root page at that site. That page then appears in your browser. Magic, huh?

You have lots of this magic in your life. If you use Novell, you have NDS. LDAP is everywhere, as is CORBA's CosNaming. You have the RMI Registry and even the file-naming scheme on your computer. They are all naming services, with each one having different specialties to handle its own specific problem domain. A wise guy once said, "The best thing about standards is that there are so many of them to choose from." This paragraph proves his point.

Each of these services plays an important role in our computing lives. It is fine that they are all written by different programmers using different design patterns (until you have to program with them, that is). Wouldn't it be nice if they all had the same programming interface?

Understanding JNDI

Enter JNDI. Sun and the Java team recognized the problem that this lack of agreement caused among programmers. Instead of producing yet another product that would compete with these existing systems, they created a committee that published a specification for an API. They then created a reference implementation to provide an example. The committee created a specification called the Java Naming and Directory Interface (JNDI), which was widely accepted.

The primary advantage of JNDI is that it flattens the learning curve. Once you have learned to program with JNDI, you will be able to program with it again, even if the underlying technology is different. This is analogous to using SQL to access databases.

JNDI is not a product, but rather a description and some classes that manage the upper layers. When you use JNDI to find a JDBC driver, you may be running different software than when you use it to find a CORBA object. But that is okay because the details are hidden from you.

JNDI is becoming the fundamental Java way of finding objects for the following technologies:

- Enterprise JavaBeans (EJB)
- Common Object Request Broker Architecture (CORBA)
- Remote Method Invocation (RMI)
- Remote Method Invocation over Internet Inter-Orb Protocol (RMI/IIOP)
- Java Message Service (JMS)
- JDBC 2.0

There are several terms that are common in the JNDI world. The most important ones are defined here:

- Context—A set of name/object pairs that occupy the same namespace. Duplicates are not allowed.
- Subcontext—A context that is a descendant of another context.
- Initial context—This is the mother of all contexts. We obtain a handle to this object first and use it to create or locate all other contexts.

Java Naming and Directory Interface (JNDI)

CHAPTER 11

407

11

JAVA NAMING
AND DIRECTORY
INTERFACE (JNDI)

- Bind—To associate a name with an object.

- Rebind—To associate a name with a different object.

- Unbind—To disassociate a name from an object.

- Binding—An association between a name and an object.

How Naming Services Work

A programming topic becomes really useful to you when you understand all the parts and the interrelationships between the parts. Until then, it is just a mass of details.

Senior programmers must understand the data flows in a system. If you can map the details into entities and data flows, they will take up less space (and will be much more interesting).

As we mentioned in the introduction, JNDI is not really a product. It is not just a description of an API, either. In truth, it is a wrapper around other products, as shown in Figure 11.1.

FIGURE 11.1
The JNDI classes sit on top of classes provided by the vendors of naming and directory products.

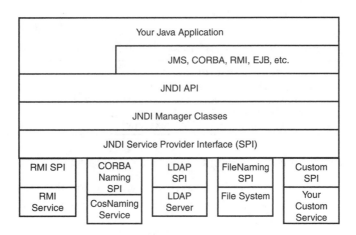

There are several parts of this figure that are interesting:

- Your Java application normally comes in contact with JNDI when you are using another API such as JMS, RMI, or CORBA. Even so, you will make some calls to JNDI to get access to the objects that you need to talk to.

- The other services may also be using JNDI for other reasons, such as security.

- The real work is always done by a service provider via a Service Provider Interface (SPI). The service provider normally, but not always, writes these interfaces. These APIs fill a role similar to that played by a JDBC driver. They form a translation layer between the JNDI object model/API and the vendor-specific programming interfaces for their naming service. We call JNDI, which calls the correct API on the vendor's naming service product to do the work we need done.

The only tricky part of the diagram is that your application may be running on a different computer than the JNDI provider. If you use the JNDI API to find objects, what will you use to find the JNDI provider objects?

The `InitialContext` Object

You must obtain the `InitialContext` object before you can use a naming service. A class file called `javax.naming.InitialContext` provides the link between your application and the naming service provider that contains the objects that you wish to find. You can create the `InitialContext` by creating a `Hashtable` object and putting values in it for the `InitialContextFactory` and the URL where the service resides.

Consider the code shown in Listing 11.1.

LISTING 11.1   The `InitialContext` Object

```
Hashtable env = new Hashtable();
env.put(Context.INITIAL_CONTEXT_FACTORY,
          "weblogic.jndi.WLInitialContextFactory");
env.put(Context.PROVIDER_URL, t3://www.xyx.com:7001);
InitialContext ic = new InitialContext(env);
```

There are several parts of this short listing that are interesting:

- The identity of the `InitialContextFactory` and its location are passed using a `HashTable`. They can also be communicated using a properties file or properties objects.

- Two pieces of information, the `ContextFactory` class and the URL of the location, are used to construct the `InitialContext` object. There is a class called `javax.naming.spi.NamingManager` that does the heavy lifting to create the `InitialContext` object. It uses the factory class and the URL and performs its work behind the scenes.

- The URL, `t3://www.xyx.com:7001`, looks a little strange. This URL doesn't have to be supported by the `java.net.URL` class, but it does have to comply with RFC 1738 and its related RFCs (which describe URLs in general terms). The `t3` is called the scheme ID. It serves the same function as `ftp` and `http` do by telling the using class the format of the information retrieved.

Java Naming and Directory Interface (JNDI)

CHAPTER 11

409

11

JAVA NAMING
AND DIRECTORY
INTERFACE (JNDI)

One of the `InitialContextFactory`'s jobs is to populate the name server with initial name/object pairs. Your application can then look up these names and obtain handles to important objects on your local machine or on a remote computer. For instance, a program using JMS needs a handle to a `QueueConnectionFactory` object so that it can connect to the queue that contains the data that it needs. Here, `ctx` is a handle to the `InitialContext`. The following code shows this:

```
qcFactory = (QueueConnectionFactory)ctx.lookup(
                    "myJMSProvider.QueueConnectionFactory");
```

This handle can now be used to access the public methods of the `QueueConnectionFactory` object. Notice that an explicit downcast is required because the object part of the name/object pair is a handle to class `Object`.

Finding the JNDI Provider

The biggest challenge of working with JNDI is locating the provider and obtaining a handle to the correct `InitialContext`. There are several techniques that can be used to do this, but they all require that, in the end, your programs have a URL and an `InitialContextFactory` class. These methods are finding by default, using a properties file, and creating a `Hashtable`. The following sections cover each of these.

Default Finding

If you are using an application server to provide your JNDI services and you are running inside the container, you can use a default `InitialContext` as shown in Listing 11.2.

LISTING 11.2   A Default URL and `InitialContext` Setup

```
package examples.jms.queue;

import java.io.*;
import java.util.*;
import javax.transaction.*;
import javax.naming.*;
import javax.jms.*;

/** This example shows how to establish a connection to the
 * InitialContext object on a WebLogic Server installation.
 * It also shows the contents of the InitialContext.
 *
 * This example runs in the same package as the JMS
 * queue examples. Copy this file to the same directory and run ant.
 * Follow the instructions that come with WebLogic Server on running
 * the examples that ship with the product on setting up the sample
 * server.
```

LISTING 11.2   continued

```
 *
 * @author Steve Potts
 */

public class ICDefaultLocator
{

   public static void main(String[] args)
   {
      try
      {
         System.out.println("The Java Unleashed ICDefaultLocator");

         //Create the InitialContext
         InitialContext ic = new InitialContext();
         System.out.println("The InitialContext object is " + ic);

         //Next find out the name of this context in its own namespace
         String myContextName = ic.getNameInNamespace();
         System.out.println("The InitialContext object's name is "
                        + myContextName);

         //Create an Enumeration of the name/object type pairs
         NamingEnumeration ne = ic.list(myContextName);
         System.out.println("The Naming Enumeration is " + ne);

         if(ne.hasMore())
         {
            System.out.println("First Element is " + ne.next());
         }else
       {
         System.out.println("Context has no elements");
       }
       }catch (NamingException e)
     {
         System.out.println("NamingException thrown " + e);
       }

   }//main
}//class
```

If a default `InitialContext` exists, you will receive a handle to it. If there isn't a default `InitialContext`, the following error message or one like it will appear:

```
The Java Unleashed ICDefaultLocator
The InitialContext object is javax.naming.InitialContext@18dfaf
```

```
NamingException thrown javax.naming.NoInitialContextException:
 Need to specify class name in environment or system property,
 or as an applet parameter, or in an application resource file:
  java.naming.factory.initialNotice
```

Notice that we get a reference to the `InitialContext` object, but that it isn't really usable. This is because JNDI uses lazy instantiation.

> **Caution**
>
> The fact that you get an `InitialContext` object reference when you first try to obtain one doesn't mean that it is valid. JNDI always returns an object, but it may not be usable. An exception will be thrown the first time you attempt to use an invalid handle.

> **Note**
>
> *Lazy instantiation* is a technique for speeding up the construction of an object. If a reference to an object that supports lazy instantiation is encountered during construction, a marker handle is placed in the object's reference. When the handle is actually used, the object is then instantiated. This technique is useful when an object might never be used, or when the construction of an object is taking too long and needs to be sped up.

IBM's WebSphere application server uses the properties file and default finding for its implementation.

Passing the Properties on the Command Line

One way of solving the problem of communicating the names of the URL and factory class to the JNDI manager classes is to pass them in as parameters on the command line. This can be done using `arg[0]` and `arg[1]`. While this will work, it creates an ugly command to start your program.

Creating a JNDI Properties File

The default `InitialContext` object can be found properly if you create a properties file that contains the proper values and place it in the classpath. To run this example correctly, we will create the following file called `jndi.properties`:

```
java.naming.factory.initial=weblogic.jndi.WLInitialContextFactory
java.naming.provider.url=t3://localhost:7001
```

Now we have the ability to run the `ICDefaultLocator` program from Listing 11.1 and get a good result:

```
The Java Unleashed ICDefaultLocator
The InitialContext object is javax.naming.InitialContext@617189
The InitialContext object's name is
The Naming Enumeration is weblogic.jndi.internal.
NameClassPairEnumeration@17a560

First Element is SubClass: weblogic.jndi.internal.ServerNamingNode
```

(The reason that we print the first binding is to make use of the `InitialContext` object to make sure that it is really functional.)

> **Note**
>
> The properties file approach is the one used by Sun in the J2EE Reference Implementation. You can locate the `jndi.properties` file in `%J2EE_HOME%\lib\classes` (as of release 1.3).

The properties file technique is a reasonable approach to providing naming services while minimizing the amount of detail present in individual programs. The main objection to this approach is that it hides too much detail from the programmers. However, properties files are commonly used and most good programmers could find the `jndi.properties` file quickly if they wanted to know the URL or factory class being used.

One disadvantage to using properties files is that in a client-deployed application, if the initial context information needs to be changed, it won't be easy to change the `jndi.properties` files on all the client machines. (This isn't something that is normally packaged with the application, but instead is usually packaged with the Java Runtime Environment. However, in server-side applications this isn't as much of an issue.)

Passing a Properties Object

We can create a properties object in our code as well. The example shown in Listing 11.3 will work without requiring us to create a `jndi.properties` file.

LISTING 11.3   A Properties Object for the `InitialContext`

```
package unleashed.ch11;

import java.io.*;
```

LISTING 11.3   continued

```java
import java.util.*;
import javax.transaction.*;
import javax.naming.*;
import javax.jms.*;

/** This example shows how to establish a connection to the
 * InitialContext object on a WebLogic Server installation.
 * It also shows the contents of the InitialContext.
 *
 *
 * @author Steve Potts
 */

public class ICDefaultLocator2
{

  public static void main(String[] args)
  {
     try
     {
        System.out.println("The Java Unleashed ICDefaultLocator2");

        java.util.Properties props = new java.util.Properties();
        props.put(Context.INITIAL_CONTEXT_FACTORY,
                        "weblogic.jndi.WLInitialContextFactory");
        props.put(Context.PROVIDER_URL, "t3://localhost:7001");

        //Create the InitialContext
        InitialContext ic = new InitialContext(props);
        System.out.println("The InitialContext object is " + ic);

        //Next find out the name of this context in its own namespace
        String myContextName = ic.getNameInNamespace();
        System.out.println("The InitialContext object's name is "
                        + myContextName);

        //Create an Enumeration of the name/object type pairs
        NamingEnumeration ne = ic.list(myContextName);
        System.out.println("The Naming Enumeration is " + ne);

        if(ne.hasMore())
        {
           System.out.println("First Element is " + ne.next());
        }else
        {
           System.out.println("Context has no elements");
        }
        }catch (NamingException e)
```

LISTING 11.3   continued

```
        {
            System.out.println("NamingException thrown " + e);
        }
    }//main
}//class
```

We declare a properties object and store the values that are needed in it. We then pass it as the argument to the constructor. We can see from the result that this will work (your implementation's output may look slightly different):

```
The Java Unleashed ICDefaultLocator2
The InitialContext object is javax.naming.InitialContext@617189
The InitialContext object's name is
The Naming Enumeration is weblogic.jndi.internal.
                              NameClassPairEnumeration@1fc2f

First Element is SubClass: weblogic.jndi.internal.ServerNamingNode
```

This approach has merit, but it keeps the connection information hard-coded in the program. It is easier to change in an updated version of code, though, because the updated information is encompassed in a new code release. Also, this hides URL information from the general public.

Creating a `Hashtable`

The final technique uses a `Hashtable` object to contain the connection parameters. It is very similar to the properties object approach. It is shown in Listing 11.4.

LISTING 11.4   A `Hashtable` InitialContext

```
package unleashed.ch11;

import java.io.*;
import java.util.*;
import javax.transaction.*;
import javax.naming.*;
import javax.jms.*;

/** This example shows how to establish a connection to the
 * InitialContext object on a WebLogic Server installation.
 * It also shows the contents of the InitialContext.
 *
 *
 * @author Steve Potts
 */

public class ICLocator
{
```

LISTING 11.4   continued

```java
public static void main(String[] args)
{
    try
    {
        System.out.println("The Java Unleashed ICLocator");

        //Specify the URL of the naming service provider. In this
        //case it is my computer
        String url = "t3://localhost:7001";
        System.out.println("The URL of the InitialContext object is "
                        + url);

        //Use the hashtable approach to getting the InitialContext
        Hashtable env = new Hashtable();

        //Specify that we want the WebLogic context factory to be run
        env.put(Context.INITIAL_CONTEXT_FACTORY,
            "weblogic.jndi.WLInitialContextFactory");
        env.put(Context.PROVIDER_URL, url);

        //Create the InitialContext
        InitialContext ic = new InitialContext(env);
        System.out.println("The InitialContext object is " + ic);

        //Next find out the name of this context in its own namespace
        String myContextName = ic.getNameInNamespace();
        System.out.println("The InitialContext object's name is "
                        + myContextName);

        //Create an Enumeration of the name/object type pairs
        NamingEnumeration ne = ic.list(myContextName);
        System.out.println("The Naming Enumeration is " + ne);

        if(ne.hasMore())
        {
            System.out.println("First Element is " + ne.next());
        }else
    {
        System.out.println("Context has no elements");
    }
    }catch (NamingException e)
    {
        System.out.println("NamingException thrown " + e);
    }

    }//main
}//class
```

The result of running this is the same as in the other examples (your output may differ slightly):

```
The Java Unleashed ICLocator
The URL of the InitialContext object is t3://localhost:7001
The InitialContext object is javax.naming.InitialContext@617189
The InitialContext object's name is
The Naming Enumeration is weblogic.jndi.internal.
NameClassPairEnumeration@17a560

First Element is SubClass: weblogic.jndi.internal.ServerNamingNode
```

> **Tip**
>
> The name of the `InitialContext` object is returned as `""`. This is not a problem because the `list()` method appears to default to the `InitialContext` as its context if it is passed an empty `String`.

The JNDI provider that you use will likely dictate the method of obtaining the `InitialContext`. The various methods described earlier were provided with the goal of removing the mystery from the process of making initial contact with the JNDI server.

JNDI and WebLogic Server

Now we can look at how WebLogic Server makes use of JNDI to do its work.

The first thing that we can do is obtain a handle to the `InitialContext` and then see what name/object pairs it contains. This code is shown in Listing 11.5.

LISTING 11.5 The WebLogic Server JNDI

```
package unleashed.ch11;

import java.io.*;
import java.util.*;
import javax.transaction.*;
import javax.naming.*;
import javax.jms.*;

/** This example shows how to establish a connection to the
 * InitialContext object on a WebLogic Server installation.
 * It also shows the contents of the InitialContext.
 *
```

Java Naming and Directory Interface (JNDI)

CHAPTER 11

417

11

JAVA NAMING
AND DIRECTORY
INTERFACE (JNDI)

LISTING 11.5   continued

```
* This example runs in the same package as the JMS
* queue examples. Copy this file to the same directory and run ant.
* Follow the instructions that come with WebLogic Server on running
* the examples that ship with the product on setting up the sample
* server.
*
* @author Steve Potts
*/

public class ICFinder
{

  public static void main(String[] args)
  {
    try
    {
        System.out.println("The Java Unleashed ICFinder");

        //Specify the URL of the naming service provider. In this
        //case it is my computer
        String url = "t3://localhost:7001";
        System.out.println("The URL of the InitialContext object is "
                        + url);

        //Use the hashtable approach to getting the InitialContext
        Hashtable env = new Hashtable();

        //Specify that we want the WebLogic context factory to be run
        env.put(Context.INITIAL_CONTEXT_FACTORY,
            "weblogic.jndi.WLInitialContextFactory");
        env.put(Context.PROVIDER_URL, url);

        //Create the InitialContext
        InitialContext ic = new InitialContext(env);
        System.out.println("The InitialContext object is " + ic);

        //Next find out the name of this context in its own namespace
        String myContextName = ic.getNameInNamespace();
        System.out.println("The InitialContext object's name is "
                        + myContextName);

        //Create an Enumeration of the name/object type pairs
        NamingEnumeration ne = ic.list(myContextName);
        System.out.println("The Naming Enumeration is " + ne);

        //list the names in the context and the object class
        // of the handles they point to
        while(ne.hasMore())
        {
            System.out.println(ne.next());
```

LISTING 11.5   continued

```
        }
    }catch (NamingException e)
    {
        System.out.println("NamingException thrown " + e);
    }
  }//main
}//class
```

The results are not surprising. This name server contains a lot of handles to a lot of different objects in WebLogic. The output that you get will depend on your installation and the program that you run to use this service:

```
SubClass: weblogic.jndi.internal.ServerNamingNode
examples: weblogic.jndi.internal.ServerNamingNode
weblogic: weblogic.jndi.internal.ServerNamingNode
eis: weblogic.jndi.internal.ServerNamingNode
xml-xslt-ContentHome_EO: weblogic.rmi.cluster.ClusterableRemoteObject
jta-jmsjdbc-ReceiveInTxHome_EO:
 weblogic.rmi.cluster.ClusterableRemoteObject
jms: weblogic.jndi.internal.ServerNamingNode
readMostly: weblogic.jndi.internal.ServerNamingNode
statelessSession: weblogic.jndi.internal.ServerNamingNode
statefulSession: weblogic.jndi.internal.ServerNamingNode
examples-dataSource-demoXAPool:
weblogic.rmi.cluster.ClusterableRemoteObject
javax: weblogic.jndi.internal.ServerNamingNode
quotes: weblogic.jms.common.DestinationImpl
jta-jmsjdbc-ReceiveInTxHome:
 weblogic.rmi.cluster.ClusterableRemoteObject
beanManaged: weblogic.jndi.internal.ServerNamingNode
xml-xslt-ContentHome: weblogic.rmi.cluster.ClusterableRemoteObject
java:comp: weblogic.jndi.internal.ServerNamingNode
containerManaged: weblogic.jndi.internal.ServerNamingNode
jconnector: weblogic.jndi.internal.ServerNamingNode
examples-dataSource-demoPool:
 weblogic.rmi.cluster.ClusterableRemoteObject
```

> **Note**
>
> The `list()` command gives the name and the class of the object. If you want the name of the object stored, use `listBindings()` instead.

As you can see from this output, WebLogic Server makes extensive use of JNDI. Interrogating a JNDI provider and learning what bindings it contains is a good way to debug naming problems.

Binding, Unbinding, and Rebinding

The real fun of a naming system is not in looking up names, but in creating your own. The process of associating a name with an object is called *binding*. Just to confuse us, the result of binding a name with an object is called a *binding*. The process of destroying a binding is called *unbinding*, the process of changing a binding is called *rebinding*, and the process of finding out what is bound to a name is called *lookup*. Listing 11.6 shows examples of all these actions.

LISTING 11.6 The Connection to the `InitialContext`

```
package unleashed.ch11;

import java.io.*;
import java.util.*;
import javax.transaction.*;
import javax.naming.*;
import javax.jms.*;

/** This example shows how to establish a connection to the
 * InitialContext object on a WebLogic Server installation.
 * It also shows the contents of the InitialContext.
 *
 *
 * @author Steve Potts
 */

public class ICBinder
{

  public static void main(String[] args)
  {
    try
    {
      System.out.println("The Java Unleashed ICBinder");

      //Specify the URL of the naming service provider. In this
      //case it is my computer
      String url = "t3://localhost:7001";

      //Use the hashtable approach to getting the InitialContext
      Hashtable env = new Hashtable();

      //Specify that we want the WebLogic context factory to be run
      env.put(Context.INITIAL_CONTEXT_FACTORY,
          "weblogic.jndi.WLInitialContextFactory");
      env.put(Context.PROVIDER_URL, url);
```

LISTING 11.6   continued

```
    //Create the InitialContext
    InitialContext ic = new InitialContext(env);

    //Create a String object
  String obj1 = new String("Mary Ann");

//Bind the String Object to the name "Girl Friend"
ic.bind("Girl Friend", obj1);

//Do a lookup on the name "Girl Friend");
    String obj2 = (String)ic.lookup("Girl Friend");
    System.out.println("The Girl Friend is " + obj2);

    //Change girlfriends
    obj1 = "Katie";
    ic.rebind("Girl Friend", obj1);

    //Do a lookup on the name "Girl Friend");
    obj2 = (String)ic.lookup("Girl Friend");
    System.out.println("The Girl Friend is now " + obj2);

    try
    {
      ic.unbind("Girl Friend");
        obj2 = (String)ic.lookup("Girl Friend");
    }catch(NameNotFoundException nnfe)
    {
        System.out.println("No name was found for Girl Friend");
    }
  }catch (NamingException e)
  {
    System.out.println("NamingException thrown " + e);
  }
 }//main
}//class
```

Several aspects of this listing are interesting:

- We obtain a handle to the `InitialContext` object, create a string, and bind it to the name `Girl Friend`. We perform a lookup that works fine.

- Next, we want to change the binding because we changed girlfriends (or maybe they changed boyfriends). We have to do a rebind here because the name is already bound. Binding will throw a `NameAlreadyBoundException` if you have a name/object pair that uses that name. You could rebind at all times, but it is a good idea to make sure that you only bind once in some cases. (The exception thrown here would be a lot easier to find than an unpredictable result would be.)

- Finally, we do an `unbind()` to prove to ourselves that this really works. Because we don't want to terminate the program right away, we catch the `NameNotFoundException` here and print out a message. This avoids the catch clause at the bottom of the page because we do not rethrow the exception.

The result of running Listing 11.6 is shown here:

```
The Java Unleashed ICBinder
The Girl Friend is Mary Ann
The Girl Friend is now Katie
No name was found for Girl Friend
```

These methods are simple to use. Once the handle to the `InitialContext` is obtained, even your boss could code it (or maybe not).

Complex Objects

The objects placed in the naming service must implement either `java.io.Serializable` or `java.io.Remote`. If these objects implement `Remote`, the requester receives a stub. If they implement `Serializable`, the requester receives a copy of the object.

Notice that, in the preceding example, the `lookup()` placed a handle in the `String` reference `obj2`:

```
obj2 = (String)ic.lookup("Girl Friend");
```

Observe also that `obj2` was never created with a `new`. The handle and the object were provided by the `lookup()` command. All you have to do is downcast it to the correct object type. Let's prove that this is always true by creating a complicated `Serializable` object example.

Caution

The JNDI provider might not have the same classpath as the client program. If your class files are not in its classpath, it will not be able to serialize your object.

We can then look up the object and discover whether we have a handle to the original object or a deep copy of the original. To do this, we will use the `Company` class and all of its subclasses as shown in Listings 11.7, 11.8, and 11.9.

LISTING 11.7   The Serialized `Employee` Object

```
package unleashed.ch11;
import java.io.Serializable;
```

LISTING **11.7**   continued

```java
import java.util.*;
/**
 *
 * @author  Stephen Potts
 * The Employee class
 */
public class Employee implements Serializable
{

    private String name;


    /** Creates Employee */
    public Employee( String name)
    {
        this.name = name;
    }

    public String getName()
    {
        return name;
    }
}
```

LISTING **11.8**   The Serializable Department Class

```java
package unleashed.ch11;
import java.io.Serializable;

/**
 *
 * @author  Stephen Potts
 * @version
 */
public class Department implements Serializable
{
    private String name;
    private Employee manager;

    /** Creates new Department */
    public Department(String name)
    {
        this.name = name;
    }

    public String getName()
```

Java Naming and Directory Interface (JNDI)

CHAPTER 11

423

11

JAVA NAMING
AND DIRECTORY
INTERFACE (JNDI)

LISTING 11.8   continued

```java
    {
        return this.name;
    }
    public Employee getManager()
    {
        return this.manager;
    }

    public void addManager(Employee e)
    {
        manager = e;
    }
}
```

LISTING 11.9   The Serialized Company Class

```java
package unleashed.ch11;
import java.util.Vector;
import java.util.Iterator;
import java.util.Set;
import java.io.Serializable;

/**
 *
 * @author  Stephen Potts
 * @version
 */
public class Company implements Serializable
{
    private String name;
    private Employee president;
    private Vector departments;

    /** Creates new Company */
    public Company(String name)
    {
        this.name = name;
        departments = new Vector();
    }

    public String getName()
    {
        return this.name;
    }

    public void addDepartment(Department dept)
    {
        departments.addElement(dept);
    }
```

LISTING **11.9**   continued

```
    public Employee getPresident()
    {
        return this.president;
    }

    public void addPresident(Employee e)
    {
        this.president = e;
    }

    public Iterator getDepartmentIterator()
    {
        return departments.iterator();
    }
}
```

The classes listed here are interesting because they contain other objects and Vectors. This makes them more difficult to serialize. The first step is to create an instance of Company that contains instances of Department that contain instances of Employee. Then we create a binding of that object to the name XYZ Company. The code that enables us to do this is shown in Listing 11.10.

LISTING **11.10**   The BindCompany Class Tests the Serialization

```
package unleashed.ch11;
import java.io.ObjectOutputStream;
import java.io.FileOutputStream;
import java.io.IOException;
import java.util.Iterator;
import java.util.Hashtable;
import javax.naming.*;


/**
 *
 * @author   Stephen Potts
 * Test to see if company is serializable
 */
public class BindCompany
{

    /** Creates new BindCompany */
    public BindCompany() {
    }
```

Java Naming and Directory Interface (JNDI)
CHAPTER 11
425

11

JAVA NAMING
AND DIRECTORY
INTERFACE (JNDI)

LISTING **11.10** continued

```java
public static void printCompanyObject(Company c)
{
    System.out.println("The company name is " + c.getName());
    System.out.println("The company president is " +
                                c.getPresident().getName());
    System.out.println(" ");

    Iterator i = c.getDepartmentIterator();
    while (i.hasNext())
    {
        Department d = (Department)i.next();
        System.out.println("   The department name is " +
                                            d.getName());
        System.out.println("   The department manager is " +
                                        d.getManager().getName());
        System.out.println(" ");
    }
}


public static void main(String[] args)
{
    try
    {
        System.out.println(
                "The Java Unleashed BindCompany");

        //Specify the URL of the naming service provider. In this
        //case it is my computer
        String url = "t3://localhost:7001";

        //Use the hashtable approach to getting the InitialContext
        Hashtable env = new Hashtable();

        //Specify that we want the WebLogic context factory to be run
        env.put(Context.INITIAL_CONTEXT_FACTORY,
          "weblogic.jndi.WLInitialContextFactory");
        env.put(Context.PROVIDER_URL, url);

        //Create the InitialContext
        InitialContext ic = new InitialContext(env);


        Company comp = new Company("The Blazer Company");
        Employee emp0 = new Employee("Leslie Waller");
        comp.addPresident(emp0);

        Department sales = new Department("Sales");
```

LISTING 11.10   continued

```
            Employee emp1 = new Employee("Grant Jackson");
            sales.addManager(emp1);
            comp.addDepartment(sales);

            Department accounting = new Department("Accounting");
            Employee emp2 = new Employee("Clay Cain");
            accounting.addManager(emp2);
            comp.addDepartment(accounting);

            Department maintenance = new Department("Maintenance");
            Employee emp3 = new Employee("Greg Hladlick");
            maintenance.addManager(emp3);
            comp.addDepartment(maintenance);
            printCompanyObject(comp);


            //Bind the String Object to the name "XYZ Company"
            ic.bind("XYZ Company", comp);


        }catch (NamingException ne)
        {
            System.out.println("NamingException thrown " + ne);
        }
    }
}
```

> **Caution**
>
> The class files for all of the serializable classes must be in the WebLogic Server's classpath as well as in the client classpath. These are not normally the same classpath.

When we run this program, everything seems fine. We want to look and see whether the name that we used in the bind() method is really in the context. We can run the ICFinder class that we defined earlier in the chapter to do this. Sure enough, in the list of bindings we find this one:

```
XYZ Company: examples.jms.queue.Company
```

Next, let's verify that we get an object from JNDI and that the object is still intact after we get it back from the naming service. The code that does this is shown in Listing 11.11.

LISTING 11.11 The LookupCompany Class

```java
package unleashed.ch11;

import java.io.ObjectInputStream;
import java.io.FileInputStream;
import java.io.IOException;
import java.util.Iterator;
import java.util.Hashtable;
import javax.naming.*;


/**
 *
 * @author   Stephen Potts
 * Test the restoration of bound objects
 */
public class LookupCompany {

    /** Creates new LookupCompany */
    public LookupCompany() {
    }

    public static void printCompanyObject(Company c)
    {
        System.out.println("The company name is " + c.getName());
        System.out.println("The company president is " +
                                        c.getPresident().getName());
        System.out.println(" ");

        Iterator i = c.getDepartmentIterator();
        while (i.hasNext())
        {
            Department d = (Department)i.next();
            System.out.println("   The department name is " +
                                                    d.getName());
            System.out.println("   The department manager is " +
                                    d.getManager().getName());
            System.out.println(" ");
        }
    }
    public static void main(String[] args)
    {
        try
        {


            System.out.println("The Java Unleashed LookupCompany");

            //Specify the URL of the naming service provider. In this
```

LISTING **11.11**   continued

```
                //case it is my computer
                String url = "t3://localhost:7001";
                System.out.println("The URL of the InitialContext object is "
                           + url);

                //Use the hashtable approach to getting the InitialContext
                Hashtable env = new Hashtable();

                //Specify that we want the WebLogic context factory to be run
                env.put(Context.INITIAL_CONTEXT_FACTORY,
                 "weblogic.jndi.WLInitialContextFactory");
                env.put(Context.PROVIDER_URL, url);

                //Create the InitialContext
                InitialContext ic = new InitialContext(env);

                //Do a lookup on the name "Girl Friend");
                Company comp = (Company)ic.lookup("XYZ Company");

                printCompanyObject(comp);


            }catch (NamingException ne)
            {
                System.out.println("NamingException thrown " + ne);
            }
        }
}
```

Now let's look at the results:

```
The Java Unleashed LookupCompany
The URL of the InitialContext object is t3://localhost:7001
The company name is The Blazer Company
The company president is Leslie Waller

   The department name is Sales
   The department manager is Grant Jackson

   The department name is Accounting
   The department manager is Clay Cain

   The department name is Maintenance
   The department manager is Greg Hladlick
```

Lo and behold, we've re-created every one of the objects contained by the Company object by simply issuing the lookup command. This miracle is really performed by the serializable functionality in the JVM. The ability to store objects of arbitrary complexity

Java Naming and Directory Interface (JNDI)
CHAPTER 11

429

11

JAVA NAMING
AND DIRECTORY
INTERFACE (JNDI)

in a naming service doesn't really seem that great until you consider that naming services can exist anywhere on the network. This means that we can use JNDI to transfer these objects from one computer to another.

Precautions When Using JNDI

At this point in the chapter you are probably excitedly thinking up ways to apply JNDI to your programs. Before you go hog-wild, however, here are a few precautions:

1. Know whether you are using JNDI locally or remotely. Local access is normally pretty fast. Remote access can be slow. If you are accessing JNDI remotely, try to access it only once, at the start of your program. You can cache the values in local variables. If the logic of your program doesn't allow you to find out what names you need to look up, at least keep the `InitialContext` object open. This will speed up future access.

2. If you are going to bind several name/object pairs to the service, do so all at once. Some implementations of J2EE allow clustering. These application servers replicate the values to every machine in the cluster every time they change. Dribbled changes are very expensive because of this.

3. A corollary of the preceding caution is that you should use JNDI for JNDI things such as object names and handles. Never use it for mundane variable storage. JNDI is designed and built so that lookups are extremely fast, but inserts and updates are expensive and slower. As such, it's usually not a good idea to use the directory as a simple holder mechanism for a lot of temporary or transient data. You shouldn't use JNDI as a replacement for a true database and JDBC.

Summary

In this chapter, we covered the inner and outer workings of the Java Naming and Directory Interface (JNDI). You learned about the role of JNDI in distributed object environments.

You learned about the `InitialContext` object and saw several ways of creating it. We looked at how to use this handle to perform operations on the data in the context.

Finally, we saw how to place a more complex object in the provider using JNDI. We retrieved it and demonstrated that a deep copy of the object is returned when we do a `lookup()`.

A good understanding of JNDI is critical to your success as a distributed object programmer. Now that you have studied the workings of JNDI, you are in a better position to design and troubleshoot your distributed systems.

Processing Speech
with Java

In the 1990s, engineers and programmers got a new dose of our favorite show in *Star Trek: The Next Generation.* When Captain Picard sat in his chair on the bridge and spoke to the starship's computers, we saw the vision of what the world would be like if voice-driven systems were to become a reality.

Ever since *2001: A Space Odyssey* premiered with its talking computer, Hal, the public has been waiting for voice-driven systems to become a reality. Who can forget the computer in *War Games* that said "Shall we play a game?" Now, after nearly 40 years of experimentation and uncountable sums of money have been expended, we are still waiting. That future is still possible, but the good news is that voice-driven systems are becoming more common. Most of us have encountered a voice-driven system that asks us to "press or say one to speak to the appointment desk." The material covered in this chapter will teach you how to write systems that can respond to the spoken word as these systems do.

In this chapter, we will learn about getting computers to accept sounds as inputs and provide them to us as outputs. To do this, we will first learn how to get a computer to speak to us. We will also learn how a computer can be made to understand our world and react to it.

Understanding Java Speech

Speech is such a common subject that whenever we bring it up as a topic of conversation, our friends look at us as if we are a little strange. We all speak, and none of us can remember a time when we didn't.

There is a lot to know about phonetics and language, and we need to understand more than a little of it if we are going to become good speech programmers. Although it is true that the software engineers at the tool vendors do much of the hard work associated with programming speech, we will not be able to take advantage of the tools they provide unless we understand the subject.

Computerized speech can be divided into two categories: speech recognition and speech synthesis. Speech recognition is the art of turning analog sound waves captured by a microphone into words. These words are either commands to be acted on or data to be stored, displayed, manipulated, and so on.

Speech synthesis is the art of taking the written word and transforming it into analog waveforms that can be heard over a speaker. When looked at in this light, the problem of teaching a computer how to listen and talk seems a little daunting.

Take yourself back mentally to the mid 1970s. Imagine for a moment that you have been given the task of taking one of the mainframe computers in the data center and teaching it to read out loud. You sit down at the computer terminal, and what do you type? What language do you write this system in? What speakers will you use? Where will you plug them in? What kind of pronunciation will you use? How will you generate the waveforms for each syllable? How will you time the output? How will punctuation be handled?

When we think about these issues, we are glad that we are living now. In the 1970s, this entire subject was in the hands of the researchers. Even now, while some commercial applications of speech synthesis have been written, it is still a fertile subject for Ph.D. and graduate students.

Our job as application programmers is much easier than it would have been in the 1970s because of two developments. The first is the creation and marketing of commercial speech products. The second is the creation of the Java Speech API by Sun, in conjunction with a number of other companies interested in this subject.

The Java Speech API is a set of abstract classes and interfaces that represent a Java programmer's view of a speech engine, but it makes no assumptions about the underlying implementation of the engine. This engine can be either a hardware or a software solution (or a hybrid of the two). It can be implemented locally or on a server. It can be written in Java or in any other language that can be called from Java. In fact, different compliant engines can even have different capabilities. One of them might have the capability to learn your speech patterns, whereas another engine might choose not to implement this. It is the engine's responsibility to handle any situations that it does not support in a graceful manner.

The Java Speech API is slightly different from other Java Extensions in that Sun Microsystems doesn't provide a reference implementation for it. Instead, Sun provides a list of third-party vendors who have products that provide a Java Speech API interface. The official Java Speech Web site (`http://java.sun.com/products/java-media/speech`) lists the following companies as providers of Java-compatible speech products:

- FreeTTS—This is an open source speech synthesizer written entirely in Java.
- IBM's Speech for Java—This implementation is based on the IBM ViaVoice product. You must purchase a copy of ViaVoice for this product to work.
- The Cloud Garden—This implementation will work with any speech engine that is based on Microsoft Speech API (SAPI) version 5.
- Lernout and Hauspie's TTS for Java Speech API—This package runs on Sun and provides a number of advanced features.

- Conversa Web 3.0—This product is a speech-enabled Web browser.
- Festival—This product comes from Scotland and is Unix based. It supports a number of programming interfaces in addition to Java.

> **Note**
>
> This list is subject to change as new products are introduced. You should consult the Web site for the latest version.

The examples in this chapter will be created using IBM's Speech for Java, which runs on top of IBM's ViaVoice product. This product was selected for this book because it is widely available both in retail stores and over the Web. Careful evaluation of the preceding products should be undertaken before choosing your production speech engine vendor. Each of them offers a different feature set, platform support, and pricing structure. Figure 12.1 shows the architecture of the Java Speech API layered on top of the IBM products.

FIGURE 12.1

The Java Speech architecture.

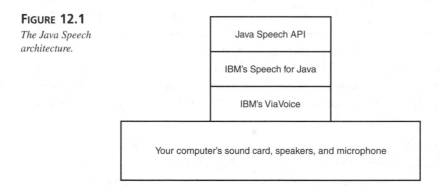

The Java Speech API is really just a layer that sits atop the speech processing software provided by the vendor, who is IBM in our case. (IBM's ViaVoice is a commercial software product that allows users to dictate letters and figures using products such as Microsoft Office.) ViaVoice, in turn, communicates with the sound card via drivers provided by the sound card manufacturer. It receives input from the microphone port on the sound card, and it provides output via the speaker port on the same sound card.

The existence of the Java Speech API is important because of the power it provides. This enables Java applications to make calls to speech processing objects as easily as it makes calls to an RMI server. This brings the portability of Java into play, as well as a shortened learning curve.

The magic of the application is really in the ViaVoice layer. In this layer, the heavy lifting is performed. We will look at what this magic entails in the sections that follow.

Creating and Allocating the Speech Engine

Let's work on an example to help us understand how to get speech to work on your machine. The first step that we need to take is to install one of the commercial products listed previously and get it running. For these examples, we installed ViaVoice and IBM Speech for Java.

Follow these steps if you are using ViaVoice on a PC. If you are on another platform, or if you are using a product other than ViaVoice, follow the vendor's directions on how to install it.

1. Install ViaVoice according to the instructions that ship with the product.

2. Download and install IBM's Speech for Java. It is free from the IBM Web site at www.alphaworks.ibm.com/tech/speech.

3. Follow the directions in Speech for Java about setting the classpath and path properly.

4. Run the test programs that ship with the IBM products to make sure that the setup is correct. If they work, you are ready to run an example.

The first step in writing an example is the creation and allocation of the Speech Engine itself. The example shown in Listing 12.1 does just that.

LISTING 12.1   The `HelloUnleashedReader` Class

```
*
 * HelloUnleashedReader.java
 *
 * Created on March 5, 2002, 3:32 PM
 */

package unleashed.ch12;

/**
 *
 * @author   Stephen Potts
 * @version
 */
import javax.speech.*;
import javax.speech.synthesis.*;
```

LISTING 12.1 continued

```java
import java.util.Locale;

public class HelloUnleashedReader
{

    public static void main(String args[])
    {
        try
        {
            // Create a synthesizer for English
            Synthesizer synth = Central.createSynthesizer(
            new SynthesizerModeDesc(Locale.ENGLISH));
            synth.allocate();
            synth.resume();

            // Speak the "Hello, Unleashed Reader" string
            synth.speakPlainText("Hello, Unleashed Reader!", null);
            System.out.println(
                "You should be hearing Hello, Unleashed Reader now");

            // Wait till speaking is done
            synth.waitEngineState(Synthesizer.QUEUE_EMPTY);

            // release the resources
            synth.deallocate();
        } catch (Exception e)
        {
            e.printStackTrace();
        }
    }
}
```

First, we need to look at the packages that are used to drive the speech engine:

```java
import javax.speech.*;
import javax.speech.synthesis.*;
import java.util.Locale;
```

The `javax.speech` package contains the `Engine` interface. Classes that extend this interface are the primary speech processing classes in Java.

The `javax.speech.synthesis` package contains the interfaces and classes that pertain to "reading" speech aloud.

The `java.util.Locale` class deals with internationalization. Because spoken language is one of the most locale dependent activities that humans participate in, very little can be done in this area without a locale specified. If you do not set a locale in your program, the default locale for your machine will be used. See Chapter 25, "Java Internationalization," for details on this package.

Before we can do anything, we need to create an object of type `Synthesizer`. `Synthesizer` is an interface, so it will be handed an object that implements it. Because the Java program has no way of knowing what the class of the actual object will be, it assigns this object to an interface handle:

```
Synthesizer synth = Central.createSynthesizer(
    new SynthesizerModeDesc(Locale.ENGLISH));
```

The `Central` class is one of those magic `Factory` classes that works behind the scenes to create a class for you that fits your specification. See Chapter 21, "Design Patterns in Java," for an explanation of the `Factory` pattern.

In this case, we are asking the `Central` class to create a `Synthesizer` that speaks English and to give us a handle to it. It is possible to create a synthesizer without specifying a locale. In this case, if an engine is already running on this computer, it will be selected as the default. Otherwise, a behind-the-scenes call is made to `java.util.Locale.` `getDefault()` to obtain the locale for the computer running the engine. The best engine for this locale will be created.

Armed with a handle, we are ready to synthesize. Before we can use our new toy, however, we have to allocate it. The `allocate()` method gathers all the resources needed to get the synthesizer running. Engines are not automatically allocated when they are created for two reasons. The first reason is that the creation of the engine is a very expensive activity (in processing terms). In order to improve performance, you have an opportunity to allocate the engine in a separate thread while you program does other work in the foreground. The second reason is that the engine needs exclusive access to certain resources such as the microphone (for recognizer applications). It is wise to allow the program to allocate and deallocate if it chooses to in order to avoid contention:

```
synth.allocate();
```

The `resume()` method is the complement of the `pause()` method. Because we are ready to play the message now, we issue the `resume()` command:

```
synth.resume();
```

The `speakPlainText()` command tells the synthesizer to say something. In this case, we tell it to say `"Hello, Unleashed Reader"`. We will discuss the specifics of the synthesis commands when we deal with speech in a later section of this chapter.

```
// Speak the "Hello, Unleashed Reader" string
synth.speakPlainText("Hello, Unleashed Reader!", null);
```

Next, we have to tell the synthesizer to wait until the queue is empty before running the rest of our program. This ensures that the resources will be held long enough to finish.

```
// Wait till speaking is done
synth.waitEngineState(Synthesizer.QUEUE_EMPTY);
```

The `deallocate()` method releases all the resources reserved for this program's use when the `allocate()` method was called:

```
synth.deallocate();
```

It is wise to deallocate the resources and allocate them again if you might not use the synthesizer for an extended period of time or if some of the exclusively held resources might be needed elsewhere.

This architecture reminds us of the way that Java itself is organized. For our programs to be portable, they must not have any concrete connection to the underlying hardware. This is the reason that abstraction layers such as the Java Speech APIs are so valuable. The same programming interface can support a number of underlying products in a very similar and sometimes identical manner.

The output of this program is audible. You should hear the phrase `"Hello Unleashed"` in your speakers or headphone. In addition, you will see the following line on the console for this application:

`You should be hearing Hello, Unleashed Reader now.`

Engine States

The engine itself moves through certain states. These states keep the engine behaving properly by allowing it to change its behavior when conditions change, as well as in response to user actions.

Four different allocation states exist that the engine passes through while doing its work: `DEALLOCATED`, `ALLOCATED`, `ALLOCATING_RESOURCES`, and `DEALLOCATING_RESOURCES`. The `ALLOCATED` state is the only one that allows any voice synthesis to be performed.

While the engine is in the allocated state, it can also have several substates. One substate is `PAUSED`, and its converse is `RESUMED`.

Another set of substates that are independent of the paused/resumed pair is the `QUEUE_EMPTY` and the `QUEUE_NOT_EMPTY` state. While there is data to be processed on the queue, the state is `QUEUE_NOT_EMPTY`. Otherwise, the state is `QUEUE_EMPTY`. These two states apply to speech synthesizing but not to recognition. Listing 12.2 shows a simple speech-synthesizing example with the states printed out.

LISTING 12.2   The `HelloUnleashedStates` Class

```java
/*
 * HelloUnleashedStates.java
 *
 * Created on March 5, 2002, 3:32 PM
 */

package unleashed.ch12;

/**
 *
 * @author   Stephen Potts
 * @version
 */
import javax.speech.*;
import javax.speech.synthesis.*;
import java.util.Locale;

public class HelloUnleashedStates
{
    private static void printState(Synthesizer synth)
    {
        System.out.println("The current States are:");
        if(synth.testEngineState(Synthesizer.QUEUE_EMPTY))
            System.out.println("State = QUEUE_EMPTY");
        if(synth.testEngineState(Synthesizer.QUEUE_NOT_EMPTY))
            System.out.println("State = QUEUE_NOT_EMPTY");
        if(synth.testEngineState(Engine.ALLOCATED))
            System.out.println("State = ALLOCATED");
      if(synth.testEngineState(Engine.DEALLOCATED))
            System.out.println("State = DEALLOCATED");
        if(synth.testEngineState(Engine.ALLOCATING_RESOURCES))
            System.out.println("State = ALLOCATING_RESOURCES");
        if(synth.testEngineState(Engine.DEALLOCATING_RESOURCES))
            System.out.println("State = DEALLOCATING_RESOURCES");


        if(synth.testEngineState(Engine.RESUMED))
            System.out.println("State = RESUMED");
        if(synth.testEngineState(Engine.PAUSED))
            System.out.println("State = PAUSED");

    }

    public static void main(String args[])
    {
        try
        {
            // Create a synthesizer for English
```

LISTING 12.2   continued

```java
        Synthesizer synth = Central.createSynthesizer(
        new SynthesizerModeDesc(Locale.ENGLISH));
        printState(synth);
        synth.allocate();
        printState(synth);
        synth.resume();
        printState(synth);

        // Speak the "Hello, Unleashed States" string
        synth.speakPlainText("Hello, Unleashed States!", null);
        printState(synth);

        // Wait till speaking is done
        synth.waitEngineState(Synthesizer.QUEUE_EMPTY);
        printState(synth);

        // release the resources
        synth.deallocate();
        printState(synth);
    } catch (Exception e)
    {
        e.printStackTrace();
    }
    }
}
```

The output from running this example is shown in the following. We can see the progression of states as the synthesizer allocates the resources, reads in the phrase, places it on the queue, processes it off the queue, and deallocates the resources:

```
The current States are:
State = QUEUE_EMPTY
State = DEALLOCATED
State = RESUMED
The current States are:
State = QUEUE_EMPTY
State = ALLOCATED
State = RESUMED
The current States are:
State = QUEUE_EMPTY
State = ALLOCATED
State = RESUMED
The current States are:
State = QUEUE_NOT_EMPTY
State = ALLOCATED
State = RESUMED
The current States are:
State = QUEUE_EMPTY
```

```
State = ALLOCATED
State = RESUMED
The current States are:
State = QUEUE_EMPTY
State = DEALLOCATED
State = RESUMED
```

In addition to the previously printed lines, the phrase `"Hello, Unleashed States"` is audible. From this example, it is clear to see how the different states are changed independently of each other.

Allocating in a Thread

Speech programs require quite a bit of processing power. This might present a problem in the perceived performance of your program. One approach that can be used to address this performance is to allocate the engine in a thread separate from the main program, thereby improving perceived performance. All you have to do is declare an anonymous inner class that runs the `allocate()` method, trap any exceptions, and execute the `start()` method as shown here in Listing 12.3.

LISTING 12.3   The `HelloThread` Example

```java
/*
 * HelloThread.java
 *
 * Created on March 5, 2002, 3:32 PM
 */

package unleashed.ch12;

/**
 *
 * @author   Stephen Potts
 * @version
 */
import javax.speech.*;
import javax.speech.synthesis.*;
import java.util.Locale;

public class HelloThread
{

    public static void main(String args[])
    {
        Engine eng;
        try
        {
            // Create a synthesizer for English
```

LISTING 12.3   continued

```java
        final Synthesizer synth = Central.createSynthesizer(
        new SynthesizerModeDesc(Locale.ENGLISH));

        new Thread(new Runnable()
        {
            public void run()
            {
                try
                {
                    synth.allocate();
                }catch (Exception e)
                {
                    System.out.println("Exception " + e);
                }
            }
        }).start();

        //Add the rest of you initialization code here


        //wait for the engine to get ready
        synth.waitEngineState(Engine.ALLOCATED);
        synth.resume();

        // Speak the "Hello, Thread" string
        synth.speakPlainText("Hello, Thread!", null);
        System.out.println(
        "You should be hearing Hello, Thread now.");


        // Wait till speaking is done
        synth.waitEngineState(Synthesizer.QUEUE_EMPTY);

        // release the resources
        synth.deallocate();
    } catch (Exception e)
    {
        e.printStackTrace();
    }
    }
}
```

There is no need to name this inner class, so we just begin the statement by declaring it with the keyword new:

```java
        new Thread(new Runnable()
        {
            public void run()
```

We perform the `allocate` on the synthesizer handle just as we did before, only this is done inside the new thread:

```
synth.allocate();
```

Because we are accessing `synth` from within another class, we have to declare it final. This is okay because we never need to reassign its value:

```
final Synthesizer synth = Central.createSynthesizer(
new SynthesizerModeDesc(Locale.ENGLISH));
```

We must coordinate the timing of the two threads for the example to work. Specifically, we must tell the main thread to wait until there is an allocated synthesizer to make calls to:

```
synth.waitEngineState(Engine.ALLOCATED);
```

The output from this application is an audible voice in your speaker or headphone, along with the following line on the console:

```
You should be hearing Hello, Thread now.
```

In an example this trivial, a separate thread is obviously overkill. In many applications though, a complex GUI could be created in the time it takes to allocate the resources needed to support the speech engine.

Speech Synthesis

Now that we are familiar with the speech engine, we can use it to do some work for our programs. The example in Listing 12.3 provided the correct audible output for a very simple sentence. As sentences become more complex, it becomes necessary for the programmer to provide direction to the synthesizer on the pronunciation of certain words and phrases. The mechanism for providing this input is called the *Java Speech Markup Language (JSML)*. To illustrate this, run the code in Listing 12.4 and listen to the result.

LISTING 12.4   The `HelloShares` Example

```
/*
 * HelloShares.java
 *
 * Created on March 5, 2002, 3:32 PM
 */

package unleashed.ch12;

/**
 *
```

LISTING 12.4   continued

```java
 * @author   Stephen Potts
 * @version
 */
import javax.speech.*;
import javax.speech.synthesis.*;
import java.util.Locale;

public class HelloShares
{

    public static void main(String args[])
    {
        try
        {
            // Create a synthesizer for English
            Synthesizer synth = Central.createSynthesizer(
            new SynthesizerModeDesc(Locale.ENGLISH));
            synth.allocate();
            synth.resume();

            // Speak the "Hello," string
            synth.speak("I own 1999 shares of stock", null);


            // Wait till speaking is done
            synth.waitEngineState(Synthesizer.QUEUE_EMPTY);

            // release the resources
            synth.deallocate();
        } catch (Exception e)
        {
            e.printStackTrace();
        }
    }
}
```

> **Caution**
>
> There is considerable difference between the operations of different synthesizers. A phrase that is rendered correctly without JSML in one synthesizer might not be rendered correctly in another.

The primary functions of a synthesizer are to manage the queue of text to be output, producing events as these functions proceed and, of course, speaking text:

```
Synthesizer synth = Central.createSynthesizer(
new SynthesizerModeDesc(Locale.ENGLISH));
```

The simplest method used to speak is called `speak()`. It considers the JSML commands and produces output. Consider this case:

```
synth.speak("I own 1999 shares of stock", null);
```

The second parameter is to pass a listener class if we want to be notified when events occur.

When you run this program, you will probably hear the phrase, "I own nineteen ninety-nine shares of stock." This sounds like the year 1999 instead of the number 1,999. We understand what this means, but it is not the natural way to say it. We need a way to provide instructions to the speech synthesizer about how a word or number should be pronounced. The Java Speech Markup Language gives us that way.

The Java Speech Markup Language (JSML)

Now that we have succeeded in getting a Java program to say a few words, we drill down to the next goal, which is to get a program to say words as naturally as possible. As with most programming topics, the concept is easy, but the details make it hard. These pesky details include the following:

- Ambiguity—Consider the sentence, "Team U.S.A. has advanced to the finals." How does the speech synthesizer know that the sentence didn't end after the *A*? How do we teach it the difference between the noun *object* and the verb *object*?

- Abbreviations—Consider the sentence, "The St. Louis Rams have won the Super Bowl." How does the synthesizer know that St. is pronounced *Saint*?

- Acronyms—Abbreviations such as IBM are never spoken as a word (that is, we say *I-B-M* rather than *ibbumm*), whereas acronyms such as UNICEF are almost never spelled out (that is, we say *unicef* rather than *U-N-I-C-E-F*). How does it know which to do?

- Dates and numbers—If the synthesizer sees the string 1999, does it pronounce it as the year 1999 or the number *one thousand nine hundred and ninety-nine*?

- Computerese—How do we teach a computer to say *A-P-I* instead of *Appi*?

- Foreign words—How does it handle foreign words such as *mahimahi* or *tsunami*?

- Jargon—How well can the synthesizer handle words such as *instantiation* or *objectify*?

One way of addressing this problem is provided in the *Java Speech Markup Language (JSML)*. This XML-based language allows the programmer or system manager to add additional markups (special tags) to the text that provide pronunciation hints to the synthesizer. This can greatly improve the accuracy of the "reading," but it requires some additional labor.

JSML is an XML-based language, and it must, therefore, conform to the requirement that its documents be well formed. It is not required that they also be validated, but it is a good idea in production applications.

The fact that a speech synthesizer can accept JSML makes it an XML application. The synthesizer contains an XML parser that is responsible for finding the XML elements in the JSML file or string. The parser extracts the values from these elements and hands them to the synthesizer. The synthesizer is responsible for handling or ignoring them. This parser is nonvalidating, so a DTD is not required. If a tag is encountered that is not understood, the parser ignores it.

You can think of the synthesizer as a kind of audible browser. A graphical browser receives an HTML document that is a combination of data and instructions. The browser parses the file, removes the instructions, and displays the data in accordance with the instructions. The synthesizer receives a JSML that is a combination of data and instructions. The synthesizer parses the file, removes the instructions, and plays the data portion in accordance with the instructions. Table 12.1 shows the element types for JSML.

TABLE 12.1 JSML Elements

Element	Description
jsml	Root element for JSML documents
div	Marks sentences and paragraphs
voice	Speaking voice for contained text
sayas	Specifies how to say the text
phoneme	Specifies pronunciation
emphasis	Emphasizes the text
break	Specifies a break in the speech
prosody	Indicates the pitch, rate, and volume
marker	Request for notification
engine	Native instructions to a synthesizer

Let's work an example that illustrates how to use JSML to improve speech output. First, we need to learn how to remove the hard-coded text from our program so that it can play different JSML documents. The easiest way to do this is by creating a new class that implements the `javax.speech.synthesis.Speakable` interface. This interface requires one method, `getJSMLText()`. It returns a string that contains JSML text. Listing 12.5 shows us an example of this class.

LISTING 12.5 The `SpeakableDate` Class

```
/*
 * SpeakableDate.java
 *
 * Created on March 12, 2002, 11:54 AM
 */

package unleashed.ch12;

import javax.speech.synthesis.Speakable;
import java.util.Date;

/**
 *
 * @author   Stephen Potts
 * @version
 */
public class SpeakableDate implements Speakable
{

    /** Creates new SpeakableDate */
    public SpeakableDate()
    {
    }

    /** getJSMLText is the only method of Speakable */
    public String getJSMLText()
    {
        StringBuffer buf = new StringBuffer();
        String todayString = "3/12/2002";

        // Speak the sender's name slower to be clearer
        buf.append("<jsml>");
        buf.append("Today is " + todayString );
        buf.append("Today is <sayas class=\"date\">"+ todayString +" </sayas>");
        buf.append("</jsml>");

        return buf.toString();
    }
}
```

This class exists to provide a JSML document to a synthesizer. Some programmers consider it more convenient to create their XML documents in a class such as this one instead of in a file. This class uses `StringBuffer` while the string is being built up because it performs better than the `String` class when it is changed frequently.

```
buf.append("Today is " + todayString );
buf.append("Today is <sayas class=\"date\">"+ todayString +" </sayas>");
```

Two separate strings are added to the JSML document. The first string simply adds the string literal. The second identifies it as a date. Listing 12.6 shows us the synthesizer class that runs this JSML.

LISTING 12.6   The `JSMLSpeaker` Class

```java
/*
 * JSMLSpeaker.java
 *
 * Created on March 5, 2002, 3:32 PM
 */

package unleashed.ch12;

/**
 *
 * @author   Stephen Potts
 * @version
 */
import javax.speech.*;
import javax.speech.synthesis.*;
import java.util.Locale;

public class JSMLSpeaker
{

    public static void main(String args[])
    {
        Speakable sAble = new SpeakableDate();
        try
        {
            // Create a synthesizer for English
            Synthesizer synth = Central.createSynthesizer(
                    new SynthesizerModeDesc(Locale.ENGLISH));
            synth.allocate();
            synth.resume();

            // Speak the string
            synth.speak(sAble, null);
            System.out.println("You are hearing the JSML output now.");

            // Wait till speaking is done
            synth.waitEngineState(Synthesizer.QUEUE_EMPTY);
```

LISTING 12.6   continued

```
        // release the resources
        synth.deallocate();
    } catch (Exception e)
    {
        e.printStackTrace();
    }
  }
}
```

This class resembles the synthesizer classes that we mentioned earlier in that it allocates and deallocates the synthesizer. It is different, though, because it expects to process a `Speakable` class instead of a string literal. The `Speakable` class is called `SpeakableDate`, and it is shown earlier in Listing 12.5.

```
    Speakable sAble = new SpeakableDate();
```

Conceptually, this is a class version of a JSML document. We can pass a handle to that class to the synthesizer's `speak()` method. This method treats it similar to an XML document that is parsed and interpreted as speech.

The output from running this program is audible and visible. The audible portion reads the date as characters with the slashes pronounced:

```
Today is three slash twelve slash two thousand two
```

The second time, the date is pronounced more like a date with the slashes omitted:

```
Today is three twelve two thousand two
```

In addition, the following visual message is written to the console:

```
You are hearing the JSML output now.
```

Listing 12.7 illustrates another example that shows some interesting JSML elements.

LISTING 12.7   The `SpeakableSlow` Class

```
/*
 * SpeakableSlow.java
 *
 * Created on March 12, 2002, 11:54 AM
 */

package unleashed.ch12;

import javax.speech.synthesis.Speakable;
```

LISTING 12.7   continued

```java
/**
 *
 * @author  Stephen Potts
 * @version
 */
public class SpeakableSlow implements Speakable
{

    /** Creates new SpeakableShares */
    public SpeakableSlow()
    {
    }

    /** getJSMLText is the only method of Speakable */
    public String getJSMLText()
    {
        StringBuffer buf = new StringBuffer();

        // Speak the sender's name slower to be clearer
        buf.append("<jsml>");
        buf.append("I own 1500 shares");
        buf.append("I own 1500 shares.");
        buf.append("<div>I own <PROS RATE=\"-20%\">1,500</PROS> shares</div> ");
        buf.append("I own <PROS RATE=\"-50%\">1500</PROS> shares");
        buf.append("</jsml>");

        return buf.toString();
    }
}
```

You can parse this document by changing the `JSMLSpeaker` class that is shown in Listing 12.6 by altering the following line:

```java
Speakable sAble = new SpeakableSlow();
```

> **Note**
>
> The code file for this modified example is available in the source code for this chapter and is named `JSMLSpeaker2.java`.

Several features are illustrated in this example. The first line is read at a normal speed. When the end is reached, it combines the first and second line and then tries to pronounce "sharesI." The first attempt to cure this problem was to add a period at the end of the next line. This causes "dot" to be uttered:

```
buf.append("I own 1500 shares");
buf.append("I own 1500 shares.");
```

Finally, the elements `<div>` and `</div>` identified the text between them as a division, and the synthesizer stopped slurring the words together. A space will work in some instances, but the explicit `<div>` tag is normally used.

Next, we added some special elements called prosody elements to slow down the speaking of the numbers. Prosody elements provide details on the rate of speech that is desired:

```
buf.append("<div>I own <PROS RATE=\"-20%\">1,500</PROS> shares</div> ");
```

The rate dropped by 20% so that the most important part of the sentence, the number of shares, would be easier to comprehend. Notice the difference between the way that the number is pronounced, depending on the presence or absence of the comma in the numerals. If the comma is present, the number is pronounced *one thousand five hundred*. Without the comma, it is pronounced like the year 1500.

You can slow the rate down even more if you choose, as we did in the last sentence:

```
buf.append("I own <PROS RATE=\"-50%\">1500</PROS> shares");
```

This will make the output sound as if it needs to take some vitamins.

The output from running this will be the phrase repeated four times with the previously mentioned variations. At the same time, the following phrase will appear on your console to prove that the program ran:

```
You are hearing the JSML output now.
```

Finally, we will create a JSML version of the HelloShares example in Listing 12.4. As you recall, the "1999" phrase was pronounced "nineteen ninety-nine" instead of "one thousand nine hundred ninety nine." The JSML version of the program is shown in Listing 12.8.

LISTING 12.8   The `SpeakableShares` Class

```
/*
 * SpeakableShares.java
 *
 * Created on March 12, 2002, 11:54 AM
 */
```

LISTING 12.8 continued

```java
package unleashed.ch12;

import javax.speech.synthesis.Speakable;
import java.util.Date;

/**
 *
 * @author  Stephen Potts
 * @version
 */
public class SpeakableShares implements Speakable
{

    /** Creates new SpeakableShares */
    public SpeakableShares()
    {
    }

    /** getJSMLText is the only method of Speakable */
    public String getJSMLText()
    {
        StringBuffer buf = new StringBuffer();
        String shareString = "1,999";

        // Speak the shareString
        buf.append("<jsml>");
        buf.append("I own 1999 shares of stock");
        buf.append("I own <sayas class=\"number\">"+ shareString
                            +" </sayas>" + " shares of stock");
        buf.append("</jsml>");

        return buf.toString();
    }
}
```

Notice that the shareString contains a comma between the first and second digits:

```java
String shareString = "1,999";
```

That, in combination with the "number" parameter in the <sayas> tag, provides an unambiguous specification for this pronunciation.

You can run this code by running the program called unleashed.ch12.
JSMLSpeaker3.java. This class is identical to the previous one except that it instantiates the SpeakableShares class. It is also included with the code download for this chapter.

The result of running this example is both audible and visual. First you will hear 1999 pronounced "nineteen ninety-nine." Next, you will hear it pronounced "one thousand nine hundred ninety nine." You will see the usual message on the console:

```
You are hearing the JSML output now.
```

> **Note**
>
> Because the Java Speech API is always running on top of a third-party speech product, the behavior that you observe might be different. For example, some products might recognize a period as a sentence ending instead of as a "dot" as we encountered in this chapter.

JSML is a very good example of how to use XML to improve your products. By embedding these controls in the JSML file, it is possible to place the specification of the pronunciation details outside the program and into the data.

Speech Recognition

The other side of Java Speech is speech recognition. As you might have predicted, the state of the art in recognition is not nearly as advanced as speech synthesis. The reason for this is simple; it is a harder topic.

If you are an English speaker, your ear might be finely tuned to the nuances of the language as the native speakers pronounce them from your region of the United States or Canada. If you relocate to another part of your country, or to another English speaking country, such as Australia, your ability to understand the language is diminished for a while. Over time, your brain learns the subtleties of the new dialect, and you once again become a fluent listener.

For a computer, the problem is similar. Recognizers receive information electronically via microphones. They then must try to determine what set of syllables to create from the set of phonemes (sounds) just received. These syllables must then be combined into words.

Recognition Grammars

A *grammar* simplifies the job of the speech recognizer by limiting the number of possible words and phrases that it has to consider when trying to determine what a speaker has said. There are two kinds of grammars: rule grammars and dictation grammars.

Rule grammars are composed of tokens and rules. When a user speaks, the input is compared to the rules and tokens in the grammar to determine the identity of the word or phrase. An application provides a rule grammar to a recognizer, normally during initialization.

Dictation grammars are built in to the recognizer itself. They define thousands of words that can be spoken in a free form fashion. Dictation grammars come closer to our ultimate goal of unrestricted speech, but, at present, they are slower than rule grammars and more prone to errors.

> **Note**
>
> There are four basic error types that recognizers suffer from regardless of the grammar employed:
> - Failure to recognize a valid word
> - Misinterpreting a word to be another valid word
> - Detecting a word where none was present
> - Failure to recognize that a word was spoken

Java Speech supports dynamic grammars. This means that grammars can be modified at runtime. After a change is made to the grammar, it must be committed using the `commitChanges()` method of the recognizer. When these changes are committed, they are committed atomically, meaning all at once. Listing 12.9 shows a simple grammar.

LISTING 12.9   A Simple Grammar

```
grammar javax.speech.demo;

public <sentence> = Hello world |
                    Hello Java Unleashed |
                    Java Speech API |
                    computer |
                    bye |
                    I program computers;
```

This rule grammar is composed of six different tokens. A recognizer that is working against this grammar will understand no other words, phrases, or parts of phrases. The reason for this is to simplify the processing and increase the likelihood that an accurate result will be obtained.

This rule grammar is formatted in the *Java Speech Grammar Format Specification (JSGF)*. Grammars formatted in JSGF can be converted logically into `RuleGrammar` objects and back again. (It might look different, but it will be equivalent.)

Armed with a grammar, we need a recognizer program to process speech against it. Listing 12.10 shows a program that will serve as a recognizer for this grammar.

LISTING 12.10   The `HelloRecognizer` Class

```
/*
 * HelloRecognizer.java
 *
 * Created on March 11, 2002, 9:53 PM
 */

package unleashed.ch12;

/**
 *
 * @author   Stephen Potts
 * @version
 */

import javax.speech.*;
import javax.speech.recognition.*;
import java.io.FileReader;
import java.util.Locale;

public class HelloRecognizer extends ResultAdapter
{

    static Recognizer recognizer;
    String gst;

    public void resultAccepted(ResultEvent re)
    {
        try
        {
        Result res = (Result)(re.getSource());
        ResultToken tokens[] = res.getBestTokens();

            for (int i=0; i < tokens.length; i++)
            {
                gst = tokens[i].getSpokenText();
                System.out.print(gst + " ");
            }
            System.out.println();

            if(gst.equals("bye"))
```

LISTING 12.10   continued

```
        {
            System.out.println("See you later!");
            recognizer.deallocate();
            System.exit(0);
        }
        }catch(Exception ee)
        {
            System.out.println("Exception " + ee);
        }
    }

    public static void main(String args[])
    {
        try
        {
            recognizer = Central.createRecognizer(
                new EngineModeDesc(Locale.ENGLISH));
            recognizer.allocate();

            FileReader grammar1 =
             new FileReader("c:/unleashed/ch12/SimpleGrammar.txt");

            RuleGrammar rg = recognizer.loadJSGF(grammar1);
            rg.setEnabled(true);

            recognizer.addResultListener(new HelloRecognizer());

        System.out.println("Ready for Input");
            recognizer.commitChanges();

            recognizer.requestFocus();
            recognizer.resume();
        }catch (Exception e)
        {
            System.out.println("Exception   " + e);
        }
    }
}
```

> **Note**
>
> The filename in the `FileReader` constructor must match the actual filename of the `SimpleGrammar.txt` file on your computer.

The creation of a recognizer is similar to the creation of a synthesizer. We use the `Central` class to create both:

```
recognizer = Central.createRecognizer(
        new EngineModeDesc(Locale.ENGLISH));
```

Once again, we have chosen English as the language for this example. Once we have a recognizer, we can load the grammar:

```
FileReader grammar1 =
 new FileReader("c:/unleashed/ch12/SimpleGrammar.txt");

RuleGrammar rg = recognizer.loadJSGF(grammar1);
rg.setEnabled(true);
```

We will load the grammar from Listing 12.8, which is stored in the `SimpleGrammar.txt` file. We create a `RuleGrammar` object, and set it to be enabled.

The event listener will do the runtime work of the program. We set the event listener here:

```
recognizer.addResultListener(new HelloRecognizer());
```

Next, we complete the initialization of the recognizer by committing the grammar, getting the focus, and putting the recognizer in the `RESUMED` state:

```
recognizer.commitChanges();
recognizer.requestFocus();
recognizer.resume();
```

When a spoken pattern is recognized as part of the grammar, a result event occurs and the `ResultAccepted()` method is called. The event object contains the information that we need to find out which phrase in the grammar was spoken:

```
Result res = (Result)(re.getSource());
ResultToken tokens[] = res.getBestTokens();
```

The `Result` interface documentation says that `getBestTokens()` guesses at the phrase that has been spoken. This is in reference to the inexact nature of the process of speech recognition. We then extract the string that the recognizer guesses is the correct one:

```
gst = tokens[i].getSpokenText();
```

For all the strings except bye, the result is echoed to the console as shown here:

```
Hello world
Hello Java Unleashed
computer
I program computers
bye
See you later!
```

Once the `bye` string is received, we print it and exit the program, adding a `See you later!` as a confirmation that we have exited.

Summary

This chapter covers the two primary functions of the Java Speech API—speech synthesis and speech recognition. In addition, you learned about the speech engine that provides services to both of these capabilities.

You learned how to synthesize speech using an implementation of the `Synthesizer` interface provided by the IBM ViaVoice product. We wrote several programs that produced speech from written input.

You also learned how to use the *Java Speech Markup Language (JSML)* to give instructions to the speech engine about how to pronounce the words, dates, and numbers that appear in the text. You saw examples of how you can use XML tags to communicate this information to the synthesizer.

Finally, we took a look at the art of recognizing speech with software. We created a simple grammar using the *Java Speech Grammar Format (JSGF)* and loaded it into a recognizer program. We then spoke into the microphone and watched as our spoken words appeared in the console. In addition, you saw how a command can be tied to a spoken word by the way the word `bye` was used to close this program.

The subject of speech in Java is larger than a single chapter can cover. This chapter provides enough information so that you will be able to get both a synthesizer and a recognizer working on your computer. Hopefully, you will be able to copy and paste these programs and enhance them to meet the requirements of your projects.

JavaMail

In This Chapter

When we think of e-mail, we think of sending pictures of the kids to grandma or getting spammed with messages selling us miracle cures for baldness. At its core, however, e-mail is just another way of sending information from one computer to another, much like JMS or RMI. The client that sends and receives messages determines what the user will see when the message arrives.

It is not surprising that Java has an API for e-mail called JavaMail. The e-mail situation is one that fits the Java API mold to a tee. There are many different e-mail protocols from *Simple Mail Transfer Protocol (SMTP)* and *Post Office Protocol (POP)* to *Internet Message Access Protocol (IMAP)*. Each of them has its own way of creating, sending, receiving, and deleting messages, but at the core, they all do mail.

The JavaMail API fits on top of these products and provides a consistent application-programming interface to Java developers. Like JDBC and JMS, you must have a provider under the covers to do the actual work. The JavaMail API allows you to program to one API regardless of what protocol is actually being used to do the heavy lifting.

In this chapter, we will look at JavaMail from a programmer's point of view. We will look at the internals of JavaMail so that we can understand how it works. Then we will get a simple send-and-receive application to work. Finally, we will get the CruiseList application to work using JavaMail to transfer the requests and responses between the CruiseList GUI and the TicketAgent.

Understanding JavaMail

The JavaMail specification includes a number of abstract classes that can be used to control a variety of messaging systems. These interfaces are `Session`, `Transport`, and `Store`. We will look at these, as well as the role that each plays in moving your e-mails around. Figure 13.1 shows the relationship between these classes.

FIGURE 13.1

The JavaMail API's system classes.

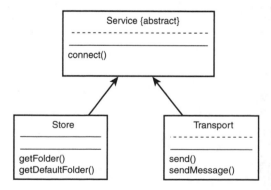

The purpose of each class is summarized here:

- The `Service` class is abstract and must therefore be extended by an actual provider. A `Service` class constructor instantiates the provider. The actual URL is passed in to the constructor and stored in this class.

- The `Transport` class extends `Service`. It is capable of moving a message from one computer to another. The *Simple Message Transport Protocol (SMTP)* is a common transport. The `Transport` class is where the methods to send messages and add listeners reside.

- The `Store` class models a provider that stores messages that have been sent to a machine. It provides methods to add listeners to the provider so that a program can retrieve messages when they arrive.

The `Session` Class

The `Session` class serves as a focal point for a messaging service. A `Session` is responsible for determining which provider is to be used for a certain type of message. It does this by examining the `providers` file. Normally, a single session can be used by all the clients in the JVM, although it is possible to have more than one.

A `Session` handle is obtained by making a call to the `getDefaultInstance()` method. This method takes a `properties` file as a parameter that normally contains the type of server to connect to. If no session of that type is active, the `getDefaultInstance()` will create one and return its handle to the client. The `Session` object is the focal point of a JavaMail application because it is the object used to create messages.

There will be as many provider classes (classes that extend `javax.mail.Transport`) on your machine as there are providers. It is the job of the `Session` object to instantiate the correct one.

The `Message` Class

The stars of our show are, of course, the classes that extend the abstract `Message` class. Messages are composed of the attributes and contents of an e-mail, along with flags that indicate its state.

Figure 13.2 shows a class diagram of the `Message` class and the `Part` interface that it implements.

13

JAVAMAIL

Figure 13.2

The Message *class diagram.*

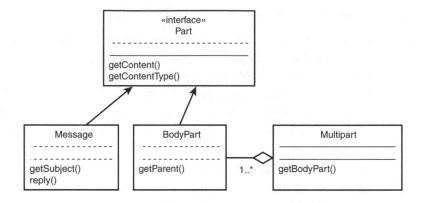

The Part interface provides several methods like getContent() and getContentType(), which are used by both the Message and the BodyPart class. The BodyPart class models one part of a message that is composed of a number of elements, such as attachments.

The normal process of sending an e-mail is to create a message, set its attributes, and then set its contents prior to handing it to the Transport.

How JavaMail Works

Let's look at what really goes on when you send an e-mail to another machine. Let's assume that you have a provider installed on your machine that is capable of acting as a transport. Let us further assume that the proper JavaMail jar files are installed on your system.

Because your e-mail provider is JavaMail-compliant, it contains a set of classes that extend the abstract class javax.mail.Transport. Your code must find a way to obtain a connection to this class.

The first thing that your program must do is provide several pieces of information:

- The name of your e-mail subscription service
- The address to send the message to
- The address that the message is sent from
- The body of the message

Your program will take the name of the e-mail service and add it to a properties file with the name mail.smtp.host. Next, it will attempt to find a Session object that can be used to send a message to this host. Session is implemented as a singleton. If one is already available, this will become your Session object. If one isn't already in memory, the Session class's static method getDefaultInstance() will create one.

In order to determine which Transport class to connect with, the Session class looks in the javamail.default.providers file (located in the J2EE.jar file currently). This file contains a mapping between the protocol and the class that extends javax.mail.Transport. This class will serve as the provider for this protocol. The contents of this file on a Windows machine are shown in Listing 13.1.

LISTING 13.1   The javamail.default.providers File Tells the Session Object Which Class File to Use to Send Messages

```
# JavaMail IMAP provider Sun Microsystems, Inc
protocol=imap; type=store; class=com.sun.mail.imap.IMAPStore;
vendor=Sun Microsystems, Inc;
# JavaMail SMTP provider Sun Microsystems, Inc
protocol=smtp; type=transport; class=com.sun.mail.smtp.SMTPTransport;
vendor=Sun Microsystems, Inc;
# JavaMail POP3 provider Sun Microsystems, Inc
protocol=pop3; type=store; class=com.sun.mail.pop3.POP3Store;
 vendor=Sun Microsystems, Inc;
```

This file is not hard to read. It contains the class names of two stores and one transport.

The Session object is now valid, so it can be used to create messages. The program proceeds to construct the message by setting its attributes such as From, Recipients, Subject, and Text.

Finally, the program calls the static send() message of the Transport class that the Session object instantiated. This Transport object does all the real work. It takes the message object and sends it to the host that was addressed.

On the receiving side, the process is even simpler. The Session object is created in the same way. This time, however, a special call to the getStore() method is made to find a handle to the store. With this handle, the program can navigate the stores folders and retrieve the messages.

Creating a Simple SMTP Application

In order to understand the JavaMail API better, let's create an example that sends a message to a real provider at a commercial site. In order to get this example to work, you will need to find out who your SMTP host is. In a later example, you will need to find out your POP3 provider. You can find out both by looking at your e-mail client. Figure 13.3 shows my settings in Microsoft Outlook.

> **Caution**
>
> Popular Web-based e-mail services such as Hotmail will not work with these examples because they do not give you access to the pop3/imap/smtp servers.

FIGURE 13.3

You can find the settings for your SMTP and POP3 hosts in your e-mail client.

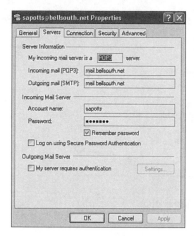

Replace the values in the setup() method with your settings to get this example to run.

The code for this example is shown in Listing 13.2.

LISTING 13.2   The SimpleSMTPClient Sends a Message to a Commercial E-mail Account

```
/*
 * SimpleSMTPClient.java
 *
 * Created on January 12, 2002, 10:44 AM
 */

package unleashed.ch13;

import javax.mail.*;
import javax.mail.internet.*;
import java.util.*;

/**
 *
 * @author  Stephen Potts
 * @version
 */
```

LISTING 13.2   continued

```java
public class SimpleSMTPClient
{
    String smtpServer;
    String to;
    String from;
    String subject;
    String body;

    /** Creates new SimpleSMTPClient */
    public SimpleSMTPClient()
    {
        setup();
        log("Constructor completed  ");

    }

    private void setup()
    {
        //This is where you put in the settings for your message
        smtpServer = "mail.bellsouth.net";
        to - "sapotts@bellsouth.net";
        from = "sapotts@bellsouth.net";
        subject = "Unleashed book example";
        body = "This is a test to see if we can send a message";
        log("Setup completed  ");

    }

    private void send()
    {
        try
        {
            log("Sending a message to " + to);

            //This is the code that does the sending of the message
            Properties props = System.getProperties();

            props.put("mail.smtp.host", smtpServer);
            Session session = Session.getDefaultInstance(props, null);

            //Create the new message
            Message msg = new MimeMessage(session);

            //Set the send from address
            msg.setFrom(new InternetAddress(from));

            //Set the to address
            msg.setRecipients(Message.RecipientType.TO,
```

13

JAVAMAIL

LISTING 13.2   continued

```java
                InternetAddress.parse(to, false));

            //Set the subject
            msg.setSubject(subject);
            msg.setText(body);

            //set the date
            msg.setSentDate(new Date());

            //send the message
            Transport.send(msg);

            System.out.println("Message was sent");
        }catch (Exception e)
        {
            log("Error sending message  " + e);
        }
    }

    private void log(String s)
    {
        System.out.println(s);
    }

    public static void main(String[] args)
    {
        SimpleSMTPClient sc = new SimpleSMTPClient();
        sc.send();
        System.out.println("SimpleSMTPClient is done ");
    }

}
```

There are several interesting lines of code in this example:

- The parameters that indicate what to send and to whom are entered in as strings in the setup() routine. They are grouped together for clarity.

- Before getting the Session object, we add all the parameters in the System object to the Properties file as shown here:

    ```java
    Properties props = System.getProperties();
    ```

- We add the name of our SMTP host to the Properties file. This gives the Session object the information it needs to create the correct Transport object:

    ```java
    props.put("mail.smtp.host", smtpServer);
    ```

- We create a `MimeMessage` object, but we assign it to a `Message` handle. The reason for this is that the methods for sending the message reside at the `Message` class in the hierarchy. The type could be changed to `MimeMessage`, and it would still work:

```
Message msg = new MimeMessage(session);
```

- The "from" and "to" are both placed inside an `InternetAddress` object before they can be assigned to the message.

- We set the recipient with a constant `RecipientType.TO`. This indicates that this recipient is the addressee of the message. Other `RecipientTypes` are "CC" for carbon copy, and "BCC" for blind carbon copy. A carbon copy is when a person is sent a copy of a message with her name in the CC list. The recipients on the blind carbon copy list don't see any of the other recipients in the message when they receive it. Carbon copy is a term left over from the typewriter days. (If you don't know what a typewriter is, ask your parents.) A black piece of paper, called carbon paper, was placed in between two sheets of white paper, causing one typing session to create two typed pages. This practice was made obsolete by the invention of the copying machine.

- The recipient parameter is run through the `parse()` method of the `InternetAddress` class prior to assignment. This is done so a single `String` object containing comma-delimited addresses can be used. The `parse()` method creates one `InternetAddress` object for each address in the string.

```
msg.setRecipients(Message.RecipientType.TO,
InternetAddress.parse(to, false));
```

- The `send()` method is a static method of the `Transport` object that was instantiated by a `Session` object. Because the method is static, you don't need an instance of the class to call the method. You can simply use the class reference:

```
sc.send();
```

When you run this program, you see the following lines on the console:

```
Setup completed
Constructor completed
Sending a message to sapotts@bellsouth.net
Message was sent
SimpleSMTPClient is done
```

This indicates, but doesn't prove, that the message was actually sent. If we look at that account in Microsoft Outlook, we will see something similar to what is in Figure 13.4.

13

JavaMail

FIGURE 13.4

A message sent via the `SimpleSMTPClient` *program will arrive in your e-mail client and look just like the other messages.*

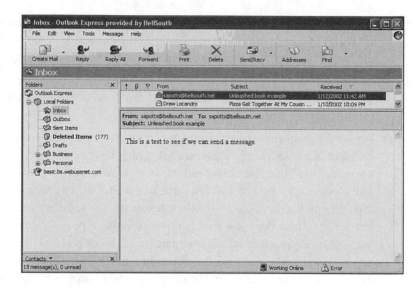

The other side of the same example is a simple program to take messages from a *store* and display them. This is essentially what your e-mail client does whenever you check messages as shown in Listing 13.3.

LISTING 13.3   The `SimplePopClient` Program Reads All the Messages in the Queue and Prints Them

```java
/*
 * SimplePopClient.java
 *
 * Created on January 12, 2002, 2:37 PM
 */

package unleashed.ch13;

import javax.mail.*;
import javax.mail.internet.*;

import java.util.*;
import java.io.*;

/**
 *
 * @author  Stephen Potts
 * @version
 */
public class SimplePopClient
```

LISTING 13.3 continued

```
{
    String server;
    String user;
    String password;

    /** Creates new SimplePopClient */
    public SimplePopClient()
    {
        setup();
    }

    private void setup()
    {
        //change these values to match your own personal settings
        server = "mail.bellsouth.net";
        user = "scoobydoo";
        password = "xyzxyz";
    }

    private void fetchMessages()
    {
        Store store1 = null;
        Folder folder1 = null;
        try
        {
            Properties props = System.getProperties();
            Session session = Session.getDefaultInstance(props, null);

            //get a handle to the pop3 store
            store1 = session.getStore("pop3");

            //connect to the store and pass the authentication
            store1.connect(server, user, password);

            //obtain the default folder handle
            folder1 = store1.getDefaultFolder();

            //get the handle to the inbox
            folder1 = folder1.getFolder("INBOX");

            //if there is no inbox, throw an exception
            if (folder1 != null)
            {
                folder1.open(Folder.READ_ONLY);
            }else
                throw new Exception("no inbox available");
```

LISTING 13.3   continued

```
            //if there are any messages, retrieve them
            Message[] messages = folder1.getMessages();
            if (messages.length == 0)
            {
                log("There are no messages to retrieve");
            }

            //print out the messages
            for (int i=0; i<messages.length; i++)
            {
                logMessage(messages[i]);
            }

        }catch (Exception e)
        {
            log("Exception thrown in fetchMessages() " + e);
        }
        finally
        {
            try
            {
                if (folder1 != null) folder1.close(false);
                if (store1 != null) store1.close();
            }
            catch (Exception ee)
            { log("Problem closing " + ee); }
        }
    }

    public void logMessage(Message message1)
    {
        try
        {
            log("-----------------------------------------");
            //get the From address
            InternetAddress ia = (InternetAddress)message1.getFrom()[0];

            //get the personal name from the message. This is the
            // name in human-readable form like Jake Snyder.
            String personalName = ia.getPersonal();
            log("The personal name is " + personalName);

            //get the addressString like jakesnyder@earthlink.com
            String addressString = ia.getAddress();
            log("The address String is " + addressString);

            //get the contents of the subject line
            String subject = message1.getSubject();
            log("The subject is " + subject);
```

LISTING 13.3   continued

```
            //Get the body of the message
            Part messagePart1 = message1;
            Object content = messagePart1.getContent();
            String contentType = messagePart1.getContentType();

            log("The content type is " + contentType);

            //If the message is plain text then you can read it with
            //a StreamReader
            if (contentType.startsWith("text/plain") ||
            contentType.startsWith("text/html"))
            {
                InputStream is = messagePart1.getInputStream();

                BufferedReader br =
                    new BufferedReader(new InputStreamReader(is));
                String line1=br.readLine();

                while (line1 != null)
                {
                    log(line1);
                    line1=br.readLine();
                }
            }
            log("-------------------------------------");
        }
        catch (Exception e)
        {
            log("Exception in logMessage " + e);
        }
    }

    private void log(String s)
    {
        System.out.println(s);
    }

    public static void main(String[] args)
    {
        //Instantiate the object
        SimplePopClient spc = new SimplePopClient();
        //get the messages
        spc.fetchMessages();
    }
}
```

There are several interesting lines of code in this example:

- Notice that we connect to the store using the server, user ID, and password.
- The store is composed of a hierarchy of folders. The default folder is used to obtain handles to the other folders.
- The folder that contains the new messages is called the INBOX. We obtain a handle to it:

```
folder1 = folder1.getFolder("INBOX");
```

- The source of the message is of type InternetAddress, so it must be cast to that type.
- The personal name is the name of the sender in human-readable form. The method getPersonal() retrieves this name.
- The e-mail address is obtained by calling the InternetAddress class's getAddress() method.
- The subject is retrieved with the getSubject() method of the Message class.
- The Part interface is the base for all the contents of a message. We use this interface to find out the type of content that the message contains.
- We also use the Part interface to retrieve the content once it is identified as shown here:

```
InputStream is = messagePart1.getInputStream();
```

When you run this example, you will see that the messages in the store will be printed to the console as shown here:

```
- - - - - - - - - - - - - - - - - - - - - - - - - - - - - - - - - - - - - - -
The personal name is null
The address String is sapotts@bellsouth.net
The subject is Unleashed book example
The content type is text/plain; charset=us-ascii
This is a test to see if we can send a message
```

Note

Without a valid user ID and password to a POP server, you will not get this result. You can get this account information from your e-mail provider.

Creating a JavaMail-Based CruiseList Application

Now that we have jumped over small hills, it is time to look at a more complex application. The CruiseList application is a GUI in which a travel agent matches a customer with a cruise. He then clicks the Book button, and a request is sent to another application called the TicketAgent.

The TicketAgent application looks up the customer in a database to retrieve her credit card number. It then calls a method that returns a `true` or `false` value for the credit card validity. If the credit card is valid, the ticket is created in the database. In either case, a message is sent back to the CruiseList GUI, telling the operator whether the request was successful.

The GUI for the CruiseList application is shown in Figure 13.5.

FIGURE 13.5

The CruiseList GUI is used by a travel agent to book cruises for his customers.

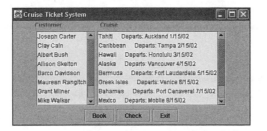

Whenever a request is answered in the affirmative, an e-mail is sent to the POP server. Clicking the Check button on the GUI will cause the messages to be retrieved and deleted after a display like the one in Figure 13.6 is shown.

FIGURE 13.6

The CruiseList GUI displays a message whenever a response is received from the TicketAgent application.

The code for the CruiseList GUI is shown in Listing 13.4.

LISTING 13.4   The CruiseList GUI Is Both an SMTP and POP Client

```java
/*
 * CruiseList.java
 *
 * Created on January 14, 2002, 4:02 PM
 */

package unleashed.ch13;

import javax.swing.*;
import java.awt.event.ActionListener;
import javax.swing.border.EtchedBorder;
import java.awt.Container;
import java.awt.BorderLayout;
import java.sql.*;
import javax.naming.*;
import javax.mail.*;
import javax.mail.internet.*;
import java.util.*;
import java.io.*;

/**
 *
 * @author   Stephen Potts
 * @version
 */
public class CruiseList extends JFrame implements ActionListener
{
    //JDBC variables
    java.sql.Connection dbConn = null;
    Statement statement1 = null;

    //JavaMail variables
    String smtpServer;
    String to;
    String from;
    String subject;
    String body;
    Session session;

    String server;
    String user;
    String password;


    //GUI Variables
    JList customerList;
    JList cruisesAvailable;
    JButton btnBook;
    JButton btnCheck;
```

LISTING 13.4 continued

```java
JButton btnExit;

//Arrays to hold database information
int[] custNums = null;
String[] lastNames = null;
String[] firstNames = null;

int[] cruiseIDs = null;
String[] cruiseDestinations = null;
String[] cruisePorts = null;
String[] cruiseSailings = null;

/** Constructors for CruiseList */
public CruiseList() throws Exception
{
    init();
}

public CruiseList(String caption) throws Exception
{
    super(caption);
    init();
}

//The init() method moves real processing out of the constructors where
//Exception handling is simpler
private void init() throws Exception
{
    try
    {
        //Obtain connections to JDBC and JMS via JNDI
        ConnectToServices();

        //configure the Frame
        setBounds(150,200,500,250);
        setDefaultCloseOperation(JFrame.EXIT_ON_CLOSE);

        //set the layout
        BorderLayout border = new BorderLayout();
        Container content = getContentPane();
        content.setLayout(border);

        //Populate the customerNames string
        String getCustomerString =
        "SELECT CustomerID, LastName, FirstName FROM CruiseCustomer";
        ResultSet custResults = statement1.executeQuery(getCustomerString);

        custNums = new int[20];
        lastNames = new String[20];
```

LISTING 13.4   continued

```java
firstNames = new String[20];
int index = 0;

while (custResults.next())
{
    custNums[index] = custResults.getInt("CustomerID");
    firstNames[index] = custResults.getString("FirstName");
    lastNames[index] = custResults.getString("LastName");
    index += 1;
}

String[] customerNames = new String[index];

for (int i=0;i<index;i++)
{
    customerNames[i] = firstNames[i] + " " + lastNames[i];
}
int numCustomers = index;
System.out.println("The number of customers " + index);

//Populate the cruises string
String getCruiseString =
"SELECT CruiseID, Destination, Port, Sailing FROM Cruises";
ResultSet cruiseResults = statement1.executeQuery(getCruiseString);

cruiseIDs = new int[20];
cruiseDestinations = new String[20];
cruisePorts = new String[20];
cruiseSailings = new String[20];
index = 0;

while (cruiseResults.next())
{
    cruiseIDs[index] = cruiseResults.getInt("CruiseID");
    cruiseDestinations[index] =
                cruiseResults.getString("Destination");
    cruisePorts[index] = cruiseResults.getString("Port");
    cruiseSailings[index] = cruiseResults.getString("Sailing");
    index += 1;
}

String[] cruises = new String[index];

for (int i=0;i<index;i++)
{
    cruises[i] = cruiseDestinations[i] +
                "        Departs: " + cruisePorts[i] +
                    " " + cruiseSailings[i];
}
```

LISTING 13.4   continued

```java
        int numCruises = index;
        System.out.println("The number of cruises" + index);


        //More GUI components
        String labelString = "                Customer";
        labelString += "                        Cruise";
        JLabel label1 = new JLabel(labelString);
        customerList = new JList(customerNames);
        cruisesAvailable = new JList(cruises);
        btnBook = new JButton("Book");
        btnCheck = new JButton("Check");
        btnExit = new JButton("Exit");
        btnBook.addActionListener(this);
        btnCheck.addActionListener(this);
        btnExit.addActionListener(this);

    JPanel bottomPanel = new JPanel();
    JPanel centerPanel = new JPanel();
    centerPanel.add(new JScrollPane(customerList,
                        JScrollPane.VERTICAL_SCROLLBAR_ALWAYS,
    JScrollPane.HORIZONTAL_SCROLLBAR_AS_NEEDED));
    centerPanel.add(new JScrollPane(cruisesAvailable,
                        JScrollPane.VERTICAL_SCROLLBAR_ALWAYS,
    JScrollPane.HORIZONTAL_SCROLLBAR_AS_NEEDED));
    bottomPanel.add(btnBook);
    bottomPanel.add(btnCheck);
    bottomPanel.add(btnExit);
    content.add(label1, BorderLayout.NORTH);
    content.add(centerPanel, BorderLayout.CENTER);
    content.add(bottomPanel, BorderLayout.SOUTH);
    setVisible(true);
}catch(Exception e)
{
    System.out.println("Exception thrown " + e);
} finally
{
    try
    {
        //close all connections
        if (statement1 != null)
            statement1.close();
        if (dbConn != null)
            dbConn.close();

    } catch (SQLException sqle)
```

13

JAVAMAIL

LISTING 13.4   continued

```java
        {
            System.out.println("SQLException during close(): " +
                                        sqle.getMessage());
        }
    }

}

private void ConnectToServices()
{
    try
    {

        //Get a connection to the datasource
         //load the driver class
        Class.forName("sun.jdbc.odbc.JdbcOdbcDriver");

        //Specify the ODBC datasource
        String sourceURL = "jdbc:odbc:CruiseTicket";

        //get a connection to the database
        dbConn =DriverManager.getConnection(sourceURL);

        //If we get to here, no exception was thrown
        System.out.println("The database connection is " + dbConn);
        System.out.println("Making connection...\n");

        //Create the statement
        statement1 = dbConn.createStatement();

        //Get a connection to the SMTP Service
        smtpServer = "mail.bellsouth.net";
        to = "sapotts@bellsouth.net";
        from = "sapotts@bellsouth.net";

        //Get a connection to POP
        server = "mail.bellsouth.net";
        user = "sapotts";
        password = "xyzxyz";


        Properties props = System.getProperties();

        props.put("mail.smtp.host", smtpServer);
        session = Session.getDefaultInstance(props, null);

        System.out.println("JavaMail Connections created");

    } catch (Exception e)
```

LISTING 13.4   continued

```java
        {
            System.out.println("Exception was thrown: " + e);
        }
    }

    /**
     * @param args the command line arguments
     */
    public static void main(String args[])
    {
        //create an instance of the GUI
        try
        {
            CruiseList mainWindow = new CruiseList("Cruise Ticket System");
        }catch(Exception e)
        {
            System.out.println("Exception in main " + e);
        }
    }

    public void actionPerformed(java.awt.event.ActionEvent ae)
    {
        try
        {
            Container c = btnExit.getParent();
            if (ae.getActionCommand().equals("Exit"))
            {
                System.exit(0);
            }

            //Try and book a ticket
            if (ae.getActionCommand().equals("Book"))
            {
                System.out.println("Book was clicked");
                int custIndex = customerList.getSelectedIndex();
                int cruiseIndex = cruisesAvailable.getSelectedIndex();

                if (custIndex == -1 || cruiseIndex == -1)
                {
                    JOptionPane.showMessageDialog(c,
                    "You must choose a customer and a cruise");
                }else
                {
                    //Pop up a dialog asking how many tickets are requested
                    String numTickets = JOptionPane.showInputDialog(c,
                    "How many tickets?");
                    int numberOfTickets = Integer.parseInt(numTickets);

                    //create a ticket request object
                    TicketRequest tickReq =
                                new TicketRequest(custNums[custIndex],
```

LISTING 13.4   continued

```
                lastNames[custIndex], firstNames[custIndex],
                cruiseIDs[cruiseIndex], cruiseDestinations[cruiseIndex],
                cruisePorts[cruiseIndex], cruiseSailings[cruiseIndex],
                numberOfTickets);

                subject = "Request";
                body = createEmailTicketRequest(tickReq);

                System.out.println(tickReq);
                //Create a message using this object

                try
                {
                    log("Sending a message to " + to);


                    //Create the new message
                    MimeMessage msg = new MimeMessage(session);

                    //Set the send from address
                    msg.setFrom(new InternetAddress(from));

                    //Set the to address
                    msg.setRecipients(Message.RecipientType.TO,
                    InternetAddress.parse(to, false));

                    //Set the subject
                    msg.setSubject(subject);
                    msg.setText(body);

                    //set the date
                    msg.setSentDate(new java.util.Date());

                    //send the message
                    Transport.send(msg);

                    System.out.println("Message was sent");
                }catch (Exception e)
                {
                    log("Error sending message  " + e);
                }

                System.out.println("Sent the ticket Request Mail Message");
            }
        }
        //See if you got a mail message back
        if (ae.getActionCommand().equals("Check"))
```

LISTING **13.4** continued

```java
            {
                //Check to see if there are any email messages for us
                fetchMessages();
            }
        }catch (Exception e)
        {
            System.out.println("Exception thrown = " + e);
        }
    }

    private String createEmailTicketRequest(TicketRequest tr)
    {
        return tr.getCustID() + "," +
        tr.getLastName() + "," +
        tr.getFirstName() + "," +
        tr.getCruiseID() + "," +
        tr.getDestination() + "," +
        tr.getPort() + "," +
        tr.getSailing() + "," +
        tr.getNumberOfTickets() ;
    }

    private void log(String s)
    {
        System.out.println(s);
    }

    private void fetchMessages()
    {
        Store store1 = null;
        Folder folder1 = null;
        try
        {
            Properties props = System.getProperties();
            Session session = Session.getDefaultInstance(props, null);

            //get a handle to the pop3 store
            store1 = session.getStore("pop3");

            //connect to the store and pass the authentication
            store1.connect(server, user, password);

            //obtain the default folder handle
            folder1 = store1.getDefaultFolder();

            //get the handle to the inbox
            folder1 = folder1.getFolder("INBOX");

            //if there is no inbox, throw an exception
            if (folder1 != null)
```

LISTING 13.4   continued

```java
        {
            folder1.open(Folder.READ_WRITE);
        }else
            throw new Exception("no inbox available");

        //if there are any messages, retrieve them
        Message[] messages = folder1.getMessages();
        if (messages.length == 0)
        {
            log("There are no messages to retrieve");
        }

        //print out the messages
        for (int i=0; i<messages.length; i++)
        {
            logMessage(messages[i]);
        }

    }catch (Exception e)
    {
        log("Exception thrown in fetchMessages() " + e);
    }
    finally
    {
        try
        {
            if (folder1 != null) folder1.close(true);
            if (store1 != null) store1.close();
        }
        catch (Exception ee)
        { log("Problem closing " + ee); }
    }
}

public void logMessage(Message message1)
{
    try
    {
        log("-----------------------------------------");
        //get the From address
        InternetAddress ia = (InternetAddress)message1.getFrom()[0];

        //get the personal name from the message.  This is the name in
        //human-readable form like Jake Snyder.
        String personalName = ia.getPersonal();
        log("The personal name is " + personalName);

        //get the addressString like jakesnyder@earthlink.com
        String addressString = ia.getAddress();
```

LISTING 13.4 continued

```
        log("The address String is " + addressString);

        //get the contents of the subject line
        String subject = message1.getSubject();
        log("The subject is " + subject);
        if (subject.equals("Response"))
        {

            //Get the body of the message
            Part messagePart1 = message1;
            Object content = messagePart1.getContent();
            String contentType = messagePart1.getContentType();

            log("The content type is " + contentType);

            //If the message is plain text then you can read it with
            //a StreamReader
            if (contentType.startsWith("text/plain") ||
            contentType.startsWith("text/html"))
            {
                InputStream is = messagePart1.getInputStream();

                BufferedReader br =
                    new BufferedReader(new InputStreamReader(is));
                String line1=br.readLine();

                while (line1 != null)
                {
                    displayResult(line1);
                    line1=br.readLine();
                }
            }
            message1.setFlag(Flags.Flag.DELETED, true);
        }
        log("----------------------------------------");
    }
    catch (Exception e)
    {
        log("Exception in logMessage " + e);
    }
}

/**
 * Message listener interface.
 * @param msg  message
 */

// MessageListener interface
```

13

JAVAMAIL

LISTING 13.4 continued

```java
    public void displayResult(String str)
    {
        try
        {
            Container c = btnExit.getParent();

            //show the message in a dialog box
            JOptionPane.showMessageDialog(c, str);
        }catch (Exception e)
        {
            System.out.println("onMessage() Exception " + e);
        }
    }
}
```

There are a number of interesting points to be made about this code:

- The application has gotten larger than it was when done in JMS or MDB. It took about 150 more lines of code to do the JavaMail version of this than it did to do the JMS version.

- This GUI has to be both an SMTP client and a POP client. The SMTP code is required to send messages, and the POP client is needed to receive them.

- The e-mail response message is deleted by the GUI after it is displayed.

- The messages that it sends are also retrieved when the Check button is clicked. This is fine because the logic is there to ignore them. In addition, the default behavior of the POP server is to allow messages to be read without being removed until explicitly deleted.

The TicketAgent application is also written in Java. The code for this class is shown in Listing 13.5.

LISTING 13.5 The TicketAgent Class

```java
/*
 * TicketAgent.java
 *
 * Created on January 14, 2002, 5:23 PM
 */

package unleashed.ch13;

/**
 *
 * @author   Stephen Potts
```

LISTING 13.5   continued

```java
 * @version
 */

import java.io.*;
import java.util.*;
import javax.transaction.*;
import javax.naming.*;

import java.sql.*;
import javax.mail.*;
import javax.mail.internet.*;

/**
 * The TicketAgent is a JavaMail and JDBC application.  It receives a Ticket
 * Request object from the CruiseList GUI.  It uses JDBC to access the database
 * to get the credit card number.  It then sends a message to the PaymentAgent
 * to request approval of a charge to the customer's credit card.  When the
 * charge is approved/disapproved TicketAgent updates the database and sends a
 * message back to the CruiseList application.
 *
 *
 * @author Steve Potts
 */
public class TicketAgent
{
    static int ticketID = 7000;
    private boolean quit = false;
    //JDBC variables
    java.sql.Connection dbConn = null;
    Statement statement1 = null;

    //JavaMail variables
    String server;
    String user;
    String password;

    String smtpServer;
    String to;
    String from;
    String subject;
    String body;


    public TicketAgent() throws Exception
    {
        init();
    }
```

LISTING 13.5   continued

```java
//The init() method moves real processing out of the constructors where
//Exception handling is simpler
private void init() throws Exception
{
    try
    {
        //Obtain connections to JDBC and JavaMail
        ConnectToServices();

    }catch(Exception e)
    {
        System.out.println("Exception thrown " + e);
    }
}

private void ConnectToServices()
{
    try
    {
        //Get a connection to the datasource
         //load the driver class
        Class.forName("sun.jdbc.odbc.JdbcOdbcDriver");

        //Specify the ODBC datasource
        String sourceURL = "jdbc:odbc:CruiseTicket";

        //get a connection to the database
        dbConn =DriverManager.getConnection(sourceURL);

        //If we get to here, no exception was thrown
        System.out.println("The database connection is " + dbConn);
        System.out.println("Making connection...\n");

        //Create the statement
        statement1 = dbConn.createStatement();



        //Get a connection to the JavaMail POP services
        server = "mail.bellsouth.net";
        user = "sapotts";
        password = "xyzxyz";

        //Get a connection to the SMTP service
        //This is where you put in the settings for your message
        smtpServer = "mail.bellsouth.net";
        to = "sapotts@bellsouth.net";
```

LISTING 13.5 continued

```
                from = "sapotts@bellsouth.net";
                subject = "Response";



            System.out.println("JavaMail Connections created");

        } catch (Exception e)
        {
            System.out.println("Exception was thrown: " + e);
        }
    }

    private void sendResponse(String s)
    {
        try
        {
            body = s;
            log("Sending a message to " + to);

            //This is the code that does the sending of the message
            Properties props = System.getProperties();

            props.put("mail.smtp.host", smtpServer);
            Session session = Session.getDefaultInstance(props, null);

            //Create the new message
            MimeMessage msg = new MimeMessage(session);

            //Set the send from address
            msg.setFrom(new InternetAddress(from));

            //Set the to address
            msg.setRecipients(Message.RecipientType.TO,
            InternetAddress.parse(to, false));

            //Set the subject
            msg.setSubject(subject);
            msg.setText(body);

            //set the date
            msg.setSentDate(new java.util.Date());

            //send the message
            Transport.send(msg);

            System.out.println("Message was sent");
```

LISTING 13.5   continued

```java
        }catch (Exception e)
        {
            log("Error sending message  " + e);
        }
    }

    public void respondToRequest(TicketRequest tr)
    {
        try
        {
            String msgText = "";

            //get the credit card number from the database
            String ccNum = getCreditCardNumber(tr.getCustID());
            System.out.println("The Credit Card Number is " + ccNum);

            //create a queue send to the Payment queue
            if (verifyCreditCard(ccNum))
            {
                createTicket(tr);
                sendTicketResponse(tr, true);
            }else
                sendTicketResponse(tr, false);

            //if the queue receives a text message to quit, the process ends
            if (msgText.equalsIgnoreCase("quit"))
            {
                synchronized(this)
                {
                    quit = true;
                    this.notifyAll(); // Notify main thread to quit
                }
            }
        }catch (Exception e)
        {
            e.printStackTrace();
        }
    }

    //This method sends a message to the response queue
    private void sendTicketResponse(TicketRequest tr, boolean isSuccessful)
    {
        try
        {
            //Create a message using this object
            String tickResp = "The ticket to " + tr.getDestination() + " for " +
            tr.getLastName();
            if (isSuccessful)
                tickResp += " was successful";
```

LISTING 13.5   continued

```
        else
            tickResp += " was not successful";

        System.out.println(tickResp);
        System.out.println("Created  the Ticket Response Message");

        //send the response
        sendResponse(tickResp);
        System.out.println("Sent the ticket Response Message");
    }catch(Exception e)
    {
        System.out.println("Exception " + e);
    }
}

private TicketRequest createTicketRequestFromEmail(String s1)
{
    log("createTicketRequestFromEmail() " + s1);
    StringTokenizer st = new StringTokenizer(s1, ",");
    String custString = st.nextToken();
    int custID = Integer.parseInt(custString);
    String lastName = st.nextToken();
    String firstName = st.nextToken();
    String cruiseIDString = st.nextToken();
    int cruiseID = Integer.parseInt(cruiseIDString);
    String destination = st.nextToken();
    String port = st.nextToken();
    String sailing = st.nextToken();
    String numTicketString = st.nextToken();
    int numTickets = Integer.parseInt(numTicketString);

    TicketRequest ticketReq = new TicketRequest(custID,
    lastName, firstName,
    cruiseID, destination,
    port, sailing,
    numTickets);
    log("ticketReq = " + ticketReq);
    return ticketReq;
}

//This method creates a database entry for the new ticket
private void createTicket(TicketRequest tr) throws Exception
{

    String insertStatement;
    ticketID += 1;
    insertStatement = "INSERT INTO CruiseTicket VALUES(" + ticketID + "," +
    Integer.toString(tr.getCustID()) + ", 'Unleashed Cruise Line'," +
    "'USS SeaBiscuit', '" + tr.getPort() + "','" + tr.getSailing() +"'," +
    "999.99," + "0,"+ "0,"+ "''")";
```

LISTING 13.5   continued

```java
        statement1.executeUpdate(insertStatement);
        System.out.println("Update was successful CustID = " + tr.getCustID());
    }

    private String getCreditCardNumber(int CustID) throws Exception
    {
        System.out.println("getCreditCard Making Database connection...\n");

        String ccNum = "";

        //Populate the creditcard string string
        String getCCString =
        "SELECT CreditCardNumber FROM CruiseCustomer " +
        "WHERE CustomerID = " + Integer.toString(CustID);

        ResultSet ccResults = statement1.executeQuery(getCCString);

        while (ccResults.next())
        {
            ccNum = ccResults.getString("CreditCardNumber");
        }

        return ccNum;
    }

    private boolean verifyCreditCard(String ccNum)
    {
        int firstNum = Integer.parseInt(ccNum.substring(0,1));

        if ( firstNum > 4)
            return false;
        else
            return true;
    }

    private void fetchMessages()
    {
        Store store1 = null;
        Folder folder1 = null;
        try
        {
            Properties props = System.getProperties();
            Session session = Session.getDefaultInstance(props, null);

            //get a handle to the pop3 store
            store1 = session.getStore("pop3");
```

LISTING 13.5   continued

```java
        //connect to the store and pass the authentication
        store1.connect(server, user, password);

        //obtain the default folder handle
        folder1 = store1.getDefaultFolder();

        //get the handle to the inbox
        folder1 = folder1.getFolder("INBOX");

        //if there is no inbox, throw an exception
        if (folder1 != null)
        {
            folder1.open(Folder.READ_WRITE);
        }else
            throw new Exception("no inbox available");

        //if there are any messages, retrieve them
        Message[] messages = folder1.getMessages();
        if (messages.length == 0)
        {
            log("There are no messages to retrieve");
        }

        //print out the messages
        for (int i=0; i<messages.length; i++)
        {
            logMessage(messages[i]);
        }

    }catch (Exception e)
    {
        log("Exception thrown in fetchMessages() " + e);
    }
    finally
    {
        try
        {
            if (folder1 != null) folder1.close(true);
            if (store1 != null) store1.close();
            log("finalize worked fine");
        }
        catch (Exception ee)
        {
            log("Problem closing " + ee);
        }
    }
}

public void logMessage(Message message1)
```

13

JAVAMAIL

LISTING 13.5   continued

```
{
    try
    {
        log("-----------------------------------------");
        //get the From address
        InternetAddress ia = (InternetAddress)message1.getFrom()[0];

        //get the personal name from the message.  This is the name in
        //human-readable form like Jake Snyder.
        String personalName = ia.getPersonal();
        log("The personal name is " + personalName);

        //get the addressString like jakesnyder@earthlink.com
        String addressString = ia.getAddress();
        log("The address String is " + addressString);

        //get the contents of the subject line
        String subject = message1.getSubject();
        log("The subject is " + subject);
        if (subject.equals("Request"))
        {
            //Get the body of the message
            Part messagePart1 = message1;
            Object content = messagePart1.getContent();
            String contentType = messagePart1.getContentType();

            log("The content type is " + contentType);

            //If the message is plain text then you can read it with
            //a StreamReader
            if (contentType.startsWith("text/plain") ||
            contentType.startsWith("text/html"))
            {
                InputStream is = messagePart1.getInputStream();

                BufferedReader br =
                    new BufferedReader(new InputStreamReader(is));
                String line1=br.readLine();

                while (line1 != null)
                {
                    log(line1);
                    //evaluate the request
                    TicketRequest tr = createTicketRequestFromEmail(line1);
                    respondToRequest(tr);
                    line1=br.readLine();
                }
```

LISTING 13.5 continued

```
                }
                message1.setFlag(Flags.Flag.DELETED, true);
            }
            log("-----------------------------------------");
        }
        catch (Exception e)
        {
            log("Exception in logMessage " + e);
        }
    }

    private void log(String s)
    {
        System.out.println(s);
    }

    /**
     * main() method.
     *
     * @exception  Exception if execution fails
     */
    public static void main(String[] args) throws Exception
    {
        try
        {
            TicketAgent ta = new TicketAgent();

            synchronized(ta)
            {
                while (!ta.quit)
                {
                    System.out.println("Starting the wait");
                    ta.wait(30000);
                    ta.fetchMessages();
                    System.out.println("Just woke up");
                }
            }
        }catch (Exception e)
        {
            System.out.println("Exception in main() " + e);
        }
    }
}
```

To run this application, open two command windows. In one of them, type

```
java unleashed.ch13.CruiseList
```

In the other window, type

```
java unleashed.ch13.TicketAgent
```

Make requests using the CruiseList GUI; then (after a few seconds, depending on you servers) click the Check button to see the results. The console windows also provide feedback on what is happening in the program.

There are several interesting parts to this listing:

- The `main()` method has to be a loop that waits for *n* seconds between checks for new messages.

- This application is both an SMTP client and a POP client. This is because it both sends and receives e-mail.

- This application uses the subject field to decide whether a message is intended for it. If so, the message is processed and then deleted. If not, the message is ignored.

- At times, the application will wake up but not be capable of reading from the POP server because CruiseList is holding a lock on it. This is no problem because the lock will be released quickly and the messages checked on the next wake-up cycle.

- Because the database is changed by this program, it is important to run `AccessJDBC2.java`, found in Appendix A, "Source Code Listings for Utility Programs Used in This Book," between sessions to reset the database to its initial state.

The `TicketRequest` class is also needed to run the code, and it is shown in Listing 13.6.

LISTING 13.6   The `TicketRequest` Contains the Data Associated with a Customer Requesting Tickets for a Cruise

```
/*
 * TicketRequest.java
 *
 * Created on January 14, 2002, 4:13 PM
 */

package unleashed.ch13;

/**
 *
 * @author  Stephen Potts
 * @version
 */
public class TicketRequest implements java.io.Serializable
{
    //information about the customer
```

LISTING 13.6   continued

```java
    int custID;
    String lastName;
    String firstName;

    //information about the cruise
    int cruiseID;
    String destination;
    String port;
    String sailing;

    int numberOfTickets;

    /** Constructor */
    public TicketRequest(int custID, String lastName, String firstName,
    int cruiseID, String destination,
    String port, String sailing, int numberOfTickets)
    {
        //set the information about the customer
        this.custID = custID;
        this.lastName = lastName;
        this.firstName = firstName;

        //set the information about the cruise
        this.cruiseID = cruiseID;
        this.destination = destination;
        this.port = port;
        this.sailing = sailing;

        this.numberOfTickets = numberOfTickets;
    }

    public int getCustID()
    {
        return this.custID = custID;
    }

    public String getLastName()
    {
        return this.lastName = lastName;
    }

    public String getFirstName()
    {
        return this.firstName = firstName;
    }

    public int getCruiseID()
    {
        return this.cruiseID;
    }
```

13

JavaMail

LISTING 13.6 continued

```java
public String getDestination()
{
    return this.destination;
}

public String getPort()
{
    return this.port;
}

public String getSailing()
{
    return this.sailing;
}

public int getNumberOfTickets()
{
    return this.numberOfTickets;
}

public String toString()
{
    String outString;
    outString = "------------------------------------------" + "\n";

    //information about the customer
    outString += "custID = " + this.custID + "\n";
    outString += "lastName = " + this.lastName + "\n";
    outString += "firstName = " + this.firstName + "\n";
    outString += "------------------------------------------" + "\n";

    //information about the cruise
    outString += "cruiseID = " + this.cruiseID + "\n";
    outString += "destination = " + this.destination + "\n";
    outString += "port = " + this.port + "\n";
    outString += "sailing = " + this.sailing + "\n";
    outString += "numberOfTickets = " + this.numberOfTickets + "\n";
    outString += "------------------------------------------" + "\n";
    return outString;
}
}
```

This example was a challenge from a number of perspectives. It took considerably more
time to code and debug than the same application done with JMS or message-driven
beans. The reason for this is that the e-mail server is not really designed to be a message

queue server, thus placing more responsibility on the shoulders of the programmer and less on the middleware.

It did produce an asynchronous application that functions well, however.

There are situations in which a JavaMail solution would have to be employed, however. If you had no budget to purchase a JMS or EJB server, but you required asynchronous processing, you wouldn't have many choices. Because most clients have e-mail services, this alternative is free (except for your salary, that is). Another situation in which a JavaMail solution might be the best choice is when messages are generated by the server and read by humans. Because e-mail was originally designed to be read by humans, this is a natural choice. Likewise, when an application needs to consume e-mail, this can be an excellent choice. Many mailing lists provide an "unsubscribe" option whereby you simply place the word unsubscribe in the subject and your name is removed from the list.

Retrieving Specific E-mail Messages

There are times when you would not want to retrieve every message that appears in your folder. One example might be if you get a lot of junk e-mail. In that case, you might want a program that only gets specific messages from the folder.

The javax.mail.search package provides a class called `SearchTerm` that allows you to specify a criteria for the messages that you want to retrieve. There are 22 different classes that you can use to specify the `SearchTerm`. Some of the more common logical operations are listed here:

- `AND` is supported by the `AndTerm` class.
- `OR` is supported by the `OrTerm` class.
- `NOT` uses the `NotTerm` class.
- The date sent is searched with the `SentDateTerm` class.
- The contents are searched with the `BodyTerm` class.
- The header can be searched with `FromTerm`, `RecipientTerm`, and `SubjectTerm`.

Listing 13.7 gives an example of searching the folder.

LISTING 13.7   The `SimplePopClientSearch` Class

```
/*
 * SimplePopClientSearch.java
 *
```

LISTING 13.7 continued

```java
 * Created on April 25, 2002, 2:37 PM
 */

package unleashed.ch13;

import javax.mail.*;
import javax.mail.search.*;
import javax.mail.internet.*;

import java.util.*;
import java.io.*;

/**
 *
 * @author   Stephen Potts
 * @version
 */
public class SimplePopClientSearch
{
    String server;
    String user;
    String password;

    /** Creates new SimplePopClient */
    public SimplePopClientSearch()
    {
        setup();
    }

    private void setup()
    {
        //change these values to match your own personal settings
        server = "mail.bellsouth.net";
        user = "sapotts";
        password = "xyzxyz";
    }

    private void fetchMessages()
    {
        Store store1 = null;
        Folder folder1 = null;
        try
        {
            Properties props = System.getProperties();
            Session session = Session.getDefaultInstance(props, null);

            //get a handle to the pop3 store
            store1 = session.getStore("pop3");
```

LISTING 13.7   continued

```
        //connect to the store and pass the authentication
        store1.connect(server, user, password);

        //obtain the default folder handle
        folder1 = store1.getDefaultFolder();

        //get the handle to the inbox
        folder1 = folder1.getFolder("INBOX");

        //if there is no inbox, throw an exception
        if (folder1 != null)
        {
            folder1.open(Folder.READ_ONLY);
        }else
            throw new Exception("no inbox available");

         //if there are any messages search for them
        SearchTerm criteria = new OrTerm( new SubjectTerm("Ch13"),
                            new SubjectTerm("Chapter 13"));

        Message[] messages = folder1.search(criteria);
        if (messages.length == 0)
        {
            log("There are no messages to retrieve");
        }

        //print out the messages
        for (int i=0; i<messages.length; i++)
        {
            logMessage(messages[i]);
        }

    }catch (Exception e)
    {
        log("Exception thrown in fetchMessages() " + e);
    }
    finally
    {
        try
        {
            if (folder1 != null) folder1.close(false);
            if (store1 != null) store1.close();
        }
        catch (Exception ee)
        { log("Problem closing " + ee); }
    }
}

public void logMessage(Message message1)
```

Listing 13.7   continued

```
{
    try
    {
        log("----------------------------------------");
        //get the From address
        InternetAddress ia = (InternetAddress)message1.getFrom()[0];

        //get the personal name from the message.  This is the name in
        //human-readable form like Jake Snyder.
        String personalName = ia.getPersonal();
        log("The personal name is " + personalName);

        //get the addressString like jakesnyder@earthlink.com
        String addressString = ia.getAddress();
        log("The address String is " + addressString);

        //get the contents of the subject line
        String subject = message1.getSubject();
        log("The subject is " + subject);

        //Get the body of the message
        Part messagePart1 = message1;
        Object content = messagePart1.getContent();
        String contentType = messagePart1.getContentType();

        log("The content type is " + contentType);

        //If the message is plain text then you can read it with
        //a StreamReader
        if (contentType.startsWith("text/plain") ||
        contentType.startsWith("text/html"))
        {
            InputStream is = messagePart1.getInputStream();

            BufferedReader br =
                    new BufferedReader(new InputStreamReader(is));
            String line1=br.readLine();

            while (line1 != null)
            {
                log(line1);
                line1=br.readLine();
            }
        }
        log("----------------------------------------");
    }
    catch (Exception e)
    {
        log("Exception in logMessage " + e);
```

LISTING 13.7   continued

```
        }
    }

    private void log(String s)
    {
        System.out.println(s);
    }

    public static void main(String[] args)
    {
        //Instantiate the object
        SimplePopClientSearch spcs = new SimplePopClientSearch();
        //get the messages
        spcs.fetchMessages();
    }
}
```

Notice that we have to add a new import statement to our code:

```
import javax.mail.search.*;
```

Next, we add the code that specifies the search:

```
        //if there are any messages search for them
        SearchTerm criteria = new OrTerm( new SubjectTerm("Ch13"),
                              new SubjectTerm("Chapter 13"));
```

First, let's run `SimplePopClient` to see all the messages that are waiting in this folder:

```
- - - - - - - - - - - - - - - - - - - - - - - - - - - - - - - - - - - - - -
The personal name is Steve Potts
The address String is stevepotts@mindspring.com
The subject is testing email
The content type is multipart/alternative;
        boundary="----=_NextPart_000_0036_01C1EC60.B7013610"
- - - - - - - - - - - - - - - - - - - - - - - - - - - - - - - - - - - - - -
- - - - - - - - - - - - - - - - - - - - - - - - - - - - - - - - - - - - - -
The personal name is Steve Potts
The address String is stevepotts@mindspring.com
The subject is Chapter 13
The content type is multipart/alternative;
        boundary="----=_NextPart_000_003F_01C1EC63.91BD8A40"
- - - - - - - - - - - - - - - - - - - - - - - - - - - - - - - - - - - - - -
- - - - - - - - - - - - - - - - - - - - - - - - - - - - - - - - - - - - - -
The personal name is Steve Potts
The address String is stevepotts@mindspring.com
The subject is Chapter 13 or Chapter 14
The content type is multipart/alternative;
        boundary="----=_NextPart_000_0048_01C1EC63.C65A03F0"
```

13

JAVAMAIL

> **Note**
>
> You need a valid user ID and password to run this example also. The contents of the output will depend on the messages that you send to your e-mail account when you run the program.

Next, we can run `SimplePopClientSearch` and look at the results:

```
----------------------------------------
The personal name is Steve Potts
The address String is stevepotts@mindspring.com
The subject is Chapter 13
The content type is multipart/alternative;
        boundary="----=_NextPart_000_003F_01C1EC63.91BD8A40"
----------------------------------------
----------------------------------------
The personal name is Steve Potts
The address String is stevepotts@mindspring.com
The subject is Chapter 13 or Chapter 14
The content type is multipart/alternative;
        boundary="----=_NextPart_000_0048_01C1EC63.C65A03F0"
```

Notice that only two messages out of the three passed the test. Note also that the subject in the second message contained more information than just the subject that we were searching for, which demonstrates that the `SearchTerm` class also looks for substrings.

Programing an Event-Driven E-mail Application

You will notice that the CruiseList example required that the operator of the GUI do an explicit button click in order to check for any e-mail messages that have been sent back by the `TicketAgent` class. On IMAP servers, it is possible to create an event listener and receive messages in an event-driven fashion. This is not possible with POP servers because of limitations of the Post Office Protocol.

If your e-mail server supports the *Internet Message Access Protocol (IMAP)*, you will be able to have your e-mail delivered to you in an event-driven manner. Listing 13.8 shows an event-driven JavaMail application that is based on IMAP.

LISTING 13.8   The `SimplePopClientEvent` Class

```
/*
 * SimplePopClientEvent.java
```

LISTING 13.8   continued

```
 *
 * Created on April 26, 2002, 2:37 PM
 */

package unleashed.ch13;

import javax.activation.*;
import javax.mail.*;
import javax.mail.internet.*;
import javax.mail.event.*;

import java.util.*;
import java.io.*;

/**
 *
 * @author  Stephen Potts, Craig Pfeifer
 * @version
 */
public class SimplePopClientEvent
{
    String server;
    String user;
    String password;
    static Folder folder1 = null;
    static Store store1 = null;
    Session session;

    /** Creates new SimplePopClient */
    public SimplePopClientEvent()
    {
        setup();
    }

    private void setup()
    {
        try
        {
            //change these values to match your own personal settings
            server = "<SERVERNAME>";
            user = "UID";
            password = "PWD";
            Properties props = System.getProperties();
            props.put("mail.imap.host", "<YOUR IMAP HOST HERE>");
            props.put("mail.smtp.host", "<YOUR SMTP HOST HERE>");
            session = Session.getDefaultInstance(props, null);

            //get a handle to the store
```

LISTING **13.8**   continued

```java
            store1 = session.getStore("imap");

            //connect to the store and pass the authentication
            store1.connect(server, user, password);

            //obtain the default folder handle
            folder1 = store1.getDefaultFolder().getFolder("Inbox");

            //if there is no inbox, throw an exception
            if (folder1 != null)
            {
                folder1.open(Folder.READ_ONLY);
            }else
            {
                System.out.println("No such folder!!");
            }
            folder1.addMessageCountListener(
                        new MyMessageCountListener());

        }
        catch (Exception e)
        {
            log("Exception thrown in setup() " + e);
            e.printStackTrace();
        }
        System.out.println(
                "Got connection to mailserver & account INBOX");
    }

    private void fetchMessages()
    {
        try
        {

        //if there are any messages, retrieve them
        Message[] messages = folder1.getMessages();
        if (messages.length == 0)
        {
            log("There are no messages to retrieve");
        }

        //print out the messages
        for (int i=0; i<messages.length; i++)
        {
            logMessage(messages[i]);
        }
        }catch (Exception e)
        {
            System.out.println("error while fetching");
```

LISTING 13.8   continued

```java
        }
    }

    public void logMessage(Message message1)
    {
        try
        {
            log("---------------------------------------");
            //get the From address
            InternetAddress ia = (InternetAddress)message1.getFrom()[0];

            //get the personal name from the message.  This is the name
            //in human-readable form like Jake Snyder.
            String personalName = ia.getPersonal();
            log("The personal name is " + personalName);

            //get the addressString like jakesnyder@earthlink.com
            String addressString = ia.getAddress();
            log("The address String is " + addressString);

            //get the contents of the subject line
            String subject = message1.getSubject();
            log("The subject is " + subject);

            //Get the body of the message
            Part messagePart1 = message1;
            Object content = messagePart1.getContent();
            String contentType = messagePart1.getContentType();

            log("The content type is " + contentType);

            //If the message is plain text then you can read it with
            //a StreamReader
            if (contentType.startsWith("text/plain") ||
            contentType.startsWith("text/html"))
            {
                InputStream is = messagePart1.getInputStream();

                BufferedReader br = new BufferedReader(
                                    new InputStreamReader(is));
                String line1=br.readLine();

                while (line1 != null)
                {
                    log(line1);
                    line1=br.readLine();
                }
            }
            log("---------------------------------------");
```

LISTING 13.8   continued

```
        }
        catch (Exception e)
        {
            log("Exception in logMessage " + e);
        }
    }

    private void log(String s)
    {
        System.out.println(s);
    }

    public static void main(String[] args)
    {
        //Instantiate the object
        SimplePopClientEvent spce = new SimplePopClientEvent();
        //get the messages
        while (true)
        {
            try
            {

                Thread.sleep(1000);
                System.out.println("woke up");
                int x  = folder1.getMessageCount();
                System.out.println("message count = "+x);

                boolean newMsgs = folder1.hasNewMessages();
                System.out.println("has new messages = "+newMsgs);
            }catch (InterruptedException ie)
            {

                try
                {
                    if (folder1 != null) folder1.close(false);
                    if (store1 != null) store1.close();
                }
                catch (Exception ee)
                { System.out.println("Problem closing " + ee); }
            }
            catch (MessagingException me)
            {
              System.out.println("Problem getting message count " + me);
            }
        }
    }
}
```

This class relies on another class, `MyMessageCountListener`, to receive notification of the change to the message count. This class is shown in Listing 13.9.

LISTING 13.9 The `MyMessageCountListener` Class

```
package unleashed.ch13;

import javax.mail.event.*;

public class MyMessageCountListener extends MessageCountAdapter
{
    public void messagesAdded(MessageCountEvent e)
    {
        System.out.println("Some messages got added : "+e.toString());
    }

    public void messagesRemoved(MessageCountEvent e)
    {
        System.out.println("Some messages got removed : "+e.toString());
    }
}
```

The only difference between this application and the POP3 application that we saw earlier is that we specify that we want to connect using IMAP:

```
//get a handle to the store
store1 = session.getStore("imap");
```

We add the `MessageCountListener` after the folder is created:

```
folder1.addMessageCountListener(
            new MyMessageCountListener());
```

The `MessageCountListener` interface is implemented by the `MessageCountAdapter` class, which is extended by our own `MyMessageCountListener` class. This class receives notification when the number of messages waiting at the server changes, allowing us to fetch them or simply to notify the application via a message. When a message arrives at your IMAP server, you will receive a message on your console telling you about it.

Summary

In this chapter, we looked at the JavaMail API from a programmer's point of view. First, we looked at the internal workings of the mail systems, and then we wrote traditional SMTP and POP client applications.

13

JAVAMAIL

Next, we looked at the JavaMail API in a different light. We wrote a complicated application that used JavaMail as a distributed processing technology. We created a GUI that placed user requests in e-mail messages behind the scenes. We wrote a simple server that sits and waits for an e-mail message to arrive, which it then parses. After updating the database, it deletes the message and sends a response back to the GUI.

Following that, you learned how to do a search on the messages waiting for you at the server without having to download them first. Finally, you learned how to use an IMAP server to receive an event notification whenever new e-mail arrives.

CHAPTER 14

Serial Port Communications

Henry Ford said that his customers could get a Model T in any color they wanted, so long as it was black. This rigidity was a prime reason that his competition at Chevrolet was able to make inroads into Ford's huge market share in the 1920s.

A computer with no peripheral devices is a lot like a Model T. It performs the basic functions, but it lacks a lot of the extras that make our computer experience so enjoyable. At one time or another, you have probably connected mouse devices, printers, digital cameras, video grabbers, modems, plotters, Palm docking stations, telescopes, or even LEGO robots to your computer via one of the communications ports. Most of the time when doing so, you are given instructions on what to plug in, where to plug it, what software to install, and so on. The end result is that the experience involves a bit of plug and play (or plug and pray).

Have you ever wondered what happens under the hood when you hook up these devices? How does the software detect the presence of the peripheral device? What type of data is being sent in and out over the wires and plugs? Have you ever wanted to connect a device to a communication port yourself and write software to communicate with it? In this chapter we will learn how to do so using Java.

You might wonder how Java can provide communication classes and methods considering the fact that it is a platform-independent language. The approach that Java uses is based on hardware abstraction. The Java Communications API, `javax.comm.*`, is the same for every platform that Java runs on. Mapping the calls in the API to actual machine instructions is the responsibility of the programmers who write the Java virtual machine (JVM) code.

As it is currently constituted, the Java Communications API supports serial and parallel port communications. There is talk of adding Universal Serial Bus (USB) support to this package, but at the time of this writing, no USB implementation has been announced. While USB support would be a powerful addition to the language, the fact that we already have two connections available to program today is a very good thing.

The Java Communications API is unusual in that it supports devices that may not be present on your computer. Some computer manufacturers don't offer serial ports on their hardware, and no amount of abstraction can overcome this deficiency.

In this chapter, we will cover the technology that is used to make serial port communications work. Following that, we will discuss how to use the Communications API to write data out and read data in through the serial port.

Understanding the RS-232 Standard

Serial port communications are built on the foundation of the RS-232 standard. To understand the origins of RS-232 communications, you have to go all the way back to the days of Samuel F.B. Morse. He is given credit for inventing the first working telegraph. Interestingly enough, Morse was not an engineer, but a portrait painter. Upon hearing of experiments in which an electrical charge was sent, almost instantaneously, over a distance of 25 miles, he recognized that intelligence could be communicated at a distance. He got to work on trying to devise a practical scheme to transmit intelligence as a sequence of electrical signals. The result of his work was the telegraph and a protocol called the Morse code.

RS-232 Hardware

When we attach a device to a computer, we are doing the same thing that was done in the nineteenth century. We are sending intelligence in the form of electrical pulses over a wire using a protocol. We send a positive voltage (normally +15 volts) called a *Logical 1* and a negative voltage called a *Logical 0*. (Low voltages [+/–3 volts] are considered noise.)

In RS-232 parlance, the computer is considered Data Terminal Equipment (DTE), and modems, Palm cradles, plotters, and so on are considered Data Communications Equipment (DCE). This distinction gives direction to each of the two sides of a connector. Some commands make sense going from DTE to DCE but others don't (and vice versa).

The serial port is different from the early telegraph in that it has more wires (25, 9 of which are commonly used), and there is usually a plug in between the DTE and DCE. Otherwise, the operation is identical: Positive voltage is applied to certain pins (which are said to be *Logical 1*) and negative voltage is applied to others (which are said to be *Logical 0*). Thus we see that RS-232 communication, at the lowest level, is not much more complicated than flipping light switches and interpreting results from the pattern that the lights form.

RS-232 is often implemented using only 9 pins (a practice started by IBM to save space on computer cards). The other 16 pins on the 25-pin connector are not commonly used. The meaning of each of the 9 commonly used pins is shown in Table 14.1, from the computer (DTE) point of view.

TABLE 14.1   The RS-232 Pin Assignments

9-Pin	*25-Pin*	*Purpose*
1	1	Frame ground
2	3	Receive data (RD)
3	2	Transmit data (TD)
4	20	Data terminal ready (DTR)
5	7	Signal ground
6	6	Data set ready (DSR)
7	4	Request to send (RTS)
8	5	Clear to send (CTS)
9	22	Ring indicator (RI)

> **Note**
>
> From this point forward, references to pin numbers in this chapter use the 9-pin connector numbering scheme.

Some of these pins serve a purpose that is electrical. The frame ground is used as the electrical ground for the circuits. The signal ground is used as a reference voltage of 0 volts. The ring indicator is on when a call is trying to come in (used mostly, but not exclusively, on modems).

The rest of the pins are used to transfer and manage the data that is going across the wire. Data is sent out on the TD pin. Data comes into the computer on RD. The computer (DTE) uses DTR to tell the external device to send data. The DTE is set to *on* to indicate that it is ready for data, or set to *off* to indicate that it is not ready. DSR is set to *on* (–15 volts, not 0 volts) by the external device to indicate that it is hooked up and ready. The computer sets the RTS pin to *on* to ask the external device whether it is ready to receive data. The external device sets the CTS pin to *on*, indicating that it is able to accept data. This way, the devices have a way of communicating with each other.

You might be wondering what happens when you hook up two devices that are both computers (DTE). Nothing. When two devices are hooked up, one of them must send on pin 3 and receive on pin 2 and the other must send on pin 2 and receive on pin 3. Otherwise, no communication can take place.

You may have connected one computer to another using a null-modem cable. This simple cable crosses wires 2 and 3 so that the problem described in the preceding paragraph is bypassed. These cables used to be popular with computer gamers before home networks and Internet-based play became common.

The actual operation of the data transfer is fairly simple. The external device is hooked up with a cable and powered on. The external device sets its DSR pin to *on* to tell the computer that it is present and powered up. If we are sending data out, the computer will set the RTS pin to *on* to ask the external device whether it can receive data. The external device turns CTS to *on*, indicating that it is ready. The computer puts the data on pin 3 and the external device takes it off pin 2 and usually places it in a buffer. This continues as long as there is data to send and the external device has room in its buffer.

If the buffer fills up, the external device turns the CTS pin to *off*, telling the computer to take a break from sending. The external device then works to clear the buffer. As soon as the buffer has enough space, it turns the CTS pin back on and the computer resumes sending data. This is called hardware flow control. Finally, when all the data has been sent, the computer turns off its RTS pin and the external device quits trying to read the data from the computer.

You have probably noticed that we are sending data one bit at a time over this wire. This is why it is called a serial port; the data is sent as a series of bits. You might ask, "Why not send data over more than one wire?" If we did, we would have parallel communication between the two devices and the port would then become a parallel port.

Communications Software

Now that the hardware part of the puzzle is in place, let's look at the data. RS-232 devices send ASCII code to communicate in character mode with the external device. There are 128 (2 to the 7th power) characters in the ASCII table, so it requires 7 bits to send one character. In addition to the bits that make up characters, we need to send some other pieces of information through pins 2 and 3 in order to make things work better. The following list names and describes the bits that are transmitted:

- Start bit—Before sending the data bits, we send a bit with synchronizing negative voltage or no voltage.

- Data bits—These 7 bits contain the ASCII character to be displayed.

- Parity bit—An extra bit, the eighth bit in the sequence, is called the parity bit. (The start bit and stop bit are not counted as data bits.) This bit is set in an attempt to provide detection of corrupt data. If the bit setting doesn't match the data bits, then an error has occurred. If your program is set to `parity=none`, this bit will always be 0. If you set it to `parity=odd`, this bit will be either 1 or 0, whichever is needed to make the total number of bits sent odd. If you set it to `parity=even`, this bit will be used to set the string even (looking at the string as a number for the sake of parity).

- Stop bit—This single bit of positive voltage is sent after a character to indicate that the character is done. It is kind of like an end-of-file marker for a character.

Caution

Don't let your confidence in the parity bit run too high. This check will only work when the bad data affects an odd number of bits. Typically, noise on lines comes in bursts, affecting many bits. Thus, this method only works part of the time.

The bit pattern is sent from one device to another at a certain number of bits per second. This is incorrectly called the baud rate of the device, but this mistake is so commonly propagated that we will continue it rather than contradict it. Common values for this rate are 9600, 38400, and 57K.

Normally we speak of the communications settings for a device using a string called the data format. For example, the string 9600-8-E-1 represents 9600 baud, 8 data bits, even parity, 1 stop bit.

Note

According to the sample string in the preceding paragraph, we are sending 8 data bits. We are really sending 7 data bits and a parity bit, as described earlier. Thus, the claim of 8 data bits is not accurate, but it is universally made.

Note

Baud rate is strictly defined as signals per second. Suppose that you created a tone for 0 and a tone for 1. Any transmission using this scheme would have the same bit rate and baud rate because every signal carries one bit of information. If, however, you used four tones, 00, 01, 10, and 11, each signal would carry two bits of information. In this case, the baud rate, or signals per second, would be half of the bit rate.

The next concept that we need to cover is flow control. We have already seen hardware flow control, in which the two devices use the RTS and CTS pins to communicate flow control to each other. One form of software flow control is to send the XON and XOFF characters (11h and 13h). XON means "please send data" and XOFF means "please hold off sending data."

The final topic that we need to talk about is delimiters. A *delimiter* is just a character or character pair that is placed at the end of a message to tell the receiver that the message is complete. The simplest and most common of these is the CR and LF pair (0Dh and 0Ah). This is a fossil left over from the typewriter era.

An alternative is the STX and ETX pair (02h and 03h). STX means "start of transmission" and ETX means "end of transmission." STX is sent to the device before any real data is sent. ETX is sent after the data transmission is complete.

You might see an ACK/NAK pair (06h and 15h) used in some software. This is rarely done anymore, but it can really improve reliability if you own both ends of the communications link. Every time a message is sent, the receiver checks it for errors. If it is error-free, it sends an ACK message. If it contains errors, it sends a NAK and the message is re-sent.

The most important thing to remember is that both sides of any communication must be set the same way or the baud rate goes immediately to zero signals per second. A few differences (such as sending with odd parity and receiving with none) can sneak by, but not much else can.

If you have trouble getting communications to work, first check the cable to make sure that it is the correct one for your arrangement. A straight serial cable works for DTE and DCE connections. A null-modem cable is required if you are attempting DTE-to-DTE communications.

The Java Communications API

The Java Communications API is built on a single abstract class called CommPort. This class has two concrete subclasses: SerialPort and ParallelPort. The CommPort class has two methods: getInputStream() and getOutputStream(). Once we've acquired handles to these streams, we can process the streams using the same I/O classes that we use to process files.

The code for this package is not installed automatically when you install a version of Java. It is considered a Standard Extension and requires a separate download from http://java.sun.com. The actual procedure that you use will depend on the platform that you are running Java on. For the Windows and Sun platforms, you will find downloads that should work right away. Other platforms may provide the implementation libraries for you to use.

> **Caution**
>
> The Windows installation instructions that are included with the download from Sun may or may not work for you. In short, you need to get three files in the correct directories: `win32com.dll`, `comm.jar`, and `javax.comm.properties`. First, try to install them to <JDK>\bin, <JDK>\lib, and <JDK>\lib, respectively. If that doesn't work, try putting them in <JDK>\jre\bin, <JDK>\jre\lib\ext, and <JDK>\jre\lib, respectively. Finally, try putting them in c:\Program Files\ JavaSoft\JRE\1.3.1\bin, c:\Program Files\JavaSoft\JRE\1.3.1\lib\ext, and c:\Program Files\JavaSoft\JRE\1.3.1\lib, respectively. If none of these works, check the Java Developer Connection at http:// developer.java.sun.com.

After installation, the first order of business is to verify that the Java Communications API is working correctly on your computer. If you are unable to get the program shown in Listing 14.1 to work, no other communications port program will work either. This program displays a list of all the serial and parallel ports that Java can find on your computer.

LISTING 14.1   The `PortFinder` Class

```java
/*
 * PortFinder.java
 *
 * Created on February 8, 2002, 4:40 PM
 */

package unleashed.ch14;
import java.io.*;
import javax.comm.*;
import java.util.*;

/**
 *
 * @author  Stephen Potts
 * @version
 */
public class PortFinder
{

    /** Creates new PortFinder */
    public PortFinder()
    {
    }
```

LISTING 14.1 continued

```java
public static void main(String[] args)
{
    Enumeration ports = CommPortIdentifier.getPortIdentifiers();

    while(ports.hasMoreElements())
    {
        CommPortIdentifier cpi =
                    (CommPortIdentifier)ports.nextElement();
        System.out.println("Port " + cpi.getName());
    }
}
}
```

This program makes use of the CommPortIdentifier class. This class is central to the operation of the communications API. It is responsible for communicating with the driver to do the following:

- Locate communications ports on a machine
- Open a communications port
- Determine port ownership
- Resolve port ownership contention
- Manage changes in port ownership status

This example runs a single static method from the CommPortIdentifier class, called getPortIdentifiers(). This method returns an enumeration of the ports, both serial and parallel, that the driver finds installed on the computer. Running this program produces results similar to these:

```
Port COM3
Port COM2
Port COM1
Port LPT1
Port LPT2
```

> **Note**
>
> Some operating systems report back all the ports that could be installed, whether or not they are really present.

Now that we are sure that we are communicating with the Java Communications port driver, we need to find out whether we are communicating with the external device.

14

SERIAL PORT
COMMUNICATIONS

> **Tip**
>
> It is critical that you learn how to troubleshoot communications applications if you want to maintain your sanity. Always verify that you have communication with the driver, that the driver can find the port, and that the port is receiving something from the external device. Only at that point does it make sense to start debugging your own code.

There are two ways to find out whether we are communicating. One way is to purchase a hardware port sniffer. (It is called this because, figuratively, it "sniffs" your data for rotten pieces.) You place it between your application and the external device using cables and connectors. This approach is needed for a certain class of problems between devices where one device is sending data that the other one can't understand or interpret.

An alternative to buying a hardware sniffer is to create a software sniffer. This sniffer is a program that reads every signal that comes from the serial port and writes the hexadecimal values of all the characters received to the screen.

The simplified version of a software sniffer is a program that simply reads everything that comes in from the serial port and dumps it to the screen. The result looks like swear words from old Sunday newspaper cartoons, but it provides proof that communication of some type is taking place. Listing 14.2 shows the code for the simplified sniffer.

LISTING 14.2 A Simple Sniffer

```
/*
 * PortSniffer.java
 *
 * Created on February 8, 2002, 4:40 PM
 */

package unleashed.ch14;
import java.io.*;
import javax.comm.*;
import java.util.*;

/**
 *
 * @author  Stephen Potts
 * @version
 */
public class PortSniffer implements Runnable, SerialPortEventListener
{
    static Enumeration ports;
```

LISTING **14.2**   continued

```
static CommPortIdentifier pID;
InputStream inStream;
SerialPort serPort;
Thread readThread;

/** Creates new PortFinder */
public PortSniffer()
{
    try
    {
        serPort = (SerialPort)pID.open("PortSniffer",2000);
    }catch (PortInUseException piue)
    {
        System.out.println("Exception " + piue);
    }

    try
    {
        inStream = serPort.getInputStream();
    }catch (IOException ioe)
    {
        System.out.println("Exception " + ioe);
    }

    try
    {
        serPort.addEventListener(this);
    }catch (TooManyListenersException tmle)
    {
        System.out.println("Exception " + tmle);
    }

    serPort.notifyOnDataAvailable(true);
    serPort.notifyOnBreakInterrupt(true);
    serPort.notifyOnCarrierDetect(true);
    serPort.notifyOnCTS(true);
    serPort.notifyOnDataAvailable(true);
    serPort.notifyOnDSR(true);
    serPort.notifyOnFramingError(true);
    serPort.notifyOnOutputEmpty(true);
    serPort.notifyOnOverrunError(true);
    serPort.notifyOnParityError(true);
    serPort.notifyOnRingIndicator(true);

    try
    {
        serPort.setSerialPortParams(9600, SerialPort.DATABITS_8,
        SerialPort.STOPBITS_1,
```

LISTING 14.2   continued

```java
            SerialPort.PARITY_NONE);
        }catch (UnsupportedCommOperationException ucoe)
        {
            System.out.println("Exception " + ucoe);
        }
        readThread = new Thread(this);
        readThread.start();
    }//Constructor

    public void serialEvent(SerialPortEvent event)
    {
        switch(event.getEventType())
        {
            case SerialPortEvent.BI:
                System.out.println("SerialPortEvent.BI occurred");
            case SerialPortEvent.OE:
                System.out.println("SerialPortEvent.OE occurred");
            case SerialPortEvent.FE:
                System.out.println("SerialPortEvent.FE occurred");
            case SerialPortEvent.PE:
                System.out.println("SerialPortEvent.PE occurred");
            case SerialPortEvent.CD:
                System.out.println("SerialPortEvent.CD occurred");
            case SerialPortEvent.CTS:
                System.out.println("SerialPortEvent.CTS occurred");
            case SerialPortEvent.DSR:
                System.out.println("SerialPortEvent.DSR occurred");
            case SerialPortEvent.RI:
                System.out.println("SerialPortEvent.RI occurred");
            case SerialPortEvent.OUTPUT_BUFFER_EMPTY:
                System.out.println(
                    "SerialPortEvent.OUTPUT_BUFFER_EMPTY occurred");
                break;
            case SerialPortEvent.DATA_AVAILABLE:
                System.out.println(
                    "SerialPortEvent.DATA_AVAILABLE occurred");
                byte[] readBuffer = new byte[20];

                try
                {
                    while (inStream.available() > 0)
                    {
                        int numBytes = inStream.read(readBuffer);
                    }
                    System.out.print(new String(readBuffer));
                }catch (IOException ioe)
                {
```

LISTING 14.2 continued

```java
                    System.out.println("Exception " + ioe);
                }
                break;
        }//switch
    }//serialEvent

    public static void main(String[] args)
    {
        ports = CommPortIdentifier.getPortIdentifiers();

        while(ports.hasMoreElements())
        {
            pID = (CommPortIdentifier)ports.nextElement();
            System.out.println("Port " + pID.getName());

            if (pID.getPortType() == CommPortIdentifier.PORT_SERIAL)
            {
                if (pID.getName().equals("COM1"))
                {
                    PortSniffer pSniffer = new PortSniffer();
                    System.out.println("COM1 found");
                }
            }
        }
    }//main()

    public void run()
    {
        try
        {
            Thread.sleep(20000);
        }catch (InterruptedException ie)
        {
            System.out.println("Exception " + ie);
        }
    }//run()
}
```

We need to obtain a `SerialPort` object. We do this by making a call to the `CommPortIdentifier`'s `open()` method and then casting the result to a `SerialPort` reference. The first parameter is simply a string that identifies who opened the port. This string can be used to identify the owner of a port in error messages to other processes that try to open the same port. The integer represents the time in milliseconds that this command will block while waiting on a port.

```java
        serPort = (SerialPort)pID.open("PortReader",2000);
```

14

SERIAL PORT
COMMUNICATIONS

The `SerialPort` class is built according to the Java event model that is described in Chapter 19, "JavaBeans and the Java Event Model." The `addEventListener()` method registers this class as one that is interested in events generated by the serial port.

```
serPort.addEventListener(this);
```

The events that can be generated by the serial port are shown in Table 14.2.

TABLE 14.2   The `SerialPort` Events

Event Code	Event Meaning
BI	Break interrupt
CD	Carrier detect
CTS	Clear to send
DATA_AVAILABLE	Data available at the serial port
DSR	Data set ready
FE	Framing error
OE	Overrun error
OUTPUT_BUFFER_EMPTY	Output buffer is empty
PE	Parity error
RI	Ring indicator

In most cases, when one of these events occurs, we will just print a string to the console telling us that it has occurred.

The event processing in the Java Communications API is more sophisticated than any that we have seen thus far. Event registration takes place in two phases. In the first phase, this event model operates like every other event-handling program in that it registers as an event listener with the object that generates the events. The communications API adds to that another level of tuning so that the program can be selective about what events it actually gets notification for, based on the type. The mechanism for doing this is a set of methods called the `notifyOnXXX()` methods. Calling these methods allows you to fine-tune the event notification. Because this is a sniffer program, we want to see them all:

```
serPort.notifyOnDataAvailable(true);
serPort.notifyOnBreakInterrupt(true);
serPort.notifyOnCarrierDetect(true);
serPort.notifyOnCTS(true);
serPort.notifyOnDataAvailable(true);
serPort.notifyOnDSR(true);
serPort.notifyOnFramingError(true);
serPort.notifyOnOutputEmpty(true);
```

```
serPort.notifyOnOverrunError(true);
serPort.notifyOnParityError(true);
serPort.notifyOnRingIndicator(true);
```

The most interesting event that we encounter is DATA_AVAILABLE. When it occurs, we read the input bytes into a buffer and then print the contents of the buffer after converting it to a String object.

In the constructor, we assigned the serial port's input to a stream called inStream:

```
inStream = serPort.getInputStream();
```

When a DATA_AVAILABLE event occurs, we use the InputStreamObject to retrieve the bytes from the stream:

```
byte[] readBuffer = new byte[20];

try
{
    while (inStream.available() > 0)
    {
        int numBytes = inStream.read(readBuffer);
    }
    System.out.print(new String(readBuffer));
}catch (IOException ioe)
{
    System.out.println("Exception " + ioe);
}
```

The only other bit code that we need to discuss is the thread. A thread is a type of lightweight process that runs in parallel with the process that created it. For more information on the operation of threads, see Chapter 24, "Multithreading Applications in Java."

In this case, the thread simply introduces a short delay between the time that the port is opened and the first attempt to get data. On some systems this is required to avoid data loss.

The only other thing that is lacking is a device to generate signals to the serial port for us to read. You can use almost any device such as a modem, a serial mouse, a digital camera with serial cable, or a Palm cradle. This code is run using a Palm IIIc cradle as the signal generator.

Now when we run the code in Listing 14.2 and press the Sync button on the Palm IIIc cradle, we get the following result:

```
Port COM3
Port COM2
Port COM1
COM1 found
```

```
Port LPT1
Port LPT2
SerialPortEvent.CTS occurred
SerialPortEvent.DSR occurred
SerialPortEvent.RI occurred
SerialPortEvent.OUTPUT_BUFFER_EMPTY occurred
SerialPortEvent.CTS occurred
SerialPortEvent.DSR occurred
SerialPortEvent.RI occurred
SerialPortEvent.OUTPUT_BUFFER_EMPTY occurred
SerialPortEvent.CTS occurred
SerialPortEvent.DSR occurred
SerialPortEvent.RI occurred
SerialPortEvent.OUTPUT_BUFFER_EMPTY occurred
SerialPortEvent.DSR occurred
SerialPortEvent.RI occurred
SerialPortEvent.OUTPUT_BUFFER_EMPTY occurred
SerialPortEvent.DATA_AVAILABLE occurred
⌐∩φ♥♥♥          SerialPortEvent.DATA_AVAILABLE occurred
§¬½ ⌐∩φ♥         SerialPortEvent.DATA_AVAILABLE occurred
♥♥  —⌐‖∈R        SerialPortEvent.DATA_AVAILABLE occurred
⌐∩φ♥♥♥          SerialPortEvent.DATA_AVAILABLE occurred
⊥‖φ⌐∩φ♥          SerialPortEvent.DATA_AVAILABLE occurred
♥♥  ↑‖φ♥         SerialPortEvent.DATA_AVAILABLE occurred
⌐∩φ♥♥♥          SerialPortEvent.DATA_AVAILABLE occurred
⌐‖«⌐⌐∩φ♥         SerialPortEvent.DATA_AVAILABLE occurred
♥♥  →‖σ┐         SerialPortEvent.DATA_AVAILABLE occurred
⌐∩φ♥♥♥          SerialPortEvent.DATA_AVAILABLE occurred
←⌐φΘ⌐∩φ♥         SerialPortEvent.DATA_AVAILABLE occurred
♥♥  ⌐┐a_        SerialPortEvent.DATA_AVAILABLE occurred
⌐∩φ♥♥♥          SerialPortEvent.DATA_AVAILABLE occurred
↔⌐‖—⌐∩φ♥         SerialPortEvent.DATA_AVAILABLE occurred
♥♥  ▲⊥ÿΣ        SerialPortEvent.DATA_AVAILABLE occurred
⌐∩φ♥♥☻ ♪         SerialPortEvent.DATA_AVAILABLE occurred
°»☺└¶
☺             SerialPortEvent.DATA_AVAILABLE occurred
☺☻  ☺┬         SerialPortEvent.DATA_AVAILABLE occurred
å■             SerialPortEvent.DATA_AVAILABLE occurred
⌐∩φ♥♥☻ ♪         SerialPortEvent.DATA_AVAILABLE occurred
°»☺└¶
☺             SerialPortEvent.DATA_AVAILABLE occurred
☺☻  ☺┬         SerialPortEvent.DATA_AVAILABLE occurred
å■             SerialPortEvent.DATA_AVAILABLE occurred
⌐∩φ♥♥☻ ♪         SerialPortEvent.DATA_AVAILABLE occurred
°»☺└¶
```

It appears that the Palm device is using the ring pin to notify the program that is listening to the serial port. Because our sniffer is listening to that port, the other program can't get access to it and answer the ring. Notice that the device generates a number of events before it starts sending data. Once the DATA_AVAILABLE events start, about 15 messages are sent. Then, it appears that the device starts a series of retries when it doesn't get the response that it expects from the computer.

Sending Data over the Serial Port

It is great to be able to detect activity on a serial port. What you probably need to do, though, is write to a serial port on one device and read from that same port on another device. To do that, we will write two programs and call them PortReader and PortWriter. A serial port reader program is a lot like a sniffer. The main difference is that the port reader is much more selective about the events that it listens for. Listing 14.3 shows the source code for a program that listens to a serial port and outputs only the data that comes over the connection.

LISTING 14.3   The PortReader Class

```
/*
 * PortReader.java
 *
 * Created on February 8, 2002, 4:40 PM
 */

package unleashed.ch14;
import java.io.*;
import javax.comm.*;
import java.util.*;

/**
 *
 * @author   Stephen Potts
 * @version
 */
public class PortReader implements Runnable, SerialPortEventListener
{
    static Enumeration ports;
    static CommPortIdentifier pID;
    InputStream inStream;
    SerialPort serPort;
    Thread readThread;

    /** Creates new PortFinder */
    public PortReader()
    {
        try
        {
            serPort = (SerialPort)pID.open("PortReader",2000);
        }catch (PortInUseException piue)
        {
```

LISTING 14.3   continued

```java
        System.out.println("Exception " + piue);
    }

    try
    {
        inStream = serPort.getInputStream();
    }catch (IOException ioe)
    {
        System.out.println("Exception " + ioe);
    }

    try
    {
        serPort.addEventListener(this);
    }catch (TooManyListenersException tmle)
    {
        System.out.println("Exception " + tmle);
    }

    serPort.notifyOnDataAvailable(true);

    try
    {
        serPort.setSerialPortParams(9600, SerialPort.DATABITS_8,
            SerialPort.STOPBITS_1,
            SerialPort.PARITY_NONE);
    }catch (UnsupportedCommOperationException ucoe)
    {
        System.out.println("Exception " + ucoe);
    }
    readThread = new Thread(this);
    readThread.start();
}//Constructor

public void serialEvent(SerialPortEvent event)
{
    switch(event.getEventType())
    {
        case SerialPortEvent.BI:
            System.out.println("SerialPortEvent.BI occurred");
        case SerialPortEvent.OE:
            System.out.println("SerialPortEvent.OE occurred");
        case SerialPortEvent.FE:
            System.out.println("SerialPortEvent.FE occurred");
        case SerialPortEvent.PE:
            System.out.println("SerialPortEvent.PE occurred");
        case SerialPortEvent.CD:
            System.out.println("SerialPortEvent.CD occurred");
        case SerialPortEvent.CTS:
```

LISTING 14.3   continued

```
                    System.out.println("SerialPortEvent.CTS occurred");
            case SerialPortEvent.DSR:
                System.out.println("SerialPortEvent.DSR occurred");
            case SerialPortEvent.RI:
                System.out.println("SerialPortEvent.RI occurred");
            case SerialPortEvent.OUTPUT_BUFFER_EMPTY:
                System.out.println(
                        "SerialPortEvent.OUTPUT_BUFFER_EMPTY occurred");
                break;
            case SerialPortEvent.DATA_AVAILABLE:
                System.out.println(
                            "SerialPortEvent.DATA_AVAILABLE occurred");
                byte[] readBuffer = new byte[20];

                try
                {
                    while (inStream.available() > 0)
                    {
                        int numBytes = inStream.read(readBuffer);
                    }
                    System.out.print(new String(readBuffer));
                 }catch (IOException ioe)
                {
                    System.out.println("Exception " + ioe);
                }
                break;
        }//switch
    }//serialEvent

    public static void main(String[] args)
    {
        ports = CommPortIdentifier.getPortIdentifiers();

        while(ports.hasMoreElements())
        {
            pID = (CommPortIdentifier)ports.nextElement();
            System.out.println("Port " + pID.getName());

            if (pID.getPortType() == CommPortIdentifier.PORT_SERIAL)
            {
                if (pID.getName().equals("COM1"))
                {
                    PortReader pReader = new PortReader();
                    System.out.println("COM1 found");
                }
            }
        }
    }//main()
```

Listing 14.3   continued

```
public void run()
{
    try
    {
        Thread.sleep(20000);
    }catch (InterruptedException ie)
    {
        System.out.println("Exception " + ie);
    }
}//run()
}
```

This program is not just trying to sample the signals that are coming in over the port; it is trying to actually read the data from the port:

```
while (inStream.available() > 0)
{
    int numBytes = inStream.read(readBuffer);
}
```

It prints the data to the console so we know that it worked:

```
System.out.print(new String(readBuffer));
```

In most situations, you would replace this `println()` with code that processes the data according to the requirements of your program.

In order to test this program, we need a program that writes data to the port. Listing 14.4 is such a program.

Listing 14.4   The `PortWriter` Class

```
/*
 * PortWriter.java
 *
 * Created on February 8, 2002, 4:40 PM
 */

package unleashed.ch14;
import java.io.*;
import javax.comm.*;
import java.util.*;

/**
 *
 * @author   Stephen Potts
 * @version
 */
```

LISTING 14.4 continued

```java
public class PortWriter
{
    static Enumeration ports;
    static CommPortIdentifier pID;
    static OutputStream outStream;
    SerialPort serPort;
    static String messageToSend = "Tell everyone what a great book this is!\n";

    /** Creates new PortFinder */
    public PortWriter()
    {
        try
        {
            serPort = (SerialPort)pID.open("PortWriter",2000);
        }catch (PortInUseException piue)
        {
            System.out.println("Exception " + piue);
        }

        try
        {
            outStream = serPort.getOutputStream();
        }catch (IOException ioe)
        {
            System.out.println("Exception " + ioe);
        }

        try
        {
            serPort.setSerialPortParams(9600, SerialPort.DATABITS_8,
            SerialPort.STOPBITS_1,
            SerialPort.PARITY_NONE);
        }catch (UnsupportedCommOperationException ucoe)
        {
            System.out.println("Exception " + ucoe);
        }
    }//Constructor

    public static void main(String[] args)
    {
        ports = CommPortIdentifier.getPortIdentifiers();

        while(ports.hasMoreElements())
        {
            pID = (CommPortIdentifier)ports.nextElement();
            System.out.println("Port " + pID.getName());
```

14

SERIAL PORT
COMMUNICATIONS

LISTING 14.4   continued

```
                if (pID.getPortType() == CommPortIdentifier.PORT_SERIAL)
                {
                    if (pID.getName().equals("COM1"))
                    {
                        PortWriter pWriter = new PortWriter();
                        System.out.println("COM1 found");
                    }
                }
            }
            try
            {
                outStream.write(messageToSend.getBytes());
                System.out.println("The message was sent");
            }catch (IOException ioe)
            {
                System.out.println("Exception " + ioe);
            }
        }//main()
}//class
```

Much of the processing of a write is the same as for a read. Instead of an `InputStream`, we ask the serial port to pass us an `OutputStream`:

```
        outStream = serPort.getOutputStream();
```

The output stream uses the `write()` method to put the string out to the serial port. Notice that the string has to be converted to a byte array before being sent:

```
        outStream.write(messageToSend.getBytes());
```

To run this program, connect two computers using a null-modem cable. Start the PortReader program on one computer and then start the PortWriter program on the other. If everything is connected properly, the result will show up in the console of the PortReader as shown here:

```
Port COM3
Port COM2
Port COM1
COM1 found
Port LPT1
Port LPT2
SerialPortEvent.DATA_AVAILABLE occurred
Tell eve         SerialPortEvent.DATA_AVAILABLE occurred
ryone wh         SerialPortEvent.DATA_AVAILABLE occurred
at a gre         SerialPortEvent.DATA_AVAILABLE occurred
at book          SerialPortEvent.DATA_AVAILABLE occurred
this is!         SerialPortEvent.DATA_AVAILABLE occurred
```

Both the `PortWriter` and `PortReader` classes can be modified to perform specific interconnection tasks. By replacing the `println()` methods with more sophisticated code, you can set up complex processing between devices.

Summary

In this chapter we examined the nature of the RS-232 hardware. You learned what each of the pins is for and how the drivers communicate information across them.

Next you learned how to use the javax.comm package to communicate with the RS-232 hardware. First we covered how to test our installation by writing a program that detects the presence of communication ports. Then we wrote a simple sniffer program that echoes all serial port activity to the console.

Finally, we wrote a program that writes to the serial port on one machine and another program that listens to the serial port on another machine. We connected the two computers with a null-modem cable and tested the programs.

Java Media Technology

Drawing with Java 2D

The next revolution in the field of user interfaces may well be based on a drastic improvement in graphics. Imagine how much more interesting computing would be if applications could get beyond buttons and frames and present users with texture-mapped graphics and animation.

The purpose of this chapter is to give you a jump-start in the area of two-dimensional graphics. You will learn about Java 2D's capabilities and will see how to create graphics that use text, shapes, and images.

We will start by discussing the creation of text on a screen. We will then discuss the value of antialiasing and will proceed to cover the creation of simple geometric shapes. Following that, we will show how to create arbitrary shapes using the GeneralPath object. Finally, you will learn how to manipulate images using Java 2D.

Understanding Java 2D

Java 2D is really an extended version of the java.awt.Graphics class. It provides a set of methods to draw objects on the screen. In addition to the usual lines, rectangles, and circles, Java 2D adds an object of arbitrary shape called the GeneralPath. A GeneralPath can have any number of edges, so you can create very complex shapes.

Java 2D also supports affine transformations with the class java.awt.geom. AffineTransform. This enables you to move, rotate, scale, and shear the objects that you create.

Two of the key concepts that you need to understand are device space and user space. Every display device has a set of characteristics including size and resolution. These characteristics are collectively called the *device space*. Each device has its own device space. This creates a problem for programmers, who must write separate programs for each device. Imagine writing a program for an ordinary 1024×768 screen and then having to alter it to work on a 1600×1600 user space being scrolled within a 400×400 sized window on a monitor set to an 800×600 resolution.

The programmer needs to be able to program in his own space using units that make sense to him. Later, these units can be translated into device-specific units for rendering. This set of characteristics is called the *user space*. It might more accurately be called the programmer space because the user never knows that it exists, but ours is not to reason why.

Another requirement for a graphics system is that it must be able to draw complex curves. This means that it has to support Bézier functions (a type of polynomial that describes the shape of a curve).

Text in Java 2D can be manipulated as well. Java 2D allows you to move text to odd angles and positions on the screen. It also enables you to create graphic documents that look like something from the advertising industry.

Java 2D also supports antialiasing. This functionality smooths the appearance of text in your drawings, especially after they have been rotated.

Java 2D supports transparency and the inclusion of images into your drawings. It also contains some filtering capabilities to blur or sharpen images.

Drawing Text on the Screen

Let's quickly create an example to provide a conversation piece for further explanations. This example will simply write a text string across a window using Java 2D. The code for this program is shown in Listing 15.1.

LISTING 15.1   The `Test2DText` Class

```
/*
 * Test2DText.java
 *
 * Created on February 21, 2002, 10:16 AM
 */

package unleashed.ch15;

import java.awt.*;
import java.awt.event.*;
import java.awt.geom.*;
import java.awt.font.*;
import javax.swing.*;

/**
 *
 * @author   Stephen Potts
 * @version
 */
public class Test2DText extends Canvas
{

    /** Creates new Test2DText */
    public Test2DText()
    {
        setBackground(Color.white);
    }

    public void paint(Graphics g)
```

LISTING 15.1   continued

```
    {
        Graphics2D g2D;
        g2D = (Graphics2D) g;

        FontRenderContext frc = g2D.getFontRenderContext();
        Font font1 = new Font("Courier",Font.BOLD, 24);
        String str1 = new String("Java Unleashed");
        TextLayout tl = new TextLayout(str1, font1, frc);
        Dimension dim1= getSize();
        g2D.setColor(Color.gray);
        tl.draw(g2D, 70, 150);
    }

    public static void main(String s[])
    {

        JFrame frame1 = new JFrame("2D Text");
        frame1.setDefaultCloseOperation(JFrame.EXIT_ON_CLOSE);

        frame1.getContentPane().add("Center", new Test2DText());
        frame1.pack();
        frame1.setSize(new Dimension(500, 300));
        frame1.show();
    }

}
```

There are several interesting pieces of this application that we should examine in detail. We create the class to extend `java.awt.Canvas`. For you server-side programmers, the `Canvas` class is just a rectangular area of the screen that you can draw on.

```
public class Test2DText extends Canvas
```

`Canvas` extends `java.awt.Component` so we can set the background using `Component`'s `setBackground()` method:

```
        setBackground(Color.white);
```

`Canvas` provides a `paint` method that is called by the JVM. It gives us a chance to place objects on the screen. It also hands us the `Graphics` handle that we need to create the `Graphics2D` handle:

```
    public void paint(Graphics g)
    {
        Graphics2D g2D;
        g2D = (Graphics2D) g;
```

The Graphics2D class provides much more extensive capabilities than its parent class java.awt.Graphics. It allows you much more control over color management, text layout, and transformations. We use a cast to assign the g2D handle to a Graphics object.

Now that we have a 2D handle, we have access to all the methods that it contains. One of these methods is getFontRenderContext(). The FontRenderContext class is a container class. It contains information needed to correctly render text. The basic activity of converting outlines of a font into pixels is complex because the point size is different from the mechanical pixel size.

```
FontRenderContext frc = g2D.getFontRenderContext();
Font font1 = new Font("Courier",Font.BOLD, 24);
```

The Font object represents the shape of a character. It is this shape that is painted on the Canvas.

In order to place the text on the screen, we create a string. Then we create a TextLayout object and pass in the string, the font, and the FontRenderContext. With this information, the TextLayout object is able to determine almost everything that will be displayed on the screen.

```
String str1 = new String("Java Unleashed");
TextLayout tl = new TextLayout(str1, font1, frc);
```

The only piece of information still missing is the color that we want to use to display the characters. We set that, then call the TextLayout object's draw function and pass in the handle to the Graphics2D object and the coordinates where we want the line printed:

```
g2D.setColor(Color.gray);
tl.draw(g2D, 70, 150);
```

In the main() method, we simply create a JFrame and then add the Test2DText class (remember that it extends Canvas) to the center of the frame:

```
frame1.getContentPane().add("Center", new Test2DText());
```

Running this example brings up the window that is shown in Figure 15.1.

FIGURE 15.1

Java 2D is capable of displaying jagged-looking text in a window.

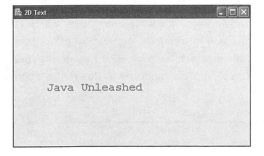

You probably have mixed feelings about this example. You are probably glad that you know how to place text on a Canvas, but you may be disappointed with the quality. Never fear, antialiasing is coming to the rescue.

Antialiasing

The pioneers in the field of computer graphics had to find a way to smooth out the jagged edges that often appear on monitors when text is displayed graphically. This effect is known as *aliasing*. Figure 15.2 shows the results from running Listing 15.1 magnified to 500% of its original size.

FIGURE 15.2

Java 2D text looks very jagged when magnified to 500%.

We can improve this situation and smooth out the text that is drawn by applying a technique called *antialiasing*.

Aliasing occurs when a continuous signal, such as a mathematical equation, is mapped into discrete space. Because pixels on a screen or in an image are discrete and finite in number, some decisions must be made about what color to make each pixel. If there are adequate pixels per inch of resolution, the problem is a small one. The problem becomes greater when the number of pixels is too small, which is very often the case. At any rate, if you continue to enlarge an image, you will see the effects of aliasing.

The antidote to aliasing is antialiasing. This is a technique by which jagged edges are smoothed. Shades of gray are used to soften the curves and make them look better. Listing 15.2 shows an example in which we have added rendering hints to specify that we want the TextLayout class to apply antialiasing to this string when it renders it.

LISTING 15.2   The Test2DtextAA Class

```
/*
 * Test2DTextAA.java
```

LISTING 15.2 continued

```
 *
 * Created on February 21, 2002, 10:16 AM
 */

package unleashed.ch15;

import java.awt.*;
import java.awt.event.*;
import java.awt.geom.*;
import java.awt.font.*;
import javax.swing.*;

/**
 *
 * @author   Stephen Potts
 * @version
 */
public class Test2DTextAA extends Canvas
{

    /** Creates new Test2DTextAA */
    public Test2DTextAA()
    {
        setBackground(Color.white);
    }

    public void paint(Graphics g)
    {
        Graphics2D g2D;
        g2D = (Graphics2D) g;

        g2D.setRenderingHint(RenderingHints.KEY_ANTIALIASING,
                        RenderingHints.VALUE_ANTIALIAS_ON);

        g2D.setRenderingHint(RenderingHints.KEY_RENDERING,
                        RenderingHints.VALUE_RENDER_QUALITY);

        FontRenderContext frc = g2D.getFontRenderContext();
        Font font1 = new Font("Courier",Font.BOLD, 24);
        String str1 = new String("Java Unleashed");
        TextLayout tl = new TextLayout(str1, font1, frc);
        Dimension dim1= getSize();
        g2D.setColor(Color.gray);
        tl.draw(g2D, 50, 150);
    }

    public static void main(String s[])
    {
```

LISTING 15.2   continued

```
        JFrame frame1 = new JFrame("2D Text");
        frame1.setDefaultCloseOperation(JFrame.EXIT_ON_CLOSE);

        frame1.getContentPane().add("Center", new Test2DTextAA());
        frame1.pack();
        frame1.setSize(new Dimension(500, 300));
        frame1.show();
    }
}
```

The two new statements add rendering instructions, called "hints," to the `Graphics2D` object. These are called hints because they may or may not actually be applied to the drawing because of the limitations of certain hardware. The first statement turns antialiasing on:

```
        g2D.setRenderingHint(RenderingHints.KEY_ANTIALIASING,
                        RenderingHints.VALUE_ANTIALIAS_ON);
```

The second hint is telling the `TextLayout` object to choose quality over speed when choosing algorithms:

```
        g2D.setRenderingHint(RenderingHints.KEY_RENDERING,
                        RenderingHints.VALUE_RENDER_QUALITY);
```

The result obtained by adding these lines is shown in Figure 15.3.

FIGURE 15.3

Java 2D is capable of displaying smooth text.

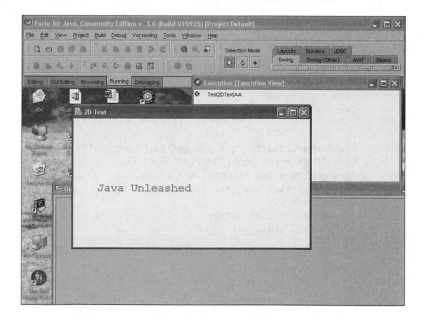

If you have difficulty seeing the difference at normal size, you won't have any trouble seeing it when the text is magnified to 500%, as it is in Figure 15.4.

FIGURE 15.4
Java 2D uses shades of gray to improve the appearance of text.

Notice the small adjustments that have been made to smooth the text. The goal is to make the viewer think that she is viewing the text at a higher resolution than she actually is.

Drawing Graphics

The next topic that we need to address is the process of drawing graphics. Java 2D enables you to draw the usual set of rectangles, circles, ellipses, and so on. In addition, it allows you to draw arbitrary shapes using the `GeneralPath` class. Listing 15.3 shows how this works.

LISTING 15.3 The `Test2DGraphics` Class

```
/*
 * Test2DGraphics.java
 *
 * Created on February 21, 2002, 10:16 AM
 */

package unleashed.ch15;

import java.awt.*;
import java.awt.event.*;
import java.awt.geom.*;
import java.awt.font.*;
import javax.swing.*;
```

LISTING 15.3   continued

```java
/**
 *
 * @author  Stephen Potts
 * @version
 */
public class Test2DGraphics extends Canvas
{

    /** Creates new Test2DText */
    public Test2DGraphics ()
    {
        setBackground(Color.white);
    }

    public void paint(Graphics g)
    {
        Graphics2D g2D;
        g2D = (Graphics2D) g;

        //draw the red rectangle
        g2D.setColor(Color.red);
        g2D.drawRect(100,100,60,40);

        //draw the blue oval
        g2D.setColor(Color.blue);
        g2D.drawOval(100,100,60,40);

        //Draw the green polygon
        GeneralPath path1 = new GeneralPath(GeneralPath.WIND_EVEN_ODD);
        path1.moveTo(0.0f, 0.0f);
        path1.lineTo(0.0f, 50.0f);
        path1.lineTo(50.0f, 100.0f);
        path1.lineTo(75.0f, 50.0f);
        path1.lineTo(75.0f, 0.0f);
        path1.closePath();
        g2D.setColor(Color.green);
        g2D.fill(path1);

        //Draw the first red polygon
        GeneralPath path2 = new GeneralPath(GeneralPath.WIND_EVEN_ODD);
        path2.moveTo(0.0f, 0.0f);
        path2.lineTo(100.0f, 300.0f);
        path2.lineTo(30.0f, 30.0f);
        path2.closePath();

        //position the first red polygon
        AffineTransform aTran = new AffineTransform();
        aTran.setToRotation(-Math.PI/10.0);
        g2D.transform(aTran);
```

LISTING 15.3   continued

```
            aTran.setToTranslation(10.0f,250.0f);
            g2D.transform(aTran);

            g2D.setColor(Color.red);
            g2D.fill(path2);

            //position and draw the red polygon again
            aTran.setToRotation(-Math.PI/5.0);
            g2D.transform(aTran);
            aTran.setToTranslation(10.0f,10.0f);
            g2D.transform(aTran);

            g2D.setColor(Color.red);
            g2D.fill(path2);

            //position and draw the red polygon for the third time
            aTran.setToRotation(-Math.PI/3.0);
            g2D.transform(aTran);
            aTran.setToTranslation(10.0f,10.0f);
            g2D.transform(aTran);

            g2D.setColor(Color.red);
            g2D.fill(path2);
        }

    public static void main(String s[])
    {

        JFrame frame1 = new JFrame("2D Graphics ");
        frame1.setDefaultCloseOperation(JFrame.EXIT_ON_CLOSE);

        frame1.getContentPane().add("Center", new Test2DGraphics ());
        frame1.pack();
        frame1.setSize(new Dimension(500, 500));
        frame1.show();
    }

}
```

Because much of the setup in this example is the same as it was in the text example, we will concentrate on the graphic elements.

Our first activity is to draw a red rectangle on the screen. All that we have to do is set the color and provide an x and y position as well as a width and height:

```
g2D.setColor(Color.red);
g2D.drawRect(100,100,60,40);
```

We can draw an oval on the screen using almost the same code that we used to draw the rectangle. (Ovals are specified by a bounding rectangle that is never drawn.) You can see in Figure 15.5 that the oval is completely enclosed by the rectangle.

```
g2D.setColor(Color.blue);
g2D.drawOval(100,100,60,40);
```

Now that we have looked at the easy shapes, we can proceed with the most interesting shape of all, the GeneralPath. This shape is arbitrary and we specify it by drawing lines from one point to the next until we are satisfied with its appearance. Finally, we close the path, set the color, and fill the path with that color. According to the Javadocs, the constant WIND_EVEN_ODD specifies that "enclosed regions of the path alternate between interior and exterior areas as traversed from the outside of the path towards a point inside the region." (Got that?) At any rate, the polygon is formed, filled, and rendered (see the upper-left corner of Figure 15.5).

```
GeneralPath path1 = new GeneralPath(GeneralPath.WIND_EVEN_ODD);
path1.moveTo(0.0f, 0.0f);
path1.lineTo(0.0f, 50.0f);
path1.lineTo(50.0f, 100.0f);
path1.lineTo(75.0f, 50.0f);
path1.lineTo(75.0f, 0.0f);
path1.closePath();
g2D.setColor(Color.green);
g2D.fill(path1);
```

The next thing that we want to do is create and reuse a polygon. To do this, we first need to describe the new polygon, an elongated red triangle:

```
GeneralPath path2 = new GeneralPath(GeneralPath.WIND_EVEN_ODD);
path2.moveTo(0.0f, 0.0f);
path2.lineTo(100.0f, 300.0f);
path2.lineTo(30.0f, 30.0f);
path2.closePath();
```

Notice that we started the path at point (0,0). This doesn't mean that we have to display it there. We can apply a transform to the shape that will move and rotate it in our drawing:

```
//position the first red polygon
AffineTransform aTran = new AffineTransform();
aTran.setToRotation(-Math.PI/10.0);
g2D.transform(aTran);
aTran.setToTranslation(10.0f,250.0f);
g2D.transform(aTran);
g2D.setColor(Color.red);
g2D.fill(path2);
```

The `AffineTransform` class performs a mapping from user space to device space in a way that keeps straight lines straight and parallel lines parallel. We'll leave it to mathematicians to explain how it does this. The fact that it works is evident from looking at Figure 15.5.

We can reuse this shape by simply translating the shape to a new position and calling the `fill()` methods over and over:

```
//position and draw the red polygon again
aTran.setToRotation(-Math.PI/5.0);
g2D.transform(aTran);
aTran.setToTranslation(10.0f,10.0f);
g2D.transform(aTran);
g2D.setColor(Color.red);
g2D.fill(path2);
```

The result of running the code in Listing 15.3 is shown in Figure 15.5.

FIGURE 15.5

Java 2D is capable of displaying a wide variety of geometric shapes.

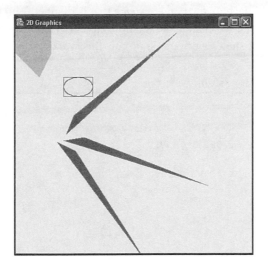

Notice how the long skinny triangle appears in three places. Notice also that it is rotated to a different orientation each time.

Manipulating Images

Armed with an understanding of how to render text and geometric shapes, you are ready to learn how to manipulate images in Java 2D. The Java Advanced Imaging (JAI) API has superseded Java 2D as the most advanced way to process images in your programs. Java 2D still has value, however, for applications with less stringent requirements.

> **Note**
>
> For an introduction to the Java Advanced Imaging API, see Chapter 17, "The Java Media Framework and the Java Advanced Imaging (JAI) API."

Java 2D's image processing capabilities allow you to perform some of the same manipulations on images that you are able to do on text and graphics. These include affine transformations and clipping. The `java.awt.image.BufferedImage` class is the main class that we will be working with in the rest of this chapter.

The first thing that we will look at is how we can display an image. Next, we will look at how we can transform images just as we can transform shapes by translating (moving), rotating, scaling, and shearing them.

An image is considered to have its own *image space* that is distinct from the user space. When we manipulate images, we change the relationship between the image space and the user space. Listing 15.4 shows an example of how this works.

LISTING 15.4   The `Test2DImage` Class

```
/*
 * Test2DImage.java
 *
 * Created on February 22, 2002, 6:47 PM
 */

package unleashed.ch15;

import java.awt.*;
import java.awt.event.*;
import java.awt.geom.*;
import java.net.*;
import javax.swing.*;

/**
 *
 * @author  Stephen Potts
 * @version
 */

public class Test2DImage extends Canvas
{

    /** Creates new Test2DText */
    public Test2DImage()
```

LISTING 15.4 continued

```java
    {
        setBackground(Color.white);
    }

    public void paint(Graphics g)
    {
        try
        {
            Graphics2D g2D;
            g2D = (Graphics2D) g;

            g2D.setRenderingHint(RenderingHints.KEY_ANTIALIASING,
            RenderingHints.VALUE_ANTIALIAS_ON);

            String fileName = "c:/unleashed/ch15/snake.jpg";

            Image img = getToolkit().getImage(fileName);

            AffineTransform aTran = new AffineTransform();
            aTran.translate(50.0f, 20.0f);
            g2D.transform(aTran);

            g2D.drawImage(img, new AffineTransform(), this);
        }catch (Exception e)
        {}
    }

    public static void main(String s[])
    {
        JFrame frame1 = new JFrame("2D Images ");
        frame1.setDefaultCloseOperation(JFrame.EXIT_ON_CLOSE);

        frame1.getContentPane().add("Center", new Test2DImage());
        frame1.pack();
        frame1.setSize(new Dimension(300, 300));
        frame1.show();
    }//main

}//class
```

This example resembles the graphics example in the setup, so we won't repeat that discussion. It begins to differ when it gets to the processing of the image. After setting the antialiasing value, we specify a filename and get the image using the ToolKit class:

```java
            String fileName = "c:/unleashed/ch15/snake.jpg";
            Image img = getToolkit().getImage(fileName);
```

The `Toolkit` class represents the platform-dependent functionality in the JVM. In AWT, almost every action is implemented using a facility on the host directly. (Swing implements much more of its functionality in Java itself.)

> **Note**
>
> The `readme` file for this chapter discusses how to deal with the C drive path of the graphic file. This file is located in the code directory.

We create a transform in order to move the image out of the upper-left corner of the `Canvas` and toward the center:

```
AffineTransform aTran = new AffineTransform();
aTran.translate(50.0f, 20.0f);
g2D.transform(aTran);
```

Finally, we are able to use the `Graphics2D` object to display the image in `this`. `this`, in our situation, means the `Canvas` object that we are extending. The only thing odd about this whole process is the creation of an anonymous `AffineTransform` object in the call:

```
g2D.drawImage(img, new AffineTransform(), this);
```

The reason for this is really fairly simple. You might remember the discussion earlier in this chapter about image space being distinct from user space. This `AffineTransform` applies to image space. As such, it will be applied before the transforms in user space. In our case, we are passing a new object that will contain no actual transforms.

The result of this process is shown in Figure 15.6.

FIGURE 15.6

Java 2D is also capable of displaying images.

Now that we have an image to play with, let's have a little fun with it. We can apply a couple of transformations that we haven't seen yet. Listing 15.5 shows an enlargement of the image and a shearing.

LISTING 15.5   The `Test2DImageTran` Class

```
/*
 * Test2DImage.java
 *
 * Created on February 22, 2002, 6:47 PM
 */

package unleashed.ch15;

import java.awt.*;
import java.awt.event.*;
import java.awt.geom.*;
import java.net.*;
import javax.swing.*;

/**
 *
 * @author  Stephen Potts
 * @version
 */

public class Test2DImageTran extends Canvas
{

    /** Creates new Test2DText */
    public Test2DImageTran()
    {
        setBackground(Color.white);
    }

    public void paint(Graphics g)
    {
        try
        {
            Graphics2D g2D;
            g2D = (Graphics2D) g;

            g2D.setRenderingHint(RenderingHints.KEY_ANTIALIASING,
            RenderingHints.VALUE_ANTIALIAS_ON);

            String fileName = "c:/unleashed/ch15/snake.jpg";
            Image img = getToolkit().getImage(fileName);

            //draw the original image
```

LISTING 15.5 continued

```
        g2D.drawImage(img, new AffineTransform(), this);
                    //move the image over
        AffineTransform aTran = new AffineTransform();
        aTran.translate(200.0f, 0.0f);
        g2D.transform(aTran);

        //adjust the scale to enlarge it
        AffineTransform imageSpaceTran = new AffineTransform();

        //set how much to shear the picture
        imageSpaceTran.setToShear(0.1f, 0.1f);

        //draw the sheared image
        g2D.drawImage(img, imageSpaceTran, this);

        //move the image over
        aTran.translate(50.0f, 0.0f);
        g2D.transform(aTran);
        imageSpaceTran.scale(1.3f, 1.3f);

        //draw the enlarged image
        g2D.drawImage(img, imageSpaceTran, this);

    }catch (Exception e)
    {}
}

public static void main(String s[])
{
    JFrame frame1 = new JFrame("2D Images ");
    frame1.setDefaultCloseOperation(JFrame.EXIT_ON_CLOSE);

    frame1.getContentPane().add("Center", new Test2DImageTran());
    frame1.pack();
    frame1.setSize(new Dimension(750, 370));
    frame1.show();
}//main

}//class
```

The interesting parts of this example are, of course, the two transforms.

First, we want to shear the image. This is shown here:

```
        AffineTransform imageSpaceTran = new AffineTransform();
        imageSpaceTran.setToShear(0.1f, 0.1f);
```

```
//draw the sheared image
g2D.drawImage(img, imageSpaceTran, this);
```

Next, we create another `AffineTransform()`. We use the `setToShear()` method to specify the amount of deformation that we want. The first number indicates how much to deform the image in the positive x direction and the second one indicates how much to deform it in the positive y direction.

The next transformation resizes the image:

```
//adjust the scale to enlarge it
imageSpaceTran.scale(1.3f, 1.3f);

//draw the enlarged image
g2D.drawImage(img, imageSpaceTran, this);
```

We don't need to declare another `AffineTransform`, as we already have one to use. We apply the `scale` method. We apply the transform to the image itself in the `drawImage()` method's parameters and not to the `Graphics2D` object as we do when we move an image. This is, once again, because we want to apply the transform to the image space, not to the user space.

The result of doing this is shown in Figure 15.7.

FIGURE 15.7

Java 2D is capable of resizing and deforming an image using the scaling and shearing functionality.

Applying these transformations on the image produces some interesting results. You can combine these transformations to produce some unique graphical displays. Java 2D also enables you to brighten, blur, and sharpen images by manipulating the pixels. In addition, you can combine text graphics and images in the same program.

Combining Text, Graphics, and Images

All the techniques that we have covered in this chapter can be combined in the same program. The result is a graphic that is similar in its appearance to a magazine cover. Listing 15.6 shows how this can be done.

LISTING 15.6   The `Test2DImageDraw` Class

```java
/*
 * Test2DImageDraw.java
 *
 * Created on February 22, 2002, 6:47 PM
 */

package unleashed.ch15;

import java.awt.*;
import java.awt.event.*;
import java.awt.geom.*;
import java.net.*;
import javax.swing.*;
import java.awt.font.*;

/**
 *
 * @author  Stephen Potts
 * @version
 */

public class Test2DImageDraw extends Canvas
{

    /** Creates new Test2DText */
    public Test2DImageDraw()
    {
        setBackground(Color.white);
    }

    public void paint(Graphics g)
    {
        try
        {
            Graphics2D g2D;
            g2D = (Graphics2D) g;

            g2D.setRenderingHint(RenderingHints.KEY_ANTIALIASING,
```

LISTING 15.6 continued

```
            RenderingHints.VALUE_ANTIALIAS_ON);

            String fileName = "c:/unleashed/ch15/snake.jpg";

            Image img = getToolkit().getImage(fileName);

            AffineTransform aTran = new AffineTransform();
            aTran.translate(50.0f, 20.0f);
            g2D.transform(aTran);

            //draw the image
            g2D.drawImage(img, new AffineTransform(), this);

            //draw the 2 red rectangles close to each other
            g2D.setColor(Color.red);
            g2D.drawRect(0,0,173,230);
            g2D.drawRect(1,1,171,228);

            //draw the white oval
            g2D.setColor(Color.white);
            g2D.drawOval(2,2,170,227);


            //add the text
            FontRenderContext frc = g2D.getFontRenderContext();
            Font font1 = new Font("Courier",Font.BOLD, 8);
            String str1 = new String("Copyright");
            TextLayout tl = new TextLayout(str1, font1, frc);
            Dimension dim1= getSize();
            g2D.setColor(Color.white);
            tl.draw(g2D, 125, 228);


        }catch (Exception e)
        {}
    }

    public static void main(String s[])
    {
        JFrame frame1 = new JFrame("2D Images ");
        frame1.setDefaultCloseOperation(JFrame.EXIT_ON_CLOSE);

        frame1.getContentPane().add("Center", new Test2DImageDraw());
        frame1.pack();
        frame1.setSize(new Dimension(300, 300));
        frame1.show();
    }//main

}//class
```

15

DRAWING WITH
JAVA 2D

This class combines images with graphics and text for a professional look. First, the image is drawn:

```
g2D.drawImage(img, new AffineTransform(), this);
```

Next, the graphics are added on top of it:

```
//draw the 2 red rectangle close to each other
g2D.setColor(Color.red);
g2D.drawRect(0,0,173,230);
g2D.drawRect(1,1,171,228);

//draw the white oval
g2D.setColor(Color.white);
g2D.drawOval(2,2,170,227);
```

Notice that two red rectangles are drawn close together to give the picture a frame. Following that, a white oval is added. Finally, the text is placed at the bottom:

```
//add the text
FontRenderContext frc = g2D.getFontRenderContext();
Font font1 = new Font("Courier",Font.BOLD, 8);
String str1 = new String("Copyright");
TextLayout tl = new TextLayout(str1, font1, frc);
Dimension dim1= getSize();
g2D.setColor(Color.white);
tl.draw(g2D, 125, 228);
```

The final result has a more polished appearance than an image displayed by itself, as shown here in Figure 15.8.

FIGURE 15.8

Java 2D allows you to draw both graphics and text on top of an image.

Notice how much better the image looks with a little trim added.

Summary

In this chapter, you learned how to use Java 2D to perform graphic processing. First, you learned how to draw graphical text on the screen. While this does not give you report-writing capabilities, it does enable you to create graphic displays that look like posters and advertisements.

Next, you learned how to draw graphics on the screen using primitive shapes as well as the path-oriented class, `GeneralPath`. This enables you to create interesting patterns on the screen, which is the real strength of Java 2D. By extending the examples in this chapter, you can produce fairly complex graphics.

Finally, you learned how to include images in Java 2D programs and how to combine images with text and graphics to produce a more professional look.

Java 3D Graphics

CHAPTER 16

Few subjects get programmers as excited as the prospect of creating models in three dimensions. The predictions that virtual reality will revolutionize computing have been around for decades. The television show *Star Trek: The Next Generation* has its holodeck, and the world as depicted in the movie *The Matrix* is one big virtual reality scene. This makes us hungry for 3D applications to become practical.

The lack of adequate CPU power is one of the reasons that 3D systems are still not as common as you might predict based on their psychological appeal. The basic truth is that it takes a lot of detail to fool humans and it takes a lot of processing power to provide this detail. Our physical world is so complex and so detailed that it is hard for us to suspend disbelief when viewing a model, even when we are trying hard to do just that.

This chapter is about Java's contribution to the three-dimensional programming world—Java 3D. We will introduce you to the governing principles of this technology. Then we will work through a few examples so that you can gain the experience you need to start planning your next model of the solar system or your next first-person shooter game.

Understanding Three-Dimensional (3D) Programming

The idea of programming in three dimensions is not a new one. Research work done in the 1970s led to the introduction of raster terminals plugged into mainframes and minicomputers in the early 1980s. By the mid-80s, solid geometric modeling systems were appearing on workstations. These systems were normally programmed using proprietary hardware-specific libraries written in C or Fortran.

As workstations became more powerful, a hardware-neutral standard called OpenGL gained popularity with C++ programmers. The implementation of OpenGL required hardware-dependent code, of course, but the API allowed programmers to ignore many of the low-level details that 3D development required previously.

Java 3D is another step up the graphics food chain. Java 3D provides yet another, higher level of abstraction that is built on top of products such as OpenGL and Direct3D. It doesn't replace them; it just provides Java programmers with a simpler API for adding 3D features to their projects.

Java 3D is a Standard Extension to the Java Development Kit (JDK). At first, programmers feared that vendors would not add support for this extension on their platforms. (Their agreements with Sun allow them to pick and choose which Standard Extensions they want to implement.) This hasn't proven to be a problem because many vendors have chosen to implement Java 3D.

The advantages of using Java 3D are many:

- Free software—Java 3D is free to download.

- High level of abstraction—As you will see in this chapter, programming in Java 3D doesn't require the creation of lines and surfaces. Instead, the programmer creates geometric objects and manages them using other objects.

- Program in Java—The Java 3D API has a look and feel similar to that of other Standard Extensions. This means that it is relatively easy for an experienced Java programmer to learn Java 3D programming.

- Performance—Java 3D has been designed with performance in mind. The runtime engine uses capability bits to optimize the structure of the objects in the Java 3D universe for maximum performance. Capability bits are your application's way of describing your objects to the Java 3D API implementation. The implementation looks at the capability bits to determine which objects can change during runtime. In addition, all objects have bounds that control when they are rendered. If the user's view is not within the bounds of an object, that object is not rendered.

- Loaders—You can use any of a number of 3D loaders to import objects into a Java 3D universe. This includes a VRML loader that can import objects created using a GUI.

- Device support—A large number of exotic devices such as headsets, wands, and data gloves are supported, as are the ever-present mouse and keyboard.

In the interest of full disclosure, we also need to point out Java 3D's disadvantages:

- High level of abstraction—The lack of low-level rendering pipeline control makes some tasks impossible. For example, you cannot use Java 3D to display reflections and reflected light on objects.

- Performance—Every level of abstraction imposes some performance penalty. If you need to squeeze every drop of performance out of a graphics subsystem, you might not be able to afford the extra layer of abstraction. In the 3D world, performance will still be a problem when we are running programs on machines that are a thousand times faster than the machines of today. In an effort to add more realism to 3D models, programmers will clog any CPU, no matter how powerful.

- Heavyweight solution—Java 3D components have a non-Java peer that actually does the rendering. If you use Swing, this puts you in the position of mixing lightweight and heavyweight components in the same application, which can be problematic.

Java 3D is not the right technology for every 3D requirement. For cases in which its disadvantages are not relevant, though, it can be a good choice.

Before we study the API, it will be helpful to list and describe a set of key concepts. This will give us a vocabulary to use when we describe the API later in the chapter.

- Universe—The root of a Java 3D model is called a universe (*world* was too limiting, perhaps). You can have more than one universe in an application, but the objects in one universe can't view the objects in other universes. One is normally all that you need.

- Locale—A universe is so big that it is organized into locales. A locale is like a neighborhood full of objects.

- View—The view represents the perspective from which you see the universe.

- Bounds—Every object has bounds. The programmer can override the default bounds if he chooses to. When the view is out of bounds, it cannot see the object (which isn't rendered). This is a performance-enhancing feature.

- Behavior—Objects can react to stimuli such as the closeness of the view (your eyes). For instance, an automatic door might open when the view is within three feet.

The Major Objects in the Java 3D API

The Java 3D API is not difficult to understand, but it contains a lot of classes and interfaces. The following is a list of the most important ones:

- Canvas3D—This class is the canvas for rendering 3D views.

- VirtualUniverse—The universe class is the container for all other objects in your model.

- BranchGroup—A branch group class is the only entity that can be moved from one location on the scene graph to another.

- Node—Every group and leaf node class is a descendant of the Node class.

- View—This is an object that contains all the information needed to view a 3D scene from one point in the universe.

- ViewPlatform—This object contains the information that the user is currently seeing.

- Shape3D—This is a leaf node that describes all geometric objects.

- Transform3D—This object controls the motion of objects in the scene graph.

- SceneGraph—This object is the common superclass for all objects in the model.

The coordinate system for Java 3D has the origin in the center of the screen. Positive y extends upward and positive x extends to the right. The coordinate system follows the right-hand rule, which means that the z-axis is positive coming from the screen toward you, as shown in Figure 16.1.

FIGURE 16.1

The coordinate system for Java 3D.

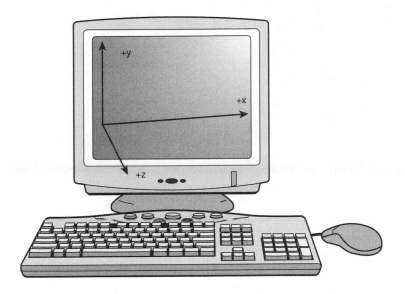

Now that we have covered Java 3D in the abstract, let's look at a concrete example. Listing 16.1 shows a simple application.

LISTING 16.1   `Minimal3D.java`: The Minimal 3D Class

```
/*
 * Minimal3D.java
 *
 * Created on March 25, 2002, 9:54 AM
 */

package unleashed.ch16;

import java.awt.*;
import java.awt.event.*;
import javax.media.j3d.*;
import com.sun.j3d.utils.geometry.Sphere;
import com.sun.j3d.utils.geometry.ColorCube;
import com.sun.j3d.utils.universe.SimpleUniverse;
```

LISTING 16.1   continued

```java
/**
 *
 * @author  Stephen Potts
 * @version
 */
public class Minimal3D extends Frame
{

    /** Creates new Minimal3D */
    public Minimal3D()
    {
        super("Minimal3D");
        setSize(400,300);
        setLayout(new BorderLayout());

        GraphicsConfiguration config =
        SimpleUniverse.getPreferredConfiguration();
        Canvas3D canvas3D = new Canvas3D(config);

        add("Center", canvas3D);
        setVisible(true);

        BranchGroup sGraph = createSceneGraph();
        sGraph.compile();

        SimpleUniverse sUniverse = new SimpleUniverse(canvas3D);

        sUniverse.getViewingPlatform().setNominalViewingTransform();

        sUniverse.addBranchGraph(sGraph);
    }//constructor

    public BranchGroup createSceneGraph()
    {
        BranchGroup root = new BranchGroup();

        Transform3D rotateX = new Transform3D();
        rotateX.rotX(Math.PI/10.0d);
        Transform3D rotateY = new Transform3D();
        rotateY.rotY(Math.PI/5.0d);
        rotateX.mul(rotateY);

        TransformGroup tGroup = new TransformGroup(rotateX);
        tGroup.addChild(new ColorCube(0.3));
        root.addChild(tGroup);

        return root;
    }//createSceneGraph()
```

LISTING 16.1   continued

```java
public static void main(String[] args)
{
    final Minimal3D m3d = new Minimal3D();
    m3d.addWindowListener(new WindowAdapter()
    {
        public void windowClosing(WindowEvent e)
        {
            m3d.dispose();
            System.exit(0);
        }
    });
}
```

One of the first things to notice when you look at this code is that it uses classes in the `javax.media.j3d` package. Another package, `com.sun.j3d.utils`, and its subpackages also provide quite a few useful classes:

```java
import javax.media.j3d.*;
import com.sun.j3d.utils.geometry.ColorCube;
```

After doing some preliminary AWT work, the constructor creates a `Canvas3D` object and adds it to the frame:

```java
GraphicsConfiguration config =
SimpleUniverse.getPreferredConfiguration();
Canvas3D canvas3D = new Canvas3D(config);

add("Center", canvas3D);
setVisible(true);
```

The primary work in all the examples in this chapter is done in the `createSceneGraph()` method. For performance reasons, we compile it:

```java
BranchGroup sGraph = createSceneGraph();
sGraph.compile();
```

The `SimpleUniverse` class is a convenience class provided in the `com.sun.j3d.utils.` `universe` package. It provides a simple way of creating a universe for your objects:

```java
SimpleUniverse sUniverse = new SimpleUniverse(canvas3D);
```

The hardest thing about creating your own universe is knowing where to stand in it when it is done. Luckily, the `setNominalViewingTransform()` provides a nice default location:

```java
sUniverse.getViewingPlatform().setNominalViewingTransform();
```

Finally, we are ready to place our scene graph in the new universe. The contents of the scene graph will change from example to example. The constructor that we have just examined will be reused with each example for the remainder of this chapter.

```
sUniverse.addBranchGraph(sGraph);
```

The `createSceneGraph()` method provides a convenient place to store all the objects that make up our universe:

```
public BranchGroup createSceneGraph()
```

We will call the main branch group, root, for obvious reasons:

```
BranchGroup root = new BranchGroup();
```

We could just add the cube here and run the example. If we do that, though, we will be looking directly at one face of the cube and all other sides will be hidden from our view. We solve that problem by rotating the cube on both the x- and y-axes:

```
Transform3D rotateX = new Transform3D();
rotateX.rotX(Math.PI/10.0d);
Transform3D rotateY = new Transform3D();
rotateY.rotY(Math.PI/5.0d);
rotateX.mul(rotateY);
```

We add a `TransformGroup` node and attach the rotation position to it:

```
TransformGroup tGroup = new TransformGroup(rotateX);
tGroup.addChild(new ColorCube(0.3));
root.addChild(tGroup);
```

We add the actual object to this group and then return the group to the constructor, where it will be attached to the universe:

```
return root;
```

Running this program is a simple matter of compiling it and using the `java` command on the command line. The result is shown in Figure 16.2.

> **Note**
>
> Because the figures in this book are rendered in black and white, they don't give you a full sense of the use of colors in this chapter's examples. Running the code from the Sams Publishing Web site (www.samspublishing.com) will enable you to see the true colors.

FIGURE 16.2

The minimal example shows a cube in 3D space.

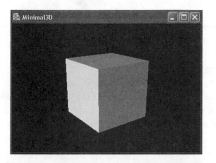

> **Note**
>
> All the examples in this chapter are identical except for the createSceneGraph()
> and other methods that it calls. The code on the Sams Publishing Web site
> (www.samspublishing.com) repeats the other methods in every listing. This chap-
> ter, however, only contains the new code.

This cube is very convenient for examples because it can be declared in one line, thus
keeping the examples relatively simple.

Adding Motion to a Java 3D Application

Having a static cube rendered in 3D is nice, but let's make it more interesting by providing some motion. Listing 16.2 causes the cube to rotate horizontally around its center
axis using a transform group class.

LISTING 16.2   The Minimal3D_1 Class's createSceneGraph() Method

```
public BranchGroup createSceneGraph()
{
    BranchGroup root = new BranchGroup();

    //do a static rotation so that we can see it better
    Transform3D rotateX = new Transform3D();
    rotateX.rotX(Math.PI/10.0d);
    Transform3D rotateY = new Transform3D();
    rotateY.rotY(Math.PI/1.0d);
    rotateX.mul(rotateY);
```

LISTING 16.2   continued

```
        TransformGroup tGroupRotate = new TransformGroup(rotateX);

        //add some spinning behavior too
        TransformGroup tGroupSpin = new TransformGroup();
        tGroupSpin.setCapability(TransformGroup.ALLOW_TRANSFORM_WRITE);

        root.addChild(tGroupRotate);
        tGroupRotate.addChild(tGroupSpin);

        // add a simple cube
        tGroupSpin.addChild(new ColorCube(0.3));

        //add the spin rate
        Transform3D  t3D = new Transform3D();
        Alpha rotateAlpha = new Alpha(-1,8000);

        RotationInterpolator rInterpolator =
              new RotationInterpolator(rotateAlpha, tGroupSpin,
                             t3D, 0.0f, (float)Math.PI*2.0f);

        //add the bounds for this behavior
        BoundingSphere bSphere = new BoundingSphere();
        rInterpolator.setSchedulingBounds(bSphere);
        tGroupSpin.addChild(rInterpolator);

        return root;
    }//createSceneGraph()
```

To get the cube to spin, we need to create another `TransformGroup` node:

```
        //add some spinning behavior too
        TransformGroup tGroupSpin = new TransformGroup();
```

For performance reasons, Java 3D requires that we provide advance notification that we intend to allow the program to change the values in this transform group while the program is running:

```
        tGroupSpin.setCapability(TransformGroup.ALLOW_TRANSFORM_WRITE);
```

Next, we add the rotation transform group to the root just as we did before, but then we add the spin transform group to the rotation group, not to the root. This is because we are doing all the transforms as a unit.

```
        root.addChild(tGroupRotate);
        tGroupRotate.addChild(tGroupSpin);
```

Next, we add the object that we want to reorient and spin to the rotation group:

```
// add a simple cube
tGroupSpin.addChild(new ColorCube(0.3));
```

To this point, we have said that we want the cube to spin, but we haven't specified how fast. To do this, we add a `Transform3D` object and an `Alpha` object:

```
//add the spin rate
Transform3D  t3D = new Transform3D();
Alpha rotateAlpha = new Alpha(-1,8000);
```

Interpolator behavior requires that a value between 0 and 1 be provided to mark the passage of time. The `Alpha` class maps time to these values, providing a timer effect:

```
RotationInterpolator rInterpolator =
        new RotationInterpolator(rotateAlpha, tGroupSpin,
                    t3D, 0.0f, (float)Math.PI*2.0f);
```

The bounding sphere tells the system when this behavior is to be active. This is a performance consideration, as it would be wasteful to spend precious CPU cycles animating something that is not visible in from your `ViewPlatform`.

```
//add the bounds for this behavior
BoundingSphere bSphere = new BoundingSphere();
rInterpolator.setSchedulingBounds(bSphere);
tGroupSpin.addChild(rInterpolator);
```

Running this program produces a result that looks like Figure 16.2 except that it is rotating slowly.

Adding Lighting to Your Java 3D Program

We can further improve our model by adding lighting. By default, the objects in our scene graph are illuminated by a light of infinite size. This produces evenly lit objects. While this might be desirable for certain models such as molecules, it certainly doesn't resemble the real world very closely.

In the real world, lights have locations. The sun is located at a point in the sky. Artificial lights have a position in a room. The appearance of an object is determined by three things: the location of the light in relation to the object, the location of the view point in relation to the object, and the material that the object is made of.

The Java 3D model uses the concept of modeled light. It doesn't attempt to capture all the light in a scene. In the real world, if two objects are located close to each other, any light hitting one may produce a shadow on the other. In addition, light reflected from one object will hit the other and will be reflected back on the original object. Obviously, we could compute endlessly to render one scene if we tried to realistically reproduce the behavior of light.

In Java 3D, you can only see the *effect* of a light source on objects around it. If you go looking for the light source itself, you will never find it. If you move it, though, you will see the changing effects on the objects in your scene graph. Listing 16.3 shows the effects of lighting on the cube that we created earlier in this chapter.

LISTING 16.3   The `Mimimal3D_2` Lighted Scene Graph

```java
public BranchGroup createSceneGraph()
{
    BranchGroup root = new BranchGroup();

    //do a static rotation so that we can see it better
    Transform3D rotateX = new Transform3D();
    rotateX.rotX(Math.PI/10.0d);
    Transform3D rotateY = new Transform3D();
    rotateY.rotY(Math.PI/1.0d);
    rotateX.mul(rotateY);

    TransformGroup tGroupRotate = new TransformGroup(rotateX);

    //add some spinning behavior too
    TransformGroup tGroupSpin = new TransformGroup();
    tGroupSpin.setCapability(TransformGroup.ALLOW_TRANSFORM_WRITE);

    root.addChild(tGroupRotate);
    tGroupRotate.addChild(tGroupSpin);

    //Add the light
    addLighting(root);

    //add the material
    Appearance mat = new Appearance();
    Color3f darkRed = new Color3f(0.9f ,0.2f, 0.1f);
    Color3f black = new Color3f(0.0f ,0.0f, 0.0f);
    mat.setMaterial(
            new Material(darkRed, black, darkRed, black, 1.0f));

    // add a simple cube
    tGroupSpin.addChild(new Box(0.3f,0.3f,0.3f, mat));

    //add the spin rate
    Transform3D  t3D = new Transform3D();
    Alpha rotateAlpha = new Alpha(-1,8000);
```

LISTING 16.3   continued

```
        RotationInterpolator rInterpolator =
              new RotationInterpolator(rotateAlpha, tGroupSpin,
                           t3D, 0.0f, (float)Math.PI*2.0f);

        //add the bounds for this behavior
        BoundingSphere bSphere = new BoundingSphere();
        rInterpolator.setSchedulingBounds(bSphere);
        tGroupSpin.addChild(rInterpolator);

        return root;
    }//createSceneGraph()

    private void addLighting(BranchGroup root)
    {
        BoundingSphere bSphere = new BoundingSphere(
            new Point3d(0.0,0.0,0.0), 100.0);
        Color3f directLightColor =
                    new Color3f(1.0f, 1.0f, 1.0f);

        Vector3f lightDirection = new Vector3f(1.0f, 0.0f, 0.0f);
        DirectionalLight dirLight =
                new DirectionalLight(directLightColor, lightDirection);
        dirLight.setInfluencingBounds(bSphere);
        root.addChild(dirLight);
    }
```

This example is very similar to the previous one, so we will only show the routines that have changed.

> **Note**
>
> The source code files that are available at www.samspublishing.com contain the examples in their entirety.

The first thing that we do in the scene graph is add some lighting:

```
        //Add the light
        addLighting(root);
```

To keep things simple, we do this in another method called addLighting(). Lights have bounding spheres just like transformations do.

```
        BoundingSphere bSphere = new BoundingSphere(
            new Point3d(0.0,0.0,0.0), 100.0);
```

Lights also have color. We define a color for our light:

```
Color3f directLightColor =
                new Color3f(1.0f, 1.0f, 1.0f);
```

Because we want to create a directional light, we need to create a direction vector. We want it to point from left to right and from above. This means that we need x to be 1 and y to be –1:

```
Vector3f lightDirection = new Vector3f(1.0f, -1.0f, 0.0f);
```

Now we can create the star of our show, the directional light:

```
DirectionalLight dirLight =
        new DirectionalLight(directLightColor, lightDirection);
dirLight.setInfluencingBounds(bSphere);
root.addChild(dirLight);
```

Because we want the light to be fixed, we simply attach it to the root of our tree.

Next, we'll add material. (The material determines the reflectivity of an object, giving it a glossy or brushed look.) To do this, we define an `Appearance` object:

```
//add the material
Appearance mat = new Appearance();
Color3f darkRed = new Color3f(0.9f ,0.2f, 0.1f);
Color3f black = new Color3f(0.0f ,0.0f, 0.0f);
```

The `setMaterial()` method takes five parameters: `ambientColor`, `emissiveColor`, `diffuseColor`, `specularColor`, and `shininess`. The shininess can be set from dull (`1.0f`) to very shiny (`128`). In this example, we want it to be dull:

```
mat.setMaterial(
        new Material(darkRed, black, darkRed, black, 1.0f));
```

We need to change our `Cube` class to a `Box` class. A `Box` object looks a lot like a `Cube` object but it also has an appearance:

```
// add a simple cube
tGroupSpin.addChild(new Box(0.3f,0.3f,0.3f, mat));
```

Figure 16.3 shows the result of running Listing 16.3.

If you were trying to simulate outer space, you would be pleased with the result. If you are trying to model something on earth, however, you need to add some ambient light to provide a more natural look. On earth, lights are normally directional. The sun is directional, but reflections from clouds and other objects on the ground produce some ambient light. In our homes, we normally place globes or shades on the lights so that we don't get a 1930s-detective-movie look dominated by shadows. Listing 16.4 shows a revised `addLighting()` method that adds ambient light to the scene graph.

FIGURE 16.3

Lighting adds to the realism of a scene.

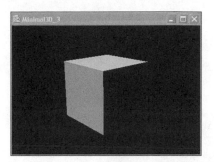

16

JAVA 3D GRAPHICS

LISTING 16.4   Minimal3D_3.java: Adding Ambient Light

```
private void addLighting(BranchGroup root)
{
    BoundingSphere bSphere = new BoundingSphere(
        new Point3d(0.0,0.0,0.0), 100.0);
    Color3f directLightColor =
                new Color3f(1.0f, 1.0f, 1.0f);

    Vector3f lightDirection = new Vector3f(1.0f, -1.0f, 0.0f);
    DirectionalLight dirLight =
                new DirectionalLight(directLightColor, lightDirection);
    dirLight.setInfluencingBounds(bSphere);
    root.addChild(dirLight);

    Color3f ambientLightColor =
                new Color3f(0.5f, 0.5f, 0.5f);

    AmbientLight ambLight = new AmbientLight(ambientLightColor);
    ambLight.setInfluencingBounds(bSphere);
    root.addChild(ambLight);
}
```

The addition of ambient light is actually simpler than the addition of directional light because there is no direction to specify, only color. The color of this light is gray, which creates the effect of low-intensity white light:

```
Color3f ambientLightColor =
                new Color3f(0.5f, 0.5f, 0.5f);

AmbientLight ambLight = new AmbientLight(ambientLightColor);
```

We use the same bounding sphere for the ambient light that we used for the directional light:

```
ambLight.setInfluencingBounds(bSphere);
```

We also attach this light to the root just as we did before:

```
root.addChild(ambLight);
```

The result is more pleasing to the eye than the box lit by the directional light alone. Figure 16.4 shows this result.

FIGURE 16.4

The ambient lighting example.

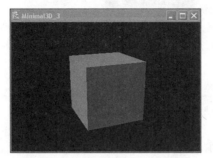

Notice that, unlike the `Minimal3D.java` color cube examples, which used primary colors to differentiate the faces of the cube, this example uses varying light intensity.

The lights don't have to be attached to the root node. They can be attached to a `TransformGroup` just as easily, as shown in Listing 16.5.

LISTING 16.5 The `Minimal3D_4.java` class's `createSceneGraph()` Method

```
public BranchGroup createSceneGraph()
{
    BranchGroup root = new BranchGroup();

    //do a static rotation so that we can see it better
    Transform3D rotateX = new Transform3D();
    rotateX.rotX(Math.PI/10.0d);
    Transform3D rotateY = new Transform3D();
    rotateY.rotY(Math.PI/1.0d);
    rotateX.mul(rotateY);

    TransformGroup tGroupRotate = new TransformGroup(rotateX);

    //add some spinning behavior too
    TransformGroup tGroupSpin = new TransformGroup();
    tGroupSpin.setCapability(TransformGroup.ALLOW_TRANSFORM_WRITE);

    root.addChild(tGroupRotate);
    tGroupRotate.addChild(tGroupSpin);

    //add the material
    Appearance mat = new Appearance();
```

LISTING 16.5   continued

```java
        Color3f darkRed = new Color3f(0.9f ,0.2f, 0.1f);
        Color3f black = new Color3f(0.0f ,0.0f, 0.0f);
        mat.setMaterial(
                new Material(darkRed, black, darkRed, black, 1.0f));

        // add a simple cube
        tGroupSpin.addChild(new Box(0.3f,0.3f,0.3f, mat));

        //Add the light
        addLighting(tGroupSpin);

        //add the spin rate
        Transform3D   t3D = new Transform3D();
        Alpha rotateAlpha = new Alpha(-1,8000);

        RotationInterpolator rInterpolator =
            new RotationInterpolator(rotateAlpha, tGroupSpin,
                            t3D, 0.0f, (float)Math.PI*2.0f);

        //add the bounds for this behavior
        BoundingSphere bSphere = new BoundingSphere();
        rInterpolator.setSchedulingBounds(bSphere);
        tGroupSpin.addChild(rInterpolator);

        return root;
    }//createSceneGraph()

    private void addLighting(TransformGroup root)
    {
        BoundingSphere bSphere = new BoundingSphere(
            new Point3d(0.0,0.0,0.0), 100.0);
        Color3f directLightColor =
                    new Color3f(1.0f, 1.0f, 1.0f);

        Vector3f lightDirection = new Vector3f(1.0f, -1.0f, 0.0f);
        DirectionalLight dirLight =
                new DirectionalLight(directLightColor, lightDirection);
        dirLight.setInfluencingBounds(bSphere);
        root.addChild(dirLight);

        Color3f ambientLightColor =
                    new Color3f(0.5f, 0.5f, 0.5f);

        AmbientLight ambLight = new AmbientLight(ambientLightColor);
        ambLight.setInfluencingBounds(bSphere);
        root.addChild(ambLight);
    }
```

All that we have to do is add the light to the spin group instead of the root:

```
//Add the light
addLighting(tGroupSpin);
```

Because of type checking, we must also alter the parameter type on the call:

```
private void addLighting(TransformGroup root)
```

Figure 16.5 shows the result. The directional light now follows the rotation of the object instead of being fixed in one place. The ambient light, however, is not affected.

FIGURE 16.5

The rotating light example.

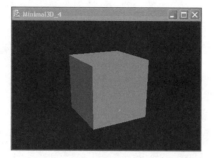

Texture Mapping in Java 3D

When you see 3D games such as *Doom* or *Wolfenstein*, you see a lot of complex-looking walls, floors, and ceilings. Bricks, stone floors, and textured ceilings create the atmosphere that makes the experience fun. If we tried to model real-world objects such as the grass on a lawn in Java 3D, we would have billions of polygons per square yard of turf, which is not practical. But in order to produce realistic-looking universes for our users, we have to find some way to represent these ultra-complex objects.

The workaround that is commonly used in 3D programming is called *texture mapping*. This technique involves taking an image of a texture (or anything else, for that matter) and "laying" it on an object, programmatically. When the viewpoint changes, the texture changes its appearance to match what you would see if you changed your viewpoint in relation to an image in the real world.

Adding texture mapping to your Java 3D programming is not terribly difficult, but there are some strict rules. Java 3D expects your image to be of a size that is a power of 2 pixels in each direction. Common sizes are 128×128 pixels and 256×256 pixels. In Listing 16.6, we will map an image to a plane. This image is a `.gif` file that is 128×128 pixels in size.

LISTING 16.6   The `TextureApp` Class

```java
/*
 * TextureApp.java
 *
 * Created on May 8, 2002, 9:54 AM
 */

package unleashed.ch16;

import java.awt.BorderLayout;
import java.awt.GraphicsConfiguration;
import com.sun.j3d.utils.geometry.*;
import com.sun.j3d.utils.universe.*;
import com.sun.j3d.utils.image.TextureLoader;
import javax.media.j3d.*;
import javax.vecmath.*;
import java.awt.*;
import java.awt.event.*;

/**
 * TextureApp demonstrates texture mapping.
 */
public class TextureApp extends Frame
{

    BranchGroup createSceneGraph()
    {
        BranchGroup objRoot = new BranchGroup();

        Transform3D transform = new Transform3D();

        QuadArray plane = new QuadArray(4, GeometryArray.COORDINATES
        | GeometryArray.TEXTURE_COORDINATE_2);

        Point3f p = new Point3f(-1.0f,  1.0f,  0.0f);
        plane.setCoordinate(0, p);
        p.set(-1.0f, -1.0f,  0.0f);
        plane.setCoordinate(1, p);
        p.set(1.0f, -1.0f,  0.0f);
        plane.setCoordinate(2, p);
        p.set(1.0f,  1.0f,  0.0f);
        plane.setCoordinate(3, p);

        Point2f q = new Point2f( 0.0f,  1.0f);
        plane.setTextureCoordinate(0, q);
        q.set(0.0f, 0.0f);
        plane.setTextureCoordinate(1, q);
        q.set(1.0f, 0.0f);
        plane.setTextureCoordinate(2, q);
        q.set(1.0f, 1.0f);
        plane.setTextureCoordinate(3, q);
```

LISTING 16.6 continued

```
Appearance appear = new Appearance();

String filename = "c:/unleashed/ch16/yasa.gif";
TextureLoader loader = new TextureLoader(filename, this);
ImageComponent2D image = loader.getImage();

if(image == null)
{
    System.out.println("load failed: "+filename);
}

Texture2D texture = new Texture2D(Texture.BASE_LEVEL, Texture.RGBA,
image.getWidth(), image.getHeight());
texture.setImage(0, image);

appear.setTexture(texture);

appear.setTransparencyAttributes(
new TransparencyAttributes(TransparencyAttributes.FASTEST, 0.1f));

Shape3D planeObj = new Shape3D(plane, appear);

// rotate  the object
Transform3D rotate = new Transform3D();
Transform3D tempRotate = new Transform3D();

rotate.rotX(Math.PI/4.0d);
tempRotate.rotY(Math.PI/5.0d);
rotate.mul(tempRotate);

TransformGroup objRotate = new TransformGroup(rotate);

TransformGroup objSpin = new TransformGroup();
objSpin.setCapability(TransformGroup.ALLOW_TRANSFORM_WRITE);

objRoot.addChild(objRotate);
objRotate.addChild(objSpin);

objSpin.addChild(planeObj);

Transform3D yAxis = new Transform3D();
Alpha rotationAlpha = new Alpha(-1, 6000);

RotationInterpolator rotator =
new RotationInterpolator(rotationAlpha, objSpin, yAxis,
0.0f, (float) Math.PI*2.0f);
```

LISTING 16.6   continued

```java
        BoundingSphere bounds = new BoundingSphere();
        rotator.setSchedulingBounds(bounds);
        objSpin.addChild(rotator);
        Background background = new Background();
        background.setColor(1.0f, 1.0f, 1.0f);
        background.setApplicationBounds(new BoundingSphere());
        objRoot.addChild(background);

        return objRoot;
    }

    public TextureApp()
    {
        super("TextureApp");
        setSize(600, 400);
        setLayout(new BorderLayout());
        GraphicsConfiguration config =
        SimpleUniverse.getPreferredConfiguration();

        Canvas3D canvas3D = new Canvas3D(config);
        add("Center", canvas3D);
        setVisible(true);

        canvas3D.setStereoEnable(false);

        SimpleUniverse u = new SimpleUniverse(canvas3D);

        u.getViewingPlatform().setNominalViewingTransform();

        u.addBranchGraph(createSceneGraph());
    }

    public static void main(String[] args)
    {
        final TextureApp ta = new TextureApp();
        ta.addWindowListener(new WindowAdapter()
        {
            public void windowClosing(WindowEvent e)
            {
                ta.dispose();
                System.exit(0);
            }
        });
    }
}
```

After we create a plane, we create four points and set them as the texture coordinates that we will use. (By changing the values, we can affix the texture upside down or sideways if we choose to.)

```
Point2f q = new Point2f( 0.0f,  1.0f);
plane.setTextureCoordinate(0, q);
q.set(0.0f, 0.0f);
plane.setTextureCoordinate(1, q);
q.set(1.0f, 0.0f);
plane.setTextureCoordinate(2, q);
q.set(1.0f, 1.0f);
plane.setTextureCoordinate(3, q);
```

Next, we create an object of type `javax.media.j3d.Appearance`. This object specifies the rendering options for the plane object that will hold the texture:

```
Appearance appear = new Appearance();
```

The file is loaded into a `com.sun.j3d.utils.image.TextureLoader` object. This object is used to prepare the image for the `Appearance` object:

```
String filename = "c:/unleashed/ch16/yasa.gif";
TextureLoader loader = new TextureLoader(filename, this);
ImageComponent2D image = loader.getImage();
```

The `javax.media.j3d.Texture2D` class defines the properties of the texture for the `Appearance` object:

```
Texture2D texture = new Texture2D(Texture.BASE_LEVEL, Texture.RGBA,
image.getWidth(), image.getHeight());
texture.setImage(0, image);
```

We set the texture in the `Appearance` object:

```
appear.setTexture(texture);
```

Next, we set the transparency attributes for the `Appearance` object. The FASTEST attribute means that we are instructing our program to use the fastest method of rendering transparency:

```
appear.setTransparencyAttributes(
new TransparencyAttributes(TransparencyAttributes.FASTEST, 0.1f));
```

Finally, we create a new `Shape3D` that combines the plane coordinates that we defined with the attributes that we set in the `Appearance` object:

```
Shape3D planeObj = new Shape3D(plane, appear);
```

The result of running this code is a rotating plane. When the plane is facing your `ViewPlatform`, you see an image of a little girl. Because the image is affixed to the front of the plane, the back of the plane is blank. Figure 16.6 shows the program running.

FIGURE 16.6

The rotating plane has a texture map affixed.

By filling your universe with texture-mapped objects, you can create an immersion experience that is superior to that provided by geometry and colors alone.

Summary

In this chapter, we examined the manipulation of 3D graphics using Java. You learned about the Java 3D API and the advantages and disadvantages of using it.

We next looked at the programming steps necessary for rendering objects on the screen. Following that, we added a rotation action to the object to demonstrate animation.

We then looked at how lighting affects the 3D experience from the user's point of view. You learned how to place both directional and ambient light in a scene. You also learned how to make the light move during the execution of the scene.

Finally, we learned how to map a texture to an object and then view the object in the Java 3D universe.

The Java Media Framework (JMF) and the Java Advanced Imaging (JAI) API

It seems that the computer has modified every device that we deal with. Our televisions, airplanes, automobiles, and watches all contain computers. Perhaps the most fun place that computers are showing up is in our cameras. Those of you who have ever practiced the black art of home-based darkroom photograph processing will remember smelly chemicals, amber lights, densitometers, lightproof bags, and two-foot-long thermometers.

The old darkrooms have been replaced by modern digital darkrooms with names like Photoshop and Paint Shop Pro. We now sit in daylight and adjust the color balance, reduce the contrast, and dodge the shadows to produce the masterpieces of the new millennium. The new technologies allow us to have all of the fun of the old days at a fraction of the cost and time commitment.

Home movies have moved into the computer also. The old Super-8 cameras were replaced by the video camcorder. Now the camcorder is in the process of being replaced by the digital video recorder. This marvelous device produces recordings of fairly high quality, but more importantly, recordings that can be easily loaded into the computer. This allows us to manipulate them using techniques that only professionals used in years past.

Imagine the possibilities if you could play video in your Java programs. What kind of program would you write if you knew how to incorporate image-editing features into your applications?

The subject of this chapter is the manipulation of media, both still and time-based, from within Java programs. The first subject that we cover is the Java Media Framework (JMF). This framework enables you to process motion video from within Java. Following that, you will learn about the Java Advanced Imaging (JAI) API. This API enables you to manipulate images to improve their appearance or to create special effects. Hopefully, you will get as much from reading it as we did from writing it.

Understanding Time-Based Media

Time-based media is data that changes as it is played or displayed. The most common forms of time-based media are sound, motion pictures, and animation. The playing of sounds from within Java programs is covered in depth in Chapter 18, "Processing Sound with Java." This chapter will concentrate mainly on the visual aspects of time-based media.

It is difficult to discuss any topic without understanding its vocabulary. Time-based media is no exception to this rule. Once you understand the concepts that govern this topic, you will be able to understand the software that is used to control its display.

The process starts with some type of capture device. A *capture device* takes its input from the real world and produces a stream of data representing what it has "seen." This data is normally stored in a file on a tape.

A file containing data that has been captured is called a *data source*. Some data sources are captured in a digital format that is ready for display. Other data sources are captured in an analog format that requires conversion to a digital format before it can be played.

The process of converting the video from an analog format to a digital format is called *encoding*. The device or program used to perform this task is called an *encoder*. The output of the conversion process is the creation of a file in a digital format.

Media data is stored in a file format called the *content-type*. Common content-types for video are QuickTime, MPEG-1, MPEG-2, and AVI. Figure 17.1 shows the process of capturing and encoding a video stream.

FIGURE 17.1
The process of capturing video and converting it to a digital format.

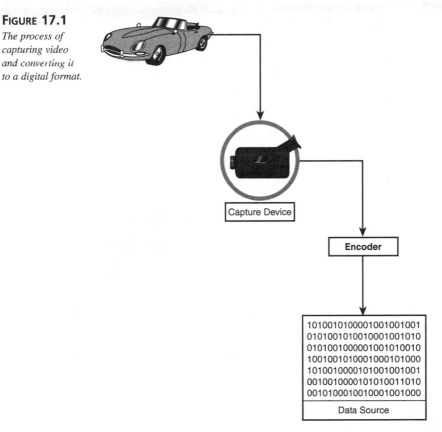

Capture Device

Encoder

1010010100001001001001
0101001010010001001010
0101001000001001010010
1001001010001000101000
1010010000101001001001
0010010000101010011010
0010100010010001001000

Data Source

The process of converting a data source into a video on a screen is referred to as *playing*, or, technically speaking, *decoding*. The hardware or software that performs this function is called a *decoder*.

A hardware decoder is normally a circuit board or peripheral device that performs the translation of the data into the series of pictures and sounds that will appear on the monitor and in the speakers. Software decoders perform the same function using the computer's CPU to do the actual transformation. In the past, software decoders were used for smaller formats such as QuickTime and MPEG-1, while hardware decoders were employed for larger formats such as MPEG-2. As the CPUs in computers have become more powerful, the need for this type of dedicated hardware has decreased. Figure 17.2 represents the decoding process.

FIGURE 17.2

The process of converting a data source into output.

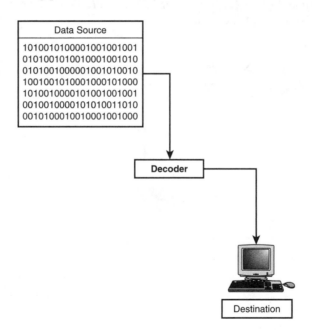

Output devices such as speakers and monitors are often called *destinations*. Occasionally you will see them referred to as *data sinks*. They serve as the primary interface to the user.

Decoding Time-Based Media with JMF

Now that we have a common vocabulary, let's look at some code. As in earlier chapters, the first example that we will work through is very simple. The name of this program is MinimalVideoPlayer and its source code is shown in Listing 17.1.

LISTING 17.1 The `MinimalVideoPlayer` Class

```java
/*
 * MinimalVideoPlayer.java
 *
 * Created on February 12, 2002, 10:49 AM
 */

package unleashed.ch17;

import javax.media.*;
import javax.media.format.*;
import javax.media.protocol.*;

import java.awt.*;
import java.awt.event.*;

/**
 *
 * @author  Stephen Potts
 * @version
 */
public class MinimalVideoPlayer extends Frame
                implements ControllerListener, ActionListener
{
    Player videoPlayer;

    String filename;


    /** Creates new MinimalVideoPlayer */
    public MinimalVideoPlayer(String s1)
    {
        super(s1);

        //handle window event handler
        addWindowListener(new WindowAdapter()
        {
            public void windowClosing(WindowEvent we)
            {
```

LISTING 17.1   continued

```
                    dispose();
                    System.exit(0);
            }
        });

        //create the menu
        MenuBar mb = new MenuBar();
        setMenuBar(mb);
        Menu fileMenu = new Menu("File");
        mb.add(fileMenu);

        MenuItem itemPlay = new MenuItem("Play");
        itemPlay.addActionListener(this);
        fileMenu.add(itemPlay);
    }

    //add the event handler
    public void actionPerformed(ActionEvent ae)
    {
        String action = ae.getActionCommand().toString();
        if (action.equals("Play"))
        {
            play();
        }
    }

    //play the video
    void play()
    {
        try
        {
            //ask the user for a filename
            FileDialog fd =
                new FileDialog(this, "Choose Video", FileDialog.LOAD);
            fd.show();

            //assemble the filename
            filename = fd.getDirectory() + fd.getFile();

            //create the player
            videoPlayer = Manager.createPlayer(
                new MediaLocator("file:///" + filename));

            //add a listener for player state changes
            System.out.println("Adding controller listener");
            videoPlayer.addControllerListener(this);

            videoPlayer.start();
        }catch (Exception e)
```

LISTING 17.1   continued

```
        {
            System.out.println("Error " + e);
        }
    }//play

    public synchronized void controllerUpdate(
                            ControllerEvent event)
    {
        System.out.println("Event: " + event);

        if (event instanceof RealizeCompleteEvent)
        {
            Component comp;

            if ((comp = videoPlayer.getVisualComponent()) != null)
            {
                add("Center", comp);
            }else
                System.out.println("Unable to get visual component");
            validate();
        }
    }

    public static void main(String[] args)
    {
        MinimalVideoPlayer mvp =
                new MinimalVideoPlayer("MinimalVideoPlayer");

        //show the frame containing the video
        mvp.show();
        //size the window
        mvp.setSize(300,300);
        mvp.setLocation(250,300);
    }
}
```

17

THE JMF AND
THE JAI API

Note

The setSize() and setLocation() values are not critical. You may alter them freely.

The class that we created is a pretty typical AWT application extending Frame and implementing ActionListener. One unique feature is that it implements the javax.media.ControllerListener interface. This interface handles asynchronous events generated by a class that implements the javax.media.Controller interface. In this case, videoPlayer will be the controller.

```
public class MinimalVideoPlayer extends Frame
              implements ControllerListener, ActionListener
```

We need a reference to the interface javax.media.Player before we can create it:

```
Player videoPlayer;
```

Here is where all the magic takes place. Notice that we never stated the content-type of the media that we want to play. The Manager class and the MediaLocator class combine to figure out the correct content-type and create a Player that can decode it.

The actual creation of a video player is done by a static method in the javax.media.Manager class called createPlayer(). The Manager class is responsible for creating the correct player for the media that is passed to it. It uses the javax.media.MediaLocator class, which is similar to a URL, as its input. The MediaLocator class and the Manager class keep trying the different players that are installed on the system. Once they find a Player that doesn't throw an error during initialization, they pass a reference to it back where it is stored in the videoPlayer handle. Notice that the videoPlayer handle is of type Player, which is an interface. Thus, any class that implements the Player interface can be returned to this handle.

```
videoPlayer = Manager.createPlayer(
    new MediaLocator("file:///" + filename));
```

Armed with a valid player for this content-type, the Player adds a special listener called the ControllerListener:

```
videoPlayer.addControllerListener(this);
```

A ControllerListener will receive the events generated by the Player. Next, we tell the Player to start. Before the player can actually place an image in the Frame, there are a number of states that it must pass through.

```
videoPlayer.start();
```

The following output (reformatted to fit this page) occurs while videoPlayer is passing through the required states:

```
Adding controller listener

Event: javax.media.TransitionEvent[source=
com.sun.media.content.unknown.Handler@5f8b99,
previous=Unrealized,current=Realizing,target=Started]

Event: javax.media.DurationUpdateEvent[source=
com.sun.media.content.unknown.Handler@5f8b99,
duration=javax.media.Time@5d88a
```

```
Event: javax.media.RealizeCompleteEvent[source=
com.sun.media.content.unknown.Handler@5f8b99,
previous=Realizing,current=Realized,target=Started]

Event: javax.media.TransitionEvent[source=
com.sun.media.content.unknown.Handler@5f8b99,
previous=Realized,current=Prefetching,target=Started]

Event: javax.media.PrefetchCompleteEvent[source=
com.sun.media.content.unknown.Handler@5f8b99,
previous=Prefetching,current=Prefetched,target=Started]

Event: javax.media.StartEvent[source=
com.sun.media.content.unknown.Handler@5f8b99,
previous=Prefetched,current=Started,target=Started,
mediaTime=javax.media.Time@7b56b1,
timeBaseTime=javax.media.Time@78968f]

Event: javax.media.EndOfMediaEvent[source=
com.sun.media.content.unknown.Handler@5f8b99,
previous=Started,current=Prefetched,target=Prefetched,
mediaTime=javax.media.Time@41b571]
```

As this output shows, the `Player` must move through the following states prior to being capable of playing a video:

- `Unrealized`—The `Player` object exists but it doesn't understand the task to be performed.

- `Realizing`—The `Player` is in the process of discovering the task to be performed and the proper `Player` to use.

- `Realized`—The `Player` is now ready.

- `Prefetching`—The `Player` is loading media data into its buffers. It needs to have a certain amount of data loaded to avoid running out. Running out causes stuttering in the playback, which is not a good thing.

- `Prefetched`—Enough data now exists in the buffers to ensure that the `Player` won't likely run out.

- `Started`—The `Player` is now displaying video and audio.

There are seven events that will occur during the life of this `Player`:

- `TransitionEvent` (`Unrealized` to `Realizing`)—The `Player` object has been created, but it is not yet ready to do any work in an `Unrealized` state. During this transition event, the `Player` moves to the `Realizing` state.

- `DurationUpdateEvent`—Now that a form of media that has duration is present, the `Player`'s duration is updated.

- RealizeCompleteEvent (Realizing to Realized)—The Player now knows what resources it needs, and what type of media it needs to decode. It can draw controls and connect to other objects in the JVM.

- TransitionEvent (Realized to Prefetching)—The Player is now loading its data into buffers and obtaining rights to exclusive-use resources.

- PrefetchCompleteEvent (Prefetching to Prefetched)—The preparations are now completed and the media is ready to be started.

- StartEvent (Prefetched to Started)—The Player is now decoding the data and displaying it in the Frame.

- EndOfMediaEvent (Started to Prefetched)—The Player has finished decoding and playing the media. It now changes its state back to Prefetched and waits for further instruction from the program.

The controllerUpdate() method is called every time the player generates an event:

```
public synchronized void controllerUpdate(
                           ControllerEvent event)
    {
        System.out.println("Event: " + event);

        if (event instanceof RealizeCompleteEvent)
```

The most interesting of the events listed here is the RealizeCompleteEvent. When this event occurs, the Player is ready to be added to the Frame. The getVisualComponent() call provides a handle to the output. This handle is placed in the Frame at the center:

```
        if ((comp = videoPlayer.getVisualComponent()) != null)
        {
            add("Center", comp);
        }
```

Validate() causes a container to lay out its components again after new ones have been added or modified.

```
        validate();
```

The main() method for this program is very simple. We create an object of type MinimalVideoPlayer, which is a Frame. We then set the size and location of the Frame, and display it on the monitor that serves as our destination.

```
        MinimalVideoPlayer mvp = new MinimalVideoPlayer("MinimalVideoPlayer");
        mvp.show();
        mvp.setSize(300,300);
        mvp.setLocation(250,300);
```

You might be surprised to see how little code is needed to play a video clip. There is a fair amount of complexity to the process, however. Figure 17.3 shows the MinimalVideoPlayer playing the file called `airboat.avi` (included with the code for this chapter).

FIGURE 17.3

The MinimalVideoPlayer produces a nice result, even if it doesn't have many controls.

Now that we have created a minimal player and learned how it works, let's create one that is worth placing in your code.

Adding the Control Panel

To do this, we need to add some controls to our example. The code that does this is shown in Listing 17.2.

LISTING 17.2   The `VideoPlayer1` Class

```
*
 * VideoPlayer1.java
 *
 * Created on February 12, 2002, 10:49 AM
 */

package unleashed.ch17;

import javax.media.*;
import javax.media.format.*;
import javax.media.protocol.*;

import java.awt.*;
import java.awt.event.*;

/**
 *
```

LISTING 17.2   continued

```java
 * @author   Stephen Potts
 * @version
 */
public class VideoPlayer1 extends Frame
implements ControllerListener, ActionListener
{
    Player videoPlayer;

    String filename;


    /** Creates new VideoPlayer1 */
    public VideoPlayer1(String s1)
    {
        super(s1);

        //handle window event handler
        addWindowListener(new WindowAdapter()
        {
            public void windowClosing(WindowEvent we)
            {
                dispose();
                System.exit(0);
            }
        });

        //create the menu
        MenuBar mb = new MenuBar();
        setMenuBar(mb);
        Menu fileMenu = new Menu("File");
        mb.add(fileMenu);

        MenuItem itemPlay = new MenuItem("Play");
        itemPlay.addActionListener(this);
        fileMenu.add(itemPlay);

        MenuItem itemStop = new MenuItem("Stop");
        itemStop.addActionListener(this);
        fileMenu.add(itemStop);

        MenuItem itemExit = new MenuItem("Exit");
        itemExit.addActionListener(this);
        fileMenu.add(itemExit);
    }

    //add the event handler
    public void actionPerformed(ActionEvent ae)
    {
        String action = ae.getActionCommand().toString();
```

LISTING 17.2 continued

```java
        if (action.equals("Play"))
        {
            play();
        }
        if (action.equals("Stop"))
        {
            stop();
        }
        if (action.equals("Exit"))
        {
            dispose();
            System.exit(0);
        }
    }

    private void stop()
    {
        if (videoPlayer != null)
        {
            videoPlayer.stop();

        }
    }


    //play the video
    public void play()
    {
        try
        {
            //ask the user for a filename
            FileDialog fd =
            new FileDialog(this, "Choose Video", FileDialog.LOAD);
            fd.show();

            //assemble the filename
            filename = fd.getDirectory() + fd.getFile();

            //create the player
            videoPlayer = Manager.createPlayer(
            new MediaLocator("file:///" + filename));

            //add a listener for player state changes
            videoPlayer.addControllerListener(this);

            videoPlayer.start();
        }catch (Exception e)
        {
            System.out.println("Error " + e);
```

LISTING 17.2   continued

```
    }
}//play

public synchronized void controllerUpdate(
ControllerEvent event)
{
    System.out.println("Event: " + event);

    if (event instanceof RealizeCompleteEvent)
    {
        Component comp;

        if ((comp = videoPlayer.getVisualComponent()) != null)
        {
            add("Center", comp);
        }else
            System.out.println("Unable to get visual component");

        if ((comp = videoPlayer.getControlPanelComponent()) != null)
        {
            add("South", comp);
        }

        validate();
    }
}

public static void main(String[] args)
{
    VideoPlayer1 vp1 = new VideoPlayer1("VideoPlayer1");

    //show the frame containing the video
    vp1.show();

    //size the window
    vp1.setSize(300,300);
    vp1.setLocation(250,300);
}
}
```

This example contains a set of controls at the bottom and a fuller menu at the top.
The addition of the controls at the bottom of the screen is accomplished very simply.
The `javax.media.Player` interface contains a method signature called
`getControlPanelComponent()`. This panel provides a prefabricated set of controls to
pause, step, resume, and mute the video clip being displayed:

```
        if ((comp = videoPlayer.getControlPanelComponent()) != null)
```

We also added a Stop button on the menu. This simply calls the stop() command in the Player. If we run the VideoPlayer1 program and choose File, Play from the menu, we will see the video player shown in Figure 17.4.

FIGURE 17.4

VideoPlayer1 is a player that has a full set of VCR-like controls to start, pause, step, and mute the video.

If you click on the filmstrip icon at the right end of the control panel, it will bring up a set of tabbed dialogs that provide quite a bit of information on the content-type being played. These dialogs are shown in Figure 17.5.

FIGURE 17.5

The Media Properties tabbed dialogs provide information about the characteristics of the video being played.

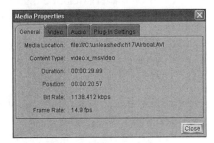

If you select the Plug-in Settings tab in this dialog, it will show a button labeled PlugIn Viewer. Clicking on this button will display a graphic that simulates the movement of data through the JMF components while the video clip is playing. This is shown in Figure 17.6.

FIGURE 17.6

The PlugIn Viewer shows a simulation of the data flowing from one component of JMF to the others.

You can provide all of these capabilities to your programs by adding a few lines of code. This is a good example of object-oriented programming—this code can be reused in any JMF player application.

Other Capabilities Within JMF

JMF provides two other capabilities that you might want to explore, depending on your requirements. These are capture (audio and video) and real-time multimedia processing. The capture classes provide ways to encode analog signals and create files on your machine. Real-time multimedia processing allows you to use JMF to display live media such as radio and television broadcasts.

Programming with the Advanced Imaging API

One of the best-kept secrets in the Java world is the Java Advanced Imaging (JAI) API. It is a huge Standard Extension to the Java platform that contains all kinds of image processing classes and methods. You can think of it as a software version of Adobe Photoshop Elements. Like the Adobe product, JAI gives you control over the brightness, contrast, size, orientation, and dozens of other characteristics of a digital image. The goal of granting you this control is to allow you to manipulate images programmatically.

When Java was first introduced in the mid-1990s, it had very little support for images. The Abstract Window Toolkit (AWT) was capable of displaying GIF and JPEG files using the `Toolkit` object, but no methods for modifying it existed.

The Java 2D API added a few image-processing methods for blurring, sharpening, and geometric transformation, but it too was very limited.

JAI provides a rich set of operators that can perform almost any image manipulation algorithm that you would normally find in products that are GUI-based. In addition, the API is highly extensible, so it can support new operations that you might add yourself in such a way that they feel like a natural part of the package.

It is not necessary to enter any special environment to use JAI. You can mix and match classes from this API with those found in other Java APIs with very few restrictions.

JAI can be used to create a GUI-based software product to compete with the familiar tools from Adobe and JASC. This is not really the intent of the API, however. You'll realize the real value of JAI when you need to integrate image processing in an application whose domain is something entirely different, such as aerial reconnaissance or crop forecasting.

There are several features of JAI that make it a valuable tool in your programming toolbox:

- Portability—Because it is a Java Standard Extension, JAI is portable. This means that an application that you create on a computer running Unix can be moved to a computer running Windows without code modification.

- Support for hardware acceleration—Many JAI implementations make use of underlying architectures such as MMX from Intel and VIS from Sun. This support is only for performance reasons, however. JAI will work on your machine even without these underlying hardware accelerations. If hardware acceleration doesn't load, a warning message may appear. The program will display properly, however.

- Object-orientation in that Java way—JAI feels as natural to Java programmers as every other Standard Extension does. This greatly increases its true availability to programmers and decreases the height of the learning curve.

- Extensibility—JAI can be extended to add processing that is not commonly needed. This allows you to add custom algorithms into a product.

- Distributability—Using functionality built on top of RMI, JAI is able to manipulate images on remote machines without moving them across the network.

- Device independence—JAI processes images using device-independent coordinates.

- Power—JAI supports large images of up to three dimensions.

JAI is based on the concept of image tiling. A tile is a rectangular section of an image. An image can be divided into rectangles of almost any size, though performance is adversely affected if the tile size is very small. The calculation of pixels takes place only when a tile is needed on the screen. Tiles are stored and processed separately, though the effect is not obvious to the user.

The tiling approach lends itself naturally to multithreaded processing. Because each tile can be processed without affecting any other tile, dividing the task among many CPUs can yield distinct performance improvements.

Armed with an understanding of what JAI is, you are now ready to see how it works. Listing 17.3 shows a sample program that we can use to discover the ruling principles of this Standard Extension.

LISTING 17.3 The JPEGResizer Class

```
/*
 * JPEGResizer.java
 *
 * Created on February 13, 2002, 1:35 PM
 */
```

17

THE JMF AND
THE JAI API

LISTING 17.3 continued

```java
package unleashed.ch17;

import java.awt.Frame;
import java.awt.event.*;
import java.awt.image.renderable.ParameterBlock;
import java.io.IOException;
import javax.media.jai.Interpolation;
import javax.media.jai.JAI;
import javax.media.jai.RenderedOp;
import com.sun.media.jai.codec.FileSeekableStream;
import javax.media.jai.widget.ScrollingImagePanel;

/**
 *
 * @author  Stephen Potts
 * @version
 */
public class JPEGResizer extends Frame
{

    /** Creates new JPEGResizer */
    public JPEGResizer()
    {
        //handle window events
        addWindowListener(new WindowAdapter()
        {
            public void windowClosing(WindowEvent we)
            {
                System.exit(0);
            }
        });

    }

    public static void main(String[] args)
    {
        JPEGResizer frame1 = new JPEGResizer();
        if (args.length != 1)
        {
            System.out.println(
            "Usage: a file parameter must be supplied");
            System.exit(-1);
        }

        FileSeekableStream fss = null;
```

LISTING 17.3   continued

```
try
{
    fss = new FileSeekableStream(args[0]);

    RenderedOp originalImage = JAI.create("stream", fss);

    Interpolation biLine = Interpolation.getInstance(
    Interpolation.INTERP_BILINEAR);

    ParameterBlock pb = new ParameterBlock();
    pb.addSource(originalImage);
    pb.add(1.5F);
    pb.add(1.5F);
    pb.add(115.0F);
    pb.add(40.0F);
    pb.add(biLine);

    RenderedOp outputImage = JAI.create("scale", pb);

    ScrollingImagePanel sip = new ScrollingImagePanel(
    outputImage, 400, 400);

    frame1.add(sip);
    frame1.pack();
    frame1.show();
}catch (IOException ioe)
{
    System.out.println("IOException " + ioe);
}
    }
}
```

Let's dissect this example and learn a little about how JAI works:

First, we declare an object `fss` of type `com.sun.media.jai.codec.`
`FileSeekableStream`. A *codec* is a class that translates content-types such as JPEG into images, and images into content-types. Notice that this class is not a `javax.media` class, but rather a `com.sun` class. This means that this package is unofficially released. By classifying this codec as unofficial, Sun encourages you to substitute codecs written by others for this one.

```
FileSeekableStream fss = null;
    fss = new FileSeekableStream(args[0]);
```

We use the `FileSeekableStream` object to create an image of type `RenderedOp`, which is a class that represents a two-dimensional image.

```
RenderedOp originalImage = JAI.create("stream", fss);
```

The `Interpolation` class specifies the algorithm that will be used to resample the image. In digital image processing, the image is represented by pixels. If we are making an image larger, as we are here, we are adding pixels where none existed. The process of deciding the color and intensity of a pixel is called *interpolation*. (In layman's terms, it is called an educated guess.) The process of adding all these pixels to an image, thereby forming a new image, is called *resampling*.

```
Interpolation biLine = Interpolation.getInstance(
Interpolation.INTERP_BILINEAR);
```

The `Interpolation` algorithm used here is called `BiLinear`. It uses four pixels in a 2×2-pixel area to determine what each of the new pixels should be.

> **Note**
>
> Shrinking an image (which requires discarding pixels) and then enlarging it (which requires interpolation to add pixels) produces an image that is not as sharp as the original.

The output image is created by a static method in the JAI class. The parameters for this operation are potentially so large that it is impractical to add them to a method signature. As an alternative, a special class called `ParameterBlock` has been provided. This class contains the kind of information normally passed in the method calls.

```
ParameterBlock pb = new ParameterBlock();
```

The first parameter is the source image, which is called `originalImage` in this program:

```
pb.addSource(originalImage);
```

These two parameters control the scaling factor of the new image as compared with the old one. The first `add()` affects the width and the second one affects the height. Here we are saying that the new image is to be 1.5 times as large as the old one:

```
pb.add(1.5F);
pb.add(1.5F);
```

The next two parameters tell the position difference between the original image and the new image in the panel. Here we are moving it over by 115 pixels and down by 40:

```
pb.add(115.0F);
pb.add(40.0F);
```

The `Interpolation` object is also passed in to specify which algorithm is to do the resampling.

```
pb.add(biLine);
```

A static method called `create()` populates the parameter vector and creates the new image:

```
RenderedOp outputImage = JAI.create("scale", pb);
```

Finally, the `outputImage` needs to be placed in a panel of some sort. The `ScrollingImagePanel` does this. The size of the panel will be 400×400 pixels:

```
ScrollingImagePanel sip = new ScrollingImagePanel(
    outputImage, 400, 400);
```

To run the program, you will need to pass in a file to process. A `.jpg` file called `snake.jpg` is included with the code for this chapter. From a command line, type the following:

```
java unleashed.ch17.JPEGResizer snake.jpg
```

The result of running this is shown in Figure 17.7.

FIGURE 17.7

This program resizes the picture to 1.5 times its original size and repositions it 115 pixels to the right and 40 pixels down.

If you open the original image using your favorite tool and compare the resolution, you will see that the enlarged image is not as sharp. This is because the extra pixels needed to make the image larger are interpolated from the surrounding pixels.

Summary

In this chapter you learned about two of the most interesting Standard Extensions, the Java Media Framework (JMF) and the Java Advanced Imaging (JAI) API.

You first learned about time-based media such as audio and video files. You learned how to create a program that uses the Java Media Framework to play video stored in a file. In addition, you learned how to make use of the controls that are built into JMF that allow you to start, pause, step, and mute the video clip being played. You also learned how to display additional information to the user about the format, encoding, and playback of the file.

You then learned about the Java Advanced Imaging API (JAI). While this chapter only scratched the surface of what can be done with this powerful set of packages, you did learn how to perform the most common tasks—resizing and moving images.

The number of image manipulation methods that are contained within JAI is staggering. A 500-page book could easily be written on this topic alone. Hopefully, the brief explanation provided here will give you a jump start on placing this kind of functionality in your own programs.

CHAPTER 18

Processing Sound with Java

In the early 1920s, filmmakers began experimenting with sound in motion pictures. Many of the leading studios considered sound a gimmick and refused to spend much money on what they thought would be a passing fad. Needless to say, those studios that were slow to catch on did a lot of work over the following few years to catch up.

Similarly, when sound cards first started to be installed on personal computers, there were detractors. Many programmers called sound and animation gimmicks and refused to study them. Although games and music dominate the sound application world presently, sound is slowly making its way into everyday computing. Around the office, we commonly hear "You've got mail" and "Printing is completed." Sound processing, if done tastefully, can be a valuable addition to many office applications. But be careful not to overuse sound—you can, after all, have too much of a good thing.

In this chapter, you will learn the principles of processing sound with the Java programming language. You will learn the difference between sampled and MIDI sound. You will also learn how to use the Java Sound API to process both of these sound types. Finally, we will work through an example of how to use the Java Sound API to both play and record sound.

The Principles of Sampled Sound

Before we get too far into the programming of sound in Java, we need to step back and get a solid understanding of how computers store and process sound. There are basically two ways that sound is recorded digitally: first, as sampled sound waves and second, as recorded MIDI events.

Microphones convert sounds (acoustical signals) into electrical signals. An analog to digital converter (often a sound card) transforms that analog signal into a series of sound samples (thus the name, sampled sound). These sound samples are recorded in a data format. The most common of these data formats is called Pulse Code Modulation. Other, less common, types include Mu-law encoding and a-law encoding. This encoded data is placed in a file along with a header. The type of header used determines the suffix of the sound file. On Windows, the .WAV file is common, .AIFF is often found on Macs, and .AU files are normally associated with Unix machines. Figure 18.1 shows a sampled sound wave.

This is a graph of the sound's amplitude plotted over time. The amplitude value of the sound wave is measured periodically at the sample rate. These discreet samples, represented by the dots on the graph, are the values stored in a file. It is clear that having more samples per unit of time would increase the fidelity of the captured sounds, but it would also increase the size of the file.

FIGURE 18.1

Sampling a sound wave.

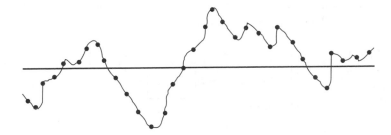

The quantization is the number of bits used to represent each sample. Obviously, the more bits stored per sample, the more faithfully the sound can be described. For instance, the compact disc standard calls for 44,100 samples/second and 16 bits/sample.

The term "sampled audio" is used in Java Sound as a synonym for "digital audio." Whereas most sampled audio is created by sampling audio input, other sampled audio is created synthetically by programs. However, this synthetic data is still called sampled audio in Java Sound documentation and in this chapter.

The Principles of MIDI Sound

The other way of capturing and playing sound in a computer is by using the *Musical Instrument Digital Interface (MIDI)*. The MIDI format records a digital equivalent of a musician's gestures. It does not record the noise being created at the time.

The MIDI standard was originally written to record the notes played by a musician on a keyboard or other MIDI hardware device. These gestures are called MIDI events. These events were stored on another hardware device called a sequencer. The sequencer was responsible for sending events to another device called a synthesizer.

This recording of events could then be played on a synthesizer that produced sounds emulating the original instrument. A common MIDI event is Note On and another is Note Off.

Over time, sequencers ceased to be separate pieces of hardware and began to appear as software. The dedicated synthesizers first became special sound cards, but now they are most often entirely written in software too. Figure 18.2 shows a graphical depiction of a sequencer sending a stream of events to a synthesizer.

MIDI data can be streamed or sequenced. Originally, MIDI 1.0 was a wire protocol— meaning that it just sent events over the wire without any timing information at all. This was based on the assumption that a musician or a MIDI device would send the event at the proper time. The synthesizer could then execute the command encapsulated by the

18

PROCESSING
SOUND WITH JAVA

event as soon as it was received. This scheme broke down when programs sent streams of events to the sequencer directly because the timing was missing.

FIGURE 18.2

Sequencers send events to synthesizers.

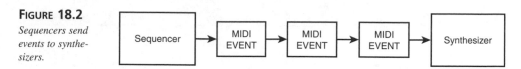

A new protocol, the Standard MIDI file, was created to send MIDI files to the sequencer with timing information added to the data. The MIDI data that includes the timing information is known as sequenced data, and the files that contain this data are known as the Standard MIDI files.

A Standard MIDI file contains a sequence. A sequence is composed of tracks. Each track represents a single instrument, so one sequence could contain all the information needed to play an arrangement with 16 instruments.

The sequencer acts similar to the orchestra conductor. It reads the Standard MIDI file and obtains the score (the sequence). It then gives instructions to the synthesizer (the musicians) to play the notes with the conductor (the sequencer) providing the timing.

A MIDI system sends messages from the sequencer (transmitter) to the synthesizer (receiver). There are three types of messages:

- ShortEvent—Channel and system messages (normal data)
- SysexEvent—Arbitrary vendor-specific data
- MetaEvent—Special events in MIDI files

For the purposes of playing MIDI files, you don't need to be able to distinguish between the types of events. Those details are handled by the sequencer and synthesizer objects that process them.

The Java Sound API

You are probably not surprised that there is a Sound API in Java. (In fact, after reading this book, you might be wondering if there is anything that doesn't have an API in Java.) Sound support has been a part of Java since its first release in the 1990s. Sound support in the early years was monaural and of telephone (low) quality. Coinciding with the release of Java 2, Sun introduced the Java Sound API as a separate download. Since the release of JDK 1.3, the Java Sound API has been included in the standard Java download.

The Java Sound API is basically a set of low-level audio processing functionality that can be called from within a Java program. This includes audio capture, mixing, and playing as well as MIDI messaging, synthesis, and sequencing.

The Sound API has, as its stated goal, the capability of playing sound better than the original classes did. It supports stereo, both sampled and MIDI sound, and a variety of file formats including .WAV, .AIFF, .AU, .MIDI, and .RMF.

The API contains two separate packages. The javax.media.sound.sampled package contains the classes and methods needed to capture and play sampled data. The javax.media.sound.midi package contains the classes and methods needed to play MIDI files.

The logical place to start our study is with the sampled sound package, javax.sound.sampled. These tasks primarily involve opening and closing input devices, managing buffers, and mixing streams of audio into one stream that can be played on your computer's speakers or headphones. The API contains methods for reading and writing various audio formats, as well as for converting between these formats.

The API can handle both streaming and buffered input, as well as in-memory data. The stream is called a *source data line* and the in-memory data is called a *clip*. A source data line provides data to the sound engine at approximately the same rate as it is played. In practice, buffers are filled and the music starts. The sound engine has no idea how long the file is; it just processes the data as it is received.

Clips are sound files that can all fit in memory at the same time. Java Sound API supports the playing of clips. Clips have the advantage of being instantaneously playable. This allows you to skip the preloading step altogether. This is critical for adding sound to games.

To play or capture sound, you need a line, a mixer, and some formatted data. Two types of formats concern us. The first is the data format that we discussed earlier. The second is the file format. The same data format, for example PCM, can be found in different file formats such as .AU and .WAV.

Let's look at the classes and interfaces that make up the javax.sound.sampled package:

- AudioFormat—This class represents a data format by containing information about the data format (normally PCM): mono or stereo, the sample rate (samples/second/ channel), bits/sample/channel, the frame rate (frames/second), the frame size (bytes), and the byte order (big-endian or little-endian). The frame contains the data for all the channels for a certain instant in time.

- AudioFileFormat—This object contains the file type (.WAV, .AU, and so on), the length of the file (bytes), the length of the data (frames), and an instance of the AudioFormat class.

- Mixer—Objects that implement this interface are considered devices. A Mixer object takes one or more streams as input and combines them into one or more streams of output. A typical case would have several incoming streams combined to produce a stereo signal to the speakers. Mixer is an interface, so it can be a handle for a variety of devices. Some sound cards serve as the implementation of the Mixer, whereas total software solutions implement this interface in other configurations.

- Port—Objects that implement this interface are normally speakers and headphones. On the input side, a port could be a line in.

- Line—Objects that implement the Line interface represent a path for moving data in and out of a mixer. These lines are similar to the wires running from the microphones into a sound-mixing console at a concert or broadway show. In the computer sound world, the inputs are ordinarily source data lines or clips. Figure 18.3 shows the interfaces that extend the Line interface.

FIGURE 18.3

The Line interfaces.

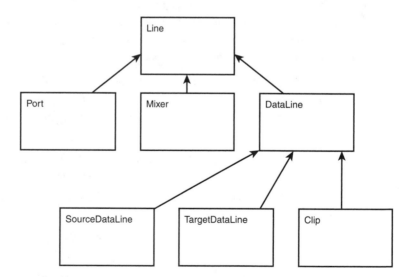

- DataLine—This interface is the parent of the SourceDataLine, TargetDataLine, and Clip. It provides an audio format, a media position, a buffer size, a volume level, a start() method , a stop() method, pause and resume logic, a flush(), and a drain(). This interface generates START and STOP events.

- SourceDataLine—Objects implementing this interface represent streams of data that provide input into a Mixer. These streams are buffered and processed according to the processing of the mixer. Many separate SourceDataLines can feed a Mixer at the same time.

- Clip—Objects implementing the Clip interface fit entirely into memory where they can be played instantaneously.

- TargetDataLine—The output from a Mixer implements this interface. A speaker receives a TargetDataLine.

Let's look at the classes and interfaces that make up the javax.sound.midi package:

- MidiSystem—This class provides access to MIDI resources such as sequencers, synthesizers, and so on.

- Sequencer—This interface is implemented by the device that sends timed events to the synthesizer.

- Synthesizer—This interface is implemented by the device that actually generates the sound.

- MidiChannel—This interface represents the events played by one "instrument."

Often, a player is written that can play either MIDI or sampled sound.

Playing Sound with Java

Now that we have a pretty good idea about what classes and interfaces control the action in this package, let's work a minimal example so that we can see how they fit together to produce sound. Listing 18.1 shows this example.

LISTING 18.1   The Simple Sound Player

```
package unleashed.ch18;


import javax.sound.midi.*;
import javax.sound.sampled.*;
import java.io.File;
import java.io.InputStream;
import java.io.FileInputStream;
import java.io.BufferedInputStream;
import java.util.Vector;
import java.net.URL;

/**
 * A simple player for sampled sound files.
```

18

PROCESSING
SOUND WITH JAVA

LISTING 18.1   continued

```java
 *
 *
 * @author Steve Potts
 */
public class SimpleSoundPlayer implements Runnable,
                    LineListener, MetaEventListener
{

    final int bufSize = 16384;

    Vector sounds = new Vector();
    Thread thread;
    Sequencer sequencer;
    boolean midiEOM, audioEOM;
    Synthesizer synthesizer;
    MidiChannel channels[];
    Object currentSound;
    String currentName;
    double duration;
    int num;
    boolean bump;
    boolean paused = false;

    String errStr;


    public void open()
    {
        try
        {
            sequencer = MidiSystem.getSequencer();

            if (sequencer instanceof Synthesizer)
            {
                synthesizer = (Synthesizer)sequencer;
                channels = synthesizer.getChannels();
            }

        } catch (Exception ex)
        { ex.printStackTrace(); return; }
        sequencer.addMetaEventListener(this);

    }


    public void close()
    {
        if (sequencer != null)
        {
```

Listing 18.1   continued

```
            sequencer.close();
        }
    }

    private void addSound(File file)
    {
        sounds.add(file);
    }


    public boolean loadSound(Object object)
    {
        duration = 0.0;

        currentName = ((File) object).getName();
        try
        {
            currentSound =
                AudioSystem.getAudioInputStream((File) object);
        } catch(Exception e1)
        {
            try
            {
                FileInputStream is = new FileInputStream((File) object);
                currentSound = new BufferedInputStream(is, 1024);
            } catch (Exception e3)
            {
                e3.printStackTrace();
                currentSound = null;
                return false;
            }
            //}
        }

        // user pressed stop or changed tabs while loading
        if (sequencer == null)
        {
            currentSound = null;
            return false;
        }

        if (currentSound instanceof AudioInputStream)
        {
            try
            {
                AudioInputStream stream = (AudioInputStream) currentSound;
                AudioFormat format = stream.getFormat();
```

LISTING **18.1**   continued

```
                    /**
                     * we can't yet open the device for ALAW/ULAW playback,
                     * convert ALAW/ULAW to PCM
                     */

                    if ((format.getEncoding() == AudioFormat.Encoding.ULAW) ||
                    (format.getEncoding() == AudioFormat.Encoding.ALAW))
                    {
                        AudioFormat tmp = new AudioFormat(
                        AudioFormat.Encoding.PCM_SIGNED,
                        format.getSampleRate(),
                        format.getSampleSizeInBits() * 2,
                        format.getChannels(),
                        format.getFrameSize() * 2,
                        format.getFrameRate(),
                        true);
                        stream = AudioSystem.getAudioInputStream(tmp, stream);
                        format = tmp;
                    }
                    DataLine.Info info = new DataLine.Info(
                    Clip.class,
                    stream.getFormat(),
                    ((int) stream.getFrameLength() *
                    format.getFrameSize())));

                    Clip clip = (Clip) AudioSystem.getLine(info);
                    clip.addLineListener(this);
                    clip.open(stream);
                    currentSound = clip;
                    //seekSlider.setMaximum((int) stream.getFrameLength());
                } catch (Exception ex)
                {
                    ex.printStackTrace();
                    currentSound = null;
                    return false;
                }
            } else if (currentSound instanceof Sequence ||
                            currentSound instanceof BufferedInputStream)
            {
                try
                {
                    sequencer.open();
                    if (currentSound instanceof Sequence)
                    {
                        sequencer.setSequence((Sequence) currentSound);
                    } else
                    {
                        sequencer.setSequence((BufferedInputStream) currentSound);
                    }
```

LISTING **18.1**   continued

```
        } catch (InvalidMidiDataException imde)
        {
            System.out.println("Unsupported audio file.");
            currentSound = null;
            return false;
        } catch (Exception ex)
        {
            ex.printStackTrace();
            currentSound = null;
            return false;
        }
    }

    duration = getDuration();

    return true;
}


public void playSound()
{
    midiEOM = audioEOM = bump = false;
    if (currentSound instanceof Sequence ||
        currentSound instanceof BufferedInputStream
            && thread != null)
    {
        sequencer.start();
        while (!midiEOM && thread != null && !bump)
        {
            try
            { thread.sleep(99); } catch (Exception e)
            {break;}
        }
        sequencer.stop();
        sequencer.close();
    } else if (currentSound instanceof Clip)
    {
        Clip clip = (Clip) currentSound;
        clip.start();
        try
        { thread.sleep(99); } catch (Exception e)
        { }
        while ((paused || clip.isActive()) && thread != null && !bump)
        {
            try
            { thread.sleep(99); } catch (Exception e)
            {break;}
        }
        clip.stop();
```

LISTING 18.1   continued

```java
        clip.close();
    }
    currentSound = null;
}


public double getDuration()
{
    double duration = 0.0;
    if (currentSound instanceof Sequence)
    {
        duration =
        ((Sequence) currentSound).getMicrosecondLength() / 1000000.0;
    }  else if (currentSound instanceof BufferedInputStream)
    {
        duration = sequencer.getMicrosecondLength() / 1000000.0;
    } else if (currentSound instanceof Clip)
    {
        Clip clip = (Clip) currentSound;
        duration = clip.getBufferSize() /
        (clip.getFormat().getFrameSize() *
            clip.getFormat().getFrameRate());
    }
    return duration;
}


public void update(LineEvent event)
{
    if (event.getType() == LineEvent.Type.STOP && !paused)
    {
        audioEOM = true;
    }
}


public void meta(MetaMessage message)
{
    if (message.getType() == 47)
    {  // 47 is end of track
        midiEOM = true;
    }
}


private void reportStatus(String msg)
{
    if ((errStr = msg) != null)
    {
```

LISTING 18.1 continued

```java
            System.out.println(errStr);
        }
    }


    public Thread getThread()
    {
        return thread;
    }

    public void start()
    {
        thread = new Thread(this);
        thread.setName("SimpleSamplePlayer");
        thread.start();
    }

    public void stop()
    {
        if (thread != null)
        {
            thread.interrupt();
        }
        thread = null;
    }

    public void run()
    {
        for (; num < sounds.size() && thread != null; num++)
        {
            if( loadSound(sounds.get(num)) == true )
            {
                playSound();
            }
            // take a little break between sounds
            try
            { thread.sleep(222); } catch (Exception e)
            {break;}
        }
        num = 0;

        thread = null;
        currentName = null;
        currentSound = null;
        System.out.println("Press <ctrl-c> to exit");
    }

    public void loadSounds(String name)
    {
```

Listing 18.1   continued

```java
        try
        {
            File file = new File(name);
            if (file != null && file.isDirectory())
            {
                String files[] = file.list();
                for (int i = 0; i < files.length; i++)
                {
                    File leafFile =
                        new File(file.getAbsolutePath(), files[i]);
                    addSound(leafFile);
                }
            }
        } catch (Exception e)
        {
            System.out.println("Exception " + e);
        }
    }

    public static void main(String args[])
    {
        //every file in this directory will be played
        String media = "c:/unleashed/ch18/sounds";

        final SimpleSoundPlayer ssp = new SimpleSoundPlayer();
        ssp.open();

        //we first load the sound file names in a vector
        ssp.loadSounds(media);


        //Then we start a thread to play the sounds
        ssp.start();

        //We have to wait for a while so that the process doesn't
        //terminate, killing the playing thread
        try
        { Thread.sleep(500000); } catch (Exception e)
        {System.out.println("Interrupted");}

        //close and exit
        ssp.close();
        System.exit(0);
    }

}
```

> **Note**
>
> The program in Listing 18.1 contains some methods that are found in Sun's JavaSoundDemo program. The right to use them is granted by Sun in the header. The full copyright statement is included in the source files for this example. It is not shown here because of its length.

This program plays all the sounds in a directory called `C:\unleashed\ch18\sounds`. This directory will be created automatically if you unzip to the `c:` drive. Otherwise, you will need to alter the filename in the `main()` method.

First, let's look at the structure of this program. The `main()` method opens the sound processor, loads all the files in the sounds directory into a vector, starts another thread with this class's `run()` method, and puts itself to sleep for a time period long enough to allow all the sound files to be processed. When the sounds finish, you can terminate the process manually, or just wait for the 500 seconds to pass. Conversely, if you add longer sound files to the directory, add more time in the sleep method parameter.

We have to sleep here because the thread that processes and plays the music is owned by the process that runs the `main()` method. If the parent process dies before the owned thread finishes, the owned thread is terminated by the JVM, and the sound stops immediately. For more information about threaded applications, see Chapter 24, "Multithreading Applications in Java."

Immediately after creating an instance of the `SimpleSoundPlayer` class, the `main()` method calls the `open()` method. The `open()` method calls the `getSequencer()` method:

```
sequencer = MidiSystem.getSequencer();
```

The `MidiSystem` class provides access to the installed sequencers and synthesizers on your system. The `getSequencer()` method returns the default sequencer. If this sequencer also contains a synthesizer, a simple cast will allow this same handle to accept synthesizer calls:

```
synthesizer = (Synthesizer)sequencer;
```

One of these calls is to the `getChannels()` method. If you recall, a channel in a MIDI device represents one instrument:

```
channels = synthesizer.getChannels();
```

Finally, the open() method adds an event handler for the MIDI Meta events. As you recall, we said that the Meta events were special events, not the ones that turn notes on and off:

```
sequencer.addMetaEventListener(this);
```

This interface has only one method, the meta() method:

```
public void meta(MetaMessage message)
{
    if (message.getType() == 47)
    {   // 47 is end of track
        midiEOM = true;
    }
}
```

In our case, the only message that we really want to know about is the end of track message.

The run() method is fired up by the starting of the thread to play the music. It is essentially one loop that steps through the sounds vector, loading and playing each file in turn:

```
for (; num < sounds.size() && thread != null; num++)
{
    if( loadSound(sounds.get(num)) == true )
    {
        playSound();
    }
    // take a little break between sounds
    try
    { thread.sleep(222); } catch (Exception e)
    {break;}
}
```

Caution

Make sure that the amount of time that you allow the thread to sleep is long enough for your file to play completely. Increase the number in the sleep() method to allow for a longer file.

The real work of the application is in loading the sound file. This is done in the loadSound() method.

After a little prep work, loadSound() tries to load the file into an AudioInputStream. If this file is not really an AudioInputStream with a specified length and format, this method will throw an exception:

```
currentSound = AudioSystem.getAudioInputStream((File) object);
```

If this happens, an attempt is made to assign the file to a buffered input stream:

```
FileInputStream is = new FileInputStream((File) object);
currentSound = new BufferedInputStream(is, 1024);
```

The next activity that must be undertaken is to get the stream in the proper format. If the format is not PCM, it must be converted:

```
AudioInputStream stream = (AudioInputStream) currentSound;
AudioFormat format = stream.getFormat();


if ((format.getEncoding() == AudioFormat.Encoding.ULAW) ||
(format.getEncoding() == AudioFormat.Encoding.ALAW))
{
    AudioFormat tmp = new AudioFormat(
    AudioFormat.Encoding.PCM_SIGNED,
    format.getSampleRate(),
    format.getSampleSizeInBits() * 2,
    format.getChannels(),
    format.getFrameSize() * 2,
    format.getFrameRate(),
    true);
    stream = AudioSystem.getAudioInputStream(tmp, stream);
    format = tmp;
}
```

Next, a `DataLineInfo` class is created to get information that will be needed to play the sound file:

```
DataLine.Info info = new DataLine.Info(
Clip.class,
stream.getFormat(),
((int) stream.getFrameLength() *
format.getFrameSize()));
```

If the sound file is an instance of `Sequence`, it is a MIDI file and it needs some preparation before it can be played:

```
sequencer.open();
if (currentSound instanceof Sequence)
{
    sequencer.setSequence((Sequence) currentSound);
} else
{
    sequencer.setSequence((BufferedInputStream) currentSound);
}
```

Finally, the duration is queried and the success indicator is returned:

```
duration = getDuration();

return true;
```

Our program is now ready to play the sounds:

If the file contained a MIDI sequence, we start the sequencer and loop until the end of

```
sequencer.start();
```

After the sequence is complete, we stop and close the sequencer:

```
sequencer.stop();
sequencer.close();
```

If the sound data contains a `Clip`, we play it with a `start()` method:

```
Clip clip = (Clip) currentSound;
clip.start();
```

After the sequence is complete, we stop and close the clip:

```
clip.stop();
clip.close();
```

The result is playing each sound stored in the directory files. If you want to play other sound files, just move them to the same directory or change the code to point to your directory. After all the files have been processed, you will see the following message:

```
Press <ctrl-c> to exit
```

Capturing Sound with Java

The final task that we need to accomplish is to capture sampled sound. (The Java Sound API can only capture sampled sound.) Listing 18.2 shows us how to do this.

> **Note**
>
> The program in Listing 18.2 contains some methods that are found in Sun's JavaSoundDemo program. The right to use them is granted by Sun in the header. The full copyright statement is included in the source files for this example. It is not shown here because of its length.

LISTING 18.2   The SimpleSoundCapture Program

```
package unleashed.ch18;


import java.awt.*;
import java.awt.event.*;
import java.awt.geom.Line2D;
```

LISTING 18.2   continued

```java
import javax.swing.*;
import javax.swing.event.*;
import javax.swing.border.*;
import java.util.Vector;
import java.util.Enumeration;
import java.io.*;
import javax.sound.sampled.*;
import java.awt.font.*;
import java.text.*;


/**
 * SimpleSoundCapture Example. This is a simple program to record
 * sounds and play them back. It uses some methods from the
 * CapturePlayback program in the JavaSoundDemo. For licensing
 * reasons the disclaimer is included in the source file.
 * @author Steve Potts
 */
public class SimpleSoundCapture extends JPanel implements ActionListener
{

    final int bufSize = 16384;

    Capture capture = new Capture();
    Playback playback = new Playback();

    AudioInputStream audioInputStream;

    JButton playB, captB;
    JTextField textField;

    String errStr;
    double duration, seconds;
    File file;

    public SimpleSoundCapture()
    {
        setLayout(new BorderLayout());
        EmptyBorder eb = new EmptyBorder(5,5,5,5);
        SoftBevelBorder sbb =
                new SoftBevelBorder(SoftBevelBorder.LOWERED);
        setBorder(new EmptyBorder(5,5,5,5));

        JPanel p1 = new JPanel();
        p1.setLayout(new BoxLayout(p1, BoxLayout.X_AXIS));

        JPanel p2 = new JPanel();
        p2.setBorder(sbb);
```

Listing 18.2   continued

```java
        p2.setLayout(new BoxLayout(p2, BoxLayout.Y_AXIS));

        JPanel buttonsPanel = new JPanel();
        buttonsPanel.setBorder(new EmptyBorder(10,0,5,0));
        playB = addButton("Play", buttonsPanel, false);
        captB = addButton("Record", buttonsPanel, true);
        p2.add(buttonsPanel);

        p1.add(p2);
        add(p1);
    }


    public void open()
    { }


    public void close()
    {
        if (playback.thread != null)
        {
            playB.doClick(0);
        }
        if (capture.thread != null)
        {
            captB.doClick(0);
        }
    }

    private JButton addButton(String name, JPanel p, boolean state)
    {
        JButton b = new JButton(name);
        b.addActionListener(this);
        b.setEnabled(state);
        p.add(b);
        return b;
    }


    public void actionPerformed(ActionEvent e)
    {
        Object obj = e.getSource();
        if (obj.equals(playB))
        {
            if (playB.getText().startsWith("Play"))
            {
                playback.start();
                captB.setEnabled(false);
                playB.setText("Stop");
```

LISTING 18.2 continued

```
        } else
        {
            playback.stop();
            captB.setEnabled(true);
            playB.setText("Play");
        }
    } else if (obj.equals(captB))
    {
        if (captB.getText().startsWith("Record"))
        {
            capture.start();
            playB.setEnabled(false);
            captB.setText("Stop");
        } else
        {
            capture.stop();
            playB.setEnabled(true);
        }

    }
}

/**
 * Write data to the OutputChannel.
 */
public class Playback implements Runnable
{

    SourceDataLine line;
    Thread thread;

    public void start()
    {
        errStr = null;
        thread = new Thread(this);
        thread.setName("Playback");
        thread.start();
    }

    public void stop()
    {
        thread = null;
    }

    private void shutDown(String message)
    {
        if ((errStr = message) != null)
        {
            System.err.println(errStr);
```

LISTING 18.2   continued

```java
        }
        if (thread != null)
        {
            thread = null;
             captB.setEnabled(true);
            playB.setText("Play");
        }
    }

    public void run()
    {

        // make sure we have something to play
        if (audioInputStream == null)
        {
            shutDown("No loaded audio to play back");
            return;
        }
        // reset to the beginning of the stream
        try
        {
            audioInputStream.reset();
        } catch (Exception e)
        {
            shutDown("Unable to reset the stream\n" + e);
            return;
        }

        // get an AudioInputStream of the desired format for playback

        AudioFormat.Encoding encoding =
                AudioFormat.Encoding.PCM_SIGNED;
        float rate = 44100.0f;
        int channels = 2;
        int frameSize = 4;
        int sampleSize = 16;
        boolean bigEndian = true;

        AudioFormat format =
                new AudioFormat(encoding, rate, sampleSize,
        channels, (sampleSize/8)*channels, rate, bigEndian);


        AudioInputStream playbackInputStream =
                AudioSystem.getAudioInputStream(format,
                                        audioInputStream);

        if (playbackInputStream == null)
        {
```

LISTING 18.2   continued

```java
        shutDown("Unable to convert stream of format " +
                audioInputStream + " to format " + format);
        return;
    }

    // define the required attributes for our line,
    // and make sure a compatible line is supported.

    DataLine.Info info = new DataLine.Info(SourceDataLine.class,
    format);
    if (!AudioSystem.isLineSupported(info))
    {
        shutDown("Line matching " + info + " not supported.");
        return;
    }

    // get and open the source data line for playback.

    try
    {
        line = (SourceDataLine) AudioSystem.getLine(info);
        line.open(format, bufSize);
    } catch (LineUnavailableException ex)
    {
        shutDown("Unable to open the line: " + ex);
        return;
    }

    // play back the captured audio data

    int frameSizeInBytes = format.getFrameSize();
    int bufferLengthInFrames = line.getBufferSize() / 8;
    int bufferLengthInBytes =
            bufferLengthInFrames * frameSizeInBytes;
    byte[] data = new byte[bufferLengthInBytes];
    int numBytesRead = 0;

    // start the source data line
    line.start();

    while (thread != null)
    {
        try
        {
            if ((numBytesRead =
                    playbackInputStream.read(data)) == -1)
            {
                break;
            }
```

LISTING 18.2 continued

```java
                    int numBytesRemaining = numBytesRead;
                    while (numBytesRemaining > 0 )
                    {
                        numBytesRemaining -=
                            line.write(data, 0, numBytesRemaining);
                    }
                } catch (Exception e)
                {
                    shutDown("Error during playback: " + e);
                    break;
                }
            }
            // we reached the end of the stream.
            //let the data play out, then
            // stop and close the line.
            if (thread != null)
            {
                line.drain();
            }
            line.stop();
            line.close();
            line = null;
            shutDown(null);
        }
    } // End class Playback


    /**
     * Reads data from the input channel and writes to the output stream
     */
    class Capture implements Runnable
    {

        TargetDataLine line;
        Thread thread;

        public void start()
        {
            errStr = null;
            thread = new Thread(this);
            thread.setName("Capture");
            thread.start();
        }

        public void stop()
        {
            thread = null;
        }
```

LISTING 18.2   continued

```java
private void shutDown(String message)
{
    if ((errStr = message) != null && thread != null)
    {
        thread = null;
        playB.setEnabled(true);
        captB.setText("Record");
        System.err.println(errStr);
    }
}

public void run()
{

    duration = 0;
    audioInputStream = null;

    // define the required attributes for our line,
    // and make sure a compatible line is supported.

    AudioFormat.Encoding encoding =
                AudioFormat.Encoding.PCM_SIGNED;
    float rate = 44100.0f;
    int channels = 2;
    int frameSize = 4;
    int sampleSize = 16;
    boolean bigEndian = true;

    AudioFormat format =
            new AudioFormat(encoding, rate, sampleSize,
    channels, (sampleSize/8)*channels, rate, bigEndian);

    DataLine.Info info = new DataLine.Info(TargetDataLine.class,
    format);

    if (!AudioSystem.isLineSupported(info))
    {
        shutDown("Line matching " + info + " not supported.");
        return;
    }

    // get and open the target data line for capture.

    try
    {
        line =
         (TargetDataLine) AudioSystem.getLine(info);
        line.open(format, line.getBufferSize());
```

LISTING 18.2   continued

```java
        } catch (LineUnavailableException ex)
        {
            shutDown("Unable to open the line: " + ex);
            return;
        } catch (SecurityException ex)
        {
            shutDown(ex.toString());
            return;
        } catch (Exception ex)
        {
            shutDown(ex.toString());
            return;
        }

        // play back the captured audio data
        ByteArrayOutputStream out =
                        new ByteArrayOutputStream();
        int frameSizeInBytes = format.getFrameSize();
        int bufferLengthInFrames = line.getBufferSize() / 8;
        int bufferLengthInBytes = bufferLengthInFrames
                                * frameSizeInBytes;
        byte[] data = new byte[bufferLengthInBytes];
        int numBytesRead;

        line.start();

        while (thread != null)
        {
            if((numBytesRead =
                    line.read(data, 0, bufferLengthInBytes)) == -1)
            {
                break;
            }
            out.write(data, 0, numBytesRead);
        }

        // we reached the end of the stream.
        //stop and close the line.
        line.stop();
        line.close();
        line = null;

        // stop and close the output stream
        try
        {
            out.flush();
            out.close();
        } catch (IOException ex)
        {
```

LISTING 18.2   continued

```
                ex.printStackTrace();
        }

        // load bytes into the audio input stream for playback

        byte audioBytes[] = out.toByteArray();
        ByteArrayInputStream bais =
                new ByteArrayInputStream(audioBytes);
        audioInputStream =
                new AudioInputStream(bais, format, audioBytes.length
                            / frameSizeInBytes);

        long milliseconds =
                (long)((audioInputStream.getFrameLength() * 1000)
                                    / format.getFrameRate());
        duration = milliseconds / 1000.0;

        try
        {
            audioInputStream.reset();
        } catch (Exception ex)
        {
            ex.printStackTrace();
            return;
        }

    }
} // End class Capture

public static void main(String s[])
{
    SimpleSoundCapture ssc = new SimpleSoundCapture();
    ssc.open();
    JFrame f = new JFrame("Capture/Playback");
    f.setDefaultCloseOperation(JFrame.EXIT_ON_CLOSE);
    f.getContentPane().add("Center", ssc);
    f.pack();
    Dimension screenSize =
                Toolkit.getDefaultToolkit().getScreenSize();
    int w = 360;
    int h = 170;
    f.setLocation(screenSize.width/2 - w/2,
                screenSize.height/2 - h/2);
    f.setSize(w, h);
    f.show();
}
}
```

> **Note**
>
> The program in Listing 18.2 will run only once. If you want to run it again, you need to restart it.

Capturing sound with the javax.sound.sampled package is reasonably straightforward, if a little long. Three classes make up this application. The first one, `SimpleSoundCapture`, is the GUI. The second one is called `Capture`, and it is a threaded application that runs while you are capturing sound. The final class is called `PlayBack`, which, as the name implies, plays the final, recorded sound for you to prove that the capture works.

All the processing in the `Capture` class is in `run()`. The first task is to create an `AudioFormat` object that will contain the details of how we are to encode the sound:

```
AudioFormat.Encoding encoding =
            AudioFormat.Encoding.PCM_SIGNED;
float rate = 44100.0f;
int channels = 2;
int frameSize = 4;
int sampleSize = 16;
boolean bigEndian = true;

AudioFormat format =
        new AudioFormat(encoding, rate, sampleSize,
channels, (sampleSize/8)*channels, rate, bigEndian);
```

The `DataLine` needs this information to create the proper file for it:

```
DataLine.Info info = new DataLine.Info(TargetDataLine.class,
format);

if (!AudioSystem.isLineSupported(info))
{
    shutDown("Line matching " + info + " not supported.");
    return;
```

If the system supports the type of line that we requested, we can create a `TargetDataLine` and open it for output:

```
line =
 (TargetDataLine) AudioSystem.getLine(info);
line.open(format, line.getBufferSize());
```

Having done that, we will prepare to play back the audio:

```
ByteArrayOutputStream out =
                new ByteArrayOutputStream();
int frameSizeInBytes = format.getFrameSize();
```

```
int bufferLengthInFrames = line.getBufferSize() / 8;
int bufferLengthInBytes = bufferLengthInFrames
                          * frameSizeInBytes;
byte[] data = new byte[bufferLengthInBytes];
int numBytesRead;

line.start();

while (thread != null)
{
    if((numBytesRead =
            line.read(data, 0, bufferLengthInBytes)) == -1)
    {
        break;
    }
    out.write(data, 0, numBytesRead);
}
```

Now we can load the audio input stream so that the playback command will work:

```
byte audioBytes[] = out.toByteArray();
ByteArrayInputStream bais =
        new ByteArrayInputStream(audioBytes);
audioInputStream =
        new AudioInputStream(bais, format, audioBytes.length
                    / frameSizeInBytes);

long milliseconds =
        (long)((audioInputStream.getFrameLength() * 1000)
                            / format.getFrameRate());
duration = milliseconds / 1000.0;
```

Finally, we reset the audioInputStream so that we can play it:

```
audioInputStream.reset();
```

Now we are ready to do the playback. Similar to the Capture class, the Runnable PlayBack class does its work in the run() method. The first thing that happens is a check to see whether an AudioInputStream is ready to play:

```
if (audioInputStream == null)
{
    shutDown("No loaded audio to play back");
    return;
}
```

Caution

The format of the audio input stream must be the same for playing as it was for recording.

Next we specify the format of the audio input stream:

```
AudioFormat.Encoding encoding =
        AudioFormat.Encoding.PCM_SIGNED;
float rate = 44100.0f;
int channels = 2;
int frameSize = 4;
int sampleSize = 16;
boolean bigEndian = true;

AudioFormat format =
        new AudioFormat(encoding, rate, sampleSize,
channels, (sampleSize/8)*channels, rate, bigEndian);


AudioInputStream playbackInputStream =
        AudioSystem.getAudioInputStream(format,
                                audioInputStream);
```

Then we create the line and open it:

```
line = (SourceDataLine) AudioSystem.getLine(info);
line.open(format, bufSize);
} catch (LineUnavailableException ex)
```

Finally, we start the line that plays the sound:

```
line.start();
```

The process of filling the buffer continues during play:

```
if ((numBytesRead =
        playbackInputStream.read(data)) == -1)
{
    break;
}
int numBytesRemaining = numBytesRead;
while (numBytesRemaining > 0 )
{
    numBytesRemaining -=
        line.write(data, 0, numBytesRemaining);
}
```

At the end, we drain the line, close it, and shut down the thread:

```
line.drain();
}
line.stop();
line.close();
line = null;
shutDown(null);
```

The GUI for this program is shown in Figure 18.4.

FIGURE 18.4

The SimpleSoundCapture GUI.

To run this program, just click the Record button and start talking. When you are done, press Stop. Finally, press Play to hear the recording played back.

Summary

In this chapter, we learned how Java supports the capture and playing of high-quality sound. We also learned how sound is recorded in files.

We learned about the important classes in the Java Sound API. Using those classes, we created an application that can play sound files in a variety of formats, including sampled sound and MIDI.

Finally, we learned how to use the API to capture sounds through a microphone. This same program was then used to play the sampled sound back to verify that it worked.

18

PROCESSING
SOUND WITH JAVA

Best Practices for Designing Java Classes

PART V

CHAPTER 19

JavaBeans and the Java Event Model

JavaBeans are Java's version of the ActiveX controls (formerly known as Visual Basic Extensions [VBXs], and later OLE Control Extensions [OCXs]). These controls, introduced around 1990, filled a niche in hiding the complexity of the Windows operating system from programmers. VBXs could be used to build graphical interfaces using Visual Basic, or included in source code using Visual C++. One senior developer was heard to say, "The day that Visual Basic was released, the high school student next door became a better Windows programmer than me!"

Beyond just hiding the Windows API from programmers (and it did need hiding), Visual Basic showed that far more programming could be done using drag-and-drop components than was previously thought possible. It created a new category of development products now known as rapid application development (RAD) tools. While RAD products still require quite a bit of hand-coding, they speed up the development of a certain category of application—GUI front ends that access and modify database tables. Attempts to go beyond these applications into game development, communications, and distributed object programming have met with mixed results.

JavaBeans are pieces of code that are represented visually in an integrated development environment (IDE). They may or may not have a visual representation at runtime.

JavaBeans have made it possible for Visual Basic–like tools such as Visual Café, JBuilder, Visual Age for Java, and Forte to come to market. These tools differ from one another in some respects, but they all have a visual development flavor to them.

In this chapter you will learn how JavaBeans are created. You will also see how the Java event model works. You will then learn how to create JavaBeans from scratch and include them into a GUI development tool.

Understanding JavaBeans

Now that you have a feel for what a JavaBean is from a manager's point of view, let's look at it from a programmer's point of view. A JavaBean is a class that is created in such a way as to conform to a tight specification. This specification dictates many aspects of the class's design, even down to the names of many of the methods.

The JavaBeans specification requires that any class aspiring to be a bean must be usable inside a visual application builder tool. This means that the bean must have the following characteristics:

- It must offer support for introspection. A bean must either follow the JavaBean naming conventions or implement the `BeanInfo` interface and provide a method that describes the bean.

- It must be serializable. The bean instances that are included in a project must be able to be saved and retrieved without any loss of state information.

- It must be usable in a visual application builder tool. This requirement implies that a toolbox icon and a design-time visual representation must exist.

- If a bean is visible at runtime, it must extend `java.awt.Component` (via a subclass such as `Canvas`).

> **Note**
>
> JavaServer Pages (JSP) documentation also contains references to JavaBeans. JSP uses a very limited subset of the JavaBeans specification to provide a simple way of creating classes that JSPs can call directly. In essence, these JavaBeans are simply Java classes with getters and setters for all the property values.

Beyond these requirements, a JavaBean is not limited in what it can perform. It can contain virtually any processing logic that can be put into other Java classes.

Programming with the Java Event Model

Graphical user interfaces (GUIs) are event-generating maniacs. Every movement of the mouse, every keystroke, every window resizing, and every window relocation generates events that your application might be interested in knowing about. The word *might* in the preceding sentence highlights the crux of the event-handling challenge.

Realistically, any single application or JavaBean is only going to be interested in a small subset of the events that are generated. If your application were notified of every event that occurs, it could easily be overwhelmed by the overhead involved in processing them all.

In Java 1.1, Sun introduced an improved event-handling strategy based on the dual concepts of event sources and event listeners. An *event source* is a class that can generate an event. (Sometimes these classes are written by the application programmer; other times the event source is the JVM.) An *event listener* is a class that implements the `java.awt.event.EventListener` interface, normally through one of the `EventListener` subinterfaces.

Each of these interfaces requires that one or more methods be written for any class that implements it. For example, the MouseListener interface requires that all five of the following methods be implemented:

```
mouseClicked(MouseEvent e)
mouseEntered(MouseEvent e)
mouseExited(MouseEvent e)
mousePressed(MouseEvent e)
mouseReleased(MouseEvent e)
```

By contrast, the ActionListener interface only requires one method:

```
actionPerformed(ActionEvent e)
```

All of these methods receive an object that is derived from java.awt.Event. Each of these derived classes contains methods specific to its needs that allow the listener to obtain more information about the nature of the event. For example, an ActionEvent class contains four methods:

- getActionCommand() returns the command string associated with this action.
- getModifiers() returns the modifier keys held down during this action.
- getWhen() returns a timestamp telling when this event occurred.
- paramString() returns a parameter string for this event.

The object generating the event is responsible for creating the Event object and populating its variables. This object is also responsible for calling the listeners whenever an event that they have registered for has occurred. Let's create an application that shows the event model in action. Listings 19.1 and 19.2 show how clicking a button causes the actionPerformed() method to be called.

LISTING 19.1   The EventCreator Class

```
/*
 * EventTest.java
 *
 * Created on January 24, 2002, 11:17 AM
 */

package unleashed.ch19;


import javax.swing.*;
import java.awt.event.ActionListener;
import javax.swing.border.EtchedBorder;
import java.awt.Container;
import java.awt.BorderLayout;
```

LISTING 19.1   continued

```java
import java.util.*;

/**
 *
 * @author  Stephen Potts
 * @version
 */
public class EventCreator extends JFrame
{
    JButton btnBook;
    JButton btnExit;

    /** Constructors */
    public EventCreator() throws Exception
    {
        init();
    }

    public EventCreator(String caption) throws Exception
    {
        super(caption);
        init();
    }

    //The init() method moves real processing out of the constructors
    //where Exception handling is simpler
    private void init() throws Exception
    {
        try
        {
            //configure the Frame
            EventConsumer ec = new EventConsumer();
            setBounds(150,200,500,250);
            setDefaultCloseOperation(JFrame.EXIT_ON_CLOSE);

            //set the layout
            BorderLayout border = new BorderLayout();
            Container content = getContentPane();
            content.setLayout(border);
            btnBook = new JButton("Book");
            btnExit = new JButton("Exit");
            btnBook.addActionListener(ec);
            btnExit.addActionListener(ec);

            JPanel bottomPanel = new JPanel();
            bottomPanel.add(btnBook);
            bottomPanel.add(btnExit);
            content.add(bottomPanel, BorderLayout.SOUTH);
            setVisible(true);
```

LISTING 19.1   continued

```
    }catch(Exception e)
    {
        System.out.println("Exception thrown " + e);
    }
}

/**
 * @param args the command line arguments
 */
public static void main(String args[])
{
    //create an instance of the GUI
    try
    {
        EventCreator mainWindow = new EventCreator("EventCreator");
    }catch(Exception e)
    {
        System.out.println("Exception in main " + e);
    }
}

}//class
```

Notice that this application contains two classes instead of one for the sake of clarity. (We could have written it with the EventCreator class serving as its own event listener.)

We had to create an instance of the EventConsumer class so that the EventCreator's buttons could call it:

```
EventConsumer ec = new EventConsumer();
```

Both buttons are of class JButton. JButton is derived from the class javax.swing. AbstractButton. One of AbstractButton's methods is addActionListener(). AbstractButton extends JComponent. JComponent is an abstract class that contains a list of all the listeners of every type. Whenever an event occurs in a program, this list is searched for the listeners to notify.

We use the addActionListener() method to add a listener to a button:

```
btnBook.addActionListener(ec);
btnExit.addActionListener(ec);
```

Whenever the buttons are clicked, the JButton code creates an ActionEvent object. It then looks at the listener list to find out who the listeners are for this component. Of the listeners on the list, the JButton chooses the ones that implement the ActionListener interface.

Listing 19.2 shows the event consumer.

LISTING 19.2   The `EventConsumer` Class

```
/*
 * EventConsumer.java
 *
 * Created on January 24, 2002, 11:31 AM
 */

package unleashed.ch19;

import javax.swing.*;
import java.awt.event.ActionListener;
import javax.swing.border.EtchedBorder;
import java.awt.Container;
import java.awt.BorderLayout;

import java.util.*;

/**
 *
 * @author  Stephen Potts
 * @version
 */
public class EventConsumer implements ActionListener
{

    JButton btnBook;
    JButton btnExit;

    /** Constructors */
    public EventConsumer() throws Exception
    {
    }

    public void actionPerformed(java.awt.event.ActionEvent ae)
    {
        if (ae.getActionCommand().equals("Exit"))
        {
            System.out.println("Exit was clicked");
        }

        //Try and book a ticket
        if (ae.getActionCommand().equals("Book"))
        {
            System.out.println("Book was clicked");
        }
    }
}//class
```

There are a few aspects of this listing that require comment:

- Whenever the buttons are clicked, the `JButton` code creates an `ActionEvent` object. It then makes a call to each one of the listeners' `actionPerformed()` method. The code in the `actionPerformed()` method is executed.

- There is only one `actionPerformed()` method for all components that can create action events in this application. This means that the `actionPerformed()` method must use the `getActionCommand()` method of the `ActionEvent` class to figure out which button was clicked. The `getActionCommand()` returns the label of the component that caused the `Event` object to be created.

The GUI for this application is shown in Figure 19.1.

FIGURE 19.1

The `EventCreator` *class uses a dialog to communicate the event to the* `EventConsumer` *event handler.*

Running this program generates the following output:

```
Book was clicked
Exit was clicked
Book was clicked
Exit was clicked
```

This example shows the basic procedure that must be followed to connect the events that one component is able to generate with the event-handling code that has been written specifically for it. There are many different event types and many different methods for handling each of them. In the end, though, they all follow the same pattern of a listener registering with an event creator.

Developing a Simple JavaBean

Armed with an understanding of the Java event model, we are ready to create a simple JavaBean class. We will create a progress bar. The code for this class is shown in Listing 19.3.

LISTING 19.3   The ProgressBar Class

```java
// ProgressBar Bean Class
// ProgressBar.java

package unleashed.ch19;

import java.awt.*;
import java.awt.event.*;
import java.beans.*;
import java.io.Serializable;

public class ProgressBar extends Canvas implements Serializable
{
    private float scaleSize;
    private float currentValue;

    //Default constructor
    public ProgressBar()
    {
        this(100, 50);
    }


    //Constructor
    public ProgressBar(float scaleSize, float currentValue)
    {
        super();

        this.scaleSize = scaleSize;
        this.currentValue = currentValue;

        setBackground(Color.lightGray);
        setForeground(Color.magenta);

        //sets the initial size of the bean on a canvas
        setSize(100, 25);
    }

    public float getScaleSize()
    {
        return scaleSize;
    }

    public void setScaleSize(float sSize)
    {
        //The scale size can never set to a value lower than
        //the current value
        this.scaleSize = Math.max(0.0f, sSize);
        if (this.scaleSize < this.currentValue)
```

LISTING 19.3 continued

```java
        {
            this.scaleSize = this.currentValue;
        }
    }

    public float getCurrentValue()
    {
        return currentValue;
    }

    public void setCurrentValue(float cVal)
    {
        //The current value can not be set negative
        //nor can it be set greater than the scale size
        this.currentValue = Math.max(0.0f, cVal);
        if (this.currentValue > this.scaleSize)
        {
            this.currentValue = this.scaleSize;
        }
    }

    //The paint method is called by the container
    public synchronized void paint(Graphics g)
    {
        int width = getSize().width;
        int height = getSize().height;

        g.setColor(getBackground());
        g.fillRect(1, 1, width-2, height-2);
        g.draw3DRect(0,0, width-1, height-1, true);

        g.setColor(getForeground());
        g.fillRect(3,3,(int)((currentValue * (width-6))/scaleSize),
        height-6);
    }

    //The grow method makes the current value larger
    public void grow()
    {
        setCurrentValue( this.currentValue + 1.0f);
    }


    //The shrink method makes the current value smaller
    public void shrink()
    {
        setCurrentValue( this.currentValue - 1.0f);
    }
}//class
```

Notice that the `ProgressBar` class inherits from the `Canvas` class and implements the marker interface `Serializable`. The `Canvas` class is a subclass of the `Container` class. It is essentially a rectangular area of a screen that can be drawn on. It contains a `paint()` method that we override to provide the bean's appearance. All JavaBeans must be serializable so that their state can be saved. Imagine placing a progress bar on your application and resizing it. How happy would you be if it returned to the default size every time you closed the GUI builder? The GUI tools serialize the components and reload them to provide the desired persistent behavior.

```
public class ProgressBar extends Canvas implements Serializable
```

This bean has only two unique properties. It has many more properties that it obtains by extending the `Canvas` class, such as foreground and background colors, height, and width. The `scaleSize` shows what value will completely fill the progress bar. The `currentValue` represents how much progress has been achieved thus far. For example, if a gas tank holds 20 gallons and you have just filled it halfway, the `scaleSize` would be set to `20` and the `currentValue` would be set to `10`.

```
private float scaleSize;
private float currentValue;
```

The default constructor sets the `scaleSize` and `currentValue` values to `100` and `50`, respectively. It is important to do this because most GUI tools will call this constructor when you pick a tool from the toolbar and drop it into an application. Manually coded applications can use either the default or the regular constructor.

```
//Default constructor
public ProgressBar()
{
    this(100, 50);
}
```

The default constructor calls the regular constructor anyway. This constructor sets the unique property values and then sets some inherited properties. Note that the initial size of the bean is set using the `setSize()` method. This size is the height and width of the bean, not to be confused with the `scaleSize` and `currentValue` of the progress bar itself.

```
        setBackground(Color.lightGray);
        setForeground(Color.magenta);

        //sets the initial size of the bean on a canvas
        setSize(100, 25);
    }
```

The paint() method is overridden here. By default, a Canvas object is just a rectangle with a background color displayed. This method provides additional visual material. It is synchronized to make it thread-safe. In essence, it translates the scaleSize and currentValue properties into the dimensions of the rectangles that visually make up this component.

```
//The paint method is called by the container
public synchronized void paint(Graphics g)
{
    int width = getSize().width;
    int height = getSize().height;

    g.setColor(getBackground());
    g.fillRect(1, 1, width-2, height-2);
    g.draw3DRect(0,0, width-1, height-1, true);

    g.setColor(getForeground());
    g.fillRect(3,3,(int)((currentValue * (width-6))/scaleSize),
    height-6);
}
```

There are two methods that other classes and components can use to cause the progress bar to grow or shrink gracefully. The only increments and decrements are by 1, so the change in size is smooth.

```
public void grow()
{
    setCurrentValue( this.currentValue + 1.0f);
}
```

Notice that this class does not inherit from any abstract JavaBean class or interface. This is because a JavaBean is more of a pattern than a subclass. It functions well using the functionality inherited from Canvas and Component classes. This functionality does not provide everything that GUI builder tools need to function. In particular, they need the toolbox icons so that users can pick them up and place them in an application. The SimpleBeanInfo class provides this functionality. In Listing 19.4, we extend the SimpleBeanInfo class and override the getIcon method.

LISTING 19.4   The ProgressBarBeanInfo Class

```
/*
 * ProgressBarBeanInfo.java
 *
 * Created on January 31, 2002, 10:27 AM
 */
```

LISTING 19.4 continued

```java
package unleashed.ch19;
import java.beans.*;
import java.awt.*;

/**
 *
 * @author  Stephen Potts
 * @version
 */
public class ProgressBarBeanInfo extends SimpleBeanInfo
{

    public Image getIcon(int iconKind)
    {
        if(iconKind == BeanInfo.ICON_COLOR_16x16)
        {
            Image img = loadImage("ProgressBarIcon16.gif");
            return img;
        }

        if(iconKind == BeanInfo.ICON_COLOR_32x32)
        {
            Image img = loadImage("ProgressBarIcon32.gif");
            return img;
        }
        return null;
    }

}
```

As mentioned earlier, the GUI builder tools can discover all the properties of the bean classes via introspection. As a result of this, we only need to override the getIcon() method. Some GUI builder tools prefer a 16×16-pixel icon, while others use a 32×32-pixel icon. The if statements enable us to provide either.

Deploying JavaBeans

The whole strategy of writing bean classes is very logical and straightforward. Unfortunately, the deployment of JavaBeans is not straightforward at all. In short, you put the classes and resources in a JAR file and place this file in a special directory. This sounds easy enough, but the devil is in the details. In addition to these resources, you must also add a special file so that the manifest can be created properly.

> **Caution**
>
> As of this book's publication date, there was no BDK installation available for Linux.

Rather than talk in generalities, we will step through the deployment of the `ProgressBar` example on a Windows machine. The process for Unix is identical except for the directory names. Follow these steps:

1. Create a directory called `c:\unleashed\ch19`.

2. Copy the following files from the downloaded code for this chapter to this directory:

   ```
   ProgressBar.java
   ProgressBarIcon32.gif
   ProgressBarIcon16.gif
   ProgressBarBeanInfo.java
   ```

3. Compile the `ProgressBar.java` and `ProgressBarBeanInfo.java` files.

4. Create a file called `ProgressBar.mf` that contains the following lines:

   ```
   Manifest-Version: 1.0

   Name: unleashed/ch19/ProgressBar.class
   Java-Bean: True
   ```

5. Use the **cd** command to move up two directory levels to `c:\`.

6. Type the following command:

   ```
   jar cfm unleashed\ch19\ProgressBar.jar unleashed\ch19\ProgressBar.mf
   ➥unleashed\ch19\*.class unleashed\ch19\*.gif
   ```

7. Look in `c:\unleashed\ch19` and confirm that a file named `ProgressBar.jar` exists. Open it with a Zip program and verify that it contains the files shown in Figure 19.2.

8. Download the JavaBeans Development Kit (BDK) from `http://java.sun.com/`. (Type **BDK** in the search box and it will take you to the download page.) Specify `c:\BDK` as the location to install to.

9. Copy the `ProgressBar.jar` file into the `C:\BDK\jars` directory.

10. Move to the `c:\BDK\beanbox` directory. Type **run**. This will bring up four windows. The first is the ToolBox window that is shown in Figure 19.3. (Notice that the topmost bean in the ToolBox is our very own `ProgressBar`.)

FIGURE 19.2

The
`ProgressBar.jar`
*file contains all
the code needed to
add this JavaBean
to a GUI develop-
ment tool.*

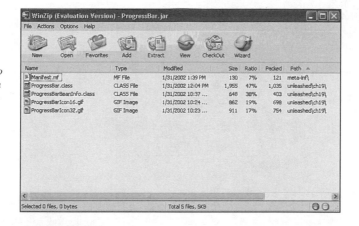

FIGURE 19.3

*The ToolBox con-
tains all the beans
that have JAR files
in* `c:\BDK\jars`.

11. Click on the `ProgressBar` icon in the ToolBox. Next, click on the middle of the BeanBox window. An instance of the `ProgressBar` bean appears in the window, as shown in Figure 19.4.

12. Examine the contents of the Properties window, which is shown in Figure 19.5. Notice that all the properties are listed, including the inherited ones. Click on the colored rectangle and look at the dialog box that appears (see Figure 19.6).

FIGURE 19.4

The BeanBox application allows programmers to test their beans before placing them into other, more complex development tools.

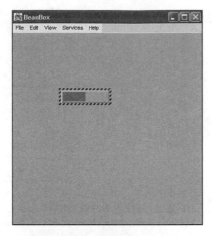

FIGURE 19.5

The Properties window provides a user interface for changing the bean-specific set of properties.

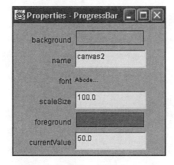

FIGURE 19.6

The Foreground property takes a Color *object as its value. A built-in property dialog exists for changing the* Color *object.*

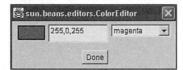

13. Observe that the color of the rectangle in the Properties dialog has changed, as has the color of the `ProgressBar` that is displayed in the BeanBox. This dialog appears automatically because the return type of the `setForegroundColor()` method is of class `Color`. Automatic property change dialogs exist for the intrinsic types, `Strings`, `Fonts`, and other common return types. If you return an object that you have defined, you will be responsible for implementing this.

Deploying the `ProgressBar` bean in another GUI building tool requires that you follow the tool's instructions for deployment. As an example, we will add the `ProgressBar` to the Forte development environment. To do so, follow this procedure:

1. Open the Forte IDE.

2. Select Tools, Install New JavaBean. The dialog shown in Figure 19.7 will appear.

FIGURE 19.7

The Install JavaBean dialog allows you to specify the location of the JAR file that holds your bean.

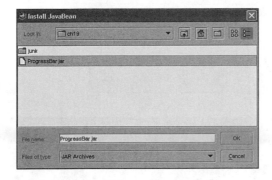

3. Select the `ProgressBar.jar` file and click OK. This will bring up the Select JavaBean dialog that is shown in Figure 19.8.

FIGURE 19.8

The Select JavaBean dialog allows you to specify the bean that you want to install.

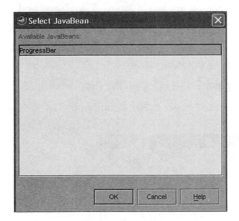

4. Select `ProgressBar` and click OK. This will bring up the Palette Category dialog box shown in Figure 19.9.

5. Select the Swing (Other) palette and select OK. `ProgressBar`'s icon is now in the Swing (Other) palette, as shown in Figure 19.10.

FIGURE 19.9

The Palette Category dialog allows you to specify the palette that your bean will reside in.

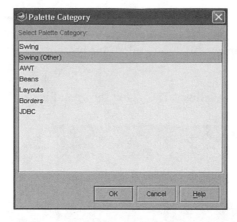

FIGURE 19.10

The Swing (Other) palette now contains the ProgressBar *bean.*

6. To use this bean, you must create a class. Choose File, New, and then Frame. Name the new class `TestProgressBar`.

7. Choose the GUI Editing tab and add a `JPanel` to the frame from the Swing palette. This will give `ProgressBar` a container.

8. Go to the Swing (Other) palette and click on the ProgressBar icon.

9. Click on the panel and see the `ProgressBar` bean appear as shown in Figure 19.11.

FIGURE 19.11

The TestProgressBar *application now contains an instance of the* ProgressBar *bean.*

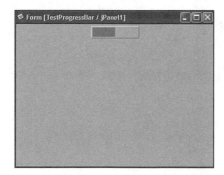

If you look at the code generated by this process, you will see an instance of the `ProgressBar` bean in the application, as shown in Listing 19.5.

LISTING 19.5 The `TestProgressBar` Class

```
/*
 * TestProgressBar.java
 *
 * Created on January 31, 2002, 2:29 PM
 */

package unleashed.ch19;

/**
 *
 * @author  Stephen Potts
 */
public class TestProgressBar extends java.awt.Frame {

    /** Creates new form TestProgressBar */
    public TestProgressBar() {
        initComponents();
    }

    /** This method is called from within the constructor to
     * initialize the form.
     * WARNING: Do NOT modify this code. The content of this method is
     * always regenerated by the Form Editor.
     */
    private void initComponents()
    {
        jPanel1 = new javax.swing.JPanel();
        progressBar2 = new unleashed.ch19.ProgressBar();

        addWindowListener(new java.awt.event.WindowAdapter()
        {
            public void windowClosing(java.awt.event.WindowEvent evt)
            {
                exitForm(evt);
            }
        });

        jPanel1.add(progressBar2);

        add(jPanel1, java.awt.BorderLayout.CENTER);

        pack();
    }

    /** Exit the Application */
    private void exitForm(java.awt.event.WindowEvent evt) {
        System.exit(0);
    }
```

19

JAVABEANS AND
THE JAVA EVENT
MODEL

LISTING 19.5   continued

```
/**
 * @param args the command line arguments
 */
public static void main(String args[]) {
    new TestProgressBar().show();
}


// Variables declaration - do not modify
private javax.swing.JPanel jPanel1;
private unleashed.ch19.ProgressBar progressBar2;
// End of variables declaration

}
```

This code, which is generated by Forte, contains an instance of the `ProgressBar` class that we created earlier in the chapter. Notice that a panel and an instance of the `ProgressBar` JavaBean were created:

```
jPanel1 = new javax.swing.JPanel();
progressBar2 = new unleashed.ch19.ProgressBar();
```

The `ProgressBar` instance is then added to the panel and the panel is added to the frame:

```
jPanel1.add(progressBar2);
add(jPanel1, java.awt.BorderLayout.CENTER);
```

From this example, we see how visual programming works. We were able to create a simple application in Forte that used a progress bar that we built by hand and integrated into the Forte IDE using tools that Forte provided.

Methods, Events, and Properties

The JavaBeans specification states that the three most important features of a JavaBean are the set of properties it exposes, the set of methods it allows other components to call, and the set of events it fires. Now that you understand the process of creating JavaBeans, let's focus on ways to take advantage of the power that comes from these three features.

Methods

Let's examine the role of methods in a JavaBean. The `ProgressBar` class contains methods to get and set the private property variables in the bean. We can also add other methods to classes. Listing 19.6 shows a class that contains a method that is neither a get method nor a set method.

LISTING 19.6 The GreenBean Class

```
/*
 * GreenBean.java
 *
 * Created on April 4, 2002, 10:41 AM
 */

package unleashed.ch19;

import java.io.Serializable;
import java.awt.*;
import java.beans.*;


/**
 *
 * @author  Stephen Potts
 * @version
 */
public class GreenBean extends Canvas implements Serializable

{
    private Color color = Color.green;

    public Color getColor()
    {
        return color;
    }

    public void setColor(Color col)
    {
        this.color = col;
    }

    /** Creates new GreenBean */
    public GreenBean()
    {
        setSize(60,40);
        setBackground(Color.green);
    }

    public void paint (Graphics g)
    {
        g.setColor(color);
        g.fillRect(20,5,20,30);
    }

    public void printoutChange(PropertyChangeEvent evt)
    {
        String changeText = evt.getPropertyName() + " := "
```

Listing 19.6 continued

```
                + evt.getNewValue();
        System.out.println(changeText);
    }
}//class
```

We kept this bean simple so that we can use it later in the chapter when we discuss the bound and `constrained` properties. In addition to the usual methods such as `paint()`, `getColor()`, and `setColor()`, it contains a method called `printoutChange()`. This method accepts a `PropertyChangeEvent` object as input. It examines the event object and obtains the information that it contains. It then prints this information to the console:

```
        String changeText = evt.getPropertyName() + " := "
                + evt.getNewValue();
        System.out.println(changeText);
```

Because this method is public, it can be called from other classes. Unlike the get and set methods, however, this method requires that you provide explicit calls to it from the other classes.

Events

Events are also an important part of JavaBean construction. There are two basic categories of events—standard and custom. A standard event is one that is generated by one of the classes that compose the JDK. These events can be low-level, such as mouse events, or they can be high-level (or semantic), such as `ActionEvent`. Custom events are those that you create yourself by extending either the `EventObject` class or the `AWTEvent` class. In the next section, you will see how one very interesting type of event, the `PropertyChangeEvent`, is communicated between JavaBeans.

Bound and Constrained Properties

In the `ProgressBar` example, you saw how properties are added to the class along with special get and set methods. These methods provide ways for development tools such as Forte to manipulate the beans in their user interfaces. There are two variations of the ordinary properties: bound properties and constrained properties.

A bound property is one that has built-in functionality to notify another JavaBean when there is a change to the property. For instance, you might consider binding a `font` property. If a container bean held six beans with text on them, it would be nice to be able to change the font on all six of them by changing the font of the container. Binding a method in each bean to the `font` property of the container bean would do this.

A constrained property goes even further. In addition to notifying the other beans when a property changes, the listener bean can veto the change. This might be useful if you wanted a container bean to maintain a consistent font in all the beans it contained. If any bean tried to change its font, the container bean would veto it.

Let's look at an example that will make use of the `printoutChange()` method that we created in the `GreenBean` example (Listing 19.6). Recall that `GreenBean` contains a method called `printoutChange()` that accepts a `PropertyChangeEvent` as its parameter:

```
public void printoutChange(PropertyChangeEvent evt)
{
    String changeText = evt.getPropertyName() + " := "
            + evt.getNewValue();
    System.out.println(changeText);
}
```

This method will accept the `Event`, get the values in its variables that pertain to the name of the property that was changed, and then get the new value of the property. When this method is called, the information contained in the `Event` object will be printed to the console. The question that remains is how to call this method when the properties change. JavaBeans that contain bound properties must be written in a special way so that `PropertyChangeEvents` can be sent whenever a bound property changes. Listing 19.7 shows a bean that is capable of sending `PropertyChangeEvents`.

LISTING 19.7   The `ButtonBean` Class

```
/*
 * ButtonBean.java
 *
 * Created on April 4, 2002, 11:38 AM
 */

package unleashed.ch19;

import java.awt.*;
import java.awt.event.*;
import java.beans.*;
import java.io.Serializable;
import java.util.Vector;

/**
 *
 * @author   Stephen Potts
 * @version
 */
public class ButtonBean extends Component implements Serializable
{
```

LISTING 19.7 continued

```java
private boolean debug;
private PropertyChangeSupport pcs=
    new PropertyChangeSupport(this);
private String label;

/** Creates new ButtonBean */
public ButtonBean()
{
    this("ButtonBean");
}

public ButtonBean(String label)
{
    super();
    this.label = label;
    setFont(new Font("Dialog", Font.PLAIN, 12));
    setBackground(Color.lightGray);
}

public synchronized void paint(Graphics g)
{
    int width = getSize().width;
    int height = getSize().height;

    g.setColor(getBackground());
    g.fill3DRect(0, 0, width-1, height-1, false);

    g.setColor(getForeground());
    g.setFont(getFont());

    g.drawRect(2, 2, width-4, height-4);

    g.drawString(label, 10, 18);
}

public void addPropertyChangeListener(PropertyChangeListener pcl)
{
    pcs.addPropertyChangeListener(pcl);
}

public void removePropertyChangeListener(PropertyChangeListener pcl)
{
    pcs.addPropertyChangeListener(pcl);
}

public void setDebug(boolean x)
{
    boolean old = debug;
    debug = x;
```

LISTING 19.7 continued

```
        pcs.firePropertyChange("debug", new Boolean(old),
        new Boolean(x));
}

public boolean getDebug()
{
    return debug;
}

public void setFontSize(int x)
{
    Font old = getFont();
    setFont(new Font(old.getName(), old.getStyle(), x));
    pcs.firePropertyChange("fontSize",
    new Integer(old.getSize()), new Integer(x));
}

public int getFontSize()
{
    return getFont().getSize();
}

public void setFont(Font f)
{
    Font old = getFont();
    super.setFont(f);
    pcs.firePropertyChange("font", old, f);
}

public void setLabel(String lab)
{
    String oldLabel = label;
    label = lab;
    pcs.firePropertyChange("label", oldLabel, lab);
}

public String getLabel()
{
    return label;
}

public Dimension getPreferredSize()
{
    FontMetrics fm = getFontMetrics(getFont());
    return new Dimension(fm.stringWidth(label) + 12,
    fm.getMaxAscent() + fm.getMaxDescent() + 8);
}
```

LISTING 19.7   continued

```
public void setForeground(Color c)
{
    Color old = getForeground();;
    super.setForeground(c);
    pcs.firePropertyChange("foreground", old, c);
    repaint();
}

public void setBackground(Color c)
{
    Color old = getBackground();;
    super.setBackground(c);
    pcs.firePropertyChange("background", old, c);
    repaint();
}
}//class
```

The `PropertyChangeEvent` is part of the java.beans package:

```
import java.beans.*;
```

`PropertyChangeSupport` is a utility class for bound properties. It will be used to hold the list of classes that are listening for this class's `PropertyChangeEvents`:

```
private PropertyChangeSupport pcs=
    new PropertyChangeSupport(this);
```

The following two methods allow other beans to register and remove their interest in being notified of changes to bound properties:

```
public void addPropertyChangeListener(PropertyChangeListener pcl)
{
    pcs.addPropertyChangeListener(pcl);
}

public void removePropertyChangeListener(PropertyChangeListener pcl)
{
    pcs.addPropertyChangeListener(pcl);
}
```

All the set methods for the bound properties have to include an additional line of code to fire the property change event. The `firePropertyChange()` method takes three parameters: the name of the property to be changed, the old value being sent, and the new value.

```
public void setFontSize(int x)
{
    Font old = getFont();
    setFont(new Font(old.getName(), old.getStyle(), x));
    pcs.firePropertyChange("fontSize",
    new Integer(old.getSize()), new Integer(x));
}
```

> **Caution**
>
> All the parameters in the `firePropertyChange()` method are sent as objects. Intrinsic types such as `int` must be sent using the object version.

The only task that remains is connecting the two beans together. This is normally done using the development tool's user interface. In this case, we will use the BeanBox application. The process of adding these beans to the BeanBox is identical to the procedure described in the "Deploying JavaBeans" section earlier in this chapter. Follow the same procedure for both the `GreenBean` and the `ButtonBean`.

Next, start the BeanBox and place one instance of `ButtonBean` in the BeanBox along with one instance of `GreenBean`. Highlight the `ButtonBean` instance. From the Edit menu choose Events, then propertyChange, then propertyChange again as shown in Figure 19.12.

FIGURE 19.12

The GreenBean *listens for changes to the* ButtonBean*'s properties and prints them to the console.*

A red line will be attached to your mouse cursor. Move your mouse cursor over the `GreenBean` and click. This signifies that you want the `GreenBean` to listen to the bound property changes generated by the `ButtonBean`. After clicking, you will see the dialog box shown in Figure 19.13.

FIGURE 19.13

printoutChange *is the* GreenBean *method that handles bound changes.*

19

JAVABEANS AND
THE JAVA EVENT
MODEL

You will see a number of methods that are inherited from GreenBean's superclasses. You will also see the printoutChange() method. Choose this method. Make the BeanBox console visible and change the properties of the ButtonBean using the BeanBox's Properties window. Output for every change you make will appear on the console. It will look similar to what is shown here:

```
debug := true
font := java.awt.Font[family=dialog,name=Dialog,style=italic,size=12]
font := java.awt.Font[family=dialog,name=Dialog,style=italic,size=14]
fontSize := 14
foreground := java.awt.Color[r=255,g=175,b=175]
label := Java Unleashed
```

You can modify this example to do work that meets your requirements by removing the println() statements in the printoutChange() method.

Summary

In this chapter we looked at the role of JavaBeans in the arsenal of Java tools that we can use to solve programming problems. You learned about why visual programming has a following and about some of the advantages that it provides.

Next, we examined the anatomy of a JavaBean and noted what makes it different from an ordinary Java class. We then created a fairly simple bean to illustrate these principles. We deployed the bean using the BeanBox application that Sun distributes to assist us in verifying that a bean is correctly created.

We put our bean into the Forte IDE, and placed it in the Swing (Other) palette. Then we created a simple application visually to see how our code was integrated into a Forte-created application.

Finally, we created a JavaBean that contained bound properties. We created another bean to listen for changes to those properties and wrote them to the console.

Architectural Models and Frameworks

Object-oriented languages have introduced new techniques for code reuse. One of these techniques is using *frameworks*—extendable, object-oriented toolkits that prescribe how to develop an application.

> **Note**
>
> Code reuse sounds like a very old idea. Over time, different techniques for code reuse have been developed. Code libraries, reusable components, and design patterns all facilitate code reuse.

In this chapter we will consider why application frameworks are necessary, what models exist, and how to use a framework. We will see how frameworks are built from the Template Method and Model-View-Controller design patterns.

We will look at Jakarta Struts as an example of a framework. Struts is an open source framework that is extendable and easy to use. Struts implements a framework for building Web applications. It provides basic structure for creating presentation pages and handling user actions. We will use Struts to build a logon application that accepts user input and decides whether the user can enter or not.

> **Note**
>
> You can see the Struts home page at http://jakarta.apache.org/struts.

The Need for Frameworks

Frameworks make our life easy. A programmer follows a set of rules that state what classes to extend, what interfaces to implement, when methods should be called, and so on. Once the programmer does all the prescribed actions, she is done—the system is functioning as expected. As software development is becoming a very competitive and demanding profession, frameworks are used to achieve the following goals:

- Code reuse is the driving force behind many practices in software engineering, including frameworks. A framework is meant to be used over and over in different projects.

- Design reuse is achieved when a framework holds an application together. In fact, the architecture of your entire project can be based on a single framework.

- Work is divided between architects and developers. A team of experienced programmers can create a framework that is followed throughout the company. Similarly, a team of industry experts can develop a framework that is followed by multiple companies in the industry.

- Frameworks allow programmers to extend an application from within by plugging in new classes and modules or by changing the behavior of the existing classes.

In short, frameworks can decrease development time and costs. However, building frameworks comes at the cost of time spent on the initial design. If subsequent projects will benefit from having a framework, designing it is a good thing.

What Is a Framework?

A framework is a set of classes that work together to achieve certain functionality or behavior. A framework targets a specific requirement in your project. However, not every requirement implementation is a framework. Frameworks provide room for growth and are flexible enough to accommodate future improvements without redesign. They may require naming conventions, package names, property names, and other rules that are to be followed when a system changes.

> **Note**
>
> Frameworks are sometimes confused with code libraries. Although both frameworks and libraries facilitate code reuse, there is a clear distinction between the two. Code libraries keep common routines and functions that your application can call. They existed long before object-oriented technologies were developed. Libraries are good for so-called *casual* code reuse. Conversely, frameworks are based on object-oriented design principles. They provide a set of rules dictating how an application can be designed. Thus, frameworks are easier to work with.

Frameworks are often based on object-oriented patterns. A framework can implement a design pattern that is well suited for a specific environment (for example, Java) and type of application (for example, Web applications). A good example of this is the Model-View-Controller (MVC) design pattern. MVC is a popular object-oriented pattern that has been implemented in many frameworks. Java Swing is a framework that is based on the MVC pattern for Java GUI applications. The MVC pattern is also implemented in some J2EE Web applications that consist of servlets and JSPs. In this chapter we will spend some time studying such a framework—Jakarta Struts.

20

**ARCHITECTURAL
MODELS AND
FRAMEWORKS**

> **Note**
>
> Chapter 21, "Design Patterns in Java," discusses Java and J2EE patterns.

Frameworks are application patterns that may be specific to a business domain. For example, a framework may describe how to write an application to sell things on the Internet. This framework may provide a set of base classes that every `sellable` object must implement. In exchange, the framework promises that every `sellable` object will be available for sale on a company Web site. Adding a new item to a Web site is easy—just implement an interface.

Regardless of the application domain or environment, all frameworks use a fundamental pattern of code reuse in object-oriented languages: the Template Method pattern. Let's go over this pattern to get a better understanding of what a framework is.

The Template Method pattern defines a way to change an individual operation without changing the algorithm. A classic example of a Template Method pattern is an application that operates on a document. The document may be a file or a database record. The application wants to treat all types of documents in the same manner without knowing how a particular document is implemented. To do this, the application defines an algorithm to perform various operations on an abstract document, deferring implementation of these methods. Figure 20.1 illustrates `Application`, `Document`, `BaseDocument`, and `ConcreteDocument` classes.

The `Application` class defines a template method `openDocument`. This method defines an algorithm for opening a document by calling various methods on the `Document` interface. The `Document` interface defines basic operations that an `Application` may call. `BaseDocument` provides a default implementation for the methods that the concrete document might consider optional. The `ConcreteDocument` class provides a concrete implementation of the required methods and can override methods from the `BaseDocument` class. Listing 20.1 shows the code for these classes.

> **Note**
>
> You can download the source code for this chapter at the Sams Publishing Web site (www.samspublishing.com).

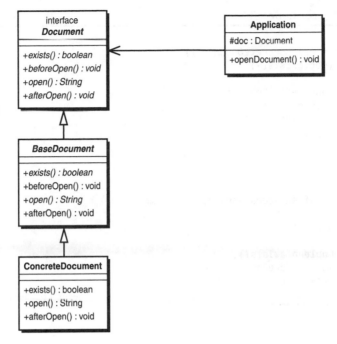

FIGURE 20.1

An example of the Template Method pattern is presented by `Application,` `Document,` `BaseDocument,` *and* `ConcreteDocument` *classes.*

LISTING 20.1 Template Method Implementation

```
package unleashed.ch20.tempmethod;

/**
* Template method pattern example.
*/
public class Application
{
    protected Document doc;

    public Application()
    {
        System.out.println("Application is created");
    }

    public static void main(String[] args)
    {
        Application app = new Application();

        app.openDocument();
    }

    //Defines algorithm to open a document.
    public void openDocument()
```

LISTING 20.1   continued

```java
    {
        doc = new ConcreteDocument();
        if (doc.exists())
        {
            doc.beforeOpen();
            doc.open();
            doc.afterOpen();
        }
    }
}

/**
* Declares required operations for a document
*/
interface Document
{
    public boolean exists();
    public void beforeOpen();
    public String open();
    public void afterOpen();
}

/**
* Provides a base implementation for a document,
* specifying primitive operations and hooks.
*/
abstract class BaseDocument implements Document
{

    public abstract boolean exists();

    public void beforeOpen()
    {
        System.out.println("BaseDocument: default hook
➡  'beforeOpen' is called");
    }

    public abstract String open();

    public void afterOpen()
    {
        System.out.println("BaseDocument: default hook 'afterOpen' is
➡  called");
    }
}

/**
* Implements a concrete document. Must implement the
* primitive operations only. May optionally implement the hooks.
```

LISTING 20.1   continued

```
*/
class ConcreteDocument extends BaseDocument
{
    //primitive operation exists implementation
    public boolean exists()
    {
        System.out.println("ConcreteDocument: primitive operation
    'exists' is called");

        //let's say that this document exists already
        return true;
    }

    //primitive operation open implementation
    public String open()
    {
        System.out.println("ConcreteDocument: primitive operation 'open'
    is called");
        return "New Document";
    }

    //example of a hook implementation
    public void afterOpen()
    {
        System.out.println("ConcreteDocument: hook 'afterOpen' is called");
    }
}
```

Application implements the skeleton of the algorithm inside the openDocument method. The Document interface declares all methods that a document can implement. BaseDocument refines it further by providing a default implementation for methods beforeOpen and afterOpen. The ConcreteDocument class extends BaseDocument, so it must only implement the abstract methods exists and open. These methods are called *primitive operations*. Additionally, ConcreteDocument may override the beforeOpen and afterOpen methods. These methods are sometimes called *hooks*. Both primitive operations and hooks are also called *callback methods*.

Listing 20.2 shows the output from running the Application class.

LISTING 20.2   Running the Template Method Example

```
Application is created
ConcreteDocument: primitive operation 'exists' is called
BaseDocument: default hook 'beforeOpen' is called
ConcreteDocument: primitive operation 'open' is called
ConcreteDocument: hook 'afterOpen' is called
```

20

ARCHITECTURAL MODELS AND FRAMEWORKS

ConcreteDocument overrides the afterOpen method. The last line of Listing 20.2 shows how ConcreteDocument is called.

> **Tip**
>
> It is not always clear which methods should be primitive operations and which should be optional hooks. Different concrete documents may take advantage of different methods. Try to minimize primitive operations so that it is easy to add a new implementation.

The Template Method pattern defines code reuse in a completely different way than it is defined by a typical code library. A library consists of classes that you can call in your code. You generally have to understand in what order you should call the methods. Using template methods, the framework calls your class—the order of calls is easily shown. Thus, the Template Method pattern defines an inverted control structure.

Template methods are so widespread in object-oriented languages such as Java that people do not always realize their importance. Nonetheless, the Template Method pattern defines how basic frameworks are built. You can find examples of this pattern in various chapters of this book, but we usually don't draw attention to it. We will study a widely used framework that uses a template method a little later in the chapter.

Overview of the MVC Pattern

Model-View-Controller (MVC) is a design pattern that has been implemented by many frameworks. Let's first go over the MVC pattern before seeing how it can be implemented in a framework.

MVC is used in so many types of architectures that it is difficult to pinpoint what it is best at. The simplest example of MVC use is probably a standalone GUI application such as Microsoft Excel. You can open a Microsoft Excel spreadsheet in different windows as a spreadsheet, a graph, a chart, and so on. All these windows present the same data, which is located in the same spreadsheet file, and they are synchronized with the data changes. Yet all the windows show the data in a unique way. The MVC pattern prescribes how multiple windows, or Views, can look at the same data simultaneously. In MVC terminology, the data is called the Model. Each Model presentation is shown in a View. The additional component that decouples the Model from the View is called the Controller. Figure 20.2 depicts MVC architecture.

FIGURE 20.2

MVC typically consists of these three modules, although View and Controller may be combined in one class in some implementations.

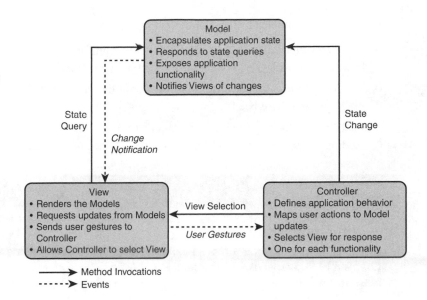

The Model represents the state of the system. The Model can be queried for its state changes by the Views. The Model can also send state change notifications to the Views.

Views present the Model in a particular way. They request updates from the Model if the Model is modified. Views also send the user actions to the Controller. Examples of user actions include button presses and mouse movements. Various Views can have different types of user actions. Further, the same data can be presented by many different Views. When a user performs an action, the appropriate View accepts it and sends a message to the Controller. Thus, the Controller does not have to know what View the message came from. Nor does the Controller have to worry about how the user expresses the action.

The Controller is effectively positioned between the Model and the Views. The Controller accepts input from the user and sends it to the Model in a uniform way.

Let's see how a GUI application can use the MVC pattern. When you open a spreadsheet in Microsoft Excel, you are essentially asking the Controller to give you a standard spreadsheet View of a certain file. The Controller creates a spreadsheet View and registers it with the Model created from the spreadsheet file. The spreadsheet View opens up and queries the Model for data. Then the View displays the data. If you enter a new cell in the spreadsheet, the View sends the new cell input to the Controller. The Controller extracts the cell number and the cell value and sends them to the Model. The Model notifies all registered Views that there is a new cell. In the simplest example, our View already knows about the data and can just ignore it. However, if you open multiple spreadsheet Views, they will need to be refreshed to show a new cell.

20

ARCHITECTURAL MODELS AND FRAMEWORKS

Our spreadsheet example has these important interactions:

- The Controller sends updates to the Model in a uniform way. The Controller knows how to work with user input controls and GUI elements.

- The Model treats Views uniformly by sending the same notification messages to all the Views that have been registered.

- Each View asks the Model for the data that it specifically needs to render itself. Adding a new View is easy because the Model does not change.

> **Note**
>
> In Figure 20.2, some interactions are shown as events and others are method calls. Technically, all the interactions could be implemented as method calls. However, events provide a more flexible and standard way to send messages. Chapter 19, "JavaBeans and the Java Event Model," discusses the event framework in Java.

The spreadsheet application is not the only example of how you can use the MVC pattern. A J2EE Web application can also take advantage of it. Of course, the nature of Web applications brings additional challenges. For example, a browser is quite limited in its ability to present material. Although Java applets are used in some applications, the most common clients are still HTML pages. An HTML page is portable, but it cannot listen for state changes from the Model as a normal View would do. This detail makes the MVC pattern in Web applications look different from other implementations of MVC.

> **Note**
>
> For the definition of a Web application in J2EE, see the J2EE BluePrints tutorial at http://java.sun.com/blueprints/guidelines/ designing_enterprise_applications/apmTOC.html. Chapter 4 of this tutorial, "The Web Tier," covers various technologies that can be used to create J2EE Web applications.

Let's go through the interaction between a user and a Web application created using the MVC pattern. Every time a user submits an HTTP request, it comes to the front Controller. The front Controller accepts all HTTP requests and decides which View should be sent back to the user as an HTTP response. The Controller is typically implemented as a Java Servlet because it does not have any presentation code. The front Controller retrieves parameters from the request and updates the Model.

> **Note**
>
> Chapter 4, "Application Development with JSP and Servlets," discusses Java Servlets and JSP. This chapter only describes how to use them within the framework of Jakarta Struts. Therefore, this chapter does not cover how a JSP can display data.

The Model classes persist the application state. To make persistence easier, they can be implemented as Enterprise JavaBeans or some other technology. As mentioned before, the Model in a Web application may not be able to notify a View because a View is an HTML page that is not capable of receiving events. So the View can only be updated when a user asks for an update.

Figure 20.3 depicts an MVC pattern in a Web application with JSPs and Java Servlets.

FIGURE 20.3

The MVC pattern in a J2EE Web application.

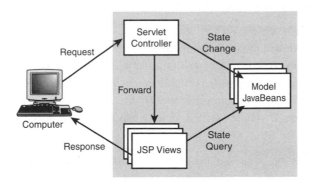

As you can see, the Controller accepts requests from the user's machine and sends back the output of View JSPs. The interactions between the View, Controller, and Model are conceptually similar to our spreadsheet example.

An MVC Implementation in the Jakarta Struts Framework

Jakarta Struts, or simply Struts, is an open source project that implements the MVC pattern in Java using Java Servlets and JavaServer Pages (JSP).

Struts is essentially one of the implementations of the MVC pattern in a J2EE Web application. It is easy to use and as a result has gained popularity among developers.

> **Tip**
>
> Although it is possible to write Web applications without any framework, big projects cannot succeed without it. Without a framework, even a small change can result in a lot of new code, making maintenance more difficult.

The Struts framework provides the following main components:

- A Controller servlet that can be configured to forward requests to Views. The Controller servlet can be configured in an XML file called `struts-config.xml`. We will see an example of this file shortly.
- Various base classes for Controller, Model, and View to assist development. In addition to the MVC classes, Struts provides utility classes to support automatic population of JavaBeans, message internationalization, and XML parsing.
- Tag libraries to display dynamic HTML in the View JSPs.

Struts also provides a blank Web application, struts-blank.war, that you can deploy in a Web container. We will use the blank application as a basis for our example application in Struts. Our example application will mimic a logon application. It will have a Welcome page, a Logon page where a user enters her username/password, and a Success page that is displayed if the logon succeeds. In this small example we will see how to configure the Struts Controller servlet, how to handle users' requests, and how to write View JSPs using the Struts tag libraries.

The blank application should be unJARred in a separate directory. Once you unJAR it, you will see that it has a `WEB-INF` directory with a `web.xml` file. the `web.xml` file is configured to use the Struts Controller servlet, so we can start writing a Struts Web application. Listing 20.3 shows the `web.xml` file that comes with the blank application.

LISTING 20.3 Logon Application `web.xml` File

```
<?xml version="1.0" encoding="ISO-8859-1"?>

<!DOCTYPE web-app
  PUBLIC "-//Sun Microsystems, Inc.//DTD Web Application 2.2//EN"
  "http://java.sun.com/j2ee/dtds/web-app_2_2.dtd">

<web-app>
```

LISTING 20.3   continued

```xml
<!-- Standard Action Servlet Configuration (with debugging) -->
<servlet>
  <servlet-name>action</servlet-name>
  <servlet-class>org.apache.struts.action.ActionServlet</servlet-class>
  <init-param>
    <param-name>application</param-name>
    <param-value>ApplicationResources</param-value>
  </init-param>
  <init-param>
    <param-name>config</param-name>
    <param-value>/WEB-INF/struts-config.xml</param-value>
  </init-param>
  <init-param>
    <param-name>debug</param-name>
    <param-value>2</param-value>
  </init-param>
  <init-param>
    <param-name>detail</param-name>
    <param-value>2</param-value>
  </init-param>
  <init-param>
    <param-name>validate</param-name>
    <param-value>true</param-value>
  </init-param>
  <load-on-startup>2</load-on-startup>
</servlet>


<!-- Standard Action Servlet Mapping -->
<servlet-mapping>
  <servlet-name>action</servlet-name>
  <url-pattern>*.do</url-pattern>
</servlet-mapping>


<!-- The Usual Welcome File List -->
<welcome-file-list>
  <welcome-file>index.jsp</welcome-file>
</welcome-file-list>


<!-- Struts Tag Library Descriptors -->
<taglib>
  <taglib-uri>/WEB-INF/struts-bean.tld</taglib-uri>
  <taglib-location>/WEB-INF/struts-bean.tld</taglib-location>
</taglib>
```

20

ARCHITECTURAL MODELS AND FRAMEWORKS

LISTING 20.3 continued

```
<taglib>
  <taglib-uri>/WEB-INF/struts-html.tld</taglib-uri>
  <taglib-location>/WEB-INF/struts-html.tld</taglib-location>
</taglib>

<taglib>
  <taglib-uri>/WEB-INF/struts-logic.tld</taglib-uri>
  <taglib-location>/WEB-INF/struts-logic.tld</taglib-location>
</taglib>

</web-app>
```

The web.xml file specifies three things: the Controller servlet, the default Welcome page, and the Struts tag libraries. The Controller servlet action has a few initialization parameters, the most interesting of which is config. The config parameter specifies a configuration file that defines the behavior of the Controller. We will go over the configuration file shortly. Suffice it to say that the configuration file is driving your Struts Web application—it defines which Views are shown to the user and when they are shown.

Next you can see the Welcome page declaration. It is index.jsp. Right under the Welcome page we have the declarations for three standard tag libraries.

> **Note**
>
> web.xml is a main descriptor for J2EE Web applications. You can study it in greater detail at http://java.sun.com/blueprints/guidelines/designing_enterprise_applications/apmTOC.html.

Creating the Controller in Struts

The Struts Controller is a front servlet that gets user requests, handles user actions, and forwards users to the next View. The Controller's behavior is defined by an XML configuration file that we have specified in the web.xml file. The Struts blank application includes a sample of this file with various sections commented out. The main purpose of the configuration file is to define mappings between URIs and action classes. Action classes are similar to event handlers that are executed when a URI is called.

The Struts configuration file acts like a traffic cop at an intersection. It decides what action is executed next and what page is displayed after the action is finished.

Listing 20.4 shows the configuration file for our logon application.

LISTING 20.4   Struts Configuration File

```xml
<?xml version="1.0" encoding="ISO-8859-1" ?>

<!DOCTYPE struts-config PUBLIC
 "-//Apache Software Foundation//DTD Struts Configuration 1.0//EN"
 "http://jakarta.apache.org/struts/dtds/struts-config_1_0.dtd">

<struts-config>

  <!-- ========== Form Bean Definitions =============== -->
  <form-beans>

    <!-- Example logon form bean -->
    <form-bean     name="logonForm"
                   type="unleashed.ch20.struts.LogonForm"/>

  </form-beans>

  <!-- ========== Global Forward Definitions =========== -->
  <global-forwards>
    <forward    name="success"     path="/logonsuccess.jsp"/>
  </global-forwards>

  <!-- ========== Action Mapping Definitions =========== -->
  <action-mappings>

    <action    path="/logon"
               type="unleashed.ch20.struts.LogonAction"
               name="logonForm"
               scope="request"
               input="/logon.jsp">
        <forward name="success"     path="/logonsuccess.jsp"/>

    </action>


  </action-mappings>

</struts-config>
```

Let's go through this file. It has three types of declarations: form-bean, forward, and action. The form-bean declaration serves as the View component, so we will discuss it a bit later. The forward declaration can be one of two types: a global forward or a local forward. Both forward type maps are expressed by the same XML element:

```xml
<forward    name="success"     path="/logonsuccess.jsp"/>
```

forward is a mapping of a name to a URI relative to the application URI. When the Controller sends a response to the user it can use a forward name instead of the actual page name. We will see how this is done in a moment.

The difference between a global and a local forward is that a global forward can be called from any action, whereas a local forward can only be called from the action to which the forward belongs. Listing 20.5 shows an action with a local forward.

LISTING 20.5   A Local Forward in the Struts Configuration File

```
<action    path="/logon"
           type="unleashed.ch20.struts.LogonAction"
           name="logonForm"
           scope="request"
           input="/logon.jsp">
      <forward name="success"       path="/logonsuccess.jsp"/>

</action>
```

The XML in Listing 20.5 shows a declaration of `action` with a local forward. `action` is a class that is called by the Controller when the user requests a URI. For example, URI `/logon` in an HTTP request tells the Controller to instantiate the `unleashed.ch20.struts.LogonAction` class and call appropriate methods on it. `action`'s attributes specify what class to instantiate and what data to pass to the action. An action class is usually interested in some data that the user entered on an HTML form. So each action can accept an `ActionForm` object that is declared by the `name` attribute. The `scope` attribute specifies that the action form exists only as long as the HTTP request lasts.

Let's look at our logon action class. An action class must extend `org.apache.struts.action.Action`, which provides the basic framework methods. Also, an action must implement the `perform` method. Listing 20.6 shows the code for the logon action.

LISTING 20.6   Logon Action Class

```
package unleashed.ch20.struts;

import java.io.IOException;
import java.util.*;
import javax.servlet.*;
import javax.servlet.http.*;
import org.apache.struts.action.*;

public class LogonAction extends Action
{

    public ActionForward perform(ActionMapping mapping,
                ActionForm form,
```

LISTING 20.6 continued

```
                HttpServletRequest request,
                HttpServletResponse response)
    throws IOException, ServletException
    {

    // Retrieve parameters from the form

        String username = ((LogonForm) form).getUsername();
        String password = ((LogonForm) form).getPassword();
        System.out.println("Username " + username + " Password " + password);

    // Forward control to the success page
        return (mapping.findForward("success"));

    }



}
```

The logon action retrieves a username and password from the action form and forwards the user to the next View, which is found using the name of a local or global forward declaration:

```
return (mapping.findForward("success"));
```

The goal of the `perform` method is to collect data, pass it to the business objects, and return an `ActionForward` object.

As you can see, the Controller servlet is just the starting point in the framework. In order to make the Controller work, a programmer has to provide the configuration file that maps URIs to actions and declares forwards. A programmer also has to write all action classes that retrieve the user input from the request, do something with it, and choose a forward.

Tip

The Struts documentation advises against putting any business logic inside the `Action` class. `Action` should always call some other classes to do the actual work. Actions should only provide navigation from a request to a View.

20

ARCHITECTURAL MODELS AND FRAMEWORKS

Creating a View in Struts

Each action can receive an object that holds user input. This object is called `ActionForm` and is really just a JavaBean with getters and setters for all the data fields. A programmer has to write an action form class to extend the `org.apache.struts.action.ActionForm` class. The action form is declared in the Controller configuration file in the `form-bean` element, as shown in Listing 20.7.

LISTING 20.7   The Logon Form Declaration in the Struts Configuration File

```
<form-beans>

  <!-- Example logon form bean -->
  <form-bean      name="logonForm"
                  type="unleashed.ch20.struts.LogonForm"/>

</form-beans>
```

The action form bean has the name `logonForm`. This name is used later in the same configuration file to specify that it will be passed to an action. Listing 20.8 shows this.

LISTING 20.8   The Form Name Is Used in the Action Declaration

```
<action   path="/logon"
          type="unleashed.ch20.struts.LogonAction"
          name="logonForm"
          scope="request"
          input="/logon.jsp">
       <forward name="success"     path="/logonsuccess.jsp"/>

  </action>
```

The action form bean has getters and setters to provide access to the data fields. Listing 20.9 shows our logon action form.

LISTING 20.9   Logon Form Class

```
package unleashed.ch20.struts;
import javax.servlet.http.HttpServletRequest;
import org.apache.struts.action.*;

public class LogonForm extends ActionForm
{
    /**
    * The password.
    */
```

LISTING 20.9 continued

```java
private String password = null;

/**
 * The username.
 */
private String username = null;

/**
 * Gets the password.
 */
public String getPassword()
{
    return password;
}

/**
 * Sets the password.
 *
 * @param password The new password
 */
public void setPassword(String password)
{
    this.password = password;
}

/**
 * Gets the username.
 */
public String getUsername()
{
    return username;
}

/**
 * Sets the username.
 *
 * @param username The new username
 */
public void setUsername(String username)
{
    this.username = username;
}

/**
 * Validates username and password.
 */
public ActionErrors validate(ActionMapping mapping,
                             HttpServletRequest request)
```

LISTING 20.9   continued

```
    {

        ActionErrors errors = new ActionErrors();
        if ((username == null) || (username.length() < 1))
            errors.add("username", new ActionError("error.username.required"));
        if ((password == null) || (password.length() < 1))
            errors.add("password", new ActionError("error.password.required"));

        return errors;

    }
}
```

The logon form bean has two fields: a password and a username. Additionally, a form
bean can provide a validate method so that the user input is validated before it gets to
the action.

> **Note**
>
> Even though action form beans keep state information, they are not considered
> the Model classes. They are only instantiated by the framework for an action to
> make it easier to get to the data. Action form beans may have a session scope,
> in which case they stay alive for the duration of the HTTP session. Yet their pur-
> pose is not the same as that of the Model.

Finally, the Struts framework provides support for creating the View portion of the MVC
pattern. Views are written as JSPs with the help of the Struts tag libraries. Struts provides
several tag libraries to display HTML and access the action form beans. The logon application has three JSP pages: index.jsp, logon.jsp, and logonsuccess.jsp. Listing
20.10 shows logon.jsp.

LISTING 20.10   Logon JSP with Struts Tags

```
<%@ page language="java" %>
<%@ taglib uri="/WEB-INF/struts-bean.tld" prefix="bean" %>
<%@ taglib uri="/WEB-INF/struts-html.tld" prefix="html" %>

<html:html locale="true">
<head>
<title><bean:message key="logon.title"/></title>
```

LISTING 20.10 continued

```
<html:base/>
</head>
<body bgcolor="white">

<html:errors/>

<html:form action="/logon" focus="username">
<table border="0" width="100%">

  <tr>
    <th align="right">
      <bean:message key="prompt.username"/>
    </th>
    <td align="left">
      <html:text property="username" size="16" maxlength="16"/>
    </td>
  </tr>

  <tr>
    <th align="right">
      <bean:message key="prompt.password"/>
    </th>
    <td align="left">
      <html:password property="password" size="16" maxlength="16"
                     redisplay="false"/>
    </td>
  </tr>

  <tr>
    <td align="right">
      <html:submit property="submit" value="Submit"/>
    </td>
    <td align="left">
      <html:reset/>
    </td>
  </tr>

</table>

</html:form>

</body>
</html:html>
```

An important line of Listing 20.10 is the one on which a form action is declared:

```
<html:form action="/logon" focus="username">
```

The action URI must appear as it is declared in the Controller configuration file. Further, the code has input tags for different HTML input types. For example, the username input type looks like this:

```
<html:text property="username" size="16" maxlength="16"/>
```

In addition to the input tags, all the messages on the page are displayed using this tag:

```
<bean:message key="logon.title"/>
```

> **Note**
>
> You can read more about tag libraries at http://java.sun.com/products/jsp/taglibraries.html.

The Struts framework uses Java resource bundles to display internationalized messages. The name of the resource bundle is specified in the web.xml file as an initialization parameter of the Controller servlet. Listing 20.11 shows this portion of the configuration file.

LISTING 20.11   Message File

```
<init-param>
    <param-name>application</param-name>
    <param-value>ApplicationResources</param-value>
</init-param>
```

In this case, the name of the resource bundle is ApplicationResources.properties, and it must be in the root directory of our classes.

All the messages that we want internationalized are stored in the resource bundle. The messages are just name/value pairs, as shown in Listing 20.12.

LISTING 20.12   Resource Bundle Where All Messages Are Stored

```
index.title=Struts Example Application
index.heading=Struts Example Application.
index.message=This example shows a simple logon application written
in Jakarta Struts.
index.logon=Logon page
prompt.password=Password:
prompt.password2=(Repeat) Password:
prompt.username=Username:
logon.title=Struts Example Logon Page
logon.success=Logon Successful!
```

Once the messages are provided in a resource bundle, you can access them from your View JSPs using the Struts tags. The messages are accessed by a tag message, as in this portion of `index.jsp`:

```
<bean:message key="logon.title"/>
```

This tag displays the value of the key `logon.title` from the resource bundle.

Creating the Model in Struts

Struts does not provide much help for the Model. Other than some general recommendations, there is no support for persistence. This is okay, though, as you are free to use any available technology to support the Model. The Struts documentation recommends using JavaBeans.

The logon application does not contain any Model classes because they would not demonstrate any Struts functionality. A developer can implement the Model classes to persist the user input to a database or do whatever the application requires.

> **Note**
>
> Struts makes a modest effort to assist you with database persistence by providing a simple connection pool. However, most commercial Web containers provide a superior implementation for a connection pool, so the Struts version is rarely used.

Running the Logon Application

To run the logon application on WebLogic 6.x you can copy the `strutsapp` directory to the deployment directory. WebLogic will deploy it automatically if hot deployment is enabled. Otherwise, you have to deploy the Web application through the administrative console. Once the application is deployed, you can point your browser to the application URL, which will take the form `http://yourserver:yourport/strutsapp`. You should see the first page, which is shown in Figure 20.4. Follow the link, enter any name and password, and press Submit to see the logon success page. The application could not be any simpler, yet it utilizes all the main features of the Struts framework.

20

ARCHITECTURAL MODELS AND FRAMEWORKS

> **Note**
>
> See the WebLogic documentation at `http://edocs.bea.com/wls/docs61/index.html` for information on how to package and deploy Web applications. Struts does not need any extra configuration to run on WebLogic 6.x. However, you should check the Struts documentation at `http://jakarta.apache.org/struts/installation.html` before you deploy it on another Web container.

FIGURE 20.4

Running the logon application.

Figure 20.4 shows the first page of the logon application. You can click on the link to see the actual logon page. Enter any text for a username and password and click Submit. You will see the final page, which says that logon was successful. Although the logon application is very simple, it demonstrates how the Struts framework works. It shows how to separate the View pages from the Controller classes. In fact, it gives you a chance to think about how the application will flow from one screen to another. At the end of the application design, all the Views and the Controller and Model classes are declared in the Struts configuration file, so it is easy to understand, document, and maintain the application.

Summary

In this chapter, you learned about development frameworks. You looked at examples of how template methods are used in frameworks. You also learned how the Struts framework is used to build Web applications. The Struts framework implements both the Template Method pattern and the Model-View-Controller pattern.

Frameworks provide a powerful technique for code reuse and extensibility. While code libraries have existed in software engineering for quite some time, frameworks are a new approach based on object-oriented principles. The Template Method design pattern is fundamental to understanding modern application models and frameworks. From the object-oriented design perspective, many application frameworks rely on the Template Method pattern as well as other design patterns. However, a framework is more than a pattern—it is a set of classes, rules, and procedures that define how to create an application.

Model-View-Controller (MVC) is a popular design pattern that has found its way into many frameworks. MVC separates data from presentation, making it easy to change one or the other without redesigning the framework. The Model keeps application data, Views are responsible for presentation, and the Controller links the two, effectively decoupling them.

While MVC is a valuable design pattern for many applications, it is not a framework. MVC does not specify what interfaces should be implemented, what environment and language should be used, and what business purpose it serves. A good framework should clearly define classes, interfaces, callback methods, and ways to extend the design.

An example of a framework that implements the MVC pattern is Jakarta Struts. Struts defines how a JSP-servlet Web application can be created. It is an open source framework that provides a front Controller servlet, base classes to handle user input, tag libraries, and other utilities for Web application development.

Good design provides for future extensions. Often an application has several frameworks built into it. Each framework should clearly define what purpose it serves. What are the interfaces, methods, and classes that define a framework? How can the existing functionality be changed, extended, or removed? Imagine yourself as somebody who will use your framework. How easy to use and elegant is it? You should address all these questions when designing a framework.

20

ARCHITECTURAL
MODELS AND
FRAMEWORKS

CHAPTER 21

Design Patterns in Java

Design patterns are reusable design practices used in object-oriented languages. Reuse of design between different projects allows us to increase productivity in software development. You can increase your development team's productivity and decrease development time by using design patterns. This is probably the biggest reason that design patterns are so popular among software architects. You can find hundreds of descriptions of similar patterns in various publications. In this chapter, we will focus on the most useful patterns, which can help you in your next project.

Generally, design patterns do not assume any specific language or environment. However, it is easy to reuse a pattern if it is described in the syntax of the relevant language. That's why we will go over the examples of the patterns written in Java. This chapter gives real examples of some of the patterns that you can reuse in your projects.

Although our examples explain how to implement patterns with simple Java objects, many design patterns are also used in the J2EE environment, where objects are remote Enterprise JavaBeans (EJB). Implementing a design pattern using EJB is different; therefore, we will show two examples of design patterns implemented in EJB: business delegate and command.

The Need for Patterns

These are some of the features that make design patterns an indispensable tool for software architects:

- Reusable design—Everybody in the software industry works under tight schedules. As competition increases, many companies are looking for ways to reuse code, designs, and even ideas. Such reuse of design has resulted in small reusable design blueprints: design patterns. This does not mean that a design pattern is a breakthrough invention; you can create your own design patterns. However, software design is often a long, iterative process that involves breaking a large system into smaller and smaller subsystems. Reusable design of these small components can dramatically increase designers' productivity.

- Tried and true—Despite our demanding schedules, we still have to create well-thought-out designs. If the system is inflexible, difficult to change, or difficult to maintain, it is going to fail and be replaced by a better design. So how does an architect know that his design is ready to withstand the test of time? He uses patterns that he and others have used many times and that are proven to be adaptable to change. Sometimes you have used these patterns yourself; often, they were used by other architects and make sense to you. In short, you can be confident that your design is based on the knowledge that was accumulated in the industry.

- Common vocabulary—During the process of creating a software system, many people collaborate to design and implement different pieces. Unobstructed communication is essential to the success of the project. The software architects must be able to clearly convey their ideas to the members of the team. Evidently, we need a common vocabulary of software design. For this, software architects use design patterns. By mentioning the name of a design pattern, you can easily explain to your peers how you are planning to implement a piece of the system. You can also use the well-known design patterns in your documentation, making it very easy for anybody to improve and maintain the system. Thus, the software design patterns give us a common vocabulary that is necessary for teamwork.

Java Patterns

This section presents some of the most commonly used design patterns in Java. Each of the following subsections talks about an individual pattern. Design patterns are usually identified by their names. Thus, every subsection is named after the design pattern that it discusses. This will enable you to use this chapter as a reference when needed. Each subsection has a completely independent example of how the design pattern is used. Feel free to reuse example code in your projects.

Singleton

Often we need to provide a central point of access to a resource. In some cases we only want one object to be the gatekeeper for a resource. An example of such a situation is a connection pool. Even though there may be many database connections, there should be only one connection pool. In this case, the connection pool class must be designed so that it does not allow multiple instances of the connection pool to coexist. The class itself must restrict access to the constructor of the connection pool.

The singleton design pattern shows how to control access to a resource. It is implemented as a class that is designed to keep track of the number of objects of its class that exist. This is achieved by restricting access to the constructors. Instead of calling class constructors, we call a static class method. Inside this method, we can control whether a new instance is created or the existing objects are reused.

Typically, the static method checks whether an object of the singleton class has already been instantiated. If there are no instances, the static method calls a protected constructor to create a new instance; otherwise, it returns an existing object. Hence, we never have more than one object in the system.

Singleton Example

The implementation of the singleton pattern in Java is straightforward: The constructors are declared protected, while a static public method is used to acquire an object of the singleton class. Listing 21.1 demonstrates a singleton connection pool class. The static method `getInstance` is responsible for controlling how many instances of the `ConnectionPool` class exist. The method calls the constructor `ConnectionPool` only if no objects have been instantiated.

LISTING 21.1   Singleton Connection Pool

```
package unleashed.ch21.singleton;

/**
* Singleton Connection Pool
*/
public class ConnectionPool
{

    //only one instance is needed
    private static ConnectionPool instance;

    private ConnectionPool()
    {
        //code to instantiate the object
        System.out.println("Creating the single instance of connection pool");
    }

    /**
    * Gets one instance of the connection pool.
    */
    public static ConnectionPool getInstance()
    {
        if(instance != null)
        {
            //give access to the existing object
            System.out.println("Getting existing instance of connection pool");
            return instance;
        }
        else
        {
            //no objects exist yet - create one
            instance = new ConnectionPool();
            return instance;
        }
    }

    public static void main(String[] args)
    {
```

LISTING 21.1 continued

```
        System.out.println("Get connection pool first time");

        ConnectionPool cPool = ConnectionPool.getInstance();

        System.out.println("Get connection pool second time");

        ConnectionPool anotherPool = ConnectionPool.getInstance();
    }
}
```

The ConnectionPool class has a static variable instance that holds a handle to the single connection pool. The getInstance method checks whether the variable instance is equal to null each time a connection pool is requested. A new connection pool is instantiated only once and is assigned to the variable instance for future calls.

The example produces this output:

```
Get connection pool first time
Creating the single instance of connection pool
Get connection pool second time
Getting existing instance of connection pool
```

It is clear from the output that a connection pool is created only once, the first time it is requested. The subsequent call to get a connection pool returns the existing pool.

Caution

The singleton class is hard to extend. The child class requires a new static method and a new constructor. If you intend to extend a singleton, you should keep the code of the getInstance method to a minimum; instead, put the logic in a separate protected method that is inherited and call it inside the child methods.

Tip

Singletons should be designed to execute concurrently, because many threads will access the same singleton object. This may produce unexpected behavior if you don't take care of synchronization. Make sure that multiple threads access resources concurrently and synchronize portions of code or methods.

This practice may lead to bottlenecks. Therefore, singletons should not contain any heavy processing. They are mere gatekeepers. If a singleton object takes substantial execution time and is not multithreaded, it will be a bottleneck.

Enumeration

Enumerations are commonly used in many programming languages to represent an object with a fixed number of states. For example, a program that models a traffic light will have three colors: green, yellow, and red. An order processing system might have fixed states to represent an order's status—for instance, order accepted, order in process, and order fulfilled. Enumerations typically define a set of valid states in which an object can exist. Typically, an enumeration is a data type built into the language. However, the Java programming language does not provide enumerations. A lot of programmers view this as a Java shortcoming. Evidently, the designers of Java felt that the enumeration type did not fit in the pure object-oriented nature of the language. To simulate enumerations, many programmers use final constants in an interface. However, the enumeration pattern suggests a better solution to this problem. It models an enumeration as a set of prede-fined objects of the same type. All the objects in the set are declared `final` so they cannot be changed by the user of the enumeration. In addition, because the enumeration states are objects, they can carry more information such as their names and descriptions. The main advantage to the interface constants is that all the states represent the same type. This can be demonstrated by an example.

Enumeration Example

Imagine a program that simulates the street traffic at an intersection. The street traffic moves or waits depending on a traffic light signal. The traffic signal can only be one of three colors: green, yellow, or red. This makes a traffic signal a perfect candidate to use the enumeration pattern. The three signals will be expressed by the enumeration class `TrafficSignal`. The `Traffic` class has a method that regulates the traffic. The code for both classes is shown in Listing 21.2.

LISTING 21.2   Enumeration Design Pattern Example

```
package unleashed.ch21.enumeration;

import java.util.*;

/**
 * Traffic Signal is an enumeration of traffic signals.
 */
class TrafficSignal
{
    private final String name;

    //Ordinal of next type is created
    private static int nextOrdinal = 0;
```

LISTING 21.2 continued

```java
    //Assign an ordinal to this type
    private final int ordinal = nextOrdinal++;

    protected TrafficSignal(String name)
    {
        this.name = name;
    }

    public String getName()
    {
        return name;
    }


    public static final TrafficSignal GREEN= new TrafficSignal("GREEN");

    public static final TrafficSignal YELLOW = new TrafficSignal("YELLOW");

    public static final TrafficSignal RED = new TrafficSignal("RED");


    /**
    * Overrides the Object equals method.
    */
    public boolean equals(Object o)
    {
        return ordinal == ((TrafficSignal)o).ordinal;
    }


}

/**
* Traffic simulator.
*/

public class Traffic
{
    /**
    * Traffic moves according to the signal.
    */
    public String move(TrafficSignal light)
    {
        if(light.equals(TrafficSignal.GREEN))
            return "Signal is green. Traffic is moving.";
        else if(light.equals(TrafficSignal.YELLOW))
            return "Signal is yellow. Traffic is stopping.";
        else if(light.equals(TrafficSignal.RED))
            return "Signal is red. Traffic is waiting.";
```

LISTING 21.2 continued

```
        else
            return "UNKNOWN SIGNAL";
    }

    public static void main(String[] args)
    {
        Traffic traffic = new Traffic();

        System.out.println("Starting the traffic signal");

        System.out.println(traffic.move(TrafficSignal.GREEN));
        System.out.println(traffic.move(TrafficSignal.YELLOW));
        System.out.println(traffic.move(TrafficSignal.RED));

        System.out.println("Shutting down the signal");


    }

}
```

The `TrafficSignal` class defines three final static objects of its type: `GREEN`, `YELLOW`, and `RED`. The constructor is declared `protected` so no other objects can be created. All three objects have names that can be used for logging and other purposes. The `Traffic` class uses the enumeration objects to decide whether the traffic should move or not. It accesses the enumeration objects as static class variables:

```
TrafficSignal.YELLOW
```

Note that the method `move` accepts one argument of type `TrafficSignal`. This ensures that nothing else will be passed to this method except for the valid enumeration objects. This type safety makes the enumeration pattern very useful, because the argument shows exactly what type of data is expected.

We get this output when we run the example:

```
Starting the traffic signal
Signal is green. Traffic is moving.
Signal is yellow. Traffic is stopping.
Signal is red. Traffic is waiting.
Shutting down the signal
```

After the traffic signal is started, the green signal is passed to the `move` method. The green signal indicates that the traffic can move. Next, the yellow signal is passed to the `move` method and the traffic prepares to stop. Finally, the traffic stands by on the red signal.

> **Note**
>
> Enumeration should not replace inheritance. If an object has a fixed set of states that are simple data fields, use the enumeration pattern. However, if the object has different kinds of states that show different types of behavior, use inheritance and polymorphism.

In the move method, the Traffic class has to compare enumeration objects to determine the method behavior. In our example, the enumeration objects can only be compared by their names:

```
if (light.getName().equals("GREEN"))
```

This operation is costly because the Traffic class needs to see the traffic signal state very often. It can be improved by using an additional field in the TrafficSignal class:

```
//Ordinal of next type is created
private static int nextOrdinal = 0;

//Assign an ordinal to this type
private final int ordinal = nextOrdinal++;
```

The static field is a counter that is increased as each new object is created. Now we can override the equals method that takes advantage of our ordinal field.

```
public boolean equals(Object o)
{
    return ordinal == ((TrafficSignal)o).ordinal;
}
```

In the method equals, comparing enumeration objects is equivalent to comparing integers.

> **Note**
>
> The enumeration design pattern has nothing to do with the Enumeration class in the java.util package. Enumeration in the java.util package is a misnamed implementation of the iterator pattern.

Factory

Imagine a Java class that needs to read a user account from a database. The type of database is still not decided. Moreover, the client is considering switching to a different database sometime after the program is in production. Therefore, the program needs two types of database connections: one for each type of database, because each database requires its own initialization for a connection. How would you design a class to easily migrate from one database to another? For this scenario the factory design pattern prescribes that each type of connection should have its own factory class that knows how to create that connection. Thus, the factory class hides the construction of an object from a client.

Factory Example

Our example shows how to use the factory pattern in a very common situation in which the client class needs to have two different types of connections to the server-side data. The client needs to connect to a database in production and to fake data during development. The database may not be available during development, so the fake connection is used. Once the database is ready, the client class is changed to use the database with minimum effort. The example has two factories, one for each type of connection. Both factories implement the same interface, so the client object can easily switch between them. Listing 21.3 shows the code for the factory pattern example.

LISTING 21.3   Factory Pattern Example

```
package unleashed.ch21.factory;

/**
* Factory pattern example
* Abstract connection factory
*/
interface DataConnectionFactory
{
    /**
    * Gets connection.
    */
    public DataConnection getConnection();

}

/**
* Abstract data storage connection.
*/
interface DataConnection
{
    /**
    * Connection can read data.
    */
    public Object readData();
```

LISTING 21.3 continued

```java
    /**
     * Connection can write data.
     */
    public void writeData(Object object);
}

/**
 * Implements connection factory to for a fake connection.
 */
class FakeConnectionFactory implements DataConnectionFactory
{
    public FakeConnectionFactory()
    {
        System.out.println("Creating fake connection factory");
    }
    //factory specific field
    protected String filename = "datafile.in";

    public DataConnection getConnection()
    {
        //open file for reading
        return new FakeDataConnection();
    }
}

/**
 * Implements connection to fake data
 */
class FakeDataConnection implements DataConnection
{
    public FakeDataConnection()
    {
        System.out.println("Creating fake data connection");
    }

    private String fakeData = "Example fake data";

    public Object readData()
    {
        System.out.println("Reading data from fake data connection");
        return fakeData;
    }

    public void writeData(Object object)
    {
        fakeData = object.toString();
    }
}
```

LISTING 21.3   continued

```java
/**
* Implements connection factory for database connection
*/
class DatabaseConnectionFactory implements DataConnectionFactory
{
    //factory-specific field
    protected String databaseConnectionURL = "database connection string";

    public DataConnection getConnection()
    {
        //code to open connection
        return null;
    }
}

/**
* Client creates a connection factory, gets connection and reads
* data from the
* connection
*/
public class FactoryExample
{

    protected static DataConnectionFactory dataFactory = new
➥ FakeConnectionFactory();

    //protected static DataConnectionFactory dataFactory = new
➥ DatabaseConnectionFactory();

    public static void main(String[] args)
    {
        //get connection to data
        DataConnection connection = dataFactory.getConnection();

        //read data
        Object mydata = connection.readData();

        //print the object
        System.out.println("Read data: " + mydata.toString());
    }
}
```

The FactoryExample class is the client that instantiates an appropriate connection factory, acquires a connection, and reads data. Both connection factories implement the DataConnectionFactory interface, so the client can easily work with either of them. Also, the example only includes the FakeDataConnection class to read data from a fake connection. The database connection is not necessary to demonstrate how the factory

pattern works. However, a new type of connection must implement the `DataConnection` interface because this interface is returned by the `getConnection` method on the `DataConnectionFactory` interface.

The example produces this output:

```
Creating fake connection factory
Creating fake data connection
Reading data from fake data connection
Read data: Example fake data
```

At compile time the client only knows the name of the factory. We can change the factory by altering a single line of code in the `FactoryExample` class as follows:

```
    //protected static DataConnectionFactory dataFactory = new
➥ DatabaseConnectionFactory();
```

In addition, if a new data storage method comes along, we will only have to add a new factory. For example, if the data is read from a file instead of a database, we can write a new factory that reads files. The client class needs to instantiate a new factory, but the rest of the client code doesn't change.

Observer

The observer pattern is often used in graphic applications such as Microsoft Excel. Microsoft Excel shows a spreadsheet in a window. This window is also called a view. The same spreadsheet can be shown in multiple views, which present the sheet in different ways. For example, one view can display the spreadsheet in a typical grid and another view can display the same spreadsheet in a chart. The views are essentially observing the data in a spreadsheet file and changing their presentation as soon as the data in the file changes. The actual object that holds the spreadsheet data is also referred to as the model. Every time the data changes, all the views must be refreshed to reflect the change. So the model triggers a refresh of the observers by sending them a notification.

In Java, a change of state is also referred to as an event. Observers are also known as listeners because they listen for specific events. Models are sometimes called notifiers because they notify listeners of their events. The Swing package in Java uses the observer pattern quite often.

Observer Example

Let's look at an example of the observer pattern. Imagine that we have a bank account from which we can withdraw funds. We can request an arbitrary withdrawal; however, the bank wants to be notified if the account does not have enough funds for the withdrawal. If an overdraft occurs, the account must notify the overdraft processor, which can take appropriate action. Listing 21.4 shows the implementation of the observer pattern.

LISTING 21.4   Observer Pattern Example

```
/**
 * Observer pattern example.
 */

package unleashed.ch21.observer;


import java.util.*;

/**
 * Overdraft event interface
 */
interface OverdraftEvent
{
    public double getOverdraftAmount();
}

/**
 * Overdraft event listener
 */
interface OverdraftEventListener
{
    public void overdraftHappened(OverdraftEvent event);

}

/**
 * Overdraft notifier
 */
interface OverdraftNotifier
{
    public void addOverdraftListener(OverdraftEventListener listener);
    public void removeOverdraftListener(OverdraftEventListener listener);
}

/**
 * Overdraft event implementation.
 */
class OverdraftEventImpl implements OverdraftEvent
{
    protected double amount;

    public OverdraftEventImpl(double amount)
```

LISTING 21.4 continued

```java
    {
        this.amount = amount;
    }

    public double getOverdraftAmount()
    {
        return amount;
    }
}

/**
 * Overdraft listener implementation
 */
class OverdraftProcessor implements OverdraftEventListener
{
    public void overdraftHappened(OverdraftEvent event)
    {
        //do something about overdraft
                System.out.println("Overdraft event happened " +
➥ event.getOverdraftAmount());
    }

}

/**
 * Account notifies of overdraft
 */
public class Account implements OverdraftNotifier
{

    //account balance
    protected double balance = 0;

    //create a vector of listeners
    protected Vector listeners = new Vector();

    public Account(double amount)
    {
        balance = amount;
    }

    public void addOverdraftListener(OverdraftEventListener listener)
    {
        listeners.add(listener);
    }

    public void removeOverdraftListener(OverdraftEventListener listener)
    {
        listeners.remove(listener);
    }
```

LISTING 21.4 continued

```java
    public void withdraw(double amount)
    {
        double newbalance = balance - amount;

        if(balance < amount)
        {
            notifyOverdraft(amount - balance);
        }

        balance = balance - amount;
    }

    public void notifyOverdraft(double overdraftAmount)
    {
        //create event
        OverdraftEventImpl event = new OverdraftEventImpl(overdraftAmount);

        //notify every listener
        for(Iterator it = listeners.iterator(); it.hasNext();)
        {
            OverdraftEventListener listener =
➥ (OverdraftEventListener)it.next();
            System.out.println("Notifying of overdraft");
            listener.overdraftHappened(event);
        }

    }

    public static void main(String[] args)
    {
        //create account with balance of 1000
        System.out.println("Creating account with balance of 1000");
        Account account = new Account(1000);

        //create overdraft listener
        System.out.println("Creating overdraft listener");
        OverdraftEventListener listener = new OverdraftProcessor();

        //add listener to account
        System.out.println("Adding listener to notifier");
        account.addOverdraftListener(listener);

        //withdraw some money
        System.out.println("Withdrawing 800");
        account.withdraw(800);
```

LISTING 21.4   continued

```
        //withdraw more money
        System.out.println("Withdrawing 300");
        account.withdraw(300);


    }
}
```

The Account class implements the OverdraftNotifier interface. Thus, Account can notify any interested observer when an overdraft event occurs. The OverdraftEvent object is created and sent to all the listeners. The example has only one listener—the OverdraftProcessor object. The observers or listeners register themselves with an account by calling the addOverdraftListener method. The main method creates an account with a balance of 1,000. After the listener is registered with the account, the code proceeds to make two withdrawals. On the second withdrawal, the account runs out of funds and sends an overdraft event to all the listeners.

It is clear in the example that we can add more listeners to the account object by calling the addOverdraftListener method. Any class that implements OverdraftListener can receive overdraft notifications from the account. This results in a clean interface between the objects that send events and the objects that are interested in these events.

This is the output of our example:

```
Creating account with balance of 1000
Creating overdraft listener
Adding listener to notifier
Withdrawing 800
Withdrawing 300
Notifying of overdraft
Overdraft event happened 100.0
```

The example in Listing 21.4 describes a so-called *push* model of sending updates, where all the state change information is sent to the observers inside the event. Even though this model is typical for Java, the opposite *pull* model may be worth considering in some cases. If your event includes a lot of data that has to be transmitted over the network, for example, you might consider just notifying the observers of the change without sending the actual data. Let the observers ask for the actual updates if they need them.

Proxy

Proxy provides access to another object while hiding the fact that the real object may not exist because it is running on a different machine or is not in memory.

In a distributed system, an object's location is transparent to the client. This means that the remote object looks as if it were local to the client. The client does not have to worry about how to find the object on the network and how to communicate with it. All the network code is hidden inside the network-aware proxy that can be generated automatically.

Another reason to have a proxy object is that the real object may be too big or too slow to be instantiated. The proxy can provide the client with the necessary view of an object and defer instantiation to a later time or prevent it altogether.

Proxy generally implements the interface of the real object that it represents. Proxy has access to the real object but defers part or all of the functionality of the real object. The real object implements the actual functionality of the system. The proxy object hides the real object from the client. The client does not know whether it is working with a proxy or the real object.

Proxy Example

Our example implements a proxy object for a property file. Imagine that we have a system with a property file that contains various system configuration parameters, for example, a configuration file for a network router. The property file happens to be so big that it is not practical to read it all into memory. There is a chance that the system will never use this property file, so keeping it in memory would be a waste of resources. To avoid loading the file, we will create a proxy object. The proxy object is used by the client to represent the property file. The proxy object decides when the property file must be loaded and unloaded from memory. Listing 21.5 shows the code for this example.

LISTING 21.5   Proxy Design Pattern Example

```
/**
 * Proxy design pattern example
 */

package unleashed.ch21.proxy;

/**
 * Property file interface
 */
interface PropertyFile
{

    public String getFileName();

    public String getPropertyValue(String propertyName);
}
```

LISTING 21.5   continued

```java
/**
* Property file real object
*/
class PropertyFileImpl implements PropertyFile
{
    protected String fileName;

    /**
    * Loads a property file
    */
    public PropertyFileImpl(String fileName)
    {
        this.fileName = fileName;
        //load property a large file from disk
        System.out.println("Creating real file and loading into memory");
    }

    /**
    * Gets file name.
    */
    public String getFileName()
    {
        return fileName;
    }

    /**
    * Gets the value of the property
    */
    public String getPropertyValue(String propertyName)
    {
        //get property value from the file
        return "Reading property value from file";
    }
}

/**
* Property file proxy, mimics property file interface
*/
class PropertyFileProxy implements PropertyFile
{
    public PropertyFileProxy()
    {
        System.out.println("Creating file proxy");
    }
    //properties file name
    protected String fileName = "properties.in";

    //real object
    protected PropertyFile realObject;
```

LISTING 21.5   continued

```java
/**
 * Gets the name of the properties file without loading it.
 */
public String getFileName()
{
    return fileName;
}

/**
 * Gets the value of a property.
 */
public String getPropertyValue(String propertyName)
{

    if(realObject == null)
    {
        //we are forced to load the file at this point
        realObject = new PropertyFileImpl(fileName);
    }

    return realObject.getPropertyValue(propertyName);

}
}

public class ProxyExample
{
    public static void main(String[] args)
    {
        ProxyExample example = new ProxyExample();

        PropertyFileProxy propertyFile = new PropertyFileProxy();

        example.usePropertyFile(propertyFile);
    }

    public void usePropertyFile(PropertyFile properties)
    {

        System.out.println("Property file name " + properties.getFileName());

        System.out.println(properties.getPropertyValue("myproperty") );

    }
}
```

The important thing in the example is that both `PropertyFileImpl` and
`PropertyFileProxy` classes implement the same `PropertyFile` interface. As a result, the

proxy object looks exactly like the real property file to the client. The `ProxyExample` class is a client that creates a property file proxy and calls `getFileName` and `getPropertyValue` methods. When the client calls the `getFileName` method, the proxy object returns the name of the file without reading the file. Obviously, reading of the file is not needed, as we only need the file's name. However, the `PropertyFileImpl` would read the file on instantiation, so the proxy object enables us to defer the memory consumption. When the client calls the `getPropertyValue` method, the proxy object has to load the property file into memory to return the value. The proxy does not manipulate the file itself; it uses the variable `realObject` to keep a handle to the `PropertyFileImpl` object.

The example produces the following output:

```
Creating file proxy
Property file name properties.in
Creating real file and loading into memory
Reading property value from file
```

The third line of the output indicates when the property file is loaded into memory.

Proxy can be used to store data temporarily. For example, our property file proxy could load a file and save the most commonly used properties in a HashMap. Then it would unload the real file to try to preserve memory.

Proxies are often created using the factory design pattern, making it impossible for the client to determine whether it creates a real object or a proxy. Sometimes at early stages you might implement a system using local objects, then swap real objects for proxies in production.

Facade

As you assemble a system from multiple subsystems, reusable components, and objects, the facade object is a clean front end that your clients see. The facade object hides the real functional components. It represents a client view of the system. A client sees and calls only the facade object instead of multiple objects. The system is easier to understand and maintain. The methods on the facade objects often mimic system use cases.

Facade is often called a workflow object because it calls other objects according to the system use cases. The facade object decides on the order in which the subcomponents are called.

Facade Example

Let's say that we have a class `Account` that is reused in our company. We just received a new requirement to write a system that transfers funds between two accounts. It is possible that the fund transfer can be done on the client; however, this is probably not a good place to put this functionality as it makes the client less flexible (not to speak of security and other concerns). Instead, we write a facade object that hides accounts from the client and has a simple, straightforward interface.

Listing 21.6 shows the code for a facade example.

LISTING 21.6 Facade Pattern Example

```
/**
 * Facade pattern example
 */

package unleashed.ch21.facade;

/**
 * Fund Transfer Facade class
 */
class FundTransfer
{
    public FundTransfer()
    {
    System.out.println("Creating fund transfer facade ");
    }
    //transfer fund use case
    public void transferFunds(double amount)
    {
        //create from account
        System.out.println("Facade: Getting FROM account");
        Account accountFrom = new Account(1000);

        //create to account
        System.out.println("Facade: Getting TO account");
        Account accountTo  = new Account(400);

        //begin atomic transaction
        accountFrom.withdraw(amount);
        accountTo.deposit(amount);
        //end atomic tarnsaction
    }
}

/**
 * Account object
 */
class Account
{
    protected double balance;
```

LISTING 21.6 continued

```java
    public Account(double amount)
    {
        balance = amount;
    }

    public void withdraw(double amount)
    {
        System.out.println("Account: withdrawing funds");
        balance = balance - amount;
    }

    public void deposit(double amount)
    {
        System.out.println("Account: depositing funds");
        balance = balance + amount;
    }
}
/**
 * Implements client to our facade.
 */
public class FacadeExample
{
    public static void main(String[] args)
    {
        //create new bank facade
        FundTransfer bank = new FundTransfer();

        //transfer funds
        System.out.println("Client: Calling the facade object");
        bank.transferFunds(100.00);


    }
}
```

The example consists of three classes: FundTransfer, Account, and FacadeExample. The Account class represents a user account. The FundTransfer is the facade object that the client knows of. Finally, the FacadeExample is the client object that calls the FundTransfer facade when it needs to transfer funds between accounts. The Account object only knows how to withdraw and deposit funds. The facade object uses both withdraw and deposit methods on the Account class to transfer funds.

The example produces the following printout:

```
Creating fund transfer facade
Client: Calling the facade object
Facade: Getting FROM account
```

```
Facade: Getting TO account
Account: withdrawing funds
Account: depositing funds
```

The client only calls the facade object; it is not aware of how funds are actually transferred. The facade object retrieves both FROM and TO accounts and calls them to withdraw and deposit the requested amount.

Facade is the result of a bottom-up design process in which the architects think of the reusable components and subsystems first. Once the functional components are designed (or bought from another company), the facade interface is implemented and provided to the client.

> **Note**
>
> Facade shields the client from the internal architecture, making it possible to provide a mockup back end in early stages of the project. The client can be developed separately from the back-end components.

EJB Design Patterns

Design patterns are not tied to any specific language or technology. They can be implemented in any object-oriented language. Therefore, it is possible to speak of design patterns without mentioning the programming language at all. However, this book takes a more practical approach by giving you examples of code that you can use in your next project. This is why we are going to discuss and implement two design patterns in the EJB environment. These patterns are implemented using EJBs although a Java object implementation is also possible.

For the sake of brevity, we will only have Java source code listings in the examples of EJB patterns. EJB deployment descriptors and build scripts are not shown but can be downloaded from the Sams Publishing Web site (www.samspublishing.com).

Business Delegate

As you build a client for an EJB project, you want to put certain things in a single place. These things include

- JNDI lookups—Your client calls multiple EJBs and does many JNDI lookups. All the lookups and EJB calls should be put in one place so that the client can be changed to call different EJBs if the business rules change.

- System exceptions—Your server-side EJBs may throw network, security, and other server-specific exceptions. The client objects should not contain any knowledge of what network or server-specific exceptions there may be. It is better to catch all server-specific exceptions in the business delegate object and rethrow them as client-specific exceptions.

> **Note**
>
> Exceptions are discussed in Chapter 22, "Exceptions and Debugging."

- Client logs and debugging and testing code—If the client has a central point to communicate to the server-side EJBs then the central point object can contain performance logs, and debugging and testing harnesses can be built into this object. When the system is ready for production, the central point object can be easily substituted for the production object that turns all the logging off.
- Server-side simulations—The client may be built before the server-side components are functional. To simulate the server-side functionality early in the project, you can build a business delegate object that represents all the server functionality. As the server side catches on, substitute the simulated code for the real back-end calls.

Typically, a set of EJBs in the middle tier is called by the clients that contain presentation logic. Instead of having each object in the client call different EJBs, it makes sense to hide all the server calls in the business delegate object. Thus, business delegate is located on the client and hides the actual calls to the back end.

In addition to hiding the back-end EJBs from the rest of the client objects, the business delegate object can perform other useful tasks such as caching EJB handles and logging. The business delegate can also simulate the back end before the back end is actually built. This can be very advantageous to the developers who are writing a client for your back-end system, because they do not have to wait until the back end is finished. They can start by presenting fake data that comes from the business delegate object. Later, when the back-end EJBs are implemented and tested, you can set the business delegate to call the real back end.

> **Note**
>
> See the complete example of the business delegate pattern in the source code for this chapter at the Sams Publishing Web site.

Business Delegate Example

Our example of the business delegate pattern shows a very simple program with one EJB
in the back end and two objects on the client side. Listing 21.7 shows the business delegate class.

LISTING 21.7   Business Delegate Class

```
package unleashed.ch21.bd;

import java.util.*;
import javax.naming.Context;
import javax.naming.InitialContext;
import javax.naming.NamingException;
import javax.rmi.PortableRemoteObject;
/**
* Business Delegate class represents a server EJB hiding it from
* the rest of the client classes
*/
public class BusinessDelegate
{

        protected String JNDI_NAME = "ServerBean";

        public String businessMethod()
        throws BusinessException
        {
            Server server = lookupServer();

            System.out.println("Business delegate is calling server");
            try
            {
                    return server.serverMethod();
             }catch(java.rmi.RemoteException e)
             {
                    throw new BusinessException(e);
             }
        }

        protected Server lookupServer()
        throws BusinessException
        {
            try
            {
                //jndi properties
                Properties h = new Properties();
                h.put(Context.INITIAL_CONTEXT_FACTORY,
                "weblogic.jndi.WLInitialContextFactory");
                h.put(Context.PROVIDER_URL, "t3://localhost:7001");
```

LISTING 21.7   continued

```
                //lookup jndi initial context
                InitialContext ctx = new InitialContext(h);

                //lookup home
                Object obj = ctx.lookup(JNDI_NAME);

                //cast home
                ServerHome home = (ServerHome)PortableRemoteObject.
➡ narrow(obj, ServerHome.class);

                //create the bean
                Object ejbObj = home.create();

                //cast the bean to our interface
                Server serverEJB = (Server)PortableRemoteObject.
➡ narrow(ejbObj, Server.class);

                return serverEJB;
            } catch (Exception e)
            {
                System.out.println(e.getMessage());
                e.printStackTrace();
                throw new BusinessException(e);
            }
        }
    }
}
```

The BusinessDelegate class has only two methods: businessMethod and
lookupServer. The lookupServer method does the JNDI lookup and creates the server-
side EJB. The lookupServer method is declared as protected and is not supposed to be
called by any other objects. This is because only the business delegate is allowed to
access the back-end EJBs. The businessMethod method is what your client objects
should call to execute the back-end beans.

Listing 21.8 shows the remote interface of the actual back-end EJB.

LISTING 21.8   Back-End EJB Remote Interface

```
package unleashed.ch21.bd;

import java.rmi.RemoteException;
import javax.ejb.EJBObject;

/**
 * Server EJB represents one of the back-end components.
 */
```

LISTING 21.8   continued

```
public interface Server extends EJBObject
{
        //declare our business method
        public  String serverMethod() throws RemoteException;
}
```

The back-end EJB has only one method on its remote interface. The serverMethod is called only by the business delegate object.

Note that the names of the EJB method (serverMethod) and the business delegate class method (businessMethod) are different. This demonstrates how the business delegate hides the actual interface of the back end. Although the business delegate interface should closely resemble the real back-end system, this is not always practical. During the course of the project, the interface of the back-end system may change to accommodate various clients. The business delegate pattern makes it easier to change the back-end interface; the clients do not have to change code in many places because only one business delegate class is affected by the change.

The server-side EJB is implemented in Listing 21.9.

LISTING 21.9   Back-End EJB Implementation

```
package unleashed.ch21.bd;

import javax.ejb.CreateException;
import javax.ejb.SessionBean;
import javax.ejb.SessionContext;
import javax.naming.InitialContext;
import javax.naming.NamingException;

/**
 * Back-end EJB implementation.
 */
public class ServerBean implements SessionBean
{

    //callback method must be implemented
    public void ejbActivate() {}
    public void ejbRemove() {}
    public void ejbPassivate() {}
    public void setSessionContext(SessionContext ctx) {}
    public void ejbCreate () throws CreateException {}
```

LISTING 21.9 continued

```
/**
* Server method implementation
*/
    public String serverMethod()
    {
        System.out.println("Server is executing");
        return "Server data";
    }
}
```

The bean implementation is quite simple. The only method prints out text to the screen and returns a string to the client.

Listing 21.10 shows a simple client class that calls the business delegate whenever it needs to execute a server-side bean.

LISTING 21.10 A Client Class That Calls the Business Delegate

```
package unleashed.ch21.bd;

/**
 * Business Delegate client.
 */

public class BusinessDelegateClient
{
    public static void main(String[] args) throws Exception
    {
      try
      {
          BusinessDelegate bd = new BusinessDelegate();
          System.out.println("Client calling business delegate");
          bd.businessMethod();
      }catch(BusinessException e)
      {
          e.printStackTrace();
      }
    }
}
```

The client instantiates a business delegate object and calls businessMethod on it. We are omitting the deployment descriptors for the server-side EJB. However, you can download the example from the Sams Publishing Web site and execute the appropriate scripts to do a fully functional build of the bean and the client classes. The build also deploys the EJB on the running WebLogic Server. After building the example, you can execute a script to run the client. The client should produce this output:

```
Client calling business delegate
Business delegate is calling server
```

If your WebLogic Server is running in a different command window, you should see this output:

```
Server is executing
```

This output is printed each time the back-end EJB method is called.

> **Tip**
>
> The business delegate object should not contain any business logic—its purpose is to hide the real server from the client classes. The business logic should be placed elsewhere.

The business delegate pattern describes how to hide the back-end EJBs from the client objects. This can be very useful for projects in which different teams create the client and the back-end EJBs. The changes on the back end do not affect the client as much because all the calls to the back end are located in the business delegate object. You might say that business delegate is no different from a proxy. In a way it is a proxy; however, proxy objects usually deal with the network plumbing code.

Command

In the beginning of your EJB project, it may not be clear exactly what operations the system will execute in the back end. Imagine that you are creating a general framework for other teams to follow and you do not want the other teams to worry about EJB details.

Also, the range of operations may be very diverse or may be expected to change in the future. You will have to support the old interface and the new one at the same time until your clients switch to the new interface.

In these cases, you should abstract from the specific interface and consider an operation as a separate object. The command pattern does this by creating a command object for each operation. When a client wants to call an operation on the server, it instantiates a command object and sends it to the command processor. The command processor is implemented as a stateless session EJB that accepts command objects and executes them. Actually, the command processor only calls the appropriate method on a command object to execute itself. When the command is finished executing, the command processor returns the result to the client. In addition to executing commands, the command processor may do logging, check whether the client is authorized to execute the command, and so on.

> **Note**
>
> See the complete example of the command pattern in the source code for this chapter at the Sams Publishing Web site.

Command Example

Let's see how the command pattern is implemented using EJBs. All command objects implement the Command interface. This interface is shown in Listing 21.11.

LISTING 21.11　The Command Interface

```
package unleashed.ch21.command;

/**
 * Command interface
 */
public interface Command extends java.io.Serializable
{
    public String execute();
}
```

A command has the execute method that is called by the command processor bean when it wants to execute the command. So, at the time of executing, the command object will be located in the back end. Therefore, it can access other EJBs, databases, and so on.

Listing 21.12 shows how a command is implemented.

LISTING 21.12　A Command Implemented by Class Operation

```
package unleashed.ch21.command;

/**
 * Command implementation
 */
public class Operation implements Command
{
    public String execute()
    {
```

LISTING 21.12 continued

```
        System.out.println("Command is executing");
        return "SUCCESS";
    }
}
```

In this example, the `Operation` class implements the `Command` interface. The `Operation` only prints a line to the screen and returns a string to the client.

The commands or operations are accepted and executed by a specialized EJB called a command processor. The command processor does not really know what a command is going to do. It calls the `execute` method on the `Command` class when it is time to execute it.

Listing 21.13 shows the remote interface of a command processor bean.

LISTING 21.13 Command Processor Remote Interface

```
package unleashed.ch21.command;

import java.rmi.RemoteException;
import javax.ejb.EJBObject;

/**
 * Command Processor.
 */
public interface CommandProcessor extends EJBObject
{
    //only execute command
    public  String executeCommand(Command command) throws RemoteException;
}
```

The `executeCommand` method accepts a `Command` object as an argument. This creates a system that can be easily extended to support new functionality. In fact, the command processor does not have to change at all, because the new functionality is implemented inside a new command object.

The command processor is implemented in Listing 21.14.

LISTING 21.14 The Command Processor Implemented by an Enterprise JavaBean

```
package unleashed.ch21.command;

import javax.ejb.CreateException;
import javax.ejb.SessionBean;
```

LISTING 21.14 continued

```java
import javax.ejb.SessionContext;
import javax.naming.InitialContext;
import javax.naming.NamingException;

/**
 * Command Processor bean implementation.
 */
public class CommandProcessorBean implements SessionBean
{

    //callback method must be implemented
    public void ejbActivate() {}
    public void ejbRemove() {}
    public void ejbPassivate() {}
    public void setSessionContext(SessionContext ctx) {}
    public void ejbCreate () throws CreateException {}


  /**
   * Facade method implementation
   */
    public String executeCommand(Command command)
    {
        return command.execute();
    }
}
```

Listing 21.14 implements a typical session bean with one executeCommand business method. Inside the executeCommand method, the command is called to execute itself. So the bean never knows what the command is to do.

> **Note**
>
> Application security in EJBs is set up by giving users permission to call specific methods. This does not work for the command pattern because all the clients call a single method on the command processor. Therefore, the command processor should check who the caller is and verify whether the caller is allowed to execute the command.

> **Caution**
>
> The disadvantage of the command pattern is that all operations in your system are passed to the back end as abstract `Command` objects. The system becomes more difficult to maintain because it is not clear from the interface of the back end what it is actually supposed to do.

Finally, the client class creates an operation and sends it to the command processor. Listing 21.15 demonstrates the client class.

LISTING 21.15   Client Implementation

```java
package unleashed.ch21.command;

import java.rmi.RemoteException;
import java.util.Properties;
import javax.ejb.CreateException;
import javax.ejb.RemoveException;
import javax.naming.Context;
import javax.naming.InitialContext;
import javax.naming.NamingException;
import javax.rmi.PortableRemoteObject;

/**
 * Command client
 */

public class CommandClient
{
    private static final String JNDI_NAME = "CommandProcessor";

    public static void main(String[] args) throws Exception
    {
        try
        {
            //jndi properties
            Properties h = new Properties();
            h.put(Context.INITIAL_CONTEXT_FACTORY,
                    "weblogic.jndi.WLInitialContextFactory");
            h.put(Context.PROVIDER_URL, "t3://localhost:7001");

            //lookup jndi initial context
            InitialContext ctx = new InitialContext(h);
```

LISTING 21.15 continued

```
            //lookup home
            Object obj = ctx.lookup(JNDI_NAME);

            //cast home
            CommandProcessorHome home = (CommandProcessorHome)
➥ PortableRemoteObject.narrow(obj, CommandProcessorHome.class);

            //create the bean
            Object ejbObj = home.create();

            //cast the bean to our interface
            CommandProcessor commandEJB = (CommandProcessor)
➥ PortableRemoteObject.narrow(ejbObj, CommandProcessor.class);

            Command operation = new Operation();

            //call bean's method
            System.out.println("Sending command to command processor bean");

            System.out.println("Command returned result: " +
➥ commandEJB.executeCommand(operation));

        } catch (Exception e)
        {
            System.out.println(e.getMessage());
            e.printStackTrace();
        }
    }
}
```

The client performs the usual chores: looking up the EJB home, creating an EJB instance, and calling the executeCommand method. You can build and deploy the command processor bean using the scripts provided at the Sams Publishing Web site. The command processor bean is deployed in the running WebLogic Server. Once you build the command processor bean, you can open another command window and run the client using the provided script. The client produces this output:

```
Sending command to command processor bean
Command returned result: SUCCESS
```

The WebLogic Server command window should have this output:

```
Command is executing
```

You can run the client multiple times without restarting the server.

> **Tip**
>
> If the back-end interface is clear and is not expected to be extended or changed, you should consider the facade pattern as an alternative to this pattern.

Your back-end EJBs may perform a large number of different operations. These operations may be called by different modules or components, which makes it necessary to have a simple, standard way to pass operations to the back end. A good way to create a flexible entry point for all the operations is to use the command pattern. The command pattern presents all operations as Command objects. The commands are accepted on the back end by the command processor EJB. The command processor may also perform security verification and logging before executing a command. After the caller is authenticated and permission is granted, the command processor calls the command to execute itself. When the command is finished executing, the command processor returns the result to the client. As a result, the command processor sets up the environment for a command and the command hides the details from the command processor. This results in an extensible back-end system.

Summary

Design patterns are small reusable design blueprints. By applying design patterns to different pieces of your system, you can increase your productivity as a designer. This gives you confidence that your future system will be based on sound, tested, and widely adopted design practices. It also makes it easy to communicate your design decisions to your fellow team members.

In this chapter, we covered various design patterns and looked at how they are used in the Java programming language. We also looked at two patterns that are widely used for EJB systems: business delegate and command.

Exceptions and Debugging

Imagine the feeling that you would get if your bank told you that it could account for 99% of your deposits from last year. What if you booked a flight on an airline that had a 99% survival rate among its passengers? Perhaps you could get a warm feeling for a post office that delivers 99% of the mail that you put in the mailbox.

All three of these businesses need to achieve a success rate approaching 100%. This means that the software that they use to run their business must be free of all critical defects. In order to maintain the public's confidence, their software also needs to be almost 100% free from cosmetic errors.

The Java language provides the functionality needed to facilitate exception handling. Using these features of the language will allow your programs to behave gracefully without burdening your code with excessive amounts of error-handling functionality.

In this chapter, you will learn how to use exception handling to improve your programs. In addition, you will learn how to create your own exception classes so that your exception handling can be clearer.

The Importance of Exception Handling

Beyond the never ending need to enhance your resume, you have a need to be taken seriously by your customers, your bosses, and by the people who find projects for you (sales types, business analysts, line managers, and so on). In addition, respect among your technical peers depends on your ability to understand difficult concepts and balance the trade-offs between proposed designs.

In our defense, creating a custom software system is much harder than building a house or even flying an airplane. (All of us have war stories that would make a marine cry.) But the truth remains that if we are going to take people's money, we'd better get used to giving them what they asked for in terms of both functionality and quality.

Java has provided us with an easy way to improve the quality of our code. The Java Exception strategy is far superior to the old ways. The following example shows us what it was like to check for exceptions in the "bad-old-days" of coding.

In the old days of C and Visual Basic programming, error checking was done by making a function call and returning a value that represented success or failure. Listing 22.1 shows the logic of how this was done.

LISTING 22.1   The `LouseyExceptionChecker` Shows How Exception Checking Used to Be Done

```
/*
 * LouseyExceptionChecker.java
 *
 */

package unleashed.ch22;

public class LouseyExceptionChecker {

    /** Creates new LouseyExceptionChecker */
    public LouseyExceptionChecker() {
    }

    private static int calculateSomethingCool()
    {
        return 5;
    }

    public static void main(String args[])
    {
     int retco = 0;

     retco = calculateSomethingCool();
        switch (retco)
        {
            case 0:
                System.out.println("Answer is good");
                break;
            case 1:
                System.out.println("Answer is too big");
                break;
            case 2:
                System.out.println("Answer is too positive");
                break;
            case 3:
                System.out.println("Answer is too negative");
                break;
            case 4:
                System.out.println("Answer is too strange");
                break;
            case 5:
                System.out.println("Answer is too goofy");
                break;
        }
    }
}
```

The output from this program is

```
Answer is too goofy
```

This example shows how tedious it can be to check for any significant number of exceptions. Producing a large system using this error-checking strategy would be overwhelming. Practically speaking, the programmer can only check for the worst errors and leave the others to chance.

First generation object-oriented languages like C++ used the modern throw-and-catch approach, but lacked the enforcement provisions of Java. In other words, a programmer was free to catch or not to catch as he chose. This limited the control that the class programmer had over those who would use his class in the future.

If we can raise our performance in the area of exception handling, we will receive greater respect from our peers and the business people who pay our invoices and sign our paychecks.

Understanding the Java Exception Strategy

The Java strategy for handling exceptions is based on the following principles:

- A guarded region is enclosed by a `try` block and at least one `catch` clause. Any exception that is thrown can be handled in the `catch` block.

- Three types of exceptions are available to programmers: `Error`, `RuntimeException`, and `Exception`. You can throw an `Error` if you do not want the exception handled. You can throw a `RuntimeException` if you want to give other classes a choice whether they want to handle it or not. Finally, you can throw a static `Exception` if you want to require users of your class to handle it.

- `Exceptions` and `Errors` are classes. You can extend these classes and create your own error-handling code.

- You can add an optional `finally` block after all the `catch` blocks associated with a `try` statement. Exceptions happen suddenly, causing the program to immediately execute the appropriate `catch` block. If there is critical code following the error, it is skipped. If there are critical resources to be released, they can be placed in a `finally` block, as shown here:

```
try
{
   ...do some work
}catch
```

```
{
    ...handle the exception
}
finally
{
    ...release critical resources
}
```

If you compare this to the paltry resources made available by C and Visual Basic, you can't help but be impressed. Perhaps the lack of facilities in older languages has lowered expectations to the point at which we just accept mystery bugs and do the best we can. It seems clear that many people are not really pleased with the situation, however, given the amount of criticism that Microsoft gets for bugs in its operating systems.

Catching Exceptions in Java Programs

The practice throughout this book is to create examples and illustrate our concepts through them. Most of the examples in this chapter can be compiled and run. At times, code fragments are sufficient to explain a concept. However, giving you the ability to borrow code and use it outweighs the disadvantage of longer listings in the chapters.

Another practice that we employ is to avoid examples using fruits, shapes, animals, and so on to illustrate concepts. It is harder to illustrate concepts using business situations, but it makes the code easier to copy and paste as the basis for your projects at work.

This chapter's example is `CantankerousCanCooker`. The pressure cooker receives cans of freshly canned food from the packing line. It raises the temperature to 210° Fahrenheit and keeps it there for some minutes. This kills all the microbes in the cans and makes it safe for humans.

If the temperature is way too low or the time is way too short, the microbes live on: The cans swell in the warehouse and can't be sold. If the temperature is a little too low or the time is a little too short, the cans don't swell, but the microbes live on and poison your customers. It is vital that we have a far greater survival rate than 99% among our customers, or we will surely get sued.

The `CantankerousCanCooker` (CCC) is made up of two major component classes:

- The `WaterTemperatureManager` class—Responsible for maintaining the correct temperature at all times.
- The `Manifest` class—Responsible for keeping track of the contents of the cooker for each cooking cycle. It gets its data from the computers on the packing line.

The WaterTemperatureManager is a black box that can be given a temperature to maintain.

- The Thermometer class—Responsible for reporting the correct temperature at all times.
- The WaterValve class—Responsible for opening and closing the hot water valve to regulate temperature.

Figure 22.1 illustrates these classes.

FIGURE 22.1

The structure of the cannery example.

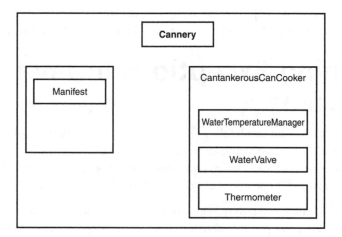

Figure 22.1 shows the relationship between the different classes in the example. The Cannery is the factory. The CantankerousCanCooker is a machine in the factory. The WaterTemperatureManager is a logic controller in the cooker. The WaterValve and the Thermometer are pieces of hardware inside the cooker, too. The code is shown in Listing 22.2.

LISTING 22.2   The CantankerousCanCooker Class

```
package unleashed.ch22;
/**
 *
 * @author  Stephen Potts
 * @version
 */
public class CantankerousCanCooker
{
    Manifest man1;
    WaterTemperatureManager wtm;
    int temperature;
```

LISTING 22.2 continued

```java
    int duration;
    boolean cooking;

    /** Creates new CantankerousCanCooker */
    public CantankerousCanCooker()
    {
        System.out.println("CantankerousCanCooker constructed");
    }

    public void cook(Manifest man1, int temperature, int duration)
    {
        this.cooking = true;
        this.man1 = man1;
        this.temperature = temperature;
        this.duration = duration;
        wtm = new WaterTemperatureManager(temperature, duration);
        wtm.startUp();
    }

    public void stop()
    {
        this.cooking = false;
    }

    public boolean isCooking()
    {
        return this.cooking;
    }
}
```

The most important method in the `CantankerousCanCooker` class is the `cook()` method. It sets a number of class variables and then creates a `WaterTemperatureManager` object and hands it a temperature and duration.

`WaterTemperatureManager` is shown in Listing 22.3.

LISTING 22.3 The `WaterTemperatureManager` Class

```java
package unleashed.ch22;
import java.util.*;

/**
 *
 * @author  Stephen Potts
 * @version
 */
public class WaterTemperatureManager
```

LISTING 22.3   continued

```java
{
    private Thermometer therm1;
    private WaterValve watValve;
    private int temperature;
    private int duration;


    /** Creates new WaterTemperatureManager */
    public WaterTemperatureManager(int temperature, int duration)
    {
        System.out.println("WaterTemperatureManager constructed");
        this.therm1 = new Thermometer();
        this.watValve = new WaterValve();
        this.temperature = temperature;
        this.duration = duration;
    }

    //Heat up the water and keep it at the temperature for the duration
    public void startUp()
    {
        try
        {
            Calendar c = Calendar.getInstance();
            boolean done = false;

            System.out.println("WaterTemperatureManager.startUP() - started");

            //get up to temperature
            this.watValve.openValve();
            while (therm1.getTemperature() < this.temperature)
            {
                System.out.println("temperature is now = " +
                                        therm1.getTemperature());
                Thread.sleep(10*60);
                therm1.increaseTemp(); //simulates the water warming up
            }
            this.watValve.closeValve();

            System.out.println(
            "WaterTemperatureManager.startup - achieved temperature of "
                + temperature);

            while (!done)
            {
                Thread.sleep(10*60);
                if (therm1.getTemperature() < this.temperature)
                    this.watValve.openValve();
                else
                    this.watValve.closeValve();
```

LISTING 22.3   continued

```
                c = Calendar.getInstance();
                System.out.print(
                    "WaterTemperatureManager.startUP() time = ");
                System.out.print(c.get(Calendar.HOUR) +":"+
                    c.get(Calendar.MINUTE) +":"+
                    c.get(Calendar.SECOND));
                System.out.println(" Temperature = "
                  + therm1.getTemperature());
                duration -= 1;
                if (duration == 0)
                    done = true;
            }
            System.out.println(
                    "WaterTemperatureManager.startUP() - ending");
        }catch (InterruptedException ie)
        {
            System.out.println("WaterTemperatureManager.startUp " + ie);
        }
    }
}
```

The startup() method controls the cooking process by opening and closing valves to regulate the temperature. It maintains the temperature for the duration that was passed into the constructor.

The Manifest class is shown in Listing 22.4.

LISTING 22.4   The Manifest Class

```
package unleashed.ch22;

/**
 *
 * The Manifest class describes the contents of one
 * load of cans in our cannery
 */
public class Manifest
{
    private int numberOfCans;
    private String contents;
    /** Creates new Manifest */
    public Manifest()
    {
        System.out.print("Manifest constructed");
        this.numberOfCans = 0;
        this.contents = "empty";
    }
```

22

LISTING 22.4   continued

```java
    public Manifest( int numberOfCans, String contents)
    {
        System.out.println("Manifest constructed");
        this.numberOfCans = numberOfCans;
        this.contents = contents;
    }

    public int getNumberOfCans()
    {
        return this.numberOfCans;
    }

    public String getContents()
    {
        return this.contents;
    }
}
```

The Manifest class describes the contents of one load of cans in our cannery. It provides a description of the material inside the cans as well as the number of cans in the load.

The WaterValve class is shown in Listing 22.5.

LISTING 22.5   The WaterValve Class

```java
package unleashed.ch22;

/**
 *
 * @author   Stephen Potts
 * @version
 * The WaterValve class controls the operation
 * of the hotwater line in the cooker
 */
public class WaterValve {

    private boolean open;

    /** Creates new WaterValve */
    public WaterValve()
    {
        System.out.println("WaterValve constructed");
    }

    public boolean isOpen()
    {
```

LISTING 22.5 continued

```
        return open;
    }

    public void openValve()
    {
        this.open = true;
    }

    public void closeValve()
    {
        this.open = false;
    }
}
```

The WaterValve Class controls the hot water line flowing into the cooker. The openValve() and closeValve() methods simulate the valve's operation.

The Thermometer class is shown in Listing 22.6.

LISTING 22.6 The Code for the Thermometer Class

```
package unleashed.ch22;

public class Thermometer
{
    private int temperature = 200;
    /** Creates new Thermometer */
    public Thermometer()
    {
        System.out.println("Thermometer constructed");
    }

    public void increaseTemp()
    {
        this.temperature += 1;
    }

    public void decreaseTemp()
    {
        this.temperature -= 1;
    }

    public int getTemperature()
    {
        return this.temperature;
    }
}
```

The Thermometer class simulates a real hardware thermometer. The increaseTemp() and decreaseTemp() methods allow the simulation to work. The getTemperature() method is called by the WaterTemperatureManager to get a reading of the current temperature.

The Cannery class is shown in Listing 22.7.

LISTING 22.7   The Code for the Cannery Class

```
/*
 * Cannery.java
 *
 * Created on December 8, 2001, 10:10 AM
 */

package unleashed.ch22;

/**
 *
 * @author   Stephen Potts
 * @version
 * The Cannery class is the factory that cans the products.
 * It contains the main() for this system
 */
public class Cannery {

    /** Creates new Cannery */
    public Cannery() {
    }

    public static void main(String[] args)
    {
        CantankerousCanCooker ccc = new CantankerousCanCooker();
        Manifest m1 = new Manifest(1000, "beef tips");
        ccc.cook(m1, 210, 5);
    }
}
```

If we run Listing 22.7 we get the following output:

```
CantankerousCanCooker constructed
Manifest constructed
WaterTemperatureManager constructed
Thermometer constructed
WaterValve constructed
WaterTemperatureManager.startUP() - started
temperature is now = 200
temperature is now = 201
temperature is now = 202
temperature is now = 203
```

```
temperature is now = 204
temperature is now = 205
temperature is now = 206
temperature is now = 207
temperature is now = 208
temperature is now = 209
WaterTemperatureManager.startUP() - achieved temperature of 210
WaterTemperatureManager.startUP() time = 0:45:59 Temperature = 210
WaterTemperatureManager.startUP() time = 0:46:0 Temperature = 210
WaterTemperatureManager.startUP() time = 0:46:0 Temperature = 210
WaterTemperatureManager.startUP() time = 0:46:1 Temperature = 210
WaterTemperatureManager.startUP() time = 0:46:1 Temperature = 210
WaterTemperatureManager.startUP() - ending
```

This output shows that the code works and that the cooker raises the temperature and holds it there until the cooking is complete. If the world were perfect, we would be done with this system. The world is not perfect, however, so we must anticipate that errors will occur. The Thermometer will fail someday, as will the hot water boiler. The operator could enter the wrong amount of time to cook. Even worse than that, someone who got sick from something else could sue us. We would need to prove that the cooking was properly done to defend ourselves in court. (Note that the times you see in your output will vary depending on the time of day.)

Common Exception-Handling Practices

If you examine the design of the Cannery System, you will see some object-oriented features. All the state variables are private, classes are used for everything, and some classes contain references to other classes as their class members.

All is not well in this design though. There is an appalling absence of exception checking. The only try...catch pair in the whole program is the InterruptedException forced by the Thread class. Is it realistic to deliver a system on the assumption that no information will be needed to diagnose and fix errors that are discovered in the field?

How will we defend ourselves if someone gets food poisoning and sues us? Is any logging being done? The System.out.println statements that you see will appear on the operator's screen and disappear when the buffer fills. Even if we redirected the output to a file and kept it for years, would it help? Could we find the information for a batch of cans that is believed to be defective?

If this were a contrived example that was not typical of what the programming world is doing, we could rest easier. Sadly, poor exception handling is the rule—not the exception.

Programmers fall into several categories when it comes to error handling:

- The Nervous Type—This programmer panics whenever the compiler tells him that he must catch an exception, so he places the exception in the throws clause of the method and breathes a sign of relief.

```
public int doLots() throws IOException, InterruptionException,
                    SocketException, MalformedURLException
```

The problem with this approach is that it doesn't provide any help in determining what has happened. He never tries to catch the exception himself, even when this method is in the best position to handle it.

- The 60s Time Traveler—This programmer thinks that exception handling is a Communist plot, so he foils them by never doing anything:

```
Public int doSomeIO()
{
try
{
  //do a bunch of i/o here
}catch (Exception e){}
}
```

That'll show them. This programmer has managed to turn back that clock to the "good old days" when we didn't need any stinking exceptions.

- The Concerned Citizen—This programmer catches everything and provides a System.out.println() for it, without regard to whether this is the logical place to handle it.

```
try
{
   //try to obtain a socket
}catch(SocketException se)
{
System.out.println("Oops");
}
//proceed just like the socket had been obtained
```

- The Literalist—This programmer provides you with "just the facts" without providing any more information about what has transpired.

```
try
{
   //try to obtain a socket
}catch(SocketException se)
{
     System.out.println("You got a socket error");
     throw se;
}
```

- The Model of Humility—This programmer would never attempt to rise above his station and presume to create his own exceptions. "That would be embarrassing. What if I don't do it right? Everyone would tease me." So, this humble servant rethrows IOExceptions to user interfaces and MalformedURLExceptions to people who have no hope of understanding what this means in his code. This results in error messages on your screen that make no sense at all. You might have been trying to buy some shoes on the Internet and gotten an ArrayOutOfBoundsException displayed on your screen.

There are a few situations where you would want to handle the exception without throwing a new one. In these cases, it is important to provide as much contextual information as possible and to target the message at the likely audience. If a socket programmer is the likely audience for a message, the message "You got a socket error" makes sense. If, however, the audience is the end user, an error message such as "The system failed to initialize. Call support at 333-987-3456" might be more appropriate.

Finally, we are ready for our heroine:

- The Very Model of a Modern Java Programmer—This noble craftsperson would never stoop to ask another programmer to clean up after her. She considers exception handling to be a major part of class design. She carefully considers what her class does from the outside—from the user's point of view. If her class uses sockets to download video and a socket error is thrown, she provides a context for the user by translating the exception into something more meaningful like a VideoServerNotAvailableException.

Ever mindful of the support staff, she is careful to preserve the call stack, type, and message from the original exception, just in case this exception indicates a much larger problem that must be addressed. In fact, she performs this amazing information-preserving feat using code that she appropriated (legally) from later in this very chapter.

The guiding principle when deciding whether to handle an exception locally or chain the exception is usability. If a system is harder to use because of local exception handling, chain the exception. Otherwise, handle it locally.

If you would like to change your errant ways and handle exceptions like our model programmer, you need only keep reading and taking to heart what is taught in this chapter.

The Right Way to Handle Exceptions

There is a right way to handle exceptions, and it is not that hard. It requires that a simple process be followed whenever you create a new class.

When you design your classes, put exception design on the list beside inheritance, method design, and member variable design. Ask yourself the question, "Given the purpose of my class, what error messages would a user expect to receive from each method in this class?" Suppose that your class processes credit card transactions. When problems occur, make your exceptions and error messages say things about credit card transactions, not about URLs, sockets, or I/O.

If your user won't be able to understand the exception that has been thrown, translate it into one that he will understand. You will need to create your own class that extends `Exception` or `RuntimeException` to do this. Populate your exception with the information that a support engineer needs to find the problem. This can include declaring member variables in your `Exception` class's definition and copying variables from your methods into these member variables during the catching process. This will hand your user a good informative object. If you create good exception objects for all your classes, your system's maintainability will increase dramatically.

Let's look at how well the Cannery System handles exceptions. Only one `try...catch` block exists in all these methods: an `InterruptedException` is caught when the `Thread` is put to sleep. What is needed is a redesign of each of the classes in our system, starting with the lowest levels and moving up. We will do that using the `Thermometer` class.

Presently, the `Thermometer` class doesn't catch or throw any exceptions. If we think about it, we will conclude that we don't want the thermometer to give us readings that are absurd. If the reading for the thermometer is below 32 degrees or above 300 degrees, we want to report a malfunction of the thermometer. We can then design our class to handle that situation as shown in Listing 22.8.

LISTING 22.8   The `ThermometerException` Class

```
package unleashed.ch22;

/**
 *
 * @author  Stephen Potts
 * the ThermometerException class is thrown when
 * a temperature is so far out of range
```

LISTING 22.8 continued

```
 * that it indicates a malfunction in the equipment
 */
public class ThermometerException extends Exception
{
    private int temperature;
    /** Creates new ThermometerException */
    public ThermometerException(){
    }

    public ThermometerException(String message, int temperature)
    {
        super(message);
        this.temperature = temperature;
    }

    public int getTemperature()
    {
        return this.temperature;
    }
}
```

There are some interesting things about this class:

- The first thing to notice is that it is a class in every way. It has a constructor and is in a package.

- We want to keep the errant temperature reading, so we define a local variable for it and an accessor method to call it with.

- We will use the message member of the Exception base class, which is set in a constructor, so we must call super() to do this.

Now we are ready to see how to use this in our system. To do this, we will modify the Thermometer class to throw the ThermometerException in Listing 22.9.

LISTING 22.9 The ThermometerE Class Simulates a Real Thermometer

```
package unleashed.ch22;

package unleashed.ch22;

public class ThermometerE
{
    private int temperature = 10000;// throw an exception immediately
    /** Creates new Thermometer */
    public ThermometerE() throws ThermometerException
    {
```

LISTING 22.9   continued

```java
        System.out.println("ThermometerE constructed");
        if ((temperature > 300) || (temperature < 32))
            throw new ThermometerException(
                    "Thermometer is malfunctioning", temperature);
    }

    public void simIncreaseTemp()
    {
        this.temperature += 1;
    }

    public void simDecreaseTemp()
    {
        this.temperature -= 1;
    }

    public int getTemperature()
    {
        return this.temperature;
    }

    public static void main(String[] args)
    {
        try
        {
            ThermometerE t1 = new ThermometerE();
            System.out.println(
                    "The temperature is " + t1.getTemperature());
        }catch(ThermometerException te)
        {
            System.out.println(
                "A problem with the thermometer has occurred");
            System.out.println(
                "The Exception message is " + te.getMessage());
            if(te.getTemperature() > 300)
                System.out.println(
                    "The thermometer shows a temperature too high");
            else
                System.out.println(
                        "The thermometer shows a temperature too low");
        }
    }//main
}
```

The output from this program is shown here:

```
Thermometer constructed
A problem with the thermometer has occurred
```

```
The Exception message is Thermometer is malfunctioning

The thermometer shows a temperature too high
```

> **Note**
>
> The simIncreaseTemperature() and simDecreaseTemperature() methods in the ThermometerE class should be ignored. They simulate a change in temperature for convenience in these examples. In reality, the thermometer hardware would send its reading through a socket or serial port. A private method in the class would write that value to the private variable temperature every *n* seconds.

There are several features of this program that deserve some attention:

- The constructor now throws ThermometerException. The purpose of creating ThermometerException is to provide a message to the calling program. If the temperature is too high at creation, the exception is thrown there.

- The constructor tested the temperature and threw the exception itself. If you create an exception, you have to throw it, or it will never be thrown.

- The constructor created an instance of the ThermometerException class before it could throw it. Exceptions in Java are objects, and objects must be created.

- The main() method that was created for testing instantiated the Thermometer object in a try...catch block. This is required because the constructor for this class stated that it *throws* this exception. If this was missing, the compiler would complain. If ThermometerException had extended RuntimeException instead of Exception, it would have been unchecked. (The compiler won't *check* that you handled it.)

- The getMessage() method was inherited from the Throwable class. It retrieves whatever message was used in the constructor to the Exception class.

- The getTemperature() method is one that we added to the ThermometerException class. It accesses the temperature variable that we added to the ThermometerException. You will see this technique used to great advantage later in this chapter.

This class now throws an exception whenever a certain abnormal condition occurs. This custom exception type is not triggered by another exception at all. The class creates it semantically.

Translating Exceptions

Custom exceptions can be useful in translating exceptions thrown by the methods that you are calling. You translate one exception into your custom exception class before sending it to your users.

For example, if you are using the `Socket` class to communicate, you have to catch a `SocketException`. This exception normally occurs when the computer you are communicating with has a problem and drops the socket connection. To your user, a `SocketException` might not be a very useful object to receive when there is a problem. You could translate the `SocketException` into a custom `ServerException` that would be meaningful to your users. This technique is illustrated here using the `WaterTemperatureManager` class:

In the original version, we weakly printed a message and continued on with the processing:

```
catch (InterruptedException ie)
{
        System.out.println("WaterTemperatureManager.startUp() " + ie);
}
```

There are several problems with this. One problem is that we continued processing even when the `WaterTemperatureManager` did not get started correctly. This can't be a good thing given that this method is the workhorse for the whole application. A second problem is that the user of this method, the `CantankerousCanCooker` thinks that it is starting a `WaterTemperatureManager`, not putting a `Thread` to sleep. Any message about a `Thread` being interrupted will be nonsense to it. This message needs to be translated into something more meaningful. This new exception class does that as shown in Listing 22.10.

LISTING 22.10   The `WaterTemperatureManagerException` Class

```
package unleashed.ch22;

/**
 *
 * @author  Stephen Potts
 * This Exception gives information about
 * problems that occur in the WaterTemperatureManager class
 */
public class WaterTemperatureManagerException extends Exception
{
    int temperature;
```

LISTING 22.10   continued

```
    /** Creates new WaterTemperatureManagerException */
    public WaterTemperatureManagerException(String message,
                     int temperature)
    {
        super(message);
        this.temperature = temperature;
    }

    public int getTemperature()
    {
        return this.temperature;
    }
}
```

Having a new exception object is better because it allows the using class to catch just one
type of exception—one that makes sense in the calling context. The same exception can
be used to translate multiple exceptions. In the constructor, it translates the
`ThermometerException` as shown in Listing 22.11. This is a code snippet, so do not try
to run it. In addition, there is no listing for it in the code on the Web site.

LISTING 22.11   The `WaterTemperatureManager` Class

```
public WaterTemperatureManager(int temperature, int duration)
                     throws WaterTemperatureManagerException
{
   try
   {
     System.out.println("WaterTemperatureManager constructed");
     this.therm1 = new Thermometer();
     this.watValve = new WaterValve();
     this.temperature = temperature;
     this.duration = duration;
   }catch (ThermometerException te)
   {
     throw new WaterTemperatureManagerException(
         "Couldn't create a WaterTemperatureManager thermometer problem." ,
             te.getTemperature());
   }
}
```

The message is specific as to the reason that an `Exception` was thrown. This same
exception class is also used to translate the `InterruptedException` that can be thrown in
the `startup()` method:

```
   }catch (InterruptedException ie)
   {
```

```
System.out.println("WaterTemperatureManager.startUp() " + ie);
throw new WaterTemperatureManagerException(
  "Couldn't start the WaterTemperatureManager " +
  "timing was interrupted by another process "
  , therm1.getTemperature());
```

```
}
```

Notice that the message portion of the exception is specific to the type of problem that occurred, even though the exception is more generic. One of the design decisions is how many different exception classes to create for each new class. A small class can often translate all exceptions to one, as we have done here. Complex classes might require the creation of several exception classes.

The hard thing about designing exception classes is that you have two constituencies: the users and the support staff. Programmers and end users are mainly concerned about problems in the context of what they are trying to accomplish with your classes and methods. They like exceptions translation because it makes more sense to them.

The support staff is different. They have to find the root cause of the problem and fix it. Any approach that masks details from them is considered a hindrance. The ideal approach would combine these two goals and provide a translated exception that still contains all the information from all the untranslated exceptions that have been thrown. This would include the type of the exception, the message, and the stack dump.

Normally, the only thing that you get from an exception object is the latest exception object thrown and the stack trace for it.

Matters only get worse when you cross machine boundaries with RMI. The stack trace is declared `transient`, and is therefore not serializable. This means that the error object you receive will have no stack trace information in it.

Exception Chaining Without Losing Information

So what can a poor programmer do? We need to serialize a custom exception class and track the bug all the way back to its source. We do this by overriding and improving the `Exception` class.

We will declare a `StackingException` class that operates much like the trusty `Exception` class except for the previously mentioned improvements as shown in Listing 22.12.

LISTING 22.12   The StackingException Class

```java
package unleashed.ch22;
import java.io.*;

/**
 *
 * @author   Stephen Potts
 * @version
 */
abstract class StackingException extends Exception
                    implements Serializable
{
    String stackBuffer = "";

    /** Creates new StackingException */
    public StackingException() {
    }

    public StackingException(String message, Exception e)
    {
        super(message);

        //turn the stack into a string
        StringWriter s = new StringWriter();
        this.printStackTrace( new PrintWriter(s));

        //if this exception is wrapping another,
        // get the old stack trace and append this
        //stack trace to it
        if (e != null && e instanceof StackingException)
        {
            StackingException se = (StackingException)e;
            stackBuffer  = se.getStackBuffer();
            stackBuffer += s.toString();
         }else
        {
            stackBuffer = s.toString();
        }

    }

    public String getStackBuffer()
    {
        return stackBuffer;
    }

}
```

Several features of this class are worth mentioning:

- The class is declared to be abstract even though it has no abstract methods. This is to prevent it from being instantiated directly.

- It has an additional member called `stackBuffer` and a method to access it. This string will contain the concatenated stacks of all the exceptions that have been translated. This string is serializable.

- The constructor uses polymorphism. The exceptions that will be handed to the constructor will all be of a class derived from `StackingException` and therefore `Exception`. Because our only interest in these classes will be to run a `printStackTrace()` call on them, we can use a handle to the base class. (If this is a bit shadowy, see Chapter 27, "Polymorphism and Inheritance.") However, we use a downcast to a `StackingException` so that we can access the `getStackBuffer()` method, which does not exist at the `Exception` class level.

- Sly bits of trickery are used to turn the `printStackTrace()` method into an assignment to a `String`. (An explanation of this can be found in Chapter 26, "Persistence and Cloning.")

Now that we have a new base class, we are in a position to create a full set of meaningful exception classes that are faithful to the virtues set forth earlier in this chapter, as shown in Listing 22.13.

LISTING 22.13 The `ThermometerException2` Class

```
package unleashed.ch22;
/**
 *
 * @author   Stephen Potts
 */
public class ThermometerException2 extends StackingException
{
    private int temperature;
    /** Creates new ThermometerException */
    public ThermometerException2(){
    }

    public ThermometerException2(String message,
                            int temperature, Exception e)
    {
        super(message, e);
        this.temperature = temperature;
    }

    public int getTemperature()
    {
```

LISTING 22.13   continued

```
        return this.temperature;
    }
}
```

Notice that `ThermometerException2` extends `StackingException`. This means that the
stack buffer will be available to any program that has a handle to this type of exception.
This will allow it to obtain all the other messages that have been generated, as well as the
temperature via the `getTemperature()` method.

The `WaterTemperatureManagerException2` class is shown in Listing 22.14.

LISTING 22.14   The `WaterTemperatureManagerException2` Class

```
package unleashed.ch22;

/**
 *
 * @author  Stephen Potts
 */
public class WaterTemperatureManagerException2 extends StackingException
{
    int temperature;

    /** Creates new WaterTemperatureManagerException */
    public WaterTemperatureManagerException2(String message,
                                        int temperature, Exception e)
    {
        super(message, e);
        this.temperature = temperature;
    }

    public int getTemperature()
    {
        return this.temperature;
    }
}
```

The `CantankerousCanCookerException2` class is shown in Listing 22.15.

LISTING 22.15   The `CantankerousCanCookerException2` Class

```
package unleashed.ch22;

/**
 *
 * @author  Stephen Potts
```

LISTING 22.15   continued

```
 * @version
 */
public class CantankerousCanCookerException2 extends StackingException
{
    int temperature;

    /** Creates new WaterTemperatureManagerException */
    public CantankerousCanCookerException2(String message,
                                           int temperature, Exception e)
    {
        super(message, e);
        this.temperature = temperature;
    }

    public int getTemperature()
    {
        return this.temperature;
    }
}
```

The CantankerousCanCookerException2 and the
WaterTemperatureManagerException2 classes are superior to the exceptions that are
thrown by the Java language or by other packages that you might be using because they
are very specific to problems in your classes. Therefore, they are more meaningful to the
users.

The user classes are shown in Listing 22.16. This version of the Cannery class uses the
getStackBuffer() method to get information from the
CantankerousCanCookerException2 object when something goes wrong.

LISTING 22.16   The Cannery2 Class

```
package unleashed.ch22;

/**
 *
 * @author  Stephen Potts
 * The Cannery class is the factory that cans the products.
 * It contains the main() for this system
 */
public class Cannery2 {

    /** Creates new Cannery */
    public Cannery2() {
    }
```

LISTING 22.16   continued

```java
public static void main(String[] args)
{
    try
    {
        CantankerousCanCooker2 ccc = new CantankerousCanCooker2();
        Manifest m1 = new Manifest(1000, "beef tips");
        ccc.cook(m1, 210, 5);
    }catch (CantankerousCanCookerException2 cce)
    {
        System.out.println("This Can Cooker is Cantankerous");
        System.out.println(
            "I don't know the problem, but here is the stackBuffer");
        System.out.println(cce.getStackBuffer());
    }
}
}
```

Notice that the `main()` method catches the `CantankerousCanCookerException2` exception. It then gets the stack buffer by calling the `getStackBuffer()` method.

The `CantankerousCanCooker2` class is shown in Listing 22.17. This version of `CantankerousCanCooker` uses the new `Exception` classes.

LISTING 22.17   The `CantankerousCanCooker2` Class

```java
package unleashed.ch22;

/**
 *
 * @author  Stephen Potts
 */
public class CantankerousCanCooker2
{
    Manifest man1;
    WaterTemperatureManager2 wtm;
    int temperature;
    int duration;
    boolean cooking;

    /** Creates new CantankerousCanCooker */
    public CantankerousCanCooker2()
    {
        System.out.println("CantankerousCanCooker constructed");
    }

    public void cook(Manifest man1, int temperature, int duration)
                        throws CantankerousCanCookerException2
```

LISTING 22.17   continued

```java
    {
        try
        {
            this.cooking = true;
            this.man1 = man1;
            this.temperature = temperature;
            this.duration = duration;
            wtm = new WaterTemperatureManager2(temperature, duration);
            wtm.startUp();
        }catch (WaterTemperatureManagerException2 wtme)
        {
            throw new CantankerousCanCookerException2(
            "Couldn't create a Cantankerous Can Cooker " +
            "WaterTemperatureManager Problem" ,
                        wtme.getTemperature(), wtme);
        }
    }

    public void stop()
    {
        this.cooking = false;
    }

    public boolean isCooking()
    {
        return this.cooking;
    }
}
```

The WaterTemperatureManager2 class is shown in Listing 22.18.

LISTING 22.18   The WaterTemperatureManager2 Class

```java
package unleashed.ch22;
import java.util.*;

/**
 *
 * @author   Stephen Potts
 */
public class WaterTemperatureManager2
{
    private Thermometer2 therm1;
    private WaterValve watValve;
    private int temperature;
    private int duration;
```

LISTING 22.18 continued

```java
/** Creates new WaterTemperatureManager */
public WaterTemperatureManager2(int temperature, int duration)
        throws WaterTemperatureManagerException2
{
    try
    {
        System.out.println("WaterTemperatureManager constructed");
        this.therm1 = new Thermometer2();
        this.watValve = new WaterValve();
        this.temperature = temperature;
        this.duration = duration;
    }catch (ThermometerException2 te)
    {
        throw new WaterTemperatureManagerException2(
        "Couldn't create a WaterTemperatureManager " +
        "thermometer problem." , te.getTemperature(), te);
    }
}


//Heat up the water and keep it at the temperature for the duration
public void startUp() throws WaterTemperatureManagerException2
{
    try
    {
        Calendar c = Calendar.getInstance();
        boolean done = false;

        System.out.println(
            "WaterTemperatureManager.startUP() - started");

        //get up to temperature
        this.watValve.openValve();
        while (therm1.getTemperature() < this.temperature)
        {
            System.out.println("temperature is now = " +
                                therm1.getTemperature());
            Thread.sleep(10*60);
            therm1.simIncreaseTemp(); // simulates the water warming
        }
        this.watValve.closeValve();

        System.out.println(
            "WaterTemperatureManager.startUP() - " +
                " achieved temperature of " +
                    therm1.getTemperature() );

        while (!done)
```

LISTING 22.18   continued

```
            {
                Thread.sleep(10*60);
                if (therm1.getTemperature() < this.temperature)
                    this.watValve.openValve();
                else
                    this.watValve.closeValve();
                c = Calendar.getInstance();
                System.out.print(
                        "WaterTemperatureManager.startUP() time = ");
                System.out.print(c.get(Calendar.HOUR) +
                    ":"+ c.get(Calendar.MINUTE) +":"+
                                c.get(Calendar.SECOND));
                System.out.println(" Temperature = " +
                                therm1.getTemperature());
                duration -= 1;
                if (duration == 0)
                    done = true;
            }
            System.out.println(
                "WaterTemperatureManager.startUP() - ending");
        }catch (InterruptedException ie)
        {
            System.out.println("WaterTemperatureManager.startUp() " + ie);
            throw new WaterTemperatureManagerException2(
                "Couldn't start the WaterTemperatureManager timing " +
                "was interrupted by another process ",
                        therm1.getTemperature(), ie);

        }
    }
}
```

Notice that the ThermometerException2 is caught. It throws the
WaterTemperatureManagerException2:

```
        }catch (ThermometerException2 te)
        {
            throw new WaterTemperatureManagerException2(
            "Couldn't create a WaterTemperatureManager " +
            "thermometer problem." , te.getTemperature(), te);
        }
```

This will cause startup()'s calling method, CantankerousCanCooker's cook() method
to catch a WaterTemperatureManagerException2.

The Thermometer2 class is shown in Listing 22.19. This version of the Thermometer
class will throw an Exception when it is instantiated.

LISTING 22.19 The Thermometer2 Class

```
package unleashed.ch22;
/**
 *
 * @author   Stephen Potts
 * @version
 */
public class Thermometer2
{
    private int temperature = 10000;
    /** Creates new Thermometer */
    public Thermometer2() throws ThermometerException2
    {
        System.out.println("Thermometer constructed");
        if ((temperature > 300) || (temperature < 32))
        {
            Exception e = null;
            throw new ThermometerException2(
                "Thermometer is malfunctioning", temperature, e);
        }
    }

    public void simIncreaseTemp()
    {
        this.temperature += 1;
    }

    public void simDecreaseTemp()
    {
        this.temperature -= 1;
    }

    public int getTemperature()
    {
        return this.temperature;
    }

    public static void main(String[] args)
    {
        try
        {
            Thermometer2 t1 = new Thermometer2();
            System.out.println("The temperature is " +
                                    t1.getTemperature());
        }catch(ThermometerException2 te)
        {
            System.out.println("Stack Buffer----------------- " );
            System.out.println( te.getStackBuffer());
            System.out.println("End of Stack Buffer----------- " );
```

LISTING 22.19   continued

```
        }
    }//main
}
```

The value added by the StackingException class can now be seen. If we include a traditional stack trace command in the catch clause of the Cannery2 class, we get the following output:

```
Manifest constructed
This Can Cooker is Cantankerous
I don't know the problem, but here is the stackBuffer
unleashed.ch22.CantankerousCanCookerException2: Couldn't create
 a Cantankerous Can Cooker WaterTemperatureManager Problem
at unleashed.ch22.CantankerousCanCooker2.cook
(CantankerousCanCooker2.java:40)
at unleashed.ch22.Cannery2.main(Cannery2.java:27)
```

This is not terrible, but it could be much better. If we use the StackingException's
getStackBuffer() method, we get a better result:

```
CantankerousCanCooker constructed
Manifest constructed
WaterTemperatureManager constructed
Thermometer constructed
This Can Cooker is Cantankerous
I don't know the problem, but here is the stackBuffer
unleashed.ch22.ThermometerException2: Thermometer is malfunctioning
        at unleashed.ch22.Thermometer2.<init>
        (Thermometer2.java:24)
        at unleashed.ch22.WaterTemperatureManager2.<init>
                (WaterTemperatureManager2.java:28)
        at unleashed.ch22.CantankerousCanCooker2.cook
                (CantankerousCanCooker2.java:35)
        at unleashed.ch22.Cannery2.main(Cannery2.java:26)
unleashed.ch22.WaterTemperatureManagerException2:
        Couldn't create a WaterTemperatureManager thermometer problem.
        at unleashed.ch22.WaterTemperatureManager2.<init>
                (WaterTemperatureManager2.java:34)
        at unleashed.ch22.CantankerousCanCooker2.cook
                (CantankerousCanCooker2.java:35)
        at unleashed.ch22.Cannery2.main(Cannery2.java:26)
unleashed.ch22.CantankerousCanCookerException2:
                Couldn't create a Cantankerous Can Cooker
                        WaterTemperatureManager Problem
        at unleashed.ch22.CantankerousCanCooker2.cook
                (CantankerousCanCooker2.java:39)
        at unleashed.ch22.Cannery2.main(Cannery2.java:26)
```

You still see the most recent stack at the bottom of the listing. In addition, you see both the other stack buffers that were saved before the next level of Exception was thrown. This provides more information to the calling classes and to the users.

Exception Chaining in JDK 1.4

Creating your own class similar to the StackingException class was the only way to avoid losing information about where your runtime exception occurred until the release of JDK 1.4. As of this release, the Throwable class has been enhanced to include two new methods: getCause() and initCause(). The initCause() method allows you to store a previous exception as the cause of the current one. The getCause() allows you to obtain this information. The printStackTrace() method has also been enhanced to display the back trace information, if the programmer has made the effort to capture it.

Additionally, two new constructors, Throwable(Throwable) and Throwable(String, Throwable), allow you to add back trace information during the creation of the new Exception.

The primary benefit of this change is that you can omit the StackingException class from your system sometimes. If you like the layout of the printStackTrace() method, you may use it directly. You may also use the getStackTrace() method to access the data in the stack trace from a program and format it yourself. Listing 22.20 shows a new Cannery3 class that uses the JDK 1.4 approach.

LISTING 22.20   The Cannery3 Class

```
package unleashed.ch22;

/**
 *
 * @author  Stephen Potts
 * The Cannery class is the factory that cans the products.
 * It contains the main() for this system
 */
public class Cannery3
{

    /** Creates new Cannery */
    public Cannery3()
    {
    }

    public static void main(String[] args)
    {
        try
```

LISTING 22.20   continued

```
    {
        CantankerousCanCooker3 ccc = new CantankerousCanCooker3();
        Manifest m1 = new Manifest(1000, "beef tips");
        ccc.cook(m1, 210, 5);
    }catch (CantankerousCanCookerException3 cce)
    {
        System.out.println("This Can Cooker is Cantankerous");
        System.out.println(
        "I don't know the problem, but here is the stack");
        cce.printStackTrace(System.out);
    }
  }
}
```

Notice that the `printStackTrace()` method is called instead of the `getStackBuffer()` method of the `StackingException` class:

```
        cce.printStackTrace(System.out);
```

If this is the only change that you make, you will not get any more information than you did using JDK 1.3. The `Exception` classes that you create must be changed also, as shown in Listings 22.21–22.23.

LISTING 22.21   The `CantankerousCanCookerException3` Class

```
package unleashed.ch22;

/**
 *
 * @author   Stephen Potts
 * @version
 */
public class CantankerousCanCookerException3 extends Exception
{
    int temperature;

    /** Creates  a new Exception */
    public CantankerousCanCookerException3(String message, int temperature,
➥Exception e)
    {
        super(message, e);
        this.temperature = temperature;
    }

    public int getTemperature()
    {
        return this.temperature;
    }
}
```

LISTING 22.22   The `ThermometerException3` Class

```
package unleashed.ch22;
/**
 *
 * @author  Stephen Potts
 */
public class ThermometerException3 extends Exception
{
    private int temperature;
    /** Creates new ThermometerException */
    public ThermometerException3(){
    }

    public ThermometerException3(String message, int temperature, Exception e)
    {
        super(message, e);
        this.temperature = temperature;
    }

    public int getTemperature()
    {
        return this.temperature;
    }
}
```

LISTING 22.23   The `WaterTemperatureManagerException3` Class

```
package unleashed.ch22;

/**
 *
 * @author  Stephen Potts
 */
public class WaterTemperatureManagerException3 extends Exception
{
    int temperature;

    /** Creates new WaterTemperatureManagerException */
    public WaterTemperatureManagerException3(String message, int temperature,
➥Exception e)
    {
        super(message, e);
        this.temperature = temperature;
    }

    public int getTemperature()
    {
        return this.temperature;
    }
}
```

These three classes are similar, so we will discuss them as a group. Notice that each class now extends the standard Java Exception class instead of the custom StackingException class. The super() call invokes the new constructor and passes the Exception that causes this one as a parameter. It also takes a message parameter just like StackingException does.

Minor changes are also required in the WaterTemperatureManager3 class, as shown in Listing 22.24.

LISTING 22.24 The WaterTemperatureManager3 Class

```java
package unleashed.ch22;
import java.util.*;

/**
 *
 * @author   Stephen Potts
 */
public class WaterTemperatureManager3
{
    private Thermometer3 therm1;
    private WaterValve watValve;
    private int temperature;
    private int duration;


    /** Creates new WaterTemperatureManager */
    public WaterTemperatureManager3(int temperature, int duration)
                throws WaterTemperatureManagerException3
    {
        try
        {
            System.out.println("WaterTemperatureManager constructed");
            this.therm1 = new Thermometer3();
            this.watValve = new WaterValve();
            this.temperature = temperature;
            this.duration = duration;
        }catch (ThermometerException3 te)
        {
             throw new WaterTemperatureManagerException3(
             "Couldn't create a WaterTemperatureManager " +
             "thermometer problem." , te.getTemperature(), te);
        }
    }


    //Heat up the water and keep it at the temperature for the duration
    public void startUp() throws WaterTemperatureManagerException3
```

LISTING 22.24   continued

```java
{
    try
    {
        Calendar c = Calendar.getInstance();
        boolean done = false;

        System.out.println(
            "WaterTemperatureManager.startUP() - started");

        //get up to temperature
        this.watValve.openValve();
        while (therm1.getTemperature() < this.temperature)
        {
            System.out.println("temperature is now = " +
                                    therm1.getTemperature());
            Thread.sleep(10*60);
            therm1.simIncreaseTemp(); // simulates the water warming
        }
        this.watValve.closeValve();

        System.out.println(
                "WaterTemperatureManager.startUP() - " +
                    " achieved temperature of " +
                        therm1.getTemperature() );

        while (!done)
        {
            Thread.sleep(10*60);
            if (therm1.getTemperature() < this.temperature)
                this.watValve.openValve();
            else
                this.watValve.closeValve();
            c = Calendar.getInstance();
            System.out.print(
                    "WaterTemperatureManager.startUP() time = ");
            System.out.print(c.get(Calendar.HOUR) +
                ":"+ c.get(Calendar.MINUTE) +":"+
                        c.get(Calendar.SECOND));
            System.out.println(" Temperature = " +
                            therm1.getTemperature());
            duration -= 1;
            if (duration == 0)
                done = true;
        }
        System.out.println(
            "WaterTemperatureManager.startUP() - ending");
    }catch (InterruptedException ie)
    {
        System.out.println(
            "WaterTemperatureManager.startUp() " + ie);
```

LISTING 22.24   continued

```
        throw new WaterTemperatureManagerException3(
            "Couldn't start the WaterTemperatureManager timing " +
            "was interrupted by another process ",
                    therm1.getTemperature(), ie);


    }
  }
}
```

Notice that the exception thrown is now changed:

```
        throw new WaterTemperatureManagerException3(
            "Couldn't start the WaterTemperatureManager timing " +
            "was interrupted by another process ",
                    therm1.getTemperature(), ie);
```

Changes are also needed to the Thermometer3 class, as shown in Listing 22.25.

LISTING 22.25   The Thermometer3 Class

```
package unleashed.ch22;
/**
 *
 * @author   Stephen Potts
 * @version
 */

public class Thermometer3
{
    private int temperature = 10000;
    /** Creates new Thermometer */
    public Thermometer3() throws ThermometerException3
    {
        System.out.println("Thermometer constructed");
        if ((temperature > 300) || (temperature < 32))
        {
            Exception e = null;
            throw new ThermometerException3(
                    "Thermometer is malfunctioning", temperature, e);
        }
    }

    public void simIncreaseTemp()
    {
        this.temperature += 1;
    }

    public void simDecreaseTemp()
```

LISTING 22.25 continued

```
    {
        this.temperature -= 1;
    }

    public int getTemperature()
    {
        return this.temperature;
    }

    public static void main(String[] args)
    {
        try
        {
            Thermometer3 t1 = new Thermometer3();
            System.out.println(
                "The temperature is " + t1.getTemperature());
        }catch(ThermometerException3 te)
        {
            System.out.println("Stack Buffer------------------ " );
            te.printStackTrace();
            System.out.println("End of Stack Buffer----------- " );

        }
    }//main
}
```

Here you can see where the original Exception is created:

```
        throw new ThermometerException3(
                "Thermometer is malfunctioning", temperature, e);
```

The three parameters contain the information that the JVM will hold until it is requested by a printStackTrace() or similar method.

The CantankerousCanCooker3 class is shown in Listing 22.26.

LISTING 22.26 The CantankerousCanCooker3 Class

```
package unleashed.ch22;

/**
 *
 * @author  Stephen Potts
 */
public class CantankerousCanCooker3
{
    Manifest man1;
    WaterTemperatureManager3 wtm;
```

LISTING 22.26   continued

```java
    int temperature;
    int duration;
    boolean cooking;

    /** Creates new CantankerousCanCooker */
    public CantankerousCanCooker3()
    {
        System.out.println("CantankerousCanCooker3 constructed");
    }

    public void cook(Manifest man1, int temperature, int duration)
                          throws CantankerousCanCookerException3
    {
        try
        {
            this.cooking = true;
            this.man1 = man1;
            this.temperature = temperature;
            this.duration = duration;
            wtm = new WaterTemperatureManager3(temperature, duration);
            wtm.startUp();
        }catch (WaterTemperatureManagerException3 wtme)
        {
            throw new CantankerousCanCookerException3(
            "Couldn't create a Cantankerous Can Cooker " +
            "WaterTemperatureManager Problem" ,
                    wtme.getTemperature(), wtme);
        }
    }

    public void stop()
    {
        this.cooking = false;
    }

    public boolean isCooking()
    {
        return this.cooking;
    }
}
```

The only real change that was made to this class was in the `catch` clause. The `Exceptions` that are thrown have changed:

```java
        }catch (WaterTemperatureManagerException3 wtme)
        {
            throw new CantankerousCanCookerException3(
            "Couldn't create a Cantankerous Can Cooker " +
```

```
    "WaterTemperatureManager Problem" ,
            wtme.getTemperature(), wtme);
```

The primary disadvantage of the JDK 1.4 approach is that the `Throwable` class is not serializable. This only comes into play when you want to communicate the error back to the client using RMI, JMS, JNDI, or a similar technology. In these cases, the `StackingException` class, which is serializable, is superior.

Summary

In this chapter, we looked at the design of our classes in the area of exception handling. You learned how the Java virtual machine behaves when an exception is thrown.

You also learned how to create meaningful custom exceptions that preserve all the debugging information handed to them. Then, you learned how to throw these exceptions in a meaningful way to improve the quality of the messages that an `Exception` object provides to the user.

Finally, you learned how to use the new `Exception` chaining methods that have been added to the `Throwable` class. This eliminates the need to create a custom class to hold stack information in cases where serialization is not important.

Java Security

CHAPTER 23

Java was started as the language in which you could write a program that was transmitted and executed on the user's machine. This feature made it absolutely necessary for Java to offer a convincing security model from the very beginning. Before Java, the idea of sending a program to another computer across a public network would have seemed crazy. What if a program carried a virus? What if it were just written so badly that it could accidentally wipe out your hard drive? Java offered ways to stop such ill-behaving applications from destroying the user's computer.

Application security is a huge topic that has many different aspects to it. We will not cover all features of Java security. However, we will cover enough for a programmer to start writing secure applications in Java. Specifically, we will talk about how to stop a program from doing what it is not supposed to. This is achieved by using the Java sandbox. We will also talk about how to securely send data over the Internet using SSL. This will prompt a use of the Java Secure Sockets Extension (JSSE).

Introduction to Java Security

You might hear from some developers, "Let's write the app first and think about security later." In fact, that is how security is treated in many languages. That is not so in Java. In Java, security features are designed in the language and implemented without exception by the Java Virtual Machine (JVM). For this reason, it makes sense to know both what is provided to you and what is required of you. This will require you to think about how your application will perform within the confines of the language's security features and restrictions from the start.

> **Note**
>
> You can download all the examples for this chapter from the Sams Publishing Web site. The source code for this chapter includes a `readme` file with instructions on how to compile and run the examples. The examples run on JDK 1.4. The Java Secure Socket Extension (JSSE) example requires a separate download from Sun's Web site at `http://java.sun.com/products/jsse/index.html` if you want to run the example on previous versions of JDK.

Overview of Application Security

Security is understood in the context of some environment. For example, in a workplace, security is needed so that an intruder cannot get in the office and steal a coffee machine. A good idea would be to ask a question such as, "Would anybody be interested in our coffee machine?" If the answer is "yes," we need to put a lock on the door to our office. Similarly, if a software system has data or resources that can be compromised, stolen, or tampered with, this system needs a set of policies that can be implemented to prevent that from happening.

Security is often implemented in hierarchical levels. The first reason for this is that security is expensive in terms of design, implementation, maintenance, and performance, and that these costs increase almost exponentially as the degree of security provided increases. In other words, you should have multiple levels of protection to safeguard assets of different values. The second reason for these separate levels is that people and applications can be divided into groups defined by the greater or lesser degree of trust you have in these people and applications. The separate levels allow you to easily restrict the more untrusted groups from having access to your more valuable assets.

> **Tip**
>
> The best computer security is achieved when the computer is turned off. This, however, would make us all lose our jobs. The key is to find a balance in which a program is reasonably secure and is still possible to use.

Efforts to increase application security should be measured by their net return. How much effort does it take to build one more level of security? Going back to our coffee machine example, we could ask if it makes sense to put the coffee machine in a bullet-proof safe to keep it from a thief.

Security Threats

In this section, we will consider two basic threats that Java must eliminate in order to be considered safe and secure:

- Any Java program might contain malicious code that can harm the user's data. At this time, we do not worry about how this malicious program got on to the user's machine in the first place. However, we do want to examine how Java's security features can prevent this program from damaging the machine. The Java designers address this threat by means of a mechanism called the Java sandbox model.

- Data transmitted over the public network might get corrupted on the way, or a malicious person might masquerade as a legitimate source and send maliciously altered data to the user's machine. To eliminate this threat, we want to be sure that the source is who it says it is. In other words, we want the other party to be authenticated. We also want to be certain that it would be impossible to change the transmitted data en route. In some cases, we might even want it to be impossible to know what we are transmitting. The Java designers address this threat by providing the Java Secure Socket Extension (JSSE) API.

Security Mechanisms in Java

Java provides a comprehensive set of mechanisms to enforce various security policies. These mechanisms can be classified by the time when they are used as follows:

- Compile-time security is provided by the Java language features that are enforced by the Java compiler. The language enforces data hiding using `private` and `protected` keywords. Also, eliminating pointers in the language improved its security.

- Class load–time security is enforced by the Java class loaders. Class loaders follow rules on how to load individual Java classes in to memory. The rules of loading classes prevent malicious classes from being used instead of the core JDK classes.

- Runtime security is enforced by the Java sandbox model mechanism. We cover the Java sandbox in a later section. In addition to the sandbox model, Java provides a mechanism to authenticate and authorize a user using Java Authentication and Authorization Service (JAAS). We cover JAAS very briefly in the next section.

- Transmission-time security is enforced when a Java program transfers data over an insecure network. The transmission-time security mechanisms include Java Secure Socket Extension (JSSE), which implements the SSL protocol, and encryption architecture that provides encryption engines. Encryption engines are used to encrypt the data, as well as generate message digests and digital signatures. We talk about encryption in the "Overview of Java Cryptography Extension" section.

Overview of Java Authentication and Authorization Service

Java Authentication and Authorization Service (JAAS) is a framework of classes that can be extended by providing implementations of various classes. The JAAS framework focuses on how to protect a system from a malicious user. The JAAS enabled application requires a user to log in and be authorized to perform certain actions. This is different from the Java sandbox in that the JAAS framework gives permissions to a user, whereas the sandbox gives permissions to Java objects.

The JAAS framework has two pieces to it: authentication of the user and authorization. Authentication is performed by a `LoginContext` object. The `LoginContext` object uses so-called login modules. The authentication mechanism is set up by a system administrator who specifies what login modules are used to authenticate a user. Every login module is essentially a set of classes that implement a way to authenticate a user. Often, a login module uses an existing authentication mechanism like an operating system. The system administrator can specify to use multiple login modules and make some modules required and some optional.

After the user is authenticated by the `LoginContext` object, she can retrieve a `Subject` object from it. `Subject` represents a user in the system and may contain multiple `Principal` objects. `Principal` object is a single identifying characteristic of a user. For example, my operating system login name and password are represented by one `Principal` object. My database login and password are represented by another `Principal` object. All the `Principal` objects represent the same user so they all are contained in one `Subject`. The `Subject` is used to call methods `doAs` and `doAsPrivileged`, passing actions that the user wants to perform. At this time, the user is being authorized to perform these actions. The authorization is done based on the JAAS policy file that looks similar to the Java sandbox policy file. The JAAS policy file grants permissions to the user to execute certain actions. So, when methods `doAs` or `doAsPrivileged` are called, the JAAS framework checks whether the subject has permission to execute this action. The action should be an object that implements the `java.security.PrivilegedAction` interface.

The JAAS framework can be extended to support a variety of authentication services. For example, JDK 1.4 provides sample login modules that can be integrated with Solaris and NT operating systems. Thus, your program can ask a user to provide a password of your NT domain for authentication.

Overview of Java Cryptography Extension

Java Cryptography Extension (JCE) is built to provide the following cryptographic operations: Encryption, Secure Key Exchanges, and Secure Message Digests. All the operations deal with how to encrypt data before it is exposed in the insecure environment.

Encryption is handled by encryption engines. An encryption engine implements a cryptographic algorithm to encrypt and decrypt a message. The engine takes input message and uses a key to encrypt it. Although the key is essential to many algorithms, some engines do not require a key. Also, some engines produce output of a smaller size than the input. An example of such engines is message digest engines.

Encryption keys are used in encryption engines. Keys come alone or in pairs. A single key is used for so-called symmetric algorithms, when the same key can be used to encrypt and decrypt a message. Pairs of keys are used in asymmetric algorithms. A pair of key consists of private and public keys. If a message is encrypted by the private key, it can be decrypted only by the public key.

A message digest is used to determine whether the data has been tampered with. It is a digital fingerprint of a stream of bytes. A digest is generated when a stream of bytes is fed through a message digest engine. It is not possible to calculate the original stream of bytes from a digest. However, if you receive a message and its digest, you can use the message to calculate the digest. Then the received digest is compared with the newly calculated one. If the two are equal, the original digest does represent the message. Thus, the recipient of the message and the digest can verify whether the message was tampered with. Of course, this does not stop a malicious source from supplying a new digest together with a corrupted message. If you receive a digest that was calculated based on the corrupted messaged, you would think that the message is good, whereas in fact you are working with a bad digest. That's why encryption keys are used to produce secure digests. If the digest is encrypted with a private key, the recipient can guarantee that the digest can only be generated by the original sender.

> **Note**
>
> A message digest that has been encrypted with a private key is called a digital signature. An encryption engine that produces digital signatures is called a digital signature engine.

JCE extends the functionality of the core Java API that deals with encryption. This includes additional encryption engines and classes to handle message digests. JCE also provides the ability to handle secret keys.

Java Sandbox Model

In this section, we consider the most basic security question: If a malicious program is running on the user's machine, what can be done to protect the system? The problem we have in addressing this question is that it is very difficult to distinguish between proper and improper behavior in a program. One approach is that we can make a list of all possible viruses and try to find them in the program. Another is that we can attempt to identify and safely contain the bad effects of a bug in a program. But, this might not be sufficient protection if a program is not a virus but connects to some bad site and downloads a virus to execute it. These less than optimal attempts to solve this difficult problem highlight the importance of the fundamental assumption that the JVM makes about each Java program. It is assumed that any program can behave badly and, therefore, there must be a way to stop it from doing so. This requirement was the motivation for the development of the sandbox mechanism. Each Java program is executed in a logically isolated area of memory called a sandbox that is defined by its access permissions. Some programs can have more permissions, and some can have less. But there is always a way to define just how much freedom is given to a program.

In this section, we will look at the underlying theories that determined the architecture of the Java sandbox model. Further, we will see how a sandbox's particular permissions are defined using Java Policy Files. Then we will see how the sandbox model can be extended to create new permissions.

Java Sandbox Architecture

Java introduced the notion of the sandbox in the very beginning. A program must execute in its own virtual sandbox. The JVM guards the rest of the system from a Java program by giving it only a specified set of permissions. When a program attempts to do something worth noting through an action of the Java API, the JVM halts it until a check is made to determine whether the program has a defined permission to perform that action.

> **Note**
>
> This section describes the sandbox model that existed in Java as of version 1.1 when the Access Controller and Policy File were added. Conceptually, the sandbox model had existed even before then; however, version 1.1 significantly improved it.

The notion of a sandbox is directly related to the idea of trust. Every program is assigned to a sandbox whose permissions are determined by the source of that program. Thus, for example, all applets downloaded from the Internet are considered untrusted. This confines them to the sandbox with the least amount of permissions.

The sandbox architecture is shown in Figure 23.1.

FIGURE 23.1
The Java sandbox model consists of a Security Manager, an Access Controller, and a Policy File.

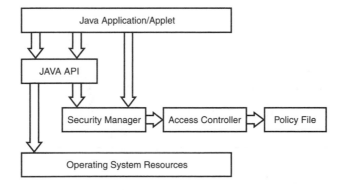

Figure 23.1 shows what subsystems and classes are called when the Java sandbox checks permission. The key players are the Security Manager, the Access Controller, and the Policy File. A Java class calls the Java API when it wants to perform a certain action—for example, to open a file. Before performing the action, the Java API checks with the Security Manager to determine if this action is permitted. The Security Manager can deny the action by throwing a `SecurityException`. However, in most cases the Security Manager does not make the final determination, but it checks with the Access Controller. The Access Controller then searches through the Policy File to determine whether this action is permitted.

A Policy File is a text file that you can edit in any text editor. You can also use the `policytool` GUI provided in the JDK to edit Policy Files.

You can see in Figure 23.1 that your application can call the Security Manager directly to check for a particular permission. This allows you to create your application to integrate with the control mechanisms of the sandbox. You can create your own application specific permissions. For example, an account access permission can be created that can be declared later in the Policy File just like any normal Java permission. We will write our own permission example later in this section.

Using Java Permissions

Let's see how the sandbox model works in a simple Java application. The example of Listing 23.1 reads the value of a system property. Reading a system property is a Java action that is controlled by the Java sandbox. Each system property has a separate permission associated with it in the Policy File.

LISTING 23.1   `JavaPermissionExample.java`—Permission Example

```
package unleashed.ch23;

/**
* Permission example
*/
public class JavaPermissionExample
{
    public static void main(String[] args)
    {
        //read property
        String prop = System.getProperty("unleashed.ch23.TestProperty");

        System.out.println("Test Property is: " + prop);
    }
}
```

The `JavaPermissionExample` class reads the value of a system property named `unleashed.ch23.TestProperty` and prints it to the screen. The class needs a permission to do that. Listing 23.2 shows the Policy File that gives this application specific permission to do that.

LISTING 23.2   `example.policy`—Policy File with Permissions

```
// Standard extensions get all permissions by default

grant codeBase "file:${java.home}/lib/ext/*" {
    permission java.security.AllPermission;
};

// default permissions granted to all domains

grant {
    // Allows any thread to stop itself using the java.lang.Thread.stop()
    // method that takes no argument.
    // Note that this permission is granted by default only to remain
    // backwards compatible.
    // It is strongly recommended that you either remove this permission
    // from this policy file or further restrict it to code sources
    // that you specify, because Thread.stop() is potentially unsafe.
    // See "http://java.sun.com/notes" for more information.
    permission java.lang.RuntimePermission "stopThread";

    // allows anyone to listen on un-privileged ports
    permission java.net.SocketPermission "localhost:1024-", "listen";

    // "standard" properties that can be read by anyone

    permission java.util.PropertyPermission "java.version", "read";
    permission java.util.PropertyPermission "java.vendor", "read";
    permission java.util.PropertyPermission "java.vendor.url", "read";
    permission java.util.PropertyPermission "java.class.version", "read";
    permission java.util.PropertyPermission "os.name", "read";
    permission java.util.PropertyPermission "os.version", "read";
    permission java.util.PropertyPermission "os.arch", "read";
    permission java.util.PropertyPermission "file.separator", "read";
    permission java.util.PropertyPermission "path.separator", "read";
    permission java.util.PropertyPermission "line.separator", "read";

    permission java.util.PropertyPermission
➥ "java.specification.version", "read";
    permission java.util.PropertyPermission
➥ "java.specification.vendor", "read";
    permission java.util.PropertyPermission "java.specification.name", "read";
```

23

JAVA SECURITY

LISTING 23.2 continued

```
    permission java.util.PropertyPermission
➥ "java.vm.specification.version", "read";
    permission java.util.PropertyPermission
➥ "java.vm.specification.vendor", "read";
    permission java.util.PropertyPermission
➥ "java.vm.specification.name", "read";
    permission java.util.PropertyPermission "java.vm.version", "read";
    permission java.util.PropertyPermission "java.vm.vendor", "read";
    permission java.util.PropertyPermission "java.vm.name", "read";
    permission java.util.PropertyPermission
➥ "unleashed.ch23.TestProperty", "read";

    //permission unleashed.ch23.MyPermission "newMyPermission";

};
```

The file can be divided into different sections based on the code base. The code base defines what directory or URL a class is loaded from. All classes loaded from the same code base are said to belong to the same protection domain. In Listing 23.2 the first protection domain has this code base:

```
grant codeBase "file:${java.home}/lib/ext/*"
```

The code base looks like a URL that can have system property variables in it. The system property `${java.home}` will be substituted at runtime for the real path, for example, `c:\jdk\jdk14`.

> **Note**
>
> In addition to the code base, the protection domain can also specify who is expected to sign the classes using digital signatures. Digital signatures in this case prove that a class has actually originated from the code base.

Java provides these standard permissions to use in a Policy File:

- File permissions control access to files.
- Property permissions control access to system properties like our `unleashed.ch23.TestProperty` property.
- Runtime permissions control various actions of the `java.lang.Runtime` class.
- Net permissions control various actions of the java.net package, such as HTTP authentication.

- Socket permissions control socket operations as follows: listen for, accept a connection to, or resolve a Java socket.

- Security permissions control actions in the `java.security` package—for example, installing a new security provider.

- AWT Permissions deal with actions in the AWT package, as in reading pixels on the screen.

- Serializable permissions allow various actions during the serialization process.

- Reflection permissions allow a program to examine private class variables through Java reflection.

- All permission is a catch permission that allows everything.

> **Tip**
>
> If your program throws an exception with Access Denied messages, there is a good chance that some permission is missing. Try giving `java.security.AllPermission` permission to this class and see if it eliminates the problem. However, do not give all permissions to your final program.

Permission in Java is represented by a descendant of the `java.security.Permission` class. For example, a permission to read `TestProperty` is given by this line in the Policy File:

```
permission java.util.PropertyPermission "unleashed.ch23.TestProperty", "read";
```

A full classname specifies the type of permission. Following the classname are two strings that specify a name of the permission and various options. A name and options are specific to the permission. In our example, the name is `"unleashed.ch23.TestProperty"` and the option is `"read"`. A property permission can have more options separated by commas (for example, `read,write`).

After compiling the example using the `compilejpe.bat` file, you can run it by executing the `runjpe.bat` file or by typing this command:

```
java -Dunleashed.ch23.TestProperty=HELLO  -Djava.security.manager
➥ -Djava.security.policy=unleashed\ch23\example.policy
➥ -classpath . unleashed.ch23.JavaPermissionExample
```

The command line specifies the property to read

```
-Dunleashed.ch23.TestProperty=HELLO
```

Further, the command specifies the use of the Security Manager and points to the Policy File that the Access Controller is supposed to use.

> **Note**
>
> One of the differences between an applet and application is that applets are always executing in a sandbox with a Security Manager. Applications do not have a Security Manager by default; you have to tell the JVM to use the Security Manager by specifying the `-Djava.security.manager` property or programmatically by calling the `System.setSecurityManager` method. If a Security Manager is not present, the sandbox essentially does not exist.

The example produces this output:

```
Test Property is: HELLO
```

Our application has successfully read the property because the Policy File explicitly allowed it to do so. You can change the Policy File to comment out the permission like this:

```
    //permission java.util.PropertyPermission
➥ "unleashed.ch23.TestProperty", "read";
```

If you run the example again, you will get an exception saying that access to the property is denied.

Writing Your Own Permissions for Java Sandbox

Java provides a large set of standard permissions for every standard application to use. However, you can create your own application permissions just as easily. To do this, you have to extend the `java.security.Permission` class. Listing 23.3 shows how to write a new permission.

LISTING 23.3 `MyPermission.java`—Writing Your Own Permission Class

```
package unleashed.ch23;

import java.security.*;

/**
 * Simple permission
 */
```

LISTING 23.3 continued

```java
public class MyPermission extends java.security.Permission
{
    /**
     * Permission name
     */
    private String name;

    /**
     * Constructor
     */
    public MyPermission(String name)
    {
        super(name);
    }

    public void checkGuard(Object object){}

    public boolean equals(Object obj)
    {
        if (obj instanceof MyPermission)
            return true;
        else
            return false;
    }

    public String getActions()
    {
      return null;
    }


    public int hashCode()
    {
        return ("MyPermission" + name).hashCode();

    }

    public boolean implies(Permission permission)
    {

        if(permission instanceof MyPermission)
            return true;
        else
            return false;
    }

    public PermissionCollection newPermissionCollection()
    {
        return null;
    }
```

LISTING 23.3   continued

```java
public String toString()
{
    return "MyPermission" + name;
}


}
```

The most important method in Listing 23.3 is the `implies` method. This method returns true if the argument to it has the same type as our permission. `implies` can contain more complicated logic; for example, it could check for a specific name or options in the argument.

Listing 23.4 demonstrates a class that behaves similarly to the way a typical Java API class checks permission before performing an action. The `doSomething` method gets the Security Manager to check for `MyPermission`. If the permission is given, the class can proceed to execute further. Otherwise, an exception is thrown.

LISTING 23.4   `MyPermissionExample.java`—Simple Permission Example Class

```java
package unleashed.ch23;

/**
 * MyPermissionExample tries to execute method doSomething() that is
 * only allowed to execute if unleashed.ch23.MyPermission permission is given.
 */
public class MyPermissionExample
{
    public static void main(String[] args)
    {
        doSomething();
    }

    public static void doSomething()
    {
        //get security manager
        SecurityManager sm = System.getSecurityManager();

        if (sm != null)
        {
            //check permission
            sm.checkPermission(new MyPermission(""), sm.getSecurityContext());
        }
        else
```

LISTING 23.4   continued

```
            throw new SecurityException("No Security Manager");


        //do the rest here -- it is allowed by security manager
        System.out.println("doSomething method is allowed to execute;");
    }
}
```

The checkPermission method throws a java.security.AccessControlException exception if the permission is not granted in the Policy File.

In order for the example to run without an exception, you need to uncomment this line in the Policy File:

```
permission unleashed.ch23.MyPermission "newMyPermission";
```

This basically gives our class MyPermissionExample a permission to execute the doSomething method.

You can compile the example by executing the compileperm.bat file. After compiling the example, you can run it using the runperm.bat file. Also, the readme file provided with the source code has all the instructions on how to compile and run the chapter examples. The runperm.bat file contains the following command to execute the example:

```
java  -Djava.security.manager
➡ -Djava.security.policy=unleashed\ch23\example.policy
➡ -classpath . unleashed.ch23.MyPermissionExample
```

The example initializes a Java sandbox by specifying the -Djava.security.manager property.

The example produces this output:

```
doSomething method is allowed to execute;
```

The doSomething method is allowed to execute because the Policy File grants the class a permission to do so.

Java Secure Sockets

Java Secure Socket Extension (JSSE) is a Java API to use with the Secure Sockets Layer (SSL) protocols associated with secure transactions over the Internet. JSSE represents an API that shields a programmer from many of the details of SSL. You will want to use

JSSE if you're writing a secure client or server that communicates over TCP. SSL is also used as the HTTPS protocol in Internet browsers. This makes SSL one of the most commonly used security protocols on the Internet.

We will briefly go over the SSL protocol to understand how the secure communication takes place. Then we will write a simple client-server application that exchanges encrypted messages.

SSL Overview

SSL is a protocol to send encrypted data over the Internet. SSL complements TCP sockets and is also known as HTTPS. Every time you see `https` in your browser URL, it means that you are using SSL. SSL is a standard protocol that is maintained by the Internet Engineering Task Force (IETF). The latest version of SSL was renamed to the Transport Layer Security (TLS) standard. However, we will use the name SSL as it is more widely accepted.

SSL is used by many online retailers for credit card transactions, so if you have bought anything online, you have most probably used SSL. A browser uses SSL if the URL has an `https` prefix. In this case, your browser plays the role of client, whereas the retailer's Web server acts as server in a secure client-server relationship. A client and a server typically go through these interactions:

1. The client tells the server what encryption mechanisms it supports.
2. The server picks the best encryption from this list and optionally authenticates itself to the client.
3. The client and the server exchange secret keys to encrypt data.
4. The client and server exchange encrypted data.

Basically, before a browser sends your credit card number to the server, it asks the server how to encrypt it so that nobody can read the data en route. Both client and server must agree on the encryption method and exchange the secret key so that nobody else knows the key. We will talk about how the key is exchanged in the next section; let's just assume that it is possible for now.

In addition to the key exchange, the client might ask the server to authenticate itself. This is required whenever the client needs assurance that it is communicating with the right Web site. The authentication is done using certificates. A certificate is like a driver's license that is issued by the state to verify that a picture and a name belong to the same person. Web certificates verify that a company name and a company Web site belong to the same company. A certificate is issued by an authorized company called a certificate authority (CA). A certificate authority can also have a certificate issued by some other CA. This is called chained certificates. The idea is that a client will check all certificates until it finds a CA that it can trust. If a trustworthy CA is found in a chain of certificates, the client can trust every certificate in this chain.

> **Tip**
>
> The key exchange and authentication happen before any data is sent over the network. This is why SSL significantly slows down the communication. Use SSL only when you are actually sending sensitive data.

Most of these details are hidden from a programmer who is using JSSE. In fact, we will see in the coming example that programming with SSL looks very similar to programming regular Java sockets.

Encryption Overview

Encryption is based on cryptology, the study of cryptanalysis and cryptography. Basic encryption algorithms were already in use in the days of the Roman Empire. In the past few decades, encryption has become a field solely owned by computers because very few humans can compete with machines in this area of mathematical operations.

Encryption works by applying one or more algorithms and keys to a message. To decrypt the message, the other party must have the right key. Two common types of encryption algorithms are as follows:

- Symmetric key encryption uses the same key to encrypt and decrypt a message. A problem with this method is that the key must remain secret among the authorized parties to the communication. If you send the secret key over the Internet in such a way that an unauthorized person can intercept it, he will be able to decrypt all your subsequent transmissions. This is commonly known as the key-distribution problem.

- Asymmetric key encryption, also known as public key encryption, uses two different keys: a public key known to everyone and a private key that is kept secret and is not distributed among the communicating parties. Asymmetric keys work only one way, meaning that if you encrypt a message by using a private key, you can decrypt only by using the public key and vice versa. Typically, in a two-party communication, one side generates a pair of keys, keeps the private key, and sends the public key to the other side. Now if the other side sends any data encrypting it with the public key, only the owner of the private key can decrypt it. The private key is never sent over the network, so the transmission is secure even over the public network. To make communication secure both ways, the two parties usually exchange their public keys. This asymmetric encryption is key to making the Internet a safe place to trade. Unfortunately, asymmetric encryption is also much slower than symmetric encryption.

As both symmetric and asymmetric methods have disadvantages, most real life protocols, including SSL, use both methods. The asymmetric encryption, because of its ability to securely distribute keys, is used first to encrypt a symmetric key. Then the encrypted key is sent over the network. Once both parties have the symmetric key, the rest of communication is done using the symmetric encryption because of its greater speed.

Client/Server with JSSE

Let's write a simple example of how a client and server would communicate using JSSE. The server class of Listing 23.5 creates a secure socket and listens on it. When a request comes along, the server starts a new thread to service that request. The thread first receives data from the client, and then sends a string back. The example looks almost like a regular Java socket program except that it communicates with SSL.

> **Note**
>
> JSSE became a part of JDK starting from version 1.4. You will need to download it separately if you want to run the examples with the previous versions of JDK.

LISTING 23.5   SSLServerExample.java—JSSE Server Class

```
package unleashed.ch23;

import java.io.*;
import java.net.*;
import java.security.*;

import javax.net.*;
import javax.net.ssl.*;

/**
 * SSL Server class runs in a separate thread. Reads the client data
 * then sends response back to the client
 */
class MySSLServer extends Thread
{
```

LISTING 23.5   continued

```
    private Socket socket;

    public MySSLServer(Socket socket)
    {
        this.socket = socket;
    }

    public void run()
    {
        try
        {
            System.out.println("Connection established");
            BufferedReader r = new BufferedReader(new
 ➧ InputStreamReader(socket.getInputStream()));

            PrintWriter p = new PrintWriter(socket.getOutputStream());

            System.out.println("Reading data");
            String data = r.readLine();
            System.out.println("Data received: " + data);

            System.out.println("Sending response");

            p.println("HELLO FROM SSL SERVER");

            p.close();

            System.out.println("Data received..closing connection");
            socket.close();

        }catch(IOException e)
        {
            System.out.println("IOException is server: " + e.getMessage());
        }
    }

}

/**
 * Server main class
 */
public class SSLServerExample extends Thread
{
    /**
     * Creates SSL socket and listens on it.
     */
    public static void main(String[] args)
    {
```

LISTING 23.5   continued

```
        try
        {
            //creates SSL socket factory
            ServerSocketFactory sf = SSLServerSocketFactory.getDefault();

            //creates SSL socket
            SSLServerSocket ss =
➡ (SSLServerSocket)sf.createServerSocket(9096);

            //enable truststore cipher suite
            enableAllCipherSuites(ss);


            System.out.println("Server started...listening");
            while (true)
            {
                //listen in a while loop
                new MySSLServer(ss.accept()).start();
            }
        }catch(Exception e)
        {
            System.out.println(e.getMessage());
            e.printStackTrace();
        }
    }

    /**
    * Enables the cipher suite that is used in the truststore.
    */
    private static void enableAllCipherSuites(SSLServerSocket ss)
    {
        String newsuites[] = new String[8];

        //read all enabled cipher suites
        String suites[] = ss.getEnabledCipherSuites();

        //overwrite the first cell with our cipher suite
        suites[0] = "SSL_DH_anon_EXPORT_WITH_DES40_CBC_SHA";

        //enable the new cipher suites
        ss.setEnabledCipherSuites(suites);

    }


}
```

The JSSE code is located in the `SSLServerExample` class. The class uses the `getDefault` method on `SSLServerSocketFactory` to create an SSL socket factory. After the factory is created, it can create a server socket on port 9096. You can use another port. Typically servers use a standard SSL port 443. Once the secure socket is created the server maintains a while loop to listen for an incoming request. The server allows the socket to accept the request and starts a new thread with this call:

```
new MySSLServer(ss.accept()).start();
```

The new thread runs the `MySSLServer` class to support all communications with the client.

To enable the correct cipher suite, the server calls the `enableAllCipherSuites` method on the socket. This method does not actually enable all cipher suites but only the one that we really need for the example to run. This is needed because we use certificates that come with WebLogic Servers. These certificates use the `SSL_DH_anon_EXPORT_WITH_DES40_CBC_SHA` cipher, which is not enabled by default in the SSL socket. To enable this cipher suite, we call the `getEnabledCipherSuites` method to get a list of all the enabled cipher suites and then put the needed cipher suite into that list. Then we call `setEnabledCipherSuites` to enable the whole list of cipher suites.

> **Note**
>
> Cipher suites are algorithms that are used to encrypt and decrypt communications. Sun's JSSE implementation supports a total of 15 different cipher suites, but not all of them are enabled by default.

The JSSE client is shown in Listing 23.6. The client also creates a secure socket and tries to connect to the server on port 9096. Once the connection is established, the client sends a string to the server and waits for a response. After the response is received, the client terminates the connection.

LISTING 23.6 `SSLClientExample.java`—JSSE Client Class

```
package unleashed.ch23;

import java.io.*;
import java.net.*;
import javax.net.*;
import javax.net.ssl.*;
```

LISTING 23.6   continued

```java
/**
* SSLClientExample creates an SSL socket to connect to local Weblogic server.
*/
public class SSLClientExample
{
    /**
    * Creates SSL socket, connects to the server,
    * sends data and receives server response.
    */
    public static void main(String[] args)
    {
        try
        {

        //create SSL socket factory
        SocketFactory sf = SSLSocketFactory.getDefault();

        //create SSL socket
        SSLSocket s = (SSLSocket)sf.createSocket
        ("localhost", Integer.parseInt("9096"));

        System.out.println("Client started");

        //enable cipher suite
        enableAllCipherSuites(s);

        //create reader
        BufferedReader br =  new BufferedReader(
            new InputStreamReader(s.getInputStream() ));

        //create writer
        PrintWriter pw = new PrintWriter(s.getOutputStream());

        System.out.println("Connection established");

        System.out.println("Sending data");

        //send data
        pw.println("HELLO FROM SSL CLIENT");

        //need to flush the buffer or the data is not sent
        pw.flush();

        System.out.println
        ("Data is sent...receiving a response from the server");

        //read the data from the server
        System.out.println("Client received data: " + br.readLine());
        System.out.println("Closing connection");
```

LISTING 23.6 continued

```
        //close socket
        s.close();

        }catch(Exception e)
        {
            System.out.println(e.getMessage());
            e.printStackTrace();
        }
    }

    /**
     * Enable the cipher suite that is used in JDK truststore
     */
    private static void enableAllCipherSuites(SSLSocket ss)
    {
        String newsuites[] = new String[8];

        String suites[] = ss.getEnabledCipherSuites();

        suites[0] = "SSL_DH_anon_EXPORT_WITH_DES40_CBC_SHA";
        ss.setEnabledCipherSuites(suites);

    }
}
```

The client of Listing 23.6 also needs to call the enableAllCipherSuites method to enable the required cipher suite.

A server and client must be run in separate JVMs. You can start a separate command window on Windows for the server and each client.

Compile the server using the compilejsseserver.bat file. Run the server using either this command or the runjsseserver.bat file provided with the example:

```
java -Djavax.net.ssl.trustStore=unleashed\ch23\truststore
➥ -Djavax.net.ssl.keyStorePassword=changeit  -classpath .
➥ unleashed.ch23.SSLServerExample
```

The command includes the path and password to access a file in which certificates are stored.

Compile the client in a separate window using the compilejsse.bat file. Then you can run the client either using the following command or calling runjsse.bat:

```
java -Djavax.net.ssl.trustStore=unleashed\ch23\truststore  -classpath .
➥ unleashed.ch23.SSLClientExample
```

When you start a client while the server is running, you will see the output of Listing 23.7 in the server window.

LISTING 23.7   JSSE Server Output

```
Server started...listening
Connection established
Reading data
Data received: HELLO FROM SSL CLIENT
Sending response
Data received..closing connection
```

Listing 23.7 shows the result of only one client connecting to the server. The same printout will be repeated for every client that connects to the server.

You can run as many clients as you want. Each client produces the output shown in Listing 23.8.

LISTING 23.8   JSSE Client Output

```
Client started
Connection established
Sending data
Data is sent...receiving a response from the server
Client received data: HELLO FROM SSL SERVER
Closing connection
```

The client prints each step it goes through: starting, connecting to the server, sending data, receiving a response back, and disconnecting.

As you can see, programming with JSSE is really not that complicated. The most complicated details are hidden from the developer. This, however, sometimes makes it difficult to debug possible problems.

Summary

Security is an important feature of Java. It was created as an integral part of the language and the JVM rather than as an add-on. Java provides security that works at compile time, class load time, and runtime.

Application security is defined as a set of enforceable policies that are designed to protect the system from ill-behaving programs. Every application developer should carefully consider the environments in which the application will be functioning in order to identify what permissions will be needed and what restrictions should be imposed. At that point, the developer will be able to document these security considerations into a security guideline for the system staff to use in tailoring the system security policy to permit proper operation of the application without causing undue exposure to the system itself.

In this chapter, we looked at Java security while trying to answer these questions: How can Java protect the user's machine from a malicious applet/application? How can Java provide secure communication between two applications over an insecure network? The Java sandbox model answers the first question. The sandbox model defines what permissions a Java program has. You can use the default permission classes or create your own. Finally, to securely transfer data across the network we studied the Java Secure Sockets Extension (JSSE) that is based on the SSL protocol. The JSSE can authenticate and encrypt the network traffic to protect system data en route.

23

JAVA SECURITY

Multithreading Applications in Java

Anybody who programs in Java is expected to have some knowledge of how to program with threads. Threads have been a core feature of the Java programming language from the beginning, so knowledge about threads is essential to becoming a good Java programmer.

Threads are an advanced topic in any programming language. They pose a challenge to even experienced programmers. They are important because they can make or break your application. Fortunately, Java provides a powerful model that helps developers create multithreaded applications.

This chapter covers the Java programming interface that allows you to create and manipulate threads. We will start by talking about what threads are and why we need them. After that, we will go over how threads are created. We will cover the methods that are provided on the Java classes for starting, stopping, and interrupting threads. The chapter also covers the problems that you may encounter when writing a multithreaded application. To illustrate the material, we will write examples to give you hands-on experience programming with threads and avoiding problems that your multithreaded application may face.

Introduction to Threads

Threads were developed as a way to improve the responsiveness of software applications many years before Java was invented. Threads are associated with operating systems, and different operating systems represent threads in different ways. We will discuss the concept of threads without getting into individual operating system details because that is how the Java language treats them.

> **Note**
>
> Threads do not make your program faster except on a multiprocessor machine. However, threads make your program *feel* faster to the user, because the GUI threads can keep the user busy looking at the progress bar while working threads do the actual work.

A *thread* is commonly defined as an execution path of a computer program. A computer program is executed by an operating system as a process that may have multiple threads. A thread may be represented by a data structure that knows what code line in the program should be executed next. Of course, a thread knows many other things, but it is in essence a type of pointer that indicates the current line of machine code to execute.

Hence, we refer to a thread as an execution path. Each process needs to have at least one execution path, so one thread is created automatically. This thread is usually called the main thread.

A multithreaded operating system allocates CPU time to execute one thread at a time. Thus, each program gets some CPU time for at least its main thread. In addition to the main thread, the application can create more threads and, possibly, receive more CPU time. This depends on how threads are scheduled by a given operating system.

A thread is a relatively lightweight object that does not take a lot of memory and can be created fast. Therefore, an application can have many threads doing different tasks. All the tasks share the same CPU but they all get a small piece of the CPU processing power. A good example of such an application is the HTTP server. A typical HTTP or Web server listens for requests from Web browsers. When a request comes in, the server needs to find a Web page and send it back to the Web browser. The HTTP server may have hundreds or even thousands requests coming in simultaneously. To handle all these requests, the server creates a thread for each request. The thread is responsible for finding the right file and sending it back to the client Web browser. After the server creates a thread for the request, it is ready to handle the next request. The thread takes care of the rest. This way, each request gets some CPU time and is serviced fairly by the server.

Another common example of a multithreaded application is an application with a graphical user interface (GUI). GUI applications have multiple visual components that should be redrawn often, even when the application is busy doing something else. For example, when a user starts a program, she expects to see a welcome screen right away. The welcome screen should be displayed while the program is preparing to execute. The best way to make this happen is to execute the welcome screen in a separate thread. Similarly, when a program is retrieving or loading information, a progress bar is usually displayed to show what percentage of the task is done. Welcome screens and progress bars do not make an application any faster but they do not prevent the application from doing its primary job because they run in separate threads and the operating system gives all the threads some of the CPU time. This makes an application seem faster to the user.

The concept of threads exists in most operating systems. However, different operating systems implement threads differently and provide different functions to call when you want to create, start, or destroy a thread. These differences make programming with threads an intimidating task.

The Java Virtual Machine (JVM) abstracts the implementation of multithreading among different operating systems. Programming threads in Java looks the same on any operating system because the JVM itself talks to the actual operating system. JVMs for different operating systems may support threads in two basic ways. Some JVMs call the underlying operating system threads. (This is referred to as using native threads.) Other JVMs implement threads only inside the JVM itself, in which case the underlying operating system does not know anything about them. Using this second technique can slow performance because all the threads share the same CPU time slice inside the JVM process. In either case, the Java programming language makes programming with threads look the same to a programmer.

> **Note**
>
> Programming with threads looks the same in Java no matter what operating system you are targeting. However, different operating systems use different algorithms to schedule threads. This may affect application behavior.

Thread Life Cycle

Every thread goes through four basic states in its life: new, runnable, blocked, and dead. The basic states are shown in Figure 24.1. The thread is in the new state when it is created but not yet started. After the thread's start method is called, it is transitioned into the runnable state. In the runnable state, the thread is ready to execute and is waiting for the scheduler to give it some CPU time. While in the runnable state, the thread can actually be running at any point the scheduler decides to let it do so. It can also be simply waiting to run. The thread stays in the runnable state until it's finished or blocked. The thread is blocked when it is put to sleep, suspended, or waiting for a resource. If the thread gets the resource or resumes, it is transitioned back into the runnable state, but this does not mean that it will actually run. The thread will only run if it is in the runnable state and the scheduler finds CPU time for it. Finally, the thread enters the dead state when it is finished running. At this point, the thread object is ready to be garbage-collected by the JVM.

FIGURE 24.1

A thread life cycle has four states: new, runnable, blocked, and dead.

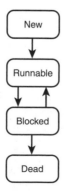

We will cover many examples of how a thread can be transitioned between the runnable state and the blocked state. But first, let's discuss the creation of threads.

Creating Threads

Java has two ways to create a thread: by extending a `java.lang.Thread` class or by implementing a `java.lang.Runnable` interface. The two ways are equally easy. Your choice whether to extend a class or implement an interface will be determined by whether your thread has to extend some other class or not. If it extends some class already, you can only implement the `java.lang.Runnable` interface because Java does not allow multiple class inheritance. Otherwise, you can extend the `java.lang.Thread` class. In both situations, you only have to implement one method—run. Listing 24.1 shows how to create a thread by extending the `java.lang.Thread` class.

LISTING 24.1 Extending the `Thread` Class

```
package unleashed.ch24;

/**
 * This thread extends Thread class.
 */
public class MyThread extends Thread
{
    public void run()
    {
        //do something
        System.out.println("MyThread running");
    }
}
```

The class implements the `run` method, which prints a message to the screen. The `run` method does not take any arguments and does not return anything. It must be public. This is the method that will be called when the JVM scheduler decides that the thread should execute.

Listing 24.2 shows how you can create a thread by implementing the `java.lang.Runnable` interface. The `run` method must be implemented in this case also.

LISTING 24.2 Implementing the `Runnable` Interface

```
package unleashed.ch24;

/**
 * This thread implements Runnable interface.
 */
```

LISTING 24.2   continued

```java
public class MyRunnable implements Runnable
{
    public void run()
    {
        System.out.println("MyRunnable running");
    }
}
```

> **Note**
>
> You can download all the examples in this chapter at the Sams Publishing Web site (www.samspublishing.com). The source code for this chapter includes a readme file with instructions on how to compile and run the examples.

You create a thread in Java by extending the class or implementing the interface. In either case, it is a matter of implementing the run method.

Coordinating Threads

After you write a thread class, you can instantiate it just like any other object in Java. When the thread is instantiated, it is put in the new state. Your program can do a variety of things to control the thread's life cycle. A thread can be started, put to sleep, interrupted, made to wait, and joined using various methods. We will study all these methods in the following sections.

Starting a Thread

The way to instantiate a thread depends on whether your thread class extends java. lang.Thread or implements java.lang.Runnable. If it extends java.lang.Thread, you can instantiate it by simply calling new on it. If it implements java.lang.Runnable, you will have to pass an instance of your class to the java.lang.Thread constructor.

Listing 24.3 demonstrates how to instantiate both a class and an interface thread implementation.

LISTING 24.3   Starting Threads

```java
package unleashed.ch24;

/**
```

LISTING 24.3 continued

```
* Starts two threads
*/
public class ThreadStarter
{
    public static void main(String[] args)
    {
        Thread thread1 = new MyThread();

        Thread thread2 = new Thread(new MyRunnable());

        thread1.start();

        thread2.start();


    }
}
```

After a thread is instantiated, you can transition it into the runnable state by calling the start method. Our threads produce this output:

```
MyThread running
MyRunnable running
```

Note that the order of the print statements is the same as the order in which the threads were started. Our threads look the same to the scheduler, so it expects that they run in the order in which they were started. This, however, is not guaranteed and can be affected by a variety of things. We will study how the order of execution can be changed in the examples that follow.

Putting a Thread to Sleep

Your program can put a thread to sleep at any time. The sleep method of the java.lang.Thread class transitions the thread from the runnable state to the blocked state. The thread can sleep for a number of milliseconds specified as an argument. You can awaken it before the end of the specified time by calling the interrupt method.

The sleep method is often used to create a timer thread that wakes up every once in a while to perform a recurrent operation. Various cleanup chores such as shopping cart expiry may be implemented by timer threads.

Listing 24.4 shows a thread calling the sleep method to put itself to sleep for 10 seconds. The sleep method may throw java.lang.InterruptedException if somebody interrupts the thread's sleep.

LISTING 24.4   Putting a Thread to Sleep

```java
package unleashed.ch24;

/**
* This example shows how to put a thread to sleep.
*/
public class SleepingThread extends Thread
{
    public void run()
    {
        boolean canRun = true;

        while (canRun)
        {
            System.out.println("SleepingThread is awake");
            try
            {
                System.out.println("SleepingThread is
➥ going to sleep for 10 sec.");
                this.sleep(10000);
            }catch(InterruptedException e)
            {
                System.out.println("SleepingThread interrupted");
                canRun = false;
            }
        }
    }

    public static void main(String[] args)
    {
        Thread sleepingThread = new SleepingThread();

        sleepingThread.start();
    }
}
```

Listing 24.4 actually shows a lot of new things, but let's concentrate only on the sleep method for now. We will come back to this example later on to study it a bit more. Calling the start method launches the thread. The thread's run method executes a while loop for as long as the canRun variable is true. Once in the while loop, the thread prints a screen message and goes to sleep for 10 seconds. After 10 seconds, it wakes up and executes the while loop again. The example produces this output:

```
SleepingThread is awake
SleepingThread is going to sleep for 10 sec.
```

This is a small portion of a very long output stream. This thread never finishes, so you will have to kill the JVM process to stop it.

Interrupting a Thread

In the preceding section, we produced a thread that cannot be stopped without killing the JVM process. Now we will see how to interrupt a thread's sleep and eventually stop it.

You can interrupt a thread's sleep by calling the `interrupt` method on the `java.lang.Thread` class. This method actually does the opposite of what you'd expect— it makes a thread resume its execution by transitioning it from the blocked state into the runnable state. In other words, the `interrupt` method interrupts the thread from doing nothing.

The example in Listing 24.5 shows the use of the `interrupt` method. The `main` method starts the `SleepingThread` from Listing 24.4. Then the main thread goes to sleep by calling the `sleep` method. When the main thread wakes up, it interrupts `SleepingThread` from its sleep.

LISTING 24.5   Interrupting a Thread

```
package unleashed.ch24;

/**
 * This example shows how to interrupt a sleeping thread.
 */
public class ThreadInterrupter
{
    public static void main(String[] args)
    {
        System.out.println("Creating SleepingThread");
        Thread thread1 = new SleepingThread();

        System.out.println("Starting SleepingThread");
        thread1.start();

        System.out.println("Putting interrupter to sleep for 30 sec.");

        try
        {
            Thread.currentThread().sleep(30000);
        }catch(InterruptedException e)
        {
            System.out.println("ThreadInterrupter interrupted!");
        }

        System.out.println("Interrupting SleepingThread");
        thread1.interrupt();
    }
}
```

24

MULTITHREADING
APPLICATIONS
IN JAVA

The thread is started using the start method:

```
thread1.start();
```

After thread1 is started, we put the main thread to sleep to give the other thread a little more time to run. We obtain a handle to the main thread using the currentThread method:

```
Thread.currentThread().sleep(30000);
```

The currentThread method returns the currently executing thread. Because it is executed by the main thread, it can only return the main thread. This is how you can get a handle to the main thread in your programs.

Finally, when the main thread wakes up, we interrupt the other thread:

```
thread1.interrupt();
```

Listing 24.6 shows the full output from the example.

LISTING 24.6   Running the Example to Interrupt a Sleeping Thread

```
Creating SleepingThread
Starting SleepingThread
Putting interrupter to sleep for 30 sec.
SleepingThread is awake
SleepingThread is going to sleep for 10 sec.
SleepingThread is awake
SleepingThread is going to sleep for 10 sec.
SleepingThread is awake
SleepingThread is going to sleep for 10 sec.
Interrupting SleepingThread
SleepingThread interrupted
```

As you can see, putting the main thread to sleep allows SleepingThread to sleep and wake up three times. Then the main thread wakes up and issues the interrupt.

Stopping a Thread

Class java.lang.Thread has stop and suspend methods. However, both methods have been deprecated. The stop method stops a thread and releases all locks even if the thread is in the middle of an operation. Therefore, using the stop method may result in invalid data and is deemed unsafe. Instead, use the safe way to stop a thread discussed in this chapter.

The suspend method stops thread execution until the resume method is called on this thread. This may result in a deadlock situation because some other threads may be waiting on the locks to be released by the suspended threads. Thus, the suspend method is also unsafe.

The safe way to stop a thread is to use a *polling loop*. Listing 24.4 contains an example of a typical polling loop in which a thread has a class variable canRun that is checked in every iteration of the while loop. The thread keeps running for as long as the variable is equal to true. However, if the thread is interrupted, the canRun variable is changed to false and the thread exits the while loop and ends.

The polling loop technique may not always be convenient, as it allows the thread to finish the current iteration before exiting. Unfortunately, there is no other, more convenient, way to stop a thread in Java at this time.

Creating Thread-Safe Applications

Creating multiple threads in Java seems like a simple thing to do. You have seen examples in which a few lines of code instantiate a thread, put it to sleep, and stop it. Creating a new thread is not the most challenging task, however. Making multiple threads work together is.

An application is considered thread-safe when it has multiple threads executing the same portions of code to produce consistent results and expected behavior over multiple executions. Coding threads to create such a robust application takes a lot of focus and experience. Sometimes problems manifest themselves in strange ways and may not be identified as a result of multithreading. In this section, we will go over some of the most common problems. We will see what methods Java provides to prevent these problems and make your application thread-safe.

The Most Common Problems in a Multithreaded Application

There are three problems that might arise in a multithreaded application:

- A *race condition* exists when two threads are racing for the same resource. The racing target may be a database connection, a file, an object, or a class variable. Race conditions often result in unexpected program behavior. Say we have a program with two threads trying to withdraw money from the same bank account. The first thread checks the available balance in the account before making a withdrawal. Then it is blocked by the system scheduler. At this time, the second thread tries to withdraw money from the same account. It also checks whether the account has enough money for the withdrawal, which it does. However, the second thread does not know that the first thread is about to make a withdrawal. So the second thread proceeds to withdraw funds. Then, the scheduler wakes the first thread. The first thread has already checked the account balance and thinks that there is enough money, so it makes the withdrawal. Because the threads did not account for each other's withdrawal, their actions may result in a negative balance. Such a race condition happens only at the rare times when the first thread is blocked just before making the withdrawal. This makes the race condition very difficult to identify and fix. It takes experience to see sections of code where race conditions exist. Such sections are called critical sections and must be delimited with the synchronized keyword. We will look at how to use the synchronized keyword in the next section.

- *Thread starvation* happens when a thread does not get enough CPU time to perform its tasks. You can see the effects of thread starvation when your program's GUI interface becomes incredibly slow—so slow that a screen does not redraw itself. You can see it happening from time to time when you start a big application. In this case, the application startup routine takes all the CPU cycles so that no other application can function properly. Running the latest programs on an older machine always seems like a painful exercise because of thread starvation.

  Thread starvation is often caused by multiple applications trying to get as much CPU time as possible. The operating system should allocate the CPU cycles fairly. However, the operating system does not always do a good job. Sometimes the operating system may decide to take all the CPU time itself to perform some heavy-duty operation such as disk defragmentation. Generally, developers cannot do much about other applications or the operating system. However, users can upgrade the machine with more memory or a faster CPU. Users can also stop other programs and even switch to a different operating system, thanks to Java.

  Thread starvation may also exist in a single application if a thread does not get the necessary CPU time because of the other threads. You can often resolve this problem by changing thread priority. We will discuss thread priority in the later sections of this chapter.

- *Deadlock* results from two threads waiting on each other. Each thread may get in the blocked state because a resource that it is waiting for is being used by the other thread. Let's say that we have two threads (thread A and thread B) and two resources (resource A and resource B). If thread A needs to use resources A and B exclusively, and thread B also needs both resources, both of the threads will try to acquire these resources. If thread A happens to get resource A first, and thread B gets resource B first, neither thread will be able to get the remaining resource to finish the operation. Thread A will block to wait for resource B, but resource B is taken by thread B. At the same time, thread B is waiting for resource A, which is held by thread A. Both threads are blocked and the application cannot proceed. Deadlocks may only manifest themselves in rare cases, which makes them very difficult to debug. I worked on a project that had a GUI application that would occasionally hang on startup. It would usually happen 1 out of 10 times. After a long night and a lot of coffee, we found that the GUI thread was waiting to connect to the server, but the server connection thread wanted the GUI thread to display a dialog to the user. Because the connection time varied from time to time, the deadlock happened only occasionally. Deadlocks are difficult to catch, so we will be talking about how to prevent them.

Java provides powerful ways to help you avoid these problems. We will see examples of them in the following sections.

> **Note**
>
> Writing a thread-safe application can be a difficult task. The EJB specification solves this problem by making the container responsible for thread cooperation. In fact, EJB developers are not supposed to use the thread API at all. This makes writing robust EJB systems much easier.

Critical Sections

Critical sections are portions of code that can only be executed by one thread at a time. Every critical section has a lock associated with it. The lock is represented by an object. Before a thread enters the critical section, it checks whether the lock is available. If it is, the thread acquires the lock and proceeds to execute the section. When the thread exits the section, the lock is released. If the lock is not available, any thread that wants to execute the section will block and wait until the lock is released.

The critical section is marked by the synchronized keyword with one argument—the object that serves as a lock for this section. The lock object is also referred to as the monitor. The monitor is implied to be this if the keyword synchronized is used in the method signature:

```
public void synchronized myMethod(){}
```

In this case, the whole method belongs to a critical section. It is identical to the following:

```
public void myMethod()
{
```

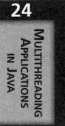

```
        synchronized(this)
        {
            //all the method code goes here
        }
}
```

Let's look at an example of how two threads can be synchronized to run a critical section in order. Listing 24.7 has a critical section in the method doSomething. The monitor object is the SynchronizedThreadExample object that is passed to both threads after they are instantiated.

LISTING 24.7   A Critical Code Section

```
package unleashed.ch24;

/**
 * Thread that is synchronized using a lock object.
 */
class SynchronizedThread extends Thread
{
    //lock object
    public Object lock;

    public void run()
    {
        doSomething();
    }

    public void doSomething()
    {
        //try to obtain a lock
```

LISTING 24.7   continued

```
            //if this line is commented multiple threads will race
            //for common resources
            synchronized(lock)
            {
                for(int i = 0; i < 100; i++)
                {
                    System.out.println("Thread " + this.getName() + "
➥ is running ");
                }
            }

    }
}


/**
 * Example creates two threads that run after one after another
 */
public class SynchronizedThreadExample
{
    public static void main(String[] args)
    {
        //create a lock object
        SynchronizedThreadExample ex = new SynchronizedThreadExample();

        //create first thread
        SynchronizedThread thread1 = new SynchronizedThread();
        thread1.lock = ex;

        //create second thread
        SynchronizedThread thread2 = new SynchronizedThread();
        thread2.lock = ex;

        //start both threads
        thread1.start();
        thread2.start();

    }
}
```

The important thing to note in this example is that the same lock object is passed to both threads. Whichever thread enters the critical section first is going to be able to finish it. The second thread will block and wait until the first thread is done. Only then will the second thread be able to enter the critical section.

Running the example produces 100 lines of output for each thread. This shows that the first thread is actually able to do a relatively long operation without the second thread doing any printing. You can see the following line printed 100 times by the first thread:

```
Thread Thread-0 is running
```

24

MULTITHREADING
APPLICATIONS
IN JAVA

The second hundred lines of output come from the second thread. All the lines look like the following:

```
Thread Thread-1 is running
```

Note

The thread numbering depends on the operating system, so you may see something like Thread-1 and Thread-2 in the output if you run the example in Listing 24.7 on your machine.

If you comment out the synchronized keyword in the doSomething method and compile and run the example again, you will see that the output from both threads will be intermingled. This means that both threads are executing the critical section at the same time. The intermingled output shows the race condition between the two threads. The threads race for the right to print out to the screen. If the threads were to change class variables, this race condition would lead to unexpected output from our program. The synchronized keyword delimits the critical sections of your code and prevents race conditions.

The critical section specifies that it can only be accessed by one thread at a time. It cannot control the order in which threads obtain the lock and execute the section. In our example, thread2 could potentially execute the critical section first even though it was started second. Java provides other means to control the order in which threads execute critical sections. We will study them in the following sections.

Tip

Making a block of code synchronized slows your program down. Make sure that you clearly identify what sections of code must be synchronized before you use this keyword.

Making a Thread Wait

In addition to using the sleep method, you can explicitly block a thread by calling a wait method on a lock object. A lock object can be any Java object. A thread can call a wait method at any time to block itself until the time when it is being notified to wake up. The `wait` method is different from the `sleep` method in that the thread must be explicitly notified to proceed. Java provides two methods to notify a thread to wake up in this case: `notify` and `notifyAll`. The `notify` method wakes only one waiting thread, whereas `notifyAll` wakes all threads that are waiting on this lock. Most of the time you will want to call the `notifyAll` method, as it guarantees that all your threads will wake up.

Listing 24.8 shows an example of two threads, one of which calls the `wait` method to wait for the other to execute a portion of code. When the second thread is finished, it calls the `notifyAll` method, which effectively wakes up the first thread.

LISTING 24.8 Making a Thread Wait on a `lock` Object

```
package unleashed.ch24;

/**
 * Thread that waits for another thread to finish
 */
class WaitingThread extends Thread
{
    public Object lock;

    public WaitingThread(String name)
    {
        super(name);
    }

    public void run()
    {
        doSomething();
    }

    public void doSomething()
    {
        //thread obtains a lock
        synchronized(lock)
        {
            try
            {
                //goes to wait until being notified
                lock.wait();
            }catch(InterruptedException e)
            {
                System.out.println("WaitingThread interrupted");
            }

            for(int i = 0; i < 100; i++)
```

LISTING 24.8   continued

```
            {
                System.out.println("Thread " + this.getName() +
➡ " is running ");
            }
        }

    }
}

/**
 * Thread that runs first and then notifies other threads that it is finished.
 */
class FirstThread extends Thread
{
    public Object lock;

    public FirstThread(String name)
    {
        super(name);
    }

    public void run()
    {
        doSomething();
    }

    public void doSomething()
    {
        //obtains a lock
        synchronized(lock)
        {
        //  Uncommenting this code will result in a deadlock
        //  both threads will wait for each other to finish

        //    try
        //    {
        //        lock.wait();
        //    }catch(InterruptedException e)
        //    {
        //        System.out.println("FirstThread interrupted");
        //    }
        //

            for(int i = 0; i < 100; i++)
            {
                System.out.println("Thread " + this.getName() +
➡ " is running ");
            }
```

LISTING 24.8 continued

```
            //notifies waiting thread that it is finished
            lock.notifyAll();
        }

    }
}

/**
 * Example creates two threads and a lock object.
 */
public class WaitingThreadExample
{
    public static void main(String[] args)
    {
        WaitingThreadExample ex = new WaitingThreadExample();

        WaitingThread thread1 = new WaitingThread("Waiting");
        thread1.lock = ex;

        FirstThread thread2 = new FirstThread("First");
        thread2.lock = ex;

        thread1.start();
        thread2.start();

    }
}
```

The `wait` method gives you some control over the order of thread execution. Imagine that you do not want your GUI thread to show a screen before a data thread connects to a database and gets the data to display. You can make your GUI threads wait until the data thread is ready. Once the data thread receives the result from the database, it notifies the GUI threads.

The example produces this output:

```
Thread First is running
Thread Waiting is running
```

The `First` thread is guaranteed to execute first because the second thread is waiting on the `lock` object. Note that the `lock` object is passed to each thread so that they both operate on the same object.

Joining a Thread

Class `java.lang.Thread` also provides the `join` method, which is similar to the `wait` method in that it also makes a thread block. The difference is that a thread that calls the join method will block until the joining is finished. Let's say that we have two threads: thread A and thread B. Thread B needs to wait until thread A exits. Then thread B can call the join method on thread A. This will effectively block thread B until thread A is finished running.

The join method is essentially a wait method without notification. The calling thread resumes its execution only when the joining thread exits. The method returns immediately if the joining thread is not running, so it is a good way for you to ensure that some thread has performed its tasks before proceeding.

The join method can be interrupted by the interrupt method. In addition, the join method accepts an argument that specifies a timeout period. The calling thread resumes in case of a timeout even if the joining thread is still running. This is a good way to avoid deadlocks if the joining thread is taking too much time to finish.

Thread Management

Some advanced multithreaded applications must provide more than just the ability to start and stop the thread. A good example of such an application is a servlet engine. Typically, a servlet engine creates a pool of threads at startup. It manages the threads in the pool throughout its lifetime and stops them when it shuts down. Every time a request comes to the servlet engine, it assigns a thread from the pool to service the request. The thread is used to run a Java Servlet for the request. When the thread is done servicing the request, it is returned to the engine pool. Thread pooling is used in various servers and is a common technique to improve server performance.

> **Tip**
>
> Java Servlets execute in multiple threads. This makes them common places to have race conditions. Carefully examine the code in your servlets for possible race conditions. Use the synchronized keyword to delimit critical sections and eliminate race conditions.

Thread pooling requires a server to instantiate multiple threads anonymously as part of a group. The number of threads in a group can be determined by a property file and a command-line argument. Your application may need to have multiple groups of threads to do different tasks such as processing user requests, retrieving data from a database, and rendering GUI components. You will learn how to create groups of threads in Java in the following section.

Thread Groups

Java provides the `java.lang.ThreadGroup` class to manage multiple threads in a thread pool. You can assign a thread to a thread group at its instantiation by passing the thread group to the thread constructor. Once a thread is assigned to a group, you can manipulate it by calling it as a part of an array. You can place all threads into an array by calling the enumerate method on a group. The enumerate method puts only active threads (threads that were started) in an array.

Listing 24.9 demonstrates the process of creating a thread group, assigning threads to it, running the threads, and, finally, stopping them.

LISTING 24.9   Thread Groups and Priorities

```java
package unleashed.ch24;

/**
 * Simple thread
 */
class GroupMemberThread extends Thread
{
    public GroupMemberThread(ThreadGroup group, String threadName)
    {
        super(group, threadName);
    }

    public void run()
    {
        boolean run = true;

        while (run)
        {
            System.out.println(this.getName() + " running");

            try
            {
                System.out.println("Putting " + this.getName() + " to sleep");
                this.sleep(1000);

            }catch(InterruptedException e)
            {
                System.out.println(this.getName() + " interrupted");
                run = false;
            }
        }
    }
}
```

LISTING 24.9   continued

```java
/**
 * This class creates a group of threads.
 */
public class ThreadGroupExample
{
    public static void main(String args[])
    {

        System.out.println("creating a thread group");
        ThreadGroup group = new ThreadGroup("My Group");

        Thread thread1 = new GroupMemberThread(group, "thread1");
        thread1.setPriority(Thread.MIN_PRIORITY);

        Thread thread2 = new GroupMemberThread(group, "thread2");
        thread2.setPriority(Thread.MIN_PRIORITY);

        Thread thread3 = new GroupMemberThread(group, "thread3");
        thread3.setPriority(Thread.MAX_PRIORITY);

        group.list();

        thread1.start();
        thread2.start();
        thread3.start();

        Thread[] threads = new Thread[group.activeCount()];

        group.enumerate(threads);


        for(int i = 0; i < threads.length; i++)
        {
            System.out.println("Interrupting thread " + threads[i].getName());
            threads[i].interrupt();
        }

    }
}
```

This example creates three threads that are assigned to one thread group. All three threads are started. Then the example creates an array to hold the threads in the group. The activeCount method returns the number of active threads in the group. Because all the threads have been started, the active count is three. The empty array is passed to the enumerate method, which puts the threads in the group into the array. Once the threads are in the array, we can loop through the array to print their names and interrupt them.

All three threads go to sleep for periods of one second until they are all stopped by the main thread.

Note that the `list` method does not return any value. It only prints the contents of the thread group to the standard output.

Listing 24.10 shows the output from the running example.

LISTING 24.10   Running the Thread Group Example

```
creating a thread group
java.lang.ThreadGroup[name=My Group,maxpri=10]
Thread[thread1,1,My Group]
Thread[thread2,1,My Group]
Thread[thread3,10,My Group]
thread1 running
thread3 running
Interrupting thread thread1
thread2 running
Putting thread1 to sleep
Putting thread3 to sleep
Interrupting thread thread2
Putting thread2 to sleep
thread1 interrupted
Interrupting thread thread3
thread2 interrupted
thread3 interrupted
```

This output shows that `thread3` executes before `thread2` but after `thread1`. We will discuss why this happened in the next section.

Thread Priority

Java provides another simple method to give the JVM a hint about the order in which threads should be executed.

Thread priority tells JVM whether a thread is more or less important than another thread. If a thread requires more CPU time, it has a higher priority. For example, GUI threads have high priority so that the screen does not freeze on the user. You can specify the thread priority using the `setPriority` method:

```
thread1.setPriority(Thread.MIN_PRIORITY);
```

In the example from Listing 24.9, `thread3` has a higher priority than the other threads. That is why in Listing 24.10 you can see that `thread3` executes before `thread2` even though it is started later.

24

MULTITHREADING
APPLICATIONS
IN JAVA

Even though we gave thread3 a higher priority, it executed after thread1, which had a lower priority. The reason is that thread1 executed before thread3 was even started.

Unfriendly threads with high thread priority may lead to thread starvation problems for threads whose priority is low. In the example from Listing 24.9, thread3 could potentially start a long operation and leave no CPU time for thread1 and thread2. You should treat thread priority with caution so that you will not produce starvation problems.

Different JVMs may have different priority minimums and maximums defined by the underlying operating system. That is why the java.lang.Thread class has final fields MIN_PRIORITY and MAX_PRIORITY. Typically, you can assign a thread's priority relative to the minimum or the maximum priorities. This way, your code will be portable across different JVMs and operating systems.

Summary

Threads are a part of every Java program. The JVM creates the main thread for a program automatically. The program can start more threads to execute for different parts of the application such as GUI components. Conceptually, a thread is an execution path that is scheduled to get a CPU time slice. This means that the CPU will execute only this thread for a period of time determined by the scheduler.

During its lifetime, every thread goes through four states: new, runnable, blocked, and dead. A thread is in the new state after it has been created. It is transferred to the runnable state in order to execute. It can also be in the blocked state when it is waiting for a locked resource. Finally, the thread is transferred to the dead state when it is finished executing.

The Java thread API enables you to create threads by extending the java.lang.Thread class or implementing the java.lang.Runnable interface. Both ways only require implementation of a run method.

A thread can be instantiated and called like any Java object. Once it is instantiated, you can manage the thread by calling the start, interrupt, sleep, wait, join and other methods on the java.lang.Thread class. An application can call these methods to coordinate different threads so that they do not conflict with each other.

Threads can be put in thread groups and assigned different priorities. The threads with high priority have a good chance of getting more CPU time because the scheduler will favor them over the threads with low priority.

CHAPTER 25

Java Internationalization

Have you ever flipped through the television channels with a remote control and come across an interesting show in a language that you did not understand? Most of us stare at the images on the screen, admire the scenery, and notice that what is going on is obviously very interesting to those who understand what is being said. After a few minutes of this, we get bored and move to the next channel—all the while wishing that we had one of those science fiction voice translation devices.

Because the Internet got its start in the United States, much of it is still American English–centric. This is curious, given the fact that less that half of the computerized population of the planet can understand English well and far fewer would prefer to view and read in English if given a choice. This is one of those classic instances in which opportunity not only knocks, but it also slaps you in the face. What if everyone, or even a larger portion of the visitors to your site, could read your site's text in their preferred language? What if they could order merchandise using their country's currency? What if they could see dates and times expressed in ways that were natural and familiar to them?

Most of us are in the computer business to make a living. We are compensated by someone who believes that we are adding value. Our goal is to add more value in the hope that this will lead to even more compensation. For most of us in the programming trade, this means getting our software in front of more people. Internationalizing our systems and Web sites is one of the best ways to do this.

Internationalization (called I18n because there are 18 letters between the *i* and the *n*) is one of the best reasons to program in Java. No other language makes supporting multiple languages as easy as Java does.

In this chapter, you will learn how to take advantage of the I18n features built into Java. You will learn how to use them to display text, dates, currency, and graphics that are sensitive to the locale of the viewer.

Fundamentals of Internationalization

Internationalization is based on the concept of a locale. A *locale* is a group of people who speak the same dialect of the same language, display their numbers in the same way, format their date and times alike, and use the same currency. Consider any two individuals; if any of the preceding criteria are different, they do not belong to the same locale.

This concept of locale is not as rigid in practice as it is in theory. Many ethnic groups conduct commerce in languages that are not their own. French Canadians can function in English, even if they prefer not to. Tahitians have long ago learned to speak French when dealing with the government. In truth, by the preceding definition, there are probably more than one million locales on the planet.

Fortunately for us programmers, a few of these locales contain so many people that it is possible to reach a significant audience by just supporting 8 or 10 different locales in your system. The number of people in each of these locales, combined with the number of others who can use these locales, is so large that most of our internationalization goals can be achieved by supporting them.

The most obvious of the locale differences is in textual language. A dog in English is a *perro* in Spanish, a *chien* in French, and a *Hund* in German.

The next most obvious difference is currency. An American uses dollars, the English use pounds, and most of the rest of Europe use the Euro. Currency is doubly challenging because it involves rates of exchange as well as formatting.

Numbers are also expressed differently in various locales. A Frenchman would understand the string of numbers 123,456 to mean one hundred twenty-three and four hundred fifty-six thousandths. In America, the same string would mean one hundred and twenty-three thousand, four hundred and fifty-six. (You would be advised to remember this when buying perfume on your next trip to Paris.) It goes without saying that mistakes in this area could be expensive.

Dates and times are also confusing. The string 01/06/55 means the sixth day of January in the year 1955 in the United States, but it means the first day of June in much of the rest of the world.

Finally, be aware that the alphabetical order of objects can also be different from locale to locale. This poses problems that go beyond formatting and requires the use of a Collator class to provide the greater-than and less-than operators for a specific locale.

Using Resource Bundles for Text

Another important concept in the world of internationalized systems is a resource. A *resource* is any piece of data that can be different from one locale to the next. We associate the same resource in all locales with the same keyword. The programmers create these keywords, ordinarily in their organization's native tongue. If an American programmer wanted a keyword for dog, he might choose the string hound. This same string would be associated with "dog" in English, "chien" in French, and "Hund" in German. Whenever the locale changes, the new locale's word for hound would be substituted in the user interface.

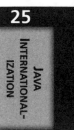

> **Tip**
>
> It is normally better not to use the same English word for the keyword as you use for the displayed name. It makes the code confusing to read. A synonym such as *hound* makes a better choice.

The process of internationalizing the text in your system is straightforward. You identify every element in your system that needs to be localized, and you create a keyword for it. After you have that list created, you obtain the translation for it in the language that you want to support. Now you are ready to get these words into your program somehow.

Java has provided incorporating these keywords and their translations through an abstract class called `ResourceBundle`. The `ResourceBundle` is always used via one of two subclasses, `PropertyResourceBundle` or `ListResourceBundle`.

The `PropertyResourceBundle` is a class that provides access to a `properties` file containing keyword/translation pairs. This is the best approach to use if you do not need to associate any images or sounds to a keyword. (The `properties` file is not capable of containing anything but text.)

The `ListResourceBundle` is a class without any `properties` file. It must provide the translation programmatically. This means that there must be a separate class file for each of the locales just as there must be a separate properties file for each of the locales that you support.

We will work with two simple examples that will make this point clearer. Listing 25.1 shows a simple program that writes strings to the console.

LISTING 25.1 The `EnglishOnly` Class

```
/*
 * EnglishOnly.java
 *
 * Created on February 6, 2002, 10:48 AM
 */

package unleashed.ch25;

/**
 *
 * @author  Stephen Potts
 * @version
 */
public class EnglishOnly
```

LISTING 25.1   continued

```
{

    /** Creates new EnglishOnly */
    public EnglishOnly()
    {
    }

    public static void main(String[] args)
    {
        System.out.println("Hello");
        System.out.println("Goodbye");
        System.out.println("Good Luck");
    }
}
```

This is a simple writing of three strings to the console. The output from running this code is boring and predictable:

```
Hello
Goodbye
Good Luck
```

> **Note**
>
> All the code and images found in this chapter can be downloaded from the Sams Publishing Web site (www.samspublishing.com). Many of the examples have filenames embedded in them. You might need to adjust these filenames depending on where you install the examples on your machine.

Now consider what we would do if we wanted a version of the program to run at our office in Paris. We would take the code and rewrite it as shown in Listing 25.2.

LISTING 25.2   The FrenchOnly Class

```
/*
 * FrenchOnly.java
 *
 * Created on February 6, 2002, 11:04 AM
 */

package unleashed.ch25;

/**
```

LISTING 25.2 continued

```
 *
 * @author  Stephen Potts
 * @version
 */
public class FrenchOnly
{

    /** Creates new FrenchOnly */
    public FrenchOnly()
    {
    }

    public static void main(String[] args)
    {
        System.out.println("Bonjour");
        System.out.println("Au revoir");
        System.out.println("Bonne chance");
    }

}
```

The output from running this code would be slightly more interesting, but only slightly:

```
Bonjour
Au revoir
Bonne chance
```

Now if you consider how many languages there are in the world, how complex your programs are going to be, and how many other issues beyond text substitution there are in internationalization, you will begin to see why we need a more automated solution.

> **Tip**
>
> When working on internationalizing programs, you will need to translate words from one language to another. An easy way to do that is to use http://www.freetranslation.com. This Web site allows you to paste or type a word in one language, submit it, and receive a response that contains the translation into one of six European languages.

Let's take the EnglishOnly application and give it that international feel. We will work an example first, and then explain it to illustrate the concepts involved. Listing 25.3 shows the code.

LISTING 25.3 The I18nOnly Class

```java
/*
 * I18nOnly.java
 *
 * Created on February 6, 2002, 11:17 AM
 */

package unleashed.ch25;
import java.util.Locale;
import java.util.*;

/**
 *
 * @author  Stephen Potts
 * @version
 */
public class I18nOnly
{

    /** Creates new I18nOnly */
    public I18nOnly()
    {
    }

    public static void main(String[] args)
    {
        String lang = "";
        String country = "";
        String variant = "";
        Locale loc;
        ResourceBundle vocabulary;

        //if they passed in a lang and country, use it. Else
        //default to US English
        if (args.length == 2)
        {
            lang = args[0];
            country = args[1];
        }

        if (args.length == 3)
        {
            lang = args[0];
            country = args[1];
            variant = args[2];
            loc = new Locale(lang, country, variant);
        }else
        {
            //Create the Locale object
            loc = new Locale(lang, country);
```

LISTING 25.3 continued

```
        }

        //get the right resource bundle for this locale
        vocabulary = ResourceBundle.getBundle(
                            "unleashed.ch25.VocabBundle", loc);

        //Print some messages from this bundle
        System.out.println(vocabulary.getString("greet"));
        System.out.println(vocabulary.getString("farewell"));
        System.out.println(vocabulary.getString("wishSuccess"));
        System.out.println(vocabulary.getString("edible"));
    }
}
```

At first blush, you might say that this program is much more complicated than the EnglishOnly one that we did earlier in this chapter. Upon further examination though, you will see that a few simple concepts dominate this and all other I18n programs.

The first interesting item that we run across is the Locale class. This class doesn't do a lot of work on its own, but rather it serves as input to tell the other internationalization classes how to behave.

```
        Locale loc;
```

The vocabulary variable is really an abstract class reference to the ResourceBundle class. Later, when we call getBundle(), it will be assigned to a concrete class of type PropertyResourceBundle or ListResourceBundle, according to what it finds when it looks for the bundle name that you specify.

```
        ResourceBundle vocabulary;
```

The actual Locale object is created with two strings. The first specifies the language preference of the program, and the second specifies the country. When we run the example, we will specify that one of our locales is the French language and the country is Haiti. This provides much more precision than specifying only a language. (French spoken in Haiti differs from French spoken in Paris, just as English spoken in New York differs from English spoken in London.)

```
        loc = new Locale(lang, country);
```

The Locale class can actually be constructed with a third parameter, the variant (not to be confused with the variant data type in some computer languages). The variant can be used to further specify the locale. It could be used, for example, to handle regionalisms. For example, VocabBundle_en_US_pa_ might signify that we want to use the phrase "gum band" instead of "rubber band" in Pennsylvania.

```
loc = new Locale(lang, country, variant);
```

A sly bit of trickery is employed by the getBundle() method. Two parameters are passed to this method: the base name of the bundle and the locale.

```
vocabulary = ResourceBundle.getBundle(
                "unleashed.ch25.VocabBundle", loc);
```

These parameters are expressions of preference on the part of the calling program. In this example, suppose that we passed in the language as French and the country as Canada. The getBundle() method would first look for a class named

```
unleashed.ch25.VocabBundle_fr_CA.class.
```

If that were not found, it would look for

```
unleashed.ch25.VocabBundle_fr.class
unleashed.ch25.VocabBundle.class
```

At that point, it would give up on classes and try to find the following properties files in this order:

```
unleashed.ch25.VocabBundle_fr_CA.properties
unleashed.ch25.VocabBundle_fr.properties
unleashed.ch25.VocabBundle.properties
```

This last file is known as the base bundle. It has no suffixes, just the base name of the bundle. If none of the six files were found, a java.util.MissingResourceException would be thrown.

> **Tip**
>
> Always provide a base bundle in your systems, which will guarantee that you will never get the java.util.MissingResourceException.

This approach is really elegant. It allows a programmer who is using classes to specify as much information about the locale as he has been able to obtain. He creates the most specific Locale object that he can and passes it to your code. Your code can be as specific as it can, but in no case does it fail to run.

Finally, we are able to output the correct language using the ResourceBundle reference and the getString() method. Both the ListResourceBundle and the

PropertiesResourceBundle classes override this method, meaning you can migrate from a design that used properties files to one that uses class files without changing this part of the code. All you would have to do is create and compile the resource classes.

```
System.out.println(vocabulary.getString("greet"));
System.out.println(vocabulary.getString("farewell"));
System.out.println(vocabulary.getString("wishSuccess"));
```

Next, we have to create the resource files for the locales that we want to support. We can run this same program with different command line parameters representing the locales and see what results appear.

Listing 25.4 shows the default resources.

LISTING 25.4   The VocabBundle.properties File

```
# I18nOnly default ResourceBundle properties file
greet=HelloD
farewell=ByeD
edible=foodD
wishSuccess=Good LuckD
```

The keywords on the left remain constant in every file. (The D at the end of each word is not needed, but was placed there so that we can see when the default properties file is being used.) Notice that we did not use the same term on the left as on the right. Using a keyword that is the same as a resource value can be confusing. The value assigned to them can vary (but doesn't have to) from locale to locale. If we execute this command, we will get the following result:

```
java unleashed.ch25.I18nOnly
```

The results are shown here:

```
HelloD
ByeD
Good LuckD
foodD
```

This program steps through the hierarchy of resources until it gets to the very bottom. Because getBundle() was not provided with any locale specific information, it drops to the bottom of the hierarchy and uses the default properties file. (The values in this file have a D appended to the end to prove to us that the default file was really used.)

If, however, we specify a bundle on the command line, that file will be used if it exists. Listing 25.5 shows the properties file values for U.S. English.

LISTING 25.5 The VocabBundle_en_US.properties File

```
# I18nOnly English US ResourceBundle properties file
greet=Hello
farewell=Bye
edible=food
wishSuccess=Good Luck
```

Next, let's run the program to display English for the United States:

```
java unleashed.ch25.I18nOnly en US
```

The following result will be displayed:

```
Hello
Bye
Good Luck
food
```

You might be wondering where the code en for English and US for the United States came from. There is an ISO standard list of languages and an ISO standard list of country codes. The standard list for languages is contained in a document called ISO 639. It can be found at

```
http://www.ics.uci.edu/pub/ietf/http/related/iso639.txt
```

Likewise, a valid list of country codes is called ISO 3166. A copy of this list can be found at

```
http://www.chemie.fu-berlin.de/diverse/doc/ISO_3166.html
```

Not all languages appear on the ISO 369 list, but there are more than 100, so the chances are good that you will find your favorite one.

If we want to use a variant, we are on our own in choosing the code. We have chosen SE for the variant representing the Southeastern United States. The properties files for this region contain some phrases not commonly used in other parts of the English-speaking world. Listing 25.6 shows the values for Southeastern U.S. English.

LISTING 25.6 This Properties File Contains the Resources for English as It Is Spoken in the Southeastern United States

```
# I18nOnly English US Southeast ResourceBundle properties file
greet=Hey
wishSuccess=Good Luck
edible=food
farewell=Take it Easy
```

Now run the program with the following command:

```
java unleashed.ch25.I18nOnly en US SE
```

The following result will be displayed:

```
Hey
Take it Easy
Good Luck
food
```

Notice that the getBundle() method had no problem finding the resource bundle for the variant.

Listing 25.7 shows the values for French.

LISTING 25.7   This Properties File Contains the Resources for French

```
# I18nOnly French ResourceBundle properties file
greet=Bonjour
wishSuccess=Bonne Chance
farewell=au revoir
edible=nourriture
```

Now run the program with the following command:

```
java unleashed.ch25.I18nOnly fr CA
```

The following result will be displayed:

```
Bonjour
au revoir
Bonne Chance
Nourriture
```

Because no properties file was provided for Canada, the request dropped down to the generic French properties file.

Listing 25.8 shows the values for Haitian French.

LISTING 25.8   This Properties File Contains the Resources for French as It Is Spoken in Haiti

```
# I18nOnly French Haiti  ResourceBundle properties file
greet=BonjourH
wishSuccess=Bonne ChanceH
farewell=au revoirH
edible=nourritureH
```

Now run the program with the following command:

```
java unleashed.ch25.I18nOnly fr HT
```

The following result will be displayed:

```
BonjourH
au revoirH
Bonne ChanceH
nourritureH
```

Note that the H was added simply to make it clearer. The generic French is not needed here because the Haitian was found.

Listing 25.9 shows the values for Tahitian French:

LISTING 25.9 This Properties File Contains the Resources for French as It Is Spoken in the Islands of French Polynesia

```
# I18nOnly French Polynesian ResourceBundle properties file
greet=Bonjour
wishSuccess=Bonne Chance
edible=ma'a
farewell=au revoir
```

Now run the program with the following command:

```
java unleashed.ch25.I18nOnly fr PF
```

The following result will be displayed:

```
Bonjour
au revoir
Bonne Chance
ma'a
```

The French in the South Pacific often substitute some local words for their French counterpart, especially if they are harder to say. Here we use *ma'a*, the Tahitian word, instead of *nourriture*, the French word.

Listing 25.10 shows the values for French Polynesian Tahitian.

LISTING 25.10 This Properties File Contains the Resources for Tahitian as It Is Spoken in the Islands of French Polynesia

```
# I18nOnly Tahitian Polynesian ResourceBundle properties file
greet=Ia Ora Na
wishSuccess=Ia Manuia
farewell=Fa'aitoito
edible=ma'a
```

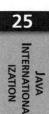

Now run the program with the following command:

```
java unleashed.ch25.I18nOnly tp FP
```

The following result will be displayed:

```
Ia Ora Na
Fa'aitoito
Ia Manuia
ma'a
```

In this case, we used the same country code as we did in the preceding listing, but the language code was different. If you were to look at the ISO 639 document in which the language codes are defined, you would not see tp as a language. In fact, Tahitian is one of the hundreds of languages that have no code. This is no hindrance to you because you can designate your own code. Take care, however, not to conflict with a code that has already been used, or you might encounter side effects when interfacing with other software.

Using ResourceBundle Classes to Store Objects

The use of PropertyResourceBundles is easy and convenient. This approach suffers from the limitation that all the objects that it handles must be strings. If you need to handle other resources such as images, you will have to use the ListResourceBundle approach and place the information in classes. Listing 25.11 contains an example of this.

LISTING 25.11   The I18nListBundleTest Class

```
/*
 * I18nListBundleTest.java
 *
 * Created on February 7, 2002, 9:13 AM
 */

package unleashed.ch25;
import java.util.*;
import javax.swing.*;

/**
 *
 * @author  Stephen Potts
 * @version
 */
public class I18nListBundleTest
```

LISTING 25.11   continued

```java
{

    /** Creates new I18nListBundleTest */
    public I18nListBundleTest()
    {
    }

    public static void main(String[] args)
    {
        String lang = "";
        String country = "";
        String variant = "";
        Locale loc;
        ResourceBundle rBundle;

        //if they passed in a lang and country, use it. Else
        //use the default resource bundle, in this case German
        if (args.length == 2)
        {
            lang = args[0];
            country = args[1];
        }

        if (args.length == 3)
        {
            lang = args[0];
            country = args[1];
            variant = args[2];
            loc = new Locale(lang, country, variant);
        }else
        {
            //Create the Locale object
            loc = new Locale(lang, country);
        }

        //Use this method to locate the correct bundle for the locale
        rBundle =
        ResourceBundle.getBundle("unleashed.ch25.ImageResources", loc);

        //Get the correct flag for this locale
        ImageIcon flagIcon = (ImageIcon)(rBundle.getObject("icon"));
        String[] options =
        {
            rBundle.getString("affirmative"),
            rBundle.getString("negative")};

            String dString = rBundle.getString("greet") + " " +
            rBundle.getString("farewell") + " " +
```

LISTING 25.11   continued

```
                  rBundle.getString("edible") + " " +
                  rBundle.getString("wishSuccess");

                  //Create an option pane to display the icon and the words
                  //in the resource bundle class
                  JOptionPane pane = new JOptionPane(
                  dString, JOptionPane.QUESTION_MESSAGE, 0, flagIcon, options);

                  //display the dialog
                  JDialog dlg = pane.createDialog(null, "Unleashed");
                  dlg.setModal(true);
                  dlg.setVisible(true);
                  String selection = (String)(pane.getValue());

                  //Exit the applications
                  System.exit(0);
      }
}
```

The most remarkable thing about this program is that it is not remarkable at all. This code looks almost exactly like the code that you used to retrieve resources from a properties file. The name of the ResourceBundle is different, but the syntax of the getBundle() call is exactly the same. In fact, the only line of code that proves you are not getting resources from a properties file is the retrieval of the ImageIcon. This flag icon must be stored in a class file because .gif files are beyond the capabilities of a properties file to hold.

```
         ImageIcon flagIcon = (ImageIcon)(rBundle.getObject("icon"));
```

Notice that an explicit cast must be made to translate the object reference that getObject() returns into a reference of the ImageIcon type.

The same bit of deception is practiced by the getBundle() method in this example. A default class is specified that is named the base name of the family of resource classes. Listing 25.12 contains the default class for the ImageResources bundle.

LISTING 25.12   The ImageResources Class

```
/*
 * ImageResources.java
 *
 * Created on February 7, 2002, 9:30 AM
 */

package unleashed.ch25;
```

LISTING 25.12 continued

```java
import java.util.*;
import javax.swing.*;

/**
 *
 * @author  Stephen Potts
 * @version
 */
public class ImageResources extends ListResourceBundle
{
    protected static Object[][] resources =
    {
        {"greet" , "Hallo"},
        {"farewell","Abschied"},
        {"edible","Speise"},
        {"wishSuccess", "Gutes Glück"},
        {"affirmative", "Ja"},
        {"negative", "Nein"},
        {"icon", new ImageIcon("c:/unleashed/ch25/germany.gif")}
    };

    protected java.lang.Object[][] getContents()
    {
        return resources;
    }
}
```

The ImageResources default class looks quite a bit different from the properties files that we saw in the first example. The resources are stored as objects in a two-dimensional array. Also notice that all are String objects, except the icon, which is of type ImageIcon.

```java
{"icon", new ImageIcon("c:/unleashed/ch25/germany.gif")}
```

The ListResourceBundle class requires that any subclasses override the getContents() method to return the array of the resource object. Your code does not call this method; it is called by getBundle() as part of its effort to identify and load the best resource bundle for a given program based on the specified locale.

To run this program, open a command window and type the following line:

java unleashed.ch25.I18nListBundleTest

Because no locale information was provided on the command line, the default bundle class will be used. The result of running this is shown in Figure 25.1.

FIGURE 25.1

Several German words and the German flag are retrieved from the class file and displayed in a dialog box.

Another interesting point is that there is no English default `ListResourceBundle` class. If you determined that your application's best alternative language is German and not English, it would make no sense to provide an English default file.

To make this example more interesting, let's suppose that some of our users are located in Switzerland, but they speak German. In this case, we could create an alternative `ListResourceBundle` class file called `ImageResources_de_CH`. We chose the `de` and `CH` instead of something campy such as `ge` and `SW` because these are the language and Locale codes for German and Switzerland, respectively.

The code for this is shown in Listing 25.13.

LISTING 25.13   The `ImageResources_de_CH` Class/*

```
 * ImageResources_de_CH.java
 *
 * Created on February 7, 2002, 9:30 AM
 */

package unleashed.ch25;
import java.util.*;
import javax.swing.*;

/**
 *
 * @author   Stephen Potts
 * @version
 */
public class ImageResources_de_CH extends ListResourceBundle
{
    protected static Object[][] resources =
    {
        {"greet" , "Hallo"},
        {"farewell","Abschied"},
        {"edible","Speise"},
        {"wishSuccess", "Gutes Glück"},
        {"icon", new ImageIcon("c:/unleashed/ch25/switzerland.gif")}
    };
```

LISTING 25.13   continued

```
protected java.lang.Object[][] getContents()
{
    return resources;
}
}
```

There are several interesting features in this code. Notice first that a different icon file is loaded. This creates and returns a different object when the getContents() method is called by the getBundle() method in your code. Notice also that not all the keywords found in the default version of this class appear here. Specifically, Ja and Nein are not shown here. This was done intentionally to illustrate that a certain sort of light inheritance is at work here. Not only is getBundle() smart enough to get the best resource bundle for your application, but it is also smart enough to create the bundle from more than one properties file or class if need be.

To run the program, open a shell or command window and type the following:

java unleashed.ch25.I18nListBundleTest de CH

This will display a dialog box like the one shown in Figure 25.2.

FIGURE 25.2

Several German words and the Swiss flag are retrieved from the class file and displayed in a dialog box.

Notice that all the words are the same, but the flag is different. This gives us a finer level of localization than we could achieve using text alone.

Internationalizing Dates and Times

Fortunately for programmers, dates and times don't vary as much as natural language does. In fact, all you have to do to format dates is to declare an object of type java.text.DateFormat and use its methods to create a string to display as shown in Listing 25.14.

LISTING 25.14   The I18nDateTimeTest Class

```java
/*
 * I18nDateTimeTest.java
 *
 * Created on February 7, 2002, 1:20 PM
 */

package unleashed.ch25;
import java.util.*;
import java.text.*;

/**
 *
 * @author  Stephen Potts
 * @version
 */
public class I18nDateTimeTest
{

    /** Creates new I18nDateTimeTest */
    public I18nDateTimeTest()
    {
    }

    static public void displayDate(Locale loc, int format)
    {
        Date today;
        String displayString;
        DateFormat df;

        //get a formatter for the date
        df = DateFormat.getDateInstance(format, loc);

        //Get the current date
        today = new Date();

        //Format the date into a string
        displayString = df.format(today);

        //Display the string
        System.out.println(displayString + " " + loc.toString());
    }


    static public void displayTime(Locale loc, int format)
    {
        Date today;
        String displayString;
        DateFormat df;
```

LISTING 25.14 continued

```java
        //Get a formatter for the time
        df = DateFormat.getTimeInstance(format, loc);

        //get the current time of day
        today = new Date();

        //create a string containing the time
        displayString = df.format(today);

        //Display the time
        System.out.println(displayString + " " + loc.toString());
    }

    public static void main(String[] args)
    {
        String lang = "en";
        String country = "US";
        String variant = "";
        Locale loc;
        ResourceBundle rBundle;

        //if they passed in a lang and country, use it. Else
        //use  en US
        if (args.length == 2)
        {
            lang = args[0];
            country = args[1];
        }

        if (args.length == 3)
        {
            lang = args[0];
            country = args[1];
            variant = args[2];
            loc = new Locale(lang, country, variant);
        }else
        {
            loc = new Locale(lang, country);
        }

        //Display the current date in a variety of formats
        System.out.println("----------------------------------------------");
        System.out.println("----------------------------------------------");
        displayDate(loc, DateFormat.DEFAULT);
        displayDate(loc, DateFormat.SHORT);
        displayDate(loc, DateFormat.MEDIUM);
        displayDate(loc, DateFormat.LONG);
        displayDate(loc, DateFormat.FULL);
```

LISTING 25.14   continued

```
        System.out.println("----------------------------------------");
        //Display the current time in a variety of formats
        displayTime(loc, DateFormat.DEFAULT);
        displayTime(loc, DateFormat.SHORT);
        displayTime(loc, DateFormat.MEDIUM);
        displayTime(loc, DateFormat.LONG);
        displayTime(loc, DateFormat.FULL);
        System.out.println("----------------------------------------");
        System.out.println("----------------------------------------");
    }
}
```

There are several interesting lines of code here. First, we display the date and time in different formats. The formats differ not only by locale, but also within a locale by providing a constant that indicates whether we want the display to be long, short, medium, and so on.

```
        df = DateFormat.getDateInstance(format, loc);
```

If we want to display a time, all we have to do is get a different formatter:

```
        df = DateFormat.getTimeInstance(format, loc);
```

Otherwise, the processing is nearly identical. Running this example with en as the language and US as the country yields the following result:

```
----------------------------------------
----------------------------------------
Feb 7, 2002 en_US
2/7/02 en_US
Feb 7, 2002 en_US
February 7, 2002 en_US
Thursday, February 7, 2002 en_US
----------------------------------------
3:10:46 PM en_US
3:10 PM en_US
3:10:46 PM en_US
3:10:46 PM EST en_US
3:10:46 PM EST en_US
----------------------------------------
----------------------------------------
```

If we run the same program with de as the language and DE as the country, we get a German version of the current date and time:

```
----------------------------------------
----------------------------------------
07.02.2002 de_DE
```

```
07.02.02 de_DE
07.02.2002 de_DE
7. Februar 2002 de_DE
Donnerstag, 7. Februar 2002 de_DE
-----------------------------------------
15:10:18 de_DE
15:10 de_DE
15:10:18 de_DE
15:10:18 EST de_DE
15.10 Uhr EST de_DE
-----------------------------------------
-----------------------------------------
```

Compare this with the work that we had to do to get text to display on a screen, and you will conclude that the Java designers have done a good job on handling dates and times.

Internationalizing Numbers and Currency

Dealing with numbers is very similar to dealing with dates. Instead of declaring an object of type `DateFormat`, you declare an object of type `NumberFormat` as shown in Listing 25.15.

LISTING 25.15   The `I18nNumberTest` Class

```
/*
 * I18nNumberTest.java
 *
 * Created on February 7, 2002, 1:20 PM
 */

package unleashed.ch25;
import java.util.*;
import java.text.*;

/**
 *
 * @author   Stephen Potts
 * @version
 */
public class I18nNumberTest
{

    /** Creates new I18nNumberTest */
    public I18nNumberTest()
    {
    }
```

LISTING 25.15 continued

```java
static public void displayNumber(Locale loc, double amount)
{
     String displayString;
     NumberFormat nf;

     //get a formatter for the number
     nf = NumberFormat.getNumberInstance(loc);


     //Format the number into a string
     displayString = nf.format(amount);

     //Display the string
     System.out.println(displayString + " " + loc.toString());
}


public static void main(String[] args)
{
     String lang = "en";
     String country = "US";
     String variant = "";
     Locale loc;
     ResourceBundle rBundle;

     //if they passed in a lang and country, use it. Else
     //use  en US
     if (args.length == 2)
     {
         lang = args[0];
         country = args[1];
     }

     if (args.length == 3)
     {
         lang = args[0];
         country = args[1];
         variant = args[2];
         loc = new Locale(lang, country, variant);
     }else
     {
          loc = new Locale(lang, country);
     }

     //Display the number in a variety of formats
     System.out.println("-----------------------------------------");
```

LISTING 25.15   continued

```
        System.out.println("-----------------------------------------");
        displayNumber(loc, 123456789);
        displayNumber(loc, 123.456);
        displayNumber(loc, 123456789.987);
        displayNumber(loc, 1234.9876543);

        System.out.println("-----------------------------------------");
        System.out.println("-----------------------------------------");
    }
}
```

The only new feature of this example is the method used to obtain a localized formatter:

```
        nf = NumberFormat.getNumberInstance(loc);
```

Running this example with en as the language and US as the country displays like this:

```
-----------------------------------------
-----------------------------------------
123,456,789 en_US
123.456 en_US
123,456,789.987 en_US
1,234.988 en_US
-----------------------------------------
-----------------------------------------
```

If we run the same program with de as the language and DE as the country, we see this:

```
-----------------------------------------
-----------------------------------------
123.456.789 de_DE
123,456 de_DE
123.456.789,987 de_DE
1.234,988 de_DE
-----------------------------------------
-----------------------------------------
```

The handling of currency is very similar. Internationalization does not deal with exchange rates because they fluctuate constantly. It is possible though, to get *n* pieces of money to display correctly on the screen. The processing that determines the value of *n* is still the programmer's responsibility. Listing 25.16 shows how currency display is done.

LISTING 25.16   The I18nCurrencyTest Class

```
/*
 * I18nCurrencyTest.java
 *
```

25

JAVA
INTERNATIONAL-
IZATION

LISTING 25.16   continued

```
 * Created on February 7, 2002, 1:20 PM
 */

package unleashed.ch25;
import java.util.*;
import java.text.*;

/**
 *
 * @author  Stephen Potts
 * @version
 */
public class I18nCurrencyTest
{

    /** Creates new I18nCurrencyTest */
    public I18nCurrencyTest()
    {
    }

    static public void displayCurrency(Locale loc, double amount)
    {
         String displayString;
         NumberFormat nf;

        //get a formatter for the number
        nf = NumberFormat.getCurrencyInstance(loc);


        //Format the number into a string
        displayString = nf.format(amount);

        //Display the string
        System.out.println(displayString + " " + loc.toString());
    }


    public static void main(String[] args)
    {
        String lang = "en";
        String country = "US";
        String variant = "";
        Locale loc;
        ResourceBundle rBundle;

        //if they passed in a lang and country, use it. Else
```

LISTING 25.16   continued

```java
//use  en US
if (args.length == 2)
{
    lang = args[0];
    country = args[1];
}

if (args.length == 3)
{
    lang = args[0];
    country = args[1];
    variant = args[2];
    loc = new Locale(lang, country, variant);
}else
{
     loc = new Locale(lang, country);
}

//Display the currency
System.out.println("-----------------------------------------");
System.out.println("-----------------------------------------");
displayCurrency(loc, 123456789);
displayCurrency(loc, 123.456);
displayCurrency(loc, 123456789.987);
displayCurrency(loc, 1234.9876543);

System.out.println("-----------------------------------------");
System.out.println("-----------------------------------------");
    }
}
```

This example uses the same logic to do its processing as the formatting of numbers did, except for the method used to get the correct formatter:

```java
nf = NumberFormat.getCurrencyInstance(loc);
```

When we run the program with en and US as the parameters, we get the following result:

```
-----------------------------------------
-----------------------------------------
$123,456,789.00 en_US
$123.46 en_US
$123,456,789.99 en_US
$1,234.99 en_US
-----------------------------------------
-----------------------------------------
```

Running this example with de and DE as the parameters returns the following result:

```
-----------------------------------------
-----------------------------------------
123.456.789,00 DM de_DE
123,46 DM de_DE
123.456.789,99 DM de_DE
1.234,99 DM de_DE
-----------------------------------------
-----------------------------------------
```

The localization features built into Java do most of the work required to handle numbers and currency.

Summary

In this chapter, we looked at the challenges of creating software systems in Java that are able to function, without modification, in any locale on earth. This is provided that you have created resources for each locale.

We learned about the role of ResourceBundles in providing internationalized text to place on the screen. We also learned how class files could be used instead of properties files when objects other than strings are needed.

Finally, we learned how to internationalize dates, times, numbers, and letters so that they appear in a way that makes sense to the users of our systems regardless of their culture and nationality.

Persistence and Cloning

Imagine purchasing a car that had electric everything—electric seat adjustments, electric mirrors, electric steering wheel adjustments, and so on. This convenience provides a lot of customer satisfaction. Imagine also that every time you shut off your car, the settings for all these would be gone and you would have to set them all over again. That would make you long for the old mechanical handles under the seats, wouldn't it? For the fancy features to be worthwhile, they need to persist between driving events. They need to be stored in a way that allows them to be retrieved correctly each time.

Many of your objects need to be persisted also. Can you imagine using a checking account program that required the reentry of every check that you ever wrote every time you started up or playing a computer game that doesn't let you save the state? Each time, you would have to begin again at the first stage.

Imagine a rental car company that was so advanced that they recorded the seat location, steering wheel setting, radio stations, and mirror positions from every car that you drive. When you rent a new car, the settings are downloaded to this car and you drive away. They have cloned the state object from your first rental and placed the copy in the second car's memory. You might need to clone objects in your code also. If you need to store an e-mail in two different folders, an exact copy can be cloned and stored. When your real-time strategy game creates another peasant, you can just clone an existing peasant and put him to work chopping wood.

Serialization is one of the fundamental technologies in the Java SDK that enables most of the remoting technologies: Remote Method Invocation (RMI), Enterprise JavaBeans (EJB), and Java Message Service (JMS) to name a few. One common form of serialization is writing an object to a database management system (DBMS). This can be a good approach if you are already using a database in you project, and if the other technologies that you are using are expecting to receive objects from the database. Many technologies such as RMI, EJB, and JMS are not expecting to deal with a database table, though, so using one would require custom programming on your part.

Java provides some clever facilities such as cloning and automatic serialization to help you persist your objects. In addition, it provides some special features that allow you to customize this process a little or a lot as your requirements dictate. In this chapter, you will learn about several of these advanced techniques, including externalization and encryption.

Object Serialization

The need to persist objects is so common that Java has a special interface to support it, the `java.io.Serializable` interface. Object Serialization is the process of saving the

state of an object as a sequence of bytes. The process of doing this translation is call
serializing. The process of reading the sequence of bytes and creating an object of identical state is called *deserializing*.

Of course, not every object can be serialized. Some objects, such as threads and sockets, are operational and are tied to a specific run of a program, not to the state of an object. In addition, not all fields in an object can be serialized, even if the object as a whole would be a good candidate. If an object contained a handle to a `Socket` object, that handle would not be meaningful after the object was read back in and re-created in memory. So, we would say that the `Socket` is not serializable.

When you deserialize a class, the class definition has to be either previously loaded or accessible by the thread's class loader; otherwise, the serialization will fail. This is most applicable in a distributed scenario (using RMI, or simply sending serialized objects over sockets).

The `Serializable` interface is a *tag interface*—it has no methods, but serves to indicate that an object is intended to be serialized. The JVM does the actual work of figuring out what needs to be stored. This work can take place automatically, manually, or as a hybrid of the two. We will look at all three of these approaches in this chapter. Serializing an object into a database is a topic in Chapter 10, " JDBC and Databases."

Automatic Serialization

The Java language comes with built-in functionality to serialize objects. All that you have to do is declare an object that implements the `Serializable` interface as shown in Listing 26.1.

LISTING 26.1 The Employee Class

```
package unleashed.ch26;
import java.io.Serializable;
import java.util.*;
/**
 *
 * @author  Stephen Potts
 * The Employee class
 */
public class Employee implements Serializable
{

    private String name;


    /** Creates Employee */
```

LISTING 26.1   continued

```
    public Employee( String name)
    {
        this.name = name;
    }

    public String getName()
    {
        return name;
    }
}
```

Notice that the class implements the `Serializable` interface:

```
public class Employee implements Serializable
```

This is required for all classes that will be serialized. We can serialize instances in this class by using the class shown in Listing 26.2.

LISTING 26.2   The `TestSerEmployee` Class

```
package unleashed.ch26;
import java.io.ObjectOutputStream;
import java.io.FileOutputStream;
import java.io.IOException;

/**
 *
 * @author   Stephen Potts
 * @version
 */
public class TestSerEmployee {

    /** Creates new TestSerEmployee */
    public TestSerEmployee() {
    }

    public static void main(String[] args)
    {
        try
        {
            String filename = "Employee.ser";

            Employee emp = new Employee("Kopack");
            FileOutputStream f  = new FileOutputStream(filename);
            ObjectOutputStream oos = new ObjectOutputStream(f);
            oos.writeObject(emp);
            oos.close();
        }catch (IOException ioe)
```

LISTING 26.2   continued

```
        {
            System.out.println("IOException thrown " + ioe);
        }
    }
}
```

The most interesting thing about this example is what is missing. No logic controls how the serialization is to take place. All we did is call the `writeObject()` method. It is quite automatic. The output of this example is the `Employee.ser` file, the contents of which are shown here:

```
¬í__sr__unleashed.ch26.Employee"ŠÉ_²·âl___L__
namet__Ljava/lang/String;xpt__Kopack
```

If you are quick, you might conclude that this file is not meant for human eyes, although some parts of it are easy to read. The rest of the data provides information to the deserializing process.

Because of your quickness, you will probably conclude that the next example will read the same file back in and create another object that has the same state as the original `Employee` object. In this you would be correct, as shown in Listing 26.3.

LISTING 26.3   The `RestoreEmployee` Class

```java
package unleashed.ch26;
import java.io.ObjectInputStream;
import java.io.FileInputStream;
import java.io.IOException;

/**
 *
 * @author  Stephen Potts
 * Test the restoration of serialized objects
 */
public class RestoreEmployee {

    /** Creates new RestoreEmployee */
    public RestoreEmployee() {
    }

    public static void main(String[] args)
    {
        try
        {
            String filename = "Employee.ser";
```

LISTING 26.3   continued

```
            Employee emp = null;
            FileInputStream f  = new FileInputStream(filename);
            ObjectInputStream ois = new ObjectInputStream(f);
            emp = (Employee)ois.readObject();
            System.out.println("The name is " + emp.getName());
            ois.close();
        }catch (IOException ioe)
        {
            System.out.println("IOException thrown " + ioe);
        }
        catch (ClassNotFoundException cnfe)
        {
            System.out.println("ClassNotFoundException thrown " + cnfe);
        }
    }
}
```

There are a few interesting points to make concerning this admittedly simple-minded example:

- The converse set of I/O classes, `FileInputStream` and `ObjectInput` stream, were used. They possess enough intelligence to discard all the metadata in the `Employee.ser` file and create an object that is indistinguishable from the one that we serialized.

- The `readObject()` method returns an object. Before we can assign this object to an `Employee` handle, we must first downcast it to be an object of that type. In a more complex program, it would be wise to use the `instanceof` operator to verify that the downcast will not throw a runtime exception. Casts fail when the object that was serialized is of a different type than the cast is trying to make it.

The result of this simple example is as you might expect:

```
The name is Kopack
```

If you are not very impressed that serialization could save and restore an `Employee` object, it is no surprise. How hard can it be to store such a simple object? The power of this feature is not apparent until we serialize a class that contains other classes as its members. You are well aware that these other classes don't really exist inside the enclosing class—the enclosing class only maintains handles to the other objects. When you do an `Object.clone()` on the enclosing class, what you get is a copy of these handles.

Serialization is smarter than that. Look at the more complex set of classes shown in Listing 26.4.

LISTING 26.4 The Company Class

```java
package unleashed.ch26;
import java.util.Vector;
import java.util.Iterator;
import java.util.Set;
import java.io.Serializable;

/**
 *
 * @author   Stephen Potts
 * @version
 */
public class Company implements Serializable
{
    private String name;
    private Employee president;
    private Vector departments;

    /** Creates new Company */
    public Company(String name)
    {
        this.name = name;
        departments = new Vector();
    }

    public String getName()
    {
        return this.name;
    }

    public void addDepartment(Department dept)
    {
        departments.addElement(dept);
    }

    public Employee getPresident()
    {
        return this.president;
    }

    public void addPresident(Employee e)
    {
        this.president = e;
    }

    public Iterator getDepartmentIterator()
    {
        return departments.iterator();
    }
}
```

We will also need to have departments for our company. Listing 26.5 provides the Department class.

LISTING 26.5   The Department Class

```
package unleashed.ch26;
import java.io.Serializable;

/**
 *
 * @author  Stephen Potts
 * @version
 */
public class Department implements Serializable
{
    private String name;
    private Employee manager;

    /** Creates new Department */
    public Department(String name)
    {
        this.name = name;
    }

    public String getName()
    {
        return this.name;
    }
    public Employee getManager()
    {
        return this.manager;
    }

    public void addManager(Employee e)
    {
        manager = e;
    }
}
```

Now we can try and serialize this complex class and see whether it re-creates an identical object. Listing 26.6 shows an example that tests this.

LISTING 26.6   The TestSerCompany Class

```
package unleashed.ch26;
import java.io.ObjectOutputStream;
import java.io.FileOutputStream;
import java.io.IOException;
import java.util.Iterator;
```

LISTING 26.6 continued

```java
/**
 *
 * @author  Stephen Potts
 * Test to see if company is serializable
 */
public class TestSerCompany
{

    /** Creates new TestSerCompany */
    public TestSerCompany() {
    }

    public static void printCompanyObject(Company c)
    {
        System.out.println("The company name is " + c.getName());
        System.out.println("The company president is " +
                                    c.getPresident().getName());
        System.out.println(" ");

        Iterator i = c.getDepartmentIterator();
        while (i.hasNext())
        {
            Department d = (Department)i.next();
            System.out.println("   The department name is " + d.getName());
            System.out.println("   The department manager is " +
                                        d.getManager().getName());
            System.out.println(" ");
        }
    }


    public static void main(String[] args)
    {
        try
        {
            String filename = "Company.ser";

            Company comp = new Company("The Blazer Company");
            Employee emp0 = new Employee("Leslie Waller");
            comp.addPresident(emp0);

            Department sales = new Department("Sales");
            Employee emp1 = new Employee("Grant Jackson");
            sales.addManager(emp1);
            comp.addDepartment(sales);
```

LISTING 26.6   continued

```
        Department accounting = new Department("Accounting");
        Employee emp2 = new Employee("Clay Cain");
        accounting.addManager(emp2);
        comp.addDepartment(accounting);

        Department maintenance = new Department("Maintenance");
        Employee emp3 = new Employee("Greg Hladlick");
        maintenance.addManager(emp3);
        comp.addDepartment(maintenance);
        printCompanyObject(comp);

        FileOutputStream f  = new FileOutputStream(filename);
        ObjectOutputStream oos = new ObjectOutputStream(f);
        oos.writeObject(comp);
        oos.close();


    }catch (IOException ioe)
    {
        System.out.println("IOException thrown " + ioe);
    }
  }
}
```

Notice how simple the serialization code is for this object:

```
        FileOutputStream f  = new FileOutputStream(filename);
        ObjectOutputStream oos = new ObjectOutputStream(f);
        oos.writeObject(comp);
        oos.close();
```

You might have expected to do more here, but the automatic serialization is able to do much of the work.

The output from running `TestSerCompany` shows the data that was written:

```
The company name is The Blazer Company
The company president is Leslie Waller

    The department name is Sales
    The department manager is Grant Jackson

    The department name is Accounting
    The department manager is Clay Cain

    The department name is Maintenance
    The department manager is Greg Hladlick
```

Now let's see what happens when we try to deserialize such a complex set of objects. Listing 26.7 shows the code needed to perform the deserialization.

LISTING 26.7   The RestoreCompany Class

```java
package unleashed.ch26;
import java.io.ObjectInputStream;
import java.io.FileInputStream;
import java.io.IOException;
import java.util.Iterator;

/**
 *
 * @author  Stephen Potts
 * Test the restoration of serialized objects
 */
public class RestoreCompany {

    /** Creates new RestoreEmployee */
    public RestoreCompany() {
    }

    public static void printCompanyObject(Company c)
    {
        System.out.println("The company name is " + c.getName());
        System.out.println("The company president is " +
                                        c.getPresident().getName());
        System.out.println(" ");

        Iterator i = c.getDepartmentIterator();
        while (i.hasNext())
        {
            Department d = (Department)i.next();
            System.out.println("   The department name is " + d.getName());
            System.out.println("   The department manager is " +
                                                d.getManager().getName());
            System.out.println(" ");
        }
    }
    public static void main(String[] args)
    {
        try
        {
            String filename = "Company.ser";
            Company comp;

            FileInputStream f  = new FileInputStream(filename);
            ObjectInputStream ois = new ObjectInputStream(f);
            comp = (Company)ois.readObject();
            printCompanyObject(comp);
            ois.close();
        }catch (IOException ioe)
        {
            System.out.println("IOException thrown " + ioe);
```

LISTING 26.7   continued

```
        }
        catch (ClassNotFoundException cnfe)
        {
            System.out.println("ClassNotFoundException thrown " + cnfe);
        }
    }
}
```

The theory is that the new object, comp, created from the stream will be in the same state as the comp object from Listing 26.6 that was serialized. That looks like a tall order when you consider the complexity of the relationships in the Company class.

Running the experiment yields the following result:

```
The company name is The Blazer Company
The company president is Leslie Waller

    The department name is Sales
    The department manager is Grant Jackson

    The department name is Accounting
    The department manager is Clay Cain

    The department name is Maintenance
    The department manager is Greg Hladlick
```

So we have proof that the Serializable interface can handle the complex case as easily as it handled the simple case in Listing 26.2.

The transient Keyword

One of the strengths of object-oriented programming is its ability to handle small differences in class design without a lot of work. Suppose, for example, that we fire the president of our company so often that we don't want to record his or her name in our serialized object. (Pretend that this company is a dot-com, and it will make sense.) We want to fill in the president's name each time we start the program. This is easily done using the transient keyword. *Transient* means that this field is temporary, and it is not to be serialized. It must be used if you have a reference to a class that is not serializable, but it can be used any time that you do not want to serialize an object. To change the Company class so that the president field is not serialized, we place the keyword in the declaration as shown here:

```
    private transient Employee president;
```

Caution

Caution must be taken if you use this keyword. The deserializing of the data
will cause the president field to exist, but it will not be populated. If you refer
to it as we did in the RestoreCompany object, you will get the following error:

```
The company name is The Blazer Company
java.lang.NullPointerException
        at unleashed.ch26.RestoreCompany.printCompanyObject
                                (RestoreCompany.java:27)
        at unleashed.ch26.RestoreCompany.main(RestoreCompany.java:49)
Exception in thread "main"
```

The Company object will be written to output just as it was before, except that the
president field data is now missing.

The moral of the story is to be careful to match what the serialization puts to the stream
and what it gets back from the stream, or errors will occur.

Serialization with Versions

The JVM is very careful to enforce the rule that the version of the class that created a
serialized stream be the same class definition when the class is read back in. Each time
an object is serialized, a *serial unique identifier (SUID)* is created. This SUID is based
on the definition of the class at the time of the serialization. If the class changes its version, even in ways that would not affect the correctness of a deserializing, the SUID difference will be detected, and the operation will fail.

This makes sense because the JVM has no way of knowing whether the serialization is
valid if the classes have changed. JVM plays it safe and refuses to honor your request.

There is an exception to every rule, so Java allows you to override this feature by obtaining the SUID for the marshaled data. You do this by issuing the following command:

```
Serialver unleashed.ch26.Company
```

In our case, we get the following response:

```
unleashed.ch26.Company:    static final long serialVersionUID =
                                5447802251683735450L;
```

Now we can modify our Company code as shown in Listing 26.8 to override the automatic
version checking.

LISTING 26.8   The Versioned Company2 Class

```java
package unleashed.ch26;
import java.util.Vector;
import java.util.Iterator;
import java.util.Set;
import java.io.Serializable;

/**
 *
 * @author   Stephen Potts
 * this version has the serversionUID set manually
 */
public class Company2 implements Serializable
{
    private String name;
    private transient Employee president;
    private Vector departments;

    private static final long serialVersionUID = 5447802251683735450L;

    /** Creates new Company */
    public Company(String name)
    {
        this.name = name;
        departments = new Vector();
    }

    public String getName()
    {
        return this.name;
    }

    public void addDepartment(Department dept)
    {
        departments.addElement(dept);
    }

    public Employee getPresident()
    {
        return this.president;
    }

    public void addPresident(Employee e)
    {
        this.president = e;
    }

    public Iterator getDepartmentIterator()
    {
```

LISTING 26.8   continued

```
        return departments.iterator();
    }
}
```

If you now run this code against the original serialized object, the exception will go away, but it will be replaced by unpredictable results. The reason for this is that changing a field from normal to transient is a material change to the version. The moral of the story is that you should try to serialize and deserialize using the same class version. If you must use the manual override that was shown here, proceed with caution.

> **Caution**
>
> Setting the SUID manually is tricky and can lead to unpredictable results. Use the same version of the class when possible.

Let common sense be your guide. Even in cases in which you understand the nuances of setting the SUID, it is still risky because of programmers who will maintain this code in the future.

Custom Serialization

In typical Java fashion, you can bypass all or part of the automatic serialization by overriding the `ObjectStream.writeObject()` and the `ObjectStream.readObject` methods as shown in Listing 26.9.

LISTING 26.9   The Company3 Class

```java
package unleashed.ch26;
import java.util.Vector;
import java.util.Iterator;
import java.util.Date;
import java.io.*;

/**
 *
 * @author   Stephen Potts
 * this version has the serversionUID set manually
 */
public class Company3 implements Serializable
{
    private String name;
```

LISTING 26.9   continued

```java
private Employee president;
private Vector departments;
private transient String dateLastMarshaled;


/** Creates new Company */
public Company2(String name)
{
    this.name = name;
    departments = new Vector();
}

public String getName()
{
    return this.name;
}

public void addDepartment(Department dept)
{
    departments.addElement(dept);
}

public Employee getPresident()
{
    return this.president;
}

public void addPresident(Employee e)
{
    this.president = e;
}

public String getDateLastMarshaled()
{
    return this.dateLastMarshaled;
}

public Iterator getDepartmentIterator()
{
    return departments.iterator();
}

//add a custom writeObject() and readObject() to do your own serialization
private void writeObject(ObjectOutputStream stream)throws IOException
{
    stream.defaultWriteObject();
    stream.writeObject(new Date().toString());
}

private void readObject(ObjectInputStream stream) throws IOException
```

LISTING 26.9   continued

```
    {
        try
        {
            stream.defaultReadObject();
            this.dateLastMarshaled = (String)(stream.readObject());
        }catch (ClassNotFoundException cnfe)
        {
            System.out.println("Class Not Found " + cnfe);
        }
    }
}
```

Several lines of code in this modified class deserve some explanation:

- We added a transient string called `dateLastMarshaled` to the state variables of the class. This was made transient for the sake of the example.

- In the overridden `writeObject()` method, we did a call to `stream.` `defaultWriteObject()`. This tells the JVM to marshal this object as always. We want to add information to the stream, but we also want the normal stream to be created.

- In the overridden `readObject()` method, we did a call to `stream.` `defaultReadObject()`. This tells the JVM to deserialize this object as always. We want to get the additional information from the stream, but we also want the normal stream read.

- We are storing the additional information in the object and accessing it just like any other method.

The `TestSerCompany2` class is identical to `TestSerCompany` class except that it creates a `Company3` object instead of a `Company` object. The `RestoreCompany2` class is identical to the `RestoreCompany` class except that it contains this line in the `printCompanyObject()` method:

```
        System.out.println("The last date marshaled is " +
                                    c.getDateLastMarshaled());
```

The output from running the `TestSerCompany2` program followed by the `RestoreCompany2` program is shown here:

```
The company name is The Blazer2 Company
The company president is Leslie Waller
The last date marshaled is Thu Dec 13 11:14:47 EST 2001

    The department name is Sales
    The department manager is Grant Jackson
```

```
The department name is Accounting
The department manager is Clay Cain

The department name is Maintenance
The department manager is Greg Hladlick
```

You can see where the re-created object now contains the date that it was last marshaled. This example was kept short intentionally, but you can easily extend the logic shown here to perform a highly customized serializing/deserializing.

Serialization Internals

Most of you are probably wondering just how good the serialization facility really is. How complex can a situation get before the serializing and deserializing get confused? The full answer to this question is beyond the scope of this book, but we can talk about a difficult problem that will provide some insights.

Suppose that we created an `Employee` and assigned him to a `secretary` field. Suppose also that the `Employee` class was now modified to allow every `Employee` to have a secretary assigned to her. If we have several employees sharing a secretary, we would have the same `Employee` handle in several of the other `Employee` classes.

If we serialize this, the serializing mechanism is smart enough to create just one object (if they were all serialized in the same pass) and make a notation in the other objects that they should all point to the same object when deserialized.

Improving Serialization Performance

Because of the work that must be done by the JVM to detect these shared objects, the process can be slow. One opportunity for performance improvement would be to replace the default serialization processing with custom processing. Because of your knowledge of your class structure, you can program the serialization in a very direct fashion. Imagine writing a method to serialize an arbitrary object. Visualize the number of different situations for which you would have to code, and you will get an idea of why it takes some measurable CPU time to serialize a complex object.

A word of caution is in order about writing extra code to speed up systems. Performance bottlenecks, or slow places in the code, are very hard for programmers to find by pondering. Don't scratch until you find an itch.

System complexity is such that running a profiling tool before gerrymandering the code is wise. Replacing undebugged serialization code in place of thoroughly debugged JVM code will have a negative impact on the schedule and reliability of your system, even as it is having a positive impact on the performance.

Object Externalization

The next greater level of persistence control is called *externalization*. If you implement the `java.io.Externalizable` interface, you will be able to control every aspect of the serializing and deserializing of your project. You might have quite a bit of extra processing that you want to do upon deserializing, or you might want to do this in an attempt to gain an improvement in performance.

The mechanics of externalizing a class are fairly simple. You create a class that implements the `Externalizable` interface, and you implement the `writeExternal()` and the `readExternal()` methods. These routines are called whenever any program attempts to serialize your objects. The calling programs need not be changed if you change the definition of your class from implementing `Serializable` to implementing `Externalizable`. Let's change our `Employee` class to prove to ourselves that this is true. This is shown in Listing 26.10.

LISTING 26.10 The `Employee2` Class

```
package unleashed.ch26;
import java.io.Externalizable;
import java.io.IOException;
import java.io.ObjectOutput;
import java.io.ObjectInput;
import java.util.*;
/**
 *
 * @author  Stephen Potts
 * The Employee class
 */
public class Employee2 implements Externalizable
{

    private String name;
    private int salary;

    public Employee2(String name, int salary)
    {
        this.name = name;
        this.salary = salary;
    }

    public Employee2()
    {
    }

    public String getName()
```

LISTING 26.10   continued

```
    {
        return name;
    }

    public int getSalary()
    {
        return this.salary;
    }

    public void writeExternal(ObjectOutput out) throws IOException
    {
        out.writeObject(this.name);
        out.writeInt(this.salary);
    }
    public void readExternal(ObjectInput in) throws
                            IOException, ClassNotFoundException
    {
        name = (String)in.readObject();
        salary = in.readInt();
    }
}
```

You will notice several differences between this class and the `Employee` class:

- The obvious one is that we have implemented `Externalizable` rather than `Serializable`.

- We have added a salary field to make the example more interesting.

- We added a default constructor. This is a requirement of Externalization, and a runtime exception will be thrown if it is not met.

- The `writeExternal()` class does not call a `defaultWriteObject()` method. `readExternal()` does not call any `defaultReadObject()` method. We have turned off the automatic portion of the reading and writing by implementing `Externalizable`.

Now we can test the class and see whether externalizing it works. First we serialize the class in Listing 26.11.

LISTING 26.11   The `TestExtEmployee` Class

```
package unleashed.ch26;
import java.io.ObjectOutputStream;
import java.io.FileOutputStream;
import java.io.IOException;
```

LISTING 26.11   continued

```
/**
 *
 * @author   Stephen Potts
 * @version
 */
public class TestExtEmployee {

    /** Creates new TestSerEmployee */
    public TestExtEmployee() {
    }

    public static void main(String[] args)
    {
        try
        {
            String filename = "Employee2.out";

            Employee2 emp = new Employee2("Jacob Snakob", 10000);
            FileOutputStream f  = new FileOutputStream(filename);
            ObjectOutputStream oos = new ObjectOutputStream(f);
            oos.writeObject(emp);
            oos.close();
        }catch (IOException ioe)
        {
            System.out.println("IOException thrown " + ioe);
        }
    }
}
```

The serialization takes place in the following code:

```
            ObjectOutputStream oos = new ObjectOutputStream(f);
            oos.writeObject(emp);
```

When the object is written to this stream, it is serialized by the JVM.

Now we can see whether externalizing worked. We deserialize the class in Listing 26.12.

LISTING 26.12   The `RestoreEmployee2` Class

```
package unleashed.ch26;
import java.io.ObjectInputStream;
import java.io.FileInputStream;
import java.io.IOException;

/**
 *
```

LISTING 26.12   continued

```
 * @author  Stephen Potts
 * Test the restoration of serialized objects
 */
public class RestoreEmployee2 {

    /** Creates new RestoreEmployee */
    public RestoreEmployee2() {
    }

    public static void main(String[] args)
    {
        try
        {
            String filename = "Employee2.out";

            Employee2 emp = null;
            FileInputStream f  = new FileInputStream(filename);
            ObjectInputStream ois = new ObjectInputStream(f);
            emp = (Employee2)ois.readObject();
            System.out.println("The name is " + emp.getName());
            System.out.println("The salary is $" + emp.getSalary());
            ois.close();
        }catch (IOException ioe)
        {
            System.out.println("IOException thrown " + ioe);
        }
        catch (ClassNotFoundException cnfe)
        {
            System.out.println("ClassNotFoundException thrown " + cnfe);
        }
    }
}
```

The most remarkable thing about Listing 26.12 is that it is so similar to the serializable version. It is a little surprising that we still use the `writeObject()` method to marshal the object and the `readObject()` method to deserialize it.

The output of Listing 26.12 is shown here:

```
The name is Jacob Snakob
The salary is $10000
```

You essentially have three choices when you want to persist an object. You can use automatic serialization, custom serialization, or externalization. Each of these gives you a different level of control over the process.

Cloning to Achieve Serialization

Cloning means to create a second object that is identical to the first. What this means depends on what the definition of "identical" is. The `Object` class provides a protected member called `clone()`, which creates a *shallow* copy of the object being cloned. A shallow copy is one that creates a literal copy of an object. If a member variable is an integer, it creates an integer. If the member is a handle to an object, it creates a handle to an object.

> **Note**
>
> This is the reason that you have to use the `.equals()` method to compare the contents of two objects. The `==` operator only does a shallow comparison of the handle values, while the `.equals()` does a deep comparison of the data itself.

This creates some interesting situations that you need to be aware of. Consider the `Employee3` class. It contains an `int` and a `String` as shown in Listing 26.13.

LISTING 26.13   The `Employee3` Class Is Declared to be Cloneable

```java
package unleashed.ch26;

import java.util.*;
/**
 *
 * @author   Stephen Potts
 * The Employee class
 */
public class Employee3 implements Cloneable
{

    private String name;
    private int salary;

    public Employee3(String name, int salary)
    {
        this.name = name;
        this.salary = salary;
    }

    public Employee3()
    {
    }
```

LISTING 26.13 continued

```java
    public String getName()
    {
        return name;
    }
    public void setName(String name)
    {
        this.name = name;
    }

    public void setSalary(int salary)
    {
        this.salary = salary;
    }

    public int getSalary()
    {
        return this.salary;
    }
}
```

Notice that `Employee3` implements the `Clonable` interface:

```java
public class Employee3 implements Cloneable
```

This means that it can be cloned if another class wants to use it.

Let's try and clone it using Listing 26.14.

LISTING 26.14 The `Cloner` Class

```java
package unleashed.ch26;

/**
 *
 * @author   Stephen Potts
 * @version
 */
public class Cloner {

    /** Creates new Cloner */
    public Cloner() {
    }

    public static void main(String[] args)
    {
        try
        {
            Employee3 e = new Employee3("Dolly", 1000);
```

LISTING 26.14   continued

```
        System.out.println(e);
        System.out.println("The employee's name is " + e.getName());
        System.out.println("The employee's pay is " + e.getSalary());

        Employee3 eClone = (Employee3)e.clone();
        System.out.println(eClone);
        System.out.println("The clone's name is " + eClone.getName());
        System.out.println("The clone's pay is " + eClone.getSalary());


    }catch (CloneNotSupportedException cnse)
    {
        System.out.println("Clone not supported");
    }
  }
}
```

This code will not compile as it is written because it makes a polymorphic call to
`Object.clone()`, which is declared to be protected. This message will appear:

```
unleashed/ch26/Cloner.java [28:1] clone() has
                  protected access in java.lang.Object
```

We need to add an access-only override of the `clone()` method in the `Employee3` class.
An access-only override adds no logic; it just relaxes the access restrictions on your
code. Remember that an overridden method cannot be more restrictive than the base
class method, but it can be less restrictive. Adding this code to the `Employee3` class
solves the problem (see Listing 26.15).

LISTING 26.15   The `clone()` Method

```
public Object clone() throws CloneNotSupportedException
{
    try
    {
        return super.clone();
    }catch (CloneNotSupportedException cnse)
    {
        System.out.println("CloneNotSupportedException thrown "+ cnse);
        throw new CloneNotSupportedException();
    }
}
```

We will call the new version of the `Employee3` class `Employee3a` and the version of
`Cloner` `Cloner3a`. Now `Cloner3a` will compile and run, giving the following results:

```
unleashed.ch26.Employee3@1fef6f
The employee's name is Dolly
```

```
The employee's pay is 1000
unleashed.ch26.Employee3@209f4e
The clone's name is Dolly
The clone's pay is 1000
```

As you would expect, the object ID is different, but the fields are identical. This means that the comparison operator, ==, will fail.

According to the rules of shallow copying, the salary field that was cloned is a new variable. The name is a string, and thus both the objects point to the same String object. Let's see what happens when we modify the clone's values and print them out again by adding these lines to main. This is done in Listing 26.16.

LISTING 26.16   The Cloner_1 Class

```java
package unleashed.ch26;

/**
 *
 * @author   Stephen Potts
 * @version
 */
public class Cloner_1
{

    /** Creates new Cloner */
    public Cloner_1() {
    }

    public static void main(String[] args)
    {
        try
        {
            Employee6 e = new Employee6("Dolly", 1000);
            System.out.println("The employee's name is " + e.getName());
            System.out.println("The employee's pay is " + e.getSalary());

            Employee6 eClone = (Employee6)e.clone();
            System.out.println("The clone's name is " + eClone.getName());
            System.out.println("The clone's pay is " + eClone.getSalary());
            eClone.setName("Polly");
            eClone.setSalary(2000);

            System.out.println("The employee's name is " + e.getName());
            System.out.println("The employee's pay is " + e.getSalary());

            System.out.println("The clone's name is " + eClone.getName());
            System.out.println("The clone's pay is " + eClone.getSalary());
```

LISTING 26.16 continued

```
        }catch (Exception e){ System.out.println("Exception " + e);}
    }
}
```

The result is shown here:

```
The employee's name is Dolly
The employee's pay is 1000
The clone's name is Dolly
The clone's pay is 1000
The employee's name is Dolly
The employee's pay is 1000
The clone's name is Polly
The clone's pay is 2000
```

Notice that both the name and the salary stayed the same on the employee and changed on the clone. You might have been predicting that both names would change, which is not the case because the `String` class is *immutable*. This means that it is never modified, but rather, it is destroyed and re-created each time it is "modified." (Performance issues might be dancing through your head at this notion, and they should be.) This gives us the desired behavior as a side effect of the way strings work. Figure 26.1 shows this graphically.

FIGURE 26.1

The original and cloned objects can't point to the same immutable object.

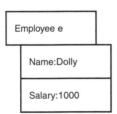

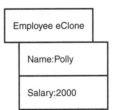

If, however, we change the data type of the name to a `StringBuffer` class, we will see the problem with shallow copying (see Listing 26.17).

LISTING 26.17 StringBuffers Are Not Immutable

```
package unleashed.ch26;

import java.util.*;
/**
 *
 * @author  Stephen Potts
```

LISTING 26.17 continued

```
 * The Employee class
 */
public class Employee4 implements Cloneable
{

    private StringBuffer name;
    private int salary;

    public Employee4(String name, int salary)
    {
        this.name = new StringBuffer(name);
        this.salary = salary;
    }

    public Employee4()
    {
    }

    public Object clone() throws CloneNotSupportedException
    {
        try
        {
            return super.clone();
        }catch (CloneNotSupportedException cnse)
        {
            System.out.println("CloneNotSupportedException thrown "+ cnse);
            throw new CloneNotSupportedException();
        }
    }

    public String getName()
    {
        return name.toString();
    }

    public void setName(String name)
    {
        this.name.delete(0, this.name.length());
        this.name.append(name);
    }

    public void setSalary(int salary)
    {
        this.salary = salary;
    }

    public int getSalary()
    {
```

LISTING 26.17   continued

```
        return this.salary;
    }
}
```

Running the same `Cloner_1 main()` against this class shows that when the class is mutable, the shallow copy does not ordinarily produce the result that you wanted. This version of `Cloner_1` is called `Cloner_1a.java`. It can be found in the source code directory for this chapter.

```
unleashed.ch26.Employee4@1fef6f
The employee's name is Dolly
The employee's pay is 1000
unleashed.ch26.Employee4@209f4e
The clone's name is Dolly
The clone's pay is 1000
The employee's name is Polly
The employee's pay is 1000
The clone's name is Polly
The clone's pay is 2000
```

Figure 26.2 shows this graphically.

FIGURE 26.2

The original and cloned objects can point to the same mutable object.

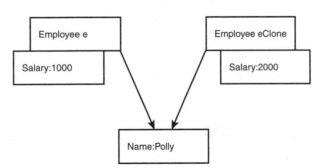

What you probably wanted was a deep copy—a duplication of the original object structure with each of the objects copied. The following section shows how to do this.

Creating Deep Copies

Creating deep copies is conceptually simple, but logistically challenging if your class structure is complex. All you have to do is clone a shallow copy and replace each of the shallow references with the creation of an object, followed by the copying of the correct fields. It sounds simple, huh? Let's look at the simple case of the `StringBuffer` version of the `Employee` class. We will modify this class to make it create a deep copy as shown in Listing 26.18.

LISTING 26.18   The `Employee5` Class

```java
package unleashed.ch26;

import java.util.*;
/**
 *
 * @author   Stephen Potts
 * The Employee5 class
 */
public class Employee5 implements Cloneable
{

    private StringBuffer name;
    private int salary;

    public Employee5(String name, int salary)
    {
        this.name = new StringBuffer(name);
        this.salary = salary;
    }

    public Employee5()
    {
    }

    public Object clone() throws CloneNotSupportedException
    {
        try
        {
            Employee5 o = (Employee5)super.clone();
            o.name = new StringBuffer(name.toString());
            return o;

        }catch (CloneNotSupportedException cnse)
        {
            System.out.println("CloneNotSupportedException thrown "+ cnse);
            throw new CloneNotSupportedException();
        }
    }

    public String getName()
    {
        return name.toString();
    }
```

Listing 26.18   continued

```java
    public void setName(String name)
    {
        this.name.delete(0, this.name.length());
        this.name.append(name);
    }

    public void setSalary(int salary)
    {
        this.salary = salary;
    }

    public int getSalary()
    {
        return this.salary;
    }
}
```

The secret of our success can be seen in these three lines of code. We did the cloning using the object version first. This worked and gave us a shallow copy. Next, we created a new `StringBuffer` object, placed the old name in it, and returned. When the Cloner program changed the name, the change took place in the new object and, therefore, did not change the original name object.

```java
        Employee5 o = (Employee5)super.clone();
        o.name = new StringBuffer(name.toString());
        return o;
```

This version of `Cloner_1` is called `Cloner_1b.java`. It can be found in the source code directory for this chapter.

The result of running this new class is shown here:

```
unleashed.ch26.Employee5@1fef6f
The employee's name is Dolly
The employee's pay is 1000
unleashed.ch26.Employee5@209f4e
The clone's name is Dolly
The clone's pay is 1000
The employee's name is Dolly
The employee's pay is 1000
The clone's name is Polly
The clone's pay is 2000
```

If you consider the amount of work that would be required to do a class structure with 30 to 40 objects in it, you begin to lose your confidence in this approach. Fortunately, another approach can save us a lot of work.

Using Serialization to Clone

You may have observed that cloning and serializing are first cousins. We can take advantage of that fact to create a cool deep-cloning program by using the serialization facilities in the JVM as shown in Listing 26.19.

LISTING 26.19   The AutoCloner Class

```java
package unleashed.ch26;
import java.util.*;
import java.io.*;

/**
 *
 * @author  Stephen Potts
 * @version
 */
public class AutoCloner implements Cloneable, Serializable
{

    /** Creates new AutoCloner */
    public AutoCloner() {
    }

    public Object clone()
    {
        Object clonedObj = null;
        try
        {
            //put the object into a byte array
            ByteArrayOutputStream baos = new ByteArrayOutputStream();
            ObjectOutputStream oos = new ObjectOutputStream(baos);
            oos.writeObject(this);
            oos.close();

            //read the stream into the copy
            ByteArrayInputStream bais =
                        new ByteArrayInputStream(baos.toByteArray());
            ObjectInputStream ois = new ObjectInputStream(bais);
            clonedObj = ois.readObject();
            ois.close();
        }catch (IOException ioe)
        {
            System.out.println("I/O exception " + ioe);
        }
        catch (ClassNotFoundException cnfe)
        {
            System.out.println("Class not found " + cnfe);
        }
```

LISTING 26.19   continued

```
        return clonedObj;

    }
}
```

Several lines of code in this example deserve some attention:

- AutoCloner is a class and not an interface. It implements both the Serializable and the Cloneable interfaces.
- A ByteArrayOutputStream is used to take the place of a file. It is more efficient to do it this way. It is also less likely to cause a runtime exception because the JVM has less interaction with the I/O services of the operating system.
- The cloned object is returned in all of its deep-copied glory. This offloads the Employee6 class considerably.

This version of Cloner_1 is called Cloner_1c.java. It can be found in the source code directory for this chapter.

The simplified Employee class is shown in Listing 26.20.

LISTING 26.20   The Employee6 Class

```java
package unleashed.ch26;

import java.util.*;
/**
 *
 * @author   Stephen Potts
 * The Employee class
 */
public class Employee6 extends AutoCloner
{

    private StringBuffer name;
    private int salary;

    public Employee6(String name, int salary)
    {
        this.name = new StringBuffer(name);
        this.salary = salary;
    }

    public Employee6()
    {
    }
```

LISTING 26.20 continued

```java
    public String getName()
    {
        return name.toString();
    }

    public void setName(String name)
    {
        this.name.delete(0, this.name.length());
        this.name.append(name);
    }

    public void setSalary(int salary)
    {
        this.salary = salary;
    }

    public int getSalary()
    {
        return this.salary;
    }
}
```

Notice that the `clone()` method is now gone, as well as all the deep-copy logic. This is not a problem because, as you can see here, the shallow-copy problem is solved by the act of serializing and deserializing the object.

```
unleashed.ch26.Employee6@1fef6f
The employee's name is Dolly
The employee's pay is 1000
unleashed.ch26.Employee6@5debc3
The clone's name is Dolly
The clone's pay is 1000
The employee's name is Dolly
The employee's pay is 1000
The clone's name is Polly
The clone's pay is 2000
```

You can see that the same correct result was achieved by using the `AutoCloner` approach.

AutoCloner and Performance

The manual deep-copy approach is at least one order of magnitude faster during execution than the `AutoCloner` approach. Conversely, the `AutoCloner` approach is at least one order of magnitude faster to code (especially if you borrow the code from this chapter, which you should).

Very often, schedule pressure dwarfs performance considerations when developing new software. Before you spend more time coding a manual deep-copy `clone()`, take the easy way out and use the `AutoCloner` class. Later, when you have completed the alpha release of your code, profile it and find the bottlenecks. If the cloning is a bottleneck, convert to a manual deep-copy clone at that time. You might find that although `AutoCloner` is slow relative to the manual approach, it is fast compared to the clock on the wall. In the end, the users measure performance by using the wall-clock metric.

Security and Serialization

When you serialize a class, you are writing private/protected member data in a well-known, unencrypted format. If this data is passed outside the application (passed via a socket or written to a disk) this is a security concern. You might say that once you deserialize the class, all the standard Java security mechanisms for protected/private data apply. This is true, but while the object is simply a file full of bytes, there are no protections or restrictions at all. Many times sensitive data is visible when the file is viewed using a text editor.

To solve this problem, we need to delve into the realm of cryptography, or secret writing. The solution to the problem of passwords, credit card numbers, and other sensitive data being shown as clear text in a file is to encrypt the sensitive fields.

Listing 26.21 shows a class that has a credit card number in its private variables.

LISTING 26.21   The `EncryptedEmployee` Class

```
package unleashed.ch26;
import java.io.*;
import java.util.*;
import javax.crypto.*;
import java.security.*;
/**
 *
 * @author  Stephen Potts
 * The EncryptedEmployee class
 */
public class EncryptedEmployee implements Externalizable
{

    private String name;
    private String creditCardNumber;
    private static SecretKey sKey;

    public EncryptedEmployee(String name, String ccn)
    {
```

LISTING 26.21   continued

```java
        this.name = name;
        this.creditCardNumber = ccn;
    }

    public EncryptedEmployee()
    {
    }

    public String getName()
    {
        return name;
    }

    public String getCreditCardNumber()
    {
        return this.creditCardNumber;
    }

    public static void setKey(SecretKey sk)
    {
        sKey = sk;
    }

    public void writeExternal(ObjectOutput out) throws IOException
    {
        try
        {
            Cipher cip = Cipher.getInstance("DES/ECB/PKCS5Padding");
            cip.init(Cipher.ENCRYPT_MODE, sKey);

            byte output[] = this.creditCardNumber.getBytes();
            byte encrypted[] = cip.doFinal(output);

            out.writeObject(this.name);
            out.writeObject(encrypted);
        }catch (NoSuchPaddingException nspe)
        {
            System.err.println("no such padding problem " + nspe);
        }
        catch (BadPaddingException bpe)
        {
            System.err.println("bad padding problem " + bpe);
        }
        catch (NoSuchAlgorithmException nsae)
        {
            System.err.println("algorithm problem " + nsae);
        }
        catch (InvalidKeyException ike)
```

LISTING 26.21   continued

```java
        {
            System.err.println("key problem " + ike);
        }
        catch (IllegalBlockSizeException ibse)
        {
            System.err.println("block size problem " + ibse);
        }
    }

    public void readExternal(ObjectInput in) throws IOException,
    ClassNotFoundException
    {
        System.out.println("readExternal() key = " + sKey);
        try
        {
            Cipher cip = Cipher.getInstance("DES/ECB/PKCS5Padding");
            cip.init(Cipher.DECRYPT_MODE, sKey);

            this.name = (String)in.readObject();
            byte encrypted[] = (byte[])in.readObject();
            byte input[] = cip.doFinal(encrypted);
            this.creditCardNumber = new String(input);
        }catch (NoSuchPaddingException nspe)
        {
            System.err.println("no such padding problem " + nspe);
        }
        catch (BadPaddingException bpe)
        {
            System.err.println("bad padding problem " + bpe);
        }
        catch (NoSuchAlgorithmException nsae)
        {
            System.err.println("algorithm problem " + nsae);
        }
        catch (InvalidKeyException ike)
        {
            System.err.println("key problem " + ike);
        }
        catch (IllegalBlockSizeException ibse)
        {
            System.err.println("block size problem " + ibse);
        }
    }
}
```

This class is a simple `Externalizable` class that implements the `writeExternal()` and `readExternal()` methods. Inside these methods we encrypt the credit card number before writing it out to a file. Using the `Cipher` class, we call the factory method to get an instance:

```
Cipher cip = Cipher.getInstance("DES/ECB/PKCS5Padding");
cip.init(Cipher.ENCRYPT_MODE, sKey);
```

We then use the `Cipher` to encrypt the string:

```
byte output[] = this.creditCardNumber.getBytes();
byte encrypted[] = cip.doFinal(output);
```

Then we write the encrypted version of the objects:

```
out.writeObject(this.name);
out.writeObject(encrypted);
```

The `readObject()` is structured similarly. We create the same `Cipher`, but this time we put it in decrypt mode:

```
Cipher cip = Cipher.getInstance("DES/ECB/PKCS5Padding");
cip.init(Cipher.DECRYPT_MODE, sKey);
```

When we read in the object, we first cast it to an array of bytes and then decrypt it:

```
byte encrypted[] = (byte[])in.readObject();
byte input[] = cip.doFinal(encrypted);
```

Finally, we convert the translated array to a string and store it in the `creditCardNumber` private variable:

```
this.creditCardNumber = new String(input);
```

We need a test class to create an instance of this class and externalize it. Listing 26.22 contains such a class.

LISTING 26.22   The `WriteReadEncryptedEmployee` Class

```
package unleashed.ch26;
import java.io.*;
import javax.crypto.*;
import java.security.*;

/**
 *
 * @author  Stephen Potts
 * @version
 */
public class WriteReadEncryptedEmployee
{


    public WriteReadEncryptedEmployee()
```

LISTING 26.22   continued

```java
    {
    }

    public static void main(String[] args)
    {
        try
        {
            KeyGenerator kg = KeyGenerator.getInstance("DES");
            SecretKey secretKey = kg.generateKey();

            String filename = "c:/unleashed/ch26/EncryptedEmployee.out";

            EncryptedEmployee emp =
            new EncryptedEmployee("Jacob Snakob",
            "1234-5678-0123");
            EncryptedEmployee.setKey(secretKey);
            System.out.println("The Secret Key is " + secretKey);
            FileOutputStream f  = new FileOutputStream(filename);
            ObjectOutputStream oos = new ObjectOutputStream(f);
            oos.writeObject(emp);
            System.out.println(
            "Finished writing EncryptedEmployee.out");
            oos.close();

            EncryptedEmployee emp2 = null;
            FileInputStream f2  = new FileInputStream(filename);
            ObjectInputStream ois = new ObjectInputStream(f2);
            emp2 = (EncryptedEmployee)ois.readObject();
            System.out.println("The name is " + emp.getName());
            System.out.println("The creditCard Number  is " +
            emp.getCreditCardNumber());
            ois.close();


        }catch (IOException ioe)
        {
            System.out.println("IOException thrown " + ioe);
        }
        catch (ClassNotFoundException cnfe)
        {
            System.out.println("ClassNotFoundException thrown " + cnfe);
        }
        catch (NoSuchAlgorithmException nsae)
        {
            System.out.println("Algorithm Exception thrown " + nsae);
        }
    }
}
```

This class is responsible for creating the private key. This key is used to "lock" and "unlock" the encrypted data:

```
KeyGenerator kg = KeyGenerator.getInstance("DES");
SecretKey secretKey = kg.generateKey();
```

We create an instance of the employee and set the key:

```
EncryptedEmployee emp =
new EncryptedEmployee("Jacob Snakob",
"1234-5678-0123");
EncryptedEmployee.setKey(secretKey);
```

Next, we create the usual streams and write the object out:

```
FileOutputStream f  = new FileOutputStream(filename);
ObjectOutputStream oos = new ObjectOutputStream(f);
oos.writeObject(emp);
```

The reading part of the class requires that we use the same key that was used in the encryption. This is accomplished by making the key static in the EncryptedEmployee class. This way, only the holder of the key can discover the credit card number. We read in the objects and cast them just as we always have:

```
EncryptedEmployee emp2 = null;
FileInputStream f2  = new FileInputStream(filename);
ObjectInputStream ois = new ObjectInputStream(f2);
emp2 = (EncryptedEmployee)ois.readObject();
```

Then we print them out to the console:

```
System.out.println("The name is " + emp.getName());
System.out.println("The creditCard Number  is " +
emp.getCreditCardNumber());
ois.close();
```

The version of this program that does not use encryption is in the download for this chapter. The employee class is called UnencryptedEmployee and the write/read class is called WriteReadUnencryptedEmployee. Running them gives the following correct result:

```
Finished writing UnencryptedEmployee.out
The name is Jacob Snakob
The creditCard Number  is 1234-5678-0123
```

The program writes a file called UnencryptedEmployee.out. It contains the following:

```
¬í__sr_"unleashed.ch26.UnencryptedEmployeeî69?T_Šw__xpt_
Jacob Snakobt__1234-5678-0123x
```

You can see the credit card number clearly using a text editor. If you run the encrypted version of this same program (Listings 26.21 and 26.22), you get a similar result (your output will vary slightly):

```
The Secret Key is com.sun.crypto.provider.DESKey@186c6
Finished writing EncryptedEmployee.out
readExternal() key = com.sun.crypto.provider.DESKey@186c6
The name is Jacob Snakob
The creditCard Number  is 1234-5678-0123
```

The improvement is clear when you look at the `EncryptedEmployee.out` file:

```
¬í__sr_ unleashed.ch26.EncryptedEmployeeO¢{û_pë___xpt
Jacob Snakobur__[B¬ó_ø__Tà___xp____»uØln?ãB" 7_Â--ýP…x
```

Notice that the credit card number is completely hidden from the reader, while the name, Jacob Snakob, is written in clear text. This is because we did not encrypt the name.

Summary

In this chapter, we looked at ways of making our objects persist beyond the life of the thread they were created in. You learned about *serialization* and the `Serializable` interface, which allows you to turn your objects into a stream of bytes that can be transmitted or persisted in a file. These streams can be used to construct a new object that is nearly as identical to the original as you, the programmer, specify. Using this stream, the virtual machine can construct a new object that behaves similarly to the old one.

Serialization, which is the mechanism that provides persistence, means more than writing objects to files and reading them back in. Technologies such as the Java Message Service (JMS) and Remote Method Invocation (RMI) are able to send any serializable object from one server to another. This gives real life to the theoretical distributed-object architectures that we have been hearing about for years.

You also learned about cloning and the `Cloning` interface. We talked about the difference between a shallow copy and a deep copy. You learned techniques for creating both. You also learned how to use serialization to accomplish the cloning automatically.

Finally, you learned how to encrypt private data when externalizing an object to a file. This protects the data from unauthorized viewing.

Polymorphism and Inheritance

A software development manager at a leading German firm once said, "I would rather hire one excellent programmer than three very good ones." When asked why, he replied that it was because excellent programmers don't write very much code. This story reminds us of Benjamin Franklin when he said that he would have written a shorter letter, but he ran out of time.

If you are reading this book, you are a highly motivated programmer who would like to become an excellent one. According to my German colleague, to do this, you need to learn to write less code. You need to deliver the same functionality in fewer lines of code by writing more intelligently and powerfully. One of the best ways to do this is to make wise use of *inheritance* and *polymorphism*.

The word *wise* is critical when discussing inheritance. To a man with a hammer, the world is a nail. After you learn how to use inheritance in your programming, you will need to quickly learn when not to use it.

This chapter assumes that you already know the nuts and bolts of inheritance and polymorphism. What is taught here is a set of tools and techniques plus a mindset that will help you make intelligent decisions and recommendations on this subject.

Why Polymorphism and Inheritance Are Important

Beyond the never-ending need to enhance your résumé, there are some sound business reasons to use inheritance and polymorphism:

- Smaller programs—As mentioned earlier, programs that make use of polymorphism tend to be smaller than those written without it. The Holy Grail of programming has always been the reuse of existing code. It is less expensive to drive the same car to work and to the movies than to own two cars—one for each purpose. Using parallel thinking, it makes sense to modify the software system that writes checks for the salaried employees to also write the checks for the hourly employees. Inheritance-based systems have fewer lines of code than procedural systems. The code is more dense and costs more per line to write, but the overall cost for the system will be lower in most cases.

- Easier modification—In the procedural programming days, this made us nervous. After all, the salaried system worked fine. If we went in and mucked with the code, all the testing that we had done would have to be redone. In those days, the decision was often made to create the hourly system from scratch or to make a copy of the code in the salaried system and transform it into a separate hourly payroll system. A company with 10 systems based on the same framework will find that the programming staff moves easily from one of these projects to the other to perform enhancements and to fix field-reported bugs. A company with 10 built-from-scratch systems will pay the learning curve costs over and over again as programmers move on to other things. In the object-oriented world, inheritance and polymorphism allow us to add new classes to process checks for the hourly employees without changing or even recompiling the original classes. Implementing the abstract methods of the base classes in the new `HourlyEmployee` classes does this.

- Lower testing costs—Whenever a program is written, it has to be tested. Many programmers lose their reputations during an outrageously long test and debug cycle. If you can extend existing code instead of writing new code, only the newly added code has to be tested. Whenever you extend existing code, you automatically test it again and provide feedback when you discover problems. Base classes and interfaces are produced and gathered together in a framework. Testing is done on the framework during the first project that uses it and 95% of the bugs are driven out. It can be safely assumed that any bugs appearing in subsequent projects are in the new code that the programmer has written. This greatly shortens the test phase of a project and lowers the risk of the project going into a death spiral. A death spiral is where fixes to bugs create more bugs, causing the total number of defects to increase until the money providers run out of time or patience.

- Software can be grown—Software development has been compared to shooting a movie because decisions made late can make it necessary for scenes shot earlier to be reshot (and paid for again). Your management would probably not have the stomach for the motion picture industry, so it is in your best interest to make this "movie shoot" that we call software development look as much like brick wall construction as you can. One way to do this is to defer decisions about details until the details have been discovered.

A common problem in commercial systems is starting development before all the analysis is complete. Traditionally, this has led to rewriting code. The problem is that we often don't know what analysis we need until we have done some development. If we code the classes as we learn about them, we can grow our project as our knowledge grows by using subclassing to handle those hidden details that always seem to emerge late in a project.

The Internals of Polymorphism

Some programmers amaze us with their ability to predict whether a design will work and whether it will perform well. They do this by reasoning through what will happen at the lower levels of the software when a system built using a proposed design is run. They have a good understanding of the internal operation of the systems that they work on, including the compiler and the *Java virtual machine (JVM)*. In this section, we will look at what happens inside the compiler and VM when polymorphism is used. Armed with this information, you will be able to amaze the next generation of programmers with your clairvoyance.

Single-threaded programs run sequentially, executing one command after another. (Multithreaded ones are just several single-threads running at the same time.) Whenever a method call occurs, this sequential execution is interrupted and the program counter offset in the CPU moves to a new "entry point" and resumes execution there. When it completes this execution, the program counter returns to the instruction following the call. During the compilation process, the compiler removes as many of these calls as it can and replaces them with inline copies of the code. If the methods are too large for a copy, a static-bind takes place that acts like a "go-to" to the correct section in the code.

With polymorphism, however, it is not possible for the compiler to know what method will be bound to a certain call. Consider a GUI in which the employee to be paid is entered and a paycheck generated on the spot. It might not be possible for the compiler to know which `calculateCheckAmount()` method to call because it is unknown at compile time what kind of employee will be entered into the GUI. In these cases, the compiler must generate code to dynamically bind the call to the method. This is called *dynamic* binding, *late* binding, or *runtime* binding because the call is bound to the method dynamically, late, and at runtime.

You might wonder how the compiler and virtual machine work this magic. Let's look at this process in more detail:

1. The compiler looks at the name of the method and determines that at least one candidate method could be called. If not, a compiler error is thrown.

2. The compiler looks at the parameter types to verify that a method of that signature exists. If not, a compile time error occurs. If exactly one method could satisfy the call, an inline substitution or a static binding is generated. In addition, if the method is private, static, or final, a static binding is added in this situation.

3. If several candidates that could be called during runtime based on the actual class type (polymorphic handle), the compiler places code to provide a dynamic binding call and moves on.

4. When your `main()` class is loaded in the virtual machine, a search is performed for all static calls. These classes are then loaded into the VM until all the statically bound classes are loaded. Next, the VM searches for all dynamically bound calls. It then builds a method table for each call that indicates which candidate methods exist for this call and the class associated with it.

5. When the VM is processing the code and runs across a dynamically bound or polymorphic call, it looks in the method table for the derived class object that is the subject of the handle. It compares the signature of the call to the signature of the calls in the method table and finds an appropriate method. The instruction pointer is given the value of the entry point for that method and execution continues.

As you can see, the virtual machine is programmed as you might predict. Seeing through the magic and thinking in terms of handles, object types, and entry points is what senior programmers learn when they look into the crystal ball. This is how they predict performance—if a design has a lot of work to do, it will be slow.

Programming with Polymorphism

The first example is a payroll system at a medium-sized company. This company is typical in that different people are paid according to different formulas based on their job classification. Sales people are on commission, union people are hourly, and executives get most of their compensation as profit-based bonuses. But in the end, everyone gets a paycheck denominated in dollars and cents that can be deposited in the bank. For simplicity, the company is located in a country where there are no income or payroll taxes and no deductions for benefits. Listing 27.1 shows this class.

LISTING 27.1   The `SimplePayroll` Class

```
/*
 * SimplePayroll.java
 *
 */

package unleashed.ch27;
import java.util.*;

public class SimplePayroll {

    /** Creates new Payroll */
    public SimplePayroll() {}

    public static void main(String[] args)
    {
```

LISTING 27.1 continued

```java
        Company c1 = new Company(5000000, 1000000, 50);
        Vector s = new Vector();
        Employee e = null;

        s.addElement( new Executive(1, "Waller", "Marshall", 10000, .02));
        s.addElement( new SalariedEmployee(2, "Sanderson", "Martha", 4000));
        s.addElement( new HourlyEmployee(3, "Ethridge", "Bennett", 20.00f));

        Iterator it = s.iterator();
        while (it.hasNext())
        {
            e = (Employee)it.next();
            System.out.println("Pay to the order of " +
                e.getFirstName() + " " + e.getLastName() +
                        " " + e.calculateCheckAmount());
        }
    }
}

class Company
{
    private static long sales;
    private static long profit;
    private static int hours;

    public Company( long sales, long profit, int hours)
    {
        this.sales = sales;
        this.profit = profit;
        this.hours = hours;
    }

    public static long getSales()
    {
        return sales;
    }

    public static long getProfit()
    {
        return profit;
    }

    public static int getHours()
    {
        return hours;
    }
}

abstract class Employee
```

LISTING 27.1 continued

```
{
    private int employeeID;
    private String lastName;
    private String firstName;

    public Employee(int employeeID, String lastName, String firstName)
    {
        this.employeeID = employeeID;
        this.lastName = lastName;
        this.firstName = firstName;
    }

    public String getFirstName()
    {
        return this.firstName;
    }

    public String getLastName()
    {
        return this.lastName;
    }

    abstract public double calculateCheckAmount();
}

class Executive extends Employee
{
    private int baseSalary;
    private double bonusPercentage;

    public Executive(int employeeID, String lastName,
                     String firstName, int baseSalary,
                              double bonusPercentage)
    {
        super(employeeID, lastName, firstName);
        this.baseSalary = baseSalary;
        this.bonusPercentage = bonusPercentage;
    }

    public double calculateCheckAmount()
    {
        double bonusAmt = Company.getProfit()*bonusPercentage;
        return baseSalary + bonusAmt;
    }
}

class SalariedEmployee extends Employee
{
```

LISTING 27.1   continued

```java
    private int baseSalary;

    public SalariedEmployee(int employeeID, String lastName,
                            String firstName, int baseSalary)
    {
        super(employeeID, lastName, firstName);
        this.baseSalary = baseSalary;
    }

    public double calculateCheckAmount()
    {
        return baseSalary;
    }
}

class HourlyEmployee extends Employee
{
    private float hourlyRate;

    public HourlyEmployee(int employeeID, String lastName,
                          String firstName, float hourlyRate)
    {
        super(employeeID, lastName, firstName);
        this.hourlyRate = hourlyRate;
    }

    public double calculateCheckAmount()
    {
        int hours = Company.getHours();
        if ( hours < 40 )
        {
                return hours*hourlyRate;
        }
        else
        {
                return 40*hourlyRate + (hours-40)*hourlyRate*1.5;
        }
    }
}
```

Notice that the creation of each object in the vector is done with the subtype:

```java
        s.addElement( new Executive(1, "Waller", "Marshall", 10000, .02));
        s.addElement( new SalariedEmployee(2, "Sanderson", "Martha", 4000));
        s.addElement( new HourlyEmployee(3, "Ethridge", "Bennett", 20.00f));
```

The polymorphic use of a handle to the base class is where the magic begins:

```java
        e = (Employee)it.next();
```

By upcasting, we are calling a method via a handle to a higher class on the inheritance chart. As we iterate through the vector, we cast the object to the base class type, not to the derived class type. Thus we leave it to the compiler to figure out the real derived type so that the proper `calculateCheckAmount()` method can be called.

Upon running this, you will find that the output looks like this:

```
Pay to the order of Marshall Waller 30000.0
Pay to the order of Martha Sanderson 4000.0
Pay to the order of Bennett Ethridge 1100.0
```

The creation of this program without polymorphism would not be as simple. You could create a vector for each derived class. Then, you could add each employee to the appropriate vector. Next, you could write the check for each class individually. Finally, you would merge the output into alphabetical order, postal code order, and so on.

But wait, it gets worse if a new type of employee is added. Suppose that you want to add another type of employee called salesman. Using polymorphism, you can create the class as we have done in Listing 27.2.

LISTING 27.2   The `SalesEmployee` Class

```
class SalesEmployee extends Employee
{
    private double commissionPercentage;

    public SalesEmployee(int employeeID, String lastName,
                  String firstName, double commissionPercentage)
    {
        super(employeeID, lastName, firstName);
        this.commissionPercentage = commissionPercentage;
    }

    public double calculateCheckAmount()
    {
        return Company.getSales()*commissionPercentage;
    }
}
```

We would have to add a new line to the main, but all the other code would remain untouched. Therefore, there would not be a need to recompile (if each class were in a separate file) or retest it.

```
    s.addElement( new SalesEmployee(4, "Rangitsch", "Thomas", .0015));
```

It is hard to overstate the impact of retesting on a company. Most software companies spend a fortune on testing, so any cost savings in the testing area is a big plus.

> **Note**
>
> The code listing for this chapter contains a class called `SimplePayroll2`, which contains a version of `SimplePayroll` with the call to the `SalesEmployee` added.

The output would then have this additional line:

```
Pay to the order of Thomas Rangitsch 7500.0
```

> **Tip**
>
> Use polymorphism and inheritance only when you have a clear is-a-kind-of relationship. Don't force it.

This example requires the use of inheritance in its solution because the subtypes clearly pass the "is-a-kind-of" test. All these subtypes are clearly true subtypes. This is not always the case, however. Take the case of a contractor. If you call a contractor an employee, you are stretching the definition. Calculating his hourly rate times hours and printing it out would be easy, but the real-world version of this system would have all types of tax tie-ins and calculations that would punish you for trying to overextend the class `Employee`. Even more punishing would be the fact that most contractors have a broker who actually gets your check and writes another one to pay the contractor.

Inheritance, Composition, or Brute Force

When we use inheritance, we are not only trying to use variables and methods that exist in another class, but we are also trying to simplify our code by the clever use of references or handles as we did in the preceding section.

If inheritance is not always the answer, what are the alternatives? In reality, you have four ways to run code in a program:

- Brute force—Write all your code in `main()` methods. This will work. In fact, it has a name: procedural programming.
- Simple instantiation—Instantiate the class in the `main()` method of your class and use it as a utility. We often use the optional Java packages in this way.

- Composition—Create a class that does the same work as a base class. Create another class that contains an instance of this class in its definition. In truth, you will only include a handle to the other class in your class definition, but the result is the same. This works well in many situations.

- Polymorphism—Inherit from a base class and use polymorphism. This is what we did in the preceding section.

As we move down the list, we gain more and more of the advantages of object-oriented programming. But wisdom is recognizing each situation, choosing the appropriate approach, and not forcing our favorite solution onto every problem. Before we can show the difference in these methods, we need to create two classes—the Vendor class and the Contractor class.

Listing 27.3 shows how a Vendor object could be used to pay a contractor.

LISTING 27.3   The Vendor Class

```
package unleashed.ch27;
public class Vendor {

    String name = null;

    double costPerHour;

    /** Creates new Vendor */
    public Vendor(String name, double costPerHour)
    {
        this.name = name;
        this.costPerHour = costPerHour;
    }

    public double getHourlyCost()
    {
        return costPerHour;
    }

    public String getName()
    {
        return name;
    }
}
```

Listing 27.4 shows a Contractor class that we can instantiate.

LISTING 27.4   The `Contractor` Class

```java
package unleashed.ch27;
public class Contractor {

    int hoursWorked;
    Vendor myBroker;
    String lastName;
    String firstName;

    /** Creates new Contractor */
    public Contractor() {
    }

    public Contractor(Vendor myBroker, String firstName,
                      String lastName, int hoursWorked)
    {
        this.myBroker = myBroker;
        this.firstName = firstName;
        this.lastName = lastName;
        this.hoursWorked = hoursWorked;
    }

    public void payBroker()
    {
        double amount = myBroker.getHourlyCost() * hoursWorked;
        System.out.println("Contractor - Pay to the order of " +
                            myBroker.getName() +" "+ amount);
    }

    public int getNumberOfHours()
    {
        return hoursWorked;
    }

}
```

In Listing 27.5, the `BillPayer` class makes use of both the `Vendor` and `Contractor` classes to illustrate the difference between brute force, simple instantiation, and composition.

LISTING 27.5   The `BillPayer` Class

```java
/*
 * BillPayer.java
 *
 * Created on December 3, 2001, 5:05 PM
 */
```

Listing 27.5 continued

```
package unleashed.ch27;

/**
 *
 * @author   Stephen Potts
 * @version
 */
public class BillPayer {

    /** Creates new BillPayer */
    public BillPayer() {
    }

    public static void main(String[] args)
    {
        double costPerHour = 75.0;
        int hoursWorked = 40;
        String vendorName = "ABC Consulting";
        Vendor v1 = new Vendor(vendorName, costPerHour);
        Contractor c1 = new Contractor( v1, "Mike",  "Kopack", hoursWorked );

        //Brute force - do the work int the main()
        double amountOfCheck = costPerHour * hoursWorked;
        System.out.println("Brute force -  Pay to the order of " +
                                        vendorName +" "+ amountOfCheck);

        //Simple Instantiation
        double amountToPay = v1.getHourlyCost() * c1.getNumberOfHours();
        System.out.println("Instantiate - Pay to the order of " +
                                        v1.getName() +" "+ amountToPay);

        //Composition - let the Contractor object do the work
        c1.payBroker();
    }
}
```

The program that is composed of the Listings 27.3, 27.4, and 27.5 is interesting in that it performs the same calculation three times using three different approaches. In the brute force section, all the logic is placed in the main() method. This short-circuits all the object-oriented features of the program. In the simple instantiation section, we instantiate objects of the correct type and query them for data that the program needs to do the calculation and display the message. In the composition section, we were still able to use an object and a high-level message to do the work. The difference between this and inheritance is that the Contractor object did not extend the Vendor class; it included it in the class definition and used it to do the work.

The results are identical in all cases:

```
Brute force - Pay to the order of ABC Consulting 3000.0

Instantiate - Pay to the order of ABC Consulting 3000.0

Contractor - Pay to the order of ABC Consulting 3000.0
```

This leads us to a rule of thumb:

> *Let the relationship dictate whether you use inheritance or composition. If you use inheritance, use polymorphism in your program.*

You might be tempted to force the use of composition on natural inheritance relationships. You might even hear this recommended:

> *If you have an inheritance relationship but you are not using polymorphism, change your code to use polymorphism, if possible.*

The existence of the inheritance relationship requires polymorphism, and you should give in most of the time. Align your design to the natural relationships that exist, and then code accordingly from that point forth.

The conclusion that you should draw is that there are several ways to accomplish the same task in Java. You can decide which one to use by following this simple rule of thumb:

> *Push all code up to the highest level that makes sense without forcing it.*

This means that we should use inheritance first, composition next, simple instantiation third, and brute force only as a last resort. This will give your code the most object-oriented flavor and normally produce the smallest code base.

Disadvantages of Inheritance and Polymorphism

It is clear that polymorphism and inheritance require more concentration and skill than the other three methods. The natural question is, "Why do it?" Because, in the right context, the advantages are huge.

Taking off the rose-colored glasses for a moment will force us to admit that there are also disadvantages to object-oriented designs. The main disadvantages are

- Learning curve steepness—Object-oriented designs are more abstract than procedural designs. They often contain base classes and interfaces such as *Throwable*,

Clonable, or one that you create such as *PoolableEntity.* In almost every case, a good argument can be made that the natural placement of the functionality in this system is in these very abstract classes and interfaces. Even when this is true, it is a problem if it makes the system difficult or impossible for a new person to learn. Most companies hire the occasional nongenius. (The supply of geniuses is finite, and geniuses will not do certain types of programming without griping continuously.) Ordinary programmers might be overwhelmed by a large number of abstract base classes. First projects using an abstract framework tend to take a long time to code.

A new hire should be able to code his first project (using your framework) in no more than double the amount of time it would take to code it without the framework.

If the 2× threshold is exceeded, you should take a long hard look at your framework's design and try to make it less abstract.

In theory, the learning curve could be attacked with better training and documentation, but that is not often present.

- Management confusion—Frameworks of base classes are very hard for the nonprogrammer to comprehend (much less pay for). Discussions of abstraction and inheritance will glaze the eyes of even the most seasoned bean counter. Care should be taken to speak in terms of the cost-reducing benefits of your framework and save the tech talk for those who will have the stomach for it.

Concrete or Abstract Base Classes

When you decide to use polymorphism, you have three choices in how you organize your code:

- Concrete base classes—Classes that contain code and can be instantiated as well as inherited from
- Abstract base classes—Classes that contain code but can never be instantiated
- Interfaces—classes that contain no code and can never be instantiated

Concrete base classes are the easiest to understand because objects of this type can exist. You might have a Manager class that is instantiated for each manager in your system. In addition, you might have a ProfitCenterManager that inherits from your Manager class, but also has methods to approve expenditures. Your system would instantiate both types of managers, but it would only use polymorphism on the methods in the base class.

Abstract base classes are not too hard either. Following the object-oriented rule to push up all code to the highest class you can, it follows that the `Employee` class could have some methods that would be concrete (such as `getNextOfKin()`) and others that would be abstract (such as the `calculateCheckAmount()` method from this chapter's earlier example). It is even possible to have an abstract class that has no abstract methods. If all the methods have meaning even when not overridden (but it makes no sense to instantiate the class itself), it could still be abstract.

Most confusion exists around interfaces—mainly because we see them used for more than just polymorphism. Interfaces are just abstract classes with all abstract methods. The syntax is simplified so that all the abstract keywords are gone, and so that the compiler can be sure that no implementation exists in the base class. This is important because classes that implement interfaces must provide the implementation of the method themselves—it cannot be in the base class (by definition). This makes the method call statically bound and therefore more efficient. Additionally, it tells the compiler that a class can implement more than one interface at the same time, giving a multiple-inheritance flavor to your class. Real multiple-inheritance is forbidden in the Java language specification.

The question of which one to use arises again.

> **Tip**
>
> During design, push all code up as high as it can naturally go. Then create the most restrictive class or interface given this design.

If the code for this design creates a concrete base class, leave it concrete. If some methods are concrete and some are abstract, make it abstract. If all are abstract, make it an interface. If you have a mix of abstract and concrete methods, you should consider making the class an abstract class. In fact, the Java language requires that if you have *any* methods in a class declared as abstract, the entire class *must* be abstract. (Because of the prohibition on multiple-inheritance in Java, you might have to force a natural abstract class into an interface.)

> **Performance**
>
> Perhaps the most important work that a senior developer does is estimate the performance of a design. When a new system is proposed and alternative designs are evaluated, the estimated performance of each design is often the deciding factor.

From our previous discussion, a couple of rules for good performance emerge:

1. Force static binding if possible. You can do this by eliminating polymorphism altogether, but then you would also lose its benefits. Make all the methods *final* if you are not going to call them polymorphically. (This is not a good option, however, if you are going to distribute your framework to others without source code.) *Final* means that the compiler will never let subclasses override the method, period. This is very restrictive. If, however, you have access to the code in the framework, and you control future changes, you can make the methods final and force static binding. You can then remove this restriction on request when someone needs to override it.

2. Use interfaces instead of abstract classes if it makes sense. The compiler knows that the implementation of the interface in your class is the correct entry point, by definition. If the class is abstract, it is harder for the compiler to be sure and can lead to some late binding.

A word of caution is in order here: Wisdom is making trade-offs well. Fanaticism is choosing one approach and slavishly applying it to all situations. You must be able to deal with subtleties and trade-offs if you want to be respected by people who do.

Type-Safe Downcasting and Inheritance

To this point, we have confined our discussion to the topic of upcasting—finding an entry point into an object via a pointer to its base class. Now we need to deal with the complementary case of downcasting a pointer to a derived class. Java allows us to assign an object of a subclass to a handle to its base class without casting because that always works. Every base-class method that could be called through the subclass can be called through the base class. When we do the opposite, though, we cannot say for certain that it will work. If an `Employee` handle refers to a `SalariedEmployee` and you try to cast it to a `HourlyEmployee`, it will pass the compiler, but it will throw an error at runtime.

Consider this example shown in Listing 27.6.

LISTING 27.6   An Illegal Cast

```
package unleashed.ch27;
public class CastAway {
```

LISTING 27.6 continued

```
/** Creates new CastAway */
public CastAway() {
}

public static void main(String[] args)
{
    Employee e = new SalariedEmployee(2, "Sanderson", "Martha", 4000);
    double amt = e.calculateCheckAmount();
    System.out.println("The first amount is " + amt);

    SalariedEmployee s = e;
    amt = s.calculateCheckAmount();
    System.out.println("The second amount is " + amt);        }
}
```

This will generate an "incompatible types" error from the compiler because this assignment is not legal without a cast. We need an explicit cast to the derived type:

```
SalariedEmployee s = (SalariedEmployee)e;
```

The result will now be

```
The first amount is 4000.0
The second amount is 4000.0
```

You might be thinking that this is wonderful. Now you can change the class of an object by casting like this:

```
package unleashed.ch27;
/**
 *
 * @author  Stephen Potts
 * @version
 */
public class BadCast {

    /** Creates new BadCast */
    public BadCast() {
    }

    public static void main(String[] args)
    {
        Employee e = new SalariedEmployee(2, "Sanderson", "Martha", 4000);
        Company c = (Company)e;
    }

}
```

In this, you would be mistaken. This example generates an "inconvertible type" error. For an object cast to work, there has to be an inheritance relationship between classes. (Primitives have conversion routines.) Because the `Employee` class is a peer of the `Company` class and not a subclass, the cast generates a compile-time error.

This helps us avoid some errors, but we are not out of the woods yet. Consider the following example:

```
package unleashed.ch27;
public class StrangeCast
{
    /** Creates new StrangeCast */
    public StrangeCast() {
    }

    public static void main(String[] args)
    {
        Employee e = new SalariedEmployee(2, "Sanderson", "Martha", 4000);
        HourlyEmployee h = (HourlyEmployee)e;
        double amt = e.calculateCheckAmount();
        System.out.println("The amount is " + amt);
    }
}
```

This example compiles just fine. When you run it, though, you get a `java.lang.` `ClassCastException`. From our discussion of the internals of the program, it is not hard to figure out why. Because a cast of an `Employee` to a `HourlyEmployee` is legal sometimes, the compiler cannot reject this action out of hand as it did when we tried to cast an `Employee` to a `Company`. Only at runtime is the information available to know what kind of a class is contained in the e handle. When the program attempted to cast the handle e to an `HourlyEmployee` type, the virtual machine sprang into action and looked up the true type of the handle e. It discovered that handle e was of type `SalariedEmployee` and wisely threw us an exception. Because the exception was uncaught, the program terminated.

The `instanceof` Solution

One way to guard against getting a `ClassCastException` is to use the `instanceof` keyword as shown in Listing 27.7.

LISTING 27.7   The `StrangeCast2` Class

```
package unleashed.ch27;
public class StrangeCast2 {

    /** Creates new StrangeCast2 */
```

LISTING 27.7   continued

```
    public StrangeCast2() {
    }

    public static void main(String[] args)
    {
        Employee e = new SalariedEmployee(2, "Sanderson", "Martha", 4000);

        if (e instanceof SalariedEmployee)
        {
            System.out.println("e is a SalariedEmployee");
            SalariedEmployee s = (SalariedEmployee)e;
        }

        if (e instanceof HourlyEmployee)
        {
            System.out.println("e is an HourlyEmployee");
            HourlyEmployee h = (HourlyEmployee)e;
        }
    }
}
```

When we run this, we find out that

```
e is a SalariedEmployee
```

This makes our program work because it catches the case in which the class types don't correspond.

> **Caution**
>
> This `instanceof` technique could easily be employed to take away all the advantages of polymorphism by turning every program into an `instanceof` and a conditional statement. This is a bad idea because it removes all the advantages of polymorphism from your program.

The `Object.getClass()` Solution

Every class in Java has the `Object` class as its superclass. One of the most common methods is the `Object.toString()`, which allows you to print any object using a `System.out.println()` statement. Following the rules of inheritance, this statement looks for the `toString()` method in your class definition. If it doesn't find `toString()`, it travels up the inheritance hierarchy until it gets to the `Object` class, where it will always find and execute the default implementation of `toString()`.

For every class in your program, the virtual machine creates a special metaclass of type `Class`. It is confusing, but you can think of it as a schema to your class's definition.

Object has a method called `getClass()` that returns a handle to the `Class` class for your class. (Say that three times fast.) Perhaps the following example shown in Listing 27.8 can help.

LISTING 27.8   Using the `getClass()` Method

```
package unleashed.ch27;
public class MetaViewer
{
    /** Creates new MetaViewer */
    public MetaViewer() {
    }

    public static void main(String[] args)
    {
            Employee e = new SalariedEmployee(2, "Sanderson", "Martha", 4000);
            Class cc = e.getClass();
            System.out.println("The name of the class is " + cc.getName());
    }
}
```

The output looks like this:

```
The name of the class is unleashed.ch27.SalariedEmployee
```

This is a convenient way to obtain a `Class` handle when you already have an object of that class. Armed with a `Class` handle, you can perform all types of magic.

The `Class.forName()` Solution

At times, you need to get a `Class` handle without an object of that type. You can do this by using the `forName()` method as shown in Listing 27.9.

LISTING 27.9   Using the `forName()` Method

```
package unleashed.ch27;
public class MetaViewer2 {

    /** Creates new MetaViewer2 */
    public MetaViewer2() {
    }

    public static void main(String[] args)
    {
```

LISTING 27.9 continued

```
        Class cc= null;
        try
        {
            cc = Class.forName("unleashed.ch27.SalariedEmployee");
        }catch(ClassNotFoundException cnfe)
    {
        System.out.println("Can't find class");
    }
        System.out.println("The name of the class is still "   +
                    cc.getName());
    }
}
```

This alternate way produces the same result:

```
The name of the class is still
unleashed.ch27.SalariedEmployee
```

Now you are able to get class information that will help you verify the downcast as shown in Listing 27.10.

LISTING 27.10 The SafeCast Class

```
package unleashed.ch27;
public class SafeCast {

    /** Creates new SafeCast */
    public SafeCast() {
    }

    public static void main(String[] args)
    {
        Employee e = new SalariedEmployee(2, "Sanderson", "Martha", 4000);

        Class cc = e.getClass();
        String className = cc.getName();

        if (className.equals("unleashed.ch27.SalariedEmployee"))
        {
            System.out.println("e is a SalariedEmployee");
            SalariedEmployee s = (SalariedEmployee)e;
        }

        if (className.equals("unleashed.ch27.HourlyEmployee"))
        {
```

LISTING 27.10 continued

```
        System.out.println("e is an HourlyEmployee");
        HourlyEmployee h = (HourlyEmployee)e;
    }
  }
}
```

The result is the same as before:

```
e is a SalariedEmployee
```

This is an alternative to using the `instanceof` operator in determining the class before a downcast.

In the interest of completeness, there is yet a third way to obtain a handle to the `Class` object for any class in your program. You can obtain the class handle by using the name of the class with the word `.class` appended to the end as shown here in Listing 27.11.

LISTING 27.11 The `MetaViewer3` Class

```
package unleashed.ch27;
public class MetaViewer3 {

    /** Creates new MetaViewer3 */
    public MetaViewer3() {
    }

    public static void main(String[] args)
    {
        Class cc= null;
        cc = SalariedEmployee.class;
        System.out.println("The name of the class is now " + cc.getName());
    }
}
```

The result is the same as always:

```
The name of the class is now
unleashed.ch27.SalariedEmployee
```

Any of the approaches used previously will accomplish your goal of guaranteeing that all of your downcasting will be done in a type-safe manner.

Polymorphic Programming with Runtime Type Identification

You can use the `Class` file for *Runtime Type Identification (RTTI)*. The `Class` class contains many more useful pieces of information about the classes in your program than just the type of the objects. After you have a handle to the `Class` object, you can find out about the classes that are running in your virtual machine. Programming through these handles is sometimes called *generic programming*. Listing 27.12 shows you some information that you can obtain.

LISTING 27.12   The `MetaViewer4` Class

```
package unleashed.ch27;

/**
 *
 * @author   Stephen Potts
 * @version
 */
public class MetaViewer4 {

    /** Creates new MetaViewer4 */
    public MetaViewer4() {
    }

    public static void main(String[] args)
    {
        Class cc= null;
        cc = SalariedEmployee.class;
        System.out.println("The name of the superclass is " +
                                        cc.getSuperclass());
        System.out.println("Is SalariedEmployee an interface? " +
                                            cc.isInterface());
    }
}
```

The result of this is shown here:

```
The name of the superclass is class
unleashed.ch27.Employee
Is SalariedEmployee an interface? false
```

You can even use the `Class` object to instantiate an object of its class. In the following example, we will instantiate a `Company` object. This technique only works with default constructors, so we have to add one to the `Company` class definition first. This `Company2` class is shown in Listing 27.13.

LISTING 27.13 The Company2 Class

```
package unleashed.ch27;

class Company2
{
    private static long sales;
    private static long profit;
    private static int hours;

    public Company2( long sales, long profit, int hours)
    {
        this.sales = sales;
        this.profit - profit;
        this.hours = hours;
    }
    public Company2()
    {
        this.sales = 1;
        this.profit = 1;
        this.hours = 1;
    }

    public static long getSales()
    {
        return sales;
    }

    public static long getProfit()
    {
        return profit;
    }

    public static int getHours()
    {
        return hours;
    }
}
```

Listing 27.14 shows how to instantiate a Company2 object using the Class object.

LISTING 27.14 The NewInstantiater Class

```
package unleashed.ch27;

/**
 *
 * @author   Stephen Potts
 * @version
 */
```

LISTING 27.14   continued

```java
public class NewInstantiater
{

    /** Creates new NewInstantiater */
    public NewInstantiater()
    {
    }

    public static void main(String[] args)
    {
        Class cc= null;
        cc = Company2.class;
        Object o = null;

        System.out.println("The name of the class is now " +
                                            cc.getName());

        try
        {
            o = cc.newInstance();


            //now we can use the handle
            Company2 comp = (Company2)o;

            System.out.println("The Company's sales total is " +
                                            comp.getSales());
            System.out.println("The Company's profit total is " +
                                            comp.getProfit());
            System.out.println("The Company's hours total is " +
                                            comp.getHours());

        }catch (InstantiationException ie)
        {System.out.println("Failed " + ie);}
        catch (IllegalAccessException iae)
        {System.out.println("Failed " + iae);}


    }
}
```

The result is shown here:

```
The name of the class is now unleashed.ch27.Company2
The Company's sales total is 1
The Company's profit total is 1
The Company's hours total is 1
```

This example illustrates that the object created behaves similar to an ordinary `Company2` object in every way.

Polymorphic Programming with Reflection

The use of the Class class is part of real-time type identification or RTTI. RTTI is a compile-time function. All the information that it is able to glean is available through the .class files at the time the code is compiled.

Increasingly, our programs are calling methods to objects that are running in another virtual machine on another server. RTTI is of no value in discovering the properties of these objects because they are unknown at compile time. For this reason, another package called java.lang.reflect has been created. The use of this package is called *reflection*. Reflection gives us visibility into objects that the VM learns about at runtime. Listing 27.15 shows how this works.

LISTING 27.15 The Reflex1 Class

```
package unleashed.ch27;
import java.lang.reflect.*;
public class Reflex1 {

    /** Creates new Reflex1 */
    public Reflex1() {
    }
    public static void main(String[] args)
    {
        Class cc= null;
        cc = Company.class;

        Method[] m = cc.getMethods();
        for (int i=0; i<m.length; i++)
            System.out.println(m[i].toString());
    }
}
```

The output from Listing 27.15 probably contains more than you expected:

```
public static int unleashed.ch27.Company.getHours()
public static long unleashed.ch27.Company.getSales()
public static long unleashed.ch27.Company.getProfit()
public native int java.lang.Object.hashCode()
public final void java.lang.Object.wait() throws
java.lang.InterruptedException
public final void java.lang.Object.wait(long,int) throws
java.lang.InterruptedException
public final native void java.lang.Object.wait(long)
```

```
throws java.lang.InterruptedException
public final native java.lang.Class
java.lang.Object.getClass()
public boolean java.lang.Object.equals(java.lang.Object)
public java.lang.String java.lang.Object.toString()
public final native void java.lang.Object.notify()
public final native void java.lang.Object.notifyAll()
```

The order of the output might vary, but you can see that in addition to the methods of the class, the methods of the Object class are listed because Company automatically extends the Object class. In addition to the Method class, a Constructor and a Field class are available in this package.

Even more surprising, there is an invoke() method on the Method object. It allows a method to be discovered and called using the following syntax:

```
Object hours = m[0].invoke(null);
```

This command is used to call the getHours() method in Listing 27.16.

LISTING 27.16   Using the invoke() Method to Act Like a Method Pointer in C

```
package unleashed.ch27;
import java.lang.reflect.*;

public class Reflex2 {

    /** Creates new Reflex2 */
    public Reflex2() {
    }

    public static void main(String[] args)
    {
        Company comp = new Company(1000, 200, 41);
        Class cc= null;
        cc = Company.class;

        Method[] m = cc.getMethods();

            System.out.println(m[0].toString());

        try
        {
            Object result = m[0].invoke(null, null);
            System.out.println("The result is " + result);
        }catch (IllegalAccessException iae){
                    System.out.println("Failed " + iae);}
```

LISTING 27.16 continued

```
        catch (InvocationTargetException ite){
                     System.out.println("Failed " + ite);}

    }
}
```

The result is as follows:

```
public static int unleashed.ch27.Company.getHours()
The result is  41
```

If your output from Listing 27.15 was different from that displayed here, m[0] could be a different method entirely. On some machines, m[0] is the getSales() method, which will cause the preceding example to display 1000.

> **Caution**
>
> Because of this varied behavior, you will want to be very careful when using this approach. The designers of Java wisely decided that method pointers were tricky and not worth the trouble. Reflection allows you to use a form of method pointer, but it doesn't get around the problems associated with finding bugs when method pointers are used.

Inheritance and Handles

Much of the power in polymorphism comes from the use of handles. Once a reference (or handle) is assigned, the JVM performs its work in accordance of the type of the handle. Listing 27.17 shows an example of how this works.

LISTING 27.17 The HandleTest Class

```
*
 * HandleTest.java
 *
 * Created on April 30, 2002, 3:33 PM
 */

package unleashed.ch27;

/**
 *
 * @author  Stephen Potts
 * @version
 */
```

LISTING 27.17   continued

```java
public class HandleTest
{

    /** Creates new HandleTest */
    public HandleTest()
    {
    }

    public static void main(String[] args)
    {
        BaseClass top = new BaseClass();
        SecondClass second= new SecondClass();
        BaseClass third = new SecondClass();

        System.out.println("The top class i= " + top.i);
        System.out.println("The second class i= " + second.i);
        System.out.println("The third class i= " + third.i);
    }
}

class BaseClass
{
    int i=1;
}

class SecondClass extends BaseClass
{
    int i=2;
}
```

We create three handles—top, second, and third:

```java
BaseClass top = new BaseClass();
SecondClass second= new SecondClass();
BaseClass third = new SecondClass();
```

Notice how the handle named `third` is of type `BaseClass`. Notice also that it was instantiated using the constructor for `SecondClass`. When we run this example, we get the following result:

```
The top class i= 1
The second class i= 2
The third class i= 1
```

Clearly, the object that is accessed is determined by the type of the handle as it was declared.

Summary

In this chapter, we have covered the advantages and disadvantages of polymorphism and its appropriate use. We next looked at the internal operation of the JVM when resolving polymorphic handles. You saw several examples that illustrated different ways to use composition and inheritance to improve your programs.

In addition, we covered the different types of base classes that support polymorphism and inheritance. We talked about how to choose between concrete classes, abstract classes, and interfaces.

Finally, we covered the topic of type-safe downcasting. You learned several ways of obtaining the `Class` object handle. You also learned how to use this handle to get information about the classes that is known at compile time via RTTI. The runtime information about classes was obtained by using reflection in the java.lang.reflect package.

CHAPTER 28

Code Organization and Deployment

The other chapters in this book are intended to make complex concepts easier to understand. This chapter's purpose is to help you understand several concepts that those of us who work with Java encounter on a daily basis, but few of us have really spent time studying.

This chapter doesn't contain difficult subject matter, but it contains material that never seems to be easy to find when you need it. The subjects covered are packages, JAR files, and Javadocs.

Every Java programmer can tell you something about packages, but almost no one can define precisely what packages are and tell you everything that they do.

JAR files are very powerful. You can't do much of anything with Enterprise JavaBeans (EJB) without knowing how to manipulate JAR files.

Most Java programmers make extensive use of the Javadocs provided by Sun. The documents provide a convenient way of locating the signature of almost any method in any package. This includes the core Java classes and the packages in the Standard Extensions. If you get in the habit of creating Javadocs in the normal course of creating your systems, you can reduce the need for other kinds of programmer documents.

Producing Javadoc files is much more interesting than creating documents in a word processor.

Understanding Packages

The most incompletely understood aspect of the Java language is the humble package. All programmers know something about packages, and most assume that they know all that they need to know.

In reality, packages are confusing because they play so many different roles in your programs. These roles are described here:

- Code location—When you create a package called unleashed.ch28 and place a package statement in your code file, you are telling the Java compiler and the JVM that the class files for this program are located in a directory called `ch28`, which is a subdirectory of a directory called `unleashed`. This directory tree must be found somewhere under an entry in the classpath, in a JAR file in the classpath, or in the `/jre/lib/ext` directory under the `JAVA_HOME` directory. We will deal with the topic of classpaths later in this section.

- Namespace—Java 1.4 contains almost 3,000 classes. Many of your systems will add hundreds more classes to this. With numbers this large, name conflicts are inevitable. The package name that you assign becomes part of the name of the class. Notice that if you try to run a program called abc.class that is in the unleashed.ch28 package, you must type the full name unleashed.ch28.abc. The package name is the namespace for this class, and therefore part of the name.

- Accessibility specification—Every class in every file in a package is compiled to a single file containing only that class. This is true for private classes as well as public classes. It is also true for inner classes, both anonymous and regular. Awareness of the fact that source for two classes resides in the same file is entirely lost once the code is compiled. The rules governing the accessibility of nonpublic classes are based on the package, not the file.

- Library creation—Most of us organize our projects according to a tree structure. We name the system ABCD and create the user interface classes, the database access classes, the utility classes, and so on. It makes perfectly good sense for us to organize these classes as abcd.ui, abcd.database, and abcd.utility. From the standpoint of the JVM, these package names have nothing to do with each other—they are as unique as if they were randomly generated strings. To humans, however, these three packages are obviously related.

- Makefile entries—Most languages are compiled using some sort of makefile. This file contains the names of all the compiled code files that the linker needs to create the executable file. Java has none of these files. All the classnames that are needed to create the main class must be referenced in the import statements. Any class files that these referenced classes need are referenced in the import statements of the source file.

- Identification—Sun recommends that you make use of a registered Web site name to create the name of your packages. Perhaps you have seen this in some of the optional classes that Sun provides that are packaged in com.sun.zyx. Because the sun.com name is unique, a package named com.sun.zyx is guaranteed to be unique if no one outside Sun uses this name. If Sun manages the names of packages carefully, every public classname in your entire system will be unique.

Now that we have enumerated the various roles that packages fill, it is not surprising that confusion is rampant on this subject. You can improve your programs by heeding the following tips when using packages:

- Never use the default package, even for experiments. Put everything in a package and call it by name.

- Reserve the use of the * in import statements to the packages provided by Sun and the Standard Extensions. If you have 10 import statements that use *, it will be nearly impossible for others to locate the definitions of classes that you use in your program. On the other hand, if you import each class individually, they can look at the imports for a class to find its package. If they don't find the class, they can assume that it is a Java class and can solve the mystery by searching `http://java.sun.com`.

- Don't think of an import statement as a Java version of `#include` from C and C++. Those languages do a compile-time substitution of every file that is listed in the includes. The Java compiler does not. It uses the import statements to find classes.

- Don't avoid using * on your package statements over concerns about compiled code size or performance. There will not be one bit of difference between the class generated whether or not you use *. (Not surprisingly, the development team that gave us anonymous inner classes is smart enough to leave out code that is not needed.)

- Realize that the names you give to packages are all unique to the JVM. It doesn't care whether your package names are carefully organized in a lovely tree arrangement. Your successor in maintaining this system will appreciate your organization, though, so don't let the JVM's indifference dissuade you.

- Name your packages (and your classes, your variables, and your children) well. If you name your son Nancy and your daughter Harry, they and the rest of humankind will be confused. By the same token, if you call your database package com.you.network and your network package com.you.gui, you will be cursed years after you quit the company.

All of the package processing depends on the value of the classpath when your program compiles and again when it runs. There are essentially four ways for your program to decide which classes will be run when you type in a program name:

- Command-line parameter—You can specify the classpath that you want used on the command line. The following three examples show how to specify a JAR file, a directory, and the current directory:

```
java -classpath /com/myco/reports.jar ReportWriter
java -classpath /com/myco/reports ReportWriter
java -classpath .;/com/myco/reports ReportWriter
```

- Environment variable—You can include a directory or JAR filename in the classpath environment variable. Whenever a class is needed, the program looks for it in the first directory or JAR file listed. If the program doesn't find the class in the first directory, it looks in the next directory listed. It proceeds in this fashion until it reaches the end of the list. At that point, it throws a file not found exception.

- Installed extensions—You can alternately move class or JAR files into the `<JavaHome>/jre/lib/ext` directory. This is a special directory in that any file, directory tree, or JAR file located in it is automatically included in the classpath.

- Download extensions—You can also alter the manifest of a JAR file to add references to other JAR files in a chained fashion. As long as the JVM locates the first JAR file in the classpath using one of the first three methods, it will find the JAR files listed in the manifest. These new JAR files are listed relative to the first JAR file.

Some software products start up using their own classpaths. This is true of some development tools and application servers. If you use a JDNI server to store serializable objects, and that server was started with a different classpath than your program was, there is no guarantee that it will be able to locate the class file for the object that you have stored in it. Be sure to consult the documentation from each product's vendor to find out how it determines the classpath.

> **Caution**
>
> Using download extensions in your JAR files is a good way to confuse anyone who is charged with maintaining your system. Forcing someone to examine the contents of a JAR file to construct a mental picture of the classpath for your application is a bad idea.

If you have a third-party package that has a class called Xyz and you are also using the name Xyz for a class in your program, you will have to indicate which Xyz class you are trying to use by fully qualifying the class with a complete package name:

`unleashed.ch28.Xyz myXyz = new unleashed.ch28.Xyz();` creates an instance of your class named Xyz.

`third.party.Xyz thirdXyz = new third.party.Xyz();` creates an instance of the third-party Xyz class.

Hopefully, this brief journey through the world of packages and classpaths has brought a touch of clarity into a sometimes-muddy subject. Being organized in your approach does take some planning and a little extra work, but no one ever complains that the systems they support are too organized.

28

CODE
ORGANIZATION
AND DEPLOYMENT

Java Archive (JAR) Files

Another subject that seems to generate a lot of questions is Java Archive files, commonly called JAR or .jar files. One reason for confusion is the great variety of uses for these files. If you think of JAR files as a software version of a Swiss Army knife, you will be close to understanding them. JAR files have the following uses:

- Compression—JAR files are created using the same lossless compression algorithm that Zip files use. This allows data stored in them to be reduced in size, saving disk space and transfer time over a network. One of the original reasons for JAR files was to speed up download time for applets. Prior to JAR files, every object/class used in an applet had to be fetched individually from the Web server. For larger applets, this meant that a huge number of connections had to be opened, serviced, and closed by the Web server. With JAR files, only a single connection needs to be opened. This makes much more efficient use of the Web server.

- Safety—A file structure stored in a JAR file is much less likely to be damaged if users accidentally delete files.

- Simplicity—An application's file structure can be fairly complex. Packaging it in a JAR file removes all of this complexity from the file system on your computer and replaces it with one file.

- Security—You can sign a JAR file so that others can determine its authorship.

- Consistency—A JAR file can be sealed, which means that any reference made to a file in a package that is designated as sealed must come from the JAR file. This reduces the errors that can come from inadvertent use of an inappropriate class.

- Versioning—You can place a version number in your JAR file that users can check.

- Standardization—The Enterprise JavaBean specification requires that JAR files be used to deploy EJBs and MDBs. This has made JAR files fashionable in enterprise software. They are also popular for use in JSP/servlets as .war files.

Let's work through a series of short examples that demonstrate how to use JAR files to perform certain tasks. For all these syntax examples, we will use the file structure shown in Figure 28.1.

The directory structure in this figure is a little bit more complex than you might think it needs to be. There is some method to the madness, though. The top two levels, unleashed and ch28, were created to store the JAR files in the same directory structure as the rest of the code in this book. The bottom three directories (code, docs, and images) contain the files that we want to place in the JAR file. The topdir directory was added to make the example more complex so that it will be more realistic. The work directory was added for convenience in creating the JAR file. A trick of the JAR trade is to create an empty directory as your root and place the directory structure that will be found in the JAR file under it. This makes the JAR creation command much simpler.

FIGURE 28.1

The directory structure has to be created correctly for some of the features of the jar *tool to work properly.*

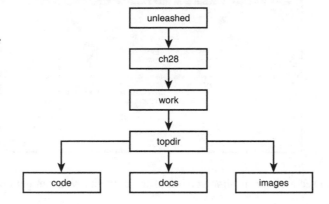

We create a subdirectory called `images` and put two graphics files containing the flags of Germany and Switzerland in it:

```
switzerland.gif
germany.gif
```

We create another subdirectory called `docs`. In it we put the documentation file:

```
Instructions.txt
```

Finally, we create a `code` subdirectory that contains the following files:

```
HelloWorld.java
HelloWorld.class
GoodByeWorld.java
GoodByeWorld.class
```

The first thing that we want to do is create a JAR file that contains the files from all three of the lowest-level directories. To do this, we need to move to the `work` directory so that the directory structure in the JAR file will be what we want:

```
C:\unleashed\ch28\work>jar cf test1.jar .
```

This is the simplest use of the `jar` command. We have simply instructed the `jar` tool to create a JAR file called `test1.jar` in the current directory. The period (`.`) after the JAR filename tells the tool to include all the files in the current directory. The `jar` tool behaves recursively. As a result, the `code`, `images`, and `docs` subdirectories are also included, along with all their contents.

The easiest way to peek inside a JAR file is to use WinZip or another tool that can display the Zip format. Figure 28.2 shows the contents of the `test1.jar` file.

FIGURE **28.2**

The jar *tool is recursive by default.*

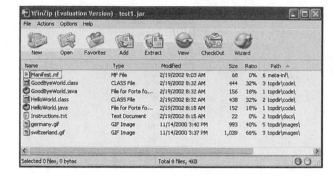

If you'd like to see a command-line version of the contents, you can get one by typing the following:

```
C:\unleashed\ch28\work>jar tf test1.jar
```

You will notice an extra directory called META-INF in the file. This stands for metadata or metainformation. It contains the manifest, which is like a table of contents for the JAR file:

```
META-INF/
META-INF/MANIFEST.MF
topdir/
topdir/docs/
topdir/docs/Instructions.txt
topdir/images/
topdir/images/germany.gif
topdir/images/switzerland.gif
topdir/code/
topdir/code/HelloWorld.java
topdir/code/HelloWorld.class
topdir/code/GoodByeWorld.java
topdir/code/GoodByeWorld.class
```

If you want to extract the contents of the file, move to the directory where you want the file system to start and issue the following command:

```
C:\extraction>jar xf c:\unleashed\ch28\test1.jar
```

You can also use the WinZip tool to provide a GUI version of this command. You just open the JAR file by double-clicking on the JAR filename. You can extract all files by not selecting any particular file and just clicking on the Extract button. The result of this is a tree structure just like the original one built under the `c:\extraction` directory.

The Manifest File

As mentioned earlier, the JAR file contains a special directory called META-INF that is created automatically (unless you specify otherwise). It contains a file called MANIFEST.MF. The word *manifest* is defined as a list of the contents of a ship or plane. A JAR file's manifest contains metadata about the contents of the file. In Java 1.1, every file in the JAR was listed in the manifest. In Java 2, the manifest contains only the information needed for special handling of the contents. Listing 28.1 shows the contents of the test1.jar default manifest.

LISTING 28.1   A Default Manifest

```
Manifest-Version: 1.0
Created-By: 1.4.0 (Sun Microsystems Inc.)
```

The only information contained in this file is a version number for the manifest and a version number for the Java that created it. The reason that it is so sparse is that we have not chosen to employ any special processing for the JAR file.

Notice that the manifest is made up of key:value pairs. These are read left to right. In this case, the value of Manifest-Version is 1.0. The value of Created-By is 1.4.0 (Sun Microsystems, Inc.).

Adding special processing to a JAR file requires that you edit the manifest. One way to do this is by adding to the manifest using the m or merge option on the jar tool command line. You first create a manifest file containing the additions that you want to make using a text editor. Let's add a command that seals a JAR file to illustrate this process.

JAR files can be sealed, which means that every class in the specified package must be contained in the same JAR file. This is a useful way to avoid calling another class file by accident. Listing 28.2 shows a file called additions.txt that contains instructions to seal this file on the package unleashed/ch25.

LISTING 28.2   additions.txt

```
Name: topdir/code/
Sealed: true
```

To merge this file into the manifest, type the following command:

```
jar umf additions.txt test1.jar
```

28

CODE
ORGANIZATION
AND DEPLOYMENT

The new `MANIFEST.MF` file is shown here:

```
Manifest-Version: 1.0
Sealed: true
Created-By: 1.4.0 (Sun Microsystems Inc.)
Name: topdir/code/
```

Running Code in a JAR File

The most powerful feature of a JAR file is that you can run the code in it without having to extract it first. There are two methods of running a JAR file's code that we need to look at. The most familiar technique to programmers is to place the JAR file in the classpath of an application. This enables the application to create instances of the classes in this JAR file and then call its methods.

The second method is to run a main class from a command line. Our desire to do this was a prime motivation for setting up the special `work` directory, which gives us a convenient current directory when running this code. Before we can run this main class in the JAR file directly, though, we have to modify the manifest once again. This time, we change the contents of the `additions.txt` file to contain only the line shown in Listing 28.3.

LISTING 28.3   The modified `additions.txt`

```
Main-Class: topdir.code.HelloWorld
```

To add this information to the manifest, we use the same command that we used to add the sealing instructions:

```
C:\unleashed\ch28\work>jar umf additions.txt test1.jar
```

The manifest now contains the main class information as well:

```
Manifest-Version: 1.0
Sealed: true
Created-By: 1.4.0 (Sun Microsystems Inc.)
Name: topdir/code/
Main-Class: topdir.code.HelloWorld
```

Now we can run the class by typing the following command:

```
C:\unleashed\ch28\work>java -classpath . -jar test1.jar
```

The `-classpath .` part of the command is needed because there is no period (`.`) in the classpath environment variable. (Some programmers consider the use of the `.` in the classpath a hindrance to really understanding what directory is current.) In keeping with our custom of showing you the results of running the code, here is the millionth occurrence of this string in a programming book:

```
Hello, World
```

Extensions

The concept of an extension is simple: Create a directory that is always in every program's classpath by default. This gets rid of the need to stuff the classpath environment variable with dozens of entries. All that we have to do to create an extension is move the JAR file to the following directory:

```
<JAVA_HOME>/jre/lib/ext
```

Once that is done, you simply run the class files just as if they were in a directory accessible from the environmental variable. One limitation is that you can't run a main class from a command line using the -jar modifier unless the <JAVA_HOME>/jre/lib/ext directory is your current directory at the time. You can, however, make calls directly to any class that has a main() method, as shown here:

```
C:\>java topdir.code.GoodByeWorld
```

Running this will produce the following result:

```
GoodBye, World
```

This section covered a few of the most useful but potentially confusing aspects of JAR files. Hopefully, the information you've learned will speed up your diagnostic skills when you are searching for missing files on your system.

The Java API Documentation Generator

The best way to climb the corporate ladder toward the coveted senior programmer status is to increase your knowledge of how things work in the world of software. The fact that you are reading this book indicates that you are well aware of that fact, and that you are acting on it.

The fastest way to move up is to communicate better the things that you already know. While increasing your vocabulary or improving your grammatical skills might take a while, documenting programs better is something that almost any programmer could do tomorrow. Most of us went into programming because we were more attracted to mathematical subjects than to literary ones. This lowers the bar considerably when it comes to written communications. You don't have to be particularly good to be an above-average documenting programmer.

Sun Microsystems has provided programmers with a tool that allows us to generate documentation that is actually worth having. Most Java programmers rely heavily on the documentation that is available for the core language and the Standard Extensions. This documentation is generated using a tool called Javadoc. This software accepts your source code files (and some others if you choose) and creates documentation that is identical in form to the documentation for the core language.

The process that you follow is much like programming. You comment your code using special syntax and tags. You then run the Javadoc tool from the command line. It generates a set of documents that display the comments you have written in a format that is controlled by the command-line options.

Figure 28.3 shows this process graphically.

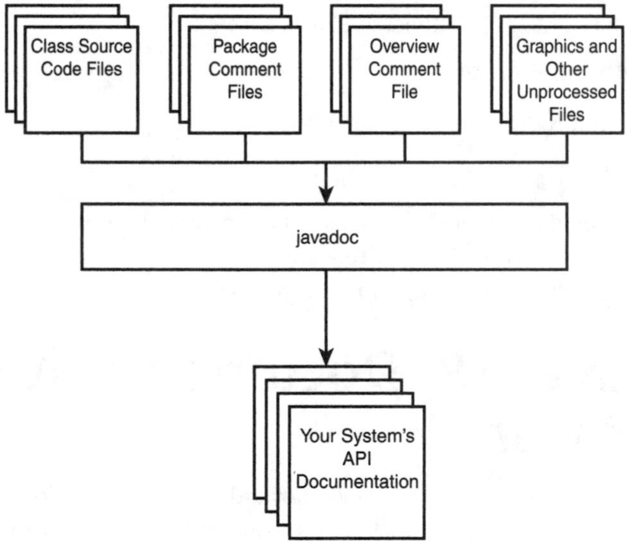

FIGURE 28.3

The Javadoc tool turns comments in your code files into quality documentation.

Without further delay, let's create an example so you can learn by doing. The first example will be a very simple one. Listing 28.4 shows an example that we will comment.

LISTING 28.4 The NewMath0 Class

```
package unleashed.ch28;

public class NewMath0
```

LISTING 28.4 continued

```
{

    public NewMath0()
    {
    }


    public int addInteger(int x, int y)
    {
        return x - y;
    }

    public int subtractInteger(int x, int y)
    {
        return x + y;
    }

    public int multiplyInteger(int x, int y)
    {
        return x * y;
    }

    public int divideInteger(int x, int y)
    {
        return x/y;
    }

    public String testDump(int x, int y)
    {
        return "Addition       = " +  addInteger(x,y) + "\n" +
               "Subtraction    = " + subtractInteger(x,y) + "\n" +
               "Multiplication = " + multiplyInteger(x,y) + "\n" +
               "Division       = " + divideInteger(x,y);
    }


    public static void main(String[] args)
    {
        NewMath0 nm = new NewMath0();

         System.out.println("Results = " + nm.testDump(100,10));
    }
}
```

28

CODE
ORGANIZATION
AND DEPLOYMENT

Those of you who possess a sharp eye will notice that there are no comments of any type in this code. This small detail shouldn't prevent us from running the Javadoc tool against it just to see what it will produce:

```
C:\>javadoc -sourcepath C: unleashed.ch28
```

We get all kinds of messages on the screen as a result:

```
Loading source files for package unleashed.ch28...
Constructing Javadoc information...
Standard Doclet version 1.4.0

Generating constant-values.html...
Building tree for all the packages and classes...
Building index for all the packages and classes...
Generating overview-tree.html...
Generating index-all.html...
Generating deprecated-list.html...
Building index for all classes...
Generating allclasses-frame.html...
Generating allclasses-noframe.html...
Generating index.html...
Generating packages.html...
Generating unleashed\ch28\package-frame.html...
Generating unleashed\ch28\package-summary.html...
Generating unleashed\ch28\package-tree.html...
Generating unleashed\ch28\NewMath.html...
Generating package-list...
Generating help-doc.html...
Generating stylesheet.css...
```

The most interesting-looking one is `unleashed\ch28\NewMath0.html`. If you open this file in a browser, you will see that it discovered quite a bit of information about our class, as shown in Figure 28.4.

FIGURE 28.4

The Javadoc tool gathers quite a bit of information from a file with no comments in it at all.

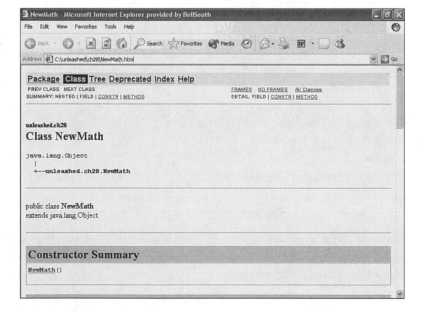

If we can get this kind of result just from the source file, imagine what we could get if we put forth a little effort. The first thing that we need to do is provide some information about the class itself. If we add the following class description to a Javadoc comment immediately preceding the class declaration, it will appear in the class description area in the generated document:

```
package unleashed.ch28;

/**
 * This is the class comment for the NewMath class.  The primary purpose
 * of the NewMath class is to provide a very simple example of a class
 * so that javadoc comments can be added to it and by consequence be
 * added to the generated documentation for this class.
 * @author  Stephen Potts
 * @version 1.0
 */
public class NewMath
```

> **Note**
>
> We generally avoid using code snippets in this book because we feel that it is important that you see entire applications and run them for yourself. In this section, because we are only adding comments, we will not repeat the code every time. At the end of the section, however, we will provide the complete listing so that you can run the code for yourself.

This code is interesting because it actually serves three functions. The first sentence is extracted from the rest of the paragraph and used as the short description of the class in the `package-summary.html` file, as shown in Figure 28.5.

The first sentence also serves as the description of the class in the `index-all.html` file, as shown in Figure 28.6.

FIGURE 28.5

The first sentence in the class comment serves as the short description of the class in the `package-summary.html` *file.*

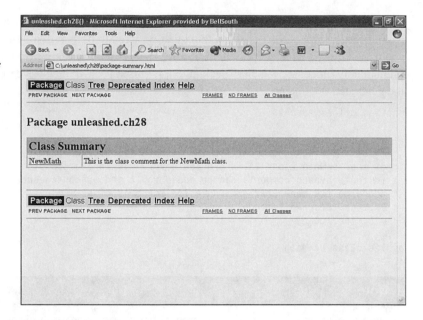

FIGURE 28.6

The first sentence in the class comment also serves as the short description of the class in the `index-all.html` *file.*

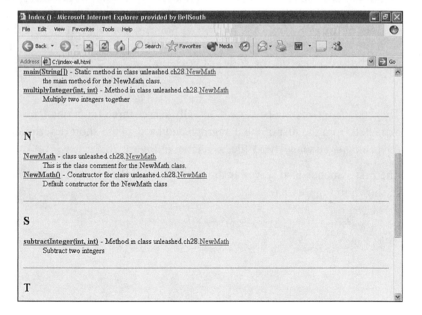

In the `NewMath.html` file, the paragraph is not truncated, but is displayed in all its glory, as shown in Figure 28.7.

FIGURE 28.7

The whole paragraph in the class comment serves as the full description of the class in the NewMath.html *file.*

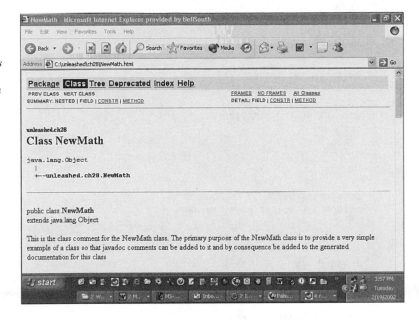

The next important step that we must take is to provide descriptions for all the methods in this class. We do this by adding comments in the following form to the source file:

```
/**
 * Default constructor for the NewMath class
 */
public NewMath()
{
}

/**
 * Add two integers together
 *@return the values when added together
 */
public int addInteger(int x, int y)
{
    return x + y;
}

/**
 * Subtract two integers
 *@return the values when subtracted
 */
public int subtractInteger(int x, int y)
{
```

```
        return x - y;
    }

    /**
     * Multiply two integers together
     *@return the values when multiplied
     */
    public int multiplyInteger(int x, int y)
    {
        return x * y;
    }

    /**
     * Divide integer x by integer y
     *@return the values when divided
     */
    public int divideInteger(int x, int y)
    {
        return x/y;
    }

    /**
     * output the data to the screen
     * @return a long string that contains newline characters
     */
    public String testDump(int x, int y)
    {
        return "Addition      = " +  addInteger(x,y) + "\n" +
               "Subtraction   = " + subtractInteger(x,y) + "\n" +
               "Multiplication  = " + multiplyInteger(x,y) + "\n" +
               "Division      = " + divideInteger(x,y);
    }

    /**
     * the main method for the NewMath class.  It instantiates the class
     * and prints the results of testDump to the screen.
     *
     */
    public static void main(String[] args)
    {
        NewMath nm = new NewMath();

        System.out.println("Results = " + nm.testDump(100,10));
    }
```

Once again, the first sentence rule applies. The first sentence of each comment is used in the index-all.html file, as shown in Figure 28.8.

FIGURE 28.8

Only the first sen-tence of each comment is used in the `index-all.html` *file.*

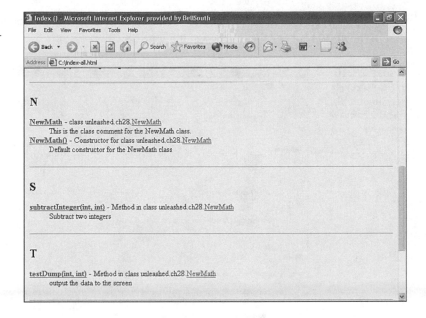

The first sentence of each comment is also used in the short descriptions found near the top of `NewMath.html`, as shown in Figure 28.9.

FIGURE 28.9

Only the first sen-tence in each comment is used in the first part of the `NewMath.html` *file.*

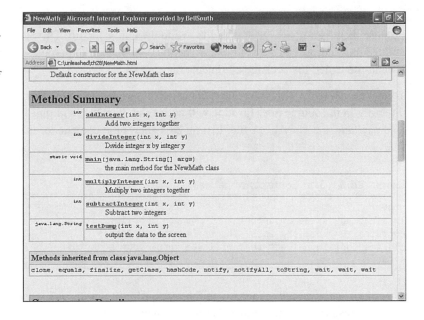

28

CODE ORGANIZATION AND DEPLOYMENT

The full paragraph is used in the detailed method descriptions that are found at the bottom of the `NewMath.html` file, as shown in Figure 28.10.

FIGURE 28.10

The bottom of the `NewMath.html` file contains complete comments.

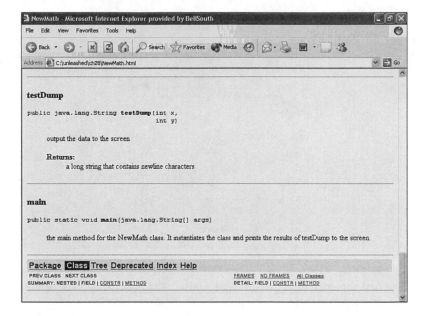

Our example is missing a description of the package. This presents a different problem because there is no package source file to add the comments to. The Sun engineers noticed this and provided a solution: Write the comments that pertain to the package in a special file called the package comments file.

To make such a file, simply create a file called `package.html` and save it to the `package` directory in the source tree. Javadoc will notice this filename and pull it into the generated `package-summary.html` file. Listing 28.5 shows the contents of the `package.html` file.

LISTING 28.5 The Contents of `package.html`

```
<body>
This package is so important that you won't believe it.  It
contains <b> lots and lots </b> of important classes.  These
classes contain methods that will <b> knock your socks off </b>.
</body>
```

This file is automatically placed with the `.java` files in the `c:\unleashed\ch28` directory. The result of rerunning the `javadoc` command is shown in Figure 28.11.

FIGURE 28.11

The contents of the package.html *file are automatically included in the generated* package-summary.html *file.*

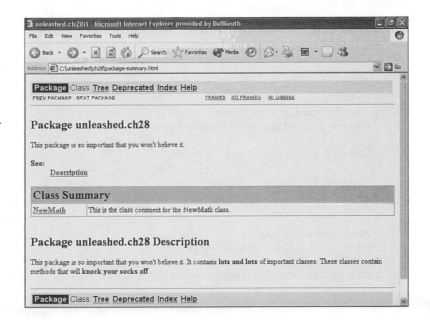

Listing 28.6 brings together the code snippets we've built and shows the commented code in its final form.

LISTING 28.6   The Final Listing for the NewMath Class

```
/*
 * NewMath.java
 *
 * Created on February 19, 2002, 10:49 AM
 */

package unleashed.ch28;

/**
 * This is the class comment for the NewMath class.  The primary purpose
 * of the NewMath class is to provide a very simple example of a class
 * so that javadoc comments can be added to it and by consequence be
 * added to the generated documentation for this class.
 * @author  Stephen Potts
 * @version 1.0
 */
public class NewMath
{
    /**
     * Default constructor for the NewMath class
     */
```

LISTING 28.6   continued

```java
public NewMath()
{
}

/**
 * Add two integers together
 *@return the values when added together
 */
public int addInteger(int x, int y)
{
    return x + y;
}

/**
 * Subtract two integers
 *@return the values when subtracted
 */
public int subtractInteger(int x, int y)
{
    return x - y;
}

/**
 * Multiply two integers together
 *@return the values when multiplied
 */
public int multiplyInteger(int x, int y)
{
    return x * y;
}

/**
 * Divide integer x by integer y
 *@return the values when divided
 */
public int divideInteger(int x, int y)
{
    return x/y;
}

/**
 * output the data to the screen
 * @return a long string that contains newline characters
 */
public String testDump(int x, int y)
{
    return "Addition       = " +  addInteger(x,y) + "\n" +
           "Subtraction    = " + subtractInteger(x,y) + "\n" +
           "Multiplication = " + multiplyInteger(x,y) + "\n" +
```

LISTING 28.6   continued

```
                "Division  = " + divideInteger(x,y);
    }

    /**
     * the main method for the NewMath class.  It instantiates the class
     * and prints the results of testDump to the screen.
     *
     */
    public static void main(String[] args)
    {
        NewMath nm = new NewMath();

        System.out.println("Results = " + nm.testDump(100,10));
    }

}
```

This section covered the most important aspects of creating Javadocs for your projects. You may need to learn about additional functionality once you get your initial Javadocs generated. This chapter, though, has taught you enough to get started. Regular use of Javadocs can help provide good documentation for a project and alleviate some maintenance nightmares down the line.

Summary

In this chapter you learned about several topics that can greatly enhance your effectiveness as a programmer. We started by discussing packages and their many uses. We took a little detour through the vagaries of classpaths along the way.

Next, we looked at the subject of JAR files in some detail. You learned how to make them more powerful by modifying the manifest. Finally, you learned how to create Javadocs for your applications. You learned that it is not very hard to generate documents that are really clear and helpful.

28

CODE
ORGANIZATION
AND DEPLOYMENT

Appendixes

IN THIS PART

APPENDIX A

Source Code Listings for Utility Programs Used in This Book

This appendix provides code listings for programs that are used in the book. These listings facilitate the running of some of the book's examples. They do not illustrate any of the concepts of the individual chapters.The files are included in the downloads for each chapter. Because they are large and are used in multiple places in the book, they are not listed in the chapters themselves. The two database loaders are complete source programs. `TicketRequest2` is just a class and contains no `main()` method.

> **Note**
>
> A readme file containing specific instructions on running the examples is included with the code for each chapter. You can download this code from www.samspublishing.com.

The WebLogic/Cloudscape Database Loader

Listing A.1 contains the WebLogic/Cloudscape version of the database loader program. It requires WebLogic Server to run. You will need to run this program whenever you need to reset the database to its original values. The following chapters use this code:

- Chapter 6, "Message-Driven Beans (MDB)"
- Chapter 7, "Java Message Service (JMS)"

LISTING A.1 The WebLogic Version of the Database Creation Program

```
/*
 * WlJDBC2.java
 *
 * Created on January 29, 2002, 9:23 AM
 */

package unleashed.ch6;

import java.sql.*;
import java.util.*;
import javax.naming.*;
import javax.transaction.*;

public class WlJDBC2
{
    public static void main(String argv[])
    throws Exception
```

LISTING A.1   continued

```
{
    java.sql.Connection dbConn = null;
    Statement statement1 = null;
    String createStatement;
    String insertStatement;

    try
    {
        // ============== Make connection to database ============
        // Obtain a Datasource conn from the WebLogic JNDI tree
        Context ctx = null;

        // Put connection properties into a hashtable.
        Hashtable ht = new Hashtable();
        ht.put(Context.INITIAL_CONTEXT_FACTORY,
        "weblogic.jndi.WLInitialContextFactory");
        ht.put(Context.PROVIDER_URL,
        "t3://localhost:7001");

        // Get a context for the JNDI lookup
        ctx = new InitialContext(ht);
        javax.sql.DataSource ds
        = (javax.sql.DataSource)
                ctx.lookup("examples-dataSource-demoPool");
        dbConn = ds.getConnection();
        System.out.println("Making connection...\n");

        //Create the statement
        statement1 = dbConn.createStatement();

        /////////////////////////////////////////////////////////////
        //     Create the tables in the database                   //
        /////////////////////////////////////////////////////////////
        try
        {
            statement1.execute("drop table CruiseReservation");
            statement1.execute("drop table CruiseCustomer");
            statement1.execute("drop table CruiseTicket");
            statement1.execute("drop table TravelAgency");
            statement1.execute("drop table CruiseBooking");
            statement1.execute("drop table Cruises");
            System.out.println("all tables dropped.");
        } catch (SQLException e)
        {
            System.out.println("table doesn't need to be dropped.");
        }

        //Add the customer data
```

LISTING A.1 continued

```
createStatement =
"CREATE TABLE CruiseReservation(resID int PRIMARY KEY,"
+ " CustomerID int, CruiseLine VARCHAR(30), "
+ "Ship VARCHAR(30), Port VARCHAR(30), "
+ "Sailing VARCHAR(30), AgencyID int, "
+ "AgentName VARCHAR(30))";
statement1.executeUpdate(createStatement);
System.out.println("Table CruiseReservation created.");
createStatement = "CREATE TABLE CruiseCustomer"
+   "(CustomerID int PRIMARY KEY, "
+ "LastName VARCHAR(30), FirstName VARCHAR(30), "
+ "MI VARCHAR(30), Address1 VARCHAR(30),"
+ " Address2 VARCHAR(30), City VARCHAR(30), "
+ "StateProv VARCHAR(30),"
+ " PostalCode VARCHAR(30), Country VARCHAR(30), "
+ "CreditCardType VARCHAR(30),"
+ " CreditCardNumber VARCHAR(30), "
+ " isGambler BIT, isDrinker BIT, "
+ "isShortTourist BIT, isPitchable BIT)";
statement1.executeUpdate(createStatement);
System.out.println("Table CruiseCustomer created.");
createStatement =
"CREATE TABLE TravelAgency(AgencyID int PRIMARY KEY,"
+ " AgencyName VARCHAR(30), Address1 VARCHAR(30),"
+ " Address2 VARCHAR(30), City VARCHAR(30),"
+ " StateProv VARCHAR(30), PostalCode VARCHAR(30), "
+ "Country VARCHAR(30),"
+ " Telephone VARCHAR(30))";
statement1.executeUpdate(createStatement);
System.out.println("Table TravelAgency created.");
createStatement = "CREATE TABLE CruiseTicket(TicketID "
+ "int PRIMARY KEY,"
+ " CustomerID int, CruiseLine VARCHAR(30),"
+ " Ship VARCHAR(30), Port VARCHAR(30),"
+ " Sailing VARCHAR(30), Price FLOAT, AgencyID int,"
+ " BookingID int, AgentName VARCHAR(30))";
statement1.executeUpdate(createStatement);
System.out.println("Table CruiseTicket created.");
createStatement = "CREATE TABLE CruiseBooking(BookingID"
+ " int PRIMARY KEY,"
+ " TicketID int, CustomerID int, Smoking BIT, "
+ "DiningPreference VARCHAR(30), "
+ "LangPref VARCHAR(30))";
statement1.executeUpdate(createStatement);
System.out.println("Table CruiseBooking created.");
createStatement = "CREATE TABLE Cruises(CruiseID int"
+ " PRIMARY KEY,"
+ " Destination VARCHAR(30), Port VARCHAR(30), "
+ "Sailing VARCHAR(30))";
```

LISTING A.1   continued

```
statement1.executeUpdate(createStatement);
System.out.println("Table Cruises created.");

//Add the cruise information
insertStatement = "INSERT INTO Cruises VALUES(3001, "
+ "'Tahiti', 'Auckland', '1/15/02')";
statement1.addBatch(insertStatement);
insertStatement = "INSERT INTO Cruises VALUES(3002, "
+ "'Caribbean', 'Tampa', '2/15/02')";
statement1.addBatch(insertStatement);
insertStatement = "INSERT INTO Cruises VALUES(3003,"
+ " 'Hawaii', 'Honolulu', '3/15/02')";
statement1.addBatch(insertStatement);
insertStatement = "INSERT INTO Cruises VALUES(3004, "
+ "'Alaska', 'Vancouver', '4/15/02')";
statement1.addBatch(insertStatement);
insertStatement = "INSERT INTO Cruises VALUES(3005, "
+ "'Bermuda', 'Fort Lauderdale', '5/15/02')";
statement1.addBatch(insertStatement);
insertStatement = "INSERT INTO Cruises VALUES(3006, "
+ "'Greek Isles', 'Venice', '6/15/02')";
statement1.addBatch(insertStatement);
insertStatement = "INSERT INTO Cruises VALUES(3007, "
+ "'Bahamas', 'Port Canaveral', '7/15/02')";
statement1.addBatch(insertStatement);
insertStatement = "INSERT INTO Cruises VALUES(3008,"
+ " 'Mexico', 'Mobile', '8/15/02')";
statement1.addBatch(insertStatement);
insertStatement = "INSERT INTO Cruises VALUES(3009,"
+ " 'South America', 'San Juan', '9/15/02')";
statement1.addBatch(insertStatement);
insertStatement = "INSERT INTO Cruises VALUES(3010,"
+ " 'Indonesia', 'Perth', '10/15/02')";
statement1.addBatch(insertStatement);


//Add the customer information
insertStatement = "INSERT INTO CruiseCustomer "
+ "VALUES(1001, 'Carter', 'Joseph', 'D', "
+ "'123 4th St.', '', 'Kennesaw', 'GA', '10064', "
+ "'USA', 'MC', '1234-1234-1234-1234',"
+ "X'0',X'0',X'0',X'0')";
statement1.addBatch(insertStatement);

insertStatement = "INSERT INTO CruiseCustomer "
+ "VALUES(1002, 'Cain', 'Clay', 'F',"
+ " '1203 5th St.', '', 'Macon', 'GA', '20064',"
+ " 'USA', 'MC', '2234-2234-2234-2234', "
+ " X'0',X'0',X'0',X'0')";
```

LISTING A.1   continued

```
statement1.addBatch(insertStatement);
insertStatement = "INSERT INTO CruiseCustomer"
+ " VALUES(1003, 'Bush', 'Albert', 'R',"
+ " '1523 6th St.', '', 'Cincinnati', 'OH', "
+ "'30064', 'USA', 'MC', '3234-3234-3234-3234', "
+ " X'0',X'0',X'0',X'0')";
statement1.addBatch(insertStatement);
insertStatement = "INSERT INTO CruiseCustomer"
+ " VALUES(1004, 'Skelton', 'Allison', 'T',"
+ " '1523 7th St.', '', 'Middletown', 'AL', '40064',"
+ " 'USA', 'MC', '4234-4234-4234-4234', "
+ "X'0',X'0',X'0',X'0')";
statement1.addBatch(insertStatement);
insertStatement = "INSERT INTO CruiseCustomer "
+ "VALUES(1005, 'Davidson', 'Barco', 'G',"
+ " '1823 8th St.', '', 'Dayton', 'OH', '50064', "
+ "'USA', 'MC', '5234-5234-5234-5234', "
+ " X'0',X'0',X'0',X'0')";
statement1.addBatch(insertStatement);
insertStatement = "INSERT INTO CruiseCustomer "
+ "VALUES(1006, 'Rangitch', 'Maureen', 'B',"
+ " '1223 9th St.', '', 'Cairo', 'KA', '60064', "
+ "'USA', 'MC', '6234-6234-6234-6234', "
+ " X'0',X'0',X'0',X'0')";
statement1.addBatch(insertStatement);
insertStatement = "INSERT INTO CruiseCustomer "
+ "VALUES(1007, 'Milner', 'Grant', 'V', "
+ "'1293 14th St.', '', 'Auberna', 'TN', '70064', "
+ "'USA', 'MC', '7234-7234-7234-7234', "
+ " X'0',X'0',X'0',X'0')";
statement1.addBatch(insertStatement);
insertStatement = "INSERT INTO CruiseCustomer "
+ "VALUES(1008, 'Walker', 'Mike', 'C',"
+ " '1223 24th St.', '', 'Spokane', 'WA', '80064', "
+ "'USA', 'MC', '8234-8234-8234-8234', "
+ " X'0',X'0',X'0',X'0')";
statement1.addBatch(insertStatement);
insertStatement = "INSERT INTO CruiseCustomer "
+ "VALUES(1009, 'Cheney', 'Michael', 'L',"
+ " '1723 25th St.', '', 'Orlando', 'FL', '90064',"
+ " 'USA', 'MC', '9234-9234-9234-9234', "
+ " X'0',X'0',X'0',X'0')";
statement1.addBatch(insertStatement);
insertStatement = "INSERT INTO CruiseCustomer"
+ " VALUES(1010, 'Pfister', 'Darlene', 'D',"
+ " '1233 9th St.', '', 'Bangor', 'MA', '10064',"
+ " 'USA', 'MC', '0234-0234-0234-0234', "
+ " X'0',X'0',X'0',X'0')";
statement1.addBatch(insertStatement);
```

LISTING A.1   continued

```
//Execute the batch
statement1.executeBatch();

//add the Travel Agents
insertStatement =
"INSERT INTO TravelAgency VALUES(2001,"
+ " 'Cruise Junction', '1233 Sego St.', "
+ "'', 'Miami', 'FL', '10064', 'USA', "
+ "'(800)242-4242')";
statement1.addBatch(insertStatement);
insertStatement =
"INSERT INTO TravelAgency VALUES(2002, "
+ "'Cruise and Snooze', '9387 Atlantic Ave.', "
+ "'', 'New York', 'NY', '00064', 'USA', "
+ "'(800)343-3434')";
statement1.addBatch(insertStatement);
insertStatement =
"INSERT INTO TravelAgency VALUES(2003, "
+ "'Pokeys Cruises', '98223 Baltic Dr.', "
+ "'', 'Los Angeles', 'CA', '20064', "
+ "'USA', '(800)565-6565')";
statement1.addBatch(insertStatement);
insertStatement =
"INSERT INTO TravelAgency VALUES(2004, "
+ "'Cruise Animal', '2345 Lester Rd.', "
+ "'', 'New Orleans', 'LA', '40064', "
+ "'USA', '(800)787-8787')";
statement1.addBatch(insertStatement);
insertStatement =
"INSERT INTO TravelAgency VALUES(2005, "
+ "'Cruisy Dot Com', '5435 Spring St.', "
+ " '', 'Atlanta', 'GA', '30064', 'USA',"
+ " '(800)879-6543')";
statement1.addBatch(insertStatement);

//Execute the batch
statement1.executeBatch();
System.out.println("All rows added successfully");
} catch (Exception e)
{
    System.out.println("Exception was thrown: "
            + e.getMessage());
} finally
{
    try
    {
        if (statement1 != null)
            statement1.close();
```

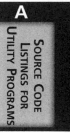

A

SOURCE CODE
LISTINGS FOR
UTILITY PROGRAMS

LISTING A.1   continued

```
            if (dbConn != null)
                dbConn.close();
        } catch (SQLException sqle)
        {
            System.out.println("SQLException during close(): "
                                    + sqle.getMessage());
        }
    }
}

}
```

The Access Version of the Database Loader

Listing A.2 contains the AccessJDBC2.java program that is used in several chapters. The code is included here as well as in the individual chapters that use it. In its current form, it requires MS Access to run. However, you can easily modify it to use any JDBC database. You will need to run this program whenever you need to reset the database to its original values. The chapters that use this code are listed here:

- Chapter 2, "Creating Applications with Remote Method Invocation (RMI)"
- Chapter 3, "Creating Applications with Java API for XML Parsing (JAXP)"
- Chapter 13, "JavaMail"

LISTING A.2   The Access Version of the Database Loader

```
/*
 * AccessJDBC2.java
 *
 * Created on January 21, 2002, 4:12 PM
 */

package unleashed.ch3;

import java.sql.*;
import java.util.*;


public class AccessJDBC2
{
    public static void main(String argv[])
    throws Exception
```

LISTING A.2   continued

```java
{
    java.sql.Connection dbConn = null;
    Statement statement1 = null;
    String createStatement;
    String insertStatement;

    try
    {
        // ============== Make connection to database ===========

        //load the driver class
        Class.forName("sun.jdbc.odbc.JdbcOdbcDriver");

        //Specify the ODBC data source
        String sourceURL = "jdbc:odbc:CruiseTicket";

        //get a connection to the database
        dbConn =DriverManager.getConnection(sourceURL);

        //If we get to here, no exception was thrown
        System.out.println("The database connection is "
                + dbConn);
        System.out.println("Making connection...\n");

        //Create the statement
        statement1 = dbConn.createStatement();

        ///////////////////////////////////////////////
        //Create the tables in the database           //
        ///////////////////////////////////////////////
        try
        {
            statement1.execute("drop table CruiseReservation");
            statement1.execute("drop table CruiseCustomer");
            statement1.execute("drop table CruiseTicket");
            statement1.execute("drop table TravelAgency");
            statement1.execute("drop table CruiseBooking");
            statement1.execute("drop table Cruises");
            System.out.println("all tables dropped.");
        } catch (SQLException e)
        {
            System.out.println("table doesn't need to be dropped.");
        }

        //Add the customer data
        createStatement = "CREATE TABLE CruiseReservation"
        + "(resID int PRIMARY KEY,"
        + " CustomerID int, CruiseLine VARCHAR(30), Ship "
```

LISTING A.2   continued

```
+ "VARCHAR(30), Port VARCHAR(30), "
+ "Sailing VARCHAR(30), AgencyID int, AgentName"
+ " VARCHAR(30))";
statement1.executeUpdate(createStatement);
System.out.println("Table CruiseReservation created.");
createStatement = "CREATE TABLE CruiseCustomer("
+ "CustomerID int PRIMARY KEY, "
+ "LastName VARCHAR(30), FirstName VARCHAR(30), "
+ "MI VARCHAR(30), Address1 VARCHAR(30),"
+ " Address2 VARCHAR(30), City VARCHAR(30), "
+ "StateProv VARCHAR(30),"
+ " PostalCode VARCHAR(30), Country VARCHAR(30),"
+ " CreditCardType VARCHAR(30),"
+ " CreditCardNumber VARCHAR(30), "
+ " isGambler BIT, isDrinker BIT, isShortTourist BIT,"
+ " isPitchable BIT)";
statement1.executeUpdate(createStatement);
System.out.println("Table CruiseCustomer created.");
createStatement = "CREATE TABLE TravelAgency(AgencyID"
+ " int PRIMARY KEY,"
+ " AgencyName VARCHAR(30), Address1 VARCHAR(30), "
+ "Address2 VARCHAR(30), City VARCHAR(30),"
+ " StateProv VARCHAR(30), PostalCode VARCHAR(30), "
+ "Country VARCHAR(30),"
+ " Telephone VARCHAR(30))";
statement1.executeUpdate(createStatement);
System.out.println("Table TravelAgency created.");
createStatement = "CREATE TABLE CruiseTicket(TicketID"
+ " int PRIMARY KEY,"
+ " CustomerID int, CruiseLine VARCHAR(30), Ship"
+ " VARCHAR(30), Port VARCHAR(30),"
+ " Sailing VARCHAR(30), Price FLOAT, AgencyID int,"
+ " BookingID int, AgentName VARCHAR(30))";
statement1.executeUpdate(createStatement);
System.out.println("Table CruiseTicket created.");
createStatement = "CREATE TABLE CruiseBooking("
+ "BookingID int PRIMARY KEY,"
+ " TicketID int, CustomerID int, Smoking BIT,"
+ " DiningPreference VARCHAR(30), "
+ "LangPref VARCHAR(30))";
statement1.executeUpdate(createStatement);
System.out.println("Table CruiseBooking created.");
createStatement = "CREATE TABLE Cruises(CruiseID "
+ "int PRIMARY KEY,"
+ " Destination VARCHAR(30), Port VARCHAR(30), "
+ "Sailing VARCHAR(30))";
statement1.executeUpdate(createStatement);
System.out.println("Table Cruises created.");
```

LISTING A.2   continued

```
//Add the cruise information
insertStatement = "INSERT INTO Cruises VALUES"
+ "(3001, 'Tahiti', 'Auckland', '1/15/02')";
statement1.addBatch(insertStatement);
insertStatement = "INSERT INTO Cruises VALUES"
+ "(3002, 'Caribbean', 'Tampa', '2/15/02')";
statement1.addBatch(insertStatement);
insertStatement = "INSERT INTO Cruises VALUES"
+ "(3003, 'Hawaii', 'Honolulu', '3/15/02')";
statement1.addBatch(insertStatement);
insertStatement = "INSERT INTO Cruises VALUES"
+ "(3004, 'Alaska', 'Vancouver', '4/15/02')";
statement1.addBatch(insertStatement);
insertStatement = "INSERT INTO Cruises VALUES"
+ "(3005, 'Bermuda', 'Fort Lauderdale', '5/15/02')";
statement1.addBatch(insertStatement);
insertStatement = "INSERT INTO Cruises VALUES"
+ "(3006, 'Greek Isles', 'Venice', '6/15/02')";
statement1.addBatch(insertStatement);
insertStatement = "INSERT INTO Cruises VALUES("
+ "3007, 'Bahamas', 'Port Canaveral', '7/15/02')";
statement1.addBatch(insertStatement);
insertStatement = "INSERT INTO Cruises VALUES("
+ "3008, 'Mexico', 'Mobile', '8/15/02')";
statement1.addBatch(insertStatement);
insertStatement = "INSERT INTO Cruises VALUES("
+ "3009, 'South America', 'San Juan', '9/15/02')";
statement1.addBatch(insertStatement);
insertStatement = "INSERT INTO Cruises VALUES("
+ "3010, 'Indonesia', 'Perth', '10/15/02')";
statement1.addBatch(insertStatement);


//Add the customer information
insertStatement = "INSERT INTO CruiseCustomer "
+ "VALUES(1001, 'Carter', 'Joseph', 'D', "
+ "'123 4th St.', '', 'Kennesaw', 'GA', '10064', "
+ "'USA', 'MC', '1234-1234-1234-1234',"
+ "0,0,0,0)";
statement1.addBatch(insertStatement);

insertStatement = "INSERT INTO CruiseCustomer "
+ "VALUES(1002, 'Cain', 'Clay', 'F',"
+ " '1203 5th St.', '', 'Macon', 'GA', '20064', "
+ "'USA', 'MC', '2234-2234-2234-2234', "
+ " 0,0,0,0)";
statement1.addBatch(insertStatement);
```

A

SOURCE CODE
LISTINGS FOR
UTILITY PROGRAMS

LISTING A.2   continued

```
insertStatement = "INSERT INTO CruiseCustomer "
+ "VALUES(1003, 'Bush', 'Albert', 'R',"
+ " '1523 6th St.', '', 'Cincinnati', 'OH', '30064',"
+ " 'USA', 'MC', '3234-3234-3234-3234', "
+ " 0,0,0,0)";
statement1.addBatch(insertStatement);
insertStatement = "INSERT INTO CruiseCustomer"
+ " VALUES(1004, 'Skelton', 'Allison', 'T',"
+ " '1523 7th St.', '', 'Middletown', 'AL',"
+ " '40064', 'USA', 'MC', '4234-4234-4234-4234', "
+ "0,0,0,0)";
statement1.addBatch(insertStatement);
insertStatement = "INSERT INTO CruiseCustomer"
+ " VALUES(1005, 'Davidson', 'Barco', 'G',"
+ " '1823 8th St.', '', 'Dayton', 'OH', '50064', "
+ "'USA', 'MC', '5234-5234-5234-5234', "
+ " 0,0,0,0)";
statement1.addBatch(insertStatement);
insertStatement = "INSERT INTO CruiseCustomer "
+ "VALUES(1006, 'Rangitch', 'Maureen', 'B',"
+ " '1223 9th St.', '', 'Cairo', 'KA', '60064',"
+ " 'USA', 'MC', '6234-6234-6234-6234', "
+ " 0,0,0,0)";
statement1.addBatch(insertStatement);
insertStatement = "INSERT INTO CruiseCustomer "
+ "VALUES(1007, 'Milner', 'Grant', 'V', "
+ "'1293 14th St.', '', 'Auberna', 'TN', '70064',"
+ " 'USA', 'MC', '7234-7234-7234-7234', "
+ " 0,0,0,0)";
statement1.addBatch(insertStatement);
insertStatement = "INSERT INTO CruiseCustomer "
+ "VALUES(1008, 'Walker', 'Mike', 'C',"
+ " '1223 24th St.', '', 'Spokane', 'WA', '80064', "
+ "'USA', 'MC', '8234-8234-8234-8234', "
+ " 0,0,0,0)";
statement1.addBatch(insertStatement);
insertStatement = "INSERT INTO CruiseCustomer "
+ "VALUES(1009, 'Cheney', 'Michael', 'L',"
+ " '1723 25th St.', '', 'Orlando', 'FL', '90064',"
+ " 'USA', 'MC', '9234-9234-9234-9234', "
+ " 0,0,0,0)";
statement1.addBatch(insertStatement);
insertStatement = "INSERT INTO CruiseCustomer "
+ "VALUES(1010, 'Pfister', 'Darlene', 'D',"
+ " '1233 9th St.', '', 'Bangor', 'MA', '10064', "
+ "'USA', 'MC', '0234-0234-0234-0234', "
+ " 0,0,0,0)";
statement1.addBatch(insertStatement);
```

LISTING A.2   continued

```
        //Execute the batch
        statement1.executeBatch();

        //add the Travel Agents
        insertStatement =
        "INSERT INTO TravelAgency VALUES(2001, "
        + "'Cruise Junction', '1233 Sego St.', "
        + "'', 'Miami', 'FL', '10064', 'USA', "
        + "'(800)242-4242')";
        statement1.addBatch(insertStatement);
        insertStatement =
        "INSERT INTO TravelAgency VALUES(2002,"
        + " 'Cruise and Snooze', '9387 Atlantic Ave.', "
        + "'', 'New York', 'NY', '00064', 'USA',"
        + "'(800)343-3434')";
        statement1.addBatch(insertStatement);
        insertStatement =
        "INSERT INTO TravelAgency VALUES(2003, "
        + "'Pokeys Cruises', '98223 Baltic Dr.', "
        + "'', 'Los Angeles', 'CA', '20064', 'USA', "
        + "'(800)565-6565')";
        statement1.addBatch(insertStatement);
        insertStatement =
        "INSERT INTO TravelAgency VALUES(2004, "
        + "'Cruise Animal', '2345 Lester Rd.', "
        + "'', 'New Orleans', 'LA', '40064', 'USA',"
        + " '(800)787-8787')";
        statement1.addBatch(insertStatement);
        insertStatement =
        "INSERT INTO TravelAgency VALUES(2005, "
        + "'Cruisy Dot Com', '5435 Spring St.', "
        + " '', 'Atlanta', 'GA', '30064', 'USA',"
        + " '(800)879-6543')";
        statement1.addBatch(insertStatement);

        //Execute the batch
        statement1.executeBatch();
        System.out.println("All rows added successfully");
    } catch (Exception e)
    {
        System.out.println("Exception was thrown: "
        + e.getMessage());
    } finally
    {
        try
        {
            if (statement1 != null)
                statement1.close();
            if (dbConn != null)
```

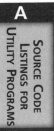

LISTING A.2   continued

```
                    dbConn.close();
        } catch (SQLException sqle)
        {
            System.out.println("SQLException during close():"
                    + sqle.getMessage());
        }
    }
}

}
```

TicketRequest2

Listing A.3 contains the `TicketRequest2` class that is used in the various CruiseList application versions that are found in the book. The following chapters use it:

- Chapter 2
- Chapter 3
- Chapter 6
- Chapter 7
- Chapter 13

LISTING A.3   The `TicketRequest2` Class

```
/*
 * TicketRequest2.java
 *
 * Created on January 19, 2002, 11:22 AM
 */

package unleashed;

/**
 *
 * @author   Stephen Potts
 * @version
 */
public class TicketRequest2 implements java.io.Serializable
{
    //information about the customer
    int custID;
    String lastName;
    String firstName;
```

LISTING A.3   continued

```
//information about the cruise
int cruiseID;
String destination;
String port;
String sailing;

int numberOfTickets;
boolean commissionable;
boolean approved;

public TicketRequest2()
{
}

/** Constructor */
public TicketRequest2(int custID, String lastName, String firstName,
int cruiseID, String destination,
String port, String sailing, int numberOfTickets,
boolean isCommissionable)
{
    //set the information about the customer
    this.custID = custID;
    this.lastName = lastName;
    this.firstName = firstName;

    //set the information about the cruise
    this.cruiseID = cruiseID;
    this.destination = destination;
    this.port = port;
    this.sailing = sailing;

    this.numberOfTickets = numberOfTickets;
    this.commissionable = commissionable;
    this.approved = false;
}

public int getCustID()
{
    return this.custID = custID;
}

public String getLastName()
{
    return this.lastName = lastName;
}

public String getFirstName()
{
```

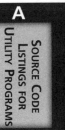

LISTING A.3 continued

```
        return this.firstName = firstName;
    }

    public int getCruiseID()
    {
        return this.cruiseID;
    }

    public String getDestination()
    {
        return this.destination;
    }

    public String getPort()
    {
        return this.port;
    }

    public String getSailing()
    {
        return this.sailing;
    }

    public int getNumberOfTickets()
    {
        return this.numberOfTickets;
    }

    public boolean isCommissionable()
    {
        return this.commissionable;
    }

    public boolean isApproved()
    {
        return approved;
    }

    public void setCustID(int custID)
    {
        this.custID = custID;
    }

    public void setLastName(String lastName)
    {
        this.lastName = lastName;
    }

    public void setFirstName(String firstName)
```

Listing A.3 continued

```
{
    this.firstName = firstName;
}

public void setCruiseID(int cruiseID)
{
    this.cruiseID = cruiseID;
}

public void setDestination(String destination)
{
    this.destination = destination;
}

public void setPort(String port)
{
    this.port = port;
}

public void setSailing(String sailing)
{
    this.sailing = sailing;
}

public void setNumberOfTickets(int numberOfTickets)
{
    this.numberOfTickets = numberOfTickets;
}

public void setCommissionable(boolean commissionable)
{
    this.commissionable = commissionable;
}

public void approve()
{
   approved = true;
}

public void disApprove()
{
   approved = false;
}

public String toString()
{
    String outString;
    outString = "------------------------------------------" + "\n";
```

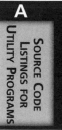

LISTING A.3 continued

```
        //information about the customer
        outString += "custID = " + this.custID + "\n";
        outString += "lastName = " + this.lastName + "\n";
        outString += "firstName = " + this.firstName + "\n";
        outString += "---------------------------------------" + "\n";

        //information about the cruise
        outString += "cruiseID = " + this.cruiseID + "\n";
        outString += "destination = " + this.destination + "\n";
        outString += "port = " + this.port + "\n";
        outString += "sailing = " + this.sailing + "\n";
        outString += "numberOfTickets = " + this.numberOfTickets + "\n";

        //information about the status
        outString += "commissionable = " + this.commissionable + "\n";
        outString += "approved? = " + this.approved + "\n";
        outString += "---------------------------------------" + "\n";
        return outString;
    }
}
```

APPENDIX B

Downloading and Installing WebLogic Server

WebLogic Server 6.1 is used in a number of chapters in this book. It provides a J2EE-compliant server that supports the creation of Enterprise JavaBeans and message-driven beans. It also provides a JMS Server, servlet, and JSP engine as well as a JNDI server.

Follow these steps to get WebLogic Server running on your machine:

1. In a browser, type **www.bea.com**.
2. When the BEA Systems home page appears, click on the Download icon.
3. Choose the BEA WebLogic Server Downloads link.
4. Scroll down to the "WebLogic Server 6.1" section of the page and navigate to the J2EE 1.2 Plus J2EE 1.3 Features drop-down list.
5. Select the platform that you run on in the Choose a Platform list. Notice that Windows NT/2000 is the only Microsoft option listed. The WebLogic Server will also work on XP Professional.
6. Click the Proceed to Download button.
7. Register or log in.
8. Agree to the license terms.
9. Click on the Download button.
10. When the download is complete, follow the directions to install.

> **Note**
>
> Web site navigation changes, so the steps listed here may be different by the time you try to use them. If the steps change, something similar will replace them, so this list will give you an idea of how to proceed in any case.

This download will run for 30 days at no charge. If you need a longer evaluation period, contact BEA. They were very cooperative when we needed extensions. You can renew the license after it expires by going to the following URL:

```
http://commerce.bea.com/eval/wls/610/index.jsp
```

You need to register and create an account with BEA (this is free). There are directions on the page describing how to apply the new license key. This key is strictly for personal/development use and contains the same five connection license restrictions as the key that was provided in your original download. As such, it should not be used for production purposes.

After you finish the installation, you can find the WebLogic Server quick start directions at

```
c:\bea\wlserver6.1\QUICK_START.HTML
```

WebLogic Server ships with an evaluation copy of the Cloudscape DBMS. The directions for running this DBMS are found at

```
c:\bea\wlserver6.1\samples\eval\cloudscape\cloudscape.html
```

(If you didn't install WebLogic Server on the c: drive, replace c:\ with the location where you installed it.)

During the installation process, you'll create a WebLogic server password. You will need this password every time you start up the WebLogic Server.

For all the examples in this book, you'll be running the examples server, *not* the default server.

INDEX

S

Other Related Titles

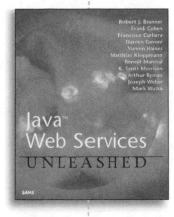